Cocoa Recipes for Mac OS X

Bill Cheeseman

 Peachpit Press

Cocoa Recipes for Mac OS X
Bill Cheeseman

Peachpit Press

1249 Eighth Street
Berkeley, CA 94710
510/524-2178
800/283-9444
510/524-2221 (fax)

Find us on the World Wide Web at: http://www.peachpit.com/
To report errors, please send a note to errata@peachpit.com
Peachpit Press is a division of Pearson Education

Editor: Cifford Colby
Production Coordinator: Connie Jeung-Mills
Copyeditor: Gail Nelson-Bonebrake
Proofreader: Eva Langfeldt
Compositor: Owen Wolfson
Indexer: Joy Dean Lee
Cover Design: Mimi Heft
Interior Design: Mimi Heft

Notice of rights

Notice of liability

Trademarks

ISBN 0-201-87801-1

9 8 7 6 5 4 3 2 1

Printed and bound in the United States of America

This book is dedicated to
David W. Walker,
who started me down this path long ago.

ACKNOWLEDGMENTS

I would like to thank many people for making this book possible through their encouragement, support, and help. Foremost among them is my wife, Sharon, who has borne up well under my obsession with computers and programming these many years, and who has always known how to bring me back to the real world when necessary. Scott Anguish's generosity in making his Stepwise Web site and his help available for the initial versions of some of these recipes has been indispensable, and I am honored to count him among my many newfound friends in the Cocoa community. The members of the Stepwise editorial team have also been immensely helpful, to me and to the entire community. In addition, although he isn't involved in Cocoa development, I want to thank Cal Simone of Main Event Software, AppleScript guru and champion, for introducing me to the world of serious software development and to my first Apple Worldwide Developers Conference. I would also like to express my appreciation for the folks involved with Cocoa at Apple Computer, who have never stood on formality or protocol in responding to my questions and requests, but who have instead willingly taken time out of their busy days to hold my hand when I needed it. Don't let anybody tell you that Apple stints when it comes to supporting its developers! It isn't fair to single out any one of the many Apple engineers and product managers who gave me assistance, but I must nevertheless thank Heather Hickman for the infectiousness of her enthusiasm for Cocoa. In addition, the participants on the Cocoa mailing lists have provided many answers, as well as many questions I would never have thought to ask. Finally, I want to thank the people at Peachpit Press—especially my editor, Cliff Colby—for their help and support on this, my first book. I especially appreciate their willingness to let me say things my way for the most part, but I also thank them for their unending efforts to rid my writing of the passive voice.

Table of Contents

Section 6: Additional Application Features 685

Section 7: Working with Mac OS X 10.2 (Jaguar) 717

Table of Topics

Introduction

Cocoa Recipes for Mac OS X is a cookbook for developing Macintosh computer applications in the Mac OS X Cocoa environment. It covers features that are new in Mac OS X 10.2 (Jaguar) as well as older versions of the operating system. It is popularly known as *Vermont Recipes* from its origins on the World Wide Web at www.stepwise.com. It takes a practical, no-nonsense, hands-on, step-by-step approach, walking you through the details of building a Cocoa application from start to finish using the Objective-C programming language. It explains in detail what the code is doing and why it works, with only as much theory about the programming language and the Cocoa frameworks as is needed to understand the approach taken. *Vermont Recipes* places a decided emphasis on getting an application to work correctly as quickly as possible.

About *Vermont Recipes*

Vermont Recipes is distinguished from other Cocoa tutorials by its single-minded dedication to creating a complete, integrated, working application. It approaches the job of writing a Cocoa application just as you would approach it in real life, starting where you would start, progressing through the steps that you would follow, and finishing up where you would end. It does not jump from one example to another to illustrate different features of the programming environment. Neither is it organized topically with a multitude of isolated discussions of narrow features of the Cocoa frameworks taken out of context. One advantage of the *Vermont Recipes* approach is that you learn how to organize an application's files and to cope with application-wide interactions that are easily overlooked in a more fragmentary presentation.

Once you have finished *Vermont Recipes*, you will be able to follow the same sequence of steps to write a full-featured application of your own. Think of *Vermont Recipes* as a detailed cookbook for a magnificent banquet, and enjoy the many other excellent Cocoa programming books that have appeared recently as side dishes and desserts, as your appetite dictates.

The emphasis here is on code. *Vermont Recipes* is not a tutorial on the finer points of Apple's development tools for Cocoa—Interface Builder and Project Builder— although the steps necessary to create an application are detailed with more than enough particularity to get you through the job. Nor does it begin by explaining all of the niceties of Objective-C syntax. Instead, it offers discussions of important features of the language, such as categories and protocols, in the Cocoa context, as they are encountered in the developing application. It is an ordered collection of do-it-yourself recipes—commented and organized code snippets, with instructions—to guide you through the process of creating classes and subclasses, objects, outlets, and actions, until you have built a fully functional Cocoa application.

Vermont Recipes is a cookbook, but it isn't the kitchen sink. The Cocoa frameworks contain over 220 classes, and this book makes no attempt to show you how to use all of them. What it does do is show you how the most important of them can be used to create a complete, working application with user controls of many kinds and other common application features. It also attempts to teach you, by example and explanation, most of the more general concepts and techniques that are used in Cocoa and Objective-C programming. In combination, what you will learn from this book should take you a long way toward an enhanced level of understanding, so that you will find it much easier to master other Cocoa classes on your own.

There is no one right way to design or code a Cocoa application. *Vermont Recipes* takes an approach that works, that is relatively easy to learn, that is consistent and therefore easy to maintain and enhance, and that is sufficiently general to adapt easily to a variety of scenarios. It conforms to conventional Cocoa practices and nomenclature. The application you will build here is a *document-based application* using Cocoa's Application Kit and Foundation frameworks, which gives it the flexibility and power to serve as a model for the widest variety of applications. Using the AppKit gives you a large part of the normal, expected functionality of any Mac OS X application "for free," without requiring any coding on your part. Conforming to the conventions of the AppKit also guarantees that you will have the greatest freedom to add Cocoa technologies to your application as they become available, with a minimum of rewriting.

An important advantage of *Vermont Recipes* stems from the fact that I began writing it while I was learning Cocoa—through careful study of Apple's initially sparse documentation and sample applications; online assistance from the NeXTstep, OpenStep, Rhapsody, and Cocoa developer community; and trial and error. It therefore covers ground that I know from personal experience would confuse and frustrate a Cocoa beginner if not spelled out in some detail. A Cocoa developer with long experience might take many issues for granted and therefore neglect to cover them.

At the same time, *Vermont Recipes* benefits from the years of experience of Scott Anguish and the Stepwise team, who graciously reviewed and commented on early versions of much of the code and text in its original incarnation on the Web. Be sure to visit the Stepwise site at www.stepwise.com for its wealth of Cocoa developer information. My thanks go to Scott and the team for helping to make this tutorial conform as closely as possible to established Cocoa techniques. Any errors are, of course, mine alone.

Vermont Recipes is written for Mac OS X version 10.2 Jaguar, released on August 24, 2002, and compatible subsequent versions. While most of the code in the book works with older versions of Mac OS X, code for the new features introduced in Jaguar requires version 10.2. If you aren't yet familiar with Mac OS X, read about it at www.apple.com/macosx.

To use *Vermont Recipes* to create the application that forms its basis, you must have the Mac OS X Developer Tools installed on your system. All Macs that ship with Mac OS X as the default operating system include them, at least in the form of disk images so you can install the Developer Tools yourself. They are also available for purchase from Apple as part of the retail Mac OS X product for older G3 and G4 Macs.

The recipes target people who have some programming experience but are Cocoa beginners. It assumes only a very modest grounding in the C programming language and at least a little familiarity with object-oriented programming concepts. Both of these can be gained by reading one or two of the many widely available introductory programming texts about C and object-oriented programming. No prior experience with Cocoa's predecessors, NeXTstep, OpenStep, and Rhapsody, is necessary, nor is any knowledge of Unix required. You don't need to know Java or C++, and some even say that knowledge of C++ is a hindrance.

Only a limited exposure to Objective-C is needed. Objective-C is nothing more than standard C with a few object-oriented extensions. Once you know C's commonly used features, you can learn the Objective-C extensions in a day or two. Having to learn a new programming language is not the obstacle to using Cocoa that some may perceive it to be.

If you already know a little C and something about object-oriented programming, the only preparation you need to undertake is this preliminary reading:

- *Inside Mac OS X: System Overview*, for essential background information on the architecture of Mac OS X. The Mac OS X Developer Tools CD includes it, and you can also browse it on the Web at http://developer.apple.com/techpubs/ macosx/Essentials/SystemOverview/index.html, download it there as a PDF file, or order it there as a book in print-on-demand form.

- *Inside Mac OS X: Object-Oriented Programming and the Objective-C Language*, Apple's Objective-C documentation. It's also part of the Developer Tools, and it is available on the Web as a PDF file at http://developer.apple.com/techpubs/ macosx/Cocoa/ObjectiveC/ObjC.pdf and as a print-on-demand book.

- Apple's developer tools documentation relating to Interface Builder and Project Builder. It is in Developer Tools and on the Web at http://developer.apple.com/tools.

After you have read these, you will be ready to start cooking with *Vermont Recipes*.

Why Cocoa?

Apple understandably emphasized Carbon development as it rolled out Mac OS X, to encourage rapid migration of existing applications from Mac OS 9 to Mac OS X. The Carbon application environment, while very complex, allows those with a long-standing investment in knowledge of the Mac OS toolbox to bring their applications to Mac OS X easily while maintaining compatibility with Mac OS 8 and 9. Apple's strategy has paid off, with virtually every major Macintosh application already available in native Mac OS X form.

But Apple has positioned Cocoa as what one might call the "real" Mac OS X of the future. The company has repeatedly urged developers of new Mac OS X applications to develop them using the Cocoa frameworks, and Apple's recommendation has grown stronger with the rollout of Mac OS X 10.0, 10.1, and now 10.2. These are mature and powerful application frameworks based on ten years or more of NeXTstep and OpenStep experience. They incorporate virtually all of Mac OS X's new functionality and the distinctive appearance of its Aqua interface. Furthermore, with Cocoa you can have it both ways: you can use the Carbon toolbox within a Cocoa application, so any feature that can be implemented in an application using Carbon can also be incorporated into a Cocoa application.

Experienced developers report that the Cocoa frameworks reduce development time by a very substantial factor. This is partly because the frameworks are so complete, giving you a vast amount of functionality without any effort on your part. Apple's Cocoa engineers are fond of demonstrating that you can build a reasonable text editor using the Cocoa frameworks—complete with multiple windows that have scrolling views, a working font panel, copy and paste, drag and drop, unlimited undo and redo, as-you-type spelling checks, and other useful features—all without having to write a single line of code yourself.

Another factor that makes Cocoa development so efficient is Cocoa's use of powerful design patterns not found in many other environments. For example, a number of the Cocoa classes employ the concept of *delegation,* where the system automatically triggers a call to a method of a delegate class when a significant event takes place, such as the user's attempting to close a window. You write the delegate method yourself, or you even decide not to implement it at all, which allows you to control whether and how your application should respond. These hooks, liberally sprinkled throughout the Cocoa frameworks, let you customize application behavior by performing additional actions or vetoing actions that the system proposes to take, depending on conditions that exist at run time. You do not have to subclass the built-in Cocoa AppKit classes to gain the benefit of these optional but powerful features. Many of the Cocoa classes also implement *notifications,* so that any class you write can learn of events as they occur elsewhere in the system and deal with them appropriately. It is vital that you learn these and other features of the 220-odd classes that make up the Cocoa frameworks. While they present a difficult learning curve, they facilitate an extraordinarily productive development experience.

The classes of the Cocoa frameworks fall into two groups, the Application Kit and Foundation. Foundation focuses on basic data types, system functionality, and other matters having nothing to do with the user interface. The AppKit concentrates on the user interface and other application features such as documents.

Many of the Foundation classes abstract the operating system, making it easy, for example, to deal with files and networking at a high level without losing access to any of the power of a lower-level approach. Others provide programming features that are always needed, such as object-oriented collection classes and data types. The NSString class, for example, is used throughout Cocoa to handle character-based data, bringing automatic support for Unicode text handling, for conversion to and from different text encodings, and for internationalization and localization.

The AppKit provides classes for implementing windows, all manner of user controls, menus, and all of the other features you need to provide a complete Aqua user interface. You can subclass all of these to create custom controls and other widgets, if you wish. The AppKit also provides fundamental classes that compose a fully integrated, document-based application, including NSApplication, NSDocument, and NSWindowController, about which you will learn much in *Vermont Recipes*.

In short, it is faster and easier to develop new applications in Cocoa, and you don't lose any power or flexibility.

Many key applications supplied with Mac OS X itself, such as System Preferences, TextEdit, Mail, Project Builder, and iPhoto, are written in Cocoa. So are many powerful, complex third-party applications, including OmniWeb, from the Omni Group, and Create, part of Stone Studio. Increasingly, existing Unix applications are also being ported because of the ease with which a Cocoa-based user interface can be added to a Unix application. With a little help from *Vermont Recipes,* you will be able to add your own application to the list much more quickly than if you first set out to learn the intricate details of Carbon.

Why Objective-C?

You can use Java and even AppleScript for Cocoa development, but most Cocoa developers seem to prefer Objective-C.

Java is not, any more than Objective-C, an answer for those who need to develop desktop applications in a cross-platform environment, because the Cocoa frameworks are not at this time officially cross-platform. Furthermore, while Apple is working hard to improve its performance, knowledgeable developers continue to express concern about Java's speed and memory requirements in a desktop environment. Finally, some features of Objective-C that are heavily used in the Cocoa frameworks are not readily reproduced in Java. Apple is nevertheless doing a good job of implementing most of Objective-C's unique features in Java, and it has marketed Cocoa as a powerful Java platform. Java may be an attractive language for Cocoa development, especially for those who already know the language, and especially if they are developing Web applications with the Java-based WebObjects 5.

Vermont Recipes is based solely on Objective-C. Objective-C is a surprisingly easy language to learn if you already know C, because it is in fact standard C with a small number of object-oriented additions. Choosing to develop Cocoa applications in Objective-C may therefore be motivated by nothing more than the wish, for C programmers, to avoid the substantial investment of time required to learn a fundamentally new language like Java.

There are more substantial reasons to use Objective-C, however. Objective-C's dynamic object-oriented extensions to standard C are flexible and powerful, making it possible to design applications in ways that are difficult or impossible using more traditional static programming languages such as C++. *Dynamic* means, among other things, that Objective C objects are bound at run time under the control of your code, so you don't have to anticipate the details of a user's actions and lock your responses into the application at compile time. It also means that you are able to inquire at run time about the capabilities of any Objective-C class (for example, whether it implements a particular method). You can do such things as assign method selectors to variables and hand them around at run time for execution in response to current conditions.

Developers learning Objective-C often report that they have experienced a magical "Aha!" moment, when their understanding of the language gels and wide new horizons of possibility suddenly become visible.

Naming Conventions

Vermont Recipes follows the naming conventions of Objective-C as they have grown up around NeXTstep and its successors. Some of these conventions—particularly the naming of accessor methods—are actually required to take advantage of built-in features of the Cocoa development and run-time environments. Others are work habits that have become more or less generally accepted in the Objective-C and Cocoa communities because they make it easier to read other developers' code. The following are the most common rules.

- Give a method that gets the value of a variable the same name as the variable it accesses. For example, method `myName` gets the value of variable `myName`.

- Give a method that sets the value of a variable a name beginning with *set* followed by the name of the variable with an initial capital letter. For example, method `setMyName:` sets the value of variable `myName`.

- Start method and instance variable names with a lowercase letter; for example, `init`.

- Start class, category, and protocol names with an uppercase letter; for example, `MyDocument`.

- Prefix class names, exported or global variable names, notification names, and defined types with two or three distinctive letters to avoid contaminating the global name space and running into naming conflicts with other software. For example, use `VR` for the Vermont Recipes application. Apple uses `NS` for most of the Cocoa classes, `WO` for WebObjects classes, `AB` for the new Address Book classes in Mac OS X 10.2, and `DR` for the new Disc Recording classes.

Apple informally reserves to itself the use of a leading underscore character (_) when naming private methods and exported functions. If developers were also to use this naming convention, they would risk unknowingly overriding private methods in Apple's frameworks, with unfortunate consequences. Apple also uses the leading underscore for private instance variables, but the compiler will probably catch instance variable naming conflicts in your code.

Newcomers to Objective-C should also be aware of the correct way to identify a method. An Objective-C method can only be uniquely identified and accurately distinguished from similarly named methods if its name, all of its parameter labels, and the colons that separate them are included (some methods take no parameters, so they have no colon). Collectively, these compose the method's name, or *signature*. For example, the `-isPartialStringValid:newEditingString:errorDescription:` method is different from the `-isPartialStringValid:proposedSelectedRange:-`

`originalString:originalSelectedRange:errorDescription:` method. It would be incorrect and misleading to refer to either of these as the `isPartialStringValid` method. This is not only an authoring guideline but a feature of the language. You will often find yourself using a method's signature in your code in ways that are not common in other programming languages, and your code will malfunction if you do not heed this advice.

A leading minus sign (-) or plus sign (+) before a method name to distinguish instance and class methods is not required when invoking a method in code, but it is part of a method's declaration and definition. It is often omitted in writing about methods, and I will omit it here.

While on the subject of naming conventions, what about the proper capitalization of NeXT and NeXTstep? Yes, the official name of the company where Cocoa's lineage got its start was NeXT Computer, Inc., and the official name of the product was NeXTstep. Although NeXT, and now Apple, registered trademarks in these names as shown here, it also claimed trademarks in the more ordinary forms Next and NextStep. You see either form, and others, in common use today.

Interface Builder and Project Builder

Cocoa applications are usually written and built using Apple's developer tools, Interface Builder and Project Builder, although a third-party tool, Metrowerks's popular CodeWarrior, can now be used in place of Project Builder.

A Cocoa beginner may perceive Interface Builder to be nothing more than a convenient interactive graphical user interface (GUI) design utility and Project Builder to be the tool for building an application. This perception would be inaccurate, but in *Vermont Recipes* you will nevertheless learn to start the application development process by using Project Builder to create a new project and to write its code. Interface Builder will mainly be used as a utility to design and build the GUI, but not to generate significant amounts of code. Interface Builder's Read Files command will periodically be used to update the internals of the Interface Builder nib files whenever outlets and actions have been added, deleted, or modified in the source code. But Interface Builder's Create Files command will rarely be used to generate code, and then generally only for prototyping the initial elements of a new class.

Greater integration of these tools in Mac OS X 10.1 and 10.2 does allow you to use Interface Builder more heavily than in prior versions, however, not just to design and build the user interface but also to generate and update the code for classes, outlets, actions, and other items automatically. If you choose Classes > Create Files in Interface Builder when your project already contains source code in the designated file, Interface Builder will launch the FileMerge application, which presents a superb interface allowing you to merge changes selectively without overwriting your existing code.

You will discover that the nib files Interface Builder generates are an integral and necessary part of a Cocoa application. A nib file describes an application's user interface more comprehensively than a simple design tool would. Interface Builder allows you, for example, to use intuitive graphical techniques to tell your code which user controls are connected to specific instance variables, or *outlets,* and which methods, or *actions,* in your code are triggered by specific user controls.

A nib file is not a collection of layout templates or generated code to be compiled along with your application code, as is the case with many interface design tools for other development systems. It is, in fact, an archived set of classes, instantiated objects, and connections that a Cocoa application loads, unarchives, and runs. In this way, Interface Builder allows you to write code in Project Builder that is more completely divorced from a specific user interface, and therefore more portable and adaptable to new interfaces. You can use Interface Builder, for example, to alter the user interface of a compiled application even if you don't have access to its source code, and conversely to prototype and test a user interface without compiling an application.

I have not found an official explanation of what the *nib* in the term *nib file* stands for. It is, of course, the file extension used to identify Interface Builder files, but what does it mean? Even the original *NeXTstep Concepts* book for version 1.0 of NeXTstep, published in 1990, refers to these files only as *interface files* or ".nib" files. Veterans of those days report that nib stands for NeXT Interface Builder.

One final note about these developer tools: Both Interface Builder and Project Builder are undergoing rapid change. Features that were temporarily dropped to facilitate porting them to Mac OS X are being added back in, and new features are being added with every release of the Developer Tools. Even the terminology used in these tools is changing. It is therefore very likely that passages in this book describing how to work with Interface Builder In Mac OS X 10.2 will grow increasingly out of date as time goes by. Reading the *Release Notes* for each new version of the tools is important to keep up with these changes.

The Vermont Recipes
Application Specification

Because the target audience of *Vermont Recipes* is a diverse group of programmers who plan to pursue a wide variety of projects, the subject of the book is a generic application implementing all of the features typically found in many applications and utilities. These include multiple documents and windows, many kinds of user controls, menus, tabbed views, and drawers, as well as standard Macintosh techniques such as drag-and-drop editing. It will not be a focused, topical application designed to serve any particular purpose, such as a music notation tool or a checkbook balancing program. Instead, it will serve simply as a showcase for common user interface devices, demonstrating not only how to build them but also how they work when completed. In this way, I hope that programmers will find information here that they can profitably use in their own applications, even though the Vermont Recipes application itself won't actually *do* anything at all.

The application is therefore specified, in broad strokes, as follows: It allows multiple documents to be open simultaneously. Each document can be saved separately with its own settings using a common file format. Each document is represented by a standard main window containing several tabbed views showcasing various categories of user controls, with an additional slide-out drawer for still more controls. Each document will also allow an additional, ancillary window to be opened, to provide a large, scrollable space for typing text. The application will incorporate additional features, such as a Help system. In short, if you're planning to create a multidocument, multi-window application, the Vermont Recipes application will provide a usable model for your own work.

You will elaborate this specification from time to time as you incorporate specific features into the application.

You, too, can tell the world your product runs on Mac OS X! The artwork, licensing requirements, and guidelines for use of the "Built for Mac OS X" badge are available on the ADC Software Licensing Web site at http://developer. apple.com/mkt/swl/agreements.html#macosx. Note that this badge cannot be used for products that launch the Classic environment.

Mac and the Mac Logo are trademarks of Apple Computer, Inc., registered in the U.S. and other countries. The "Built for Mac OS X" graphic and the Mac Badge are trademarks of Apple Computer, Inc., used under license.

Installing the Downloadable Project Files

You can download the Vermont Recipes application project's source files from the Web to follow along with the book, if you prefer not to type all the code yourself. The URL for the download is http://graphics.stepwise.com/Articles/VermontRecipes/VermontRecipesProj.dmg. Declarations and definitions in the source files are annotated with references to the Recipes and Steps of the book that describe them. If you are a nonlinear thinker, you can start with the source files and look up the explanations in the book.

To use the project files, you must have the Mac OS X Developer Tools. All Macs that ship with Mac OS X as the default operating system include them. The Developer Tools are also included with the retail version of Mac OS X.

The download of the Vermont Recipes application project files comes in the form of a standard Macintosh disk image file. After downloading it, you will find a file in your download folder or on the desktop named VermontRecipesProj.dmg. If it does not mount automatically as a virtual disk and open, double-click the image file to mount it and double-click the mounted disk icon to open it. Then drag the Vermont Recipes folder that it contains to the place where you keep your development files (for example, in your home Documents folder).

To mount the disk image, you may have to drag the image file to the Mac OS X version of Disk Copy, if this is the first time you have used that utility. If you double-click the image file instead, the Mac OS 9 version of Disk Copy in the Classic environment may open it, and then it may refuse to install. You'll find the Mac OS X version of Disk Copy in your /Applications/Utilities folder. Once the image is mounted, you will see it either on your desktop or by clicking the Computer toolbar button in any Finder window.

You can also download the completed application and run it on your computer to see all the features that are covered in the book. The URL is http://graphics.stepwise.com/Articles/VermontRecipes/VermontRecipesApp.dmg.

About the Author

Bill Cheeseman is a retired Boston lawyer of some notoriety (did you read or see *A Civil Action*?) now living in Quechee, Vermont. He first experienced the joy of computing when, in 1964, his Harvard roommate was programming the PDP-1 at the Cambridge Electron Accelerator in Fortran, and they played the original Space War daily for a year. He began writing programs himself in the mid-1970s, first on the HP-25 programmable calculator, followed by the HP-41C. As a member of the national HP-41C users group, he wrote the first compiler of undocumented HP-41C commands. He subsequently programmed extensively in AppleSoft Basic, UCSD Pascal, Modula-2 and 6502 assembler on the original Apple][and the Apple //e; Business Basic and UCSD Pascal on the Apple ///; and a wide variety of languages, including Basic, Pascal, Object Pascal, Modula-2, C, and C++, on a long succession of Macintosh computers. He is well known in the AppleScript community as Webmaster of The AppleScript Sourcebook (www.AppleScriptSourcebook.com), and in the Cocoa community as the author of these *Vermont Recipes* (www.stepwise.com/Articles/VermontRecipes). Having retired from the practice of law at the end of 1999, he is now beginning the new millennium with a second career, programming full-time in Objective-C in the Cocoa environment of Mac OS X.

Building an Application

Vermont Recipes *is based upon a single application, used throughout the book to provide a consistent and familiar foundation for all of the Cocoa features I will discuss. As you proceed through the recipes and explore Cocoa's myriad capabilities, adding new features to the application a step at a time, you will never be in any doubt regarding the underpinnings of a particular task, because you will have built them yourself. By following the linear path traced in the recipes, you will see how to assemble a working, feature-complete application from start to finish. Once you have made it all the way through* Vermont Recipes, *you will be able to follow a similar process to build a complete application to your own specification.*

In Section 1, you will build the skeleton of the application to the point where it has almost everything a typical application requires, but it won't have any meat on its bones. It will have a menu bar with all of the standard menus and menu items; an About window; the ability to create, save, and reopen documents and to revert to the last saved version of a document; windows with working tab view items; unlimited undo and redo; and double-clickable application and document icons. But it will have only one simple user control and one data item that you can save, just enough to give you a hint of the riches to come. Now would be a good time to review the Vermont Recipes *application specification in the introduction, to remind yourself of what it is you are about to build.*

The skeleton of the application is created in a single long recipe, composed of many steps. In it, you will become familiar with the basic operation of the tools used for Cocoa development, Project Builder and Interface Builder.

A Multidocument, Multiwindow Application

In the first recipe, you will start by creating a new project in Project Builder, setting up the initial source files, nib files, and other resources, as well as the correct folder structure for your project. You will then turn to Interface Builder to begin laying out the basic features of the application's graphical user interface (GUI) and even generating a little code. Finally, you will return to Project Builder to write code that will complete the implementation of your initial user interface and begin implementing the application's substantive functions. When you have completed Recipe 1, you will have a working Cocoa application, complete with its own icons, which you can double-click in the Finder; an About window; support for multiple documents and their windows; a tabbed view with user controls; unlimited undo and redo; and the ability to save, open, and revert documents.

The Vermont Recipes application is a document-based application relying on the Cocoa Application Kit. Like most Cocoa document-based applications, it adopts the Model-View-Controller (MVC) paradigm, which originated in the Smalltalk-80 language from which the Objective-C extensions to C were derived. This is mainstream Cocoa application design, embodying the approach recommended by Apple for typical Cocoa applications and accounting for much of the simplicity and efficiency of Cocoa development.

If you haven't done so already, read about MVC and the Cocoa application architecture generally in the Program Design topic under Programming Topics in Apple's Cocoa Developer Documentation, available on your computer under Cocoa Help in the Project Builder Help menu. You can find the most recent version of this important document on the Cocoa Developer Documentation Web site at http:// developer.apple.com/techpubs/macosx/Cocoa/CocoaTopics.html.

The Model-View-Controller Paradigm

In the MVC paradigm, the *model* is where the application's data resides, including behaviors and logic relating directly to the data. It is typically represented in a Cocoa application by one or more model objects, usually designed to be as independent as possible of all other aspects of the application. In particular, the code for the model should be completely independent of the user interface, not depending in any way on knowledge of how any item of data in the model is represented onscreen. The NSDocument class, which you will subclass for the Vermont Recipes application, usually serves to manage these model objects and should not normally be thought of as a model itself. The Cocoa frameworks, particularly NSDocument, already do much of the work of managing your model objects for you, such as providing the underpinnings of multiple undo and redo. They enable you to focus on writing the code that implements the application's unique data structures and logic.

The *view* is where the GUI lives. Most classes in the Cocoa AppKit are view classes, and they do most of the work of drawing and manipulating windows, panels, and user controls for you. You will add views to the application using Interface Builder, which requires relatively little coding in Project Builder. What little code you might write for the views will be independent of the model's data structures, having no knowledge of how the data represented by a view is structured or where it exists.

The *controller* acts as an intermediary between the model and the view, allowing the application to maintain a complete separation between the data and the user interface. It is typically represented in Cocoa by the NSWindowController class, which you will subclass for Vermont Recipes and instantiate once for each window that the user opens. The application's views tell the window controller that the user has done something—such as clicking a control—generally by sending an action message to the window controller. The window controller in turn tells the model to adjust its data accordingly. Likewise, when the model's data is modified—for example, by an AppleScript command or the user's choosing the Undo or Redo menu item—the model notifies the window controller, which in turn tells the affected views to update their visual state. The controller is where you must do most of your coding, since the interaction between the application's data and its user interface is complex and unique and cannot be anticipated in the Cocoa frameworks. You can write a simple Cocoa application without subclassing NSWindowController, but the greater complexity of Vermont Recipes, as with most Cocoa applications, requires that you customize it.

There can be many kinds of controllers in a Cocoa application, and they aren't always identified by the term *controller* in the class name. For example, you can think of NSDocument as a controller responsible for managing a document's model objects. Another that you will encounter in your reading is the built-in NSDocumentController class, which, among other things, manages some aspects of a document's relationship with the file system. Don't let naming issues confuse you, but focus instead on the role the Cocoa classes play in the overall structure of an application.

Designing your application in conformity with the MVC paradigm will pay big dividends. You should not think of it as a gimmick that you can safely ignore. Cocoa—particularly in the AppKit's document-based application classes—is designed on the assumption that you will conform to the MVC paradigm, and it makes capabilities available to you that are easy to implement only if you have followed the rules. For example, if you meet Cocoa's MVC expectations, multiple undo and redo support will become part of your application with little effort on your part. Similarly, adding AppleScript support to your application will be much easier if you follow the MVC paradigm.

Don't treat the MVC paradigm as a straitjacket, though. A simple application, for example, can combine its data with document management in a single subclass of NSDocument. Similarly, a graphics application can often usefully combine aspects of the model and the view in a single object, since a graphics object should know how to draw itself. It is essentially both model and view at once.

Documentation

PBOverview, a "welcome" note on your computer at /Developer/Documentation/ReleaseNotes/PBOverview.html, is a brief introduction to Project Builder and related tools. It serves as a simple road map for other Project Builder documentation.

For general information about Project Builder and other developer tools, read *Developer Tools Overview* at /Developer/Documentation/DeveloperTools/DevToolsOverview.html. A convenient road map for all of the developer tools appears at /Developer/Documentation/DeveloperTools/devtools.html.

With the release of the most recent versions of Mac OS X, the best place to learn how to use Project Builder in detail is the *Inside Mac OS X* volume, *Project Builder Help*. It is found in PDF form on your computer at /Developer/Documentation/DeveloperTools/ProjectBuilder/ProjectBuilder.pdf and in HTML form from the Help menu in Project Builder. This document explains the use of just about every window, pane, and control in Project Builder, including overviews of how to set up build phases, how to use the debugger facilities, and how the CVS version-control system works.

The Project Builder *Release Notes*, available from the Help menu in Project Builder itself, are useful sources of new as well as older information about changes to Project Builder. The most recent *Release Notes* are must-read documents every time Apple releases a new version of Project Builder. Examples with which to practice your skills are described on your computer at /Developer/Documentation/DeveloperTools/ProjectBuilder. Later, you will want to read *Project Builder Build Settings* at /Developer/Documentation/ReleaseNotes/PBBuildSettings.html and the other debugging information detailed in Step 10 below, but for now it is far too advanced to be of much use to you.

For the latest versions of any of these documents, check on the Web at http://developer.apple.com/techpubs.

For an even fuller understanding of Project Builder, it is still worth reading the old *Tools & Techniques Book*, if you can find it. Its detailed, step-by-step instructions on the use of Project Builder remain useful if you want to get the most out of the application. It is a legacy document from the days of NeXTstep and OpenStep and therefore doesn't reflect Project Builder's current features in every respect. It is no longer installed with Developer Tools in Mac OS X 10.2.

Step 1: Create the Project Using Project Builder

Project Builder, commonly referred to as PB, is the core of the Mac OS X Integrated Development Environment (IDE) supplied by Apple for building Cocoa and other applications. Through it, you access the code editor, the debugger, the compiler, the linker, and other tools.

Typically, the first step in developing a Cocoa application is to set up the project files. Let's get to work.

1. Launch Project Builder. A window with tabs and panes opens. You will find it useful to enlarge this window as much as possible on your screen. Although Project Builder 2 allows you to turn this one window into multiple windows to help you focus on specific tasks, you should leave it in the default configuration while you are learning how to use Project Builder.

2. Choose File > New Project. The New Project Assistant opens, listing many templates with which you can start to develop an application, bundle, or framework using the Cocoa frameworks with Objective-C, Java, or AppleScript. If you prefer, you can use a Carbon application template or any of several templates to build a kernel extension, plug-in, or tool.

3. In the New Project Assistant, click the Cocoa Document-based Application template under the Application heading to select it. The Next button is enabled (**Figure 1.1**).

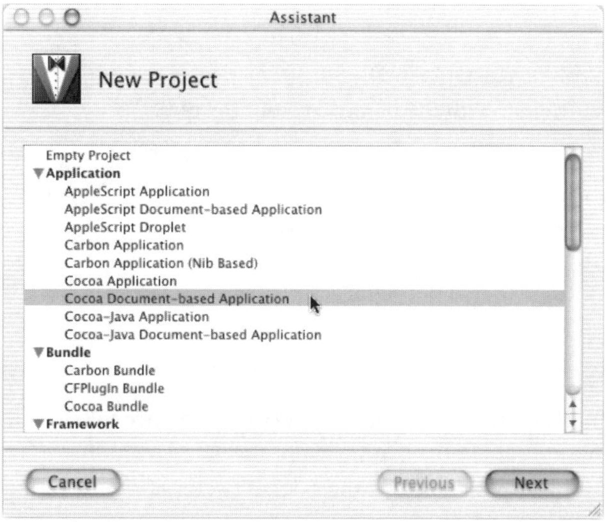

FIGURE 1.1 Using Project Builder's New Project Assistant.

4. Click Next. The next panel of the New Project Assistant appears. Here you can name the project and specify its location. The current user's home directory is provided as the default location.

5. Type **Vermont Recipes** in the Project Name text field. This will be the name of your new project folder.

6. Click Choose to set the new project folder's location, which you may find easier than typing its path. A sheet is presented in which you can navigate to any folder. Select the folder where you keep development projects (your home folder will be preselected, but your Documents folder may be more appropriate), and click Choose. The sheet closes and the Finish button in the New Project Assistant is enabled (**Figure 1.2**).

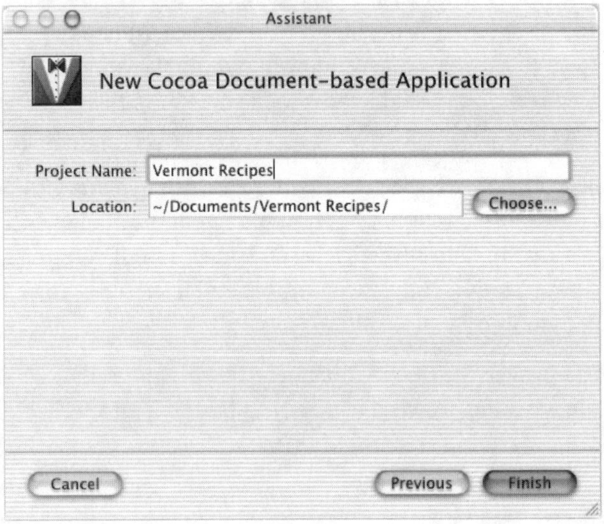

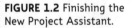

FIGURE 1.2 Finishing the New Project Assistant.

7. Click Finish. The New Project Assistant closes and, after a pause, the project window opens in Project Builder with the name Vermont Recipes.

8. Select the Files tab, if it isn't already selected, to open the Groups & Files pane at the left side of the project window, then click the disclosure triangle next to the Classes folder icon to expand it. You see that the Classes group holds two source files, MyDocument.h and MyDocument.m. Drag the border between the left and right panes to the right to see the full filenames, if necessary. Project Builder created these files for you. They are templates containing code to get you started on your new Cocoa document-based application.

9. To see the text of the template header file, click MyDocument.h once to select it. The text of the header file appears in the main pane of the project window, if you've left your Project Builder preferences at their default values (**Figure 1.3**).

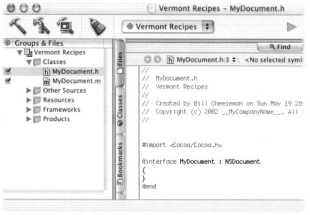

FIGURE 1.3 The MyDocument.h template in a project window.

10. To see the text of the template source file, double-click MyDocument.m. The text of the source file appears in a new editing window. Opening separate windows by double-clicking the filename allows you to view multiple files side by side and to drag text between them (**Figure 1.4**). Close the MyDocument.m window for now.

FIGURE 1.4 The MyDocument.m template in an editing window.

11. Click the disclosure triangle next to the Resources group folder icon to see that it contains several items, including one called MyDocument.nib. MyDocument.nib is the nib file you will work with in Interface Builder in Step 2 of this recipe to design your application's main document window. The other nib file, MainMenu.nib, is the application's main nib file, containing its menu bar with standard menus and menu items. Both nib files are provided as part of the Cocoa Document-based Application template.

12. Click the other disclosure triangles to see what they contain. The main.m file in the Other Sources group contains a standard C main function, which you will rarely need to modify for a Cocoa application. The Frameworks group contains links to the Cocoa umbrella framework and to the Foundation and AppKit frameworks; you may add other frameworks here if your application requires them. The Products group is where your built application will reside, if you've left your Project Builder preferences at their default values (**Figure 1.5**).

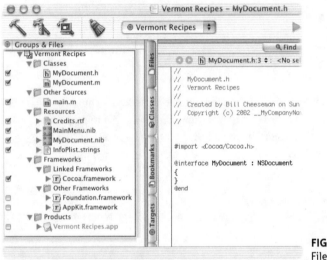

FIGURE 1.5 The Groups & Files pane fully expanded.

13. Bring the Finder to the front and open the Vermont Recipes folder, wherever you created it, to examine its contents. What you see is the standard folder structure created by the Cocoa Document-based Application template. In addition to the two MyDocument files and the main.m file, you see an English.lproj folder where nib files and other localized information are kept. Depending on your preference settings, you may see other language folders as well. You also see a build folder, where Project Builder normally stores intermediate and final build products, including your finished, executable application. Finally, you see the project file itself, Vermont Recipes.pbproj. This is actually a bundle; you can examine its constituent parts by holding down the Control key and, from the contextual menu, choosing Show Package Contents (**Figure 1.6**).

Notice that the folder structure in the Finder bears no relationship to the group structure in the Groups & Files pane of the project window. You can reorganize the Groups & Files pane in any way you find convenient, without moving any of the files or folders in the Finder.

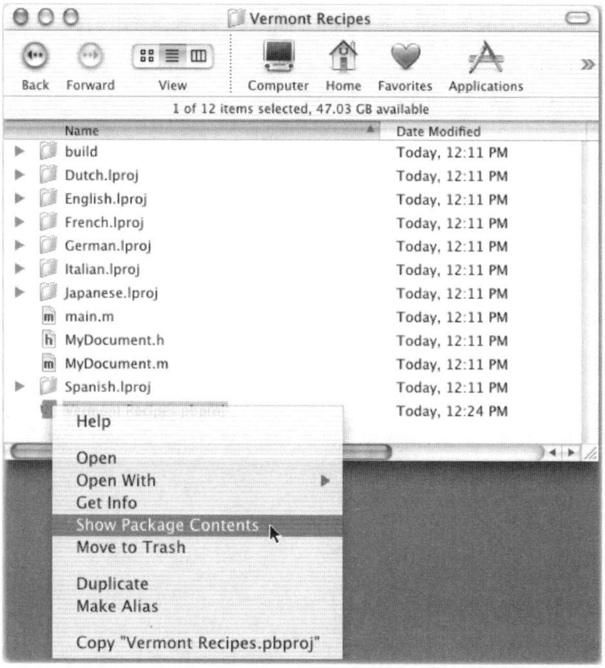

FIGURE 1.6 The Vermont Recipes project folder in the Finder.

14. MyDocument is a rather mundane and commonplace class name. It would be more fitting to brand this class with initials relating to the name of your application bundle. Consistently with the naming convention for classes described in the introduction, use the initials VR (for Vermont Recipes) instead of My. Click the file MyDocument.h in the Groups & Files pane and choose Project > Rename to select its text for editing. You must use a menu command to enable editing of group and filenames in the left pane of the project window because, as you learned in Instruction 10, above, double-clicking opens the file in a new window. Type **VRDocument.h** to change its name, then repeat the process with MyDocument.m and MyDocument.nib, naming them **VRDocument.m** and **VRDocument.nib**, respectively.

You will defer further setup of the project for now and turn directly to interface design.

Step 2: Design and Build the GUI Using Interface Builder

The name of the Interface Builder application, commonly referred to as IB, suggests that it is a tool for designing and building a GUI. It's all that, and more. In the course of designing the GUI for the Vermont Recipes application, you will see that the nib file created by Interface Builder contains a significant amount of information that the application will use at run time. Unlike many GUI design utilities, which generate uncompiled code, and unlike ResEdit, used in Mac OS 9 and earlier to create layout templates, Interface Builder allows you to create classes and objects, as well as connections between them and their methods, and to archive them for loading directly into your application at run time.

You can examine some of the information contained in a nib file now, although you haven't yet launched Interface Builder. Launch Property List Editor in /Developer/Applications, choose File > Open, and open the classes.nib component of the VRDocument.nib bundle, which is in the English.lproj subfolder of the project folder. You see an expandable outline showing the Cocoa classes and related information already known to the nib file simply from setting up the project files. If you look deep enough, you will see a reference to the MyDocument class, although you renamed it in Step 1; you will update this reference to VRDocument later. You will add more information to the nib file in Step 2, but much of the information in a finished Cocoa nib file will be in the form of archived Cocoa classes that Property List Editor can't read (**Figure 1.7**).

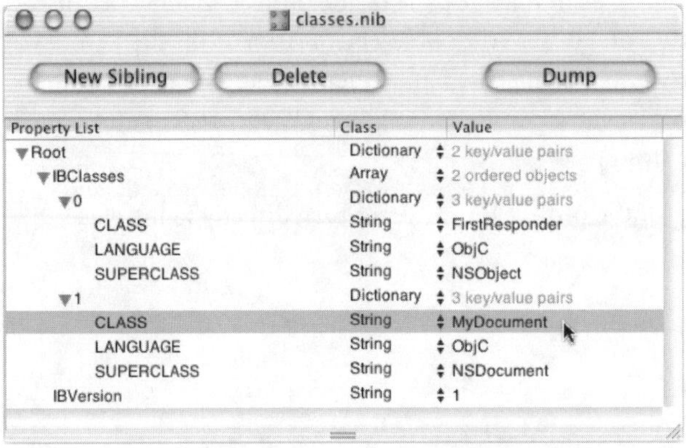

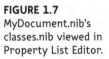

FIGURE 1.7
MyDocument.nib's classes.nib viewed in Property List Editor.

Documentation

The best place to begin reading about Interface Builder is in its Help files, FAQ, and *Release Notes*, all available directly from Interface Builder's Help menu.

You'll find several example projects for practicing your skills on your computer at /Developer/Examples/InterfaceBuilder. Most of them are about designing Interface Builder palettes or using Interface Builder for Carbon applications, but the SimpleMultiWindow example is an important Cocoa example. Another example project is described at /Developer/Documentation/DeveloperTools/InterfaceBuilder/Converter.pdf.

The old *Tools & Techniques Book* contains detailed step-by-step instructions for using Interface Builder that are still valuable, though out of date. It is no longer installed as part of the Developer Tools on Mac OS X 10.2, so you may have difficulty finding it.

When you reach the point of writing code for the application, you will discover one reason why the nib file's internal information is important. Many seemingly essential items are omitted from the Project Builder source files. For example, you will declare some instance variables in code, referring to user control objects, yet you will write no code telling the application which user controls the instance variables point to. Similarly, you will implement some methods in code, telling the application what actions to take when particular user controls have been clicked, yet you will write no code telling the application which action methods specific controls should invoke. In addition, often you will not write code to set the default values of user controls.

Interface Builder's nib files, which the application will open at an appropriate time, supply the omitted items. As you design the GUI for the application, you create outlets and actions and connect them to appropriate objects using Interface Builder. *Outlets* are instance variables declared in code that you can connect to objects in the nib file—you use Interface Builder to draw a connection from an object containing an outlet to the associated user control, then specify which of the object's instance variables to connect. *Actions* are action methods you implement in code. Again, you use Interface Builder to draw a connection from a user control to the target object that implements the control's action method, then specify which of the target's action methods is to be invoked when the user clicks that control. Cocoa will automatically invoke the correct method at run time whenever the user clicks the control, with little or no further coding on your part. You will also use Interface Builder to set the default values and attributes of many user controls.

As you use Interface Builder to create these outlets, actions, connections, defaults, and attributes, the information is stored in the nib file. The nib file is an integral part of the application, and the information in it is used at run time to pull everything together.

Outlets and Actions

You will see in Step 2 that Interface Builder relies to some extent on an electrical metaphor. Objects have outlets, and you plug other objects into them by stringing wires between objects that have outlets and the objects to be plugged into them. Interface Builder even uses a little electric outlet symbol to identify outlets.

In programmer's terms, an outlet is an instance variable declared in a class header. Typically, a document class or a window controller class, for example, declares numerous outlets identifying other objects with which it needs to communicate, including not only user controls but any kind of object. The outlet is simply a pointer to the object.

In Step 2.6.1, you will see how you can also wire user interface objects with a sort of control circuit, connecting each user control object to a specific action method in a target object, to be invoked when the user control is turned on or off. This implements the target-action design pattern, which lies at the heart of Cocoa. Typically, a user control is connected to an action method implemented in a window controller object.

In this way, Interface Builder allows you to divorce your user interface code from your substantive code to a much greater extent than is true of other programming environments. One of Interface Builder's functions is to let your application know at run time what is connected to what, so you don't have to lock this information into your code at compile time. Interface Builder does much more than its name suggests.

2.1 Create the Main Document Window

It will be convenient to design and build the essential elements of the user interface for the application's main document window next. To start, you must create the window and connect its wiring.

2.1.1 Open the main document window's nib file.

In Project Builder, expand the Resources folder in the Groups & Files pane of the project window and double-click VRDocument.nib. Interface Builder launches and opens the nib file. Alternatively, you can launch Interface Builder and use it to open the nib file.

Two windows and a palette appear. The nib file window is in the lower-left corner of your screen, entitled VRDocument.nib. It initially contains the File's Owner, First Responder, and Window icons. The main document window is in the center of your screen. Initially called Window, it contains a string reading "Your document contents here." The Cocoa Palette window is in the upper-right corner of your screen. From it, you will drag various user controls to the VRDocument.nib window and to the main document window when you begin designing it. The Palette window is hidden whenever you bring another application to the front.

The Info Panel, formerly known as the Inspector, appears when you choose Tools > Show Info. Its content changes when you select different items in the nib file window or the main document window. You use the Info Panel for many purposes, including to set a user control's default properties or attributes and to select targets for a variety of connections. Like the Palette window, it is hidden whenever you bring another application to the front. You can change Interface Builder's preferences so the Info Panel opens automatically when the application is launched. This is so convenient that you should do this now.

2.1.2 *Examine the default nib file.*

Explore the default instances and classes that have been set up for you. The full meaning of what you find will become clear later.

1. Select the main document window by clicking its title bar, then choose Tools > Show Info if you haven't already done so. In the NSWindow Info Panel, use the pop-up menu at the top to select the Connections pane, if necessary, and click the **delegate** connection at the bottom. A line appears, extending from the main document window's title bar to the File's Owner icon in the VRDocument.nib window (**Figure 1.8**). This indicates that the Window object delegates some of its functionality to your VRDocument.nib file's owner. You don't yet know what object is the file's owner, but you will learn in a moment. Delegation is an important Cocoa concept that you will learn more about later.

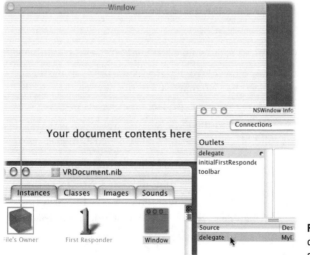

FIGURE 1.8 File's Owner delegate connection shown in Interface Builder.

2. Click the File's Owner icon in the VRDocument.nib window. The line disappears and the Info Panel automatically becomes the File's Owner Info Panel. You never have to close the Info Panel and reopen it to see information about another object; it is a chameleon that constantly changes its colors to match its surroundings.

3. Click the `window` connection in the connections area at the bottom of the Connections pane of the File's Owner Info Panel. A line appears, extending from the File's Owner icon to the main document window's title bar. This indicates that the default file's owner in your project—you still don't know what object it represents—has an outlet, or instance variable, named window, and that it points to an NSWindow object named Window.

4. Choose Custom Class in the pop-up menu at the top of the File's Owner Info Panel. A list of all available classes appears, with MyDocument selected near the top. This indicates that the file's owner of VRDocument.nib is a class called MyDocument. Obviously, the nib file isn't yet aware that you renamed the class VRDocument in Step 1; you will set this straight a little later, in Step 2.4.

Step 2.5 will explain the concept of a nib *file's owner* in Cocoa in some detail. For now, think of it simply as the object that will load the nib file at run time. In this case, when a new document is created while the application is running, the document will load this nib file to obtain the document's main window.

5. Select the Classes tab in the VRDocument.nib window. A list of all available classes appears. Most of them are dimmed, indicating that they are built-in Cocoa classes that you cannot edit.

You can toggle this list between a columnar format and an outline format by clicking the leftmost button above the list. The Column View was new in Mac OS X 10.1.

6. Scroll down until the NSDocument class comes into view, if necessary, and click the disclosure triangle in Outline View to expand it or click the class name in Column View to select it. Beneath the class name or in the next column to the right, you see MyDocument. This is the same MyDocument class you encountered in the File's Owner Info Panel a moment ago, when you learned that it is the file's owner. Its name is solid black, indicating that it is a custom class you can edit (**Figure 1.9**).

A shortcut to find a class in the Classes pane is to double-click the class's icon in the Instances pane of the main Interface Builder window. Try it: Select the Instances tab and double-click the File's Owner icon. The window automatically switches back to the Classes pane and shows the MyDocument class selected.

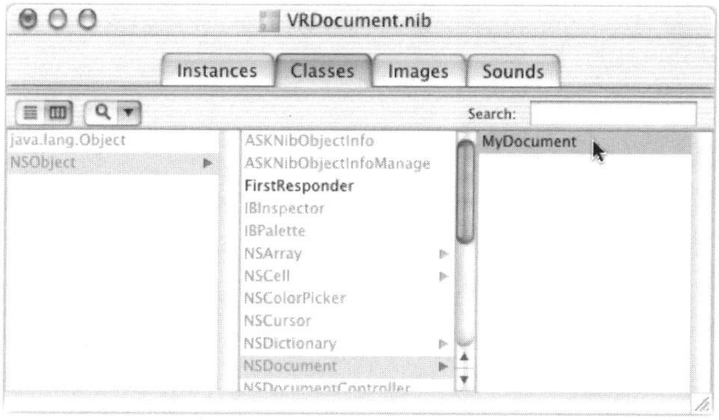

FIGURE 1.9 The VRDocument.nib window showing the columnar view in the Classes pane.

7. Select the Instances tab in the VRDocument.nib window. The absence of a VRDocument icon in the Instances pane indicates that no object of the custom VRDocument class has been instantiated. This is as it should be, because you want documents to be instantiated only at certain times—when, for example, the user chooses File > New or File > Open while the application is running. For now, just remember that opening the Classes tab is the way you can examine classes known to your nib file even though they have not been instantiated.

To visit the final stop in your introductory Interface Builder tour, look at the little button that appears at the top of the vertical scroll bar in the VRDocument.nib window when the Instances pane is showing. This may look like two buttons, but, like the button that toggles between columnar and outline format, it is a single button that toggles the Instances pane between Icon mode and Outline mode. Click it to switch to Outline mode. You see an expandable outline listing the three objects whose icons you saw in Icon mode.

Click the disclosure triangle to the left of the NSWindow (Window) entry. It expands to show you the NSView (Content View) that every window contains. Expand the Content View, and you see the one NSTextField object currently visible in the document's main window, together with the field's contents ("Your document contents here"). Later, after you add more user controls, you will see them in the expanded outline as well.

Next, click one of the wedges enabled in the right pane of the VRDocument.nib window. Lines appear, showing all of the incoming and outgoing outlets related to that object. You will find this view very useful during Cocoa development, because it lets you see at a glance all of the connections among interface objects in your application (**Figure 1.10**).

Return now to the Icon mode of the window's Instances pane.

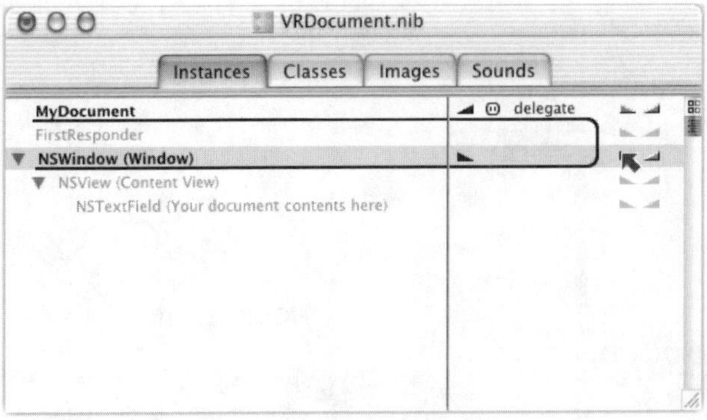

FIGURE 1.10 The VRDocument.nib window showing connections in the Instances pane.

2.1.3 *Create a window with a drawer.*

The Vermont Recipes application specification tells you that the application's main document windows will have a drawer. To meet this requirement, you must alter VRDocument.nib so that it implements a window with a drawer, rather than the simple window provided by the Cocoa Document-based Application template. For the time being, you will leave the original window object in the nib file to remind you of its connections, some of which might have to be duplicated in the new window object you will now create. You will not actually work with the drawer until Recipe 16, but you can avoid a lot of extra work at that time if you set the stage for it now.

If you plan to build an application based on Vermont Recipes but using a simple document window without drawers, just skip the instructions here that relate to creating a window with drawers. Everything in Vermont Recipes relating to the parent window will work the same way in a simple window.

To implement a window with a drawer, you will for the first time use the Cocoa Palette window. The Palette window has a standard Mac OS X toolbar at the top, with a number of icons you can use to display individual palettes containing various categories of user interface objects. It has a pane at the bottom to display the objects in any one palette. By default, the toolbar shows icons only.

Unless you are quite familiar with Interface Builder, you will find it helpful to add text labels to the icons in the toolbar. Choose Tools > Palettes > Customize Toolbar, and use the Show pop-up menu at the bottom of the sheet that is presented to choose Icon & Text. After you click Done to close the sheet, you will see a textual label that supplements the toolbar icons. It is important that you display the icons' text labels, because I will refer to them by name hereafter. (I can't refer to them by position, because their positions can be changed by dragging and by adding and deleting palettes.)

1. In the toolbar at the top of the Palette window, click the Windows icon to show the Cocoa Windows palette. If the Palette window has been resized to make it very narrow or if additional panes have been added to it, you may find Windows in the overflow menu at the right end of the toolbar.

If you haven't displayed text labels and are in doubt about which icon represents the palette you want, just hold the mouse pointer over an icon for a moment. A Help tag appears, displaying its name. Then you can move the mouse pointer from icon to icon without pausing to see the Help tag for each in turn. Help tags also identify the class of individual items in the Palette window (**Figure 1.11**).

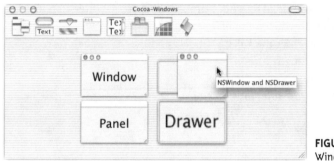

FIGURE 1.11 The Cocoa Windows palette.

2. Drag the icon representing a window with an open drawer (the NSWindow and NSDrawer icon) and drop it into the VRDocument.nib nib file window (don't use the icon labeled Drawer; it's for adding additional drawers to an existing window). Three new icons appear in the nib file window: an NSDrawer icon, a DrawContentView icon, and a Parent Window icon (**Figure 1.12**). A new, empty window entitled Window and a new window entitled DrawContentView also appear on the desktop. Drawers do not have title bars in a running application; the title bar you see on the DrawContentView window is only an Interface Builder convenience to let you move it around on the screen. DrawContentView is short for Drawer Content View; the term has nothing to do with drawing.

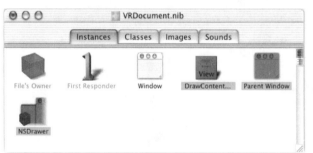

FIGURE 1.12 The VRDocument.nib window after adding a window and drawer.

You could have added a drawer to the existing main document window by dragging the Drawer icon and a custom view object to the document window, but you would have had to create all the required connections yourself. Using the composite window and drawer object from the Cocoa Windows palette gives you all the required connections prewired, as you will see in a moment.

3. You can determine which window is associated with which icon in the VRDocument.nib window by double-clicking an icon to bring its associated window to the front. Bring the parent window to the front by double-clicking the Parent Window icon. Notice that it doesn't come with a "Your document contents here" text field.

4. The window is a little too small for your purposes, so drag the lower-right corner to make it about an inch wider and taller. If necessary, drag the window to the left to pull it out from under the Palette window and the Info Panel. You can resize and reposition it at any time.

2.1.4 Examine the modified nib file.

Explore the new objects you just created.

1. Click the NSDrawer icon to select it. In the NSDrawer Info Panel's Connections pane, you see that two outlets, `contentView` and `parentWindow`, are already connected, the former to an NSView object and the latter to an NSWindow object.

2. Click the `contentView` connection in the connections area at the bottom of the NSDrawer Info Panel. A line appears, extending from the NSDrawer icon to the DrawContentView icon in the VRDocument.nib window. This indicates that it is the content area to which the outlet is connected (**Figure 1.13**).

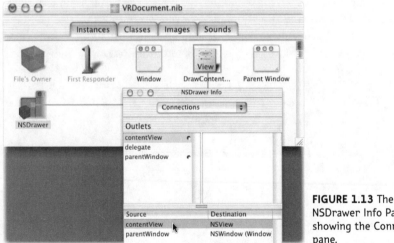

FIGURE 1.13 The NSDrawer Info Panel showing the Connections pane.

3. Click the `parentWindow` outlet connection in the NSDrawer Info Panel. A line appears, extending from the NSDrawer icon to the title bar of the parent window. This outlet will enable the drawer to talk to its parent window.

4. The DrawContentView and Parent Window icons have no connections at this point, although they do have outlets. You saw above that the original window had a connection from its delegate outlet to the MyDocument class, but you will not duplicate that connection in the parent window because you will create a different delegate connection in Step 2.6.3.

2.1.5 Set the new window's attributes.

Whenever you're creating a new object in Interface Builder, it is important to examine the Attributes pane of the object's Info Panel to determine whether any of the default attributes need to be changed.

The documentation does not always adequately assist you in understanding what behaviors the listed attributes control. Eventually, Help tags will likely be added to Interface Builder to provide some information. In the meantime, you must figure it out for yourself. In most cases, the wording alone makes the use of an attribute obvious. In other cases, the wording is downright misleading. In case of doubt, the best course is to examine the class reference document and look for a method with a similar name, then read up on what it does. It is generally, but not always, the case that a setting in the Attributes pane is simply a convenient way to set an instance variable's value or to provide a return value for a method, saving you the trouble of doing it explicitly in your code. If you are stuck, it is a good idea to read the legacy OpenStep *Tools & Techniques* book, if you can find it. It provides more details on the many attributes that have survived from earlier days.

Let's examine a mistake I made in early versions of the Vermont Recipes application, to see what light it may shed on the importance of understanding these attributes.

To be consistent with the *Aqua Human Interface Guidelines,* the latest version of which is available at http://developer.apple.com/techpubs/macosx/Essentials/AquaHIGuidelines, a new, untitled window should open when the application is launched and, of course, whenever the user opens a new document. An untitled window should also open when the application is already running and a user brings it to the front, for example, by clicking its icon in the Dock, unless a window owned by the application is already open (minimized or not). Knowing this, I wanted to make sure I took care of this detail at the outset.

Clicking the new Parent Window icon in the VRDocument.nib window to select it, then selecting the Attributes pane of the NSWindow Info Panel from the pop-up menu at the top, I saw the "Visible at launch time" checkbox in the Options area (**Figure 1.14**). From its wording, I concluded that Interface Builder gives us a choice in the matter. It was not checked by default, however, which seemed odd in light of the *Guidelines.* In retrospect, I should have recognized this as a clue that this attribute does not control the behavior in which I was interested, because Interface Builder generally does a good job of enforcing the *Guidelines*. However, I took the description, "Visible at launch time," as a pretty obvious reference to the requirement to open a new window when the application launches. I therefore selected this setting in Interface Builder.

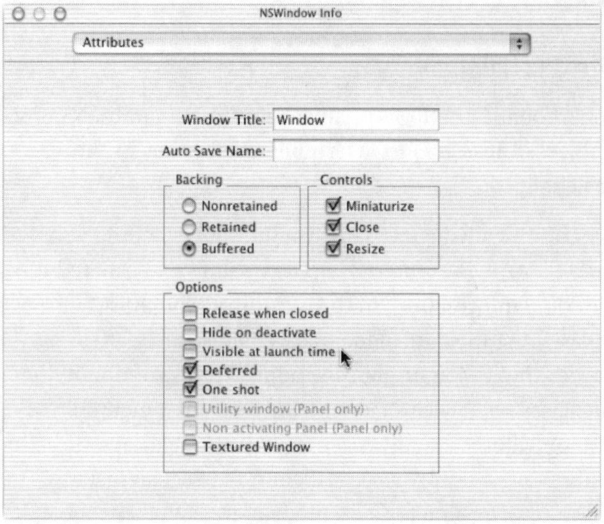

FIGURE 1.14 The NSWindow Info Panel showing default attribute settings.

I was simply wrong. I now know that this Interface Builder attribute does not control whether a new, untitled window opens when an AppKit-based application launches. That behavior is controlled instead by the return value of a delegate method in NSApplication, aptly called `applicationShouldOpenUntitledFile:`, which defaults to opening a new document when the application is launched, as one would expect. The "Visible at launch time" setting in the NSWindow Info Panel controls a different aspect of window behavior: namely, whether a window becomes visible as soon as its nib file is loaded, instead of at some later time. It defaults to unchecked because applications usually don't want new windows to become visible until they have had an opportunity to update the appearance of the controls they contain, which may not be fully defined in the nib file.

How did I figure this out? After a lot of research into the Cocoa documentation, I finally found it in the legacy OpenStep document, *Tools & Techniques,* confirming the ongoing value of this ancient document. It says on page 47, "The window should appear when the nib file is loaded." However, my research was too thorough, and I also found an even older legacy document, the NeXTstep 3.3 Interface Builder manual, on the Web at www.channelu.com/NeXT/NeXTStep/3.3/nd. It says, "The window should appear when the application is launched." These two statements are inconsistent, so I consulted the research tool of last resort, the Cocoa developer mailing lists. There, I learned from Apple engineers that the more recent OpenStep *Tools & Techniques* book is correct. I was told that "after the nib file is loaded into memory and all of the connections have been established, the windows in the nib file that have the 'Visible at launch time' flag turned on are ordered front." A more accurate name for the attribute would therefore be "Visible at nib load time."

I also found an old NeXTstep version of the Currency Converter tutorial, which contains a remark that likely explains why the modern Currency Converter tutorial recommends turning on this option. This is apparently a leftover from the days when leaving it off could cause a noticeable delay in the window's appearing onscreen. This is no longer an issue for modern hardware, so you can safely leave this option off unless you are confident that your nib file fully defines the state of a window.

Now that I understand it, my advice is to leave this attribute in its default unchecked state for the Vermont Recipes application. Cocoa will automatically make the window visible a little later, after the application has had a chance to update its interface. For a window that has complex, code-controlled content, turning this setting on in Interface Builder risks allowing the user to see the contents of a window in the process of updating under some circumstances (see Step 4.3 for more information). You would prefer to present them all at once, fully configured, for a more polished appearance.

In general, Interface Builder's Info Panel gives you a lot of control over initial attribute settings without requiring that you set them explicitly in code. For example, you should now uncheck the Resize control setting in the Attributes pane, because the main document window will be designed to have a fixed, unchangeable size. You can leave other settings as they are. If you don't understand them, now you know where to look.

The Attributes pane is not the only pane to examine in the Info Panel of a new object. If you switch to the Size pane of the NSWindow Info Panel, for example, you see that you can set the initial size and location of the window, minimum and maximum size constraints, and how controls within the window respond to resizing the window. You will explore the Size attributes in Recipe 16, Step 2, when you configure the drawer.

2.1.6 Connect the new window to the nib file's owner.

You must change the connection between the file's owner and its window object, because it is currently a connection to the original simple window created by the Cocoa Document-based Application template. You will soon discard this simple window.

1. Click the File's Owner icon to select it, then choose the Connections pane of the File's Owner Info Panel from the pop-up menu at the top. The Connections pane for the window opens.

2. Click the window connection in the connections area at the bottom of the File's Owner Info Panel. You see, as before, that its `window` outlet is connected to the title bar of the original window. The Disconnect button is enabled.

3. Click Disconnect. The connection is broken.

4. Hold down Control and drag from the File's Owner icon to the Parent Window icon in the VRDocument.nib window. A line is drawn from the File's Owner icon to the Parent Window icon as you drag. When you release the mouse button, the `window` outlet in the connections area of the File's Owner Info Panel is selected and the Connect button is enabled.

5. Click Connect. The new connection appears in the connections area at the bottom of the File's Owner Info Panel. To verify it, you can click in a blank area of the VRDocument.nib window to make the line disappear, if necessary, then click the File's Owner icon again and click the new connection in the File's Owner Info Panel. This time, a line appears from the File's Owner icon to the title bar of the window associated with the Parent Window icon.

2.1.7 *Delete the original, default window.*

Now you can delete the original window object provided by the Cocoa Document-based Application template. Click the Window icon (not the Parent Window icon) in the VRDocument.nib window to select it, then choose Edit > Delete or press Delete. The Window icon and the original main document window disappear. No confirmation dialog is presented to let you cancel this action, but you can undo it by choosing Edit > Undo Delete if you made a mistake.

2.1.8 *Save the nib file.*

Save your work in the nib file by choosing File > Save.

If you look now in the English.lproj subfolder of your project folder, you will see not only the VRDocument.nib file but also a VRDocument~.nib file. The latter is a backup file that Interface Builder automatically creates. You can reset a preference item in Interface Builder Preferences if you don't want backup files. (In versions of Mac OS X older than 10.1, the tilde [~] appeared at the end of the .nib extension. To use such a backup file in Mac OS X 10.1 and up, you must move the tilde immediately before the dot, or to the end of the file name if you are hiding file extensions.)

In the next step, you will insert some text, a tab view, and a checkbox user control into the parent window and set them up.

2.2 Add a Tab View and User Controls to the Main Document Window

The Vermont Recipes application specification tells you that the application's main document window will contain a tab view to permit the user to switch among multiple panes within the one window. The window also needs several controls to let the user edit the document's settings and data. In this step, you will create some static text in the upper-left corner of the main document window to identify the document; a tab view with two tabs filling most of the rest of the window; and a single user control, a checkbox, in the second pane. In Recipe 2, you will add additional tabbed panes and user controls using the same techniques.

Start where you left off at the end of Step 2.1. Launch Interface Builder and open VRDocument.nib, if necessary.

2.2.1 *Bring the main document window to the front.*

In the VRDocument.nib window, double-click the Parent Window icon. The empty document window associated with the Parent Window icon comes to the front.

Tab Views

Tab views have become a common element of Macintosh user-interface design. They are particularly suitable in Mac OS X, because it places increased emphasis on minimizing the multiwindow desktop clutter characteristic of Mac OS 9 and earlier. Tab views offer an intuitive and efficient way to increase the amount of information that a single window can usefully contain.

It is somewhat easier to include a tab view at the outset, before you put a lot of user controls in the window, than it is to add one later and then move existing controls into it. You will therefore start by creating a tab view here. You will discover that using a tab view adds almost no complexity to a Cocoa application's code, because the built-in NSTabView and NSTabViewItem Cocoa classes do almost all of the work. In fact, the application's code would be almost identical in an application free of tab views. This is but one example of the many application features you get at almost no cost when you use the Cocoa frameworks.

Part of the reason for this is that a Cocoa document window without a tab view is not without any view at all. In fact, every window has an implicit view to hold its contents. That implicit content view performs many of the functions that an explicit tab view or other view performs, particularly with respect to embedded user controls.

2.2.2 *Add static text to the window.*

The main document window needs some static text to tell the user what it is.

1. In the toolbar of the Palette window, select the Views icon. The Cocoa Views palette appears in the bottom pane.

2. Drag the System Font Text NSTextField item (it was Message Text in older versions of Interface Builder) from the Palette window and drop it in the upper-left corner of the empty main document window. As you drag it over the window, a focus ring appears around the window's content area, showing you that the area will accept the drop. When you drag the icon near the upper-left corner, vertical and horizontal guides appear. Drop it while the guides are visible to ensure that it is placed in accordance with the *Aqua Human Interface Guidelines.* This is an ordinary NSTextField view, with its font and font size preset to comply with the *Guidelines* for message text in sheets and dialogs. It is suitable as is for the use you will make of it here. Selection knobs surround it, indicating that the NSTextField object is selected and can be resized or dragged to a new position.

3. You must edit the text field's content. If the text field has become deselected because you clicked outside it after dropping it in the window, reselect the text for editing by double-clicking to highlight it. Type `Vermont Recipes, My First Cocoa Application` over the selected text. The text field does not expand to accommodate the new contents as you type. Drag one of the selection knobs on the right to enlarge it.

    Suppose you now decide the name is too trite. Select the text for editing again, if necessary, add the word `The` at the beginning, and delete everything after Vermont Recipes. The field does not contract after you delete the text. You can resize the field again manually by dragging any of its knobs while the field (not its text) is selected.

    As an alternative to resizing a user control by dragging its selection handles, you can resize it to precisely contain its content by choosing Layout > Size to Fit while either the field or the content is selected. Do this now, after changing the control's size for testing purposes. You see the border and handles demarking the object move until they just fit around the text. Click in an empty area of the window to deselect the NSTextField object.

4. If you inadvertently repositioned the text field while resizing it, reselect the field (not its content) and drag it to the vicinity of its final location near the upper-left corner of the window. You can click and drag in one motion. Leave room above it for another text field, which you will add shortly.

5. Next, examine its attributes. While the NSTextField object is selected, click the NSTextField Info Panel to bring it to the front, then choose the Attributes pane using the pop-up menu at the top. Make sure the Editable and Selectable checkboxes in the Options area are deselected, since this is intended to be static text that should not be changed by the user and there is no need to allow the user to select and copy it.

Using the techniques you just learned, drag the Small System Font Text (formerly Informational Text) item in the Cocoa Views palette to create another static text field immediately above the first, and edit it to read `Cocoa Recipes for Mac OS X`. Drag as necessary to position it in the top-left corner of the window, above The Vermont Recipes, relying on the horizontal and vertical guides for its exact position. Then reposition The Vermont Recipes immediately below it, using the vertical guide to align the left ends of the two text fields the proper distance from the left edge of the window. You should normally use the spacing recommended by the horizontal guide that appears as you drag The Vermont Recipes up under the upper text field, but these two lines are closely related and I find they look better when they are squeezed a little closer together.

If you prefer to center The Vermont Recipes beneath the upper text field, select the upper text field, Shift-click the lower text field to add it to the selection, and choose Layout > Alignment > Align Vertical Centers. Don't forget to select the Attributes pane of the NSTextField Info Panel while the lower text field alone is selected, then change its attributes to the same settings you just used for the first text field.

2.2.3 *Add a tab view to the window.*

Next, you will install a tab view in the main document window.

If you plan to adapt Vermont Recipes to an application that does not utilize tab views, just skip the instructions that relate to tab views. Almost everything else in Vermont Recipes will remain applicable, without change.

1. In the toolbar of the Palette window, select the Containers icon. The Cocoa Containers palette appears in the bottom pane.

2. Drag the NSTabView item from the Palette window and drop it in the main document window immediately below the two static text fields you just added. Use the guides to align it horizontally with the left end of the topmost static text item and vertically the correct distance below the bottommost static text item (**Figure 1.15**). Resize the tab view by dragging its bottom-right selection knob almost to the bottom and right edges of the window. Guides appear to help you place it. Beginning with Mac OS X 10.2, you can place the tabs on any of the four edges of the tab view, but here you use the default, the top edge.

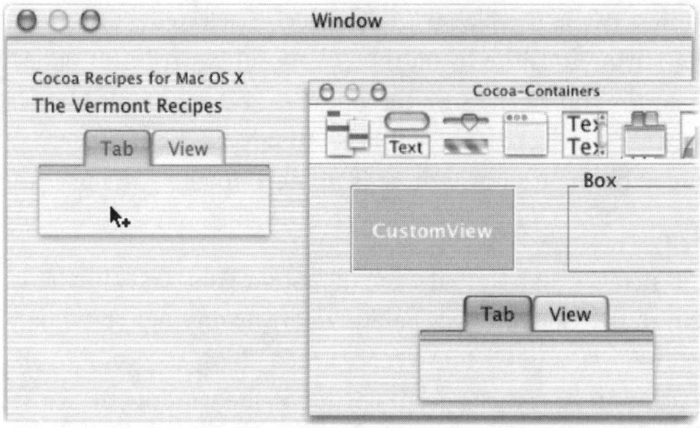

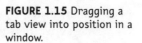

FIGURE 1.15 Dragging a tab view into position in a window.

3. There are currently two tabs on the tab view, each representing a separate pane, or tab view item, within the tab view. Neither tab has the title you want. To change the text of a tab's title, start by double-clicking anywhere in the tab view to select the tab view item that has a highlighted tab. A border appears around the tab view, indicating that the tab view item, as opposed to the tab view, is selected. Then double-click the text in the first or leftmost tab to create a text entry area where you can type its title. Type **Text Boxes**. Then deselect the text entry area by pressing Return or Enter or by clicking outside the tab view. The tab widens automatically to fit the text.

4. Using the technique you just learned, type **Buttons** on the second tab. Leave the Buttons tab highlighted for Step 2.2.4.

`2.2.4` *Add a checkbox to the window.*

Assume the application specification requires that the main document window contain a checkbox user control. In Interface Builder, a checkbox is referred to as a Switch, but *Vermont Recipes* will refer to it as a checkbox control except when referring to its icon in the Interface Builder Palette window.

1. In the toolbar of the Palette window, select the Views icon. The Cocoa Views palette appears in the bottom pane.

2. Drag the Switch NSButton item from the Cocoa Views palette and move it over the tab view area in the main document window. Keep holding down the button while you drag the item over various parts of the window and observe what happens. As you drag the item over the window, a focus ring surrounds the window's content area. As you drag farther over the tab view area, a focus ring surrounds the tab view content area. As you drag up and pause over the tab that is not highlighted, it becomes highlighted. Using this behavior, you can drop the item in the desired tab view item without having to select it in advance.

This behavior was new in Mac OS X 10.1. In older versions, it was necessary to select the target tab view item in advance with a series of clicks and double-clicks. Now, when you drag an icon from the Palette window over a container, whether or not you've selected it, Interface Builder automatically places a focus ring around the deepest container under the mouse, and that container will accept the drop.

3. Drop the item into the second, or rightmost, tab view item, after ensuring that it is selected by pausing over the Buttons tab until it highlights. A border appears around the entire tab view area, indicating that Interface Builder has automatically selected the Buttons tab view item as you performed the drop. Place the control near the upper-left corner of the tab view item, where the guides indicate.

4. Select the control so you can edit its label. If you can't see it because the wrong tab view item is currently selected, you can toggle back and forth between the tab view items by pressing Tab and Shift-Tab or the left and right arrow keys. You can also use the stepper control at the top of the Attributes pane of the NSTabViewItem Info Panel. Try all of these techniques now just to see how they work.

5. Instead of using the double-click technique you learned previously to select and edit the label of a control, you can, if you prefer, use the NSButton Info Panel. While the control is selected, select the NSButton Info Panel to bring it to the front. In the Attributes pane, edit the Title (Switch) to read **Checkbox**. When you tab or click outside of the Title field or press the Return or Enter key, the label of the checkbox in the main document window changes to Checkbox. You can use this technique to edit the label of most user controls. If the control does not enlarge automatically to show the new title in its entirety, choose Layout > Size to Fit while the control is selected.

6. Help tags, sometimes called tool tips, can be useful aids to users of your application. With the newly renamed checkbox control selected, select the Help pane of the NSButton Info Panel. In the Tool Tip box, type `Toggle checkbox` and press the Enter key. In a real application, of course, you would provide more useful information in the Help tag, or you might choose not to provide a Help tag at all if the control's use were obvious. You will provide additional forms of online help in Recipe 20.

2.2.5 Test the window.

You can test the document window at any time to make sure the controls are working. Choose File > Test Interface. The Interface Builder windows disappear, leaving only your document's main window, as if you were actually running the completed application. Click once in the main document window to make sure it is frontmost. Select the two tabs alternately to see that one and then the other pane appears, with the checkbox control visible only in the Buttons pane. Click the checkbox control in the Buttons pane repeatedly to see that a check mark appears and disappears. Leave the mouse pointer over the control for a moment to see that the Help tag appears (**Figure 1.16**). When you move the pointer away, the Help tag slowly fades away.

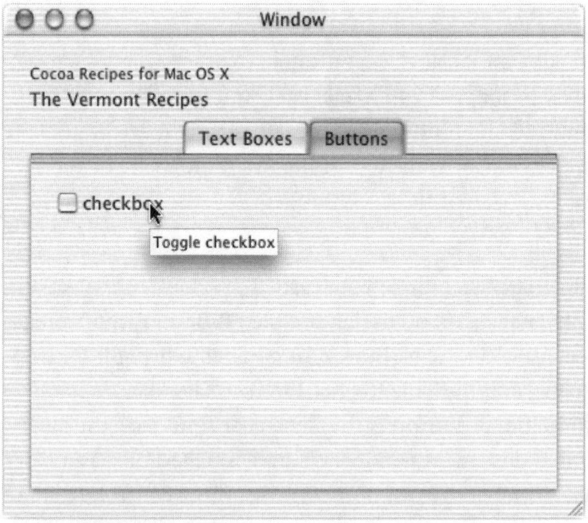

FIGURE 1.16 Testing the finished window with a checkbox control and a Help tag.

To return to editing mode, choose Interface Builder > Quit Interface Builder. Interface Builder does not quit but instead switches out of test mode, and the Interface Builder windows reappear for more editing.

2.2.6 Save the nib file.

Save your work in the nib file by choosing File > Save.

In the next step, you will use Interface Builder to create a window controller class that will act as an intermediary between the application's data and its user interface.

2.3 Create a Subclass of the Window Controller Class

You know from the Vermont Recipes application specification that this application will allow many documents to be open at once, each supporting more than one kind of window. In Vermont Recipes, each kind of window will have its own nib file archiving its unique set of user controls and connections, such as the main window you created in Step 2.1. You will also create a window controller for each kind of window—in other words, a window controller for each nib file.

Since these window controllers will perform many functions unique to the Vermont Recipes application, you should subclass NSWindowController in order to add custom functionality. You will do so once for each kind of window. In this step, you will create VRMainWindowController, an NSWindowController subclass for a Vermont Recipes document's main window.

The Window Controller Class

In a document-based Cocoa application using the MVC paradigm, the window controller class is especially important.

In a sense, the window controller is the least standardized of the MVC classes, because it must keep a unique set of models and views synchronized and tell them how to perform the unique functions of the application. In essence, a window controller manages a window on behalf of the document. A model class representing the application's data should know nothing about the GUI, and the view classes, such as windows, tab views, and user controls, should know nothing about the specific data they represent. You don't have to subclass NSWindowController for a very simple application, but in a typical document-based application you usually do.

Only the controller class knows how the model and the views interact. The document tells the controller when data has changed (perhaps the user has reverted to the document's saved state or chosen Undo or Redo from the Edit menu, or an AppleScript has altered some data), and the controller then tells the views to change their state to reflect the new data. Similarly, the views tell the controller when the user has changed the state of a user control (perhaps the user has clicked on a checkbox control), and the controller then tells the model to update its data stores accordingly. For these reasons, you will likely write much more custom code for the controller than for the model or the views.

(continues on next page)

The Window Controller Class *(continued)*

Modern computer science offers many reasons why an application's data and user interface should be factored out into separate classes in this fashion. It has mostly to do with keeping concepts clear and easing maintenance and upgrades.

But there are also specific reasons relating to the way the Macintosh works. In particular, the GUI is not the only interface of most Macintosh applications. There is also a scripting interface, for example. Using AppleScript, a user can command an application to alter its data without touching a user control. In doing so, AppleScript does not need to know anything about the GUI; it can communicate directly with the document's model objects, and it may do so without requiring that a window be open. By keeping the model separate from the views and relying on the controller to mediate between them, Cocoa's AppKit can give you AppleScript support almost for free. Just as the user's reverting a document to its saved state causes the model to tell the window controller to update any affected views, so does a script's alteration of the model's data invoke the same methods, with the same effect on the views.

Another important feature of a window controller is its role as a delegate of other classes. In the Cocoa environment, many classes perform their work by invoking *delegate methods,* which you as application designer can choose to implement in your subclasses. This is one of the abilities that allows Cocoa to provide so much precoded functionality while preserving the flexibility to let the application designer create unique applications. Your NSWindowController subclass is one class that plays an important role as a delegate in the Cocoa scheme of things, as you will see.

Documentation

Choose Cocoa Help from Project Builder's Help menu to browse the detailed class reference documentation provided with the Developer Tools, such as the "Document-Based Applications" section of the "Program Design" topic and the NSDocument and NSWindowController class reference documents.

The class reference documents provide detailed explanations of every method declared in each Cocoa class. Don't overlook the function, protocol, and other references near the bottom of the overall AppKit and Foundation tables of contents; they are important, but they aren't yet well integrated into the class reference documents. Also be sure to look at the bottom of individual class reference documents for the list of delegate methods that appear in some of them. For more concept- and task-oriented help, read the articles in the "Programming Topics" section. The latest versions of all of these are on the Web at http://developer.apple.com/techpubs/macosx/Cocoa/CocoaTopics.html.

In late 2001 and again in 2002, the Cocoa documentation was substantially rewritten and reorganized to make it more complete and bring it up to date. In the process, a lot of general conceptual and architectural material and task-oriented instructions were moved from key class reference documents into the *Programming Topics* documents. It is therefore advisable to read the appropriate *Programming Topics* document before turning to a class reference document for detailed information about the methods needed to carry out a particular task.

The class reference documents remain an extremely important source of information about the proper way to use the Cocoa classes. Along with the comments often included in the class header files, the class reference documents may be the only source of information available to guide you in designing and coding important features of a Cocoa application. You should not use any features of a Cocoa class without first becoming familiar with its class reference and in many cases its header file.

Remember also that Cocoa frameworks are object oriented, with many classes inheriting functionality from their superclasses. You must therefore read the superclasses' reference documents as well for a full understanding of what any one class can do. Links to the superclasses usually appear at the top of each class reference document. Overlooking these is a very common beginner error.

You'll also find the class reference documents on your computer in both HTML and PDF format. The actual location of a class reference is deep within the System Library's Frameworks folder. The current documentation for an AppKit class, for example, is located in the most recent subfolder of the Versions folder in AppKit.framework. You can be assured of reading the most recent version by opening the Current subfolder at the same level, which is actually a symbolic link to the most recent subfolder. Within the most recent subfolder, the header files are in the Headers folder and the class reference documents are located deep in the Resources folder, in the Documentation subfolder of the English.lproj folder.

A convenient shortcut to find the HTML and PDF versions of the class reference documents is this:

/Developer/Documentation/Cocoa/Reference/ApplicationKit/Obj-C_classic

This documentation is available to you directly in Project Builder while you are writing code. Read *Project Builder Help* for instructions.

In the /Developer/Documentation folder, you'll notice many other subfolders containing important documentation, and you shouldn't forget to look at the many developer examples provided in /Developer/Examples. Cocoa development involves a fair learning curve, but familiarity with the provided documentation will ease you through it quickly.

Start where you left off in Step 2.2. Launch Interface Builder and open VRDocument.nib, if necessary.

1. In the VRDocument.nib window, select the Classes tab. A list of all available classes appears. In Column View, you have to move the scroller at the bottom to see the class hierarchy spread out horizontally in multiple columns. In Outline View, you have to scroll up and down, expanding and collapsing outline items until you find the place in the class hierarchy where the item you're looking for is located.

2. Navigate into the NSResponder class hierarchy and click the NSWindowController class to select it. The line on which NSWindowController appears is highlighted.

3. Choose Classes > Subclass NSWindowController. A new subclass named MyWindowController appears on a new line, indented under NSWindowController or in the column to its right. Its text is solid black, not gray, to indicate that it is a custom class that you can edit, and it is selected.

4. Rename the MyWindowController subclass by double-clicking its name and typing `VRMainWindowController`. Press Return to commit the new name (**Figure 1.17**).

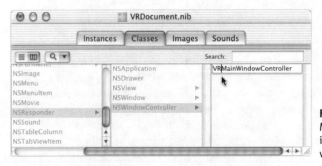

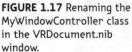

FIGURE 1.17 Renaming the MyWindowController class in the VRDocument.nib window.

5. At this point in the process of creating a new subclass in Interface Builder, it is possible to instantiate an object based on the new subclass by selecting it and choosing Classes > Instantiate VRMainWindowController. However, you should not instantiate the VRMainWindowController subclass at this time, because this is to be a multidocument, multiwindow application. You will want a new instance of the window controller to be created programmatically every time a new, empty document is created when the application is launched and again each time the user requests a new document at run time, because there is a one-to-one correspondence between a window and its controller. Later, in Step 3.3, you will write code so that your application can create window controller instances at appropriate times.

Interface Builder nevertheless needs to know about the class now, because when the time comes to define connections among VRMainWindowController, its main window, and its window's user controls, you must be able to include VRMainWindowController at one end of the connections you will draw. To do this, in Step 2.5 you will designate the VRMainWindowController subclass as the file's owner of the VRDocument.nib file, enabling you to draw connections to and from the File's Owner icon. The File's Owner icon in Interface Builder is a sort of proxy or stand-in for a class that is not instantiated in the nib file but programmatically, allowing you to use Interface Builder to create connections between that class and other objects.

6. Save your work in the nib file by choosing File > Save.

In the next step, you will use Interface Builder to examine your nib file's document subclass and finish renaming it VRDocument.

2.4 Finish Renaming the Existing Subclass of the Document Class

The user's work in your application's document windows must eventually be saved to nonvolatile, or persistent, storage, such as a hard disk, so that it can be recovered and used at a later time or by other users. The live data that is maintained in an application's internal data structures in RAM while a user is editing a document window is saved to storage in a specific file format periodically and when the associated document is closed. The word *document* generally refers to both the file on disk and its live data representation in RAM. Document in this sense is not to be confused with the NSDocument class, which is normally a controller rather than a repository of data in a Cocoa document-based application.

A subclass of Cocoa's NSDocument class is required in a document-based application. A new instance of the subclass will be created whenever the user creates a new document or opens an existing document from storage. The required document subclass was automatically provided to you in the Cocoa Document-based Application template files MyDocument.h and MyDocument.m, which you renamed VRDocument.h and VRDocument.m in Project Builder in Step 1. The VRDocument class must have a corresponding entry in VRDocument.nib so that appropriate outlets can be connected to it using Interface Builder.

In this step, you will take a closer look at its representation in the nib file and you will rename it VRDocument to correspond to the name of the source files.

The Document Class

Every document-based Cocoa application must subclass NSDocument. As mentioned in Step 2.3, the document subclass controls the application's data model. It is considered a controller class in the MVC paradigm. You must subclass NSDocument, among other reasons, to provide access to data variables in model objects that hold your document's data, to provide accessor methods that enable other objects to get and set the data values, and to tell the window controller when the data has changed so the user interface can be updated. Your document subclass usually does all this by controlling other model objects that you create and link to the document. The document is also the primary entry point for scripting.

Cocoa also has an NSDocumentController class, but it is almost never necessary to subclass it. NSDocumentController handles document behaviors relating to the file system that are common to all document-based applications, such as opening documents when needed and reporting on various properties of the application. When customization of NSDocumentController is required, it is usually preferable to use an application delegate.

Start where you left off in Step 2.3. Launch Interface Builder and open VRDocument.nib, if necessary.

1. In the VRDocument.nib window, select the Classes tab. The view of all available classes you worked with in the previous step appears.

2. Scroll down or across the Classes list, in Outline or Column View, until you find the NSDocument class, and you will see indented under it or listed to its right the MyDocument subclass.

   The hierarchical relationship between NSDocument and MyDocument revealed in Outline or Column mode shows you graphically that MyDocument is a subclass of NSDocument. You already knew that MyDocument is a subclass of some other class, because it does not contain the NS prefix that identifies most built-in Cocoa classes. The declaration of the subclass in the VRDocument.h header file that you created using Project Builder in Step 1 specifically identifies NSDocument as its superclass.

   The original prefix for NeXTstep classes was NX. This was changed to NS, for NeXTstep, when the Foundation frameworks were made available, before the OpenStep protocols were released. It represents the core Cocoa frameworks, Foundation and AppKit. A prefix of some sort is recommended for all classes in publicly distributed frameworks, to minimize the chance of global name space collisions.

You should not instantiate the MyDocument class in Interface Builder, as you learned in Step 2.1, because a new instance of the document must be created each time the user requests a new document at run time in a multidocument application. Cocoa will create a connection between the new document and its associated window controller at that time, so that your window controller can talk to the document, for example, to set or get the data it controls.

3. Now you can rename the MyDocument class VRDocument in the nib file. Simply double-click MyDocument in the Classes pane to select it for editing and type **VRDocument** in its place. Press Return to commit the change (**Figure 1.18**). You will complete the process of changing the name of the class in the Project Builder source files shortly, in Step 3.3.

FIGURE 1.18 Renaming the MyDocument class in the VRDocument.nib window.

Normally, as you will learn later, it is better to use Interface Builder's Classes > Read Files menu item to inform the nib file about the Project Builder classes it uses. This is because the Read Files command reads not only the name of the class declared in the header file into the nib file but also all of its outlets and actions declared in the header file. However, you haven't yet declared any custom outlets or actions in VRDocument.h, so it is acceptable simply to rename the class in Interface Builder. It wouldn't do to read the header file into the nib file yet, anyway, because you haven't yet changed the name of the class as it is declared in the header file but have changed only the name of the file.

4. When you changed the class name to VRDocument in the nib file, you may have noticed that the Info Panel became the VRDocument Class Info Panel. Click VRDocument in the Classes pane of the VRDocument.nib window to select it now, if necessary, then examine the VRDocument Class Info Panel. The Info Panel contains two tab view items, one for Outlets and one for Actions, each containing a scrollable list. Examining these, you see that the VRDocument class currently has one outlet and no actions. The dimmed entry in the Outlets list indicates that the VRDocument class, which you know is the file's owner, declares a built-in outlet, **window**. This is the same window instance variable you encountered in the File's Owner Info Panel in Step 2.1, where you learned that it is connected to the NSWindow object.

5. Save your work in the nib file by choosing File > Save.

   You might find it comforting to reexamine the nib file in Property List Editor. Follow the instructions for using Property List Editor in Step 2.1. You will see that what the nib file originally thought was a MyDocument class is now your VRDocument class, due to the change you just made.

In the next step, you will use Interface Builder to designate a new file's owner for the nib file.

2.5 Designate a New File's Owner for the Nib File

VRDocument.nib needs a file's owner to take responsibility for loading the nib file into memory when a document is opened.

The Cocoa Document-based Application template gives you a nib file that makes a subclass of NSDocument the default owner of the nib file. This is because the template is designed for a simple application having only one kind of document represented in a single kind of window.

However, you should normally create multiple subclasses of NSWindowController in cases where a document will have multiple kinds of window, or where you need to customize the built-in behavior of NSWindowController. It is convenient to make a subclass of NSWindowController the owner of the document's nib file in such an application, to facilitate a one-to-one correspondence between the document's main window and its window controller. Later, when you create other kinds of windows for the document, each will be given its own nib file and another window controller subclass to manage it.

Start where you left off in Step 2.4. Launch Interface Builder and open VRDocument.nib, if necessary.

1. Click the File's Owner icon in the Instances pane of the VRDocument.nib window to select it. The File's Owner Info Panel appears.

2. Select the Custom Class pane of the File's Owner Info Panel. VRDocument is already selected as the default owner. Click VRMainWindowController, just below VRDocument in the list, to select VRMainWindowController as the new owner of VRDocument.nib (**Figure 1.19**).

   If you have gotten ahead of me and already created some connections to the old file's owner, an alert appears, warning you that this step will break existing connections. Click OK, because you want to break any existing connections between objects in VRDocument.nib and its old owner, VRDocument.

3. Save your work in the nib file by choosing File > Save.

In the next step, you will use Interface Builder to create outlets and actions and connect them to objects.

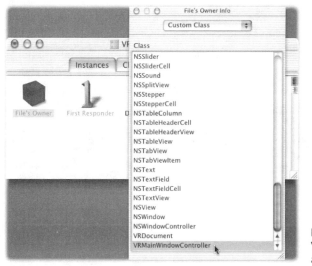

FIGURE 1.19 Designating VRMainWindowController as File's Owner.

File's Owner

The File's Owner icon in an Interface Builder nib file is a proxy for whatever object owns the nib file.

A proxy is used because the nib file's owner cannot be instantiated in the nib file. It's a chicken-and-egg problem. The application must be launched first; only then can it load the nib file. But for this to happen, an object that knows how to load the nib file must already exist in RAM inside the application. That object is the nib file's owner, and you usually create it programmatically. You might say the file's owner is the chicken and the nib file it owns is the egg.

Every application has another nib file, its main nib file, whose owner is the application object, NSApplication. The application loads its main nib file at launch time. In a typical application, the main nib file is MainMenu.nib, which is responsible for the application's menu bar and potentially other interface objects.

As discussed in Step 2.3, a new document is instantiated programmatically at run time using hard-wired Cocoa code, every time the user calls for a new document. You write your document subclass in either of two ways.

(continues on next page)

In a simple application, the document loads the nib file directly, in which case the document is the file's owner. In a typical, more complex application, the document instantiates a window controller, which in turn loads the nib file. In that case, the window controller is the file's owner. Either way, the owner of the nib file must exist in memory as an instantiated object before it can load the nib file. The owner is in this sense external to the nib file that archives the window.

When you create the nib file in Interface Builder, you must have some means of communication between the file's owner and the window defined in the nib file. The File's Owner stands in for the owning object for this purpose. Its icon is used to draw the necessary connections between it and other objects when you are designing the program. When the nib file is loaded at run time, Cocoa takes care of instantiating the connections to the real file's owner object, using the information it finds in the nib file.

2.6 Create Actions, Outlets, and Connections

The application needs to know how the various objects and classes you have created relate to one another, so that one object can send messages to another at run time. In this step, you will create an action message to be sent by your checkbox control when a user selects or deselects it and you will create outlets in some of the objects to enable them to talk to other objects. You will also create connections among them. You will do this in Interface Builder. Although you could do it in code in Project Builder, Interface Builder is usually vastly more convenient.

Start where you left off in Step 2.5. Launch Interface Builder and open VRDocument.nib, if necessary.

2.6.1 *Create an action and connect it to its target.*

An action, as you learned in Step 2.1, can be described as a message sent by a user control to a target object. In Cocoa, the action is implemented as a method in the target object. Cocoa will automatically invoke this method when the user changes the control's state—for example, by clicking it. The target of the message is known as the *receiver,* and the user control sending the message is the *sender.* In this step, you will create an action method in the receiver, VRMainWindowController, to be invoked when the user clicks the sender, the checkbox control.

How does Cocoa know where to find the action method it must call when the user clicks a control? The answer, as you will see in a moment, is that you will draw a connection in Interface Builder between the user control and its target, the intended receiver of the message.

You learned in Step 2.3 that the role of VRMainWindowController is to mediate between the data controlled by its associated document and the user controls in its associated window. Each user control in the main document window will invoke an action method in VRMainWindowController when the user changes the state of the control, so that VRMainWindowController can in turn tell the document to update its data structures to reflect the user's action. The application knows where to find the proper action method because you will wire them together using Interface Builder. At this point, you have only one interactive user control in the main window, so only one action method need be implemented.

1. In the VRDocument.nib window, select the Classes tab. A list of all available classes appears.

2. Navigate to NSWindowController. Expand the NSWindowController topic in Outline mode or look in the next column in Column mode, and click VRMainWindowController to select it. The Info Panel becomes the VRMainWindowController Class Info Panel.

3. In the Attributes pane of the VRMainWindowController Class Info Panel, select the Actions tab, then click the Add button to add a new action. Alternatively, you can choose Classes > Add Action to VRMainWindowController. Above the built-in action `showWindow:`, a new action appears named `myAction:`. Its text is selected, ready to be edited.

   Notice that the names of actions end with a colon, indicating that they are Objective-C methods that take a single parameter. All action methods take `sender` as a parameter, giving the target, or receiver, a means to identify the control that sent the action message.

4. Type to rename the new action `checkboxAction:`. Include the trailing colon indicating that this is a method. Press Return to accept the new name (**Figure 1.20**).

5. Bring the main document window to the front and choose the Buttons pane of the tab view, if necessary, to show the checkbox control. Then hold down Control and drag from the checkbox toward the VRDocument.nib window. While you drag, a line is drawn from the checkbox and follows the moving mouse pointer. The VRDocument.nib window automatically switches to the Instances pane as your drag extends over it. Release the mouse button over the File's Owner icon in the VRDocument.nib window to complete the drag (drag to an edge of the window, if necessary, to scroll the File's Owner icon into view). The NSButton Info Panel automatically appears and comes to the front, with the Connections pane showing.

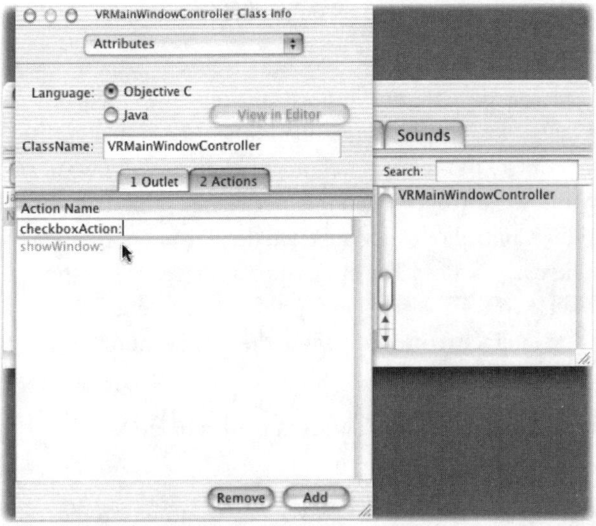

FIGURE 1.20 Renaming myAction: in the VRMainWindowController Class Info Panel.

6. Click the **target** outlet in the left column of the Outlets pane of the NSButton Info Panel to select it, if necessary. The **target** outlet is normally a method that is already declared in the Cocoa frameworks, which returns the value of the **target** instance variable. Then click the new **checkboxAction:** method in the right column to select it. The Connect button at the bottom of the Info Panel is enabled. Finally, click Connect. Your new connection appears in the bottom pane of the Info Panel (**Figure 1.21**).

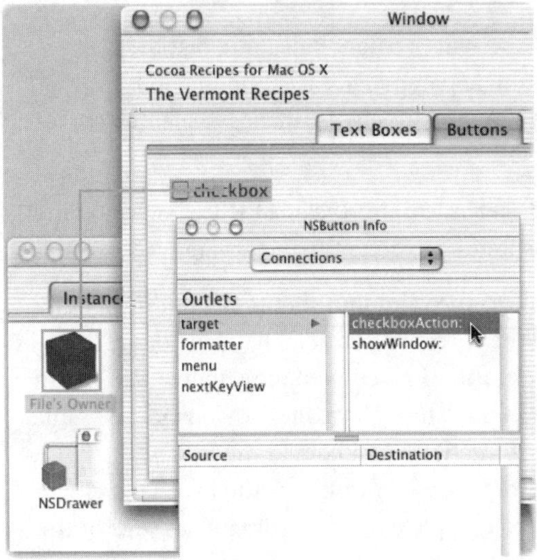

FIGURE 1.21 Connecting the checkbox control to File's Owner.

Here, you created an action in Interface Builder, but you haven't written any code for it yet. You will add code to the project in Step 3.5 and Step 3.6 to complete your work and implement this action. More commonly, in the remainder of Vermont Recipes, you will write an action method in Project Builder, then read it into the nib file using Interface Builder. Either technique is perfectly appropriate.

Before writing the code for the action method, you will create some more outlets and connections in Interface Builder.

2.6.2 *Create outlets and more connections.*

Some of your application's objects need outlets to other objects so they can send messages to and obtain information from the latter. To finish wiring the user action you just created, for example, you need an outlet in your main window's controller to its document, so that the window controller can tell the document to alter the data it controls and to retrieve the value of the data. You also need an outlet from the window controller to the checkbox control in the main window, so the window controller can tell the control to alter its appearance to reflect the state of the document's data.

It turns out, however, that Cocoa has already done some of this work for you.

2.6.2.1 AN OUTLET FROM THE WINDOW CONTROLLER TO THE DOCUMENT ALREADY EXISTS.

In Step 2.6.1, you created an action method, **checkboxAction:**, so that the checkbox control can tell the file's owner, VRMainWindowController, when the user has changed the state of the control. When a VRMainWindowController object receives such a message at run time, it must be able in turn to tell its associated document to change its data structures to reflect the user's action. The window controller must also at times be able to obtain data from the document, in order to alter the user interface to correspond to the state of the document and for other purposes. To do all this, VRMainWindowController must have a way to talk to VRDocument.

In fact, however, the window controller class already has a means to converse with its associated document. When you examine the header files and documentation for the NSWindowController class from which VRMainWindowController descends, you will find that it has a method, called **document**, that returns the window controller's associated document object. Recall that a document object is created at run time whenever the user requests a new document or opens an existing document. At the time of the document's creation, NSWindowController sets up the **document** method for you as part of the process of creating your window controller. You can't connect it in advance in Interface Builder for the same reason that you could not instantiate an NSDocument object in Interface Builder: A new document is created only at run time in response to the user's request for one.

You will find that many Cocoa classes automatically provide such connections when you need them, so that you don't have to create an explicit outlet yourself. The only way you can know whether you need to create your own outlet is to become familiar with the Cocoa classes. A common beginner's error is to create custom outlets without realizing that they are already built into the Cocoa frameworks.

2.6.2.2 AN OUTLET FROM THE WINDOW CONTROLLER TO THE USER CONTROL MUST BE CREATED.

To complete the network of actions and outlets involving the checkbox control, you must create an outlet from the VRMainWindowController subclass to the control, so that the control can be told to change its appearance when appropriate. This outlet is not provided in the NSWindowController superclass because the Cocoa frameworks could not have known in advance that you would create this particular user control for your application.

1. In the VRDocument.nib window, select the Classes tab. A list of all available classes appears.

2. Navigate to NSWindowController and click VRMainWindowController to select it. The Info Panel becomes the VRMainWindowController Class Info Panel.

3. Select the Attributes pane of the Info Panel. You see two tabs listing one outlet and two actions.

4. Select the Outlets tab and click the Add button, or choose Classes > Add Outlet to VRMainWindowController. A new outlet appears in the Outlets section, named myOutlet. Its text is selected, ready to be edited.

5. Type to rename it **checkbox** and then press Return.

   Notice that the new outlet does not have a trailing colon. This is because outlet methods do not take any parameters but merely return the value of the associated instance variable.

   In Mac OS X 10.2, Interface Builder allows you to set an outlet's type by choosing it from a pop-up menu (**Figure 1.22**). However, leave it as type **id** for now so you can see how to set the type programmatically using Project Builder in Step 3.4.

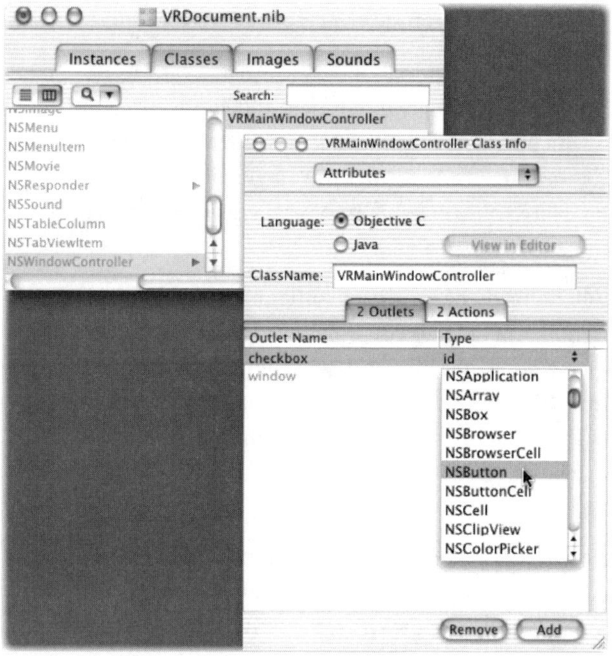

FIGURE 1.22 Renaming myOutlet: in the VRMainWindowController Class Info Panel.

6. In the VRDocument.nib window, select the Instances tab. Make sure the Buttons pane is showing in the main document window's tab view. Then hold down Control and drag from the File's Owner icon to the checkbox control in the Buttons pane. While you drag, a line is drawn from the File's Owner icon and follows the moving pointer. Release the button over the control to complete the drag. The File's Owner Info Panel automatically appears and comes to the front, with the Connections pane showing and the **checkbox** outlet selected. The Connect button is enabled at the bottom of the Info Panel.

7. Click Connect. The new connection appears in the bottom pane of the Info Panel.

You will add code to the project in Step 3.4 to complete your work on this outlet.

2.6.3 *Connect other outlets.*

You will need to connect a number of additional outlets to permit various objects to talk to one another. You go about deciding what outlets and connections are needed by thinking through which objects must be able to control or obtain information from other objects. If you forget something, you can create more actions, outlets, and connections later. Here you will confirm or make several connections on built-in outlets.

1. VRMainWindowController already has a `window` outlet provided by the Cocoa Document-based Application template, so you don't need to create it. You already connected it to the parent window in Step 2.1.6, while you were substituting a window with a drawer for the window originally provided by the template. To verify this, select the Instances tab of the VRDocument.nib window, click the File's Owner icon, click the `window` connection in the bottom section of the Connections pane in the File's Owner Info Panel, and see where the line leads.

2. Control-drag to draw a connection from the Parent Window icon in the VRDocument.nib window to the File's Owner icon, which now represents the window controller. When you complete the drag, the NSWindow Info Panel comes to the front. This time, select the existing `delegate` outlet and click Connect. This appoints VRMainWindowController as the Parent Window's delegate, which will permit built-in Cocoa window routines to delegate various tasks to VRMainWindowController objects at run time. You will see an example of delegation in use later, in Step 6.1. Many AppKit classes have built-in `delegate` outlets; you will connect them to other objects at your option, depending on whether you want to take advantage of delegated functionality.

3. You should also connect the `initialFirstResponder` outlet in the parent window, so the application will know, when a new window is opened, which one of its user controls has the keyboard focus or is *key*. Control-drag from the Parent Window icon in the VRDocument.nib window to the checkbox control in the Buttons tab view item of the main window, select `initialFirstResponder` in the NSWindow Info Panel, and click the Connect button. You will learn how to connect key view loops in windows and tab view items in Recipe 5, Step 1, to ensure correct tabbing order among controls.

4. Save your work in the nib file by choosing File > Save.

In the next step, you will create source files for the window controller you have created in Interface Builder.

2.7 Create the Source Files

You are now ready to generate the window controller source files. You could instead continue working in Interface Builder to add more user controls to the main window, and you could also use Interface Builder to create a user interface and connections for the DrawContentView object and additional drawers and windows. In a typical Cocoa development process, you would proceed in exactly this way—not only to take maximum advantage of Interface Builder's ease of use in building the user interface but also to create a prototype of your planned user interface. However, for learning purposes, you will add more controls later in source code using Project Builder to see how you would accomplish these tasks in code.

In this step, you will use Interface Builder to generate source files for the VRMainWindowController subclass. You will also try to generate source files for VRDocument, even though the Cocoa Document-based Application template has already provided starter files for this subclass (under the name MyDocument), just to see what Interface Builder produces.

Now that the code generation features of Interface Builder and Project Builder are more fully integrated than they used to be, you can use Interface Builder to merge new instance variables, outlets, and actions created in Interface Builder into your existing Project Builder header and source files without fear of inadvertently over-writing existing code. The FileMerge utility in the /Developer/Applications folder will automatically be launched to present you with a side-by-side comparison of the old and the new files, with all changes prominently marked. This will enable you to place new instance variables into the existing header file and stub declarations for new outlets and actions into the existing source files. Using FileMerge, it is remarkably easy to pick and choose which old lines to retain and which new lines to substitute into the finished file. If, after developing code for additional outlets, actions, and other routines using Project Builder, you decide to create additional user controls and their outlets and actions in Interface Builder, you will be able to do so.

Start where you left off in Step 2.6. Launch Interface Builder and open MyDocument.nib, if necessary.

1. In the VRDocument.nib window, select the Classes tab. A list of all available classes appears.

2. Navigate to VRMainWindowController and click to select it.

3. Choose Classes > Create Files for VRMainWindowController. A sheet opens, letting you select a location in which to create the files; the Vermont Recipes folder is already conveniently selected. You also see in the "Create files" area two check-boxes in which to confirm that you want to create VRMainWindowController.h

and VRMainWindowController.m, and they are checked by default. (The box may be too small to see the full filenames, but it is safe to take it on faith that this is what they are.) If the project is still open in Project Builder at this point, you also see a checkbox in the "Insert into targets" area in which to confirm that the files should be inserted into the Vermont Recipes target (**Figure 1.23**).

FIGURE 1.23 Creating source files for the VRMainWindowController class in Interface Builder.

4. Normally, you would leave this last checkbox checked to assure that the generated files were not only placed in the project folder but were also added to the list of files in the Groups & Files pane of the project window in Project Builder. But for present purposes, uncheck this checkbox. Leave the checkboxes for creating the two source files checked, click the Vermont Recipes folder to confirm that this is where the files should be placed, and click the Choose button. As you will see in Instruction 9 below, the two new files are created in the Vermont Recipes folder, but you will have to merge them into the project manually because you told Interface Builder not to do it for you.

Because files with the names VRMainWindowController.h and VRMainWindowController.m do not already exist in the folder, no error messages are generated.

5. Now turn to the VRDocument class. Navigate through the Classes list in the VRDocument.nib window and click VRDocument.

6. Choose Classes > Create Files for VRDocument. A sheet opens as before, letting you select a location in which to create the files, and the checkboxes confirming that you want to create VRDocument.h and VRDocument.m are checked.

7. This time, check the Vermont Recipes target in the "Insert into targets" area. You can see in the file list that the Vermont Recipes folder already contains files named VRDocument.h and VRDocument.m where you created them earlier, but go ahead and start the process of generating new files by clicking Choose. You are immediately presented with an alert, warning you that the VRDocument.h file already exists and giving you the option to overwrite the existing file, merge the new temporary file with it, or cancel. A similar alert regarding the VRDocument.m source file appears underneath it.

8. Click the Merge button. If you checked the button to insert the files into the Vermont Recipes target, you will be presented with another alert, warning you that there has been an error because the file is already in the target. Click OK when you get the chance. In the meantime, the FileMerge application launches and comes to the front displaying a side-by-side comparison of the contents of the old and new header files.

Neither the VRDocument.h header file you are creating in Interface Builder and FileMerge nor the MyDocument.h header file the Project Builder template provided, which you renamed VRDocument.h in Step 1, contains any code. You created no outlets or actions for the VRDocument class in Interface Builder, and the Project Builder template contains none, either.

However, there are some differences between the two header files, and the FileMerge utility finds all of them for you. You see at a glance that the initial comments and copyright notice are missing from the newly generated header file, replaced by a single comment showing the name of the new class. More importantly, Interface Builder knew that the @interface directive in the new header should declare a class named VRDocument, not MyDocument.

You can make choices in FileMerge about which changes to keep and which to reject. To do so, you would select a change by clicking its numbered arrow in the center column, then choose an action from the Actions command pop-down menu at the bottom of the window. However, you will make the changes in Project Builder instead of FileMerge for present purposes, so just quit FileMerge now and leave the original template files undisturbed.

9. Using the Finder, navigate to the Vermont Recipes folder. You find the two new VRMainWindowController files you created in Instruction 3. Open them. You see that they are very simple, with stubs for the action method and each of the outlets you created in Step 2.6, but not much else. Don't be discouraged; the nib file contains essential additional information behind the scenes that will greatly simplify the work remaining. Remember also that if you had used Interface Builder to create a prototype for a very complex application, one whose main document

window would contain a great many user controls, the generated instance variables and stub methods would have saved you a fair amount of typing.

In the next step, you will finish merging the source files into the project.

2.8 Merge the Source Files into the Project

Assuming you did not select the Vermont Recipes target in the "Insert into targets" pane in Instruction 4 of Step 2.7, you now have to merge the two new VRMainWindowController files into the project. This step is spelled out here only to show you how to do it. Normally, you will find it much easier to select the checkbox that makes this happen automatically.

Start where you left off in Step 2.7. Launch Project Builder, if necessary.

1. In the Finder, confirm that VRMainWindowController.h and VRMainWindowController.m were saved in the main Vermont Recipes folder when you generated them in Interface Builder. If you saved them somewhere else in the previous step, drag them into the folder now. It is important to place files in their proper locations in the Finder before adding them to the project.

2. In Project Builder, choose Project > Add Files. A sheet opens in which you can select files to add.

3. In the sheet, navigate to the Vermont Recipes folder. Select VRMainWindowController.h and VRMainWindowController.m, holding down the Shift or Command key to select both at once. Click the Open button. Another sheet opens, in which you can set options.

4. In the Options sheet, you normally check the "Copy into group's folder (if needed)" checkbox to ensure that the files are copied into the project folder in the Finder. You have already done this manually in Instruction 1, above, but it does no harm to get in the habit of checking this checkbox. The setting of the other controls in the Options sheet doesn't matter at this stage; leave them as you find them. Click the Add button. Both files are added to the left pane of the project window, entitled Groups & Files.

5. In the project window, drag both files into the Classes group in the Groups & Files pane of the project window, if necessary. This does not move the files on disk or in the Finder, but it does organize the Groups & Files pane according to the conventions of Cocoa development. You are free to rearrange the Groups & Files pane in any way that you find convenient.

You are just about ready to begin coding the application.

Step 3: Set Up the Project Source Files Using Project Builder

3.1 Set Up the Project Target and Resources

At some point, you must set up the application's Finder-related information and other settings, such as its CFBundlePackageType, CFBundleSignature, and CFBundleDocumentTypes. It is a good idea to get these out of the way up front.

Launch Project Builder and open the project, if necessary.

3.1.1 Set up the Info.plist Entries.

The settings you provide in the Info.plist Entries section of the Targets pane of the project window are installed into an Info.plist file in the application's bundle when you use Project Builder to build your application. In Mac OS X 10.0 and later, Project Builder creates the application as a *new-style bundle,* automatically saving the Info.plist file in XML property list format. In earlier versions, the Info.plist file was saved as a traditional property list containing key-value pairs in plain text, and some of the information was also saved in a versions.plist file in the application bundle.

Cocoa uses the Info.plist file for a variety of purposes, including providing the short application name that appears in the menu bar when the application is running; telling the system where the application and document icons are located; providing the version, copyright, and other strings used in the Finder's Show Info window, the About window, and other dialogs and alerts; and providing recognized document types used to tell the desktop to open the application when the user double-clicks one of the application's document icons. Project Builder also places the type and creator code for your application into a file named PkgInfo in the compiled application bundle, which the Finder uses to cache this information for performance reasons.

1. In the project window, select the Targets tab. A pane slides into view on the left side of the main project window. In Mac OS X 10.2, it was redesigned as an expandable outline containing the project's targets, build styles, and executables (**Figure 1.24a**).

FIGURE 1.24a
Project Builder Targets,
Build Styles, and
Executables outline.

Documentation

The "Software Configuration" chapter of Inside Mac OS X: System Overview in /Developer/Documentation/Essentials/SystemOverview explains the function and format of the Info.plist and InfoPlist.strings files found in application packages and other bundles. The "Software Configuration" chapter includes an explanation of these files, and "Appendix A" lists and explains all of the keys. Also read the "Bundles" and "Application Packaging" chapters for information about localizable strings and other resources. System Overview is also available on disk as a PDF file, in the same folder. Be sure to check the Cocoa Documentation Web site for the latest version of System Overview, at http://developer.apple.com/techpubs/macosx/Essentials/SystemOverview.

The *Information Property List* release note at /Developer/Documentation/ReleaseNotes/InfoPlist.html contains important information about new features of the Info.plist file introduced in Mac OS X 10.0. Also search on Info.plist or any of its individual items in the Developer Help Center of the Apple Help Center for additional information.

For more information on localizable strings, read the "Internationalization" chapter of *System Overview*.

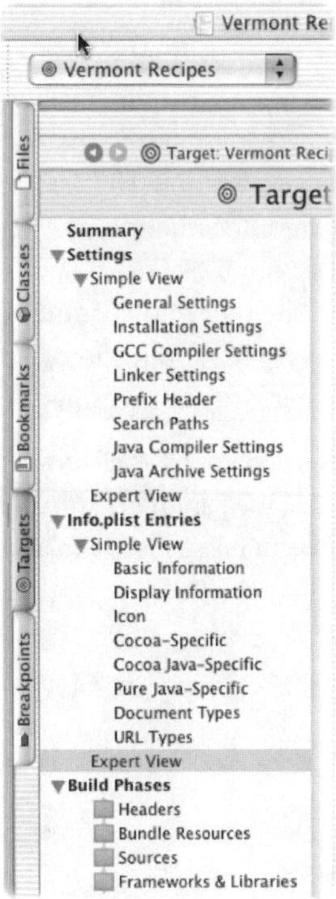

2. Click Vermont Recipes under the Targets item in the left pane. The project's main Targets pane appears, with an expandable outline at its left where you can select a summary, certain settings, the Info.plist entries, and build phases. The Targets pane was completely redesigned for Mac OS X 10.2 (**Figure 1.24b**).

3. Expand the Info.plist Entries item, if necessary, and click the Expert View item. You will change only some of the default settings found here. (The Simple View item is left as an exercise for the reader. Note that there are Help tags associated with some of the fields in the Simple View to help you identify their purpose.)

FIGURE 1.24b
Project Builder
Targets pane outline.

4. Click the disclosure triangle to expand CFBundleDocumentTypes, then expand element **0**, then expand CFBundleTypeExtensions and CFBundleTypeOSTypes.

- For CFBundleTypeExtensions **0**, double-click the series of question marks (????) to select the field for editing, drag-select to select the existing text, if necessary, then replace the existing text with your document's four-character type. For Vermont Recipes, type **VRd1**. In the arbitrary locution I use here, *VR* stands for *Vermont Recipes* and *d* stands for *document*. The 1 stands for the first released version of the finished Vermont Recipes application.

- For CFBundleTypeName, replace DocumentType with **Vermont Recipes document**. Later, in Step 4.2.1, you will code a variable using this same string in VRDocument.m, and your application will not work correctly if the strings are not identical.

- For CFBundleTypeOSTypes **0**, replace ???? with **VRd1**.

- For NSDocumentClass, replace MyDocument with **VRDocument**.

- Leave the rest of the CFBundleDocumentTypes as you find them. They are correct for the application you are building. You can specify a MIME type as a document type, but Vermont Recipes does not use MIME types. You can save documents with HFS type and creator codes, although this is not the Cocoa default. Instructions for doing so appear in the "Saving HFS Type and Creator Codes" article in the "Document-Based Applications" section of the "Programming Design" topic in *Cocoa Developer Documentation*.

5. Change CFBundleSignature from ???? to your application's creator. For Vermont Recipes, type **VRa1** (the *a* stands for *application* in my arbitrary usage).

This creator code has been registered with Apple Computer. For your own applications, you should register your creator code with Apple to ensure that it is, and remains, unique. This is easy to do at http://developer.apple.com/dev/cftype/. Be sure to register your application for free inclusion in Apple's product listings, as well, at http://guide.apple.com/.

6. Change CFBundleVersion to **1** to specify the build number, since this is the first build of what will become version 1.0.0 of the application.

If you don't also specify CFBundleShortVersionString, informally known as the marketing version number and described in Step 3.1.2, below, CFBundleVersion should not be used as a build versioning mechanism but should instead be set to 1.0.0d1 and used as the primary versioning mechanism. I prefer to take advantage of both.

When used as a build number, CFBundleVersion is typically incremented at every build, even while the marketing version number remains unchanged. In the standard Cocoa About window, the CFBundleShortVersionString, if present, and the CFBundleVersion are combined so that, given the values prescribed here, the line would read 1.0.0d1 (v1). The next build would read 1.0.0d1 (v2), and so on. Eventually, you might get to an alpha version 1.0.0a1 (v1), a beta version 1.0.0b1 (v1), a final candidate version 1.0.0fc1 (v1), and a release version 1.0.0 (v1).

7. Click the New Sibling button. Type over the New Item name to create an item named CFBundleIdentifier. Click in the empty space in the Application Settings pane to let the new item move to its alphabetical place in the list. Double-click the Value column opposite the new item to select it for editing, then type com.stepwise.VermontRecipes. This is the application's domain, which Mac OS X uses for various purposes that you will learn about later, including locating the application's preference files.

8. All the other settings are correct, so you're done with the Info.plist Entries pane for now (**Figure 1.24c**). Select the Files tab of the project window and choose File > Save.

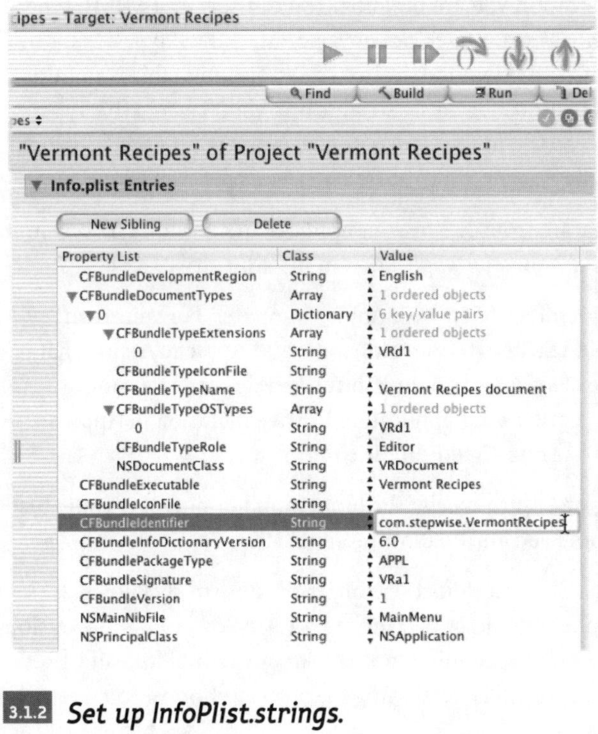

FIGURE 1.24c Finished Info.plist Entries in Project Builder.

3.1.2 Set up InfoPlist.strings.

An InfoPlist.strings file can be used to provide localizations for many settings, including some that might otherwise be placed only in the Info.plist file that you just finished setting up. Localization files are saved as key-value pair property lists, often with comments to help localization contractors identify the use and purpose of the strings. Some of these strings are used, for example, in the application's About window and some by the Finder.

I give instructions here for specifying several items in the InfoPlist.strings file, as advised in current Cocoa documentation. However, not all of these have worked properly as localizations in every release of Mac OS X. For example, in Mac OS X 10.1 and 10.2, the CFBundleGetInfoString localized value does not appear as the version of the application in the Finder's Show Info window, as it should. This is still broken in Mac OS X 10.2.1.

Note that some localized InfoPlist.strings keys do not belong in Info.plist. The NSHumanReadableCopyright entry, for example, works only if specified in the InfoPlist.strings file.

Mac OS X 10.2 introduced a new capability for localizing the display of folder and file names. To localize your application's document names, add a CFBundleDisplayName item to Info.plist and a localized version of it to InfoPlist.strings. A couple of new Cocoa methods support retrieving the localized display name for a file system entity. See the AppKit release notes for additional requirements. The release notes recommend not implementing this unless your application is localized, for performance reasons, so you will not implement these items in Vermont Recipes.

Place all of the keys described below except NSHumanReadableCopyright in the Info.plist file by adding them to the Info.Plist Entries pane using the technique described in Step 3.1.1, above. Also add them to the InfoPlist.strings file as described here to the extent that you anticipate localizing any of them. Those that work correctly as localized strings will override the Info.plist settings; those that don't will have to be localized directly in the Info.plist file until Apple fixes the problem.

1. Select the Files tab in the project window to return to the Groups & Files pane. Expand the Resources group and click InfoPlist.strings. Several settings appear in the main pane of the project window, most of which need to be edited.

   - Change CFBundleName to `Vermont Recipes` if it is not already set to that string. This appears as the application's name both in the standard About window and as the title of the application menu in the Finder. If you were to localize the application, you might decide to translate Recipes to its equivalent in the local language.

   - Change CFBundleShortVersionString to `1.0.0d1`. This appears as the primary, or marketing, version number in the standard About window.

   - Change CFBundleGetInfoString to `Vermont Recipes 1.0.0d1, Copyright © 2000–2002 Bill Cheeseman.`. This is supposed to appear as the application's version in the Finder's Show Info window.

The standard copyright symbol (©) is Option-G on the U.S. keyboard. The dash should be an en dash (–) in correct typographical usage; hold down Option and type a hyphen (-).

- Change NSHumanReadableCopyright to **Copyright © 2000-2002 Bill Cheeseman.\nAll rights reserved.**.

    The \n is an escaped new-line character, which forces a line break when used in InfoPlist.strings.

2. Mac OS X 10.0 introduced a new InfoPlist.strings requirement, as described in the *Information Property List* release note referenced in the documentation note, above. The CFBundleTypeName entry you created for the Info.plist file in Step 3.1.1, above, is now displayed by the Finder as the Kind string for documents. It often requires localization because it usually includes language-specific words such as *document*. To ensure that a localized string is displayed by the Finder for Vermont Recipes documents, add the entry shown below at the end of InfoPlist.strings. The InfoPlist.strings key must be the *value*, not the *key*, used in Info.plist, because the Info.plist file specifies multiple CFBundleTypeName entries in an array.

```
"Vermont Recipes document" = "Vermont Recipes document";
```

The quotation marks around the key on the left and the value on the right must be included, and the semicolon at the end is also required (**Figure 1.25**).

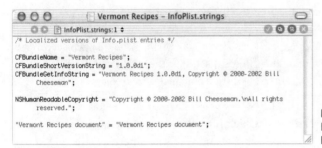

FIGURE 1.25 Finished InfoPlist.strings in Project Builder.

3. Choose File > Save.

3.1.3 *Set up Credits.rtf.*

The contents of Credits.rtf are shown in the application's About window.

1. Click Credits.rtf in the Groups & Files pane of the project window and make appropriate changes to the dummy text provided by the template. It should come as no surprise that I credit myself for everything. I give thanks to Scott Anguish and the Stepwise team because of their important contributions to the success of the Vermont Recipes venture. It is common to add text at the top of the file describing your application briefly.

2. You don't have to follow the Rich Text Format (RTF) model provided by the template. Provision was added in Mac OS X 10.1 to use an HTML file. Any HTML links in Credits.html will become clickable links in the application's About window. If you have a Web site for your product, you should certainly include a link in the About window. Credits.html will take precedence over Credits.rtf if both are present. Including an RTF copy is required if your application will run under Mac OS X 10.0.

Copy and paste the contents of your modified Credits.rtf file into a new HTML file created in your favorite Web authoring tool. Save it into the project folder's English.lproj subfolder as Credits.html, and add it to the project using the Project > Add Files menu item. Include in the file the standard HTML tags to link to the Vermont Recipes Web site at www.stepwise.com/Articles/VermontRecipes/ and the Peachpit Press Web site at www.peachpit.com.

3. Choose File > Save.

3.1.4 *Set up Localizable.strings.*

A Localizable.strings file should be added to the project for each localized or language-specific version of the application. It contains key-value pairs specifying string values for any localizable string used in the application—for example, menu item names, button names, and the like. Localizable.strings is the conventional name for the file if you have only one. The application can contain many similar files with other names and, by convention, the .strings extension. All .strings files for a given language belong in that language's .lproj folder. The files take the form of property lists containing key-value pairs in plain text, with comments to assist localization contractors. Here you will create a Localizable.strings file for the English.lproj folder.

Specifying strings in localizable, or internationalized, form in your code is so easy that you should always do it. At any place in the application's code where you would normally use the @"this is a string" form to provide fixed user-viewable text, you should instead use the NSLocalizedString() function, or, if you have .strings files with names other than Localizable.strings, the NSLocalizedStringFromTable() function. These functions are defined in the NSBundle header in the Foundation framework, which call NSBundle's localizedStringForKey:value:table: method on the application's main bundle. In the NSLocalizedString() function, you pass two parameters specifying the key and a comment string explaining what you are doing. The comment is not used at run time but exists only to force you to document your code for your localization contractor. It should be descriptive and should be repeated verbatim as a comment in the Localizable.strings file or a similar file to assist your localization contractor. In the NSLocalizedStringFromTable() function, you pass three parameters specifying the key, the name of the .strings file in which the key and its paired value are found, and a comment string. For examples of the use of the NSLocalizedString()

function to name menu items and to compare names of menu items, see Step 5.2 and Step 6.

Typically, when your application is turned over to localization contractors, they will add a new .lproj folder for another language. Among other things, they will place in it a copy of the Localizable.strings file and any other .strings files you provide, using the same keys but localized string values. They will also localize the application's nib files, using Interface Builder, as well as provide localized images, sounds, and perhaps other resources. The localization contractors will not have to touch the application's code, because when you use these functions, Cocoa automatically uses the resources in the .lproj folder corresponding to the language for which a particular computer is set up.

Whenever you insert the `NSLocalizedString()` function or the `NSLocalizedString-FromTable()` function into your code, you should also remember to return to the Localizable.strings file and similar files to provide a suitable key-value pair and comment to match. Fortunately, in case this is too demanding for you, Apple provides the genstrings command-line tool, which automates the process. Launch the Terminal application and type `genstrings` for help. A similar command-line tool, nibtool, is provided for localizing strings in nib files; enter `nibtool` in Terminal for help.

1. Choose File > New File in Project Builder.

2. Select Empty File at the top of the list in the New File Assistant, and click the Next button.

3. In the New Assistant, set the name of the file to Localizable.strings, set its location to the English.lproj folder in the Vermont Recipes project folder, and click the Finish button.

4. In the Groups & Files pane, drag the new Localizable.strings item into the Resources group, if necessary.

5. If you wish (this is not required), click Localizable.strings to open the new, empty file in the right pane and type a descriptive heading such as `/* English strings for Vermont Recipes */`.

6. Choose File > Save.

In the next series of steps, you will begin coding the application.

3.2 Import the Cocoa Umbrella Framework

You are finally ready to begin writing code. The application you will create in these recipes is, as you know, a document-based application. If you have not already done so, you should now read some background documentation on basic concepts.

Older versions of Interface Builder and Project Builder generated templates that contained directives importing the Application Kit framework, and some of the templates available through the File > New File command in current versions of Project Builder (such as the Cocoa Objective-C class template) import Foundation. However, *Inside Mac OS X: System Overview* recommends that Cocoa application classes import the Cocoa umbrella framework instead. This framework imports both AppKit and the Foundation framework, and it may from version to version import other headers possibly required for Cocoa development. For example, in the Public Beta release of Mac OS X, it imported AppKitScripting.h for AppleScript support, although the AppleScript frameworks are now imported as part of the Cocoa umbrella framework.

Launch Project Builder and open the project, if necessary.

1. Open all of the header files in the Classes group in the Groups & Files pane of the project window by clicking each in turn.

2. In each, if necessary, replace a line such as `#import <AppKit/AppKit.h>` with `#import <Cocoa/Cocoa.h>`.

Documentation

For more information about localization of Mac OS X applications, see Apple's *Localization on Mac OS X* Web page at http://developer.apple.com/intl/localization.html, and "Internationalizing Cocoa Applications—A Primer for Developers and End Localizers," an article by Andrew Stone in the September 2001 issue of *MacTech* magazine.

A good technical overview of what you have to do to create a document-based application appears in the "Document-Based Applications" section of the "Program Design" topic on Apple's Cocoa Developer Documentation Web site at http://developer.apple.com/techpubs/macosx/Cocoa/CocoaTopics.html. It is accessible on your computer in the Cocoa section of the Developer Help Center in the Apple Help Center, available from the Help menu in Project Builder.

The "Program Design" topic in *Cocoa Developer Documentation* is an updated version of the legacy document *Application Design for Scripting, Documents, and Undo,* which is no longer included in Developer Tools.

3.3 Replace the Document's Nib File Methods Provided by the Template

The MyDocument class implemented in the MyDocument.m source file provided by the Cocoa Document-based Application template is a subclass of a built-in Cocoa class, NSDocument. Out of the box, the source file, which you have renamed VRDocument.m, contains four methods that override methods built into NSDocument. As override methods, they are invoked automatically at appropriate times by the Cocoa frameworks. Your overrides of them are passive, in a manner of speaking. You rarely or never call these override methods yourself; instead, you modify them so that when Cocoa calls them, they will provide custom information to Cocoa that is unique to your application, such as the name you give to the nib file for the document's main window.

These four methods are the minimum that must be overridden to build a working, customized Cocoa document-based application. In fact, if you were willing to live with the minimal capabilities of these methods as provided in the template, you could have built and run the Vermont Recipes application before changing the names of the document and nib files supplied by the template, without writing any code of your own. You would have discovered that it actually works, up to a point. For example, when you launched the application, it would have automatically opened the main document window you designed in Step 2. If you chose File > New, it would have opened another, identical document window. You wouldn't have been able to save the setting of the checkbox control, but you'll deal with that issue later.

This would be a short tutorial if you were satisfied with the template as is, however, so you will make many changes to it in Vermont Recipes. In this step, you will rework the first two of the supplied override methods, `windowNibName` and `windowControllerDidLoadNib:`, both of which have to do with the way the application loads and uses the nib file you created in Step 2. Because this is the first real Cocoa code you will write, I will spend more than a little time explaining what is going on.

First, note that MyDocument.m, now named VRDocument.m, includes a comment specifically advising you to remove its first method, the override method `windowNibName`, in certain circumstances. It tells you to override `makeWindowControllers` instead in the case of an application that subclasses Cocoa's NSWindowController class or that allows a document to have more than one window open at once. In this step, you will make this change because the Vermont Recipes application meets both conditions.

The template contemplates an application in which only one window can be opened for each document and in which the built-in services of NSWindowController do not require customization. Accordingly, its first method overrides NSDocument's `windowNibName` method, which is designed to work with such an application. This method returns the name of a document's sole nib file (without the .nib extension), which you supply in your override of the method. In the template, the name supplied is, of course, MyDocument; you would change it to VRDocument if you were to use this method in the Vermont Recipes application. NSDocument calls this method automatically in an application that is designed to use it, using the name that it returns to instantiate a single window controller for the document.

Because the Vermont Recipes application specification dictates that a document can have multiple windows, you will override NSDocument's `makeWindowControllers` method instead. You won't actually implement this capability in Vermont Recipes, although you will learn how. Overriding the `makeWindowControllers` method now will make it easy to implement this feature yourself, and in the meantime it does no harm. By opening multiple windows onto a document, a user would be able to view two or more different tab view items onscreen simultaneously. Unlike a window with a scroll view, a window based on a tab view doesn't let a user see two different parts of a document in separate tab view items by splitting it into two panes.

You also override this method instead of `windowNibName` because you need to subclass NSWindowController to add custom features to it. The `makeWindowControllers` method will instantiate a window controller from your subclass, not from NSWindowController itself, as Cocoa does when `windowNibName` is used. Every nib file containing at least a main window requires its own controller. The `makeWindowControllers` override method will add each controller it instantiates to a list maintained by the document using Cocoa's `addWindowControllers` method.

The comments in the MyDocument.m template also suggest that you need not implement the second method in this template source file, `windowControllerDidLoadNib:`, although you can do so if there is something your application needs to do just after the nib file is loaded. This is a delegate method, which under certain circumstances Cocoa calls automatically right after a nib file is loaded. There is more than one way to skin this particular cat in a document-based application, however. You won't need `windowControllerDidLoadNib:` in Vermont Recipes, so you will delete it.

You may wonder why Apple bothers to provide you with the Cocoa Document-based Application template, if you have to delete half its provided methods to use it. The answer is that it is designed for a simple application, and for that purpose it is perfectly appropriate. Apple does not provide a template for more complex document-based applications such as Vermont Recipes, perhaps because they can take so many different forms. Once you understand how these applications can be built and have settled on some favorite techniques of your own, you can write your own template and add it to the Project Builder templates at /Developer/ProjectBuilder Extras/Project Templates/Application (or, better yet, in a user-domain version of that folder, to avoid overwriting it when you install a new version of the Developer Tools).

Launch Project Builder and open the project, if necessary.

1. Click the header file VRDocument.h in the Classes group of the Groups & Files pane of the project window. The full text of VRDocument.h appears in the main pane. Change `@interface MyDocument : NSDocument` to `@interface VRDocument: NSDocument`. This is required because you changed the name of the main document subclass from MyDocument to VRDocument in Step 1 and Step 2.4.

    At the same time, you might want to take this opportunity to settle upon a standardized comment block identifying your header and source files. You might add comments at the top listing items such as the name of the application, the name of the file, the author's name, copyright information, explanatory material, disclaimers, and licensing information regarding any restrictions on its use. I use the following in the VRDocument.h header file:

    ```
    /*
    Vermont Recipes
    VRDocument.h
    Copyright © 2000-2002 Bill Cheeseman. All rights reserved.

    Comments like "r1s5.1" refer to a Recipe and Step in Vermont Recipes,
    on the Web at www.stepwise.com/Articles/VermontRecipes, and available
    in expanded form as Cocoa Recipes for Mac OS X - The Vermont Recipes
    (Peachpit Press 2002, www.peachpit.com).
    */
    ```

2. Click the source file VRDocument.m in the Classes group of the Groups & Files pane of the project window. The full text of VRDocument.m appears in the main pane. Change `#import "MyDocument.h"` to `#import "VRDocument.h"` and change `@implementation MyDocument` to `@implementation VRDocument`.

    Now is also a good time to place a standardized comment block at the top of the source file. I use the same block that I used in the header file as shown in Instruction 1, modifying the filename with the .m extension for Objective-C implementation files. I also include a long legal disclaimer, cribbed from Apple's Cocoa example files in the grand old lawyers' tradition of reusing precedents whenever possible.

3. Add this line to VRDocument.m, after `#import "VRDocument.h"`:

    ```
    #import "VRMainWindowController.h"
    ```

    Without this, the override of `makeWindowcontrollers` in Instruction 5, below, would generate compiler warnings because the compiler wouldn't see a declaration for that method.

4. Delete the first two methods from VRDocument.m, **windowNibName** and **windowControllerDidLoadNib:**, which were generated by the Cocoa Document-based Application template but aren't needed for the Vermont Recipes application.

5. Replace the first of the deleted methods with the following:

```
#pragma mark WINDOW MANAGEMENT

- (void)makeWindowControllers {
    VRMainWindowController *controller =
        [[VRMainWindowController alloc] init];
    [self addWindowController:controller];
    [controller release];
}
```

As instructed in Step 2.3, you did not instantiate a window controller in Interface Builder because you knew your application might have to open many windows at run time. Now you have closed this gap by placing code in your VRDocument class that Cocoa will invoke automatically to instantiate and initialize a window controller every time Cocoa creates a new document object in response to user commands. The second statement in the method body inserts the new window controller object into the built-in NSDocument window controllers array, providing access to all open windows associated with a particular document. If you look at the **addWindowController:** method's documentation in the NSDocument class reference document, you will see that it automatically calls NSWindowController's **setDocument:** to set up the window controller's link back to the document.

DECLARING METHODS IN THE HEADER FILE. You do not need to declare the **makeWindowControllers** method in the header file MyDocument.h. It will not be called explicitly from your code. It merely overrides a built-in NSDocument method that the Cocoa frameworks will invoke for you at the proper time. As an override method, it is already declared in the NSDocument header.

Whether to declare override methods in the header file is a matter of personal preference. Many programmers add matching declarations for all methods that are defined in their source, or implementation, file. The header file can then easily be used as a table of contents for the source file, listing every method that has an implementation. Others prefer to declare only override methods that aren't routinely overridden, as **init**, for example, is. Here, on a general principle of parsimony, I suggest you choose not to declare override methods at all. This makes it easy to see, with a glance at the header file, all of the custom methods you have written; you aren't forced, in order to distinguish override methods from your original methods, to try to remember whether a particular method signature exists in the built-in Cocoa frameworks. I once conducted an informal online poll of Cocoa developers, and they were evenly divided between these camps.

CODE NAVIGATION. The line `#pragma mark WINDOW MANAGEMENT` takes advantage of a new facility in Project Builder that greatly improves navigation within your source files. This line causes a marker to appear in the function pop-up menu at the top of the code pane in the project window. Normally, the function pop-up menu allows you to jump quickly to any method declaration or definition in the file. Now you can add your own custom markers, which are useful for dividing your code into meaningful sections. The Navigation pane in the Project Builder Preferences window controls which items generate markers.

In versions of the Developer Tools prior to April 2002, this technique could not be used in header files because it caused compilation to fail when the header was imported into another class. In Mac OS X 10.2 the technique works across the board, as it did in Mac OS X 10.1 if you had installed the April 2002 Developer Tools. You can include `#pragma mark` in header files compiled under older versions, but comment them out or enclose them in a preprocessor command that prevents their compilation to work around the bug.

INSTANTIATING AND INITIALIZING NEW OBJECTS. This is your first encounter with the standard technique to instantiate and initialize objects using Objective-C in Cocoa, so I will explain in considerable detail what this code does and why. This discussion applies generally to the creation of objects in Cocoa, something you will do many times over.

The first line in `makeWindowControllers` combines the allocation of memory for the new object with an invocation of a method to initialize it, all in a single line of code. This is common Cocoa practice. It is important to get in the habit of doing it this way, because some objects' initialization methods may substitute a different object for the one you allocated. This technique helps you to make sure you use the object that is actually returned by the `init` method. You could end up working with the wrong object if you first assigned the result of an `alloc` or `allocWithZone:` method to your instance variable, then in a separate statement sent the `init` message to that instance variable.

Depending on the object, it may have a variety of initialization methods, and it is important to invoke and obtain a return value from the one that is relevant to the purpose at hand. Usually, this will be the so-called *designated initializer,* which should be identifiable from its documentation or comments in its header file. Invoked here is the designated initializer for VRMainWindowController, its `init` method. You will see later in this step that its `init` method will call a built-in Cocoa method that initializes the window controller and makes it the owner of the nib file.

MEMORY MANAGEMENT (`release` and `autorelease`). Immediately before initializing the window controller, this method allocates memory for it. You could have used `allocWithZone:` instead of `alloc`. The former was originally intended to improve efficiency by allocating memory for the new object in the same area where the receiver is located. The best current advice from Apple, however, is always to use `alloc` initially and to experiment later with `allocWithZone:` only if performance testing reveals a bottleneck. The sophisticated virtual memory paging mechanisms of recent versions of Mac OS X can cause `allocWithZone:` to become less efficient than `alloc` in many circumstances.

This is not the place to delve too deeply into the difficult subject of reference counting and the autorelease pool, and when to use `release` and `autorelease` in your code. Take it on faith for now that the memory for the window controller object that is allocated here was automatically retained by the invocation of the `alloc` method, as it also would have been had you used `allocWithZone:`, `copy:`, or `copyWithZone:` instead. When an object is *retained*, a reference counter associated with it is incremented. Any object that you created by calling `alloc`, `allocWithZone:`, or one of the copy methods, is said to be *owned* by you; that is, you are responsible for releasing it when the application has no further use for it. When an object is *released*, or sometime after it is *autoreleased*, its reference counter is decremented. When the reference counter reaches 0, Cocoa deallocates the object and makes its memory available for reuse.

Reference counting is a creature of the Cocoa architecture, not an integral feature of the Objective-C language. The theory behind Cocoa's approach to memory management is that reference counting is more efficient at run time than automatic garbage collection, but miscounting while writing an application presents a lurking danger and must be avoided. Any attempt to use a deallocated object is likely to lead to a crash sooner or later when the memory location being accessed suddenly contains something new, and any failure to deallocate an object that is no longer needed is a waste of memory—a leak that can, if it accumulates, lead to your application's running out of free memory.

Here, in your `makeWindowControllers` method, you release the new object right away, in the last line of the same method that allocated it. It is quite common in Cocoa to release an object in the same method in which it is allocated. It is safe to release it here, even though it is being added to the document's window controller array and the window will remain open. As a general rule, a Cocoa method such as `addWindowController:`, which adds an object to a *collection* (here, an array), calls its own `retain` on the object. You are no longer the sole owner of the object once it is inserted into the array, and you should release it if you, as opposed to the array, no longer need it. In a document-based application such as Vermont Recipes, Cocoa will eventually release it again automatically when the window is closed and its window controller is removed from the array, at which time its retain account will become 0.

Confused? So is almost everybody at this stage, so don't worry about it. Basically, invoking an object's **retain** method simply increments its reference counter by 1. Invoking the object's **release** or **autorelease** method does not actually deallocate the object, but decrements its reference counter by 1. As long as its reference counter is greater than 0, the object survives. Very shortly after its reference counter becomes 0, probably when the current iteration of the application's main run loop terminates, the memory will be deallocated. In the method under discussion here, when the window closes, the two releases will have balanced the two retains and the object will go away, thus avoiding a memory leak.

6. Click the header file VRMainWindowController.h and the source file VRMainWindowController.m in the Groups & Files pane of the project window, in turn. Add your standardized identifying comments and disclaimers at the top of each, with appropriate changes to identify the files.

7. Whenever a new window controller is created, it must, like any object, initialize itself in response to an initialization message from the object that creates it. If, in addition, it allocates memory for an object, it must also release that memory when it is destroyed. In deciding whether a subclass needs a method to release memory, you must take into account whether it allocates memory, as well as other issues.

Documentation

Apple provides excellent documentation about memory management, in the "Memory Management" section of the "Program Design" topic in the Cocoa Documentation material on disk and on the Cocoa Developer Documentation Web site at http://developer.apple.com/techpubs/macosx/Cocoa/CocoaTopics.html.

To learn more about memory allocation and deallocation, reference counting, retain, release, and autorelease, read "Very Simple Rules for Memory Management in Cocoa," a 2001 article by mmalcolm crawford; "Memory Management with Cocoa/WebObjects," a 1999 article by Manulyengar; and "Hold Me, Use Me, Free Me," a 1997 article by Don Yacktman; all are available on the Stepwise site at www.stepwise.com.

In VRMainWindowController.m, insert the following two methods after @implementation VRMainWindowController:

```
#pragma mark INITIALIZATION

- (id)init {
    self = [super initWithWindowNibName:@"VRDocument"];
    return self;
}

- (void)dealloc {
    [[NSNotificationCenter defaultCenter] removeObserver:self];
    [super dealloc];
}
```

You will modify the init method in the next instruction, but keep it simple for now.

In Instruction 5, above, you arranged for a new window controller to be allocated and initialized every time a new document is created. The init message that you told your VRDocument object to send to the window controller is defined here as the window controller's init method. It in turn invokes a method implemented by its superclass, NSWindowController, called initWithWindowNibName:. The name passed as a parameter to initWithWindowNibName: is the name of the VRDocument.nib file, without the .nib extension. The initWithWindowNibName: method has the effect, among other things, of making the new window controller the owner of this nib file. When Cocoa loads the nib file in response to this statement, the application will acquire knowledge of all the classes and subclasses, the windows, and the user controls that you created in Interface Builder in Step 2.

MEMORY MANAGEMENT AND NIB FILES. Although I have barely introduced you to the basic rule of Cocoa memory management and the use of release and autorelease, I must already mention an exception to the rule. You learned in Instruction 5 that when any object retains another object or creates another object using alloc, copy, or certain other methods, the former becomes the latter's owner and is responsible for releasing the latter.

The Cocoa Document-based Application template came with a Window object—an instance of the NSWindow class—already instantiated in the MyDocument.nib nib file. In addition, as you work through Vermont Recipes, you will use Interface Builder to instantiate several other objects at what is called the top level of the nib file, which you have renamed VRDocument.nib. All top-level objects loaded from any nib file are retained. Who is responsible for releasing them?

Normally, the nib file's Files's Owner must release top-level nib file objects. This is considered an exception to the alloc/copy/retain rule, since your application does not call any of these methods to create the top-level objects in the nib file. Fortunately, there is only one other exception to the rule in Cocoa, so you shouldn't have trouble remembering this one.

There is an exception to the exception, however. When NSWindowController loads a nib file, as it did in the `init` method you just wrote, NSWindowController itself became responsible for releasing all top-level objects in the nib file, no matter what object is the File's Owner. NSWindowController will release them when it is deallocated. This is one of many conveniences provided by the AppKit when you write a Cocoa document-based application. The top-level objects own any lower-level objects in the nib file and will therefore release them.

The `dealloc` method you just wrote in VRMainWindowController is therefore correct in not releasing the Window object in the nib file.

String constants. The syntax used to pass the nib file's name to the `initWithWindowNibName:` method, `@"VRDocument"`, is the standard Objective-C technique for inserting string constants into an application's code. You will make very, very frequent use of this technique. In Cocoa, strings are usually implemented as NSString objects because this enables the use of Cocoa's extensive internal implementation of Unicode and other object-oriented string functionality. The @ symbol indicates this is a compiler directive that identifies the string as an NSString constant, as opposed to a C string.

You will shortly see how to resolve localization issues raised by the use of fixed or hard-coded strings like this. Localization is not an issue here, however, because this string is the name of a source file that will have the same, fixed name in every country and region.

The override of NSWindowController's `dealloc` method takes care of a notification center issue that you don't yet need to understand (see Step 6.3). It is included here just to emphasize the need to remember to do this. Then it calls its superclass's `dealloc` method to release any memory that the superclass allocated. Later, when you add instance variables to the window controller, you will consider releasing them here, as well.

Now, every time your application opens a new document, it will automatically create a corresponding window controller instantiated from the VRMainWindowController subclass, which will in turn open that document's main window. When the document is closed, the window controller will be deallocated.

8. You know from the application specification that every document will optionally be able to open one or more separate windows. One of these separate windows

will be ancillary to the main document window, containing information that is not identical to that displayed in the main window. It will be appropriate to close this ancillary window automatically when a document's main window is closed. That is, the document itself should close and take its ancillary window with it when its main window is closed. You should take care of this detail now.

The default Cocoa setting is not to close a document when one of its windows closes. You will therefore revise your brand-new **init** method in MyWindowController.m by adding a line invoking a built-in NSWindowController method to reverse this NSWindowController default. Doing this requires a slight change to the structure of the **init** method that you just wrote. It is useful to do this here to illustrate an important point of object initialization, although you won't get around to coding the ancillary window itself until Recipe 17.

Replace the **init** method with the following new version:

```
- (id)init {
    if (self = [super initWithWindowNibName:@"VRDocument"]) {
        [self setShouldCloseDocument:YES];
    }
    return self;
}
```

INITIALIZATION CONVENTIONS. An initialization method must always return an object, usually the super's **self**, if it succeeds; if it fails, it should always return **nil**.

Note that **nil**, **Nil**, and **NULL** are not the same thing. In Objective-C, **nil** is a null object pointer. The value of the pointer is **0**; that is, it points to memory address **0**. It is not the same as an empty object. For example, an empty NSString object is a real object having a location somewhere in memory, although its contents are empty. **Nil** (note the initial capital letter) is a null class pointer. It is rarely used. The **NULL** keyword is a standard C symbolic constant optionally used in place of **0** when describing pointer values. You will run into trouble if you don't keep these distinctions straight.

The test at the beginning of this method ensures that initialization of the super-class has succeeded before an attempt is made to use the **setShouldClose-Document:** method of NSWindowController. By convention, a **nil** value will have been returned if initialization of the superclass failed. The test is not neces-sary, as you might think, in order to avoid a crash as a result of sending the **setShouldCloseDocument:** message to **nil**, because in Objective-C, unlike in many other languages, sending a message to a **nil** object does not cause an immediate error. Instead, it does nothing. The test is performed here simply to provide a place where you can safely put statements that do depend on the success of the attempt to allocate the object. Notice that the `nil` value of `self` will be returned to the `init` method's caller, which can also respond accordingly.

This statement is tricky, but it is the standard Objective-C way to perform this task. It combines in one line the assignment of the return value of the super's `initWithWindowNibName:` method to `self` and a test to see whether the result is `nil`, indicating a failure to initialize the superclass. Don't mistake this for a direct comparison of `self` with the result of the `[super initWithWindowNibName:-@"VRDocument"]` message, which would require the `==` operator. Here, the assignment in parentheses is executed first; then, if `nil` was assigned to `self`, the `if` test evaluates the `nil` value as `NO` and the `[self setShouldCloseDocument:YES]` message is not sent. Your `init` method then returns the `nil` value of `self`, as it should by convention because the allocation of the superclass has failed. If the initialization of the superclass succeeded, then of course the new object is returned. It is common in Cocoa and Objective-C to test whether an object is `nil` by using `if` and interpreting the instance variable's value as the Boolean value `YES` or `NO`, depending on whether it points to an existing object or to memory address `0`.

This is the standard and safest way to design an initialization method for sub-classes. Although it often isn't necessary, you should get in the habit of doing it this way to avoid surprises in those cases where it is necessary.

9. It seems to be customary in some circles to declare an `init` method in the header file even though it is an override method, but not to declare a `dealloc` override method. Others consider it silly to declare methods such as `init` and `dealloc` that everyone knows are commonly overridden, while still others think it important to declare every method that is implemented. In Vermont Recipes, I do not declare `init` or `dealloc` methods in header files because both are override methods.

If you wish to follow the practice of declaring `init` methods, click the header file VRMainWindowController.h in the Groups & Files pane of the project window. The text of VRMainWindowController.h appears in the main pane. Add the following line after the `@interface VRMainWindowController` block (that is, outside the curly braces):

- (id)init;

If you wish to declare the `dealloc` method, too, follow a similar process.

You will not be reminded hereafter to save your work at the end of each step.

3.4 Implement an Accessor Method in the Window Controller for the User Control Outlet Created in Interface Builder

In Step 2.6.2.2, you used Interface Builder to create an outlet from the VRDocument.nib file's owner, VRMainWindowController, to the checkbox user control in the main document window. You must now see to it that this outlet is correctly implemented in Project Builder.

Launch Project Builder and open the project, if necessary.

1. Click the header file VRMainWindowController.h in the Groups & Files pane of the project window. VRMainWindowController.h appears in the main pane.

2. You see that the interface declares an object, **checkbox**, of generic object type **id**, with the **IBOutlet** prefix. Interface Builder created this declaration when you used its Classes > Create Files command. If you were later to read VRMainWindowController.h back into Interface Builder to update the nib file, Interface Builder would recognize this as an outlet even without the **IBOutlet** prefix, because it thinks all instance variables of type **id** are outlets. However, you will gain the benefit of stricter type checking at compile time if you change it to an object of type NSButton. When you do this, you must, for the benefit of Interface Builder, explicitly identify it as an Interface Builder outlet; you must therefore use the **IBOutlet** prefix.

Beginning with Mac OS X 10.2, Interface Builder is able to create typed outlets. You could therefore have arranged in Interface Builder to declare this outlet of type NSButton, instead of waiting to do it in Project Builder, as you saw in Step 2.6.2.2.

Delete the line **IBOutlet id checkbox;** in VRMainWindowController.h and replace it with the following lines:

```
@private
IBOutlet NSButton *checkbox;
```

COMPILER DIRECTIVES. You have seen several compiler directives already. You encountered one in the previous step, when you used the **@"string"** directive to insert an NSString constant. You have seen others in the form of the **@interface**, **@implementation**, and **@end** directives. Compiler directives in Objective-C are identified by the @ symbol.

You use the **@private** directive here to ensure, at least theoretically, that both unrelated subclasses and any subclasses of MyWindowController.h will be denied direct access to the instance variable. It signals that they should instead use the accessor methods that you will provide shortly. Declaring instance variables private to limit their scope to the declaring class in this fashion is optional. If other classes honor this directive, it gives you the ability in the future to change the way the checkbox object is coded without invalidating any other classes that access the data through accessor methods. In reality, subclasses can still access these variables using Objective-C techniques, so the effect is more one of moral suasion than full security.

Instead of **@private**, you could have used the **@protected** directive to enlarge the scope of instance variables to this class and its subclasses, or **@public** to remove limitations on their scope. The default is **@protected**.

FORWARD DECLARATIONS. You might think, from a first reading of the Objective-C documentation, that you need to add the line **@class NSButton;** before **@interface** in VRMainWindowController.h to tell the compiler that you intend to refer to an object of type NSButton. However, in this case you do not need such a line because your header file already imports the Cocoa.h umbrella header, which indirectly imports NSButton.

You must either import a class into the header or, if that might create a circular reference, use the **@class** directive to avoid an undefined type error when compiling and linking your project with respect to any type referenced in the header. If you use **@class** in a header file for a custom class, you must import the class in the source file if you use it there. You will have several occasions to use **@class** in the Vermont Recipes application, but you don't need it here.

3. You created the checkbox outlet in the first place because you anticipated that your document object might have to send a message to the user control to modify its visible state from time to time, or at least to read its state. For example, the application might have to select it or deselect it (that is, check it or uncheck it) to keep it synchronized with the underlying data, perhaps because a menu command was used to set or clear an underlying Boolean data item.

    ACCESSOR METHODS. One way the application could read or manipulate the checkbox control's state would be to send a message to the **checkbox** instance variable.

    However, to isolate your application's underlying implementation of the control as much as possible from the code that reads and manipulates its state, you should instead add an accessor method to get a reference to the control. By doing this, you give yourself the freedom to change the innards of the application without altering the declaration of the accessor methods in the header file. In this fashion, you avoid forcing clients that use the header file to recompile when you make changes to the code. You would only revise the implementation of your accessor methods in the source file to accommodate the change. The use of accessor methods is a commonplace of Cocoa development for this reason, among others.

This is true to such an extent that Cocoa is actually written to look for accessor methods conforming to certain conventions. To take full advantage of the benefits conferred by Cocoa, you should always honor these conventions. In summary, an accessor method that gets the value of an instance variable should have the same name as the instance variable and simply return its value. An accessor method that sets the value of an instance variable should have the same name as the instance variable, but with its first letter capitalized, preceded by `set` as a prefix. Thus, the accessor methods for an instance variable named `myWidth` would be `myWidth` and `setMyWidth:`. Obeying this convention is even more important for your application's data values than it is for the user controls and other view objects.

You can warn clients of your class to rely only on the accessor methods by declaring the associated instance variable private, as described above. Still, it is a peculiarity of Objective-C that instance variables are visible and accessible in the header file despite the `@private` compiler directive. If you want to get really fancy, you can keep clients completely ignorant of your methods by declaring them in a separate category declared in your source file, but this is an advanced technique and it is not available for instance variables.

Here, as with most instance variables that refer to a user control as opposed to a data value, you will implement only a `get` accessor. You don't need a `set` accessor because you are not going to create multiple checkbox controls in code. You do want a `get` accessor, because you will access the control very frequently to obtain a reference to its visible state so you can retrieve or change its appearance. Changing the visible state of a user control only requires a get reference to the control, because this enables you to access and manipulate its state using built-in Cocoa methods designed for this purpose. Strictly speaking, it isn't even necessary to declare get accessor methods for instance variables referring to built-in Cocoa user controls, because their representations are not likely to change. You could simply refer to them through their instance variables. You will take a somewhat pedantic approach and declare accessor methods for them anyway, at the expense of adding to the heft of the application's source code.

Add the following to VRMainWindowController.h, immediately before the `checkboxAction:` method that Interface Builder put there:

```
#pragma mark ACCESSORS - Buttons tab view item


- (NSButton *)checkbox;
```

Review the discussion of code navigation in Step 3.3 regarding the `#pragma mark` technique for creating organizational markers in your code files. There are many possible ways to organize Cocoa code files, but I use this method because I like the convenience of having markers in the pop-up menu. The window controller in particular will grow very large and unwieldy, and it cries out for organizational aids. You will start to organize it now: first by marking groups of methods, such as Accessors and Actions, based on their basic function; then by adding subcategories within each functional section.

In this connection, now is a good time to add a similar comment immediately before the declaration of the **checkboxAction:** method as well:

```
#pragma mark ACTIONS - Buttons tab view item
```

4. Switch to the source file VRMainWindowController.m and add the following lines before the **checkboxAction:** stub:

```
#pragma mark ACCESSORS - Buttons tab view item

- (NSButton *)checkbox {
    return checkbox;
}
```

Now, whenever you need to send a message to the window controller's associated checkbox object, you will be able to write something like [[[self myWindowController] checkbox] doSomething] from any object that has an outlet connected to the window controller.

This would be a good time to place a marker above the **checkboxAction:** method that Interface Builder added in the source file VRMainWindowController.m:

```
#pragma mark ACTIONS - Buttons tab view item
```

Accessor methods are a standard feature of any Objective-C Cocoa application. Your code will be full of accessor methods that look like this in no time at all. Later in *Vermont Recipes*, you will learn more about different kinds of accessor methods and their role in memory management.

3.5 Set Up a Model Class to Hold and Manage the Application's Data

In Step 2.6.1., you used Interface Builder to create an action that will be invoked every time the user clicks the checkbox user control. When you subsequently used Interface Builder's Classes > Create Files command to generate the source files for the project, it created a stub method for this action in VRMainWindowController. Interface Builder left it to you to provide the code to make this stub method work, however. Since the user's clicking the checkbox control should initiate a change in the state of the application's data, and the application should remember its new state, you must provide some architecture that the application can use to store the associated data.

In short, you are now forced to make some decisions about data representation in the application.

This is a very big issue, and it will take you on a long digression before you can finally return to implement the action method in Step 3.6. Decisions you make now about how to represent data in the application will have a significant effect on the ease with which additional settings can be implemented and on the efficiency of the application itself. In normal software development, this is one of the most important elements of the application specification. You'll avoid a lot of false starts during coding if you have settled in advance on a data representation that will meet all of the application's eventual needs.

In general, the MVC paradigm contemplates that an application's data and the data's behaviors will be encapsulated in one or more separate model objects, each devoted solely to the representation and management of the application's data or some subset of it. You will therefore now create a separate class to hold the data value that is set and reset from time to time when the user clicks the checkbox control. You can give this new class any name in your applications. You will call it VRButtonModel here, implying that this model object will hold data and methods to manage data relating to the Buttons tab view item of the main window's tab view.

In later recipes, you will add variables and methods to it, and you will create additional model objects to hold data and methods relating to other tab view items. There is no reason why your model objects have to be organized to correspond to tab view items. This technique is used here simply as a convenient way to show how multiple model objects can be implemented for one document.

You will create a simple Boolean instance variable in the VRButtonModel object to hold the data value associated with the checkbox control, along with a few methods by which other objects, such as the window controller, can access it. In the course of doing this, you will have to arrange to instantiate and initialize the new model object.

Then, in the remainder of Recipe 1, you will implement all the additional elements of the application needed to make this design work, such as finally filling in the action method; writing methods to undo and redo changes to the data value, to save the data value to disk, and to read it back in; and devising a way to revert a changed data value to its saved state. Later, in Recipe 2, you will add additional tab view items, additional model objects, and new user controls, all using the same approach.

Launch Project Builder and open the project, if necessary.

3.5.1 *Create a new model class using Project Builder.*

In Step 1 and Step 2, you created files for two new classes: first, VRDocument, created from a Project Builder template while setting up a new project, and second, VRMainWindowController, created using Interface Builder's Create Files command. Now you will create a file for a new class using a third technique, from scratch in Project Builder. The process is very similar to what you did in Step 3.1.4 to create the Localizable.strings file.

1. Choose File > New File in Project Builder.

2. Select the Cocoa Objective-C class template under the Cocoa heading in the New File Assistant, and click the Next button.

3. Set the name of the file to **VRButtonModel.m** in the New Objective-C Class Assistant, and check the checkbox to create VRButtonModel.h as well.

4. Click the Set button to open a navigation sheet and, if necessary, click the Vermont Recipes folder to set the new files' location to the Vermont Recipes project folder. Then click the Choose button.

5. After verifying the project and target, click the Finish button.

6. In the Groups & Files pane, drag the new VRButtonModel.h and VRButtonModel.m file icons into the Classes folder, if necessary.

7. Click VRButtonModel.h to open the new header file in the right pane, then type over the comments at the top provided by the template to insert your own standard comments. Do the same with VRButtonModel.m.

8. In VRButtonModel.h, replace **#import <Foundation/Foundation.h>** with the following:

   `#import <Cocoa/Cocoa.h>`

9. Choose File > Save.

Data Representation and Model Classes

The cardinal rule of data representation in document-based Cocoa application development is that you should represent the data in a model object.

Among other things, this means you should not write an application in such a way that it depends upon the current visual state of a user control as a permanent record of the state of the application's data. It may seem that reliance on whether, for example, a checkbox is checked is the most efficient way to know whether the setting represented by the checkbox is true or false. After all, Cocoa already contains routines that allow you to read the current visual state of the checkbox, so why not keep things simple by taking advantage of work already done? Indeed, conventional Mac applications sometimes use this technique, at least temporarily while, for example, a dialog is being presented for user interaction.

The chief practical problem with such a shortcut is that a typical application offers more than one interface device to alter its data, some of which may have the ability to change the state of the data without altering the visible state of the user control. For example, you may want to add a menu command as an alternative interface to let the user change the underlying data. Or you may (as you should) include AppleScript support in your application, and a user may run a script that changes the data without displaying a window. In either of these cases, you would have to write additional code to change the visual state of the checkbox to reflect the data change made by the menu command or the AppleScript command. The AppleScript issue is particularly serious, since scripts often should access an application's data without wasting time and bothering the user by activating the GUI.

Centralizing the representation of the data in one place makes it far easier to keep all these interfaces synchronized. It even makes it easier to add new functionality such as saving and reading the data, undo and redo, and revert. It also pays dividends in code maintenance in the future, when you might want to add entirely new functionality related to the existing data or add completely different data sets with their own functionality.

Note that the document object in Cocoa is not a model object, as you might expect. Instead, the document object is a controller devoted to managing the application's data in a larger sense. For example, you will shortly place the application's generic, abstracted methods for storing and retrieving data into the document object, VRDocument. Not all controllers in Cocoa include the word *controller* in their names, although you might think the function of NSDocument would have been clearer if it were named NSDataController. Also, don't be confused by the fact that there is a separate class in Cocoa called NSDocumentController; that, too, is a controller class, but it controls documents within the context of an application and its file system—for example, the opening and closing of documents.

Therefore, you should not, as you might initially assume, place specific data definitions and accessor methods in the document class. Instead, you should put them in a separate class or classes devoted specifically to that purpose.

3.5.2 *Initialize the model object.*

The template file you chose in the preceding step makes the new VRButtonModel class a subclass of Cocoa's NSObject class. This is appropriate, because as a model class VRButtonModel has no need to inherit capabilities from any but this most basic of Cocoa objects. Almost all classes in Cocoa inherit ultimately from NSObject.

Like most new objects, a VRButtonModel object requires initialization beyond that provided by the NSObject class from which it inherits. It will have two initialization methods, one of which will be its *designated initializer,* the initializer that should normally be invoked when a new VRButtonModel object is created. It is common for Objective-C classes to have more than one initializer, although many offer only an override of the basic init method inherited from NSObject as a way to initialize instance variables to default values. If there is nothing to initialize, however, there is no reason to provide any initializer at all, because the super's init method will serve. It is a good idea to get object initialization routines in place early in the process of writing a new class.

The designated initializer for VRButtonModel will be used by the document object that creates this model object to pass in a reference to the document's **self**. This is a common technique in Objective-C and other object-oriented languages, to give a newly created object the ability to communicate back to the object that created it. You will see later that this back reference, among other things, is needed so that the model object can tell the document object that created it that some data has changed, and the document object can then pass the news along to the window controller and eventually to affected user controls. You will learn that a link from VRButtonModel to VRDocument is also needed so that the model object can share the document object's undo manager.

1. In the header file VRButtonModel.h, add the following compiler directive and instance variable between the braces after **@interface VRButtonModel**:

   ```
   @private
   VRDocument *document;
   ```

2. Before **@interface VRButtonModel**, add this:

   ```
   @class VRDocument;
   ```

   This forward reference is needed so the compiler will know you intended to use the custom VRDocument type in the header.

3. Add the following method declaration after the **@interface VRButtonModel** block:

   ```
   #pragma mark INITIALIZATION

   - (id)initWithDocument:(VRDocument *)inDocument;
         // designated initializer
   ```

Object Initialization and the Designated Initializer

Initialization of Cocoa objects is governed by a well-defined programming convention that all Cocoa applications must follow. The convention is best described in the class reference document for NSObject, a fundamental class declared in the Foundation framework, in the section documenting NSObject's init method; I urge you to read it. Since most Cocoa classes inherit from NSObject (and the principal one that doesn't, NSProxy, nevertheless follows the NSObject protocol), reliance upon this convention is implicit throughout the Cocoa frameworks. If your application doesn't honor this convention, it probably won't work.

NSObject's init method does nothing except return self. This init method is available in every object that inherits from NSObject. Most such classes override the init method and possibly provide one or more alternatives to do additional initialization. Because there can be many intermediate classes in the inheritance chain, a convention is needed to ensure that an appropriate initialization method of every object in the chain is called when a new object of any class is created. If initialization fails, a class's initialization method must release the object and return nil to signal failure.

To assure that the initialization methods of classes intermediate between NSObject and the class are called, one of the initialization methods of the class must begin by invoking an appropriate initialization method of its immediate superclass. This is the designated initializer. If the super's initializer returns a valid reference to the new object (as opposed to nil, indicating failure somewhere up the chain), then the new object knows that all classes above it in the chain have been successfully initialized, and it can go ahead with initialization of its own variables.

The designated initializer typically contains more parameters than any of the other initializers, allowing clients to pass as many unique values as possible to a new object. Other initializers are often provided in custom classes for special purposes, setting a variety of instance variables to default values and therefore requiring fewer parameters. Each of them must call the class's designated initializer, directly or indirectly, through a message to self, passing the default values and any parameter values to parameters of the designated initializer. This guarantees that the variables of the class are initialized to appropriate values and that all intermediate classes higher in the hierarchy are initialized, and it avoids circular initialization references.

Typically, a class that inherits directly or indirectly from NSObject declares an init method as well as alternative, more complicated initialization methods that take arguments to set the initial values of variables declared in the class. The initialization method that takes the most arguments—that is, the one capable of most completely setting up the object's initial state—is usually the designated initializer. Only the designated initializer actually sets any instance variable values; the others call the designated initializer to do this for them. In most circumstances, an application will find it convenient to initialize a new instance of the class by calling the designated initializer.

It is the developer's obligation to identify the designated initializer by a comment in the header file, so that clients of the class can know which initialization method to call.

A simple `init` method will be defined shortly in the source file, but in accordance with your practice it is not declared here in the header file, because it is an override method. The `initWithDocument:` method is a custom method and must be declared.

Note that `initWithDocument:` could have been written with the same name as `init` and a trailing colon, namely, `init:`. This would not make it an overloaded method in the sense used in other programming languages, because, although it would use the same word as the `init` method, it would have a different signature by virtue of taking a parameter, indicated by the colon. Objective-C would recognize that they are two separate methods by the presence or absence of the colon. It is customary in Cocoa, however, for separate initialization methods to be given different names. Usually, additional initialization methods are named initWith, followed by a name suggesting the additional parameter's type: here, Document.

This method is a designated initializer, which means that other objects should normally call it when instantiating a VRButtonModel object. It is guaranteed to call the initialization methods of all classes from which it inherits. In this way, a newly created VRButtonModel object will always be correctly set up and have the information it needs to locate its associated document. As a matter of practice, you should always include a comment indicating which method is the designated initializer.

4. In the source file VRButtonModel.m, add the following initialization methods after @implementation VRButtonModel:

```
#pragma mark INITIALIZATION

- (id)init {
    return [self initWithDocument:nil];
}


- (id)initWithDocument:(VRDocument *)inDocument {
        // designated initializer
    if (self = [super init]) {
        document = inDocument;
    }
    return self;
}
```

The simple `init` method invokes the designated initializer, passing `nil` as its parameter. It may be called automatically by Cocoa in certain circumstances and should be provided, even though you aren't likely to call it yourself. The document object will invoke the designated initializer when it instantiates a new model object and initializes it by passing in the document object.

This method utilizes the standard Objective-C technique that you first saw in Step 3.3 for initializing a subclass of another class. Notice again the tricky test in the first line.

5. Back in the header file VRButtonModel.h, add the following accessor method declaration after the Initialization section:

```
#pragma mark ACCESSORS


- (VRDocument *)document;
```

6. In the source file VRButtonModel.m, add the following accessor method definition after the Initialization section:

```
#pragma mark ACCESSORS


- (VRDocument *)document {
    return document;
}
```

7. In VRButtonModel.m, also add the following after `#import "VRButtonModel.h"` so that it will compile:

```
#import "VRDocument.h"
```

3.5.3 Enable the document to instantiate the model object and access its data.

VRButtonModel is now a complete class in the project, but nobody yet instantiates an object of this class. A VRButtonModel object will serve strictly to hold and manage data associated with the document, so a document object is the obvious candidate to fill this role. Every document will have one and only one associated VRButtonModel object, and the VRButtonModel object will exist for the life of the document.

You will therefore arrange for VRDocument to instantiate a VRButtonModel object immediately when any document is instantiated and to release the VRButtonModel object when its associated document is released. You will create an instance variable and accessor method in VRDocument so that the document can access its data.

1. You must create an instance variable in VRDocument to hold a VRButtonModel object. In VRDocument.h, add the following within the curly braces in the `@interface VRDocument` block:

```
@private
VRButtonModel *buttonModel;
```

2. To prevent the compiler from complaining about an unknown VRButtonModel type, add the following above `@interface VRDocument`:

```
@class VRButtonModel;
```

3. Add the following accessor method declaration after the `@interface VRDocument` block:

```
#pragma mark ACCESSORS

- (VRButtonModel *)buttonModel;
```

You will define this accessor in Instruction 7, below.

You do not need a `setButtonModel:` accessor method for now, because a VRButtonModel object will be instantiated only once, in VRDocument's initialization method, and you don't want to invite anybody else to instantiate a VRButtonModel object. (Later, in Recipe 12, you will discover that you need a `set` accessor, too, after all.)

4. Still in the header file VRDocument.h, you may declare an `init` method after `@interface VRDocument`—but only do this if you feel a need to declare override methods that are commonly overridden anyway:

```
- (id)init;
```

5. In the source file VRDocument.m, add the following definition to initialize the document object by setting its `buttonModel` instance variable, after `@implementation VRDocument`:

```
#pragma mark INITIALIZATION

- (id)init {
    if (self = [super init]) {
        buttonModel = [[VRButtonModel alloc]
                initWithDocument:self];
    }
    return self;
}
```

This method again utilizes the standard Objective-C technique that you first saw in Step 3.3 for initializing a subclass of another class. Notice again the tricky test in the first line.

Its allocation of the VRButtonModel object utilizes the standard Objective-C technique, which you have also seen before, for allocating memory for a new object and initializing it, all in one line. As noted in Step 3.5.2, above, this invokes the model object's designated initializer to pass in a reference to the document.

6. Immediately after the `init` method, add the following `dealloc` method override in VRDocument.m:

```
- (void)dealloc {
    [[self buttonModel] release];
    [super dealloc];
}
```

As you know, it is a general rule of Cocoa programming that any object you allocate by calling `alloc` or certain other methods must be explicitly released by you when it is no longer needed. You have just made sure that your document releases its associated model object when the document itself is deallocated. Because only one VRButtonModel object is created by each document, this takes care of the issue.

You encountered this issue previously, in Step 3.3, when you arranged for the document to release its window controller immediately after creating it. There, however, the window controller continued to live because it was added to the document's array of window controllers, which will eventually take care of releasing it for you when the document is closed. Here, your VRButtonModel object is a custom object entirely under your ownership and control, and you therefore release it only when the document itself is being deallocated.

7. In VRDocument.m, add the implementation of the `buttonModel` accessor method following the INITIALIZATION section:

```
#pragma mark ACCESSORS

- (VRButtonModel *)buttonModel {
    return buttonModel;
}
```

8. To prevent the linker from complaining when it finds invocations of methods from VRButtonModel, add the following after `#import "VRDocument.h"`:

```
#import "VRButtonModel.h"
```

3.5.4 *Define a data variable and accessors in the model object.*

Recall that Interface Builder has already supplied the declaration and a definition stub of the `checkboxAction:` method in VRMainWindowController, complete with the `IBAction` type specification so that it will be recognized as an action method if you later read the header file back into Interface Builder. You will fill in the missing contents of the action method's definition shortly. To do that, you must first implement a variable to hold the data, as well as accessors to set it and get it.

In this and several following recipes, data variables will be declared using standard C data types, such as int, and the special Objective-C Boolean data type BOOL, for simplicity. Later, in Recipe 5, you will learn how to use data typed as Cocoa objects.

1. In the header file VRButtonModel.h, declare a variable to hold the value represented by the checkbox control. Insert the following within the @interface VRButtonModel block (that is, between the curly braces), after the declaration of the document instance variable:

```
BOOL checkboxValue;
```

In a real application, this variable would be named to describe the item whose on/off or true/false state it records, such as speechEnabled or isEnrolled.

2. Declare accessor methods in the header file VRButtonModel.h to set and get the value of the variable. One of them, toggleCheckboxValue, will engender further discussion in a moment. Add these lines at the end of the ACCESSORS section:

```
- (void)setCheckboxValue:(BOOL)inValue;
- (BOOL)checkboxValue;
- (void)toggleCheckboxValue;
```

3. Switch to the source file VRButtonModel.m and implement the accessor methods by adding these lines at the end of the ACCESSORS section:

```
- (void)setCheckboxValue:(BOOL)inValue {
    checkboxValue = inValue;
}

- (BOOL)checkboxValue {
    return checkboxValue;
}

- (void)toggleCheckboxValue {
    [self setCheckboxValue:([self checkboxValue] ? NO : YES)];
}
```

These accessor methods are very simple, to the point where you might think it silly to use methods at all. You will start to see the reason for using them later in this recipe, when you will add support for undo and redo to the set accessor, setCheckboxValue: in Step 6. Later still, in Recipe 4, you will learn that accessor methods play an important role in memory management when the values they access are objects, as opposed to the simple C data type used here.

The last of these accessors, `toggleCheckboxValue`, is a red herring. It illustrates how a developer coming from some other programming tradition might initially think to implement a convenience method using the C ternary operator to set the value of `checkboxValue` to the reverse of its current value. In a moment, in Step 3.6, you will have second thoughts and eliminate this ill-considered method.

Before axing it, however, let's learn something from it. The `toggleCheckboxValue` method could have been written to obtain the value of the variable directly for simplicity, as follows: `checkboxValue = (checkboxValue ? NO : YES);`. Although different programmers might make different decisions on this point, Vermont Recipes will not use this shorter technique, instead always accessing variables through accessor methods. As you will see later, this decision will make it much easier to implement undo and redo, and it will also make it easier to add AppleScript functionality. For this reason, Cocoa applications generally use accessor methods. (The parentheses around the C ternary operator are not required by C or Objective-C syntax. They are included here, as elsewhere in Vermont Recipes in a variety of contexts, only because it makes the code easier to read.)

Now, any objects that may need to obtain the data value associated with the checkbox control can invoke the VRButtonModel accessor method `checkboxValue`, and they can set the value by invoking `setCheckboxValue:`.

3.5.5 Link the window controller to the model object through the document.

There is still something missing. The `setCheckboxValue:` and `checkboxValue` accessor methods are located in the VRButtonModel class where the instance variable holding the data is located, but the action method that will invoke `setCheckboxValue:` to set the data value is located in the VRMainWindowController object. These two objects do not yet know how to talk to one another. You must supply this final missing link now.

1. The first step is to link VRMainWindowController to VRButtonModel. You will do this indirectly, through the document object acting as an intermediary. This illustrates what I meant when I said earlier that the document object is a controller of the model object that holds and manages the data.

    In the header file VRMainWindowController.h, add the following method declaration at the top of the "Accessors – Buttons tab view item" section:

    ```
    - (VRButtonModel *)buttonModel;
    ```

2. Also add the following above @interface `VRMainWindowController` so the compiler will recognize that you meant to use the VRButtonModel type for the return value of the `buttonModel` accessor method:

```
@class VRButtonModel;
```

3. In the source file VRMainWindowController.m, define the new `buttonModel` accessor method by adding the following at the top of the "Accessors – Buttons tab view item" section:

```
- (VRButtonModel *)buttonModel {
    return [[self document] buttonModel];
}
```

Notice that this accessor method does not return an instance variable that was declared in the same object, as you have done previously. Instead, it simply invokes its associated document's `buttonModel` accessor method, completing a chain of links from VRMainWindowController through VRDocument to VRButtonModel. You learned in Step 2.6.2.1 that Cocoa's NSWindowController class already declares an accessor method, `document`, which is how the first link of this chain was established. You inherit that reference in the subclass VRMainWindowController. Declaring accessor methods as chained links in this fashion is very common in Cocoa.

There are at least two other ways in which you could have given VRMainWindowController access to the VRButtonModel object.

You could have declared a `buttonModel` instance variable in VRMainWindowController, as you did in VRDocument, and set it to the value of the document's link to VRButtonModel. However, this would require setting aside additional memory for the instance variable, which might grow out of hand if you followed this practice routinely in a large application. In general, you should avoid intermediate instance variables such as this whenever possible.

As a second alternative, you could have dispensed with the accessor method and simply used chained references through the document object every time VRMainWindowController needs access to a VRButtonModel value. However, the window controller will eventually acquire jurisdiction over a lot of additional user controls, and you would have to invoke a message such as [[[self document] buttonModel] checkboxValue] for each of them. The shorter form of reference allowed by the accessor method in VRMainWindowController, [[self buttonModel] checkboxValue], is a convenient shortcut. It will also make it easier to change the relationship between the document object and the model object, if that should prove necessary in the future. You'll only have to change one statement in VRMainWindowController.m instead of changing code throughout the file.

4. In VRMainWindowController.m, add the following line after **#import** **VRMainWindowController.h**:

```
#import "VRButtonModel.h"
```

Without this, the compiler will complain that VRMainWindowController doesn't understand the **buttonModel** command.

That was a lot to swallow in one meal, but you now have a working model class to manage the data associated with user controls in the Buttons tab view item of the main document window, as well as the infrastructure required to make it accessible to the window controller via the document object. In the next step, you will reap the reward for all your efforts by finally implementing the window controller's action method that will change the value of the data when the user clicks the checkbox control.

3.6 Implement the Action Created in Interface Builder

Now that the VRButtonModel object knows how to store and fetch the data value represented by the checkbox control and the window controller can talk to the VRButtonModel object, you can return to VRMainWindowController's action method and enable it to mediate between the data and the user interface. This is the role prescribed for a window controller in the MVC paradigm.

In the source file VRMainWindowController.m, for a first attempt, insert the following in the stub **myCheckboxAction:** method provided by Interface Builder:

```
[[self buttonModel] toggleCheckboxValue];
```

Normally, an action method would make some use of its reference to the **sender**, a parameter that is always passed with an action message so the action method can know what object initiated the action. But you didn't do that here. You might have thought that you could get away without referring to the state of the **sender**, on the premise that anytime the user clicks a checkbox it always reverses its state. On this assumption, the data value in memory could simply be toggled, too.

However, for a variety of reasons, you should not do it this way. Among other things, to ensure that the data in VRButtonModel does not fall out of sync with the state of the control in the user interface due to an error somewhere else, it would be safer and make debugging easier to replace the statement you just typed with the following:

```
[[self buttonModel] setCheckboxValue:([sender state] == NSOnState)];
```

This new implementation of the action method reads the visual state of the user control object `sender`—which has already changed due to the user's having just clicked it—then asks whether it is `NSOnState`. `NSOnState` is a constant declared in the Cocoa frameworks to describe the state of a button object; another such constant is `NSOffState`. If you look at the declaration of these constants in Cocoa's NSCell.h header file, you will see that `NSOnState` is equated to `1` and `NSOffState` to `0`. This means you can code them as integer or Boolean values, whichever you prefer. The action method sets the data value accordingly, to either `YES` or `NO`.

You will see later that there is another reason not to toggle a checkbox control between either of two states. Checkbox controls can have three states, and you will sometimes want to use the third state, represented by the Cocoa constant `NSMixedState`, equated to `-1`. Your new version of the action method lends itself more readily to being modified to handle three-state checkboxes. You will do this in Recipe 2.

Having settled upon an action method implementation, you should now delete the `toggleCheckboxValue` method from the VRButtonModel header and source files. You no longer need it, since the `setCheckboxValue:` method is a safer and more general means to accomplish the same thing.

Wrap up Step 3. This ends Step 3, the first step in which you added real Objective-C code in Project Builder to the application whose interface you designed and built in Step 2 using Interface Builder. To celebrate, build and run the application now. Building it will allow you to catch and fix any typographical errors you might have made while typing the code. Running it might help to catch any incipient bugs or at least remind you of things you haven't yet implemented.

Click the "Build active target" button in the top-left corner of the project window to compile and link the application. If any errors appear in the Build pane, fix them. If I have done my job right, you will not encounter any build errors other than typos, so you can probably click any error to go directly to the offending line for correction. Then click the "Build and run active executable" button near it to run the application. You can skip the Build button and use the Run button to accomplish both steps, if you prefer, but first you'll have to choose View > Customize Toolbar to add the Run button to the project window's toolbar.

When you run the application, the window you designed in Step 2 will open. You can select tabs to switch panes, and you can click the checkbox control to select and deselect it, making its checkmark appear and disappear. You can also pull down menus. But you are a long way from finished, and many things don't yet work. For example, you can't save the document to disk. You'll tackle that issue next.

Step 4: Provide for Data Storage and Retrieval in Property List Format

It is all well and good to be able to hold and manage data in memory while your application is running, but this obviously isn't enough. Your application must also be able to save its data to persistent storage, typically on a disk of some kind, and to read it back from storage when a document is opened or reverted to a previously saved state. In this step, you will add routines for data storage and retrieval to the application.

After some preliminary setup, you will implement the two data storage override methods provided to you by the Cocoa Document-based Application template, `dataRepresentationOfType:` and `loadDataRepresentation:ofType:`, simply because they are there. These are known, in Cocoa parlance, as *data-based primitives,* and they are frequently used in Cocoa applications. In Step 5, however, you will remove these two override methods and substitute two other override methods known as *location-based primitives.* You can use either technique in a Cocoa application, but not both of them at once. Also, you will save documents in universal XML format in Step 5, instead of the traditional Cocoa property list format used in Step 4, although this is not a necessary consequence of choosing location-based over data-based primitives.

Steps 4 and 5 were initially written before Apple introduced keyed archiving in Mac OS X 10.2. At that time, ordinary archiving without keys was available, but it suffered a few shortcomings that are now cured with the arrival of keyed archiving. Steps 4 and 5 are still included in Vermont Recipes because the techniques they teach serve as a good introduction to the basic framework for persistent storage in Cocoa. At the same time, they also introduce the concepts of paired keys and values that is very common in Cocoa. You will learn how to implement the new keyed archiving technology in Recipe 12, where much of the infrastructure you are about to build in Steps 4 and 5 will be reused.

In Mac OS X 10.1, Apple introduced the concept of hiding filename extensions. Don't think I have overlooked it just because I don't talk about it here. Cocoa handles the new rules for filename extensions and other metadata automatically in document-based applications, so you don't have to pay any attention to the issue. (Well, that's not quite true. You should always use NSFileManager's `displayNameAtPath:` method to obtain the names of files when displaying them in your user interface. This will ensure that your application honors your users' preferences regarding the display of filename extensions.) The new policies are written up in detail in current Cocoa documentation.

4.1 Initialize the Data

Before coding the application's storage routines, you should set up the default value of the data represented by the checkbox user control when a new document is created from scratch. For now, you will simply initialize a new document so that the initial setting of the `checkboxValue` variable in VRButtonModel is `YES`. Later, in Recipe 19, you will implement a full-fledged Cocoa preferences system to let the user determine the default data values for a new document.

Launch Project Builder and open the project, if necessary.

In the source file VRButtonModel.m, add the following statement at the end of the `if` block in the designated initializer, `initWithDocument::`

```
[self setCheckboxValue:YES];
```

If you don't provide an initialization value for a variable, Cocoa will initialize it to `0` (or `NO`, or `nil`, or any value represented internally as `0`). For this reason, it is common practice to omit initialization of data values altogether when they should start life with one of these empty values. I provide a nonempty value here arbitrarily to show you that it works.

Here, the initialization method initialized the `checkboxValue` variable to `YES`. As written, this will apply to both new documents and documents opened from storage. In the latter case, however, the value will be reset to the value read from the saved document, using routines you will write in Step 4.2. You'll tolerate this redundancy for now, since you will replace this default initialization later with a more formal preferences system.

Notice that you have initialized the `checkboxValue` instance variable by calling the `setCheckboxValue:` accessor method. You will encounter an issue with this later. In Step 6, you will add code to the accessor method to register the change in the variable's value with Cocoa's undo manager, so that changes to the data can be undone and redone. You will want to make sure that the initialization of the variable will *not* be registered with the undo manager, however, because there is no point to undoing the default value of a variable in a newly created document. A tempting solution would be to set the instance variable directly by assigning it the value `YES`, like so: `checkboxValue = YES;`. However, it is better to stick to the general advice to use accessor methods everywhere. Go ahead and invoke the accessor method here, as shown. In Step 6, you will learn a convenient technique to avoid registering initialization of the variable with the undo manager.

Finally, notice that a `dealloc` method is not provided for VRButtonModel. At this point, the application does not allocate any objects in VRButtonModel, so it has nothing to release. The Cocoa frameworks will call its super's `dealloc` method, in NSObject, without touching the VRButtonModel object's layer. A `dealloc` method may become necessary in VRButtonModel or its sibling model objects later, as you proceed to add functionality to the application.

4.2 Implement the Document's Data Representation Methods Provided by the Template

VRDocument.m includes two stub methods provided by the Cocoa Document-based Application template related to storing data and reading it back from storage. The role that one of them, `dataRepresentationOfType:`, plays in a Cocoa application is to convert your document's data from its live, internal format, or representation, into an NSData object suitable for storage. An NSData object is nothing fancier than a byte stream or buffer (a stream of characters of any kind). Cocoa doesn't know anything about your document's data structures in advance, of course, so it provides only a stub method. You must fill it in with code that returns an NSData object encoding your document's data, and Cocoa will then store it for you by calling this method at an appropriate time. The second stub method, `loadDataRepresentation:ofType:`, reads data from storage as a byte stream and converts it back to your document's internal storage representation in RAM. You must implement both methods by providing statements that accomplish the data conversion based on the document's data structures.

You will implement these methods in such a way that a document is saved in traditional Cocoa property list format, consisting of key-value pairs in plain text conforming to certain conventions regarding the representation of Cocoa objects such as dictionaries. Any application that knows how to parse property list files, such as Apple's Property List Editor, will be able to read and edit the file. In Step 5, you will revisit this technique and make a couple of simple changes to save the document in a more universal format, XML, instead.

The methods you will write here and in Step 5 are suitable for storing and retrieving individual items of data represented as C data types, such as the Boolean variable `checkboxValue`. Later, in Recipe 5, you will learn how to store and retrieve data represented as Cocoa objects. Eventually, in Recipe 12, you will rewrite the methods discussed here in order to serialize the model objects' data, including its data objects, using a Cocoa technique known as keyed archiving, new in Mac OS X 10.2. For now, though, you will tackle basic concepts.

Be forewarned that the code in this step is dense. It merits close study because, among other things, it is your first exposure to the Cocoa NSDictionary class, which is used frequently throughout Cocoa. It implements the key-value technology to which you have already been exposed.

Launch Project Builder and open the project, if necessary.

4.2.1 *Convert the document's internal data to its external storage representation.*

1. In the header file VRDocument.h, add a declaration before **@end**, as follows:

```
#pragma mark STORAGE

// Saving information to persistent storage

- (NSDictionary *)dictionaryFromModel;
```

2. Switch to the source file VRDocument.m and replace the stub method dataRepresentationOfType: with the following definition:

```
#pragma mark STORAGE

// Saving information to persistent storage

- (NSData *)dataRepresentationOfType:(NSString *)type {
    if ([type isEqualToString:VRDocumentType]) {
        return [[[self dictionaryFromModel] description]
                dataUsingEncoding:NSUTF8StringEncoding];
    } else {
        return nil;
    }
}
```

You will define the **VRDocumentType** variable shortly.

3. In VRDocument.m, define the **dictionaryFromModel** method you just declared immediately following **dataRepresentationOfType:**.

```
- (NSDictionary *)dictionaryFromModel {
    NSMutableDictionary *dictionary =
        [NSMutableDictionary dictionary];
    [dictionary setObject:NSStringFromClass([self class])
        forKey:VRDocumentClassKey];
    [dictionary setObject:[NSString stringWithFormat:@"%d",
        VRDocumentVersion] forKey:VRDocumentVersionKey];
    [[self buttonModel] addDataToDictionary:dictionary];
    // Insert calls to other model objects'
        addDataToDictionary: methods here.
    return dictionary;
}
```

This routine also contains some variables you have not yet defined.

There is a lot going on here. You are urged, as always, to read the documentation for each of the Cocoa methods invoked in these subroutines. The key point is that the custom `dictionaryFromModel` method you just wrote uses key-value pairs to set up a Cocoa-standard temporary mutable dictionary representing the document's data in memory as an intermediate representation of the data before streaming it to persistent storage.

The `dictionaryFromModel` method returns the document model's data in the form of a Cocoa dictionary. It is used by the `dataRepresentationOfType:` method as the source for generating an NSString object (namely, a property list, using the dictionary's built-in `description` method) that is immediately converted to an NSData object—that is, a byte stream—suitable for writing to disk. In a previous version of the Vermont Recipes application, the conversion to an NSData object was accomplished using ASCII encoding; in the present version, it is done using UTF8 encoding to match Cocoa's recent change to that encoding for property lists. The application's override of the NSDocument `dataRepresentationOfType:` method then returns this byte stream to Cocoa, which writes it to persistent storage at an appropriate time.

Dictionaries

Cocoa frameworks and applications frequently use temporary *dictionary* objects as a fast, efficient, and standardized way to encapsulate data and make it available to the application.

A dictionary is a collection of key-value pairs. The keys are usually strings that label the corresponding values, and they are often kept in variables in a running application for easy use. In the dictionary, the keys are organized into a hash table for fast lookup of the matched values.

A dictionary's keys are arbitrary values, unique within any one dictionary. Unlike an array's indices, a dictionary's keys are constant; they do not change value as entries are added or removed.

The values in a dictionary are unordered. Unlike a set's members, a dictionary's values are always associated with a matching key.

A number of convenient methods are provided in NSDictionary and NSMutableDictionary for managing dictionaries, freeing you from the tribulations of hash tables. The most frequently used methods may be those for adding an entry to a dictionary, setObject:forKey:, and for retrieving a value from a dictionary, objectForKey:. Another often-used method is description, which returns the entire dictionary as a string formatted as a standard Cocoa property list. NSDictionary, like many collection classes in Cocoa, also implements methods to write its contents to persistent storage and read them back.

In **dictionaryFromModel**, you first create an empty temporary mutable dictionary, using the NSDictionary convenience method, **dictionary**, and assign it to a local variable named **dictionary** so you can refer to it in other statements within this method. The **dictionary** method is a so-called *class method*, an Objective-C method that you can call without first having instantiated an instance of the class. Unlike C++ and other languages, Objective-C classes are real objects with methods you can call. Class methods are distinguished from instance methods by their leading plus (+) character.

Cocoa is full of *convenience methods* such as **dictionary**, which allocates and initializes a temporary empty dictionary for use in situations like this. Convenience methods return autoreleased objects to you. If you need to use them beyond the current run loop, you must **retain** them and eventually **release** them. Here, although you return the dictionary as a method result, it will immediately be used in the calling method to generate a string object, after which the dictionary object is no longer needed. It therefore does not require a **retain**. It also doesn't require an explicit release, because Cocoa gave it to you autoreleased, which means that it will be deallocated automatically after this method exits.

The **dictionaryFromModel** method uses a mutable dictionary, because it will add entries to the dictionary. It invokes the new dictionary's **setObject:forKey:** method, a workhorse that you will use frequently in Cocoa programming. Here, the first two invocations add strings to the dictionary that identify the class of the object whose data is to be written to storage and an integer number defining the version of the document format being used. The latter will come in handy if you revise your document format and wish to provide for backward compatibility. Because the dictionary will no longer be used after the data is saved to persistent storage, there are no performance-related reasons to convert the mutable dictionary to a more efficient nonmutable dictionary when it is returned.

Finally, you pass the dictionary to an **addDataToDictionary:** method yet to be written in VRButtonModel, where one or more model data values will be added to the dictionary before returning it to you here. You will write that method in Step 4.2.3, below, where you will invoke **setObject:forKey:** for a third time. That method will initially represent the value of the **checkboxValue** variable as a dictionary entry and pass the dictionary back to the document here.

The important point to understand is that later, when you add additional variables to the VRButtonModel object, you will simply add them to the dictionary that VRButtonModel returns to the document object in its **addDataToDictionary:** method, without having to make any changes to the document object. In other words, by setting up the document's storage routines in this fashion, you have isolated the internals of the VRButtonModel data representation so successfully that the document object needn't know about them.

Furthermore, when you add additional model objects to your document, you will only have to add one line for each model object to the document's `dictionaryFromModel` method, such as `[[self anotherModel] addDataTo-Dictionary:dictionary];`. The `dictionary` local variable will accumulate entries from all of them. Take note that it is up to you to make sure all keys declared in the document's several model objects are unique, because dictionaries do not accept duplicate keys (they replace the old entry with the new entry if you add an entry that uses an existing key).

4. Define the new variables referenced in Instructions 2 and 3, above, by inserting the following in VRDocument.m at the top of the STORAGE section:

```
// Keys and values for dictionary

static NSString *VRDocumentClassKey = @"Class";
static NSString *VRDocumentVersionKey = @"Version";
static NSString *VRDocumentType = @"Vermont Recipes document";
static int VRDocumentVersion = 1;
```

The VRDocumentType variable must be assigned the same string that you entered as the CFBundleTypeName in the first element of the CFBundleDocumentTypes array in the target's Application Settings in Step 3.1.1. This is vital; if you get it wrong, your application won't work.

4.2.2 *Convert the document's stored data to its internal representation.*

1. In the header file VRDocument.h, add a declaration before `@end` as follows:

```
// Loading information from persistent storage

- (NSDictionary *)dictionaryFromStorage:(NSData *)data;
```

2. Switch to the source file VRDocument.m and replace the stub method `loadDataRepresentation:ofType:` with the following:

```
// Loading information from persistent storage

- (BOOL)loadDataRepresentation:(NSData *)data
        ofType:(NSString *)type {
    if ([type isEqualToString:VRDocumentType]) {
        NSDictionary *dictionary =
                [self dictionaryFromStorage:data];
        [[self buttonModel]
                restoreDataFromDictionary:dictionary];
        // Insert calls to other model objects'
```

```
        restoreDataFromDictionary: methods here.
        return YES;
    } else {
        return NO;
    }
}
```

The `loadDataRepresentation:ofType:` method invokes the VRButtonModel object's `restoreDataFromDictionary:` method, which you will write shortly. The VRButtonModel's `restoreDataFromDictionary:` method plays a role similar to that played by its `addDataToDictionary:` method, invoked in `dictionaryFromMemory` in Step 4.2.1, above. It allows the VRButtonModel object to take a dictionary, which was just read from persistent storage as a byte stream and converted to a dictionary by `dictionaryFromStorage:`, and to extract data from it in the form required by the data variables in VRButtonModel. Again, the document's data storage routines do not need to know anything about the data format implemented in VRButtonModel.

As in Step 4.2.1, this scheme can accommodate multiple model objects if you simply add one line for each model object, such as `[[self anotherModel] restoreDataFromDictionary:dictionary];`, to the document's `loadDataRepresentation:ofType:` method. The dictionary may contain values destined for other model objects as well, but each model object knows which values belong to it by their keys. Take care to ensure that all keys in the document's model objects are unique.

This is what I meant earlier when I said that VRDocument is a controller, not a model object. It simply controls what will soon become a whole bunch of model objects, saving them to disk and retrieving them as needed, without knowing anything about their internal data representation. By encapsulating the data representation in each model object, you make maintenance and enhancement of your application vastly easier.

3. In VRDocument.m, implement the method whose declaration you added in Instruction 1, above, immediately following `loadDataRepresentation:ofType::`

```
- (NSDictionary *)dictionaryFromStorage:(NSData *)data {
    NSString *string = [[NSString alloc]
            initWithData:data encoding:NSUTF8StringEncoding];
    NSDictionary *dictionary = [string propertyList];
    [string release];
    return dictionary;
}
```

This method goes to the trouble of converting the NSData object that was read from persistent storage into a string allocated and released in this method for only one reason: to take advantage of the built-in NSString method **propertyList**. This is the counterpart of the NSDictionary **description** method you used in the **dataRepresentationOfType:** method in Step 4.2.1 to encode the dictionary as a string formatted as a property list for storage. As it is used here, **propertyList** parses the string and returns it as an NSDictionary object to be returned to **loadDataRepresentation:ofType:**, where it will be used to restore the data to the appropriate model object.

4.2.3 Implement the model object's data conversion methods.

1. In the VRButtonModel.h header file, insert the following declarations:

```
#pragma mark STORAGE

// Saving information to persistent storage:

- (void)addDataToDictionary:(NSMutableDictionary *)dictionary;

// Loading information from persistent storage:

- (void)restoreDataFromDictionary:(NSDictionary *)dictionary;
```

2. In the VRButtonModel.m source file, insert the following definitions:

```
#pragma mark STORAGE

// Keys and values for dictionary

static NSString *VRCheckboxValueKey =
    @"VRButtonModelCheckboxValue";

// Saving information to persistent storage:

- (void)addDataToDictionary:(NSMutableDictionary *)dictionary {
    [dictionary setObject:[NSString stringWithFormat:@"%d",
        [self checkboxValue]] forKey:VRCheckboxValueKey];
}

// Loading information from persistent storage:

- (void)restoreDataFromDictionary:(NSDictionary *)dictionary {
    [self setCheckboxValue:(BOOL)[[dictionary
        objectForKey:VRCheckboxValueKey] intValue]];
}
```

The Boolean value for the **checkboxValue** setting is converted and returned as a string in **addDataToDictionary:**, after which it will be stored as a byte stream. This is accomplished here with another workhorse Cocoa method, **stringWithFormat:**. It uses standard C `printf` codes (with some modifications) to convert values, here taking the Boolean value returned by the **checkboxValue** accessor method and converting it to a string representation of an integer. The **restoreDataFromDictionary:** method does the reverse, taking the integer value of the string and casting it to a Boolean value. In Recipe 2 onward, you will add many similar statements to this method to convert other data values to string format for storage. Note that any data that is already in string format does not have to be converted using the **stringWithFormat:** method, but can instead be installed directly into the dictionary. Note also that it is not necessary to populate a dictionary with string values; you can also use values consisting of Cocoa objects. You use strings here because of the ease with which it allows you to stream the dictionary to disk.

The key defined for use with the NSDictionary **setObject:forKey:** and **objectForKey:** methods is rather long: **@"VRButtonModelCheckboxValue"**. The length is of no concern from a performance viewpoint—in fact, it is an advantage, which is why you tend to see very long strings used as keys in Cocoa applications—because it will be hashed in the dictionary. You should include the name of the model object in the key as an aid to help you ensure that all keys in all of the document's model objects are unique.

Notice that the **checkboxValue** variable is set indirectly using the **setCheckboxValue:** accessor method in **restoreDataFromDictionary:**. This is consistent with the decision you made in Step 4.1 to hew to the advice to always use accessor methods to access instance variables, even in data initialization situations. Reading data from disk is a form of initialization, but you will learn a technique in Step 6 to avoid registering with the undo manager here.

These two methods belong in the VRButtonModel object, a model object, because they involve direct manipulation of the object's internal data structures. The outside world, including the document object, should know nothing of these internal data structures. All the document needs to know is that they return or accept a dictionary, which the document can store or retrieve without knowing its contents. As you add more data variables to VRButtonModel, you will simply add lines to these two methods to convert the individual variables to and from the dictionary object without having to make any changes to the document object.

4.3 Display the Document's Data

You have now initialized the document's internal data variable `checkboxValue` to a default value of `YES` when a new document is created, and you have written routines to set the variable from data that was read in from storage when an existing document is opened or reverted. But you have written nothing yet to enable VRMainWindowController to tell the window to show the value held in `checkboxValue` to the user in either event.

In most Cocoa applications, this is the job of the `awakeFromNib` method, which you must override. Cocoa sends an `awakeFromNib` message whenever a nib file is loaded and unarchived. The message is sent to every object at the top level of the nib file, including the nib file's owner, which is represented in the nib file by the File's Owner proxy. Any such object that overrides the `awakeFromNib` method receives and acts on this message. This is the first point at which the object can count on all its nib file's connections having been instantiated, initialized, and connected, so that they are ready to go to work. For example, any windows in the nib file have now been loaded and connected, although their contents are not yet visible.

Launch Project Builder and open the project, if necessary.

Add the following to the source file VRMainWindowController.m before the ACTIONS section:

```
#pragma mark WINDOW MANAGEMENT

- (void)awakeFromNib {
    [[self checkbox] setState:([[self buttonModel] checkboxValue]
            ? NSOnState : NSOffState)];
    if (![[self document] fileName]) {
        [[self window] center];
    }
}
```

This method implements a Cocoa informal protocol, so it is not necessary to declare it in the header file. The `awakeFromNib` method is declared in the header file NSNibLoading.h in what is called *an informal protocol* or *category* on the NSObject named NSNibAwaking. You don't need to understand informal protocols or categories yet. The effect is that every Cocoa object descended from NSObject (which means almost but not quite all of the objects used in Cocoa) will recognize the `awakeFromNib` message if they override it, even if they don't declare it in their interfaces.

In earlier versions of the Vermont Recipes application, I used NSWindowController's `windowDidLoad` delegate method instead of `awakeFromNib`. As in the case of `awakeFromNib`, Cocoa invokes `windowDidLoad` automatically after the document's nib file has been loaded and all of its internals have been initialized, and the two are generally interchangeable in a document-based application. However, I noticed that if the window's "Visible at launch time" attribute is turned on in Interface Builder's Info Panel, as mentioned in Step 2.1.5, using `windowDidLoad` instead of `awakeFromNib` has the effect of showing the updating of the checkbox control's visible state a fraction of a second after the window itself becomes visible. In a window with many controls, the effect would be a cascade of user controls updating onscreen, one after the other, at least in the case of controls whose initial value is set to something other than their empty or deselected state. You can avoid this unsightly effect by using `awakeFromNib` instead, no matter what the setting of the "Visible at launch time" attribute.

Now, whenever the window loads, whether as a new document that has never been saved or as a document that was just loaded from storage, the checkbox control in the Buttons pane of the main document window will immediately be updated to reflect the internal state of the VRButtonModel variable `checkboxValue`, just before the window becomes visible.

You will deal later, in Step 7, with the case where the user chooses the Revert menu item, which does not reload the nib file and therefore does not cause the `awakeFromNib` method to be invoked.

Since the `awakeFromNib` method is where almost all code is called that affects the appearance of a window just before it becomes visible, you should take this opportunity to make sure the first new untitled window is centered on the main screen, in accordance with the *Aqua Human Interface Guidelines*. You check first to see whether the document has a filename; if not, you know it is a new untitled window and tell it to center itself. Subsequent new windows will automatically be staggered below and to the right. You will deal later with the position of windows for existing documents opened from disk.

WRAP UP STEP 4. You have now finished Step 4. Build and run the application, because for the first time you should be able to make it do something arguably useful—namely, save and retrieve data.

When the application finishes launching and the main document window opens, its checkbox control should be selected (that is, checked), reflecting the default YES value you gave to it in code. This proves that your `awakeFromNib` method is correctly updating the user interface to correspond to the model object's data. Click the control to deselect it. Then choose File > Save As and use the sheet that is presented to save the document somewhere on disk under any name you like. Then close the window, and choose File > Open or File > Open Recent to reopen the document. When its window opens, the control should still be deselected, proving that the document's YES value was changed to NO and saved to disk and that the document's data was properly retrieved from disk and displayed.

Check out the document's format. First, select it in the Finder and choose File > Get Info, then select the Info window's Name & Extension pane. You should see that your saved document was given the file extension you specified in Application Settings: namely, VRd1. Next, drag the saved document's icon onto the TextEdit application icon. A window will open, showing you the contents of your document in plain text property list format. You should recognize the three items in the document. You can also launch Property List Editor and, from its File menu, open the document into that application's outline format.

Congratulations! But you can't rest on your laurels yet, because you haven't yet implemented many of the required Mac OS X application behaviors. For example, you might have noticed that the top-left button in the document's window did not acquire a dot when you changed the value of the checkbox control to indicate that it was "dirtied," or changed, and requires saving. And when you closed the window after changing the control's setting, you were not given a chance to save the document. Also, undo and redo didn't work. You should get back to work and fix these problems, but first you will pause in the next step to tinker with the data storage routines.

Step 5: Provide a Better Way to Save Data, in XML Format

Having just implemented data storage routines, you will now immediately take a brief detour to implement a better way of doing it.

In Step 4.2, you learned one way to save a document's data to persistent storage and retrieve it. There, you used a dictionary object as a vehicle to save the data in Cocoa's old property list format, a text format that consists of a list of key-value pairs, each separated by an equal sign (=). Now, in this step, you will learn how to save a document in XML format. Calling this a better way to save data is a bit of an exaggeration, as the way you did it originally is a perfectly viable method for saving data in appropriate circumstances. But XML has many uses, and this is a good opportunity to learn one utterly painless way to save your data in XML format.

XML (Extensible Markup Language, a W3C Recommendation at www.w3.org/XML/) has taken the digital world by storm because it is a generalized computer-readable markup format for structured data. The old Cocoa property list format is more readable for humans, because your eyes don't have to sift through a lot of angle-bracketed XML tags with less than obvious meanings. XML is a universal format for storing computer data in text form, amenable to automated parsing by XML utilities and easy integration with data obtained from other sources. Once a document type definition (DTD) for a particular XML data set is publicly available, as the Cocoa property list DTD is on your computer at /System/Library/DTDs/PropertyList.dtd, any XML utility can read and manipulate its data.

For example, in Mac OS X, you can use Late Night Software's free XML Tools scripting addition to parse data files saved by your application in XML format and extract individual items using AppleScript. This makes your application a better citizen of the Mac OS X world even if it is not itself scriptable. If you're curious as to how this might work, examine the Lookup Vermont Recipes Key script in the listing at the end of this step; this script uses XML Tools to look up a value in a Vermont Recipes data file, given a valid key. (The script is specially designed to understand the specific Vermont Recipes XML data format used in this step; it is not a generalized XML parser.)

Mac OS X is acquiring even more support for the XML format as time goes by. Your application may gain a wider market if potential customers know that its data will be accessible in this fashion. Of course, you will sacrifice the economic advantages that a proprietary data format gives to a product that already enjoys market dominance in its class. Even if you are lucky enough to have a product in this category, XML might be a good data interchange format for your application.

Cocoa's NSDocument class contains facilities that allow a document-based application to save data to persistent storage by overriding built-in methods at various levels. In Step 4.2, you took the easy path, overriding the `dataRepresentationOfType:` method that the Cocoa Document-based Application template placed in your VRDocument class when you first created the Vermont Recipes project files. Cocoa also allows you to override another built-in method, `writeToFile:OfType:`, as one data storage alternative. The documentation describes the former as a *data-based primitive* and the latter as a *location-based primitive*. You can use either, and in this step you will choose the location-based primitive.

Your `writeToFile:ofType:` method will simply invoke a method with a similar name declared in Cocoa's NSDictionary class. Methods with the name `writeToFile:-atomically:` exist in the Cocoa collection classes NSArray, NSData, NSDictionary, and NSString for just this purpose—namely, to let you call them in your document class's override of the NSDocument `writeToFile:OfType:` method. The NSDictionary implementation is just what you want here, because the AppKit *Release Notes* for Mac OS X 10.0 disclose that, with that release, these methods now write their data in XML format by default.

NSDocument also contains a `readFromFile:ofType:` method, and the collection classes contain methods such as NSDictionary's `dictionaryWithContentsOfFile:` class methods that let you read XML files back into memory from persistent storage.

1. You don't want to throw away work already undertaken, in case this new technique doesn't pan out. So, for the time being, comment out the existing code in

VRDocument.m that you will be replacing. In the "Saving information to persistent storage" subsection of the STORAGE section, bracket the implementation of the `dataRepresentationOfType:` method with a pair of comment brackets, /* and */. Keep the `dictionaryFromModel` method, however, because you need it to set up your document's data in RAM as a temporary dictionary, which will then write itself to persistent storage in XML format.

2. In VRDocument.m, add the following override method after the method that you commented out:

```
- (BOOL)writeToFile:(NSString *)fileName
      ofType:(NSString *)type {
   if ([type isEqualToString:VRDocumentType]) {
      return [[self dictionaryFromModel] writeToFile:fileName
            atomically:YES];
   } else {
      return NO;
   }
}
```

You needn't declare this method in VRDocument.h, since it is an override method.

The key statement is in the middle of the method: `return [[self dictionary-FromMemory] writeToFile:fileName atomically:YES];`. This simply tells the dictionary object that you created in `dictionaryFromMemory` to write itself to persistent storage, which as of Mac OS X 10.0 it does in XML format. It automatically uses UTF-8 encoding. Since you have overwritten the document's `writeToFile:ofType:` method in its entirety without calling its super, this completely replaces the built-in behavior of the Cocoa version of this document method, relying on the dictionary's `writeToFile:atomically:` method for actual disk access.

You will recognize the rest of the code in this method as having been stolen from your old `dataRepresentationOfType:` override method, which used it to make sure the document being written to persistent storage was of the right type and, if so, to return the document's data in the form of a byte stream in traditional Cocoa property list format. The method you wrote there returned `nil` if the document was of the wrong type, because the `dataRepresentationOfType:` method is supposed to return an object. The method you are writing here returns `NO`, because the `writeToFile:OfType:` method is supposed to return a Boolean value. If the document is of the correct type, you return the `YES` or `NO` value returned by the dictionary's `writeToFile:atomically:` method, instead of the NSData object returned by the `dataRepresentationOfType:` method. A `NO` return value will result in Cocoa's presenting an alert telling you that it could not save the file.

The `atomically` parameter specifies whether the file should be fully written to persistent storage before the old version of the file is deleted. You normally want to pass `YES` to this parameter to ensure against loss of data due to power failures and the like.

One final comment: The data-storage technique that you just abandoned invoked a built-in NSDictionary method, `description`, to generate the text for the key-value pairs that you then saved to persistent storage. One frequently asked question is why the `description` method wasn't updated in Mac OS X 10.0, as `writeToFile:OfType:` was, to provide an XML rendition of the data instead of a list of equated key-value pairs. The answer is that virtually every Cocoa class implements a `description` method whose principal purpose is to assist you in debugging your applications. The debugger used in Project Builder does not provide a GUI for reading the current values of the instance variables declared in an object, but this is information that would be very useful to you when debugging. What you do is to use the print object or po command in the debugger, which calls the object's `description` method, if it has one, and shows you its instance variables' values. Because the point of the `description` method is to provide readily human-readable text for debugging, it would not make sense to have it return an XML rendition.

3. If you were to compile and run the application at this point, you might be surprised to discover that you could stop here if you wanted to. Try it. Once the initial, untitled Vermont Recipes document is visible onscreen, save it as is and close its window. Then, in the Finder, drag the document's icon onto the TextEdit application icon to see what it looks like. Sure enough, you see the telltale tag-filled text of an XML document, complete with elements telling you what version of the XML standard is used and where the property list DTD can be found. That isn't the surprise, though—after all, you expected this to work, didn't you? The surprise comes when you then return to the Vermont Recipes application and try to open the document you just saved. It works! How could this be? You haven't yet revised your code to *read* XML documents, but only to *write* them.

    The explanation lies in the NSString `propertyList` method you used in your `dictionaryFromStorage:` method in Step 4.2.2 to convert the file's data to dictionary form after it is read back in from persistent storage. It already knows how to interpret XML data as well as old-style property list data.

4. However, there is value in symmetry, and the methods you wrote previously to read the file from persistent storage were not as efficient as they might be, so you will now revise the methods that read a Vermont Recipes document to correspond to the pattern you just used to save it to persistent storage.

For the time being, comment out the existing code in VRDocument.m that you will be replacing. In the "Loading information from persistent storage" subsection of the STORAGE section, bracket the entire implementation of the **loadDataRepresentation:ofType:** and **dictionaryFromStorage:** methods with a pair of comment delimiters, /* and */. You must also comment out the declaration of **dictionaryFromStorage:** in the header file, VRDocument.h.

5. In VRDocument.m, add the following override method after the methods that you commented out:

```
- (BOOL)readFromFile:(NSString *)fileName
      ofType:(NSString *)type {
   if ([type isEqualToString:VRDocumentType]) {
      NSDictionary *dictionary = [NSDictionary
            dictionaryWithContentsOfFile:fileName];
      [[self buttonModel]
restoreDataFromDictionary:dictionary];
      // Insert calls to other model objects'
         restoreDataFromDictionary: methods here.
      return (dictionary != nil);
   } else {
      return NO;
   }
}
```

You needn't declare this method in VRDocument.h, since it is an override method.

Notice that this method retrieves the data from persistent storage using NSDictionary's **dictionaryWithContentsOfFile:** class method. This built-in Cocoa method takes the place of the custom **dictionaryFromStorage:** method you wrote in Step 4.2.2. In general, many of Cocoa's Foundation classes, not just NSData, include methods for reading data directly into an instance of the class from persistent storage, just as many of them include methods for writing their data directly to persistent storage.

6. Before deleting the code you commented out, compile and run the application, write a file to persistent storage, and read it back to make sure these routines are working. If all is well, delete the commented-out code from VRDocument.h and VRDocument.m.

7. As long as you're improving the application's data storage routines, why not arrange for automatic maintenance of backup files? It is as simple as overriding NSDocument's **keepBackupFile** method to return **YES** instead of the default **NO**.

Add the following to VRDocument.m at the top of the "Saving information to persistent storage" section:

```
- (BOOL)keepBackupFile {
    return YES;
}
```

Now, every time you choose File > Save to save recent changes to a Vermont Recipes document, the old version will be retained instead of being deleted after the new version is successfully written to disk. The old version, now serving as a backup, retains the original name except for a tilde (~) appended at the end of the filename just before the file extension. Subsequent saves will delete the last backup file and replace it with the new backup file, so you will never have more than one backup file on your disk at a time. This is an awfully limited backup scheme, but it's a lot better than none at all, and it gives you a layer of protection that goes one step beyond the Revert command.

WRAP UP STEP 5. Perform the same tests you performed at the end of Step 4 to verify that the data is still saved and retrieved successfully, this time in XML format. In addition, change the value of the checkbox user control and resave the file. This time, open the backup file to verify that the previous value of the control was retained as a backup.

You have now substituted a more useful file format, XML, for the old-style property list format in which Vermont Recipes documents were originally saved. In the process, you have provided for a system of automatic backup files to protect your data against loss. In the next step, you will begin to implement additional features of a Cocoa document-based application, starting with undo and redo support.

```
(*
 * Lookup Vermont Recipes Key
 * version 1.0.1, 02-02-04
 * Bill Cheeseman


 * This script asks you to choose a Vermont Recipes file
 * and to provide a key to look up, then it displays the
 * value associated with the key, if any.
 *
 * The script is written to work with a file saved by the
 * Vermont Recipes application as specified in Recipe 1.
 * It should continue to work with files saved by later
 * versions of Vermont Recipes, until we begin to save
 * values in collection classes such as arrays or dictionaries
 * or to save nonstring values. In Recipe 1, the Vermont
 * Recipes document format is a specialized property list in
```

```
  * XML form consisting of a list of entries, each of which is
  * a key-value pair, in a top-level dictionary. Keys and
  * values are strings.
  *
  * The script requires the XML Tools scripting addition
  * from Late Night Software:
  *      <www.latenightsw.com/freeware/XMLTools2/>

  * Some lines are wrapped using the AppleScript line
  * continuation character ("¬").
  *)

choose file with prompt "Choose a Vermont Recipes document"
tell application "TextEdit"
    open result
    get text of document 1
end tell
set XMLdoc to parse XML result ¬
    -- requires XML Tools 2.2 scripting addition

display dialog "Key to search for:" default answer ""
set searchKey to text returned of result
set foundValue to SearchXMLdoc(XMLdoc, searchKey)
beep
display dialog searchKey & " = " & foundValue ¬
        buttons {"OK"} default button "OK"

to SearchXMLdoc(aDoc, aKey)
    (* Returns a string value associated with the string 'aKey'
    in 'aDoc'; the 'aDoc' parameter is the text of an XML
    document after parsing by the XML Tools scripting addition.
    This handler tests 'aDoc' to make sure it appears to be from
    a valid XML property list document, then hands off the search
    to subroutine handlers. Generates errors number 5000-5003 if
    document is not a proper XML property list. *)

    tell aDoc
        if class of it is XML document then
            if XML doctype name is "plist" then
                if XML tag is "plist" then
                    tell item 1 of XML contents
(
```

(continues on next page)

```
                    if XML tag is "dict" then
                        return my SearchPListDict ¬
                            (XML contents, aKey)
                    else
                        error "Property list does not contain ¬
                            a dictionary" number 5003
                    end if
                end tell
            else
                error "Document does not contain a ¬
                    property list" number 5002
            end if
        else
            error "Document is not an XML property ¬
                list document" number 5001
        end if
    else
        error "Document is not an XML document" number 5000
    end if
    end tell
end SearchXMLdoc


to SearchPListDict(aDict, aKey)
    (* Returns a string value associated with the string 'aKey'
    in 'dict'; the 'dict' parameter is a dictionary element of
    an XML pList document. Generates error number 5006 if key
    is not found. *)

    tell aDict
        count
        repeat with idx from 1 to result by 2
            my SearchPListEntry({item idx, item (idx + 1)})
            if PListKey of result is aKey then ¬
                return pListValue of result
        end repeat
        error "Not found" number 5006
    end tell
end SearchPListDict


to SearchPListEntry(aEntry)
    (* Returns an AppleScript record in the form
```

```
{pListKey:<string>, pListValue:<string>}; the 'aEntry'
parameter is a list of two items, where item 1 is a
pList key and item 2 is the associated pList value
(which is a string). Generates errors number 5004-5005
if the key-value pair is ill-formed. *)

local pair
tell aEntry
    tell item 1 — process key
        if XML tag is "key" then
            set pair to {PListKey:item 1 of XML contents}
        else
            error "Ill-formed property list: missing key" ¬
                    number 5004
        end if
    end tell
    tell item 2 — process value
        if XML tag is "string" then
            set pair to pair & {pListValue:item 1 of XML contents}
        else
            error "Ill-formed property list: missing value" ¬
                    number 5005
        end if
    end tell
end tell
return pair
end SearchPListEntry
```

Step 6: Implement Undo and Redo

In Step 4 and Step 5 you wrote methods to convert the document's internal data to a representation suitable for storage. However, although the Save and Save As menu items can now be used to save a modified document, the application does not yet have a means to know when the document needs to be saved. It cannot tell when data in the model object has been altered. You need to add routines to make a dot appear in the document window's Save button, signifying that the document has been changed; to cause an alert to appear if the user attempts to close a modified document; and to enable the Revert menu item to restore the previously saved data when a document has been modified.

In Cocoa, you can keep track of document changes explicitly, but in a document-based application, it will be accomplished automatically if you implement the Cocoa AppKit's built-in undo and redo capability. The undo manager necessarily tracks changes made by the user, and Cocoa uses this information to implement the proper window and menu behaviors. Undo and redo support should be part of every Macintosh application, so you will now take advantage of this labor-saving feature by implementing undo and redo. As a side benefit, you will be able to dispense with tracking document changes yourself.

The basic operating principle behind Cocoa's undo and redo support is that changes to the application's state initiated by the user, especially changes to a document's data, should be registered or recorded with the appropriate undo manager. The undo manager can automatically revert or restore the change later, when the user chooses Undo or Redo from the Edit menu, by using information provided at the time of registration or recording.

It normally makes sense to register a change to a document's data in a *primitive* accessor method, which, like `setCheckboxValue:` in VRButtonModel, performs the operation by directly altering an instance variable. Every other method that invokes the primitive method will thereby gain the benefit of Cocoa's undo and redo support. As noted previously, every operation that changes the value of the variable should do so through this method.

Extended methods, which invoke a primitive method to effect a change indirectly, should not register with the undo manager because the primitive method will do it for them. An example of an extended method is `toggleCheckboxValue`, which you briefly implemented in Step 3.5; it invoked the primitive method, `setCheckboxValue:`, to do its work and therefore would not have needed to register with the undo manager itself.

Also recall from Step 4.1 that initialization of an instance variable should not be undoable. You can nevertheless safely implement undo registration in a primitive method because toward the end of this step you will modify the application's initialization routines to suppress undo registration, enabling the application to use the primitive accessor method to set data variables even during initialization.

At this point, the only action you need to deal with for undo and redo is the user's clicking the checkbox control to change the VRButtonModel's `checkboxValue` variable. This change is implemented by the `setCheckboxValue:` accessor method in VRButtonModel. Therefore, you should implement undo and redo registration in that method.

After you have implemented undo and redo for the document's data, you will attend to the wording of the Undo and Redo menu items and consider how the application should update its user interface to remain synchronized with the changed data.

6.1 Register Data Changes with the Document's Undo Manager

Launch Project Builder and open the project, if necessary.

1. In the source file VRButtonModel.m, change the `setCheckboxValue:` primitive accessor method to the following:

```
- (void)setCheckboxValue:(BOOL)inValue {
    [[[self undoManager] prepareWithInvocationTarget:self]
        setCheckboxValue:checkboxValue];
    checkboxValue = value;
}
```

The invocation of the undo manager's `prepareWithInvocationTarget:` method causes the document to create an undo manager object "lazily," if one does not already exist. That is, the application will never waste time and effort to create an undo manager object unless and until it is needed.

The statement records, or saves in memory, the `setCheckboxValue:` method, as if it were being called now using the current state of the `checkboxValue` variable—that is, its state before the user clicked the checkbox control. This recorded version of the call will automatically be played back from the undo manager's undo stack when the user chooses Undo from the Edit menu to restore the variable to this recorded value. At the same time, it will record a new undo action with the old value and place it on the undo manager's redo stack. Cocoa will play this back from the redo stack when the user chooses Redo.

2. VRButtonModel does not have a way to talk to the undo manager, so you must add one. The undo manager will be associated with the document object, so you will create a chained accessor method, just as you did in Step 3.5.5 to enable the window manager to access the VRButtonModel object. In the header file VRButtonModel.h, add this declaration in the Accessors section, after the **document** accessor method:

```
- (NSUndoManager *)undoManager;
```

In the source file VRButtonModel.m, add this definition in the Accessors section, after the **document** accessor method:

```
- (NSUndoManager *)undoManager {
    return [[self document] undoManager];
}
```

Delegation

Cocoa makes heavy use of delegation as a means for one object to carry out actions or respond to events on behalf of another object. This is an important factor in the power and flexibility of Cocoa, since it allows a simple Cocoa application to behave appropriately, while at the same time allowing Cocoa developers to create more complex applications by altering chosen aspects of default Cocoa behavior. It is often easier to implement a delegate method in a delegate class than it is to subclass a Cocoa class.

An object that can hand off some of its responsibilities to a delegate always includes a standardized mechanism to appoint a delegate, the setDelegate: method. This sets up an instance variable that gives the delegator the ability to talk to the delegate. Typically, however, a developer of a new class uses Interface Builder to connect the delegate to the delegator's delegate outlet instead.

The developer of a class that can appoint a delegate tries to anticipate all events that a delegate could usefully handle and declares for each such event a *delegate method.* When a relevant event occurs at run time, the delegating object first checks to see whether a delegate has been appointed and, if so, whether the delegate implements the delegate method. If so, the delegating object calls the delegate method as implemented by the delegate.

Before writing a subclass to react to an event, you should always consider whether an object exists that already calls appropriate delegate methods in connection with the event. If so, you can implement the delegate method in a delegate class instead. The delegate method will be called automatically by the delegator when the triggering event occurs. There isn't any rule against writing subclasses in Cocoa; it's just that implementing a delegate method is often a simpler and more direct way to accomplish something.

Many delegate methods in Cocoa use *will, should,* or *did* in their names. By convention, the delegator invokes a will delegate method when the event is about to be handled; the delegate's implementation of the delegate method can cause the delegator to do something beforehand. The delegator invokes a should delegate method before the event is handled; the delegate's implementation can, however, prevent anything from happening in response to the event, or veto it, as well as altering what would normally happen. The delegator invokes a did delegate method just after the event has been handled.

You, too, can write classes that employ delegates. Designing appropriate delegate methods may seem like a black art, but all it requires is a design with good class structure and an understanding of how delegates could make use of it. Implementation is trivial; just check whether a delegate has been appointed and has implemented a particular delegate method before calling it.

3. The application must know how to locate the relevant undo manager stack when the user chooses the Undo or Redo menu item. Cocoa handles this in the same way it handles most menu items, by walking the responder chain from the current first responder until it finds a responder that knows how to handle the command. It is possible that the application will encounter an undo manager object before reaching the top of the responder chain; for example, one might have been implemented in a custom view object that handles undo and redo commands itself. If the application reaches the window object at the top of the chain without encountering an undo manager object, it asks the window object's delegate for a reference to an undo manager object. If a delegate exists that implements the `windowWillReturnUndoManager:` delegate method, Cocoa calls it. If there is no delegate or the delegate method is not found, the window creates its own undo manager and uses that. Here, the word *will* embedded in the name of this method indicates that the window manager is about to return an undo manager to the application. By implementing the delegate method in your window controller, you alter Cocoa's default behavior, causing the window to return an undo manager of your choosing instead of returning the undo manager it would otherwise create itself.

Recall that VRMainWindowController was designated as the window's delegate in Interface Builder, in Step 2.6.3. In document-based applications, the model is supposed to handle all of the undo chores, and the window controller therefore should return the document's undo manager. To ensure that the application finds the document's undo or redo stack at this point, add the following delegate method to the source file VRMainWindowController.m, after the ACCESSORS section.

```
#pragma mark UNDO MANAGEMENT


- (NSUndoManager *)windowWillReturnUndoManager:
        (NSWindow *)window {
    return [[self document] undoManager];
}
```

It is not necessary to declare this method in the header file VRMainWindowController.h, because it is a delegate method.

Documentation

To understand what delegation is all about, read "Delegating Authority—Cocoa Delegation and Notification," a 1999 article by Erik Buck on the Stepwise site at www.stepwise.com.

4. You should clear the undo and redo stacks for the document when it is saved because, in the Vermont Recipes application, saving a document is regarded as committing all changes. You could write an application to allow undo beyond the last save, as is done, for example, in Project Builder, but that is a complication you don't need at this stage of the learning process. Add the following line at the beginning of the if test in the `writeToFile:ofType:` method in the source file VRDocument.m:

```
[[self undoManager] removeAllActions];
```

5. Back in Step 4, you were twice promised a technique to avoid registration with the undo manager when the VRButtonModel's `setCheckboxValue:` accessor method was called in data initialization situations.

It turns out that Cocoa provides an easy way to suppress registration with the undo manager: the `disableUndoRegistration` and `enableUndoRegistration` methods declared in NSUndoManager. If you bracket a call to the `setCheckboxValue:` accessor method with invocations of these two NSUndoManager methods, the accessor method will not register the change with the undo manager.

You will now use this technique in the initialization of the data variable associated with the checkbox control when a new document is created. In VRButtonModel.m, surround the line of the `initWithDocument:` method that initializes the `checkboxValue` instance variable with these two calls, so that it looks like this:

```
[[self undoManager] disableUndoRegistration];
[self setCheckboxValue:YES];
[[self undoManager] enableUndoRegistration];
```

You also need to take care to avoid registering with the undo manager when you load the `checkboxValue` instance variable from disk upon opening an existing document or reverting a document to its saved state, which are forms of initialization. The cure is identical. In VRButtonModel.m, replace the contents of the `restoreDataFromDictionary:` method with the following:

```
[[self undoManager] disableUndoRegistration];
[self setCheckboxValue:(BOOL)[[dictionary
        objectForKey:VRCheckboxValueKey] intValue]];
[[self undoManager] enableUndoRegistration];
```

Later, in Recipe 2, accessor methods to initialize additional instance variables will always be inserted between the `disableUndoRegistration` and `enableUndoRegistration` calls.

6.2 Set the Undo and Redo Menu Item Titles with Localized Strings

Applications that implement undo and redo should provide descriptive titles for the Undo and Redo menu items to give the user a fairly specific idea of what will happen when they are chosen. This is particularly important in a Cocoa application, where multiple undo and redo are the norm. A user could easily get lost if faced with a succession of Undo menu items all titled simply Undo.

1. In the source file VRMainWindowController.m, insert the following lines at the end of the **checkboxAction:** method:

```
if ([sender state] == NSOnState) {
    [[[self document] undoManager]
            setActionName:NSLocalizedString(@"Set Checkbox",
            @"Name of undo/redo menu item after checkbox control
            was set")];
} else {
    [[[self document] undoManager]
            setActionName:NSLocalizedString(@"Clear Checkbox",
            @"Name of undo/redo menu item after checkbox control
            was cleared")];
}
```

This invocation of the undo manager's **setActionName:** method will cause the Undo or Redo menu item's title to change whenever this user action has been invoked.

The documentation recommends that the **setActionName:** method be invoked in an action method, as you have done here, rather than in the primitive accessor method that actually changes the data value in the model object—here, **setCheckboxValue:** in VRButtonModel. There are a couple of reasons for this. For one thing, the primitive method might also be called for other purposes, and a change to the Undo and Redo menu items might not be appropriate for all of them. More important, the titles of the Undo and Redo menu items should reflect the nature of the user action that will be undone or redone, not the nature of the underlying primitive operation that alters the data. By changing the menu item titles in the action method, you leave open the possibility of using other menu item titles if the same change to the document were effected, say, by a menu command or an AppleScript command instead of by clicking the checkbox control. Several times in the course of implementing new features in the Vermont Recipes application in later recipes, you will see the benefits of doing it this way.

2. This is the first time you have written code for a localizable string. I explained the use of the **NSLocalizedString()** convenience function to extract a localized string from the Localizable.strings resource in Step 3.1.4. Here, you see it in use to make sure the Undo and Redo menu items appear in the native language of the location where the application is being run (assuming the application has been localized for that language).

To make this work, you must add the following key-value pairs to the Localizable.strings file in the Resources group in the Groups & Files pane. It is customary but not required to word the key identically to the value used for the locale of the developer; here, it's English. Don't forget the trailing semicolons; if you do forget them, this will appear to work but Cocoa will in fact be using the name of the key instead of the localized value and therefore won't pick up any different strings provided by the localization contractors.

```
/* Undo/Redo menu item names */


    /* Checkbox */
/* Name of undo/redo menu item after checkbox control was set */
"Set Checkbox" = "Set Checkbox";
/* Name of undo/redo menu item after checkbox control was
        cleared */
"Clear Checkbox" = "Clear Checkbox";
```

6.3 Update the User Interface

Finally, undoing and redoing changes to the application's data is all well and good, but you must update the user interface as well. In this step, you will devise a means by which the VRButtonModel object lets the window controller know when the user interface needs to be updated to reflect the new, undone or redone state of the data.

The Sketch example application supplied by Apple deals with this problem using brute force. If applied here, that technique would require every primitive method that changes a data value, such as **SetCheckboxValue:** in VRModelObject, to invoke a custom method, called something like **invalidateData**. This method would in turn invoke a custom window controller method, called something like **invalidateUI**, to instruct all of the window's user controls to change state to match the new state of the document's data.

There is a serious problem with applying this brute force solution here. It would require the window controller to update every user control in the window, even though the user had only undone or redone a change to a single data value. While this is not a problem for a window containing only one or a few user controls, it could introduce a noticeable delay if the window contained many complex controls.

Also, it would result in a user control's being updated twice when clicked; once when the user clicks the control, and again when the `invalidateData` method is invoked and in turn invokes `invalidateUI` to update the user control.

There are at least two available techniques to solve these problems. One is to have the window controller's action method pass to the model object's `SetCheckboxValue:` method the selector for a specific method to update the visible state of the checkbox user control. The `SetCheckboxValue:` method would then invoke that selector using the NSObject protocol's `performSelector:` method to update the user control. Although the window controller's action method already knows how to update its user control, the point is that this process would also be registered with the undo manager, to be played back when the user chooses Undo or Redo from the Edit menu.

Here, however, you will use another important Cocoa technique: notifications, the standard Cocoa solution to this issue. Every primitive accessor method that changes a data value, such as `setCheckboxValue:`, will post a notification describing the change to the default notification center. The notification center will in turn immediately broadcast that notification to every other object that has registered to receive it. The VRMainWindowController object will register to receive such a notification for every user control it manages. When it receives the notification, it will invoke a method to update the specific user control whose associated data value triggered the notification. This process will also be registered with the undo manager, so the same notification will be broadcast again when the user chooses Undo or Redo from the Edit menu.

As a result, the model object will not need an outlet to the window controller object, and when the window controller receives a notification because Undo or Redo was chosen, the one, and only the one, user control will be updated. Notifications are posted and sent synchronously, so the GUI is updated immediately. As a bonus, any other object in the application can register to receive notification when a specific data item changes, and it can take action accordingly without requiring any further changes to the model object's code.

Documentation

To understand what notification is all about, read "Delegating Authority—Cocoa Delegation and Notification," a 1999 article by Erik Buck on the Stepwise site at www.stepwise.com.

Notifications

The Cocoa AppKit creates by default a notification center, which an application object can use to post and send notifications to any other objects that register to receive them.

The notification technique differs from delegation in several respects and is useful in different situations. For one thing, multiple objects can register to receive a single notification; that is, an object can have many observers, whereas it can have only one delegate. Notifications are therefore useful when an object does something that affects the application in a way that many other objects need to know about and respond to—for example, to synchronize their state with that of the sending object.

For another, notification does not require the notifier to know anything about the observer or even that there are any observers, and an observer need not know anything about the notifier. They only need to share knowledge of the existence and nature of the notification mechanism. This makes notification a more flexible technique than delegation. For example, a developer can add new functionality to an application without altering the notifier in any way or even knowing anything about it. It is not necessary for an observer to have access to a notifier through an instance variable or accessor method, as a delegate must in order to become the notifier's delegate; it is necessary only to register with the notification center to observe the notification. Optionally, notifications can include information about the notifying object that observers can use to understand the notification in greater detail.

A limitation of notifications is that, unlike delegates, an observer cannot interfere in any way with the notifying object. The observer cannot, for example, prevent the event that is the subject of the notification from happening, as some delegate methods can.

There is some processing overhead associated with notifications, but in general they are very efficient and can be used in most situations without concern regarding performance. Cocoa itself makes extensive use of notifications.

You will solve the problem of redundant updating of a user control when a user clicks it by the simple expedient of testing its state first. If its state already corresponds to its associated data value, the window controller will not let it update. This will save whatever time would have been required to redraw the control on the screen.

1. It is customary to assign the notification's name to an external variable in the originating class and to use the variable in every class where it is needed. External variables are a common C syntax; if you don't understand their use here, consult any good C reference. The variable name should be given a unique prefix to avoid contamination of the global name space; here, you use VR for Vermont Recipes. In addition, because these are external variables available and used in the window controller, which may refer to several model objects, you refer to the model object by name in the variable name as well as its value to help assure that both are unique within the window controller. In the header file VRButtonModel.h, after **@end**, declare the following external variable:

```
extern NSString *VRButtonModelCheckboxValueChangedNotification;
```

2. In the source file VRButtonModel.m, define the variable as follows, before **@implementation VRButtonModel**:

```
NSString *VRButtonModelCheckboxValueChangedNotification =
    @"ButtonModel checkboxValue Changed Notification";
```

3. In the source file VRButtonModel.m, insert the following at the end of the **setCheckboxValue:** accessor method:

```
[[NSNotificationCenter defaultCenter] postNotificationName:
    VRButtonModelCheckboxValueChangedNotification
    object:[self document];
```

The role of the object: parameter will be explained shortly.

4. In the header file VRMainWindowController.h, declare the following methods before the ACTIONS section:

```
#pragma mark INTERFACE MANAGEMENT - Generic updaters

- (void)updateTwoStateCheckbox:(NSButton *)control
    setting:(BOOL)inValue;

#pragma mark INTERFACE MANAGEMENT - Buttons tab view item
    updaters

- (void)updateCheckbox:(NSNotification *)notification;
```

In addition, because you anticipate adding many user controls to the application in Recipe 2, add the following declaration above the Interface Management section of VRMainWindowController.h. It will be used to accumulate all of the specific view updaters that you will write later, simply as a convenience when you need to call all of them at once (as you will in just a moment).

```
#pragma mark WINDOW MANAGEMENT

- (void)updateWindow;
```

5. In the source file VRMainWindowController.m, define the first two of these
methods as follows before the ACTIONS section:

```
#pragma mark INTERFACE MANAGEMENT - Generic view updaters

- (void)updateTwoStateCheckbox:(NSButton *)control
        setting:(BOOL)inValue {
    if (inValue != [control state]) {
        [control setState:(inValue ? NSOnState : NSOffState)];
    }
}


#pragma mark INTERFACE MANAGEMENT - Buttons tab view item
        updaters

- (void)updateCheckbox:(NSNotification *)notification {
    [self updateTwoStateCheckbox:[self checkbox] setting:
        [[self buttonModel] checkboxValue]];
}
```

Still in VRMainWindowController.m, define the third method as follows in the
WINDOW MANAGEMENT section after the **awakeFromNib** method:

```
- (void)updateWindow {


    // Buttons tab view item
    [self updateCheckbox:nil];
}
```

Notice that you are directly calling a method that was designed to be invoked
by a notification method. There is nothing wrong with this. Just pass the
notification parameter as **nil**. If the notification method were written so as
to make use of any of the notification's parameters—as you will eventually do
in Recipe 12, Step 5—you would test for **nil** before accessing them.

Finally, in the **awakeFromNib** method definition in MyWindowController.m, replace
the first line with an invocation of the new **updateWindow** method as follows:

```
[self updateWindow];
```

You have to update the visible state of every control in the window in awakeFromNib, to force the window to reflect the initial state of the document model's data. Thereafter, individual user controls will update whenever the model's associated accessor method sends a notification indicating that the data has changed.

The updateCheckbox: method is specific to this one checkbox; it will be invoked by the notification that you are about to register with the default notification center. The updateTwoStateCheckbox:setting: method is generic; it may eventually be called by many specific checkbox controls, passing in the control and its underlying data setting for each distinct control, as is done in updateCheckbox:.

The specific updateCheckbox: method fetched the setting parameter from the model object. It would have been possible to include this information in the notification itself by using its userInfo parameter, freeing the window controller from the necessity of looking up the setting in the document object. Including information in a notification is in many circumstances preferred to maintain a full separation between the object originating the notification and an object receiving it. Here, however, it is the window controller's primary function to talk to the model object, so there is no harm for the moment in looking the value up. This does, however, limit the ability of other classes to use the notification; they must know about the model object, as VRMainWindowController does. You will have an opportunity to pass data in a notification's userInfo parameter in later recipes, including Recipe 12, Step 5.

Don't be concerned about the apparent mixing of integer, Boolean, and enum data types in the updateTwoStateCheckbox:setting: method. It is common in Cocoa programming to treat Boolean values as integers whenever this promotes convenience, and the same goes for enumeration types, which are of course implemented as integers. The NSButton class reference document is explicit about this in the case of the setState: method, saying, "Although using the enumerated constants is preferred, value can also be an integer. If the cell has two states, zero is treated as NSOffState, and a nonzero value is treated as NSOnState. If the cell has three states, zero is treated as NSOffState; a negative value, as NSMixedState; and a positive value, as NSOnState." You cast the setting parameter to a Boolean value here only to capture the traditional notion that a two-state checkbox is either on or off, true or false; Cocoa allows a checkbox to assume only these two states by default. You will learn how to implement mixed-state (or three-state) checkboxes in Recipe 2, Step 2.4, where the setting parameter will be cast to an integer value to allow the use of three states.

6. All that is left is to register the window controller with the default notification center as an observer of the notification. Anticipating again that Recipe 2 will bring a slew of additional controls to the Vermont Recipes application, you should plan ahead and create a separate method to collect all notification registrations in one place for the sake of convenient code maintenance.

In VRMainWindowController.h, at the beginning of the WINDOW MANAGEMENT section, declare a new `registerNotificationObservers` method:

```
- (void)registerNotificationObservers;
```

In VRMainWindowController.m, define it as follows in the WINDOW MANAGEMENT section, after `awakeFromNib`:

```
- (void)registerNotificationObservers {

    // Buttons tab view item

    [[NSNotificationCenter defaultCenter] addObserver:self
            selector:@selector(updateCheckbox:)
            name:VRButtonModelCheckboxValueChangedNotification
            object:[self document]];
}
```

The NSNotificationCenter class registration method you called here passes four pieces of information to the default notification center: the identify of the observer, the selector the observer should be told to invoke when the notification is posted, the name of the notification to be observed, and an object contained in the notification. The first three of these are easy to understand. The new observer is **self**, the document's window controller. When the observer receives the notification, it will invoke its **updateCheckbox:** selector. The name of the notification being observed is the string assigned to the **VRButtonModel-CheckboxValueChangedNotification** external variable you just defined.

The fourth parameter, **object:**, can be a source of confusion, however. It looks at first as if it plays two roles in Cocoa's notification mechanism, acting both as a filter to limit the circumstances under which the observer will respond to a notification and as a source of information for the selector the notification will invoke when the observer does respond. In fact, it plays only the role of a filter.

As a filter, the **object:** parameter works together with the notification name. If the name is present but the object is **nil**, the observer will respond to all notifications with the given name no matter what object is contained in a particular notification. If the object is defined, the observer will only respond to a notification with the given name if it also contains the specified object. Either configuration, as well as others, is useful in appropriate circumstances, but you must take care to be sure you understand which configuration you need.

When you do pass an object in the `object:` parameter, nothing is done with it other than to test it as a filter. Every notification contains an object, usually the object that sent it. When any notification is received, its contained object can be accessed by the responding selector whether or not the object was specified as a filter in the registration method.

In other words, when registering an observer, you do not have to specify an object in order to give the selector access to it, because the selector will always have access to the notification's object. You only have to be concerned about whether your observer should respond only to notifications containing a specified object, or instead to all notifications with the given name.

Here, you constrained the observer so that it would respond to the named notification only if the notification also contained the `document` object associated with this window controller. In Instruction 3, above, the `set` accessor set the notification's object to this `document` object, so the window controller will respond to the notification. I will explain why it was important to specify the `document` object in a moment. Before delving further into this issue, continue with the registration code. It will elucidate some consequences of using the `document` object as a filter.

7. In the `awakeFromNib` method definition in VRMainWindowController.m, call the new `registerNotificationObservers` method immediately before sending the [`self updateWindow`] message, as follows:

[`self registerNotificationObservers`];

You might have been tempted to register the window controller as an observer in the VRMainWindowController `init` method instead, but this would involve a subtle error, common among Cocoa beginners. NSWindowController, the parent object, does not set its `document` instance variable until the document invokes its `addWindowController:` method. Thus, at the point when the window controller initializes itself, its `document` instance variable is still `nil`. Your notification registration method's [`self document`] message would therefore return `nil` if registration were accomplished in the window controller's `init` method.

Vermont Recipes would appear to function correctly with a single window open. However, it would not function correctly with multiple windows open, and it would be very difficult to debug the problem. To avoid errors, the window controller must be registered with the notification center in the window controller's `awakeFromNib` method, after the document object has been initialized and can be passed to the notification center. As noted above, this means you must also explicitly update all the controls in the window in `awakeFromNib` so their visible states match the initial data values.

It is important to understand exactly why you should not register observers of data changes in the window controller's `init` method. You want your notifications to go only to the update method in the particular instance of VRMainWindowController that is associated with this document object and its window, not in some other document. If you were to register your observer in the window controller's `init` method, you would effectively pass `nil` in the object parameter for the reason just stated, even though that wasn't your intent. As explained above, passing `nil` causes the notification to be broadcast too widely, to every window controller of every open document. If the notification were broadcast to all instances of VRMainWindowController, then the same user control in every open window would update, potentially causing pending edits in those windows to be aborted behind the user's back. It is important to ensure that the notification observer registration specifies an object, as well as a notification name, so the window controller will only receive notifications of the given name if they also specify the given object.

In general, you have to be very careful what you do in your window controller's `init` method, because many objects aren't yet in existence or hooked up when it is invoked. For example, objects instantiated in the nib file do not yet exist. For this reason, many operations must be deferred to the `awakeFromNib` method, or to an override of NSDocument's `windowControllerDidLoadNib:` method, or, in a document-based application such as Vermont Recipes, to an override of NSWindowController's `windowDidLoad` method.

A final point: Back in Instruction 7 of Step 3.3, you removed VRMainWindowController from the list of notification center observers when VRMainWindowController was `deallocated`, without understanding why. Now you know: Here you have added VRMainWindowController to the list of observers, and removing it later is a necessary part of the object's cleanup process. This is easy to forget, so add it to your checklist of things to do in every window controller's `dealloc` method; it is almost always required because window controllers almost always register to receive notifications.

8. Now return to the question of what object to pass in the notification registration method's `object:` parameter.

You just learned that you must pass something in this parameter, because if you pass `nil`, every open document's window controller will respond to the notification. It is only this document that is affected by the change in this data, so only this document's window controller should respond.

Therefore, pass [`self document`]—the document associated with this window controller—in the `object:` parameter. Doing so will prevent other documents' window controllers from responding. Furthermore, by specifying the notification name, you have already ensured that only a user control associated with this data item will respond, because only this user control's associated accessor method posts a notification with this name.

Defining the `object:` filter too narrowly—as you would, for example, if you set it to a specific `buttonModel` object instead of to the document at large—would generate a hard-to-detect error in later stages of the application's development. To be specific, you will learn in Recipe 12 that implementing keyed archiving to store and retrieve the document's data requires creating a new `buttonModel` object and substituting it for the current `buttonModel` object. That new `buttonModel` object won't be the same object as the current `buttonModel` object, which posts this notification. The window controller therefore wouldn't respond to the notification during unarchiving, because you would have specified the old `buttonModel` object as a filter. Your document would receive the new data value as it was unarchived from disk, but your user interface wouldn't reflect the change.

As written, the `set` accessor and the registration method together ensure that the user control in the window associated with this window controller's document—and only this document—will be updated when the document's checkbox data item is changed. In addition, the window controller will respond to the notification even during unarchiving or any other operation that substitutes a new model object for the current model object.

The cumulative effect of the code you wrote in this step is that whenever an item of data in the application is changed by any operation, including an undo or redo operation, the window controller gets wind of it and updates the associated user control to match. This is all managed in such a way that the model object does not have to know what user interface objects exist, or even that a window controller exists. You could take the same model object, unchanged, and tack a completely different user interface onto it.

WRAP UP STEP 6. That's all there is to implementing undo and redo support in the application. You should compile, link, and run the application now. Try clicking the checkbox control several times in succession. Then try undoing these changes from the Edit menu. You will discover that you can repeatedly undo the changes until the Undo menu item finally dims. This is because Cocoa's undo is unlimited by default; it lets you undo each of your clicks until the control finally reverts to its original state. At any point, you can also choose the Redo menu item repeatedly until all of the undos have been reversed and the Redo menu item finally dims.

Best of all, by implementing undo and redo, the application automatically gained the ability to know when a document has been modified and needs to be saved. You can test this by clicking the checkbox in the window to change its state. The dot in the window's close button appears, signifying that the document has been dirtied. Then close the window. A sheet will open, advising you that the document has been modified and asking whether to save it. If you cancel and choose Edit > Undo, the dot in the close button disappears and you are able to close the document without seeing this sheet, because the document knows that it is no longer modified from its previously saved state.

In the next step, you will deal with a related subject, the Revert menu.

Step 7: Tinker with Revert

The Revert menu item in the Vermont Recipes application already works. It is one of the bonuses the Cocoa Document-based Application template gives you for free when you implement undo and redo. You can therefore skip immediately to Step 8 if you're in a hurry to finish the application.

However, I included this step here for two reasons: one, to walk you through the somewhat circuitous route that brought the application to this happy state of affairs; and two, to show you that the behavior of the Revert menu item in Mac OS X isn't the same as it was in Mac OS 9 and earlier—and to show you how to subvert it if you don't like the new approach.

7.1 How to Make the Revert Menu Item Work

In an early version of the Vermont Recipes application, I had difficulty making the Revert menu item work. I dealt with the problem of suppressing undo notification in initialization situations by directly assigning an initial value to the `checkboxValue` instance variable in VRButtonModel, bypassing the `setCheckboxValue:` accessor method that you implemented in Step 4. Only later did I realize that there is a provision in Cocoa to allow initialization to use accessor methods while suppressing undo registration, as you saw in Step 6. Once I implemented that technique and switched back to accessor methods when opening saved documents, I discovered that doing so magically enabled the Revert menu item to work. The lesson is clear: Use accessor methods to set the value of variables, because Cocoa depends on it in this and many other ways.

The story of how I went astray and eventually found the true path has elicited favorable reviews from readers of earlier versions of *Vermont Recipes*. It is a programmer's

detective story that illustrates how to go about researching and solving a problem in Cocoa development. It was written at a time when Cocoa documentation was very incomplete and even obsolete. You may find it enlightening, even though the documentation is now much better.

When I reached this point in Recipe 1, I noticed that the Revert menu item didn't seem to work correctly. For example, I saved a file with its checkbox control checked. Then I closed and reopened that document, unchecked the checkbox, and chose File > Revert. The checkbox did not appear to revert to its checked state, as it should have.

Using the Project Builder debugger, I discovered that the value of the `checkboxValue` variable in VRButtonModel had nevertheless returned to `YES`, confirming that the Revert command did in fact read the document back into memory from disk. When I traced the logical flow of control in the source code, I realized that there was no code in the application to tell the checkbox control to conform its visible state to that of the `checkboxValue` variable when the document reverted to its saved state.

Here are the steps I followed to figure out one way to resolve this issue.

The first step was to determine how Revert works. Checking the documentation and using the debugger to trace what happens when the Revert menu item is chosen, I discovered that Cocoa automatically invokes a built-in NSDocument action method called `revertDocumentToSaved:`, which in turn invoked my override of the NSDocument `loadDataRepresentation:ofType:` method. This makes sense, because `loadDataRepresentation:ofType:` is a method that is invoked to obtain data from disk when you open a document, and you also want to obtain data from disk when you revert. Looking at the code in an earlier version of the override of `loadDataRepresentation:ofType:`, I saw that I had already included a means to set the `checkboxValue` variable via the VRButtonModel object. This is what set the value of the document's data to match what was found on disk, as I saw in the debugger.

This therefore seemed like a possible place to add a statement to make the checkbox control's visible state match the value of the data. However, this also seemed a very awkward place to do anything that is limited to reverting the document. The same routines in the code were also invoked when a document was being opened, but the `awakeFromNib` method in VRMainWindowController already updated the user interface in that case. To handle Revert here would have required that I somehow detect whether the Open or the Revert menu item was being handled.

So I needed to investigate further. I had already discovered that NSDocument includes an action method for the Revert menu item, `revertDocumentToSaved:`. This might be just the ticket, I thought, since it is invoked only to revert a document, not to open a document. Still, I felt a little discomfort about overriding a built-in Cocoa action method for fear of breaking something else, so I kept looking.

As a last resort, I examined the NSDocument header file in /System/Library/ Frameworks/AppKit.framework/headers. I hit pay dirt! Cocoa has a method, revertToSavedFromFile:ofType:, which the class reference document did not document at that time, but a comment in the header indicated that the Revert menu item's action method calls it. The comment explicitly told me that this is the appropriate place to detect when a document is being reverted and to take additional actions, if desired. Therefore, I decided to override this method in VRDocument.m and use it as a springboard to tell the window controller object that the document is reverted and the user interface needs to be updated.

These are the instructions that I followed to do this at the time, and it worked. *But don't do it!* You have already done it the right way. Just read this for whatever lessons it may teach.

1. Add the following override method to VRDocument.m, immediately after the makeWindowControllers method:

```
- (BOOL)revertToSavedFromFile:(NSString *)fileName
      ofType:(NSString *)type {
   if ([super revertToSavedFromFile:fileName ofType:type]) {
      [[self windowControllers] makeObjectsPerformSelector:
            @selector(documentDidRevert)];
      return YES;
   } else {
      return NO;
   }
}
```

This is an override method, so it does not require declaration in VRDocument.h.

It first invokes the method's super, to make sure any necessary changes are made to the document's internal structure. If successful, it informs the built-in window controller array windowControllers that the document has reverted to its saved state by invoking the window controller's documentDidRevert method, which you are about to write.

2. In the header file VRMainWindowController.h, after the ACCESSORS section, add the following:

```
- (void)documentDidRevert;
```

3. In the source file VRMainWindowController.m, after awakeFromNib, define the method as follows:

```
- (void)documentDidRevert {
    [self updateTwoStateCheckbox:[self checkbox]
           setting:[[self buttonModel] checkboxValue]];
}
```

You have seen this same statement before, in Step 6.3, where you used it to
update the checkbox control after an undo or redo operation.

The application could now update the user interface when a new document is created
or a saved document is opened, using the awakeFromNib method, and when a changed
document is reverted to its saved state, through the documentDidRevert method, both
of which call a single generic method to update the checkbox. The awakeFromNib and
documentDidRevert methods gave me a good general framework for handling user
interface updating when a user chooses the Save, Open, and Revert menu items, as
well as Undo and Redo, no matter how many user controls we might add later.

At this point, I was pleased to think that I had achieved my goal, a working application that maintains a good separation between the model object's single data item
and its single user control in the user interface. The window controller object is used
to mediate between the data and the view when a change takes place in either. When
the user changes the interface by clicking the control, Cocoa tells the window controller to send an action method to the model object so that it can decide how to
update its data. And when the user changes the document's data by choosing the
New, Open, or Revert menu item, Cocoa tells the model object or its document to
inform the window controller that it needs to decide how to update the state of the
user interface.

Later, I figured out that using the setCheckboxValue: accessor method in initialization situations would solve the problem independently. Here is a paraphrase of how
I reported the discovery:

Now, a remarkable thing happens. By using the accessor method to initialize the
data variable, it becomes possible to update the checkbox when a document is
reverted to its saved state by taking advantage of the fact that the accessor method
posts a notification. The specific view updater method you wrote in Recipe 1, Step 6.3,
is a notification method that is registered to receive and act upon this notification.
The checkbox control will therefore update automatically onscreen when it receives
the notification, not only when the user invokes the Undo or Redo menu items, but
also when the user reverts a document to its saved state. You no longer need to
invoke the generic updater method explicitly in VRMainWindowController's
documentDidRevert method. In fact, you no longer need the documentDidRevert
method at all nor the revertToSavedFromFile:ofType: override method that you
added to VRDocument.m. You can simplify your code by removing these two methods.

However, you still need to update the checkbox control explicitly in VRMain-WindowController's `awakeFromNib` method. When you initialize the data variable in the VRButtonModel object's initialization method or when a document is being created or opened, its accessor method posts its notification before the control's update method in the VRMainWindowController object has been registered as an observer. The checkbox user control doesn't yet even exist, because a document that is being created or opened is initialized before its window appears or its window controller object is instantiated. The posting of the notification when nobody is yet observing it is harmless, but you do have to update the user control yourself later, when the window and its controller are created.

7.2 How to Alter the Behavior of the Revert and Save Menu Items

Returning to the present, you might have noticed that the Save and Revert menu items in the File menu do not behave as a Mac OS 9 user would expect. The Save menu item in Cocoa remains enabled at all times after the first change is made to the document, even after a document is saved, reverted, or opened. In Mac OS 9, the Save menu item would become disabled at these times, and it would remain disabled until the user makes another change to the document. The Revert menu item in Cocoa behaves just like Save, except that it remains disabled for a new document until the document has been saved once (because there is nothing to revert to before then). In Mac OS 9, a Revert menu item is normally disabled at the same time Save is disabled.

This is the way these menu items are supposed to behave in Cocoa. The theory is that Mac OS X is inherently multiprocess and multiuser in nature, so there is always a chance that another application has changed the document behind the back of the current application. Because of this possibility, the Save and Revert menu items are kept available at all times, to let the application at any time update the document on disk to its current representation in RAM or to revert your representation in RAM to its current state on disk, in case another user—say, on a network—has altered it since you last saved your own changes. That is, it allows you to decide at any time whether to conform your version of the document to a concurrent user's version, or to force the concurrent user's version to conform to yours, or to choose Save As to create a separate copy for your own use.

Cocoa's default behavior may leave you feeling somewhat uncomfortable. It could be considered irresponsible to allow a concurrent user to change a document's representation on disk without first warning other active users about what is happening. An application could at least, as Project Builder does, allow you to decide what to do by raising an alert when you bring it to the front after a concurrent user has changed the document. Applications might also implement some form of document locking or record locking to prevent concurrent users from making changes while you are using the document. Ideally, Cocoa would implement one or more standard mechanisms for dealing with this situation. The current default, allowing a user to save or revert at any time, seems incomplete and unsatisfactory.

You will not implement record locking or other devices here because it is a complicated task. However, you can, if you wish, implement a simple change to the application at this point that will cause it to adopt the standard Mac OS 9 menu behavior, disabling the Save and Revert menu items unless you yourself have made a change to the document's representation in RAM. This may provide a small measure of safety, because it will make it slightly harder for you to overwrite changes saved to storage by others since you last saved your own changes. Note, however, that it still allows you to save your own changes even though other users may also be making changes to the document.

You should normally follow Apple's official interface guidelines and practices, because Mac OS X users will come to expect all Mac OS X applications to behave alike. This is one of the Mac's great strengths. *You are therefore advised not to make the changes described here.* They are presented only to show you how it could be done and to introduce you to some standard Cocoa techniques for enabling and disabling menu items.

Launch Project Builder and open the project, if necessary.

In the source file VRDocument.m, add the following method before the STORAGE section:

```
#pragma mark MENU MANAGEMENT
```

```
- (BOOL)validateMenuItem:(NSMenuItem *)menuItem {
    if ([[menuItem title] isEqualToString:
            NSLocalizedString(@"Save",
            @"Name of Save menu item")]) {
        return ([self isDocumentEdited] ? YES : NO);
    } else if ([[menuItem title] isEqualToString:
            NSLocalizedString(@"Revert",
            @"Name of Revert menu item")]) {
        return ((([self fileName] != nil) &&
                ([self isDocumentEdited])) ? YES : NO);
    } else {
        return [super validateMenuItem:menuItem];
    }
}
```

This overrides the default NSDocument implementation of `validateMenuItem:`, so you do not need to declare it in VRDocument.h.

Note that the override method invokes its super's method only if it is not being called on the Save or Revert menu items. Invoking the super's method is necessary to ensure that Cocoa is able to validate other menu items. However, the override method prevents NSDocument's standard `validateMenuItem:` from being invoked on Save or Revert. The standard method would enable the menu item when a document exists on disk and has ever been edited, even if it has since been saved. If the standard method is not overridden, the user can choose Revert on a document that is not currently dirtied—that is, a document that may have been modified but that you have since saved—but there will be no response; that is, the standard revert sheet, saying that the document has been edited and asking if you want to undo the edits, does not open. This is correct behavior under the circumstances, but a user may find it confusing.

Testing whether the document's name is `nil` is a standard way to test whether it has ever been saved to storage.

You use the `NSLocalizedString()` convenience function to make sure you are comparing the menu item title to its localized name in the language where the computer is being used, as described in Step 3.1.4, above.

To make this work, you must add these key-value pairs to the Localizable.strings file in the Resources folder.

```
/* Name of Save menu item */
"Save" = "Save";


/* Name of Revert menu item */
"Revert" = "Revert";
```

Only a few details remain to complete Recipe 1 and your first version of a working Cocoa application. You need to create application and document icons and also revise your application's menu bar so it discloses the name of your application to the user in appropriate menu items.

Step 8: Add Application and Document Icons

No application is complete without an application icon and document icons. The system shows these on the desktop, in the Dock, in the Finder's info window, and in various alerts and dialogs. Also, the application normally shows its icon in its About window.

This is not a tutorial on the details of using image-editing applications to create images suitable for use as icons, so you will have to create or find your own graphics to serve as icons using whatever applications are available to you. You may find it convenient to use a drawing program, a scanner or a digital camera to acquire the images, and an image-editing application to edit them. A variety of native Mac OS X applications has become available for the purpose.

For the Vermont Recipes icons, the cover and a page from an antique Vermont cookbook whose copyright has expired were scanned into Photoshop. Each image was then reduced in size and placed on a 128-by-128-pixel canvas. The areas outside the image were erased to transparent. Finally, each image was saved in PNG-24 format with transparency using the Save for Web command in Photoshop. If you are a perfectionist, you will want to repeat the process until you have saved the images in four sizes—16, 32, 48, and 128 pixels square, each optimized to look good at its size.

There was at one time a controversy in some circles over whether it is best to use Apple's Mac OS X icon style—an angled view of a stylized, photo-illustrative three-dimensional object, as described in the "Icons" chapter of *Inside Mac OS X: Aqua Human Interface Guidelines*—or a more traditional abstract, flat graphic. Like many early controversies regarding Mac OS X departures from Mac OS 9 and earlier expectations, this issue has pretty much blown over. The Vermont Recipes choice of a flat but photo-realistic icon does not reflect a considered position on the issue, but only a deficit of artistic talent. If you're serious about your application, hire a professional artist.

In this recipe, you use icon tools provided with Mac OS X to install the icons from whatever images you have found or created. More powerful commercial applications are available.

Once you have the image files for each icon in hand, you are ready to turn them into icons for the application.

Launch IconComposer (in the /Developer/Applications folder). Also launch Project Builder and open the project, if necessary.

1. Using an untitled IconComposer window, drag each image onto the empty square in the first column matching its size. You can get away with using only a 128-by-128-pixel icon.

2. If each of the three smaller images is dragged onto its square, an alert may appear, asking you whether to extract a 1-bit mask from the data. Click No if the mask is already present; otherwise, click Yes.

3. Choose File > Save As, give the icon file a name, designate any location to which to save it, and click Save. The file is automatically given the required .icns extension.

4. The icon is saved as an icns Browser document, so you can double-click the icon file to open it in the icns Browser application and examine it. If it contains only a thumbnail icon (128 by 128 pixels), it will still work fine.

5. If you did not already save the icon files into the root level of the project folder in Instruction 3, above, drag them there now. For Vermont Recipes, name the application icon **VRApplicationIcon.icns** and the document icon **VRMainDocument.icns**. These go in the root project folder rather than the English.lproj folder because icons cannot be localized.

6. In Project Builder, select the Targets tab of the project, click the Vermont Recipes target in the left pane, select the Info.plist Entries item, and click the Expert item.

7. On the CFBundleIconFile line, type **VRApplicationIcon** without the .icns extension.

8. Expand the disclosure triangle for CFBundleDocumentTypes, then expand element **0**. On the CFBundleTypeIconFile line, type **VRMainDocumentIcon** without the .icns extension.

9. Select the Files tab of the project and expand the Resources disclosure triangle. Then choose Projects > Add Files, select the two new icon files, click Open, then click Add in the next sheet. The two new icons appear in the Groups & Files pane. Drag them into the Resources group, if necessary.

When you compile and run the application, you will see the new icons in all the expected places. You may have to move the application from the project's build folder to the Mac OS X Applications folder, or log out and in, or shut down and restart, to see the icons in the Finder and the Dock.

Step 9: Revise the Menu Bar

Before you finish, you should perform a little cosmetic surgery on your application's menu bar.

Launch Project Builder and open the project, if necessary.

1. In the Groups & Files pane of the project window, double-click MainMenu.nib in the Resources group. MainMenu.nib opens in Interface Builder.

2. In the MainMenu window, double-click the NewApplication menu title to select its text for editing, and edit it to read **Vermont Recipes**. Press Return when you're done to commit the change.

3. Click the newly edited Vermont Recipes menu title. The menu opens.

4. Double-click the About NewApplication menu item to select its text for editing, and edit it to read **About Vermont Recipes**. Press Return to commit the change.

5. Double-click the Hide NewApplication menu item, and edit it to read **Hide Vermont Recipes**.

6. Click the Quit NewApplication menu item to select it, and edit it to read **Quit Vermont Recipes** (**Figure 1.26**).

FIGURE 1.26 Editing the Quit menu item in Interface Builder.

7. Choose the Help menu and click the MyApp Help menu item to select it. Edit it to read **Vermont Recipes Help**.

8. In the Interface Builder menu bar, choose File > Save.

Compile, link, and run the application. You will find the compiled application in the build folder of your project folder, unless you altered your build settings in Project Builder. Try moving the application to your /Applications folder and running it from there, if icons don't appear properly.

Step 10: Debug the Application and Build It for Deployment

You have come all this way with only an occasional reference to the debugging capabilities of Project Builder. Now that you are about to begin adding more features to the Vermont Recipes application, it is time to learn a little about the subject. There apparently aren't any bugs in the application yet, but learning about debugging will serve you well as you move through the remainder of Vermont Recipes and on to your own applications.

You may find it useful to think of *debugging* as having two separate meanings. In one usage, *debugging* signifies an activity: namely, running your application in the debugger. As the application runs and you do things with it, such as clicking user controls and choosing menu items, you can stop execution and examine the current state of the application and its variables. In the second usage, *debugging* denotes placing special instructions in your source files that control the build process. Before building the application, you add text to the source that tells the preprocessor, the compiler, or the linker to do things in particular ways. One common use of debugging statements in source is for conditional compilation—that is, including a section of code when compiling for development that will enhance the debugging process, perhaps by generating additional messages. These sections of the code are isolated from the build process when you build for deployment, in order to improve the run-time performance of the application.

10.1 Step Through the Application with Breakpoints

The first line of defense against bugs, and the easiest debugging technique to use, is stepping through your code one line at a time while it is running. Even without the use of the other available debugging features in Project Builder, this is invaluable for detecting the exact location in your code where a problem first appears. Experienced developers will tell you that this often isn't the location of the bad code but only where it first manifests itself to you. But it is a good way to start thinking about the problem.

Documentation

Introductory information regarding the activity of debugging, such as stepping and other ways to use the debugger, is found in the "Debugging" topic in *Project Builder Help*, available from the Help menu in Project Builder and as a separate volume of *Inside Mac OS X* in PDF form at /Developer/Documentation/DeveloperTools/ProjectBuilder/ProjectBuilder.pdf. It is also a good idea to read a short tutorial, *DebugApp: Debugging an Application with Project Builder*, a PDF document on your disk at /Developer/Documentation/DeveloperTools/ProjectBuilder/Debugger.pdf. It is based on debugging a Carbon application, but most of the information in it translates well to Cocoa.

The most detailed and up-to-date Macintosh-specific technical information about using the debugger is *Getting Started with GDB*, Apple's Technical Note TN2032 (December 7, 2001) at http://developer.apple.com/technotes/tn/tn2032.html. If you're familiar with debugging in Mac OS 9 and earlier, also read *GDB for MacsBug Veterans*, Technical Note TN2030, at http://developer.apple.com/technotes/tn/tn2030.html.

On your disk at /Developer/Documentation/DeveloperTools/gdb you will find several technical documents describing the GNU Source-Level Debugger used by Project Builder, including the *Debugging with GDB* document and *Quick Reference Card* listing the commands you can enter at the (gdb) prompt.

In addition to using the debugger, it is often helpful to include debugging commands in your source code, such as preprocessor directives and the NSLog() and NSAssert() macros in Foundation. An introduction to code optimization and the use of the preprocessor is found in the "Compiling C, C++, and Objective-C Files" topic in *Project Builder Help*. The use of NSLog() and NSAssert() is documented in the "Assertions and Logging" section of the "Program Design" topic under "Programming Topics" in the *Cocoa Developer Documentation*, available in Cocoa Help in the Help menu in Project Builder. For a discussion of advanced debugging, see the "Exceptions" section.

For details regarding the role of the preprocessor when compiling an application, including the use of preprocessor macros, there are several important sources of information. First, much of this is standard C technology, described in any good C programming book. For Mac OS X specifics, see *The GNU C Preprocessor* on your disk at /Developer/Documentation/DeveloperTools/Preprocessor, and *The Objective-C Compiler* at /Developer/Documentation/DeveloperTools/Compiler. It is also a good idea to read both the current and older Project Builder *Release Notes*, which describe some major feature changes to the build process that aren't yet well documented elsewhere. For a complete list of compiler macros with brief explanations of each, see *Project Builder Build Settings* at /Developer/Documentation/ReleaseNotes/PBBuildSettings.html.

To see how stepping works, do the following:

1. When debugging, you should first make sure your build styles are set to development, not deployment. To do this, select the Targets tab. A pane slides out from the left where you find an item entitled Build Styles. Expand this item and click the Development radio button, then select the Files tab to return to your Groups & Files pane.

    Be sure to click the radio button, not the name of the build style, Development. Clicking the name selects the Development build style for editing in the main pane of the project builder window, but it does not turn the Development build style on. For that, you must click directly on the radio button.

2. In the Groups & Files pane, click VRMainWindowController.m. Its source code becomes visible in the main pane.

3. Scroll to the bottom of the source, then click in the narrow vertical area that forms the left margin of the pane, adjacent to the first line in the outer block of the `checkboxAction:` method. An arrow appears in the margin. It is generally a good idea to place breakpoints on executable lines of code: that is, opposite a statement between the curly braces delimiting a method's executable code, not opposite its function prototype or method signature or a comment.

4. Select the Breakpoints tab. The Breakpoints pane slides out from the left, showing you a list of all current breakpoints. You can turn one on or off without removing it by clicking its arrow symbol or clicking the Use column adjacent to its line number, and you can delete one by selecting it and pressing Delete. You can also delete a breakpoint by dragging its arrow symbol out of the margin of the source code listing.

5. Click the Build and Debug button. After building, the application runs and an untitled main document window appears in front of the Project Builder window, just as it does when you click Build and Run. In the Project Builder window in the background, the Debug pane instead of the Run pane slides down from the top.

6. Click the project window to bring it to the front. Make sure the Debug pane is large enough by dragging its lower edge until it fills the top half of the project window. In addition, drag the lower edge of the Console pane down within the Debug pane until it fills about half the Debug pane.

7. Click the Vermont Recipes application icon in the Dock to bring its main document window back to the front, then click the checkbox control. After a moment, Project Builder returns to the front, and the line where you set the breakpoint scrolls into view and is highlighted. In addition, both halves of the Debug pane fill with information (**Figure 1.27**).

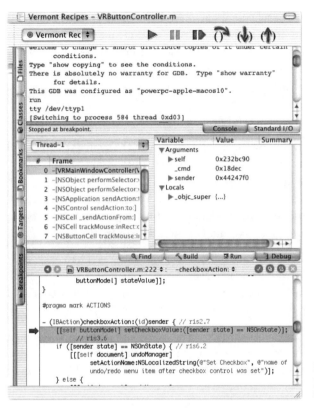

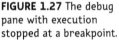

FIGURE 1.27 The debug pane with execution stopped at a breakpoint.

8. Execution of the application has now stopped at the breakpoint, and the information in the Debug pane shows the state of various items within the application. In the left pane, you see all pending frames in the call chain, with the most recent, **checkboxAction:**, selected. You can click any frame to see its status. You can also select any thread from the pop-up menu, although only one thread is running now. In the right pane, you see the variable list, an outline showing arguments to the current method and its local variables. There is a Project Builder menu item that allows you to see types, as well.

9. Click the Step Into button, the downward-pointing arrow on the toolbar in the upper-right corner of the project window. The arrow that was superimposed on the breakpoint moves down one line, indicating that execution has proceeded one step further, and the information in the Debug pane may change to reflect the new state of the application. If any variables changed in this step, they appear in red instead of black text. (You could have clicked the Step Over button in the toolbar, but you may find it useful to get in the habit of using the Step Into button most of the time to make sure you don't accidentally skip a subroutine in which you are interested.)

10. Control-click the `self` variable nested under Arguments in the variable list and choose Print Description to Console in the contextual menu. A message appears in the Console pane telling you that it is printing a description of `self`. In the following line, the description appears, telling you that `self` is an instance of the VRMainWindowController class and giving its address in memory. You could have accomplished the same thing by entering **po self** following the (gdb) prompt in the Console; *po* stands for *print object*.

11. Click the Step Into button a few more times, and watch the source window scroll and switch to other source files as you step through a succession of accessor methods, until you end up at the first line of the `setCheckboxValue:` accessor in VRButtonModel. In the Debug pane under Arguments, you see the `inValue` parameter with its associated value, 0'\000', indicating that the accessor is being told to set the data value associated with the checkbox control to `NO`.

12. Click the Step Into button again a few times, until just after you have stepped through the line, `checkboxValue = inValue;`. Control-click `self` again in the Debug pane and choose Print Description to Console. You see that `self` is now an instance of the VRButtonModel class.

13. Now expand `self` and look at its `checkboxValue` instance variable. You can drag the column divider to the right, if necessary, to see its full name. You see that the value of this instance variable has successfully been set to `NO` (**Figure 1.28**).

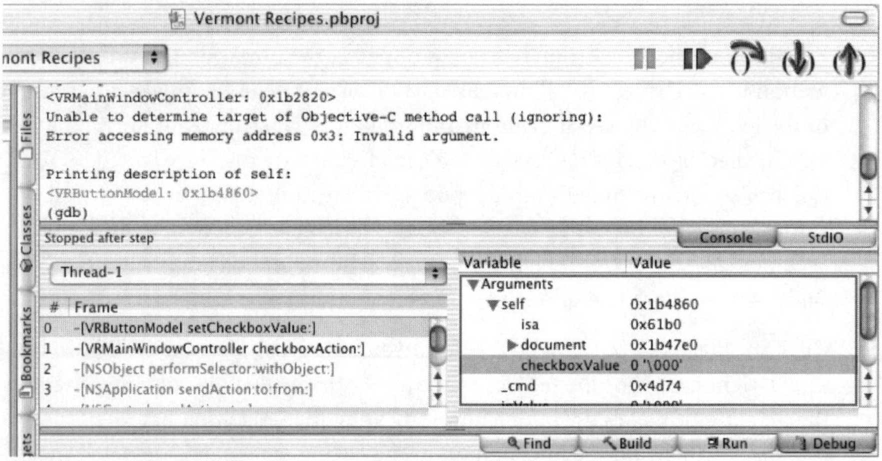

FIGURE 1.28 The debug pane showing a printed object description.

14. You've seen enough to get the drift. You can do much more with the debugger than this, but for now click the Stop button to quit debugging the application. To clean up, click the breakpoint in the Breakpoints pane to select it and press Delete to remove it.

There is another way to use the Breakpoints pane that is very useful when you can't figure out where to place an explicit breakpoint. In the Breakpoints pane, click New and type the following symbolic breakpoint: -[NSException raise]. Now when you run your application in the debugger, it will break wherever an exception is raised due to a programming error in your code. When you click the most recent stack frame in your code at the left side of the Project Builder debugging pane, an arrow appears in the bottom pane beside the line where the exception was raised, and you can explore the state of variables as described above. Of course, the condition that set the stage for the exception may have been created earlier in the flow of your code, but this information will help you pinpoint your mistake. You can also set symbolic breakpoints on any other message.

10.2 Use NSLog()

If you know that you will want to track the state of an instance variable such as VRButtonModel's checkboxValue every time you run the application in Project Builder, you can arrange to have its value printed to the Console or StdIO automatically using Foundation's NSLog() macro. This way you won't have to set a breakpoint and waste time interrupting execution in the debugger.

1. Return to the setCheckboxValue: accessor method in VRButtonModel.m and insert the following line at its end:

    ```
    NSLog(@"\n\tExiting [VRButtonModel setCheckboxValue:],
        checkboxValue:%d\n", checkboxValue);
    ```

    This is equivalent to the following:

    ```
    NSLog([NSString stringWithFormat:
        @"\n\tExiting [VRButtonModel setCheckboxValue:],
        checkboxValue:%d\n", checkboxValue]);
    ```

    Notice that you do not send a [self checkboxValue] message to get the value of the checkboxValue instance variable but instead access the instance variable directly. I suggest you do this primarily because in Step 10.4 you will place another debugging macro in the checkboxValue accessor method and you don't want to trigger it here. Doing so would print multiple messages to StdIO and cause unnecessary confusion. It might be advisable in general to access instance variables directly in NSLog() macros, to avoid any errors that might exist in the accessor method.

    You first saw the stringWithFormat: class method in Step 4.2.3. Here you use escaped new-line and tab characters to format the output to StdIO, and you use the %d printf-style placeholder to return the checkboxValue instance variable's value as an integer. Returning it as an integer instead of a human-readable

Boolean string is a quick-and-dirty approach, typical of NSLog() calls that may be removed from the application for deployment.

This is a tutorial, however, so I should teach you to do things the right way. Fix this call now to return a Boolean as a string in human-readable form. This is easy to do using a conditional expression with the standard C ternary operator, like so:

```
NSLog(@"\n\tExiting [VRButtonModel setCheckboxValue:],
     checkboxValue:%@\n", (checkboxValue ? @"YES" : @"NO"));
```

You needn't bother with internationalizing the string used here because as the developer you will debug it in your own language. Of course, if you are part of a multilingual development team, internationalizing this might be useful. You will learn how to do it with NSString's localizedStringWithFormat: method later.

2. Build and run the application. In the Run pane, you see an entry something like this:

```
2002-02-06 13:34:01.896 Vermont Recipes[5817]
     Exiting [VRButtonModel setCheckboxValue:]
     checkboxValue:YES
```

Your log entry has been printed to StdIO. If you had built and debugged the application instead of running it, you would have seen the same output in the Console pane or the StdIO pane, whichever was selected.

3. With the Vermont Recipes application's main document window in front, click the checkbox control to deselect it. You see a similar log entry in StdIO, but this time it tells you that checkboxValue = NO. Evidently the first value reported was that resulting from the instance variable's being initialized to YES as the application was launched.

You can use the NSLog() macro anywhere in your application to report information you might find useful during development. For example, developers often use it to report that a particular method has been called, to verify the flow of the application's logic.

10.3 Insert a Description Method

In Step 10.1, you learned how to use the Print Description to Console command in the contextual menu in Project Builder. You may not have recognized it at the time, but this command literally prints the value of the NSString object returned by the description method that is implemented in most Cocoa classes. NSDictionary's description method, for example, was explained in Step 5.

You will make debugging your applications easier if you provide a `description` method in all of your custom classes as well, at least if they declare any instance variables. You do this by overriding the super's `description` method. Let's add a `description` method to VRButtonModel. A `description` method can get quite messy if you have lots of instance variables, because you must not only print the values of each of them but also attend to formatting for readable output in stdIO using escaped control characters. Fortunately, there is only one instance variable in VRButtonModel at this point.

1. In VRButtonModel.m, add the following method definition. You don't need to declare it in the header file because it is an override method.

    ```
    #pragma mark DEBUGGING

    - (NSString *)description {

            return [NSString stringWithFormat:
                    @"%@\n\tcheckboxValue:%@\n", [super description],
                    (([self checkboxValue]) ? @"YES" : @"NO")];

    }
    ```

    This uses the now familiar `stringWithFormat:` class method to return a formatted string containing two placeholders, the first filled by the return value of the super's `description` method, and the second filled by the value of VRButtonModel's `checkboxValue` instance variable. The latter is obtained using the `checkboxValue` accessor method, and its result is converted to a human-readable Boolean value in string form, YES or NO, using a conditional expression. Output formatting is accomplished using escaped new-line and tab characters.

    When you add additional instance variables to VRButtonModel, you should remember to add them to this `description` method.

2. Set a breakpoint on the third line of VRButtonModel.m's `setCheckboxValue:` method, then build and debug the application. The application runs until it stops with the third line highlighted.

3. Control-click `self` under Arguments in the variable list, and choose the Print Description to Console command. You see this output in the StdIO pane:

    ```
    <VRButtonModel: 0x1b7860>
            checkboxValue:YES
    ```

    NSObject's `description` method supplied the class name and its address, through the [`super description`] message in the first parameter.

You now have a convenient way to test the value of the `checkboxValue` instance variable at any point in execution where a VRButtonModel object is instantiated.

4. Clean up by removing the breakpoint.

5. You now also have a simpler way to write the `NSLog()` call that you learned about in Step 10.2. All you have to do is this:

```
NSLog(@"\n\t%@", self);
```

The `self` parameter in an `NSLog()` call will return the string value returned by the new `description` method. You shouldn't do this in the `setCheckboxValue:` accessor method, however, because in Recipe 2 you will add a number of additional instance variables to the class and their values won't be relevant in this accessor method. So leave the existing `NSLog()` call in `setCheckboxValue:` as you wrote it in Step 10.2, and place the new `NSLog()` call at the end of the `if` block in the `initWithDocument:` designated initializer. Now, every time you open a new document, the status of all of VRButtonModel's instance variables immediately after initializing the object will be printed to stdIO. This could be a useful sanity check as you enhance the application.

10.4 Use NSAssert()

Another useful debugging macro is `NSAssert()`, which is similar to `NSLog()` but raises an exception and prints a message to StdIO only if a defined test condition is false. You define the condition in a Boolean parameter to the macro, along with the message.

There are several different versions of the assertion macro. For example, `NSAssert()` is for use when the message contains no printf-style placeholders, `NSAssert1()` when the message contains one placeholder `NSAssert2()` for two placeholders, and so on.

1. In VRButtonModel.m, at the end of the `checkboxValue` accessor method, insert the following statement:

```
NSAssert(checkboxValue, @"checkboxValue is not YES");
```

This test consists of a simple Boolean instance variable, but the test can be as complex as you like as long as it returns a Boolean value.

2. Build and run the application, then select the checkbox control and immediately deselect it. You see something like this reported in StdIO:

```
2002-02-07 06:13:42.631 Vermont Recipes[1048]
    *** Assertion failure in -[VRButtonModel checkboxValue],
    VRButtonModel.m:66
```

```
2002-02-07 06:13:42.632 Vermont Recipes[1048]
    Exception raised during posting of notification.
    Ignored.  exception: checkboxValue is not YES
```

Why was the message printed? Trace the logic: The **checkboxAction:** action method in VRMainWindowController was called when you clicked the checkbox control to deselect it. The action method in turn called the **setCheckboxValue:** accessor method in VRButtonModel to change the data value associated with the control. After that accessor method posted a notification that the data value had changed, the **updateCheckbox:** method in VRMainWindowController was triggered when the notification was broadcast. It called the **checkboxValue** accessor method while preparing to call the **updateTwoStateCheckbox:setting:** method, to see whether the checkbox control's visible state needed updating (it did not, because Cocoa had automatically deselected it when you clicked it). At the time when the **checkboxValue** accessor method was called, the value of **checkboxValue** had already been changed to **NO** in the **setCheckboxValue:** method. **NSAssert()** expected the value to be **YES**, so it reported an assertion failure.

An accessor method is not ordinarily a sensible place for an assertion macro that tests the value of the instance variable. It would be more useful to call an assertion macro at some place in the logic where you are concerned that a fatal or incorrect condition may arise, and you need to catch it if and when it happens. An assertion failure is annoying enough without having it reported repeatedly in the correct execution of the application. I just put it here to show you how it works. But don't remove it just yet, because I will use it to illustrate another aspect of Cocoa debugging in Step 10.5. You will see a useful invocation of NSAssert() in Recipe 4, Step 1.

Exceptions

Exceptions are a powerful and advanced debugging technique. Cocoa supports them with several macros defined in Foundation and the NSException class. They are beyond the scope of this book. Read about their use in the materials referenced in the Documentation note, above.

10.5 Build the Application for Deployment

Up to this point, you have paid no attention to some important features in Project Builder. It is now time to explore one of them, the Build Settings pane. This pane is one of the places where you set up the application's build target. You already worked with another target pane, Info.plist Entries, in Step 3.1.

Project Builder has long supported the use of Build Settings to control many features of the preprocessor, compiler, and linker that can be changed to achieve different effects for development and deployment. These include various levels of code optimization for improved speed or memory usage (which very often involve trade-offs between one and the other), as well as support for different kinds of debugging.

You can achieve many if not all changes to build settings in your source files, but it is extremely awkward to have to change various flags in every source file in a large project every time you want to build it. You can instead change them in the Build Settings pane once for all files that compose a build target, a giant step forward in convenience. And here's another step toward convenience: You can define multiple targets for a build, each with its own settings. You will not do this in Vermont Recipes, but it is quite easy: Just choose Project > New Target, select the new target in the Targets pane, and set its unique Build Settings. Then, anytime you want to build the project with different settings, you can choose a different target.

In the newest versions of Project Builder, the build system has been enhanced to achieve still more convenience. You can use all the other techniques, but now you have the Build Styles facility layered on top of them. You can create new build styles by choosing Project > New Build Style, but in Vermont Recipes you will work with the two that come as defaults, Development and Deployment. In this version of Project Builder, the Build Settings pane for a particular target determines the settings that will apply to all builds of the project by default. If you don't use any build style, or if you use the Deployment build style, these are the settings that will be used (plus any additional settings in the Deployment build style, if you select it). These settings will in fact be used for all builds except to the extent that you override or supplement particular settings in the selected build style.

To build for development, therefore, you can leave the Build Settings as they are, designed for deployment, but define additional or different settings in the Development build style and select it for building. This is the technique Apple recommends for normal use, and this is the way you will do it in Vermont Recipes.

Configure the Build Settings to compile Vermont Recipes for deployment. You want to suppress `NSAssert()` and `NSLog()` messages to StdIO, and you want the application to be lean and fast.

1. Select the Targets tab, click Vermont Recipes in the Targets item in the left pane to select it, expand the Settings item if necessary, and select the Simple View item. A scrollable list of settings appears in the project window, ready for editing.

2. Configure the GCC Compiler Settings for the medium built-in level of optimization, choosing "More optimizations (-O2)" in the Optimization level pop-up menu, and for no profiling code or debugging symbols by deselecting both checkboxes.

   The Release Notes for the compiler recommend Level 2 optimization for deployment of most applications built using GCC 3.1, the default compiler in Mac OS X 10.2, to achieve the best balance between speed and application size. If your application places a premium on speed or size, try one of the Level 3 settings. Choose a higher level of optimization only after profiling the performance of Level 2, then profile the higher levels to see whether they actually improve performance. It is important to be scientific about this. Read the documentation for information about specific optimization settings that go beyond Level 3.

3. Click the Expert View item on the left to see the Build Settings text box (**Figure 1.29**). These settings consist of a list of flags or macros, only some of which are equated to values (sometimes their values are used, and sometimes it is enough to know whether they are defined at all). To get some idea of how this text box works, click the Generate Profiling Code and Generate Debugger Symbols checkboxes under GCC Compiler Settings, and watch what happens in Build Settings. If the first checkbox started out deselected and the second was selected, and you just reversed these settings by clicking the checkboxes, you now see a new setting in the Build Settings text box named `PROFILING_CODE`, equated to `YES`, and you see the existing setting, `DEBUGGING_SYMBOLS = NO`, disappear. Deselect the two Compiler Settings checkboxes, because you don't want either of them selected for deployment builds. (If your deployment build will incorporate a system in which customers' crashes are automatically emailed to you with debugging information, however, you had better leave `DEBUGGING_SYMBOLS` set to `YES` even for deployment.)

4. Click the Deployment build style in the Build Styles item in the left pane of the project window to select it. The project window now shows a single text box, Build Settings. This is where you enter additional items to override or add to the base Build Settings for deployment. You see one already defined here by default, `COPY_PHASE_STRIP = YES`.

   You don't want to change any deployment build style items yet. You can return to the main Build Settings pane by choosing the Vermont Recipes target.

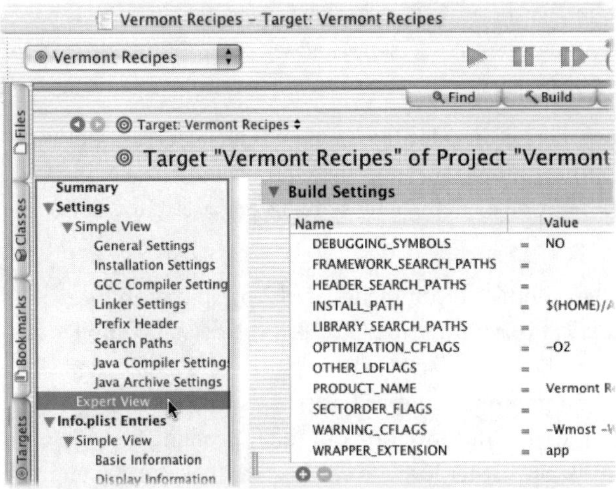

FIGURE 1.29 The Build Settings pane.

5. Click the Development build style in the Build Styles item. Again you see a single Build Settings text box for this build style. This one has two items defined, `COPY_PHASE_STRIP = NO` and `OPTIMIZATION_CFLAGS = -O0.` The `O0` stands for Optimization level zero; this overrides the Optimization level setting of the pop-up menu in the main Build Settings pane, which you set to 2 in Instruction 2, above. You want optimization to be at the lowest level for development because it gives you the greatest debugging power.

6. You also want debugging symbols turned on for development, but you turned them off in the base build settings in Instruction 3, above. To turn them back on for development, insert the associated flag you saw in Instruction 3. In the Development build style pane, click the + button. You see a new item appear, with the dummy name `BUILD_SETTING` selected for editing. Type `DEBUGGING_-SYMBOLS` over it, then press Return to force the list to alphabetize itself. Then move to the Value column to type the new setting, `YES`.

7. Select Deployment in the Build Styles item (be sure to click the Deployment radio button; if you click the title instead, you will select this build style for editing but the radio button won't be selected and it won't compile using this build style). Clean the target by clicking the "Clean active target" button; you must always clean the target before compiling it when changing build styles. Then build and run the application in Project Builder and click the checkbox control to deselect it. The messages from `NSLog()` and `NSAssert()` still appear in StdIO, even though you built for deployment, because these are C macros defined in Foundation and the build style settings you have defined so far don't affect them. You need some additional settings for deployment.

8. Start with **NSAssertion()**. The documentation for Cocoa assertions tells you that defining **NS_BLOCK_ASSERTIONS** will do the trick. Therefore, in the Deployment build style, click the + button, type **OTHER_CFLAGS** in the Name column, click the = button in the middle column to change it to +=, and type **-DNS_BLOCK_-ASSERTIONS** in the Value column. The D between the leading dash and the first N defines the flag. You aren't required to click the = button to change it to += because there are no other C flags defined in the main Build Settings pane, but it is always a good idea to do this in any build style to preserve other C flags in the event that you ever do define this key in the main Build Settings. Also, you don't have to set **NS_BLOCK_ASSERTIONS** to **1** or **YES**, because the mere fact of defining it makes it work. For the same reason, you *cannot* enter it as **-DNS_-BLOCK_ASSERTIONS=0** in the Development build style, where you want assertion failures to be reported, because the definition alone would suppress assertions.

9. Clean the target, then build it using the Deployment build style (make sure to click the Deployment radio button, not its title). Compilation will take much longer than usual, and you will see many warnings, because the precompiled Cocoa headers can't be used with this flag defined. You can ignore the warnings (they're harmless), and the extra compile time won't matter because you won't often build for deployment.

10. Run the application in Project Builder to verify that the assertion failure is not reported in StdIO. After you recompile for development, the assertion failure will once again appear. Using the **NS_BLOCK_ASSERTIONS** flag, you get the benefit of conditional compilation without having to use the preprocessor operator in your source files.

11. Now deal with **NSLog()**. The documentation does not identify a counterpart to **NS_BLOCK_ASSERTIONS** for **NSLog()**. Suppressing log messages is nevertheless almost as easy as suppressing assertion failure messages.

   You will define another C flag in the Deployment build style with the value **-DVR_BLOCK_LOGS** (*VR* for *Vermont Recipes,* of course). In the Deployment build style, double-click the existing value of **OTHER_CFLAGS** to select it for editing, and, after the existing value **-DNS_BLOCK_ASSERTIONS**, type **-DVR_BLOCK_LOGS**. As you see, multiple values are defined for one key just as they are on Terminal's command line, by typing them one after another, separated by white space, each preceded by a dash. Again, you are defining a new C flag without assigning a value to it.

12. If you were to clean and compile for development now and run the application, all of the log messages would still appear. The new flag does not have a predefined use in Project Builder, as **NS_BLOCK_ASSERTIONS** does. You must therefore modify your code files to give it effect.

If you are experienced with C, you are no doubt already familiar with the pre-processor operator, #. You should use it now to bracket both of the calls to NSLog() in VRButtonModel in #ifndef VR_BLOCK_LOGS blocks. #ifndef <name> is shorthand for #if !defined (<name>), just as #ifdef <name> is shorthand for #if defined (<name>). In initWithDocument:, change the line that calls NSLog() to the following:

```
#ifndef VR_BLOCK_LOGS
        NSLog(@"\n\t%@", self);
#endif
```

Similarly, in setCheckboxValue:, change the line that calls NSLog() to this:

```
#ifndef VR_BLOCK_LOGS
        NSLog(@"\n\tExiting [VRButtonModel setCheckboxValue:],
              checkboxValue:%@\n", (checkboxValue ? @"YES" :
              @"NO"));

#endif
```

As a result of these changes, whenever you build for deployment, Project Builder will find that the VR_BLOCK_LOGS flag is defined and it will not compile the lines calling NSLog() because the if test is false (the flag is not undefined). When you build for development, however, it will find the VR_BLOCK_LOGS flag and compile these lines because the if test is true (the flag is undefined). To switch back and forth between these two build styles, you do not have to change flag definitions in your source files but can simply click a radio button once.

13. Clean and build the target for deployment and run it. StdIO displays neither log messages nor assertion failures. You have achieved your objective.

14. Clean up before moving on.

The NSAssert() call in the checkboxValue accessor method is really annoying, as I pointed out at the end of Step 10.4. Move it near the end of initWithDocument:, before return self. Now it will generate an assertion failure only if the designated initializer fails to initialize the checkboxValue instance variable to YES, which will happen only if you remove the initialization code that sets it to YES. The next time you run the application in a development build after doing that, you will be reminded that you have departed from the teaching of Recipe 1.

Set up a facility now that may come in handy later. It is very common when programming in many languages to define a DEBUG flag for development builds. Then you can sprinkle #ifdef DEBUG blocks throughout your source to isolate code snippets that should only be compiled into development builds. In the development build style, add an OTHER-CFLAGS item using the technique you learned in Instruction 8, above, and give it the value -DDEBUG. If you want to test it (or if you just don't like the VR_BLOCK_LOGS flag you created earlier), change the two #ifndef VR_BLOCK_LOGS tests to #ifdef DEBUG tests and run the application in development and deployment builds, noticing the difference in StdIO output.

Finally, reselect the Development build style in the Target tab and clean the target so that you will have the benefit of the NSLog() and NSAssert() messages while continuing to work on Vermont Recipes. As you enhance the Vermont Recipes application, you will add more definition methods and NSLog() calls, and possibly even a few NSAssert() calls. You will want these to generate messages to help you when you're debugging.

Wrap up Step 10. In this step, you learned four different ways to ascertain the value of the checkboxValue instance variable in VRButtonModel at run time using standard debugging techniques: stepping and reading the value in the variable list, logging the value to StdIO, printing a description of the entire object to the Console, and reporting the value to StdIO as an assertion failure. These skills should be enough to get you through the rest of Vermont Recipes.

You also learned how to build the application for deployment, which is, after all, your ultimate goal.

Conclusion

Run the application and try out all its features.

To ensure that Mac OS X adds your new document format to its database, don't run the application from within Project Builder. Instead, open the build folder in the Vermont Recipes folder, move the compiled and linked application to the Mac OS X Applications folder, and run it by double-clicking it there. This is necessary to allow the system to recognize the application as the owner of its saved documents, so that double-clicking a document will automatically open it in the application, and it may also be necessary to ensure that its icons appear in the Dock and elsewhere. If you run the application from within Project Builder before running it independently, you may find that these features of Mac OS X don't work properly and you might not be able to minimize it to the Dock.

A few things don't work yet, such as drawers and online help, and you haven't yet created any new menus or menu items. But an amazing number of standard application features now work perfectly, and getting to this stage required remarkably little effort on your part.

For example, the About Vermont Recipes menu item opens an About window with information about your application, including the copyright notice you supplied. The window minimizes and zooms as expected, both from the buttons in the window title bar and from the Window menu. Other commands in the Window menu work, for example, to bring any of multiple open windows to the front. The keyboard equivalents work just like their associated menu items. Saving changes to an existing document, or reverting it to its last saved state, opens appropriate confirmation sheets. And so on.

And all of the features you added in this first recipe work flawlessly. Go ahead: Exercise the New, Save, and Open commands repeatedly, working with a dozen documents open at once, if you like. Make changes to saved documents and revert them. Use the Undo and Redo menu commands to see that they count multiple changes and undo and redo them as they should.

You are ready now to turn to Recipe 2, where you will begin implementing a large variety of standard Mac OS X user controls. Subsequent recipes will deal with menus and menu items, sheets, drawers, Apple Help, and a myriad other topics of interest to Cocoa developers.

User Controls

In Section 2, you will flesh out the skeleton of the Vermont Recipes application by adding a large number of user controls.

This is the natural task to tackle next in almost any document-based application development project. You can't do much with a typical application if you can't set and view the data it's designed to manage. Its user controls—buttons, sliders, text fields, and the like—are the most visible and varied devices for doing this. It is important that you learn at an early stage how to create the many kinds of user controls available and how to fit them into the overall operation of an application and its data.

In addition, prototyping the user interface is the quickest way to get a sense of the application's overall look and feel, as well as its usability. The user interface consists mostly of user controls, and it is easy to create and test them in Interface Builder and to tinker with them until they meet your requirements.

Each basic category of user control covered in Section 2 is the subject of a separate recipe—a recipe for buttons, a recipe for sliders, and so on. Since Vermont Recipes targets programmers, I will categorize controls by Cocoa view type. In some cases, this may seem odd from an end user's point of view; for example, checkboxes and pop-up menus are NSButtons, so they appear in the Buttons recipe.

Within each of this section's recipes, I devote separate steps to many of the common variants of a single category. The steps of Recipe 2, for example, which is devoted to buttons, show you how to create and use more complicated checkboxes, radio buttons, and even some controls you might not think of as buttons, such as pop-up menus and command pop-down menus (formerly known as pull-down menus). Although each step within a recipe focuses on a particular control, the recipe may cover other related controls, especially where their interaction is important.

Following Recipe 2, you will learn about other kinds of controls. For example, Recipe 3 covers sliders, including techniques for linking sliders and other controls. After learning how to implement bare-bones text fields in Recipe 4, you will digress in several subsequent recipes to learn about a number of text field extras, including alert sheets in Recipe 5 to communicate with your users while they are working in a text field; formatters in Recipe 6 to filter out invalid characters and generate correctly formatted text automatically on the fly; undo and redo in text fields in Recipe 7; and drag-and-drop editing in Recipe 8.

You won't find every control known to humankind in Section 2, but you will find the most important standard Macintosh user controls, including a few variants. Some of the controls will interoperate—for example, by disabling or enabling other controls or rapidly updating a number in a text field as the user drags a slider back and forth.

Each step of these recipes covers both the Interface Builder and the Project Builder aspects of creating and using the controls it covers. After Step 1 of Recipe 2 teaches you how to prepare the project files, Step 2 provides a very detailed road map of the process for implementing an interrelated group of checkboxes. Step 2 serves as a checklist of fundamental tasks for implementing almost any kind of control. Subsequent steps and recipes through the remainder of Section 2 follow the same model, providing less detail to avoid repetition, but always flagging new and interesting techniques and explaining them in depth. This organization should make it possible to use Section 2 as a reference when implementing controls in your own application.

Along the way, Vermont Recipes will continue to introduce you to other features of Cocoa as the need arises, in the natural flow of developing a complete Cocoa application. In Recipe 3, for example, you will learn how to add tab view items to the tab view you created in Recipe 1, as well as how to navigate between and within tab view items using the keyboard.

As you work your way through Section 2, you should pay close attention to the Aqua Human Interface Guidelines. They are very detailed, prescribing specific dimensions for buttons, position and spacing of controls in dialogs, and similar details. The success of the Macintosh platform depends in part on the fact that users can expect things to look and work more or less the same in all applications. Interface Builder is a great help, because it lets you apply many of the guidelines automatically, particularly with the introduction of Aqua guides in Mac OS X 10.0. When you have completed Section 2, each tab view item in the running application will serve as a demonstration of how the variants of that tab's category of controls work, and you want to be sure they work correctly.

Once you have completed Section 2, you will have a good grasp of how to implement any kind of user control and integrate it into the overall workings of your own application.

RECIPE 2

Buttons

In Recipe 2, you will implement several different kinds of buttons. From a Cocoa programmer's perspective, buttons include checkboxes, radio buttons, pop-up menus, command pop-down menus, and other controls, as well as traditional push buttons, all of which inherit from Cocoa's NSButton class.

All of the buttons will appear on the Buttons tab view item that you created in Recipe 1. When you have finished Recipe 2, the contents of the Buttons pane will appear as shown in **Figure 2.1**. (The figure shows other features, such as renamed and rearranged tab view items and a Notes button, that you will create in later recipes.)

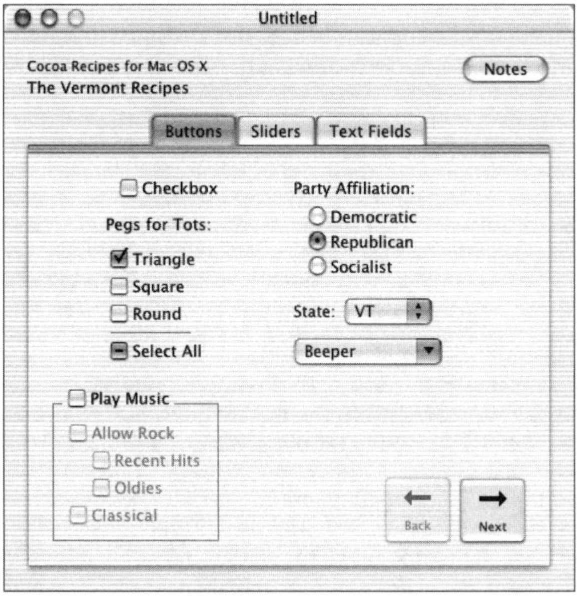

FIGURE 2.1 The finished Buttons tab view item.

Step 1: Prepare the Project for Recipe 2

Before getting into the meat of Recipe 2, you will change some of the application's settings in Step 1 to reflect the fact that you are updating its features. You will also learn how to break the window controller subclass into separate files as a convenient means to organize what would otherwise eventually become one very large and unwieldy file.

`1.1` Update the Application Settings

Very few changes need be made to the Info.plist Entries that you originally set up in Recipe 1, Step 3.1. You will bump up the application's build version to indicate that you're rebuilding it for Recipe 2, while leaving the application version at 1.0.0d1. Also, the new data items you will add in this recipe require a new file format, so you will change the document version code in VRDocument.m. If this were a second release version of the application, you would include routines using the document version code to make sure the newer version of the application does not attempt to access data that was unavailable in older documents left over from the previous version.

Documentation

The primary source for Mac OS X human interface guidelines is *Inside Mac OS X: Aqua Human Interface Guidelines*, a downloadable PDF document at http://developer.apple.com/techpubs/macosx/Essentials/AquaHIGuildelines/AquaHIGuidelines.pdf. It is also available on your disk in both PDF and HTML form at /Developer/Documentation/Essentials/AquaHIGuidelines, but you should occasionally check the Web version. Substantial additions and many changes to this document have appeared since the initial release of Mac OS X. Serious developers will want to keep close tabs on its status.

The *Guidelines* are written as addenda to the older human interface guidelines, which remain in effect to the extent that they are not inconsistent with the Mac OS X document. The older documents are available on the Web as the downloadable PDF files *Macintosh Human Interface Guidelines* and *Mac OS 8 Human Interface Guidelines* at http://developer.apple.com/techpubs/mac/pdf as HIGuidelines.pdf and HIGOS8Guidelines.pdf, respectively. Both are also available as Web documents at http://developer.apple.com/techpubs/macos8/HumanInterfaceToolbox/HumanInterfaceGuide/humaninterfaceguide.html.

In subsequent recipes, you will routinely change the build version, as well as the document version code if the document format changes.

1. In the Finder, duplicate the Vermont Recipes folder and move the original to a safe backup or archival location for safekeeping. I suggest that you rename the backup something like `Vermont Recipes 1` to avoid confusion. It is a good idea to give the top-level project folders different names to reflect different builds and make it easy to distinguish them, especially if you keep both of them in an active location.

    In the backup Vermont Recipes 1 folder, you needn't rename the Vermont Recipes.pbproj bundle. There is no need to change this name every time you build a new version. Even with multiple versions open at once in Project Builder, you will be able to tell them apart by their paths, which you can access by Command-clicking the project name in the project window's title bar.

2. To reduce the size of the backup before you store it away, drag its entire build folder to the Trash using the Finder. Cocoa will create a new one the next time you build the application from this folder, should you later wish to revert to the older version. You can reduce the size of the folder still more by trashing the backup copies of the nib files in the English.lproj subfolder; the backups are the files with a tilde (~) in their filenames. You should also perform these steps before sending a project folder to someone electronically or posting it on the Web; they'll reduce the transmission or download time.

3. In the active Vermont Recipes folder, double-click Vermont Recipes.pbproj to open the project in Project Builder.

4. Select the Targets tab, click the Vermont Recipes target, then expand the Info.plist Entries item and click its Expert item. Change CFBundleVersion to 2. This is the new build version.

5. Select the Files tab, expand the Classes group, and open VRDocument.m. A little over halfway down, in the "Keys and values for dictionary" section, change VRDocumentVersion to 2. This value will be saved in every document. In real-world development, backward-compatibility routines would use it to identify the format of the document when opening it. You only need to change it if the document format changes from one build to another.

6. If it makes you comfortable, build and run the application to confirm that it is working as expected before proceeding with the rest of Recipe 2. Choose About Vermont Recipes from the application menu, and you see that the version is now given as 1.0.0d1 (v2).

If you wish, you can change many of the other items in the Info.plist Entries, such as the application's creator code and its document file type. There is no good reason to do so during development of one version of an application, however. This sort of change is generally reserved for updates that will be released to the public. If you do make such changes, make any corresponding changes required in other files, such as the VRDocument.m source file and the InfoPlist.strings file.

1.2 Create a Category to Simplify Source Code Management

You should take a moment now to think about how your files are organized.

Placing the declarations and definitions of each class in its own pair of header and source files is certainly a helpful organizing principle. You have already seen the benefits of using separate classes in an object-oriented application. You set up a model class, VRButtonModel, in Recipe 1 strictly to manage data relating to user controls that will appear on the Buttons tab view item. You will create separate model classes for controls that appear on other tab view items in Recipe 3 and those that follow.

You also used another organizational device, `#pragma mark` directives, to identify separate sections of code within their respective header and source files. You did this partly to organize the markers pop-up menu for easier navigation but also to impose order on the text in some files that may become very long.

The VRMainWindowController class is bound to need some organizational structure beyond mere `#pragma mark` directives. Think about how much code you have already placed in that class and how much more code you will have to add to it as you create additional user controls in recipes yet to come. You would be justified in fearing that textual compartmentalization of the VRMainWindowController class, particularly its source file, will not be good enough.

It would be nice if you could break the window controller apart into some sort of master controller that is in charge of separate, subsidiary controllers for the user controls within each tab view item. In concept, this would be similar to the document controller and its several model objects. However, there isn't the same difference in kind between these window controller methods as there is between the methods in a document controller such as your VRDocument class and those in the model objects it manages. Furthermore, controller classes are not likely to be candidates for reuse in other applications to the extent that model classes are. You might therefore think it advantageous to keep all of the controller methods in a single class, while still breaking the class into separate files.

Fortunately, Objective-C offers a solution. Here, you will learn another common device, the Objective-C *category*, which can be used as an organizing tool, among other things.

Categories

Categories are a powerful feature of the Objective-C language not commonly found in other programming languages. Categories can be used in a variety of ways.

In their most interesting use, categories allow you to extend and enhance the functionality of any class, even if you don't have access to its source code, by adding new methods to the base class or reimplementing existing methods it already implements. When what you want to do is add a few methods to an existing class, categories may be a good substitute for subclassing it even if you do have access to its source code. New methods implemented in a category become available to all clients of the base class, and they are indistinguishable at run time from methods implemented in the base class. You can add both class methods and instance methods in a category. However, you cannot add new instance variables, and when you redeclare an existing method in a category, you cannot access the original method as you could by sending a message to super if you had subclassed the base class.

Categories on one class are often declared and implemented within header and source files for other classes, usually because the methods in the category relate to the function of the class in whose files they appear. You can see many examples of this in the Cocoa frameworks by browsing their header files.

Multiple categories on one class can also be declared and implemented in the same file as the base class, as a device to break the class into convenient topical sections. You can use categories in this way to partition the implementation of a single class into separate source files, as you will do here. You import the common class header in each of the source files. This is particularly convenient for managing a large, complex class.

Another use of categories is to declare *informal protocols*, a subject you will learn about later.

Finally, you can declare and implement a category in files of its own. For example, the category on NSString that you will create in Step 2.7 is declared and implemented in separate header and source files, which could serve as the beginning of a reusable custom string library for your private use.

As described in the note about categories, you can use categories purely and simply as a device to organize files, although they also have other, more powerful uses. Here, you will move the method declarations and definitions you wrote for the checkbox user control in the VRMainWindowController class—its **accessor**, **update**, and **action** methods—into a separate category on that class devoted solely to the controls that appear in the Buttons tab view item. You will name the category VRButtonController. In Recipe 3 and following, you will write additional categories on VRMainWindowController for the controls in new tab view items.

The declarations will be left in the main VRMainWindowController.h header file, but they will be moved into the interface parts of new categories declared at the end of that file. Header files are relatively short and needn't be broken into physically separate files.

The definitions of these methods will likewise be moved into the new categories' implementation parts. However, instead of placing the categories' implementation parts at the end of the VRMainWindowController.m source file, you will place them in new, separate category source files. In this recipe, you will use VRButtonController.m. In Recipe 3 and following, you will create separate controller source files for the implementations of new categories for additional tab view items.

By breaking the VRMainWindowController class implementation into separate files, you will make the source code for the user controls in each tab view item far easier to manage. This requires no change to the code of any of these methods. All that is required is to use the correct **#import** directives to make sure each file knows how to find the interface declarations it needs. In all respects, Objective-C considers all of the methods in these categories to be an integral part of the VRMainWindowController class.

Remember that your use of tab view items to organize these files is arbitrary and meant only for instructional purposes. It works as an organizing principle here, but in your own applications, you may find it more sensible to use some other logical principle for categorizing your window controller's methods.

1. In the VRMainWindowController.h header file, *after* the **@end** directive at the end of the text, insert the following:

```
@interface VRMainWindowController (VRButtonController)
@end
```

This specifies a new category, VRButtonController, named within the parentheses, which adds functionality to the existing VRMainWindowController class. You do not declare it as a descendant of some other class, as you would when creating a new class, because the inheritance chain for VRMainWindowController is already defined in your application. The category is part of the existing VRMainWindowController class. You cannot declare new instance variables in a category either, so there are no curly braces. The instance variables are declared in the main class declaration, as usual.

2. Cut the existing **buttonModel**, **checkbox**, **updateCheckbox:**, and **checkboxAction:** method declarations and paste them into the new category at the end of the VRMainWindowController.h header file, between the **@interface** directive and its corresponding **@end** directive. Move the **#pragma mark** and other section headings with them, because you will still find it useful to keep the new category navigable and organized in this fashion.

3. You will move the implementation of these four methods into the new category as well, but you will place the implementation part of the category in a separate file.

   You have created new files several times by now, so I won't belabor the details. Begin by choosing File > New File in Project Builder using the Objective-C class template under the Cocoa heading. After clicking the Next button, name the new file **VRButtonController.m**. This time, deselect the "Also create 'VRButtonController.h'" checkbox, because you don't need a separate header file. A single new file will be created in your project folder. Use Project Builder's Project > Add Files command to get the new file into the Groups & Files pane, and place it in the Classes group. Click VRButtonController.m in the Groups & Files pane to open it in the editing pane, and add your usual leading comments and disclaimers.

4. After the comments, add the following at the end of the VRButtonController.m source file:

   ```
   @implementation VRMainWindowController (VRButtonController)
   @end
   ```

5. Cut the definitions of the same four methods—**buttonModel**, **checkbox**, **updateCheckbox:**, and **checkboxAction:**—from the VRMainWindowController.m source file and paste them into the category in the new VRButtonController.m source file, between the **@implementation** directive and its corresponding **@end** directive. Move the **#pragma mark** and other headings with them as appropriate.

6. Immediately before the **@implementation** directive, add these two **#import** directives so the methods you just moved can find the header declarations they need:

   ```
   #import "VRMainWindowController.h"
   #import "VRButtonModel.h"
   ```

7. You could stop here, but it would improve the usability of these files still more if you also declared two methods in the new category, corresponding in function to the **registerNotificationObservers** and **updateWindow** methods in the main body of the VRMainWindowController class.

   In the VRMainWindowController.h header file, after the **ACCESSORS** section of the VRButtonController category, add the following new method declarations:

   ```
   #pragma mark WINDOW MANAGEMENT

   - (void)registerNotificationObserversForButtonsTab;

   - (void)updateButtonsTab;
   ```

8. In the VRButtonController.m category source file, after the **ACCESSORS** section, insert these definition method stubs:

```
#pragma mark WINDOW MANAGEMENT

- (void)registerNotificationObserversForButtonsTab {
}

- (void)updateButtonsTab {
}
```

Then fill in both of these stub method definitions by cutting the existing contents of the `registerNotificationObservers` and `updateWindow` methods from the VRMainWindowController.m source file and pasting them into the two corresponding stub methods you just created in the VRButtonController.m category source file.

9. Turn to VRMainWindowController.m. In the now empty `registerNotification-Observers` and `updateWindow` methods, substitute calls to the two new category methods, so they look like this:

```
- (void)registerNotificationObservers {
    [self registerNotificationObserversForButtonsTab];
}

- (void)updateWindow{
    [self updateButtonsTab];
}
```

10. One final simplification is now possible. You no longer have to import the VRButtonModel.h header file into the VRMainWindowController.m source file, because every statement that has to know something about the buttons model has now been moved into the VRButtonController.m source file. Therefore, remove the `#import "VRButtonModel.h"` directive from VRMainWindowController.m. Not only have you reorganized the project's files for convenience but you've also achieved some real compartmentalization of its logic.

If you wanted to push optimization still further, you could now consider whether it makes sense to pull the methods controlling the Buttons tab view item into an altogether separate class rather than into a category. You will not do so here because you need to move on to creating new user controls. However, in a large, complex application, it might improve the user experience if you were to load methods relating to hidden tab view items *lazily;* that is, you'd defer loading them into memory until the user actually selected their tabs—which, after all, the user might never do. The application would launch more quickly and would take up less memory initially, because it wouldn't have to load the code for more than one of what could eventually amount to half a dozen tab view items. It would instead defer loading the code for them until they were needed, if ever. Performing this optimization would not be simple, because you would need to add logic to load the various tab view controllers at appropriate times, but it might be worth the effort.

In general, efficient software development entails writing an application as simply as is reasonably possible first, then testing it under real-world conditions to identify any optimizations that might be required to achieve satisfactory responsiveness. Often, an optimization that looks attractive in theory proves to be wholly unnecessary in practice, and you can save yourself a lot of coding time by deferring this decision as long as possible.

11. Compile and build the application, then test it to make sure everything is working just as it did at the end of Recipe 1.

You are now ready to begin adding user controls to the application.

Step 2: Create Checkboxes (Switch Buttons) in a Borderless Group Box

The Switch button—or checkbox, as I call it in *Vermont Recipes*—that you implemented in Recipe 1 is sometimes known as a *two-state checkbox,* because it can be either on (selected or checked) or off (deselected or unchecked). You can also create *mixed-state checkboxes,* which have the familiar checked and unchecked states but also have

HIGHLIGHTS:

Creating a mixed-state checkbox

Using an Objective-C category to enhance a built-in Cocoa class

an indeterminate or mixed state indicated by a dash inside the checkbox. The *Mac OS 8 Human Interface Guidelines* (which applies in Mac OS X except as revised in the *Aqua Human Interface Guidelines*) describes a mixed-state checkbox as follows:

> There is a mixed state for checkboxes, which shows that a selected range of items has some in the on state and some in the off state. For example, a text formatting checkbox for bold text would be in the mixed state if a text selection contained both bold and non-bold text....

> Checkboxes differ from radio buttons in that they are independent of each other, even when they offer related options. Any number of checkboxes can be on, off, or mixed at the same time.

For purposes of demonstrating how to implement a mixed-state checkbox, you will create three independent but related two-state checkboxes in a titled group box, and the box will contain a fourth, mixed-state checkbox at the bottom that can be used to turn all three of the two-state checkboxes on or off at once. The mixed-state checkbox will assume the mixed state when one or more but not all of the other three checkboxes have been turned on separately, but the user cannot create a mixed state by clicking this checkbox.

The checkboxes in this step will be grouped because all of them relate to a single subject, but the group will not contain a visible border. The *Aqua Human Interface Guidelines* recommends that bordered group boxes be used sparingly, if at all, expressing a preference for the use of white space to separate a group of related controls visually from other interface items and groups. This differs from the Mac OS 9 and earlier interface guidelines, which encouraged the use of enclosing borders to group related items. In Mac OS X, the trend is to retreat from the overbusy user interfaces that have become common in older applications. In Step 3 you will implement a similar group of checkboxes using a visible bordered box, which the guidelines still permit when it serves usability.

Adding a new control and its associated data variable to an application can be a surprisingly tedious affair, as you will discover in this step. There are a great many details to take care of. However, the object-oriented structure of a Cocoa application allows you to organize the process into a fixed set of steps, no matter what kind of user control is involved, so you can adopt a routine practice to reduce the chance of errors. This way, you can easily take care of features such as multiple undo and redo and data storage. Before turning to the details, here is a checklist of what you must do.

- **Control.** Use Interface Builder to draw controls, then turn to Project Builder to code them.

- **User control outlet variables and accessors.*** Add outlet variables and accessor methods to the window controller so the state of new controls can be accessed.

- **Data variables and accessors.** Add data variables and accessor methods to the model object so the values represented by new controls can be accessed; the **set** accessor methods will also register data changes with the undo manager and post notifications to signal to observers that the data has changed.

- **Notification variables.** Declare notification variables in the model object so it can notify the window controller when the data changes.

- **Graphical user interface (GUI) update methods.*** Add methods to the window controller to update the visible state of new controls in response to notifications that the data has changed.

- **NOTIFICATION OBSERVERS.*** Register the window controller as a notification observer so it will receive notifications that the data has changed.

- **ACTION METHODS.*** Add action methods to the window controller to change the data in the model object when the user clicks new controls; also provide the undo and redo menu item titles here.

- **LOCALIZABLE.STRINGS.** Update the Localizable.strings file with the new undo and redo menu item titles.

- **INITIALIZATION.** Initialize the data variables in the model object to default values, if desired.

- **DATA STORAGE.** Add keys and devise methods in the model object to save and retrieve the data to and from persistent storage.

- **GUI UPDATE METHOD INVOCATIONS.*** Add invocations of the control updaters so the window controller's `updateWindow` method will update the visible state of the new controls.

- **DESCRIPTION METHOD.** Add the values of the new data variables in the model object to its `description` method for use in debugging and for other purposes.

- **HELP TAGS.** Add Help tags to controls, if appropriate.

- **INITIAL FIRST RESPONDER AND NEXT KEY VIEW.** Insert every new control into its containing view's key view loop to enable the user to tab from one control to the next. This includes not only text fields but also all user controls. You will learn how to do this in Recipe 4, Step 2.

- **NIB FILE.** Use Interface Builder to read the code files into the nib file to capture the new outlets and actions, then connect them with the new controls and set any required delegate connections.

It took all of Recipe 1 to cover these steps for one checkbox control, along with the basics of creating the application. Here, you will do it for the new mixed-state checkbox and its associated two-state checkboxes in a single step. The checklist above will serve you well as a road map in steps and recipes to come, where you will create many more controls. After you work through this road map in detail, shortened instructions in subsequent steps and recipes will help you focus on what is unique about each control.

Five items in the checklist are marked with an asterisk. The new methods contemplated for each of these five items will be declared and defined in a category on VRMainWindowController for convenience, and the implementation part of the category will be placed in a separate controller source file. In this recipe, you will use the VRButtonController category you created in Step 1.2.

The routine steps for implementing these controls are covered in Steps 2.1 and 2.2. The more interesting material—the methods to update the mixed-state checkbox and its action method, and another brief foray into the land of Objective-C categories— is covered in Steps 2.3 and following.

2.1 Create a Borderless Group Box and Checkboxes in Interface Builder

Use Interface Builder to create several new checkboxes grouped in a box, using the techniques you learned in Recipe 1, Step 2.2. When you are done with this, the group should look like that shown in **Figure 2.2**.

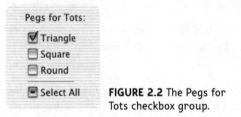

FIGURE 2.2 The Pegs for Tots checkbox group.

1. Open VRDocument.nib in Interface Builder and select the Buttons tab view item, if necessary. Its tab highlights when it is selected.

   In the latest versions of Interface Builder, it is no longer necessary to select a tab view item to ensure that a control dropped on it from the Cocoa palette doesn't fall through into the underlying view object. You don't even have to preselect the correct tab view item to ensure that the control drops into the Buttons tab view item, since dragging a control over a tab will select that tab view item on the fly. It is nevertheless often easier to select the intended tab view item before dragging. You can verify that a tab view item is selected by checking the Info Panel, which should show the NSTabViewItem Info Panel, not the Info Panel for the underlying NSView or NSWindow.

2. Drag an NSBox object from the Containers palette onto the Buttons pane and position it below the existing checkbox control, using the guides to establish the correct distance beneath the checkbox and to the right of the tab view's left edge. Drag its lower-right resize handle downward and to the right to make it a little larger (**Figure 2.3**).

   In older versions of Interface Builder, the NSBox object was located on a different palette. Furthermore, it wasn't necessary to drag it from the palette at all, since a Group in Box command was available in the Layout menu to surround selected controls with a box. The Group in Box function is still available, now as Layout > Make subviews of > Box. Its former position in the Layout menu has been taken over by Group and Ungroup menu items, which function more like the typical group and ungroup commands in graphics applications.

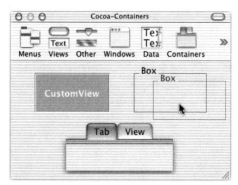

FIGURE 2.3 Dragging a Box item from the Cocoa Containers palette.

Although you can still select some existing user controls and group them in a box, it is easier to create the box first and then drop user controls into it. Among other things, you gain the benefit of Aqua guides for positioning the controls within the box.

If the box you are using here were to be untitled as well as borderless, you might think you could have used the new Group command instead of a box. However, the Group command is not intended to establish a group of controls for human interface design purpose, but only to keep the grouped controls together when moving them. Positioning a grouped set of controls using the Aqua guides would result in their being placed immediately below the existing Checkbox control, with no extra white space to distinguish them as a separate group. Here, you want a title for the group anyway, so the use of a box is required.

3. From the Views palette, drag three Switch controls into the new box in succession and position them in accordance with the guides. As you drag them over the box, you see a line appear around it indicating that the controls will be dropped into the box, effectively grouping them within it when you drop them. If you drag the box around in its tab view item now, the checkboxes will move with it.

4. Rename the three new checkboxes **Triangle**, **Square**, and **Round**, respectively.

5. From the Views palette, drag the horizontal line below the radio buttons into the box, placing it beneath the three new checkboxes where indicated by the guides.

6. From the Views palette, drag another Switch control into the box and position it beneath the dividing line where the guides suggest. Rename it **Select All**.

7. Some of the checkbox titles may be too long for the width of the box. If so, select the box and drag the appropriate resize handle to the right until a guide-line shows you the correct position for the right edge of the box relative to the ends of the checkbox labels.

8. Double-click the title Box and type over it to change it to `Pegs for Tots:` (with a trailing colon because the box's border will be made invisible). This title may be a little too long for the width of the box, so drag a resize handle to widen the box again, if necessary, to the proper size as indicated by the guides.

9. This box is to be borderless, so in the Attributes pane of the NSBox Info Panel, click the button designating a borderless group box. If you watch closely, you'll see that the individual controls within the box change position slightly, automatically conforming to a different set of spacing guidelines (**Figure 2.4**).

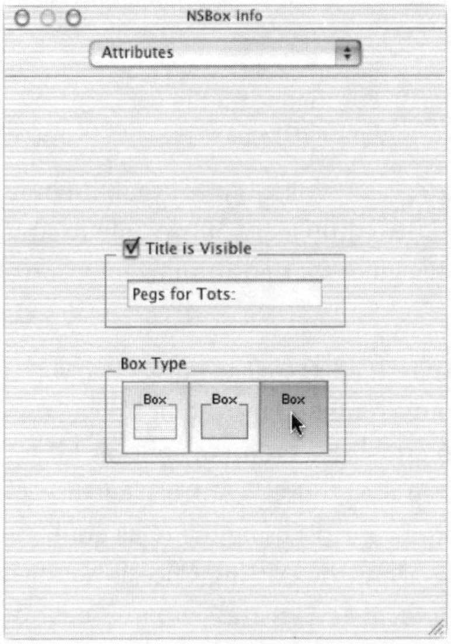

FIGURE 2.4 The NSBox Info Panel.

10. All of these changes may require repositioning the entire group. Do so now in accordance with the guides, and you are done.

11. If you want to reposition the items in the box manually, you can experiment with a variety of potentially useful tools, as follows:

- Choose Layout > Alignment > Alignment Panel to open the Alignment Panel, then select the three topmost checkboxes in the box. In this panel, you can use the pop-up menu to select the Left/Top set of buttons, then click the top-left button to align the left edges again, if necessary. Other menu commands and buttons are available for a variety of other alignment options. For example, you can use the bottom-right button to spread them out or close them up vertically with appropriate spacing—after, say, entering 7 pixels for checkboxes, to achieve the recommended 20-pixel spacing between the baselines of their titles. Or, after selecting the checkboxes, you can use the same button to adjust the vertical position of the divider so that it is, say, 8 pixels below the Round checkbox and move the Select All checkbox so that it is, say, 8 pixels below the divider.

- If you don't like the resulting appearance, drag the checkboxes and the divider individually within the group box. You'll notice that guides appear, suggesting internal placement for items within the box.

- Click one of the checkboxes to select it, then hold down the Option key as you move the pointer (without holding down the mouse button) over several other controls and out into the empty part of the window. You see arrows showing the exact number of pixels between various elements of the window.

- Select the group box and use the Layout > Size to Fit command to shrink the box around the controls. You see that all of the controls close up and the border shrinks around them.

- Turn to the NSBox Info Panel and see what tools it offers to change the spacing and appearance of the group box. The only choice for the group title is to have a visible title or not. You can use the Format menu to change the font and style, but the *Aqua Human Interface Guidelines* do not encourage you to depart from the defaults. You have a choice of three Box Type buttons, but for this step you have specified borderless.

By now, you've probably thoroughly messed up the spacing and position of the group box and its items. The easiest way to restore them is to start with the top-most item in the group box and drag each item in turn to the position indicated by the Aqua guides.

Examine the *Aqua Human Interface Guidelines* to satisfy yourself that you have complied with its arrangement, sizing and spacing recommendations. One issue to note is that Mac OS X favors a center-biased dialog layout. At the end of this Recipe you will adjust the horizontal placement of items in the Buttons tab view item to comply with this recommendation.

2.2 Write the Code for the Checkboxes in Project Builder

Use Project Builder to write the code required to make the three new two-state checkboxes work, and to implement the simpler features of the fourth, mixed-state checkbox. The Triangle, Square, and Round checkboxes will be coded exactly as the first checkbox control was coded in Recipe 1, each new checkbox acting independently of the other to set an associated variable in the VRButtonModel model object.

The mixed-state Select All checkbox will have new functionality, setting or clearing all of the other checkboxes when it is checked or unchecked. It will in turn be checked, cleared, or left in the mixed state, as appropriate, when any of the other checkboxes in the group is checked or unchecked. You will defer the more interesting code involving the mixed-state checkbox to Step 2.3, below.

1. **USER CONTROL OUTLET VARIABLES AND ACCESSORS.** Each of the four new checkboxes will be represented by an outlet variable in VRMainWindowController, so that the window controller can tell the controls to change their visible states when the data changes or obtain the states when that information is needed. In Recipe 1, Step 2.6.2.2, you created an outlet for the Checkbox control in Interface Builder. You could do it that way here, too, because the FileMerge application would be invoked and allow you to preserve the existing code in VRMainWindowController. However, it is easier to type in the code, since you have to type a great deal of code that Interface Builder can't supply, anyway. You will do so now, following the model of Recipe 1, Step 3.4.

Near the top of the header file VRMainWindowController.h, declare four new outlets after the **checkbox** declaration, as follows:

```
// Pegs switch button group
IBOutlet NSButton *trianglePegsCheckbox;
IBOutlet NSButton *squarePegsCheckbox;
IBOutlet NSButton *roundPegsCheckbox;
IBOutlet NSButton *allPegsCheckbox;
```

Still in VRMainWindowController.h, also declare accessor methods for these outlets after the **checkbox** accessor method in the VRButtonController category at the bottom of the header file, as follows:

```
// Pegs switch button group
- (NSButton *)trianglePegsCheckbox;
- (NSButton *)squarePegsCheckbox;
- (NSButton *)roundPegsCheckbox;
- (NSButton *)allPegsCheckbox;
```

Turn to the new category source file VRButtonController.m and define the accessors after the **checkbox** accessor, as follows:

```
// Pegs switch button group

- (NSButton *)trianglePegsCheckbox {
    return trianglePegsCheckbox;
}

- (NSButton *)squarePegsCheckbox {
    return squarePegsCheckbox;
}
```

```
- (NSButton *)roundPegsCheckbox {
    return roundPegsCheckbox;
}

- (NSButton *)allPegsCheckbox {
    return allPegsCheckbox;
}
```

Now that you've gone to all that trouble, let us say once again that using accessor methods to get user controls may be overkill. Everybody recommends using accessors for data variables in your model object, but the justifications for doing so don't necessarily extend to user controls. The implementation of user controls, unlike your application's data structures, is pretty much built into Cocoa. It is unlikely to change in ways you would want to hide from your header files. Your code would be simpler if you just accessed user controls by their instance variables directly.

Nevertheless, on the theory that tutorial code should be conservative, you will continue to use accessors for user controls throughout the Vermont Recipes application. It may even turn out that there is a payoff down the line, when you start to think about automating the GUI of Vermont Recipes using AppleScript.

2. **DATA VARIABLES AND ACCESSORS.** Three of the new checkboxes require corresponding variables in VRButtonModel to hold the data they represent. The fourth checkbox is used only to affect or reflect the state of the other three as a group, so it does not require an independent data variable. You can determine the values of the three as a group by testing all of them at once, and this avoids the risk that a fourth variable to track the value of the group might fall out of sync.

You will now create the three new data variables in VRButtonModel, along with their accessors, following the model of Recipe 1, Step 3.5.4. You will include in the set methods the undo manager and notification center statements you learned in Recipe 1, Steps 6.1 and 6.3, to ensure that changing the values of these data variables will be undoable and will be reflected in the GUI.

In the header file VRButtonModel.h, declare three new variables after the checkboxValue variable, as follows:

```
// Pegs
BOOL trianglePegsValue;
BOOL squarePegsValue;
BOOL roundPegsValue;
```

In VRButtonModel.h, also declare the corresponding accessor methods after the checkboxValue accessor, as follows:

```
// Pegs

- (void)setTrianglePegsValue:(BOOL)inValue;
- (BOOL)trianglePegsValue;

- (void)setSquarePegsValue:(BOOL)inValue;
- (BOOL)squarePegsValue;

- (void)setRoundPegsValue:(BOOL)inValue;
- (BOOL)roundPegsValue;
```

Turn to the source file VRButtonModel.m and define the accessor methods after the checkboxValue accessor, as set forth below. Although they aren't shown here, you can also add an NSLog() call to each set accessor, bracketed by preprocessor directives, on the model of Recipe 1, Step 10.2, if you wish to follow this practice as a debugging aid.

```
// Pegs

- (void)setTrianglePegsValue:(BOOL)inValue {
    [[[self undoManager] prepareWithInvocationTarget:self]
          setTrianglePegsValue:trianglePegsValue];
    trianglePegsValue = inValue;
    [[NSNotificationCenter defaultCenter] postNotificationName:
          VRButtonModelTrianglePegsValueChangedNotification
          object:[self document]];
}

- (BOOL)trianglePegsValue {
    return trianglePegsValue;
}

- (void)setSquarePegsValue:(BOOL)inValue {
    [[[self undoManager] prepareWithInvocationTarget:self]
          setSquarePegsValue:squarePegsValue];
    squarePegsValue = inValue;
    [[NSNotificationCenter defaultCenter] postNotificationName:
          VRButtonModelSquarePegsValueChangedNotification
          object:[self document]];
}

- (BOOL)squarePegsValue {
```

```
        return squarePegsValue;
}


- (void)setRoundPegsValue:(BOOL)inValue {
    [[[self undoManager] prepareWithInvocationTarget:self]
        setRoundPegsValue:roundPegsValue];
    roundPegsValue = inValue;
    [[NSNotificationCenter defaultCenter] postNotificationName:
        VRButtonModelRoundPegsValueChangedNotification
        object:[self document]];
}


- (BOOL)roundPegsValue {
    return roundPegsValue;
}
```

3. **NOTIFICATION VARIABLES.** Return to the header file VRButtonModel.h to declare at the bottom the notification variables used in the **set** methods to cause the window controller to update the GUI when the data is changed, as follows:

```
// Pegs
extern NSString
        *VRButtonModelTrianglePegsValueChangedNotification;
extern NSString
        *VRButtonModelSquarePegsValueChangedNotification;
extern NSString
        *VRButtonModelRoundPegsValueChangedNotification;
```

You will end up with a lot of these notification variables at the bottom of the header file. To make them easier to find, insert **#pragma mark NOTIFICATIONS** before the existing declaration of **VRButtonModelCheckboxValueChanged-Notification.**

Turn back to the source file VRButtonModel.m, near the top, to define the notification variables as set forth below and also to insert **#pragma mark NOTIFICATIONS** before the existing definition of **VRButtonModelCheckboxValue-ChangedNotification:**

```
// Pegs
NSString *VRButtonModelTrianglePegsValueChangedNotification =
        @"ButtonModel trianglePegsValue Changed Notification";
NSString *VRButtonModelSquarePegsValueChangedNotification =
        @"ButtonModel squarePegsValue Changed Notification";
NSString *VRButtonModelRoundPegsValueChangedNotification =
        @"ButtonModel roundPegsValue Changed Notification";
```

4. **GUI update methods.** Go now to the header file VRMainWindowController.h to declare methods to update the GUI in response to these notifications, after `updateCheckbox:` in the "INTERFACE MANAGEMENT - Specific updaters" section of the VRButtonController category, as follows:

```
// Pegs
- (void)updateTrianglePegsCheckbox:
        (NSNotification *)notification;
- (void)updateSquarePegsCheckbox:
        (NSNotification *)notification;
- (void)updateRoundPegsCheckbox:
        (NSNotification *)notification;
```

In the category source file VRButtonController.m, define these specific update methods, after `updateCheckbox:` in the corresponding section, as follows:

```
// Pegs

- (void)updateTrianglePegsCheckbox:
        (NSNotification *)notification {
    [self updateTwoStateCheckbox:[self trianglePegsCheckbox]
            setting:[[self buttonModel] trianglePegsValue]];
}

- (void)updateSquarePegsCheckbox:
        (NSNotification *)notification {
    [self updateTwoStateCheckbox:[self squarePegsCheckbox]
            setting:[[self buttonModel] squarePegsValue]];
}

- (void)updateRoundPegsCheckbox:
        (NSNotification *)notification {
    [self updateTwoStateCheckbox:[self roundPegsCheckbox]
            setting:[[self buttonModel] roundPegsValue]];
}
```

It is not necessary to declare a new generic checkbox updater for these three update methods, because they call the generic checkbox updater you created in Recipe 1, Step 6.3. That generic method handles two-state checkboxes, and that's what these checkboxes are.

Notice, however, that you have not implemented an update method for the Select All checkbox. You will have to do so, obviously, but you will defer this task for now. The Select All checkbox updater will require more careful thought, because it must reflect the state of all three of the new data variables in combination. Among other things, it must be able to display the dash that characterizes a mixed-state checkbox. To do this, you will have to write a new generic update method to handle mixed-state checkboxes. You will return to this issue in Step 2.4.

5. **NOTIFICATION OBSERVERS.** Now register the window controller as a notification observer of the notifications that will trigger these updaters, by inserting the following statements in the `registerNotificationObserversForButtonsTab` method of the category source file VRButtonController.m, after the existing registration:

```
// Pegs
[[NSNotificationCenter defaultCenter] addObserver:self
        selector:@selector(updateTrianglePegsCheckbox:)
        name:VRButtonModelTrianglePegsValueChangedNotification
        object:[self document]];
[[NSNotificationCenter defaultCenter] addObserver:self
        selector:@selector(updateSquarePegsCheckbox:)
        name:VRButtonModelSquarePegsValueChangedNotification
        object:[self document]];
[[NSNotificationCenter defaultCenter] addObserver:self
        selector:@selector(updateRoundPegsCheckbox:)
        name:VRButtonModelRoundPegsValueChangedNotification
        object:[self document]];
```

6. **ACTION METHODS.** Next, you must add action methods that will be triggered when the user checks or unchecks any of the new controls, to update the data variables on the model of Recipe 1, Step 3.6. Again, you could now create stubs for these action methods using Interface Builder's Create Files command, as you did for the checkbox action method in Recipe 1, Step 2.6.1, but as a practical matter it is easy enough to do it here by typing it into the code files. In the header file VRMainWindowController.h, after the existing **checkboxAction:** method in the VRButtonController category at the end, add the following:

```
// Pegs
- (IBAction)trianglePegsAction:(id)sender;
- (IBAction)squarePegsAction:(id)sender;
- (IBAction)roundPegsAction:(id)sender;
```

In the category source file VRButtonController.m, define these action methods, after the existing **checkboxAction:** method at the end, as follows:

```
// Pegs

- (IBAction)trianglePegsAction:(id)sender {
    [[self buttonModel]
            setTrianglePegsValue:([sender state] == NSOnState)];
    if ([sender state] == NSOnState) {
        [[[self document] undoManager]
            setActionName:NSLocalizedString
            (@"Set Triangle Pegs", @"Name of undo/redo menu \
            item after Triangle checkbox control was set")];
    } else {
        [[[self document] undoManager]
            setActionName:NSLocalizedString
            (@"Clear Triangle Pegs", @"Name of undo/redo \
            menu item after Triangle checkbox control was \
            cleared")];
    }
}


- (IBAction)squarePegsAction:(id)sender {
    [[self buttonModel]
            setSquarePegsValue:([sender state] == NSOnState)];
    if ([sender state] == NSOnState) {
        [[[self document] undoManager]
            setActionName:NSLocalizedString(@"Set Square \
            Pegs", @"Name of undo/redo menu item after \
            Square checkbox control was set")];
    } else {
        [[[self document] undoManager]
            setActionName:NSLocalizedString(@"Clear Square \
            Pegs", @"Name of undo/redo menu item after \
            Square checkbox control was cleared")];
    }
}


- (IBAction)roundPegsAction:(id)sender {
    [[self buttonModel]
            setRoundPegsValue:([sender state] == NSOnState)];
    if ([sender state] == NSOnState) {
```

```
              [[[self document] undoManager]
                      setActionName:NSLocalizedString(@"Set Round Pegs",
                      @"Name of undo/redo menu item after Round \
                      checkbox control was set")];
      } else {
          [[[self document] undoManager]
                      setActionName:NSLocalizedString(@"Clear Round \
                      Pegs", @"Name of undo/redo menu item after \
                      Round checkbox control was cleared")];
      }
}
```

Notice that you have not implemented an action method for the Select All checkbox. You will defer this, too, to Step 2.3. It will require more careful thought, because it must change the state of all three of the new data variables in combination.

7. **LOCALIZABLE.STRINGS.** When you add user controls, you generally also add action methods, and action methods generally name undo and redo menu items. These are strings that must be localizable. So don't forget to update the Localizable.strings file by adding all of the localizable strings used in the previous instruction ("Set Triangle Pegs" and so on), along with their comments. Follow the model of the localized strings you added to the file in Recipe 1, Step 6.2 for the original checkbox control.

8. **INITIALIZATION.** In Recipe 1, Step 4.1, you initialized the value of the checkboxValue variable to YES. To assist in testing, you will now set the value of the trianglesValue variable to YES as well. You will not initialize the other new data variables, and Objective-C will therefore initialize them to the default value NO. Some programmers prefer to initialize values to 0 or equivalent explicitly for the sake of clarity. You won't do that here because you can in fact rely on Objective-C to do this for you, and in any event you will learn how to implement a full-blown preferences system in Recipe 19.

In the source file VRButtonModel.m, add this line to the initWithDocument: method, after the initialization of checkboxValue:

```
[self setTrianglePegsValue:YES];
```

You can do something new in this connection. Return to Interface Builder; select the Triangle checkbox; and, in the Options area of the NSButton Info Panel's Attributes pane, check the Selected checkbox. A check will appear in the Triangle checkbox. Now, when the application launches and a document opens, the Triangle checkbox will appear in its default on state without delay or flicker because the nib file and the default data value are the same. As long as you're in

Interface Builder, you might as well do the same with the original checkbox from Recipe 1, since it is also initialized to YES.

9. **DATA STORAGE.** You must attend to persistent storage of the new data variables. Thanks to the architecture you set up for this in VRButtonModel, this task is extremely easy. These are all Boolean values, and your code is essentially identical to that used to save and load the Boolean value of the **checkBoxValue** variable in Recipe 1, Step 4.2.3.

At the end of this step, however, you will return to this code and improve it. To preview the change, notice that the Boolean values for these variables are saved as integers: 1 for YES and 0 for NO. In the event that you ever examine Vermont Recipes documents using a utility that can read property lists, it may be difficult to distinguish actual integer values in the file from Booleans masquerading as integers. In Step 2.7, below, you will learn a remarkably convenient way to save Booleans as the strings "YES" or "NO", improving the human readability of your documents. For the moment, go ahead and do it the old way.

In the source file VRButtonModel.m, define these keys in the "Keys and values for dictionary" subsection of the STORAGE section:

```
// Pegs
static NSString *VRTrianglePegsValueKey =
        @"VRButtonModelTrianglePegsValue";
static NSString *VRSquarePegsValueKey =
        @"VRButtonModelSquarePegsValue";
static NSString *VRRoundPegsValueKey =
        @"VRButtonModelRoundPegsValue";
```

Immediately after that, add these lines at the end of the **addDataToDictionary:** method:

```
// Pegs
[dictionary setObject:[NSString stringWithFormat:@"%d",
        trianglePegsValue] forKey:VRTrianglePegsValueKey];
[dictionary setObject:[NSString stringWithFormat:@"%d",
        squarePegsValue] forKey:VRSquarePegsValueKey];
[dictionary setObject:[NSString stringWithFormat:@"%d",
        roundPegsValue] forKey:VRRoundPegsValueKey];
```

Add these lines near the end of the **restoreDataFromDictionary:** method. Take care to place them inside the bracketing [[self undoManager] disableUndo-Registration] and [[self undoManager] enableUndoRegistration] messages:

```
// Pegs
[self setTrianglePegsValue:[[dictionary
        objectForKey:VRTrianglePegsValueKey] intValue]];
[self setSquarePegsValue:[[dictionary
        objectForKey:VRSquarePegsValueKey] intValue]];
[self setRoundPegsValue:[[dictionary
        objectForKey:VRRoundPegsValueKey] intValue]];
```

10. **GUI UPDATE METHOD INVOCATIONS.** Add calls to the user control update methods to the window controller, so that the controls will be drawn to reflect the data correctly when the document is created or opened. In the category source file VRButtonController.m, add the following calls at the end of the **updateButtonsTab** method:

```
// Pegs
[self updateTrianglePegsCheckbox:nil];
[self updateSquarePegsCheckbox:nil];
[self updateRoundPegsCheckbox:nil];
```

You will have to come back in a moment to update the **allPegsCheckbox** control, too.

11. **DESCRIPTION METHOD.** Revise the description method that you added to VRButtonModel.m in Recipe 1, Step 10.3, so that it reads as set forth below. The backslash at the end of each line within the long string value acts as a line continuation character, allowing you to break the string into separate lines for readability in the source file.

```
- (NSString *)description {
    return [NSString stringWithFormat:@"%@\
    \n\tcheckboxValue:%@\
    \n\ttrianglePegsValue:%@\
    \n\tsquarePegsValue:%@\
    \n\troundPegsValue:%@\n",
        [super description],
        ([self checkboxValue] ? @"YES" : @"NO"),
        ([self trianglePegsValue] ? @"YES" : @"NO"),
        ([self squarePegsValue] ? @"YES" : @"NO"),
        ([self roundPegsValue] ? @"YES" : @"NO")];
}
```

12. **HELP TAGS.** Use the Help pane of the Info Panel for each of the four new checkboxes in Interface Builder to add a Help tag to each: "Include triangle pegs," "Include square pegs," "Include round pegs," and "Include all pegs" will do.

2.3 Implement an Action Method for a Mixed-State Checkbox

You have left until the end the most interesting parts of this step, implementing a method to update a mixed-state checkbox and implementing its action method. You will tackle the action method first because it is easier.

In the header file VRMainWindowController.h, declare the action method in the VRButtonController category at the end of the file, as follows:

```
- (IBAction)allPegsAction:(id)sender;
```

Then, in the category source file VRButtonController.m, define it at the end of the file, as follows:

```
- (IBAction)allPegsAction:(id)sender {
    int newState;

    if ([sender state] == NSMixedState) {
        [sender setState:NSOnState];
    }
    newState = [sender state];

    [[self buttonModel] setTrianglePegsValue:newState];
    [[self buttonModel] setSquarePegsValue:newState];
    [[self buttonModel] setRoundPegsValue:newState];

    if (newState == NSOnState) {
        [[[self document] undoManager]
                setActionName:NSLocalizedString(@"Set All Pegs",
                @"Name of undo/redo menu item after Select All \
                checkbox control was set")];
    } else {
        [[[self document] undoManager]
                setActionName:NSLocalizedString(@"Clear All Pegs",
                @"Name of undo/redo menu item after Select All \
                checkbox control was cleared")];
    }
}
```

There are some subtleties here. When a user clicks a control, Cocoa updates the control's state before invoking its action method. Thus, when the action method is called, it has access to the new state of the control through the **sender** parameter.

In the case of a mixed-state checkbox, the default progression of states as the user clicks the control repeatedly is from NSOnState to NSOffState to NSMixedState, then back to NSOnState, and so on. While you want this checkbox to be able to display the mixed state when you click other associated checkboxes so as to leave some on and some off, it makes no sense to allow the user to select the mixed state by clicking the mixed-state checkbox. Therefore, this action method first reads the new state of the control, then forces it to NSOnState if its new state is found to be NSMixedState.

The action method then saves the control's new (possibly altered) state in the newState local variable, to use it for setting the new value of all three of the other checkboxes to match. It is prudent to use a variable to preserve the new state, because the actual state of the checkbox may change in response to the notifications that the other three checkboxes issue when their states are changed by this action method. The details of this issue are discussed in Step 2.4, below.

When the user clicks the allPegsCheckbox control, the action method tells the model object to set the three associated data variables, trianglePegsValue, squarePegsValue, and roundPegsValue, to match the new on or off state of the control, all at once. Each of the three set methods invoked here automatically sends a notification that its associated data value has changed, and the corresponding checkbox view updaters are already registered to receive those notifications. They will therefore update the three controls' visible states automatically. The Undo/Redo menu item will read either Set All Pegs or Clear All Pegs, as appropriate.

Note that the last point confirms the wisdom of your decision in Recipe 1, Step 6.2 to follow Apple's recommendation that you set the name of the Undo/Redo menu item in the action method instead of the accessor method. If you did this in the accessor method instead, the menu item would not have been assigned a name appropriate to the user's action.

Before you go on, don't forget to add two new strings from this action method to the Localizable.strings file, on the model of those you added in Instruction 7 of Step 2.2, above.

2.4 Implement an Update Method for a Mixed-State Checkbox

Now for the update method.

1. Designing a generic method to update the appearance of a mixed-state control is simple, so you will do that first.

   In the header file VRMainWindowController.h, declare the generic method as follows after updateCheckbox::

```
- (void)updateMixedStateCheckbox:(NSButton *)control
     setting:(int)inValue;
```

In the source file VRMainWindowController.m, define the generic method as follows after **updateCheckbox:**:

```
- (void)updateMixedStateCheckbox:(NSButton *)control
     setting:(int)inValue {
   if (inValue != [control state]) {
      [control setState:inValue];
   }
}
```

This is so simple because the **inValue** value passed in the **setting** parameter will always be one of **NSOnState**, **NSOffState**, or **NSMixedState** or one of their integer equivalents (0 for **NSOffState**, positive for **NSOnState**, and negative for **NSMixedState**).

2. The implementation of the specific method to update this particular mixed-state checkbox is more complex. It must get the values of the three associated data variables, then set the control's visible state to one of three values depending on whether all are **YES**, all are **NO**, or some are **YES** and others **NO**. You will obtain the desired state in a separate utility method, because this information has to be gathered in more than one place.

In the header file VRMainWindowController.h, declare the utility method as follows after **updateRoundPegsCheckbox:** at the end of the "INTERFACE MANAGEMENT - Specific updaters" section in the VRButtonController category:

```
- (int)wantAllPegsCheckboxState;
```

In the category source file VRButtonController.m, define the utility method as follows after **updateRoundPegsCheckbox:** in the corresponding section:

```
- (int)wantAllPegsCheckboxState {
   if ([[self buttonModel] trianglePegsValue] == YES &&
         [[self buttonModel] squarePegsValue] == YES &&
         [[self buttonModel] roundPegsValue] == YES) {
      return NSOnState;
   }
   else if ([[self buttonModel] trianglePegsValue] == NO &&
         [[self buttonModel] squarePegsValue] == NO &&
         [[self buttonModel] roundPegsValue] == NO) {
      return NSOffState;
   }
   else {
```

```
            return NSMixedState;
        }
    }
```

3. Now you are ready to write the specific updater method. In the header file VRMainWindowController.h, declare the specific method as follows in the VRButtonController category after `wantAllPegsCheckboxState`:

```
- (void)updateAllPegsCheckbox:(NSNotification *)notification;
```

In the category source file VRButtonController.m, define the specific method as follows after `wantAllPegsCheckboxState`:

```
- (void)updateAllPegsCheckbox:(NSNotification *)notification {
    [self updateMixedStateCheckbox:[self allPegsCheckbox]
            setting:[self wantAllPegsCheckboxState]];
}
```

4. You now face a tough question: How does the **updateAllPegsCheckbox:** method get invoked? The answer is simple, when you think it through. The Select All checkbox must potentially be updated to reflect the state of the three data values as a group whenever any one of them is changed. You have already provided for notifications to be posted whenever any one of them is changed. Therefore, a straightforward solution is to have the **updateAllPegsCheckbox:** method respond to all of these notifications. To do this, the **updateAllPegsCheckbox:** method must be registered to receive notifications from any of them. It is permissible to have more than one method in a class receive the same notification. In the category source file VRButtonController.m, add the following lines to the **registerNotificationObserversForButtonsTab** method, following the other notification registrations:

```
[[NSNotificationCenter defaultCenter] addObserver:self
        selector:@selector(updateAllPegsCheckbox:)
        name:VRButtonModelTrianglePegsValueChangedNotification
        object:[self document]];
[[NSNotificationCenter defaultCenter] addObserver:self
        selector:@selector(updateAllPegsCheckbox:)
        name:VRButtonModelSquarePegsValueChangedNotification
        object:[self document]];
[[NSNotificationCenter defaultCenter] addObserver:self
        selector:@selector(updateAllPegsCheckbox:)
        name:VRButtonModelRoundPegsValueChangedNotification
        object:[self document]];
```

5. This solution, however, raises a new issue when the user checks or unchecks the mixed-state checkbox itself. In this case, the `allPegsAction:` action method invokes all three of the data accessor methods to change their values. An issue arises because the three accessor methods in turn post three separate notifications that their values have changed, so that the visible states of the three controls will update. Unfortunately, the `updateAllPegsCheckbox:` notification method also executes three times in succession because it, too, is observing these notifications. It doesn't need to be called at all in this case, because Cocoa updated the mixed-state checkbox when the user clicked it. These three redundant calls do not cause a significant delay in Vermont Recipes, where only three accessor methods are invoked, but a better solution might be required if a larger number of user controls were at issue. You should fix this issue now, so it doesn't come back to bite you later if you revise this part of the interface.

The simplest solution is to create a state variable in VRMainWindowController and test it in the `updateAllPegsCheckbox:` notification method. It can be a reusable variable, available to any routine that, like the `allPegsAction:` method, controls the state of other checkboxes in a group, so it should not be hidden away in a category. In outline, this is the strategy: Name the state variable `controlUpdatingDisabled`. In the `allPegsAction:` action method, call a `disableControlUpdating:` method at the beginning to disable processing of the notification temporarily, and call its opposing method `enableControlUpdating` at the end of the action method to reenable processing of the notification. The notification will still be posted so that the other three checkboxes in the group can update, but when the `updateAllPegsCheckbox:` notification method receives the notification, nothing will happen.

Some programmers may be uncomfortable with the use of a state variable in the window controller for this purpose, but there is no obvious way to avoid it here. The notifications must be posted by the data accessor methods so their associated controls will be updated, and the `allPegsCheckbox` updater must be registered as an observer of those notifications to update itself in cases where the user clicks one of the other checkboxes in the group. Cocoa does not provide a built-in means to suspend registration of notification observers on a per-selector basis, so you have to resort to a state variable to jury-rig your own routine to disable the effect of the notification on this one selector temporarily.

In the header file VRMainWindowController.h, declare the state variable after the existing outlet declarations:

`NSControl *controlUpdatingDisabled;`

This variable is typed to hold an NSControl object, so that any method testing its value can determine whether a specific user control's updating has been disabled. A `nil` value will indicate that no control's updating is currently disabled. The variable need not be initialized explicitly, because Objective-C will initialize it to `nil`, which should be the default value.

Also declare its accessor methods in the header file VRMainWindowController.h, at the end of the **ACCESSORS** section:

```
- (void)setControlUpdatingDisabled:(NSControl *)inValue;
- (NSControl *)controlUpdatingDisabled;
```

In the source file VRMainWindowController.m, define the accessor methods in the corresponding section:

```
- (void)setControlUpdatingDisabled:(NSControl *)inValue {
    controlUpdatingDisabled = inValue;
}


- (NSControl *)controlUpdatingDisabled {
    return controlUpdatingDisabled;
}
```

Now, in the header file VRMainWindowController.h, declare **disableControl-Updating:** and **enableControlUpdating**, the methods that will be invoked in one or more action methods as shown below, just before the "INTERFACE MANAGEMENT - Generic updaters" section. You create and use these two additional methods in case you find a better way to disable and enable control updating later. If so, you will be able to redefine these methods and eliminate the state variable and its accessors.

```
#pragma mark INTERFACE MANAGEMENT - View update utilities


- (void)disableControlUpdating:(NSControl *)control;
- (void)enableControlUpdating;
```

Define these two methods in VRMainWindowController.m, as follows, in the corresponding location:

```
#pragma mark INTERFACE MANAGEMENT - View update utilities


- (void)disableControlUpdating:(NSControl *)control {
    [self setControlUpdatingDisabled:control];
}

- (void)enableControlUpdating {
    [self setControlUpdatingDisabled:nil];
}
```

In the allPegsAction: action method in the category source file
VRButtonController.m, invoke these two methods to bracket the calls to the
data accessor methods for the other three checkboxes in the group, so that
this section of the action method reads as follows:

```
[self disableControlUpdating:sender];
[[self mySettings] setTrianglePegsValue:newState];
[[self mySettings] setSquarePegsValue:newState];
[[self mySettings] setRoundPegsValue:newState];
[self enableControlUpdating];
```

Finally, rewrite the updateAllPegsCheckbox: notification method in the
VRButtonController category in VRMainWindowController.m to test the state
of the new state variable, like this:

```
- (void)updateAllPegsCheckbox:(NSNotification *)notification {
    if ([self controlUpdatingDisabled] !=
            [self allPegsCheckbox]) {
        [self updateMixedCheckbox:[self allPegsCheckbox]
                setting:[self wantAllPegsCheckboxState]];
    }
}
```

2.5 Update the User Interface

The GUI must be updated when a document is created or opened. As noted in
Instruction 10 of Step 2.2, above, you must therefore update the visible state of the
allPegsCheckbox control. In the category source file VRButtonController.m, add
the following call at the end of the updateButtonsTab method:

```
[self updateAllPegsCheckbox:nil];
```

2.6 Turn On the Three-State Capability of the Mixed-State Checkbox

In addition, you must set up the allPegsCheckbox control to serve as a mixed-state checkbox. By default, checkboxes are two-state; in response to an attempt to set the state of
a two-state checkbox to the mixed state, it displays as checked, which is not what you
want here. You will set up the allPegsCheckbox control as a mixed-state checkbox in the
awakeFromNib method instead of the window controller's init method, because you can't
be sure the checkbox is ready to be set up at initialization time. Add the following
line at the beginning of the awakeFromNib method of VRMainWindowController.m:

```
[[self allPegsCheckbox] setAllowsMixedState:YES];
```

2.7 Create a Category on NSString to Convert Between Booleans and Strings

There is one other thing you should consider doing here, in anticipation of adding a number of user controls as the Vermont Recipes application grows in size and functionality. Many of the controls in this or any other application are used to set Boolean values, and those Boolean values need to be saved and retrieved from persistent storage. Initially, you wrote your storage routines so that they save Booleans as string representations of integers, integers being their native internal representation. As previewed in Instruction 9 of Step 2.2, above, however, it may be more useful to save them as the human-readable strings "YES" and "NO". This requires changing the **addDataToDictionary:** and **restoreDataFromDictionary:** methods in VRButtonModel so that they work with strings representing the Objective-C Boolean values **YES** and **NO**.

While this could easily enough be done by changing the code in those two methods to use inline C conditionals with the ternary operator, you will use a much cleverer and perhaps more efficient technique here, implementing another Objective-C category, this time to serve a purpose different from that served by the category you created in Step 1.2. You will create a new header file and a new source file containing the interface and implementation parts, respectively, of the new category VRStringUtilities. This new category will add two new methods to Cocoa's built-in NSString class, one of them a class method that returns an NSString object when passed a Boolean value as a parameter, and the other an instance method that returns a C Boolean value equivalent to the NSString object's string value. Once this category is available, your VRButtonModel class can call the two new methods as if they were built-in NSString methods.

Some would consider this a hack; others, a creative use of the capabilities built into the Objective-C language. However you view it, creating categories on Cocoa classes does create a potential for name space conflicts with private methods declared in Cocoa, now or in a future release of Mac OS X. You should test for this possibility and consider prefacing your category methods with VR or two or three other initials to minimize the risk.

While the use of a category here is trivial, it illustrates the potential the language gives you to simplify more complex operations and make them clearer. For example, in Step 4.3, you will learn how to use this technique to represent enumeration constants as human-readable strings instead of integers. This should prove quite helpful when you use these category methods on NSString to print object descriptions to StdIO during debugging.

Later, in Recipe 12, you will learn how to read and write data using Cocoa's new keyed archiving methods. There, you will handle conversion of data for storage differently, using objects rather than standard C data types, with conversion to human-readable property list form happening automatically. These NSString category methods will not be necessary then in connection with data storage, although they will remain useful for debugging.

1. First, you must create two files for the new category. Choose File > New File in Project Builder to create the source and header files for the new category, using the Objective-C class template under the Cocoa heading, and name them NSString+VRStringUtilities.h and NSString+VRStringUtilities.m, respectively. Names such as these are common in Cocoa programming to make it clear that these files hold custom Vermont Recipes additions to the existing Cocoa NSString class.

2. These are specialized files, so it might be useful to create a subgroup called Categories in the Groups & Files pane in the project window to hold these and any similar utility categories you might create. Select the Classes group, then choose Project > New Group. A new folder icon appears, nested under the Classes folder icon. Name the new subgroup **Categories**, then drag the two new files into it. The actual files will remain at the root level of your project folder in the Finder.

    Although VRButtonController is a category, too, its source file is part of the VRMainWindowController universe, and I prefer to keep it out of the Categories group.

3. In NSString+VRStringUtilities.h, add your standard comments at the beginning and make sure the import directive imports at least <Foundation/NSString.h>. There is no need to import the Cocoa umbrella framework here, because you are working solely with a Foundation class. You don't even have to import the whole of <Foundation/Foundation.h>, because the only material you use is from the NSString class header file.

4. The interface directive supplied by the template must be changed to read `@interface NSString (VRStringUtilities)`. This specifies that you have created the category VRStringUtilities, adding functionality to the existing NSString class. You do not declare it as a descendant of some other class, as you do when creating a new class, because the inheritance chain for NSString is already defined in the Foundation frameworks. You cannot declare new instance variables in a category, so there are no curly braces.

5. Declare the two new NSString methods in NSString+VRStringUtilities.h, following the model of a number of existing NSString methods, as shown below. Notice that the first is a class method, like other NSString **stringWith...** methods, as denoted by the leading plus (+) sign.

```
+ (id)stringWithBool:(BOOL)inValue;
- (BOOL)boolValue;
```

6. In NSString+VRStringUtilities.m, change the implementation directive to read **@implementation NSString (VRStringUtilities)**.

7. Define the two new NSString methods as follows:

```
+ (id)stringWithBool:(BOOL)inValue {
    return [NSString
            stringWithString:(inValue ? @"YES" : @"NO")];
}

- (BOOL)boolValue {
    return ([self isEqualToString:@"YES"] ? YES : NO);
}
```

The **stringWithBool:** method uses an NSString class method, **stringWithString:**, as a convenient substitute for allocating and initializing a string to represent the incoming Boolean value. The **boolValue** method uses NSString's **isEqualToString:** instance method to compare the contents of the string object for equality with the string constant **@"YES"**. Note that you could use the NSObject protocol's **isEqual:** method for this purpose, but **isEqualToString:** is faster when you know both objects are strings.

8. It is that easy to add functionality to any existing class, even without having access to its source code. This new NSString functionality will be available to you throughout the Vermont Recipes application. You don't even have to import it into other files, although compiler warnings will be generated if you do not import a category that adds new methods not declared in the base class. Here, you want to use the new methods in VRButtonModel, so add the following line to the source file VRButtonModel.m after the existing import statements to suppress compiler warnings:

```
#import "NSString+VRStringUtilities.h"
```

9. Now all that remains is to use the new methods. In VRButtonModel.m, return to the **addDataToDictionary:** method and replace the statements you wrote in Instruction 9 of Step 2.2 with the following:

```
[dictionary setObject:
        [NSString stringWithBool:[self trianglePegsValue]]
        forKey:VRTrianglePegsValueKey];
[dictionary setObject:
        [NSString stringWithBool:[self squarePegsValue]]
        forKey:VRSquarePegsValueKey];
[dictionary setObject:
        [NSString stringWithBool:[self roundPegsValue]]
        forKey:VRRoundPegsValueKey];
```

Replace the lines you wrote at the end of the **restoreDataFromDictionary:** method with the following:

```
[self setTrianglePegsValue:[[dictionary objectForKey:
        VRTrianglePegsValueKey] boolValue]];
[self setSquarePegsValue: [[dictionary objectForKey:
        VRSquarePegsValueKey] boolValue]];
[self setRoundPegsValue: [[dictionary objectForKey:
        VRRoundPegsValueKey] boolValue]];
```

10. As an exercise, change the statements that save and retrieve the **checkBoxValue** variable in the same way.

2.8 Read the Source Files into the Nib File and Connect Outlets and Actions

Before you can run the revised application and expect it to work correctly, you must inform the nib file about the new outlets and actions you have created in the code files, then connect them to the new checkboxes. If you don't do this, clicking any of the Triangle, Square, or Round checkboxes will fail to update the Select All checkbox, and vice versa. It is easy to forget to do this; when new additions to your application don't appear to work correctly, this should be near the top of your troubleshooting checklist.

1. In Interface Builder, select the Classes tab in the nib file window, then choose Classes > Read File. In the resulting dialog, select the one Vermont Recipes header file in which you have created outlets or actions, VRMainWindow-Controller.h, then click the Parse button.

If in the next instruction you don't see the outlets you expected to see, you probably failed to save the header file before reading it into the nib file. As a general rule, it is a good idea to get into the habit of building the project before you read its header files into the nib file, to make sure that the files have been saved and that their syntax is correct.

2. Select the Instances tab and look at the File's Owner icon. It has a little badge in its lower-left corner, which indicates that it is not fully connected. Hold the pointer over the icon, and a Help tag appears to show you the outlets that are not connected. Control-drag from the File's Owner icon to each of the four new checkboxes in turn, each time clicking its outlet name and then clicking the Connect button in the Connections pane of the File's Owner Info Panel. When you are done, the warning badge will have disappeared.

3. Control-drag from each of the four new checkboxes to the File's Owner icon in turn, each time clicking the target in the left pane and the appropriate action in the right pane of the Outlets area in the Connections pane of the NSButton Info Panel, then clicking the Connect button.

2.9 Build and Run the Application

Build and run the application to test the interactions among the four new checkboxes. Note that the StdIO pane now reports the default values of all four instance variables. Explore how undo and redo work, and make sure changes can be saved to disk, restored, and reverted properly. If you implemented NSLog() calls, you will also see their reports in the StdIO pane every time you click a checkbox. It is particularly interesting to click the Select All checkbox, which generates reports from all three of the other Pegs checkboxes.

Launch the Property List Editor application that comes with Cocoa, open a file saved by Vermont Recipes, and verify that the Boolean values appear as the strings "YES" and "NO", not integers. Also note that the document format's Version code has been updated to 2.

You have now created several new user controls in the Buttons tab view item, using a convenient checklist to make sure you implemented every detail required to make the controls work as desired. In the next few steps of Recipe 2 and in the next few recipes, you will make use of this checklist to implement a variety of additional user controls.

Step 3: Create Checkboxes (Switch Buttons) in a Bordered Group Box

HIGHLIGHTS:

Using a control as a group box title

Disabling and enabling controls

In this step, you will implement five more standard two-state checkboxes. This step differs from the previous step in three respects: First, the topmost checkbox serves as the title of the group. Second, the same checkbox enables and disables the rest of the controls in the group, and another of the checkboxes enables and disables a subgroup. Finally, the group is surrounded by a box with borders because this makes its function clearer to the user. Boxes are permitted in these circumstances by the *Aqua Human Interface Guidelines.*

You will specify this group of checkboxes as a control center for the sound system in an office lobby. The title of the group, Play Music, is the on/off switch; if it is unchecked, no music is available and the other checkboxes, controlling the kinds of music that will be played, are disabled (dimmed or grayed out). One of the other checkboxes in the group, Allow Rock, controls whether rock music is to be played, assuming the overall control is turned on; if it is unchecked, the two subcategories of rock, Recent Hits and Oldies, are disabled. In that case, the only available option is Classical.

The routine code in this step is very similar—nearly identical—to much of the code in the previous step. The explanations will therefore be kept to a minimum, simply showing the code to insert. When in doubt about the reason for any code snippet, refer to the corresponding instruction in Step 2.

The routine steps needed to implement these controls are covered in Step 3.2. The interesting material is covered in Step 3.1 and in Steps 3.3 and following. Here, the interesting material has to do with turning a control into a group box title in Interface Builder and using Project Builder to code the enabling and disabling of the remaining user controls.

3.1 Create a Bordered Group Box and Checkboxes in Interface Builder, with a Checkbox for the Group Box's Title

Use Interface Builder to create several new checkboxes grouped together in a bordered group box. When you are done, the group should look like **Figure 2.5**.

FIGURE 2.5 The Play Music checkbox group.

1. Open VRDocument.nib in Interface Builder and select the Buttons tab view item, if necessary.

2. Drag an NSBox item from the Containers palette onto the Buttons pane of the main document window, and place it in the lower-left corner, beneath the borderless group box that you created in the previous step. The box starts with both a border and a title superimposed on the top border. You will keep the border this time, but the title is text and you would like to change it into a checkbox control.

   Unfortunately, Interface Builder doesn't let you turn the built-in title of a group box into a user control, although the *Aqua Human Interface Guidelines* expressly allow the use of a checkbox label or the text of a pop-up menu as a group box title, in addition to static text. Presumably, Interface Builder will eventually be updated to make this possible directly, but in the meantime you must devise a technique of your own.

   Your first thought about how to create a title consisting of a checkbox might be to use a group box without a title and simply drag a checkbox into the place where the title would normally appear. If you do this, however, the top border of the box will show through.

   You must therefore resort to a kludge to accomplish the desired effect. Drag a Switch control from the Cocoa Views palette onto an empty area of the Buttons tab. (You can't drag it over the top border of the box you just created, because it would probably end up inside the box and become partially obscured if you then tried to drag it up where it belongs, straddling the top border.) Rename the new checkbox **Play Music** (without a trailing colon). Drag it again until it is located a pixel or two above the default title of the NSBox object (Box), with the left edge of the checkbox lined up vertically with the left edge of the leading B in Box.

You won't get any help from the standard Aqua guides in doing this, nor can you use the Alignment commands, because Interface Builder doesn't treat the box's title as a separate object. If you need help with alignment, choose Layout > Guides > Add Vertical Guide to create a custom manual guide and drag it to the left edge of the B in Box; then drag the Play Music checkbox until its left edge also butts up against the custom guide. Select the NSBox title, Box, for editing, and type over it with space characters until they take up precisely as much room horizontally as the Play Music checkbox and its label require, leaving the obligatory small blank space at each end of the title. Then select the Play Music checkbox again and use the arrow keys on your keyboard to nudge it downward until the baseline of its label is even with the baseline of the NSBox title. If it would be helpful to you, choose Layout > Guides > Add Horizontal Guide and drag the manual guide until it is directly on top of the top border of the group box.

If you need to adjust the length of the title by inserting or deleting spaces, you may have to send the Play Music checkbox back using the Layout > Send to Back command, so that you can select the NSBox title for editing, instead of the Play Music checkbox. When you finish adding or deleting spaces and press Enter to stop editing the title, it will resize automatically (don't use the Layout > Size to Fit command, because it will resize the group box, not its title). Congratulations! Now you have a checkbox as a title for a group box. To preserve their alignment, select both items at the same time and choose Layout > Group. To get rid of the two manual guides, drag them out of the window.

Some NeXTstep and OpenStep developers' tricks were invented long ago to make the checkbox opaque, so you didn't need a dummy title composed of spaces. One was to group the control in a borderless, untitled box, then drag it over the top border. You could also create a noneditable, nonselectable, nonbordered text field with no content besides a suitable background color to obscure the top border of the group box. While one or another of these tricks may continue to work indefinitely in Mac OS X, the dummy title with spaces is easier to implement.

3. From the Cocoa Views palette, drag four more Switch controls onto the Buttons pane of the main document window. This time, drop them into the NSBox object, arranging them approximately as shown in Figure 2.3, with the top and bottom checkboxes aligned to the left inside the box using the guides, and the two middle checkboxes indented to the right. The guides won't give you any help with the amount of indentation. If necessary, resize the bottom edges of the box, the tab view, and the window to make room.

4. Rename the new checkboxes, from top to bottom, `Allow Rock`, `Recent Hits`, `Oldies`, and `Classical`. Now you can select the box and choose Layout > Size to Fit to make sure the box is the right size.

You don't have to worry about disrupting the box and the checkboxes it contains when you move it, because they are effectively grouped by being placed inside the box. Drag the box, and the checkboxes will all move with it (you already grouped it with its new title). In older versions of Interface Builder, you had to group them explicitly because the checkboxes were not subviews of the box.

3.2 Write the Code for the Checkboxes in Project Builder

Use Project Builder to write the code, guided by the checklist you developed in Step 2.

1. **USER CONTROL OUTLET VARIABLES AND ACCESSORS.** In the header file VRMainWindowController.h, declare five new outlets to access each of the new checkboxes, after the "Pegs switch button group" near the top of the file, as follows:

```
// Music switch button group
IBOutlet NSButton *playMusicCheckbox;
IBOutlet NSButton *rockCheckbox;
IBOutlet NSButton *recentRockCheckbox;
IBOutlet NSButton *oldiesRockCheckbox;
IBOutlet NSButton *classicalCheckbox;
```

Still in the header file, also declare accessors for the outlets after the "Pegs switch button group" in the ACCESSORS section of the VRButtonController category near the bottom of the file, as follows:

```
// Music switch button group
- (NSButton *)playMusicCheckbox;
- (NSButton *)rockCheckbox;
- (NSButton *)recentRockCheckbox;
- (NSButton *)oldiesRockCheckbox;
- (NSButton *)classicalCheckbox;
```

In the category source file VRButtonController.m, define the accessors after the "Pegs switch button group" in the ACCESSORS section, as follows:

```
// Music switch button group

- (NSButton *)playMusicCheckbox {
```

(continues on next page)

```
    return playMusicCheckbox;
}

- (NSButton *)rockCheckbox {
    return rockCheckbox;
}

- (NSButton *)recentRockCheckbox {
    return recentRockCheckbox;
}

- (NSButton *)oldiesRockCheckbox {
    return oldiesRockCheckbox;
}

- (NSButton *)classicalCheckbox {
    return classicalCheckbox; }
```

2. **DATA VARIABLES AND ACCESSORS.** All of the new checkboxes require corresponding Boolean variables in VRButtonModel to hold the data they represent. The first checkbox (Play Music) is used to determine whether music is turned on or off—that is, whether the other checkboxes should be enabled or disabled—so this value must be preserved. The second checkbox (Allow Rock) is used to control whether playing of rock music is allowed, so it needs a data variable for the same reason. The remaining three switches record what kinds of music have been selected for play and must also be preserved.

In the header file VRButtonModel.h, declare four new variables after the Pegs section, as follows:

```
// Music
BOOL playMusicValue;
BOOL rockValue;
BOOL recentRockValue;
BOOL oldiesRockValue;
BOOL classicalValue;
```

In VRButtonModel.h, also declare the corresponding accessor methods after the Pegs subsection of the ACCESSORS section, as follows:

```
// Music

- (void)setPlayMusicValue:(BOOL)inValue;
- (BOOL)playMusicValue;
```

```
- (void)setRockValue:(BOOL)inValue;
- (BOOL)rockValue;

- (void)setRecentRockValue:(BOOL)inValue;
- (BOOL)recentRockValue;

- (void)setOldiesRockValue:(BOOL)inValue;
- (BOOL)oldiesRockValue;

- (void)setClassicalValue:(BOOL)inValue;
- (BOOL)classicalValue;
```

Turn to the source file VRButtonModel.m and define the accessor methods after
the Pegs subsection of the ACCESSORS section, as set forth below. Again,
although I don't show them here, you can also add an NSLog() call to each set
accessor method, bracketed in preprocessor directives, on the model of Recipe
1, Step 10.2. In fact, now that you have written the stringWithBool: class
method in the VRStringUtilities category, you should go back to all of your
NSLog() calls in the ACCESSORS section of VRButtonModel.m and change
them to this model: NSLog(@"\n\tExiting [VRButtonModel setClassicalValue:],
classicalValue:%@\n", [NSString stringWithBool:classicalValue]);.

```
// Music

- (void)setPlayMusicValue:(BOOL)inValue {
    [[[self undoManager] prepareWithInvocationTarget:self]
        setPlayMusicValue:playMusicValue];
    playMusicValue = inValue;
    [[NSNotificationCenter defaultCenter] postNotificationName:
        VRButtonModelPlayMusicValueChangedNotification
        object:[self document]];
}

- (BOOL)playMusicValue {
    return playMusicValue;
}

- (void)setRockValue:(BOOL)inValue {
    [[[self undoManager] prepareWithInvocationTarget:self]
        setRockValue:rockValue];
    rockValue = inValue;
    [[NSNotificationCenter defaultCenter] postNotificationName:
```

(continues on next page)

```objc
                VRButtonModelRockValueChangedNotification
            object:[self document]];
}


- (BOOL)rockValue {
    return rockValue;
}


- (void)setRecentRockValue:(BOOL)inValue {
    [[[self undoManager] prepareWithInvocationTarget:self]
        setRecentRockValue:recentRockValue];
    recentRockValue = inValue;
    [[NSNotificationCenter defaultCenter] postNotificationName:
        VRButtonModelRecentRockValueChangedNotification
        object:[self document]];
}


- (BOOL)recentRockValue {
    return recentRockValue;
}


- (void)setOldiesRockValue:(BOOL)inValue {
    [[[self undoManager] prepareWithInvocationTarget:self]
        setOldiesRockValue:oldiesRockValue];
    oldiesRockValue = inValue;
    [[NSNotificationCenter defaultCenter] postNotificationName:
        VRButtonModelOldiesRockValueChangedNotification
        object:[self document]];
}


- (BOOL)oldiesRockValue {
    return oldiesRockValue;
}


- (void)setClassicalValue:(BOOL)inValue {
    [[[self undoManager] prepareWithInvocationTarget:self]
        setClassicalValue:classicalValue];
    classicalValue = inValue;
    [[NSNotificationCenter defaultCenter] postNotificationName:
        VRButtonModelClassicalValueChangedNotification
        object:[self document]];
}
```

```
- (BOOL)classicalValue {
    return classicalValue;
}
```

3. **NOTIFICATION VARIABLES.** Return to the header file VRButtonModel.h, at the bottom of the file, to declare the notification variables used in the **set** accessors, as follows:

```
// Music
extern NSString
    *VRButtonModelPlayMusicValueChangedNotification;
extern NSString
    *VRButtonModelRockValueChangedNotification;
extern NSString
    *VRButtonModelRecentRockValueChangedNotification;
extern NSString
    *VRButtonModelOldiesRockValueChangedNotification;
extern NSString
    *VRButtonModelClassicalValueChangedNotification;
```

Turn back to the source file VRButtonModel.m, near the top of the file, to define the notification variables, as follows:

```
// Music
NSString *VRButtonModelPlayMusicValueChangedNotification =
    @"ButtonModel playMusicValue Changed Notification";
NSString *VRButtonModelRockValueChangedNotification =
    @"ButtonModel rockValue Changed Notification";
NSString *VRButtonModelRecentRockValueChangedNotification =
    @"ButtonModel recentRockValue Changed Notification";
NSString *VRButtonModelOldiesRockValueChangedNotification =
    @"ButtonModel oldiesRockValue Changed Notification";
NSString *VRButtonModelClassicalValueChangedNotification =
    @"ButtonModel classicalValue Changed Notification";
```

4. **GUI UPDATE METHODS.** Go now to the header file VRMainWindowController.h to declare methods to update the GUI in response to these notifications, after the Pegs subsection of the "INTERFACE MANAGEMENT - Specific updaters" section of the VRButtonController category, as follows:

```
// Music
- (void)updateRecentRockCheckbox:(NSNotification *)notification;
- (void)updateOldiesRockCheckbox:(NSNotification *)notification;
- (void)updateClassicalCheckbox:(NSNotification *)notification;
```

You will also need update methods for the Play Music and Allow Rock checkboxes, but these will be used to enable and disable the other checkboxes and require a new approach. They will be deferred to Step 3.4, below.

In the category source file VRButtonController.m, define these specific update methods, after the Pegs subsection of the "Specific view updaters" section, as follows:

```
// Music

- (void)updateRecentRockCheckbox:
        (NSNotification *)notification {
    [self updateTwoStateCheckbox:[self recentRockCheckbox]
        setting:[[self buttonModel] recentRockValue]];
}

- (void)updateOldiesRockCheckbox:
        (NSNotification *)notification {
    [self updateTwoStateCheckbox:[self oldiesRockCheckbox]
        setting:[[self buttonModel] oldiesRockValue]];
}

- (void)updateClassicalCheckbox:
        (NSNotification *)notification {
    [self updateTwoStateCheckbox:[self classicalCheckbox]
        setting:[[self buttonModel] classicalValue]];
}
```

5. **NOTIFICATION OBSERVERS.** Now register the window controller as an observer of the notifications that will trigger these updaters, by inserting the following statements in the **registerNotificationObserversForButtonsTab** method of the category source file VRButtonController.m, after the Pegs registrations:

```
// Music
[[NSNotificationCenter defaultCenter] addObserver:self
        selector:@selector(updateRecentRockCheckbox:)
        name:VRButtonModelRecentRockValueChangedNotification
        object:[self document]];
[[NSNotificationCenter defaultCenter] addObserver:self
        selector:@selector(updateOldiesRockCheckbox:)
        name:VRButtonModelOldiesRockValueChangedNotification
        object:[self document]];
[[NSNotificationCenter defaultCenter] addObserver:self
        selector:@selector(updateClassicalCheckbox:)
```

```
name:VRButtonModelClassicalValueChangedNotification
object:[self document]];
```

The Play Music and Allow Rock observers will be dealt with in Step 3.4, below.

6. **ACTION METHODS.** Next, you must add action methods. In the header file VRMainWindowController.h, after the Pegs section of the VRButtonController category at the end, add the following:

```
// Music
- (IBAction)recentRockAction:(id)sender;
- (IBAction)oldiesRockAction:(id)sender;
- (IBAction)classicalAction:(id)sender;
```

You will also need action methods for the Play Music and Allow Rock checkboxes, but these will be deferred to Step 3.3, below, because both require some new techniques.

In the category source file VRButtonController.m, define these action methods, after the Pegs section at the end, as follows:

```
// Music

- (IBAction)recentRockAction:(id)sender {
    [[self buttonModel] setRecentRockValue:
            ([sender state] == NSOnState)];
    if ([sender state] == NSOnState) {
        [[[self document] undoManager] setActionName:
                NSLocalizedString(@"Set Recent Hits",
                @"Name of undo/redo menu item after Recent Hits \
                checkbox control was set")];
    } else {
        [[[self document] undoManager] setActionName:
                NSLocalizedString(@"Clear Recent Hits",
                @"Name of undo/redo menu item after Recent Hits \
                checkbox control was cleared")];
    }
}


- (IBAction)oldiesRockAction:(id)sender {
    [[self buttonModel] setOldiesRockValue:
            ([sender state] == NSOnState)];
    if ([sender state] == NSOnState) {
        [[[self document] undoManager] setActionName:
```

(continues on next page)

```
                NSLocalizedString(@"Set Oldies",
                @"Name of undo/redo menu item after Oldies \
                checkbox control was set")];
        } else {
           [[[self document] undoManager] setActionName:
                NSLocalizedString(@"Clear Oldies",
                @"Name of undo/redo menu item after Oldies \
                checkbox control was cleared")];
        }
    }


    - (IBAction)classicalAction:(id)sender {
        [[self buttonModel] setClassicalValue:
                ([sender state] == NSOnState)];
        if ([sender state] == NSOnState) {
           [[[self document] undoManager] setActionName:
                NSLocalizedString(@"Set Classical",
                @"Name of undo/redo menu item after Classical \
                checkbox control was set")];
        } else {
           [[[self document] undoManager] setActionName:
                NSLocalizedString(@"Clear Classical",
                @"Name of undo/redo menu item after Classical \
                checkbox control was cleared")];
        }
    }
```

7. **LOCALIZABLE.STRINGS.** Don't forget to update the Localizable.strings file with the undo and redo menu titles in the previous instruction.

8. **INITIALIZATION.** Don't initialize any of your new variables. When a new document is opened, the Play Music checkbox will be unchecked and all of the other checkboxes will be unchecked and disabled.

9. **DATA STORAGE.** Take care of persistent storage of the new data variables. In the source file VRButtonModel.m, define these keys at the end of the "Keys and values for dictionary" subsection of the STORAGE section:

```
// Music
static NSString *VRPlayMusicValueKey =
        @"VRButtonModelPlayMusicValue";
static NSString *VRRockValueKey =
        @"VRButtonModelRockValue";
static NSString *VRRecentRockValueKey =
```

```
        @"VRButtonModelRecentRockValue";
static NSString *VROldiesRockValueKey =
        @"VRButtonModelOldiesRockValue";
static NSString *VRClassicalValueKey =
        @"VRButtonModelClassicalValue";
```

Add these lines at the end of the **addDataToDictionary:** method, using the new
methods from the VRStringUtilities category that you created in Step 2:

```
// Music
[dictionary setObject:[NSString stringWithBool:
        [self playMusicValue]] forKey:VRPlayMusicValueKey];
[dictionary setObject:[NSString stringWithBool:
        [self rockValue]] forKey:VRRockValueKey];
[dictionary setObject:[NSString stringWithBool:
        [self recentRockValue]] forKey:VRRecentRockValueKey];
[dictionary setObject:[NSString stringWithBool:
        [self oldiesRockValue]] forKey:VROldiesRockValueKey];
[dictionary setObject:[NSString stringWithBool:
        [self classicalValue]] forKey:VRClassicalValueKey];
```

Add these lines near the end of the **restoreDataFromDictionary:** method,
before the [[self undoManager] enableUndoRegistration] message, also using
the new VRStringUtilities methods:

```
// Music
[self setPlayMusicValue:[[dictionary
        objectForKey:VRPlayMusicValueKey] boolValue]];
[self setRockValue:[[dictionary
        objectForKey:VRRecentRockValueKey] boolValue]];
[self setOldiesRockValue:[[dictionary
        objectForKey:VROldiesRockValueKey] boolValue]];
[self setClassicalValue:[[dictionary
        objectForKey:VRClassicalValueKey] boolValue]];
```

10. **GUI UPDATE METHOD INVOCATIONS.** Add calls to the control update methods to the
Buttons tab controller category. In VRButtonController.m, add the following
calls at the end of the **updateButtonsTab** method:

```
// Music
[self updateRecentRockCheckbox:nil];
[self updateOldiesRockCheckbox:nil];
[self updateClassicalCheckbox:nil];
```

You will deal with the Play Music and Allow Rock checkboxes in Step 3.5, below.

11. **Description method.** Add the new data values to the **description** method in VRButtonModel.m so that it reads as set forth below. Now that you have written a **stringWithBool:** method in the new VRStringUtilities category that you created in Step 2.7, you use it here in place of the C conditional statements you used in the **description** method initially.

```
- (NSString *)description {
    return [NSString stringWithFormat:@"%@\
\n\tcheckboxValue:%@\
\n\ttrianglePegsValue:%@\
\n\tsquarePegsValue:%@\
\n\troundPegsValue:%@\
\n\tplayMusicValue:%@\
\n\trockValue:%@\
\n\trecentRockValue:%@\
\n\toldiesRockValue:%@\
\n\tclassicalValue:%@\n",
        [super description],
        [NSString stringWithBool:[self checkboxValue]],
        [NSString stringWithBool:[self trianglePegsValue]],
        [NSString stringWithBool:[self squarePegsValue]],
        [NSString stringWithBool:[self roundPegsValue]],
        [NSString stringWithBool:[self playMusicValue]],
        [NSString stringWithBool:[self rockValue]],
        [NSString stringWithBool:[self recentRockValue]],
        [NSString stringWithBool:[self oldiesRockValue]],
        [NSString stringWithBool:[self classicalValue]]];
}
```

12. **Help tags.** Add Help tags to the five new checkboxes in Interface Builder from top to bottom, as follows: "Turn on music programs," "Allow rock 'n roll selections," "Play recent rock hits," "Play rock oldies," and "Play classical music."

3.3 Implement Action Methods for the New Checkboxes

You have left until the end the most interesting part of this step, implementing the means to disable and enable various groupings of checkboxes.

1. You will start with the two subsidiary checkboxes controlled by the Allow Rock checkbox, the Recent Hits and Oldies checkboxes.

First, go back to Interface Builder. Select in turn the Recent Hits and Oldies checkboxes. In the NSButton Info Panel, under Options, deselect the Enabled checkbox for each, so that they will start up in a default disabled state.

Then, in the header file VRMainWindowController.h, declare a new action method as follows, at the top of the Music subsection in the ACTIONS section of the VRButtonController category:

```
- (IBAction)rockAction:(id)sender;
```

Then turn to the definition of this action method, which disables and enables the two subsidiary checkboxes, the Recent Hits and Oldies checkboxes. In the category source file VRButtonController.m, define its action method at the top of the Music subsection in the ACTIONS section, as follows:

```
- (IBAction)rockAction:(id)sender {
    [[self buttonModel] setRockValue:
            ([sender state] == NSOnState)];
    //[[self recentRockCheckbox]
            setEnabled:[[self buttonModel] rockValue]];
    //[[self oldiesRockCheckbox]
            setEnabled:[[self buttonModel] rockValue]];
    if ([sender state] == NSOnState) {
        [[[self document] undoManager] setActionName:
                NSLocalizedString(@"Set Allow Rock",
                @"Name of undo/redo menu item after Allow \
                Rock checkbox control was set")];
    } else {
        [[[self document] undoManager] setActionName:
                NSLocalizedString(@"Clear Allow Rock",
                @"Name of undo/redo menu item after Allow \
                Rock checkbox control was cleared")];
    }
}
```

Consider the second and third statements in the body of this method, which have been commented out. They are shown here to introduce you to the notion that the visual state of other, subsidiary user controls may have to be altered because the user clicks a primary user control. It is feasible to do this here, in the primary control's action method, but this has the disadvantage of putting the setting of data values and the updating of the user interface in the same place. In the context of the Vermont Recipes application architecture, it is cleaner to deal with the user interface in update methods. You will do this in Step 3.4, below.

Note one point regarding the commented-out methods, however. You could have tested the visible on/off state of the Allow Rock checkbox to determine whether to enable or disable the two subsidiary checkboxes, instead of testing the state of the rockValue data variable. It is generally safer, however, to be consistent about relying on a data variable whenever one exists, to minimize the possibility of the application's data and its user interface getting out of sync. (You will encounter an exception to this rule of thumb in Recipe 3, Step 3, where two user controls are intended to display a single underlying data value. In such cases it is more efficient to use built-in Cocoa facilities to take one control's state directly from a linked control's state—for example, where moving a slider causes an associated text field to update a number rapidly.)

Don't forget to provide for the localizable Undo and Redo menu item names in Localizable.strings.

2. The action method for the Play Music checkbox is more complicated. Analyze it first in the context of the user interface. While considering whether to enable and disable the subsidiary checkboxes in the entire group box, it must take into account the enabled or disabled state of the Allow Rock checkbox with respect to its own subsubsidiary switches. It will take several lines of code to enable or disable all of the subsidiary checkboxes in the Play Music group. To keep the logic clear, you first create a utility method to accomplish this task.

In the header file VRMainWindowController.h, add the following declaration at the top of the Music subsection of the "INTERFACE MANAGEMENT - Specific updaters" section of the VRButtonController category:

```
- (void)enableMusicGroup:(BOOL)flag;
```

In the category source file VRButtonController.m, define the utility method at the top of the Music subsection of the "INTERFACE MANAGEMENT - Specific updaters" section:

```
- (void)enableMusicGroup:(BOOL)flag {
    [[self rockCheckbox] setEnabled:flag];
    [[self recentRockCheckbox]
        setEnabled:flag && [[self buttonModel] rockValue]];
    [[self oldiesRockCheckbox]
        setEnabled:flag && [[self buttonModel] rockValue]];
    [[self classicalCheckbox] setEnabled:flag];
}
```

As you see, the subsidiary Recent Hits and Oldies checkboxes are updated on the basis of the data values displayed by both the Play Music checkbox, passed in as the **flag** parameter, and the Allow Rock checkbox. If the Allow Rock checkbox is off, for example, then setting the Play Music checkbox should not enable the subsidiary rock categories.

Now you can turn to the **playMusicAction:** method itself. In the header file VRMainWindowController.h, declare a new action method as follows, at the top of the Music subsection in the ACTIONS section of the VRButtonController category:

```
- (IBAction)playMusicAction:(id)sender;
```

Add the following at the top of the Music subsection of the ACTIONS section of the category source file VRButtonController.m:

```
- (IBAction)playMusicAction:(id)sender {
    [[self buttonModel]
        setPlayMusicValue:([sender state] == NSOnState)];
    //[self enableMusicGroup:[[self buttonModel] musicValue]];
    if ([sender state] == NSOnState) {
        [[[self document] undoManager] setActionName:
            NSLocalizedString(@"Set Play Music",
            @"Name of undo/redo menu item after Play \
            Music checkbox control was set")];
    } else {
        [[[self document] undoManager] setActionName:
            NSLocalizedString(@"Clear Play Music",
            @"Name of undo/redo menu item after Play \
            Music checkbox control was cleared")];
    }
}
```

Again, the line that calls the **enableMusicGroup:** method is commented out, because this will be more appropriately done in the corresponding update method, but I show it here to illustrate the user interface consequences that must somewhere be made to flow from the user's action.

The default state of the Play Music checkbox will be off, so return to Interface Builder and uncheck the Enabled checkbox in the Options section of the NSButton Info Panel for the Allow Rock and Classical checkboxes.

Finally, make sure the localizable Undo and Redo menu item names have been provided for in Localizable.strings.

3.4 Implement Update Methods to Enable and Disable Subsidiary Checkboxes

Now for the update methods.

1. The implementation of the Play Music update method is very simple because of the utility method you created in Step 3.3, above. In addition to doing what an update method normally does—setting the state of its checkbox to on or off— it need only invoke the utility method to enable or disable all of the other checkboxes in the group.

    In the header file VRMainWindowController.h, declare the update method as follows, at the top of the Music subsection of the "INTERFACE MANAGE-MENT - Specific updaters" section of the VRButtonController category:

    ```
    - (void)updatePlayMusicCheckbox:(NSNotification *)notification;
    ```

    In the category source file VRButtonController.m, define the update method as follows, at the top of the Music subsection of the "INTERFACE MANAGE-MENT - Specific updaters" section:

    ```
    - (void)updatePlayMusicCheckbox:(NSNotification *)notification {
        [self updateTwoStateCheckbox:[self playMusicCheckbox]
                setting:[[self buttonModel] playMusicValue]];
        [self enableMusicGroup:[[self buttonModel] playMusicValue]];
    }
    ```

    This updates the visible state of the Play Music checkbox in response to a notification posted by the associated **set** accessor method, indicating that the data value in the model object has changed. Then, as you noted above, it passes this new data value to the **enableMusicGroup:** method you just created, in its **flag** parameter, to update the visible state of the rest of the checkboxes in the group box. It is much more appropriate to do this in an update method than in an action method.

    Now make sure the **updatePlayMusicCheckbox:** method gets called when its data value is changed. In the category source file VRButtonController.m, add the following to the **registerNotificationObserversForButtonsTab** method, at the beginning of the Music section:

    ```
    [[NSNotificationCenter defaultCenter] addObserver:self
            selector:@selector(updatePlayMusicCheckbox:)
            name:VRButtonModelPlayMusicValueChangedNotification
            object:[self document]];
    ```

2. Do the same with the Allow Rock checkbox.

In the header file VRMainWindowController.h, declare the update method as follows, after the **enableMusicGroup:** method in the Music subsection of the "INTERFACE MANAGEMENT - Specific updaters" section of the VRButtonController category:

```
- (void)updateRockCheckbox:(NSNotification *)notification;
```

In the category source file VRButtonController.m, define the update method as follows, after the **enableMusicGroup:** method in the corresponding location:

```
- (void)updateRockCheckbox:(NSNotification *)notification {
    [self updateTwoStateCheckbox:[self rockCheckbox]
            setting:[[self buttonModel] rockValue]];
    [[self recentRockCheckbox] setEnabled:
            [[self buttonModel] rockValue] &&
            [[self buttonModel] playMusicValue]];
    [[self oldiesRockCheckbox] setEnabled:
            [[self buttonModel] rockValue] &&
            [[self buttonModel] playMusicValue]];
}
```

You might initially think that the **updateRockCheckbox:** method doesn't need to test the status of the Play Music checkbox when updating the two subsidiary rock checkboxes, because if the Play Music checkbox is unchecked, the Allow Rock checkbox will be disabled and the user can't select it to invoke this method. However, you must always keep in mind that there are other interfaces, such as AppleScript, that might be able to do things without paying attention to GUI constraints (even if that might be a bug). Code defensively, and test the state of all conditions on which updating a user control depends.

Now make sure the **updateRockCheckbox:** method gets called when its data value is changed. In the category source file VRButtonController.m, add the following to the **registerNotificationObserversForButtonsTab** method, after the **VRButtonModelPlayMusicValueChangedNotification** registration:

```
[[NSNotificationCenter defaultCenter] addObserver:self
        selector:@selector(updateRockCheckbox:)
        name:VRButtonModelRockValueChangedNotification
        object:[self document]];
```

3.5 | Finish Updating the User Interface

One thing remains: The GUI must be updated when a document is created or opened. As noted in Instruction 10 of Step 3.2, above, you must therefore update the visible state of the Play Music and Allow Rock checkboxes. In the category source file VRButtonController.m, add the following calls at the beginning of the Music section in the updateButtonsTab method:

```
[self updatePlayMusicCheckbox:nil];
[self updateRockCheckbox:nil];
```

3.6 | Read the Source Files into the Nib File and Connect Outlets and Actions

Before you run the revised application, you must inform the nib file of the new outlets and actions you have created in the code files, then connect them to the new checkboxes.

1. In Interface Builder, select the Classes tab in the VRDocument.nib window, then choose Classes > Read Files. In the resulting dialog, select the one header file in which you have created outlets or actions, VRMainWindowController.h, then click the Parse button.

2. Select the Instances tab. You see a badge next to the File's Owner icon, indicating that required connections are missing. Control-drag from the File's Owner icon to each of the five new checkboxes in turn, each time clicking its outlet name, then clicking the Connect button in the Connections pane of the File's Owner Info Panel.

   You might encounter a problem when attempting to connect the File's Owner icon to the Play Music checkbox. If you left the Play Music checkbox layered behind the NSBox object when creating the group in Instruction 2 of Step 3.1, above, you can't select it now when ending the Control-drag operation. Instead, you select the box itself. A message appears in the File's Owner Info Panel telling you that the Play Music checkbox must be of type NSButton, and the Connect button isn't enabled. The cure is simple. Select the box, then choose Layout > Send to Back. Now the Play Music checkbox is in front of it, and you can successfully Control-drag to get to the checkbox.

3. Control-drag from each of the five new checkboxes to the File's Owner icon in turn, each time clicking the target in the left pane and the appropriate action in the right pane of the Outlets section in the Connections pane of the NSButton Info palette, then clicking the Connect button.

▌3.7▐ Build and Run the Application

Build and run the application to test the five new checkboxes and their interactions. Check their default values when a window is first opened, and make sure the checkboxes within the group box are disabled at first. Click checkboxes in various combinations to test their enabling and disabling behavior. Explore how undo and redo work, and make sure changes can be saved to disk, restored, and reverted properly. Finally, notice that the Help tags appear even over disabled checkboxes, allowing you to get help about them at all times.

Take this opportunity to reconsider the user interface. You decided early in this step that it was advisable to place this set of controls in a boxed group with a border, but is the border really necessary? To explore this question, go into Interface Builder, select the NSBox object by clicking in an empty area near one of the checkboxes, and, in the NSBox Info Panel, click the borderless Box Type button. Save, build, and run the application. It may be a close question, but a group with a checkbox for its title and subgroups within the main group seems clearer with a border—at least with all the other checkboxes arranged as they are in the tab view item. There are examples in the *Aqua Human Interface Guidelines* showing borderless group boxes with checkboxes for titles, and they appear to work well because of the overall design of their windows. Set this group box back to its bordered state for now and move on to the next step.

Step 4: Create a Radio Button Cluster

Radio buttons always come in clusters. A two-button cluster is sometimes preferred over a checkbox because it allows you to name both states; for example, the choice between red and green is more meaningful than the choice whether to turn red on or off. Having more than two radio buttons in a cluster is very common. The *Aqua Human Interface Guidelines* put the recommended maximum at about seven; more than that, and you should consider using a pop-up menu (see Step 5, below).

HIGHLIGHTS:

Using tags and an enumeration type to manage a radio button cluster

Raising an exception to catch a programming error

Interestingly, no matter how many radio buttons are in a cluster, only one variable is needed to store their value. This follows from the fact that only one button in the cluster can be selected at a time. You can therefore specify the value of the cluster with an integer representing the ordinal index of the selected button, starting with **0** for the first. It is customary, though not necessary, to use the C enumeration type to assign meaningful names to each of the integer values.

Cocoa implements radio clusters and certain other grouped controls using matrices whose component cells can be assigned tags. Each button in a radio button cluster is a separate cell in an NSMatrix object. You can use the NSMatrix Info Panel in Interface Builder to assign each button a unique tag value, which you can use in your code to specify a particular button. These tags can be any value, such as arbitrary numeric codes or even strings, in any order, giving you great flexibility. A common technique is to equate each tag to its cell's **0**-based ordinal position within the matrix, either horizontally or vertically. Click the Tags = Positions button to accomplish this for all the cells at once (recent versions of Interface Builder do this for you automatically). Alternatively, you can select each button in turn and set the tags manually using the NSButton Info Panel. It is generally preferable to use tag or index values to identify user interface items in your code, instead of using their titles, because localization may change the titles.

This step is remarkably simple, yet interesting techniques and code appear throughout.

4.1 Create a Radio Button Cluster in Interface Builder

Use Interface Builder to create a cluster of three radio buttons with a title. When you are done with Step 4.1, the group should look like **Figure 2.6**.

FIGURE 2.6 The Party Affiliation radio button cluster.

1. From the Cocoa Views palette, drag the two-button radio button group to the upper-right area of the Buttons pane, leaving room to insert a title between the cluster and the top of the tab view item.

2. Select the cluster by clicking anywhere in it. There are two ways in which you can create a third button. Using the NSMatrix Info Panel, change the number of rows from 2 to 3 by typing in the R: cell of the Row/Col form at the bottom right. The easier method is to Option-drag the bottom border of the matrix and watch as new buttons appear before your eyes. Using either technique, create a third button.

3. Rename the three buttons **Democratic**, **Republican**, and **Socialist**, respectively. (Bernie Sanders is the socialist—er, Independent—Congressman from Vermont. Local tub-thumping will hopefully be forgiven in the Vermont Recipes.) Choose Layout > Size to Fit to get the proper size and spacing.

4. Drag the System Font Text text field item onto the Buttons pane, placing it above and a little to the left of the radio buttons. Use the Aqua guides to position the baseline of the text at the same level as the baseline of the original checkbox control's label. Then drag the radio button cluster, using the guides to position it the proper distance below the System Font Text item and indented slightly to the right.

5. Rename the text field **Party Affiliation:** (note the trailing colon). You may have to choose Layout > Size to Fit to make the new text fully visible.

6. In the NSTextField Info Panel, make sure the Selectable and Editable Options are not selected. This text field holds static text—that is, a heading that the user should not be able to edit, select, or copy to the clipboard.

4.2 Write the Code for the Radio Button Cluster in Project Builder

Use Project Builder to write the code.

1. **USER CONTROL OUTLET VARIABLES AND ACCESSORS.** In the header file VRMainWindowController.h, declare a new outlet to access the radio button cluster, after the "Music switch button group" near the top of the file, as follows:

```
// Party radio button cluster
IBOutlet NSMatrix *partyRadioCluster;
```

Still in the header file, also declare the accessor for the outlet, after the "Music switch button group" at the end of the ACCESSORS section of the VRButtonController category, as follows:

```
// Party radio button cluster
- (NSMatrix *)partyRadioCluster;
```

In the category source file VRButtonController.m, define the accessor after the "Music switch button group" in the ACCESSORS section, as follows:

```
// Party radio button cluster

- (NSMatrix *)partyRadioCluster {
    return partyRadioCluster;
}
```

2. **DATA VARIABLES AND ACCESSORS.** The variable that will hold the data value associated with the radio button cluster can be a simple C integer type, and its accessors and other methods can accept and return integers. However, the use of the C enumeration type to substitute constants for integers often promotes more understandable code.

In the header file VRButtonModel.h, declare a new type immediately following the `#import` directive, as follows:

```
#pragma mark TYPEDEFS

typedef enum {
    VRDemocratic,
    VRRepublican,
    VRSocialist
} VRParty;
```

Now you can declare the data variable as type **VRParty** instead of type **int**. You will see an example of how to do this in Instruction 8, below.

When you use **typedefs** like this, you should generally prefix them with unique initials to avoid possible naming conflicts with third-party frameworks that you might use, just as you did earlier (and will continue to do) with the notification names.

In the header file VRButtonModel.h, declare the variable to access the data value associated with the radio button cluster, after the Music section, as follows:

```
// Party
VRParty partyValue;
```

In VRButtonModel.h, also declare the corresponding accessor methods after the Music subsection of the ACCESSORS section, as follows:

```
// Party

- (void)setPartyValue:(VRParty)inValue;
- (VRParty)partyValue;
```

Turn to the source file VRButtonModel.m and define these accessor methods after the Music subsection of the ACCESSORS section, as set forth below. If you have been following the practice of adding **NSLog()** calls to your data accessor methods, do so here as well, on the model of Recipe 1, Step 10.2. Note that the **partyValue** instance variable holds an integer enumeration value, rather than a Boolean. You will learn how to convert this to a string in the VRStringUtilities category in Step 4.3, below, and this will provide a convenient way to log the value here.

```
// Party

- (void)setPartyValue:(VRParty)inValue {
    [[[self undoManager]
            prepareWithInvocationTarget:self]
            setPartyValue:partyValue];
    partyValue = inValue;
    [[NSNotificationCenter defaultCenter] postNotificationName:
            VRButtonModelPartyValueChangedNotification
            object:[self document]];
}

- (VRParty)partyValue {
    return partyValue;
}
```

3. **NOTIFICATION VARIABLES.** Return to the header file VRButtonModel.h, at the bottom of the file, to declare the notification variable used in the **set** method, as follows:

```
// Party
extern NSString *VRButtonModelPartyValueChangedNotification;
```

Turn back to the source file VRButtonModel.m, near the top of the file, to define the notification variable, as follows:

```
// Party
NSString *VRButtonModelPartyValueChangedNotification =
        @"ButtonModel partyValue Changed Notification";
```

4. **GUI UPDATE METHODS.** Now you need a method to update the GUI in response to this notification. First, however, since you are dealing with a new kind of control, you must devise a new generic method to update radio button clusters. In the header file VRMainWindowController.h, declare the following method at the end of the "INTERFACE MANAGEMENT - Generic updaters" section:

```
- (void)updateRadioCluster:(NSMatrix *)control
        setting:(int)inValue;
```

Because this is a generic method that must be able to update many different radio button clusters, the second parameter must be typed as an integer rather than as the enumeration type you have created for this particular button.

Now define this method in the corresponding location in VRMainWindow-Controller.m, as shown below. Here you see how matrix-based groups of controls can express their values, namely, by reporting the value of the currently selected cell's tag. By the same token, such a control's view is updated by selecting the cell whose tag corresponds to the integer value passed to it.

```
- (void)updateRadioCluster:(NSMatrix *)control
        setting:(int)inValue {
    if (inValue != [control selectedTag]) {
        [control selectCellWithTag:inValue];
    }
}
```

Now you can declare the specific updater in the header file VRMainWindow-Controller.h, after the Music subsection of the "INTERFACE MANAGEMENT - Specific updaters" section of the VRButtonController category, as follows:

```
// Party
- (void)updatePartyRadioCluster:(NSNotification *)notification;
```

In the category source file VRButtonController.m, define this specific update method, in the corresponding location, as follows:

```
// Party

- (void)updatePartyRadioCluster:(NSNotification *)notification {
    [self updateRadioCluster:[self partyRadioCluster]
            setting:[[self buttonModel] partyValue]];
}
```

5. **NOTIFICATION OBSERVERS.** Now register the window controller as an observer of the notification that will trigger this updater, by inserting the following statement in the **registerNotificationObserversForButtonsTab** method of the category source file VRButtonController.m, after the Music registrations:

```
// Party
[[NSNotificationCenter defaultCenter] addObserver:self
        selector:@selector(updatePartyRadioCluster:)
        name:VRButtonModelPartyValueChangedNotification
        object:[self document]];
```

6. **ACTION METHODS.** Next, you must add an action method. In the header file VRMainWindowController.h, after the Music subsection in the ACTIONS section of the VRButtonController category at the end of the file, add the following:

```
// Party
- (IBAction)partyAction:(id)sender;
```

In the category source file VRButtonController.m, define the action method, after the Music subsection of the ACTIONS section at the end, as shown below. Here again, you see the use of a cell's tag in a matrix-based user control. Since there may be multiple values associated with multiple radio buttons in the cluster, you must use a C switch statement or chained if/else statements.

```objc
// Party

- (IBAction)partyAction:(id)sender {
    [[self buttonModel]
            setPartyValue:[sender selectedTag]];
    switch ([[sender selectedCell] tag]) {
    case 0:
        [[[self document] undoManager] setActionName:
                NSLocalizedString(@"Select Democratic Party",
                @"Name of undo/redo menu item after \
                Democratic radio button was selected")];
        break;
    case 1:
        [[[self document] undoManager] setActionName:
                NSLocalizedString(@"Select Republican Party",
                @"Name of undo/redo menu item after \
                Republican radio button was selected")];
        break;
    case 2:
        [[[self document] undoManager] setActionName:
                NSLocalizedString(@"Select Socialist Party",
                @"Name of undo/redo menu item after \
                Socialist radio button was selected")];
        break;
    }
}
```

Using a C switch statement in this fashion to set the undo and redo menu item name is convenient, but it is not a fully object-oriented approach. For greater flexibility should you need to add or reorder menu items in the future, you might wish you had connected a separate action method to each individual menu item. You will see how to do this in Step 6. When you use tags, or the menu items' indices as you will do in Step 5, you must be alert to the possible necessity of rewriting the entire switch statement. This problem is somewhat eased by using unique tag values for each menu item, because the tags stay with their menu items even if you change their order.

7. **LOCALIZABLE.STRINGS.** Update the Localizable.strings file with these undo and redo menu titles.

8. **INITIALIZATION.** To give you an example of how to use the enumeration type you defined in Instruction 2, above, you will now set the initial default value of the `partyValue` variable to `VRRepublican`, which is one of the constants you defined there.

   In the source file VRButtonModel.m, add this line to the `initWithDocument:` method, after the initialization of `trianglePegsValue`:

   ```
   [self setPartyValue:VRRepublican];
   ```

   Also return to Interface Builder to make sure the initial appearance of the radio button cluster is correct. Select the Republican radio button. To do this, you must first select the entire cluster by clicking it, then double-click the Republican radio button. Then, in the Options area of the NSButtonCell Info Panel's Attributes pane, check the Selected checkbox. You will see the Republican radio button become selected immediately. It is not necessary to uncheck the Democratic radio button, because selecting the Republican radio button did this for you automatically. Now, when the application launches and a document opens, the Republican radio button will appear selected by default.

9. **DATA STORAGE.** Deal now with persistent storage of the new data variables. In the source file VRButtonModel.m, define this key at the end of the "Keys and values for dictionary" subsection of the STORAGE section:

   ```
   // Party
   static NSString *VRPartyValueKey = @"VRButtonModelPartyValue";
   ```

   Add these lines at the end of the `addDataToDictionary:` method:

   ```
   // Party
   [dictionary setObject:[NSString stringWithFormat:@"%d",
       [self partyValue]] forKey:VRPartyValueKey];
   ```

   Add these lines near the end of the `restoreDataFromDictionary:` method, before the `[[self undoManager] enableUndoRegistration]` message:

   ```
   // Party
   [self setPartyValue:(VRParty)[[dictionary
       objectForKey:VRPartyValueKey] intValue]];
   ```

   Notice that you are saving and retrieving integer values here. You could instead add methods to the VRStringUtilities category that you implemented in Step 2 to save the enumeration constants as strings. This would make the file more readable for anyone examining it with a general file utility. This is so interesting, if not very useful, that instead of leaving it as a challenge, I will do it in Step 4.3, next.

10. **GUI UPDATE METHOD INVOCATIONS.** Finally, add an invocation of the control update method to the window controller. In the category source file VRButtonController.m, add the following call at the end of the **updateButtonsTab** method :

```
// Party
[self updatePartyRadioCluster:nil];
```

11. **DESCRIPTION METHOD.** Add the new data value to the description method in VRButtonModel.m so that it reads as set forth below. You will again use the **stringWithBool:** method you wrote in the VRStringUtilities category in Step 2.7. In a sneak preview, you will also use the **stringWithVRParty:** method that you are about to write in Step 4.3, below.

```
- (NSString *)description {
    return [NSString stringWithFormat:@"%@\
/n/tcheckboxValue:%@\
/n/ttrianglePegsValue:%@\
/n/tsquarePegsValue:%@\
/n/troundPegsValue:%@\
/n/tplayMusicValue:%@\
/n/trockValue:%@\
/n/trecentRockValue:%@\
/n/toldiesRockValue:%@\
/n/tclassicalValue:%@\
/n/tpartyValue:%@\n",
        [super description],
        [NSString stringWithBool:[self checkboxValue]],
        [NSString stringWithBool:[self trianglePegsValue]],
        [NSString stringWithBool:[self squarePegsValue]],
        [NSString stringWithBool:[self roundPegsValue]],
        [NSString stringWithBool:[self playMusicValue]],
        [NSString stringWithBool:[self rockValue]],
        [NSString stringWithBool:[self recentRockValue]],
        [NSString stringWithBool:[self oldiesRockValue]],
        [NSString stringWithBool:[self classicalValue]]
        [NSString stringWithVRParty:[self partyValue]]];
}
```

12. **HELP TAGS.** Add Help tags to the three new radio buttons in Interface Builder, as follows from top to bottom: "Register to vote in the Democratic primary," "Register to vote in the Republican primary," and "Register to vote in the Socialist primary."

4.3 Add to the Category on NSString to Convert Between Enumeration Types and Strings

In Instruction 9 of Step 4.2, above, I promised to show you how to add methods to the VRStringUtilities category that will let you save and retrieve party affiliation values as strings corresponding to the enumeration constants **VRDemocratic**, **VRRepublican**, and **VRSocialist**. The following additions to the VRStringUtilities category work on the same principle as the original methods taught in Step 2.7 and require no further explanation.

This is not as useful, to be sure, as the Boolean methods you added to NSString earlier, because there are fewer occasions to use the enumeration type. It is almost as easy to code this in a separate method, or even inline in the one or two places where it might be used.

1. At the end of the header file NSString+VRStringUtilities.h, declare these two methods:

   ```
   + (id)stringWithVRParty:(int)inValue;
   - (int)VRPartyValue;
   ```

2. At the end of the source file NSString+VRStringUtilities.m, define the two methods as set forth below. You provide dummy values (an empty string in **stringWithVRParty:** and **-1** in **VRPartyValue**) in the event that an unrecognized value is encountered. It might be preferable to generate an exception here, since a bad parameter evidences a programming error. I don't cover the use of Cocoa's NSException class in *Vermont Recipes,* but the simplest way to raise an exception at run time to catch programming errors is shown in these two methods. You just call an NSException class method, **raise:format:**, passing it a Cocoa or custom exception name and an explanatory string. The lines returning a dummy value are included to suppress compiler warnings.

   ```
   + (id)stringWithVRParty:(int)inValue {
       switch (inValue) {
           case 0:
               return [NSString stringWithString:@"VRDemocratic"];
               break;
           case 1:
               return [NSString stringWithString:@"VRRepublican"];
               break;
           case 2:
               return [NSString stringWithString:@"VRSocialist"];
   ```

```
                break:
            default:

                [NSException raise:NSInvalidArgumentException
                        format:@"Exception raised in \
                        NSString+VRStringUtilities \
                        +stringWithVRParty: - attempt to \
                        pass parameter (%d) other than \
                        VRDemocratic (0), VRRepublican (1), \
                        or VRSocialist (2)", inValue];
                return [NSString string]; // empty string
                break;

        }
    }


    - (int)VRPartyValue {
        if ([self isEqualToString:@"VRDemocratic"]) {
            return 0;
        } else if ([self isEqualToString:@"VRRepublican"]) {
            return 1;
        } else if ([self isEqualToString:@"VRSocialist"]) {
            return 2;
        } else {
            [NSException raise:@"VRInvalidValueException"
                    format:@"Exception raised in \
                    NSString+VRStringUtilities -VRPartyValue - \
                    found string (%@) other than VRDemocratic, \
                    VRRepublican, or VRSocialist", self];
            return -1; // treat as error
        }
    }
```

3. Now you can rewrite the data storage methods. Substitute these lines for the previous version at the end of the **addDataToDictionary:** method in the source file VRButtonModel.m:

```
// Party
[dictionary setObject:[NSString stringWithVRParty:
        [self partyValue]] forKey:VRPartyValueKey];
```

Add these lines near the end of the **restoreFromDictionary:** method, before the [[self undoManager] enableUndoRegistration] method:

```
// Party
[self setPartyValue:
        [[dictionary objectForKey:VRPartyValueKey] partyValue]];
```

4.4 Read the Source Files into the Nib File and Connect Outlets and Actions

You must inform the nib file of the new outlet and action you have created, then connect them to the new radio button cluster.

1. In Interface Builder, select the Classes tab in the nib file window, then choose Classes > Read Files. In the resulting dialog, select the one header file in which you have created an outlet and an action, VRMainWindowController.h, then click the Parse button.

2. Select the Instances tab and see the badge on the File's Owner icon indicating that connections need to be made. Control-drag from the File's Owner icon to the new radio cluster and click its outlet name, then click the Connect button in the Connections pane of the File's Owner Info Panel. Take care that the entire radio cluster is enclosed in the square at the end of the line while you are drawing the connection. If you aren't careful, you will end up selecting one of the individual radio buttons, which is not what you want.

3. Control-drag from the new radio cluster to the File's Owner icon and click the target in the left pane and the appropriate action in the right pane of the Outlets section in the Connections pane of the NSButton Info Panel. Then click the Connect button. Again, make sure you start the drag with the entire radio cluster, not one of the individual radio buttons.

4.5 Build and Run the Application

Build and run the application to test the interactions among the new radio buttons, explore how undo and redo work, and make sure changes can be saved to disk, restored, and reverted properly. If you haven't done so already, try changing a few of the controls you created in Steps 2 and 3 in between changing radio button selections, then undo all your actions in turn to confirm that multiple undo unwinds your actions in the same order no matter which controls or groups of controls are involved. Use Property List Editor on a saved file to make sure the party affiliation was saved as a string value rather than as an integer.

Step 5: Create a Pop-Up Menu Button

A pop-up menu button (also known as a pop-up list) is very similar in function to a radio button cluster. It allows you to choose one among multiple listed options. It takes up much less screen real estate than a radio button cluster, but the user has to click it to see all of the options it offers. The current choice appears in the button as its title, and when you expand the list by clicking it, the list extends above and below the button as far as needed to allow the current choice to remain positioned where it was, over the button. As far back as the *Mac OS 8 Human Interface Guidelines,* Apple has recommended that radio button clusters max out at approximately 7 options. If you offer more than 5 options, according to the latest *Aqua Human Interface Guidelines,* you should consider using a pop-up menu button instead, but a pop-up button should not present more than 12 mutually exclusive choices. Use a scrolling list for more than 12. You can also use a pop-up menu button when there are fewer options, as space or design considerations may dictate, but not fewer than 5.

HIGHLIGHTS:

Using an index and an enumeration type to manage a pop-up menu button

As in the case of a radio button cluster, only one variable is needed to store the value of a pop-up menu button. You can specify the value of the button in your code with a unique tag you assign, possibly using Interface Builder, as in the case of radio buttons, or as an integer index representing the 0-based positional index of the currently selected menu item. It is customary, though not necessary, to use the C enumeration type to assign meaningful names to each of the integer values. At times tags are more useful, as when you will continually realphabetize the menu items. Here, however, you will use index values to see how it is done.

Because the selected menu item in the pop-up menu button here will be identified by its index, it is not necessary to override the values Interface Builder automatically gives their tags. Except for using the index instead of the tag, coding a pop-up menu button is virtually identical to coding a radio button cluster. As is the case with radio button clusters, it is possible to use the titles of the separate items to select and obtain the selection of a pop-up menu button, and Cocoa provides methods to convert among index, tag, and title.

5.1 Create a Pop-Up Menu Button in Interface Builder

Use Interface Builder to create a pop-up menu button. When you are done with Step 5.1, the result should look like **Figure 2.7** and **Figure 2.8**.

FIGURE 2.7 The State pop-up menu button.

FIGURE 2.8 The State pop-up menu button expanded.

1. From the Other palette, drag the pop-up menu button to the Buttons pane, some distance below the Party Affiliation radio button cluster. The pop-up menu button is distinguished by the double arrows at its right end.

   Aqua guides aren't available to you to decide how much space to leave between the Party Affiliation cluster and your new pop-up menu button, because you did not place the radio button cluster and its title in a borderless group box. In retrospect, it might have been a good idea to do so, but another technique is available. With the new pop-up menu button selected, hold down Option and move the mouse over the Socialist radio button. Arrows appear showing you how many pixels separate them. Now use the arrow keys on your keyboard to nudge the new button until it is 20 pixels below the bottommost radio button. Don't line it up vertically with the leftmost edge of the radio button cluster's title, however, because you will shortly add a label to the left of the button.

2. Double-click the new button. Three menu items appear superimposed over it. Add two more menu items to this list. You do this by selecting the Cocoa Menus palette in the upper-right quadrant of your screen, then drag the menu item named Item to the bottom of the pop-up menu button's menu item list twice.

3. Rename the five menu items ME, MA, NH, RI, and VT, respectively. If you rename the VT menu item last, it appears with a checkmark beside it. This is what you want, because you will make VT the default initial choice in the pop-up menu (Vermont is one of the five New England states; local tub-thumping again). However, if you prefer to choose another default, simply click it, and a checkmark appears in front of it. An alternative way to do this is to use the arrow keys on your keyboard. Once you have chosen a default, click outside the menu to close its item list.

4. Drag the System Font Text text field onto the Buttons pane, placing it to the left of the pop-up menu button.

5. Rename the textfield **State:** (note the trailing colon), and choose Layout > Size to Fit to shrink it. Drag it to align with the left edge below the title of the radio button cluster, using the Aqua guides for precise positioning. Then drag or nudge the pop-up menu button, using the guides so its text baseline ends up on the baseline of the text field and it is the proper distance to the right of the text field.

6. Using the Options area of the NSTextField Info Panel, make sure the text field is not Editable or Selectable but is Enabled.

7. Select the pop-up menu button and choose Layout > Size to Fit to size the new button appropriately relative to its longest menu item.

5.2 Write the Code for the Pop-Up Menu Button in Project Builder

Use Project Builder to write the code.

1. USER CONTROL OUTLET VARIABLES AND ACCESSORS. In the header file VRMain-WindowController.h, declare a new outlet to access the pop-up menu button, after the "Party radio button cluster" section near the top of the file, as follows:

```
// State pop-up menu button
IBOutlet NSPopUpButton *statePopUpButton;
```

Still in the header file, also declare the accessor for the outlet, after the "Party radio button cluster" subsection of the ACCESSORS section in the VRButtonController category, as follows:

```
// State pop-up menu button
- (NSPopUpButton *)statePopUpButton;
```

In the category source file VRButtonController.m, define the accessor after the "Party radio button cluster" subsection of the ACCESSORS section, as follows:

```
// State pop-up menu button

- (NSPopUpButton *)statePopUpButton {
    return statePopUpButton;
}
```

2. **DATA VARIABLES AND ACCESSORS.** Create the variable that will hold the data value associated with the pop-up menu button and a related C enumeration type.

In the header file VRButtonModel.h, declare a new type following the party enumeration type, as follows:

```
typedef enum {
    VRMaine,
    VRMassachusetts,
    VRNewHampshire,
    VRRhodeIsland,
    VRVermont
} VRState;
```

Still in the header file, declare the variable to access the data value associated with the pop-up menu button, after the Party section, as follows:

```
// State
VRState stateValue;
```

Also declare the corresponding accessor methods after the Party section, as follows:

```
// State

- (void)setStateValue:(VRState)inValue;
- (VRState)stateValue;
```

Turn to the source file VRButtonModel.m and define these accessor methods after the Party section, as follows, and add an **NSLog( )** call if you are following that practice:

```
// State

- (void)setStateValue:(VRState)inValue {
    [[[self undoManager] prepareWithInvocationTarget:self]
        setStateValue:stateValue];
    stateValue = inValue;
    [[NSNotificationCenter defaultCenter] postNotificationName:
        VRButtonModelStateValueChangedNotification
        object:[self document]];
}

- (VRState)stateValue {
    return stateValue;
}
```

3. **NOTIFICATION VARIABLES.** In the header file VRButtonModel.h, at the bottom of the file, declare the notification variable used in the **set** method, as follows:

```
// State
extern NSString *VRButtonModelStateValueChangedNotification;
```

In the source file VRButtonModel.m, at the end of the notification definitions near the top, define the notification variable, as follows:

```
// State
NSString *VRButtonModelStateValueChangedNotification =
    @"ButtonModel stateValue Changed Notification";
```

4. **GUI UPDATE METHODS.** You are dealing with a new kind of control, so you must again define a new generic method to update pop-up menu buttons. You will use the index of its selected menu item. In the header file VRMainWindow-Controller.h, declare the following method at the end of the "INTERFACE MANAGEMENT - Generic updaters" section:

```
- (void)updatePopUpButton:(NSPopUpButton *)control
        setting:(int)inValue;
```

Because this is a generic method that must be able to update many different pop-up menu buttons, the second parameter must be typed as an integer rather than any specific enumeration constant.

Now define this method in the corresponding location in VRMainWindow-Controller.m, as shown below. Here you see that the button reports the value of the index of the currently selected menu item. By the same token, such a control's view is updated by selecting the menu item whose index corresponds to the integer value passed to it.

```
- (void)updatePopUpButton:(NSPopUpButton *)control
        setting:(int)inValue {
    if (inValue != [control indexOfSelectedItem]) {
        [control selectItemAtIndex:inValue];
    }
}
```

Now you can declare the specific updater, after the Party subsection in the "INTERFACE MANAGEMENT - Specific updaters" section of the VRButtonController category in VRMainWindowController.h, as follows:

```
// State
- (void)updateStatePopUpButton:(NSNotification *)notification;
```

In the category source file VRButtonController.m, define this specific update method, after the Party subsection of the "INTERFACE MANAGEMENT - Specific updaters" section, as follows:

```
// State

- (void)updateStatePopUpButton:(NSNotification *)notification {
    [self updatePopUpButton:[self statePopUpButton]
            setting:[[self buttonModel] stateValue]];
}
```

5. **NOTIFICATION OBSERVERS.** Register the window controller as an observer of the notification that will trigger this updater, by inserting the following statement in the **registerNotificationObserversForButtonsTab** method of the category source file VRButtonController.m, after the Party registration:

```
// State
[[NSNotificationCenter defaultCenter] addObserver:self
        selector:@selector(updateStatePopUpButton:)
        name:VRButtonModelStateValueChangedNotification
        object:[self document]];
```

6. **ACTION METHODS.** Add an action method. In the header file VRMainWindow-Controller.h, after the Party subsection of the ACTIONS section at the end of the VRButtonController category, declare it as follows:

```
// State
- (IBAction)stateAction:(id)sender;
```

In the category source file VRButtonController.m, define the action method, after the Party subsection of the ACTIONS section at the end of the file, as shown below. Here again, you see the use of the menu item's index.

```
// State

- (IBAction)stateAction:(id)sender {
    [[self buttonModel] setStateValue:
            [sender indexOfSelectedItem]];
    switch ([sender indexOfSelectedItem]) {
    case 0:
        [[[self document] undoManager] setActionName:
                NSLocalizedString(@"Select ME",
                @"Name of undo/redo menu item after Maine \
                pop-up menu button was selected")];
        break;
```

```
    case 1:
        [[[self document] undoManager] setActionName:
                NSLocalizedString(@"Select MA",
                @"Name of undo/redo menu item after \
                Massachusetts pop-up menu button was selected")];
        break;
    case 2:
        [[[self document] undoManager] setActionName:
                NSLocalizedString(@"Select NH",
                @"Name of undo/redo menu item after New \
                Hampshire pop-up menu button was selected")];
        break;
    case 3:
        [[[self document] undoManager] setActionName:
                NSLocalizedString(@"Select RI",
                @"Name of undo/redo menu item after Rhode Island \
                pop-up menu button was selected")];
        break;
    case 4:
        [[[self document] undoManager] setActionName:
                NSLocalizedString(@"Select VT",
                @"Name of undo/redo menu item after Vermont \
                pop-up menu button was selected")];
        break;
    }
}
```

The use of a switch statement here to set the undo and redo menu item title, like its use in the previous step with menu item tags, is not the most object-oriented approach. Furthermore, the indices will change if you reorder, insert, or delete menu items, so it presents a more difficult code maintenance issue.

7. **LOCALIZABLE.STRINGS.** Update the Localizable.strings file with these undo and redo menu titles.

8. **INITIALIZATION.** Set the value of the stateValue variable to VRVermont, which is one of the constants you defined in the VRState enumeration type. In the source file VRButtonModel.m, add this line to the initWithDocument: method, after the initialization of partyValue:

```
[self setStateValue:VRVermont];
```

You already set up the Interface Builder selection in Step 5.1, above.

9. **Data storage.** Deal now with persistent storage of the new data variables. In the source file VRButtonModel.m, define this key at the end of the "Keys and values for dictionary" subsection of the STORAGE section:

```
// State
static NSString *VRStateValueKey = @"VRButtonModelStateValue";
```

Add these lines at the end of the **addDataToDictionary:** method:

```
// State
[dictionary setObject:[NSString stringWithVRState:
    [self stateValue]] forKey:VRStateValueKey];
```

Add these lines near the end of the **restoreDataFromDictionary:** method, before the [[self undoManager] enableUndoRegistration] message:

```
// State
[self setStateValue:
    [[dictionary objectForKey:VRStateValueKey] stateValue]];
```

You saved and retrieved string equivalents of integer enumeration values here, but you haven't yet added the methods required to do this to the VRStringUtilities category on NSString. Follow the procedure you established in Step 4.3 to add **VRState** string utilities to the category. The changes required to the code you wrote in Step 4.3 are very minor and I will not spell them out here.

10. **GUI update method invocation.** Add invocations of the control update method to the window controller. In the category source file VRButtonController.m, add the following call at the end of the **updateButtonsTab** method:

```
// State
[self updateStatePopUpButton:nil];
```

11. **Description method.** Add the new data value to the description method in VRButtonModel.m so that it reads as set forth below. You use the new **stringWithVRState:** method that you just finished writing in the VRStringUtilities category.

```
- (NSString *)description {
    return [NSString stringWithFormat:@"%@\
    \n\tcheckboxValue:%@\
    \n\ttrianglePegsValue:%@\
    \n\tsquarePegsValue:%@\
    \n\troundPegsValue:%@\
    \n\tplayMusicValue:%@\
    \n\trockValue:%@\
    \n\trecentRockValue:%@\
```

```
\n\toldiesRockValue:%@\
\n\tclassicalValue:%@\
\n\tpartyValue:%@\
\n\tstateValue:%@\n",
    [super description],
    [NSString stringWithBool:[self checkboxValue]],
    [NSString stringWithBool:[self trianglePegsValue]],
    [NSString stringWithBool:[self squarePegsValue]],
    [NSString stringWithBool:[self roundPegsValue]],
    [NSString stringWithBool:[self playMusicValue]],
    [NSString stringWithBool:[self rockValue]],
    [NSString stringWithBool:[self recentRockValue]],
    [NSString stringWithBool:[self oldiesRockValue]],
    [NSString stringWithBool:[self classicalValue]],
    [NSString stringWithVRParty:[self partyValue]],
    [NSString stringWithVRState:[self stateValue]]];
}
```

12. HELP TAGS. Add a Help tag to the new pop-up menu button in Interface Builder: "Where do you live?" You cannot use Interface Builder to add Help tags to individual menu items.

5.3 Read the Source Files into the Nib File and Connect Outlets and Actions

You must inform the nib file of the new outlet and action you have created, then connect them to the new pop-up menu button.

1. In Interface Builder, select the Classes tab in the nib file window, then choose Classes > Read Files. In the resulting dialog, select the one Vermont Recipes header file in which you have created an outlet and an action, VRMainWindow-Controller.h, then click the Parse button.

2. Select the Instances tab and Control-drag from the File's Owner icon to the new pop-up menu button and click its outlet name, then click the Connect button in the Connections pane of the File's Owner Info Panel.

3. Control-drag from the new pop-up menu button to the File's Owner icon and click the target in the left pane and the appropriate action in the right pane of the Outlets section in the Connections pane of the NSButton Info Panel. Then click the Connect button.

5.4 Build and Run the Application

Build and run the application to test the new pop-up menu button. Explore how undo and redo work, and make sure changes can be saved to disk, restored, and reverted properly.

Step 6: Create a Command Pop-Down Menu Button

HIGHLIGHTS:

Issuing commands from menu items in a command pop-down menu button

Using a timer to delay an operation for a fixed time interval

A command pop-down menu button (formerly known as a pull-down menu or list) is an NSPopUpButton object configured as a pull-down menu button. Its appearance, behavior, and function are slightly different from those of a pop-up menu button. It has a single down-pointing arrow at the right end, signifying that it only pulls down, instead of two arrows pointing in opposite directions. Like a pop-up menu button, it allows you to choose one of multiple listed options. However, the button's title never changes, and the current choice thus isn't visible except when the list is expanded. This behavior makes it suitable for choosing options in a constrained environment, where the context is fixed and readily apparent, and in a constricted space, where a label can't appear beside it. It can also be used to choose and execute commands, since each menu item can have its own action method.

Here, you will create a command pop-down menu button whose menu items simply beep the indicated number of times. The beeps are for demonstration purposes only, of course; they are stand-ins for whatever actions you might want to perform in your application. It is good to know, however, that there is an `NSBeep()` function in the AppKit (declared in NSGraphics.h, of all places), which you can use at any time to play an alert sound based on the user's system preferences. Since the command pop-down menu is purely action oriented, you will not need to provide storage for a data value or support for undo, redo, save, open, or revert. All you need is action methods.

This step differs from the previous step in that you will work with the two individual menu items, rather than the command pop-down menu button itself.

6.1 Create a Command Pop-Down Menu Button in Interface Builder

Use Interface Builder to create a command pop-down menu button. When you are done with this instruction, the results should look like **Figure 2.9** and **Figure 2.10**.

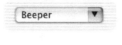

FIGURE 2.9 The Beeper command pop-down menu button.

FIGURE 2.10 The Beeper command pop-down menu button expanded.

1. From the Other Cocoa Views palette, drag the pop-up menu button item to the Buttons pane, placing it below the State pop-up menu button. You will change the new button to a command pop-down menu button in a moment.

2. Double-click the button. Three menu items appear superimposed over it. Select the topmost item for editing, and name it `Beeper`. Name the next two items `Beep Once` and `Beep Twice`. The topmost menu item, at index `0,` will become the fixed title when you change the button to a command pop-down menu button, and the first menu item that the user can choose will be at index `1`.

3. Click outside the button to close the menu items, then select the button itself by clicking it once. In the NSPopUpButton Info Panel, click the PullDown radio button. You will see the button change appearance to that of a command pop-down menu button.

4. If necessary, choose Layout > Size to Fit to size the new button appropriately relative to its longest menu item and position it in the pane according to the Aqua guides.

6.2 Write the Code for the Command Pop-Down Menu Button in Project Builder

Use Project Builder to write the code.

1. **USER CONTROL OUTLET VARIABLES AND ACCESSORS.** If you were planning to implement some means to disable the two menu items, Beep Once and Beep Twice, you would need to create two new outlets in VRMainWindowController, using the same technique you used in Step 5.2. You might call these new outlets `beep1MenuItem` and `beep2MenuItem`. Their type would be NSMenuItem. You would need to declare the variable and the accessor method in the header file and define the accessor method in the source file.

However, since you aren't going to let the user disable these menu items, you don't need outlets or accessor methods for them. You also don't need to create a data variable, because there is no data value associated with the command pop-down menu button, nor do you need a C enumeration type. For the same reason, you don't need notifications to update the control or an observer. All you need is action methods.

2. **ACTION METHODS.** You will create two action methods to carry out the commands issued by each of the two menu items in the command pop-down menu button. In the header file VRMainWindowController.h, after the State subsection of the ACTIONS section of the VRButtonController category, declare these two action methods and a timer method:

```
// Beeper
- (IBAction)beep1Action:(id)sender;
- (IBAction)beep2Action:(id)sender;
- (void)beepAgain:(NSTimer *)timer;
```

In the category source file VRButtonController.m, define the action methods and the timer method, after the **State** subsection at the end of the **ACTIONS** section, as shown below. **NSBeep()** is a Cocoa function that beeps using the user's preferred system alert sound.

Note that you create a separate action method here for each menu item, instead of relying on a C switch statement in a single action method connected to the menu button as a whole, as you did in the previous two steps. It may be advisable generally to use separate action methods.

```
// Beeper

- (IBAction)beep1Action:(id)sender {
    NSBeep();
}

- (IBAction)beep2Action:(id)sender {
    NSBeep();
    [NSTimer scheduledTimerWithTimeInterval:0.5
            target:self
            selector:@selector(beepAgain:)
            userInfo:nil
            repeats:NO];
}
```

```
- (void)beepAgain:(NSTimer *)timer {
    NSBeep();
    [timer invalidate];
}
```

In earlier versions of Mac OS X, multiple beeps in succession worked; that is, if you coded two calls to NSBeep() in succession, you would hear both beeps, one after the other. In recent versions of Mac OS X, this has stopped working. Stepping through the code in the debugger shows that both calls to NSBeep() executed, at least in the debugger environment, but at run time you heard only one. The same problem affected multiple successive beeps using AppleScript at the same time, so I suspect a system-level change is at work here. Nothing has been documented, however, so I'm not sure that it's a bug nor do I know that it will be fixed. I have therefore written a workaround here, using an NSTimer object to fire the second beep.

This is a very simple example of an NSTimer at work. When the user chooses Beep Twice from the pull-down menu, the beep2Action: action method beeps once, then it creates a timer object that will fire half a second later. When it fires, the timer object sends a beepAgain: message to the window controller (self), sending itself as the message's sole parameter so that the beepAgain: method has access to the timer. This is similar to the way an action message sends the sending user control or menu item as the sender parameter to the action method. The beepAgain: method beeps again, then it calls the timer's invalidate method to remove the timer. You actually don't need the invalidate command here, because nonrepeating timers invalidate themselves.

This was so easy, in fact, that Cocoa's NSobject provides a method that does it for you, performSelector:withObject:afterDelay:.

Providing a delay interval of half a second may be unsatisfactory in practice, in that it disregards the relative speeds of various machines and the relative lengths of various system alert sounds. But it is a simple solution for a problem that might go away, so you can live with it.

There are no undo or redo strings to be updated in the Localizable.strings file, nor is there any data to initialize, describe, or store or control update methods to invoke.

3. **HELP TAGS.** Add a Help tag to the pull-down menu button: "Test sound output." You cannot attach Help tags to individual menu items in Cocoa.

6.3 Read the Source Files into the Nib File and Connect the Actions

You must inform the nib file of the new actions you have created, then connect them to the new pull-down menu button's menu items.

1. In Interface Builder, select the Classes tab in the nib file window, then choose Classes > Read Files. In the resulting dialog, select the header file in which you have created the actions, VRMainWindowController.h, then click the Parse button.

2. Double-click the pull-down menu button to reveal its two menu items. Control-drag from each of the new menu items to the File's Owner icon in turn, and click the target in the left pane and the appropriate action in the right pane of the Outlets section in the Connections pane of the NSButton Info Panel. Then click the Connect button.

6.4 Build and Run the Application

Build and run the application to test the new pull-down menu button, listening for the beeps.

Step 7: Create Bevel Buttons to Navigate a Tab View

HIGHLIGHTS:

Placing an image and text on a bevel button

Creating a navigation button that appears on every tab view item in a tab view

Using a delegate method to disable navigation buttons when the first or last tab view item is selected

Bevel buttons are ordinary buttons, except that they are square, with or without rounded corners, and come in any size. Bevel buttons with square corners are useful when lined up to simulate a button bar. Bevel buttons usually hold an image or icon, and they can also contain text, generally placed below the image. The *Aqua Human Interface Guidelines* specify Label font for the button's text, which is 10-point Lucida Grande Regular.

In this step, you will create two rounded-corner bevel buttons that behave as push-buttons. They highlight momentarily when clicked but do not alter their permanent appearance, as a sticky button does. They will function as navigation buttons to take the user back to the previous pane or forward to the next pane in the tab view.

Two interesting techniques are used in this step.

First, you will make a single pair of navigation buttons, named Back and Next, appear as if they were separate buttons in each of the tab view items. This is done by the simple expedient of dropping them into the window instead of onto the tab view. You could place them to one side of the tab view, but by placing them in the same space occupied by the tab view and layering them in front of it, you can make it appear as if there are buttons in every tab view item.

Second, a delegate method is implemented, taking advantage of the ability of NSTabView to tell its delegate when a new tab view item has been selected and is about to come to the front. You need some means to disable the Back button when the first tab view item is selected, and to enable it when another tab view item is selected. Similarly, you need a means to disable the Next button when the last tab view item is selected, and to enable it when another tab view item is selected. Because tab view items can be selected in ways that don't involve clicking a navigation button—for example, by clicking any tab—you might think that disabling and enabling the navigation buttons would require adding code in more than one place. However, you can harness the power of delegation to do it all in a single, short method in the window controller. This will be your first significant encounter with a delegate method. Pay close attention, because it is an extraordinarily useful technique, used heavily throughout Cocoa.

7.1 Create Bevel Buttons in Interface Builder

Use Interface Builder to create two bevel buttons. When you are done with Step 7.1, they should look like **Figure 2.11** (their images may be different, depending on where you find suitable arrow images).

FIGURE 2.11 The bevel buttons for tab view item navigation.

1. From the Cocoa Views palette, drag the square-shaped, round-cornered bevel button bearing a Mac face to the main document window, then do it again so you have two of them. Don't drop them over the tab view. Instead, drop them in the empty area near the bottom-right corner of the window, to the right of the tab view. Their Mac faces will disappear along the way.

    In current versions of Interface Builder, the only way to install the buttons in the window where you want them is to drop them into an empty part of the window. Dropping them over the tab view instead would now force them to end up grouped in the selected tab view item, instead of falling through into the window as they used to do.

2. Now that they are in the window, drag both buttons to the left and drop them over the tab view so they end up side by side near its bottom-right corner. Because they reside in the window, not the tab view, you will not see Aqua guides to help you position them relative to the bottom and right edges of the tab view. However, if you select the rightmost bevel button and then hold down the Option key while moving the pointer toward the edges of the tab view, you will see markers disclosing its distance in pixels from every object. Memorize how far away it is from the right and bottom edges of the tab view and nudge it using the arrow keys until it is 20 pixels from each of these edges. Then drag the leftmost bevel button next to the first, using the Aqua guides to help you line it up with the other button and to determine how far apart they should be.

    While you're working in design mode, the buttons will disappear if you select either tab view item. But they will reappear and be available for editing if you select the window or if you select the tab view itself by clicking in the area to either side of the tabs near the view's top. When you choose File > Test Interface to test the window as if the application were running, you will see that both buttons remain visible no matter which tab view item you select. This is because you created them after you created the tab view, so they are layered in front of the tab view within the window. If you were to select them and choose Layout > Send to Back, they would no longer be visible while the application was running. If this happens, you can again change the layering order and bring them back into view by selecting the tab view and choosing Layout > Send to Back.

3. Find or create images of left and right arrows. They can be TIFF or PNG images (or GIF, which have more limited capability and present potential licensing issues) or any of a number of other graphic types. Consult the *Aqua Human Interface Guidelines* regarding the dimensions of the images. If you have nothing more suitable handy, use the two TIFF images in the Vermont Recipes downloadable project files.

    To install the images in your project, first save or drag the image files into the Vermont Recipes project folder in the Finder. Then choose Project > Add Files in Project Builder and add them to the Resources group in the Groups & Files pane of the main project window.

    If the images might require localization, you can place them in the appropriate language subfolder in the project folder instead, and a localization contractor can substitute other images in other language subfolders.

    In Mac OS X Public Beta and earlier, it was common to store images in the nib file, and you can still do this by setting an Interface Builder preference. It is now recommended, however, that you always store images in the project folder.

4. By adding the image files to the project, you made them automatically available to Interface Builder in the Images tab of the VRDocument.nib window. Drag the left arrow and right arrow images in turn from the Images pane of the VRDocument.nib window and drop them onto the left and right bevel buttons, respectively.

5. Select each button in turn and select the Attributes pane of the NSButton Info Panel. First make sure the lower-right button is selected in the Icon Position area of the Info Panel, in order to place the image near the top of the button to make room for the text you are about to add. Then make sure the centered button is selected in the Alignment area. Finally, type **Back** as the title for the left button and **Next** as the title for the right button. The text will appear in the buttons, below the arrow images.

6. Select the Back and Next text for editing in each button in turn. Choose Format > Font > Show Fonts to open the Fonts dialog, and verify that the font size of the button text is 10 points.

7.2 Write the Code for the Bevel Buttons in Project Builder

Use Project Builder to write the code.

1. **USER CONTROL OUTLET VARIABLES AND ACCESSORS.** Create two new outlets in VRMainWindowController, calling them **backButton** and **nextButton**. In the header file VRMainWindowController.m, declare them as follows:

```
// Navigation push buttons

IBOutlet NSButton *backButton;
IBOutlet NSButton *nextButton;
```

Still in the header file, declare accessor methods for these two instance variables as set forth below, at the top of the main **ACCESSORS** section. Do not declare them in the VRButtonController category because their use is not limited to the Buttons tab view item.

```
// Navigation push buttons

- (NSButton *)backButton;
- (NSButton *)nextButton;
```

Finally, in the source file VRMainWindowController.m, define the accessor methods as set forth below. You do not define them in the VRButtonController.m category source file for the reason just stated.

```
// Navigation push buttons

- (NSButton *)backButton {
    return backButton;
}

- (NSButton *)nextButton {
    return nextButton;
}
```

You don't need to create a data variable, because there is no data value associated with these buttons. For the same reason, you don't need a C enumeration type, a description method, notifications to update the buttons, or observers.

You will need to create two action methods, one to carry out the commands issued by each of the two navigation buttons. The action methods will tell the tab view to select the previous or next tab view item, respectively.

However, you haven't created an instance variable to enable you to talk to the tab view. You'll have to do that now, along with a related accessor method.

In the header file VRMainWindowController.h, above the **checkbox** variable declaration, add the following:

```
IBOutlet NSTabView *tabView;
```

Also in the header file, declare the accessor method above the **checkbox** accessor declaration at the top of the main ACCESSORS section, as follows:

```
- (NSTabView *)tabView;
```

In the source file VRMainWindowController.m., above the **checkbox** accessor definition at the top of the main ACCESSORS section, add this definition:

```
- (NSTabView *)tabView {
    return tabView;
}
```

2. **ACTION METHODS.** Now you can create the navigation button action methods. In the header file VRMainWindowController.h, at the end of the main class declarations section just before the VRButtonController category, add the following:

```
#pragma mark ACTIONS

// Navigation
- (IBAction)backAction:(id)sender;
- (IBAction)nextAction:(id)sender;
```

In the source file VRMainWindowController.m, define the action methods at the end of the file, as shown below. Again, these do not belong in the VRButtonController.m category source file.

```
#pragma mark ACTIONS


// Navigation


- (IBAction)backAction:(id)sender {
    [[self tabView] selectPreviousTabViewItem:sender];
}


- (IBAction)nextAction:(id)sender {
    [[self tabView] selectNextTabViewItem:sender];
}
```

NSTabView's `selectPreviousTabViewItem:` and `selectNextTabViewItem:` methods do nothing if there is no previous or next tab item, so you never have to worry about an error if the Back button is clicked while the first tab item is selected or if the Next button is clicked while the last tab item is selected.

Note that NSTabView implements a full set of methods for navigation among panes in a tab view, including methods to select the first tab view item, the last tab view item, and any tab view item by its index.

7.3 Implement a Delegate Method to Enable and Disable Bevel Buttons

Although the action methods will not cause an error if an attempt is made to navigate past the first or last tab view item, it is good user interface design to disable either button when the user can't navigate any farther in one direction or the other. To do this, you will implement in VRMainWindowController a delegate method provided for in NSTabView, `tabview:willSelectTabViewItem:`. If you haven't worked with the delegation capability of Objective-C before, you will find it to be an eye-opening and powerful feature of the language.

This delegate method is declared in NSTabView, because the designers of the Cocoa frameworks anticipated that developers might need to know when the user tries to switch to another tab view item. Whenever the user selects a new tab view item by any means—selecting a tab, choosing a pull-down menu item, or clicking a button, for example—this delegate method, built into NSTabView, will be invoked just before the selected tab view item is made visible. NSTabView, among other things, checks to see whether a delegate has been appointed and, if so, whether that delegate implements the `tabview:willSelectTabViewItem:` delegate method. If neither condition is met, the delegate method is not called. If, however, NSTabView discovers that a delegate has been appointed and that the delegate implements this method, then it is invoked. You, the developer, can use Interface Builder to appoint a delegate for NSTabView (here, you will appoint VRMainWindowController as the delegate), and you can implement the delegate method in this delegate and code it to do anything that will be useful when a user selects a new tab view item.

What your delegate method will do here, of course, is test whether the newly selected tab view item is the first or last and disable or enable one or both of the navigation buttons accordingly. Because of the power of delegation, you will only have to write one simple method, and Cocoa will see to it that it is invoked every time the user chooses a new tab view item by any means.

In the source file VRMainWindowController.m, define the delegate method at the end of the `WINDOW MANAGEMENT` section, as follows:

```
- (void)tabView:(NSTabView *)theTabView
      willSelectTabViewItem:(NSTabViewItem *)theTabViewItem {
   if (theTabView == [self tabView]) {
      [[self backButton] setEnabled:
            ([theTabView indexOfTabViewItem:theTabViewItem]
            > 0)];
      [[self nextButton] setEnabled:
            ([theTabView indexOfTabViewItem:theTabViewItem]
            + 1 < [theTabView numberOfTabViewItems])];
   }
}
```

You do not have to declare a delegate method in the header file, because Cocoa declares and invokes it for you.

This method first tests to make sure this is the same tab view. Your application might eventually include two or more tab views in the same window, and you want to know that Cocoa called the delegate method because it was this tab view in which the user selected a new tab view item.

It then calls the NSButton `setEnabled:` method twice. The `setEnabled:` method takes a Boolean parameter, enabling the control if the parameter's value is `YES` and disabling it if its value is `NO`. You want the Back button to become disabled when the user selects the leftmost tab view item, and to become enabled (in case it was in a disabled state) whenever the user selects any other tab view item. This is accomplished by testing the index of the selected tab view item to see whether it is greater than 0 (that is, it's not the leftmost tab); if so, `YES` is passed to `setEnabled:`, otherwise, `NO`. Similar logic applies to the Next button, but the selected tab view item's index is tested against the total count of tab view items to determine whether it is not the rightmost tab.

The beauty of all this is that it will continue to work without requiring any modification of the code after you add additional tab view items in any position within this tab view.

That's all there is to it, except for connecting things in Interface Builder. There are no undo or redo strings to update in the Localizable.strings file, there's no data to initialize or store, and there are no control update methods to invoke.

7.4 Read the Source Files into the Nib File and Connect the Actions

You must inform the nib file of the new outlets and actions you have created, then connect them to the associated objects.

1. In Interface Builder, select the Classes tab in the nib file window, then choose Classes > Read Files. In the resulting dialog, select the header file in which you have created outlets and actions, VRMainWindowController.h, then click the Parse button.

2. Control-drag from the tab view to the File's Owner icon in the VRDocument.nib window, select the built-in **delegate** outlet in the NSTabView Info Panel, and click the Connect button. When dragging, take care to drag from the tab view, not from any of the controls. Start the drag from any empty part of the tab view or from the open area beside the first or last tab in the area at the top of the tab view.

3. Control-drag from the File's Owner icon to the tab view, click its outlet name, **tabView**, in the NSButton Info Panel, and click the Connect button. When dragging to the tab view, be careful to end in the tab view, not one of the controls. Do this by ending the drag in any empty part of the tab view or the open area beside the first or last tab at the top of the tab view.

4. Control-drag from the File's Owner icon to each of the new bevel buttons in turn, and click its outlet name, **backButton** or **nextButton**, in the Info Panel, then click the Connect button.

5. Control-drag from each of the new bevel buttons to the File's Owner icon in turn, and click the target in the left pane and the appropriate action, **backAction** or **nextAction**, in the Info palette, then click the Connect button.

6. If the Buttons tab is going to be the initially selected tab when the document window is opened, the Next button should be disabled at the outset as long as

the Buttons pane is the last tab view item. Select the Next button and, in the NSButton Info Panel, uncheck Enabled. You will come back to change this later, when you add another tab view item.

7. Finally, since you have now fully populated the Buttons pane of the document window, step back and consider its overall arrangement. It's pretty ugly, but that's mainly because this is a set of disparate examples; there isn't a unifying theme or function to the pane.

However, you should do one thing to finish your effort so it complies with human interface guidelines. Mac OS X dialogs are supposed to gravitate toward the center, horizontally. So drag the original checkbox and the Pegs group box to the right until their right edges align with the right border of the Music group box; the Aqua guides make this especially easy. It's still ugly, but you'll do better in your real applications.

7.5 Build and Run the Application

Build and run the application. To test the new Back button, click it and note that the Text Boxes pane is selected. Then click the Next button and note that the Buttons pane is selected. In each case, confirm that the navigation buttons are disabled and enabled appropriately.

Conclusion

You are now done with Recipe 2. There are still more variants of buttons you can use in your application, but this recipe has given you enough of a start so that you can figure out how to create additional buttons in your application without help from me.

Although you have finished populating the Buttons tab view item with user controls, there is one important thing you haven't done with it: namely, setting the tab order of its several controls. You need to do this in every view that contains multiple user controls, because Mac OS X supports a system preference to use the keyboard for setting controls and navigating among them. However, the topic of tab order among controls is easier to visualize with text fields, because the tab order determines where the insertion point will appear. I will therefore defer this topic for the time being, taking it up in Recipe 4, Step 2.

In the next recipe, you will learn how to create a variety of sliders.

RECIPE 3

Sliders

This recipe is the second in a series of recipes dealing with user controls. In Recipe 2, you implemented a bunch of buttons. Here, you will learn about some slick sliders and you will get a brief introduction to text fields and alert sheets in the bargain.

Sliders are fun, in addition to being useful. They have a much more interactive and realistic feel than other controls, probably because of their graphical complexity and the continuous visual feedback they give you as you drag them back and forth or up and down. Also, they give you an instantaneous sense of scale that pure numbers lack. If a slider is set toward one end, you immediately sense that it represents something that is at, say, a fifth or a quarter of the range of available values. Where absolute precision doesn't matter, it is much easier to set a slider approximately where you want it than it is to type a number. With the addition of tick marks and the use of a discrete slider—one that snaps to integer values, say—you can also achieve accuracy easily.

Sliders provide the best of both worlds if you link them to a text field. The text field can report the slider's setting in exact numbers, and you can type a specific number in the text field and see the slider instantly snap to that setting. Cocoa provides a linking mechanism that causes the numbers in the text field to spin rapidly as you drag the slider, creating an extraordinarily responsive feel. You can also link sliders to buttons and other user controls. For example, you can provide buttons that instantly set the slider to its minimum and maximum positions or, say, to one-third and two-thirds positions. In this recipe, you will create some of these examples. When you have finished Recipe 3, the contents of a new Sliders tab will appear as shown in **Figure 3.1**. (The figure shows the tabs as they will be rearranged and renamed in Recipe 4.)

Before turning to Step 1, you should prepare your Info.plist Entries for Recipe 3. Simply change the build version to 3, as detailed in Recipe 2, Step 1.2. You should also change the `VRDocumentVersion` variable in VRDocument.m to 3, since you will change the document format to hold additional data values associated with the new controls.

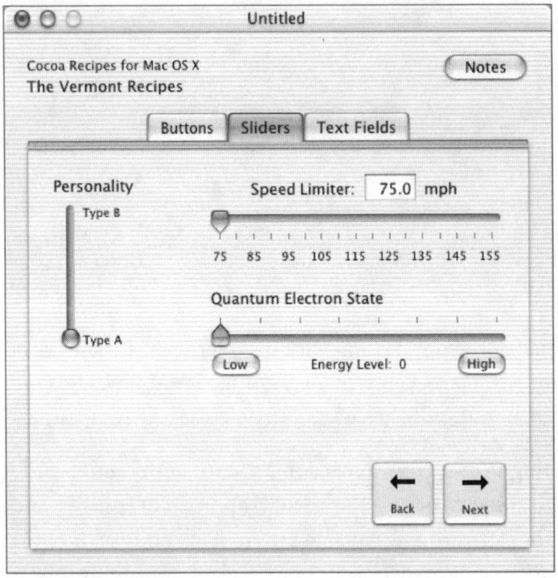

FIGURE 3.1 The finished Sliders tab view item.

Step 1: Create a Simple Slider

HIGHLIGHTS:

Adding a tab view item using Interface Builder

Adding a new model object and controller category

Presenting a simple document-modal sheet

Concatenating strings and formatting numbers using localized formatting conventions

In Step 1, you will create a simple vertical slider that returns a floating point value within a defined range after you drag it to a new setting. It will be adorned with a title and labels at top and bottom, but it will have no tick marks. The slider will describe a personality in a continuous range from Type A to Type B (never mind whether psychologists recognize a B+ or an A- personality type). You will add this control using the road map adopted in Recipe 2, Step 2.

You'll place the slider in a new tab view item that will hold the various sliders you'll create in Recipe 3. The technique for adding a tab view item in Interface Builder is described in Step 1.1, below. One interesting thing to note is that you do not have to update the code for disabling and enabling the navigation buttons you wrote in Recipe 2, Step 7—they work as is, without revision, no matter how many tab view items you might add.

You will also add a new model object to the project in Step 1.2, below, to continue the process begun in Recipe 1, Step 3.5, of compartmentalizing the application's code according to the tab view item in which a set of user controls appears. For the same reason, you will create a new category on VRMainWindowController to contain accessor, update, and action methods relating to the new controls, as you did for the Buttons tab view item in Recipe 2, Step 1.2.

So you can verify that the slider returns an appropriate value when you finish dragging it, the application will present a sheet reporting its final value. This is not something you would necessarily want to do in a real-world application; instead, you might provide a text field to present the value, as you will do later, in Step 2, or you might simply rely on the slider itself as a sufficient presentation of the data. Here, however, a sheet will give you an introduction to the topic of alert sheets in Cocoa, in addition to giving you some reassurance that the slider is working correctly. The code for the sheet appears in Step 1.3, below. It makes use of an important Cocoa method, the NSString `localizedStringWithFormat:` method, which you will use frequently throughout your applications.

1.1 Create a New Tab View Item and a Slider in Interface Builder

Use Interface Builder to add a tab view item to the existing tab view and place a new vertical slider in it with a title and labels. When you are done with Step 1.1, the group should look like that shown in **Figure 3.2**.

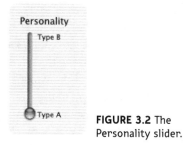

FIGURE 3.2 The Personality slider.

1. Using VRDocument.nib in Interface Builder, select the tab view (not a tab view item) in the document window by clicking in empty space anywhere in the tab view or on either side of the existing tabs. In the NSTabView Info Panel, type **3** in the Number of Items box and press Enter. A third tab appears to the right of the two existing tabs. Double-click the new tab twice to edit its label, then type **Sliders**. When you press Enter or click elsewhere in the window, the tab resizes so the new label will fit, and the three tabs center themselves as a group. Click once outside the tab view, and the two navigation buttons you created in Recipe 2 appear. The Next button remains disabled; you might as well leave it that way for now.

2. With the new Sliders tab view item selected, drag the rightmost vertical slider from the Other palette onto the Sliders pane and place it in the upper-left corner. Leave room above it for a title. In the NSSlider Info Panel, leave all but one of the Attributes set as you find them, including a range from **0.0** to **100.0** and the number of tick markers set to **0**. However, you should uncheck the Continuous option. There is no need for this control to send its action method continuously as the slider is dragged up and down; it only needs to set its associated instance variable when the drag is completed. Also, in Step 1.3, below, you will add a statement to the slider's action method to present a sheet, and you want the sheet to appear only after the drag is completed.

3. Drag the System Font Text item from the Views palette and place it above the slider, using the guides to place it in the top-left corner of the tab view item. Type **Personality** and choose Layout > Size to Fit. Make sure that the Editable and Selectable checkboxes in the Options area of the NSTextField Info Panel are unchecked and that the Enabled checkbox is checked.

4. Drag the Label Font Text item from the Views palette and place it to the right of the slider at its bottom, using the Aqua guides to position it properly. Rename it **Type A** and choose Layout > Size to Fit. For vertical sliders, the minimum value is always at the bottom. Uncheck the Editable and Selectable checkboxes and check the Enabled checkbox, if necessary.

5. Duplicate the Type A label by Option-dragging a copy of it to the top of the slider, and rename it **Type B**.

6. Reposition all the new items to comply with human interface guidelines. First, drag each label and position it, according to the guides, relative to the top and bottom of the slider. Next, select both labels and the slider and choose Layout > Group. Finally, select the title, Shift-click to add the slider group to the selection, and choose Layout > Alignment > Align Vertical Centers to center the slider group beneath its title.

7. Select all the new items, then choose Layout > Ungroup, immediately followed by Layout > Group. Now you can drag the new items as a group without selecting them individually and without disrupting their relative positions.

1.2 Create a New Model Class for Sliders

Before writing the code for the slider, you have to create a new model class and a new controller category. Start with the model class, following the pattern of the first three instructions in Recipe 1, Step 3.5, and some instructions that came later in Recipe 1.

1. Following the instructions in Recipe 1, Step 3.5.1, create a new class and name it **VRSliderModel**.

   Now you have two header files and two source files for models, and you will create still more in later recipes. To help keep everything straight in the project and in your mind, create a new group called Models within the Classes group in the Groups & Files pane, using the Project > New Group command, and drag both the VRButtonModel and the VRSliderModel header and source files into it.

2. Following the instructions in Recipe 1, Step 3.5.2, write initialization code into the VRSliderModel class. The code in both the header and the source files should be identical to that used in VRButtonModel.

   You may want to include the **NSLog()** call, bracketed in preprocessor directives, that you learned about in Recipe 1, Step 10.2.

3. In addition to the document accessor method, you must also add an **undoManager** accessor method in both the header and the source file of the VRSliderModel class, as you did for the VRButtonModel class in Recipe 1, Step 6.1.

4. Following the instructions in Recipe 1, Step 3.5.3, write code in the VRDocument class to instantiate a VRSliderModel object whenever a new document is created. You will, of course, write all references to a model object in the new code as references to the new VRSliderModel object. Simply add one line to the **init** and **dealloc** methods to allocate and deallocate the Slider model object, just as you did with the Button model object.

1.3 Create a New Window Controller Category for Sliders

Next, create a new category on VRMainWindowController following the relevant instructions in Recipe 2, Step 1.2, calling it **VRSliderController**. There isn't yet any code for the new slider you added in Step 1.1, above, so ignore any instructions you find in Recipe 2 regarding controller methods.

1. Your principal tasks here are to declare the interface part of a new controller category in the existing VRMainWindowController.h header file and to create a new source file for the VRSliderController implementation part, called VRSliderController.m. Remember, you do not need a VRSliderController.h header file because all of the window controller categories' declarations are combined in VRMainWindowController.h. You should replace any references to VRButtonModel and VRButtonController that you find in Recipe 2, Step 1.2, with references to VRSliderModel and VRSliderController.

2. Be sure to import the correct header files. Also insert the window management methods described in Instructions 7, 8, and 9 of Recipe 2, Step 1.2, but refer to the Sliders tab view item instead of the Buttons tab view item.

3. Add code to the VRSliderController category to allow it to communicate with the new VRSliderModel model object, using the instructions in Recipe 1, Step 3.5.5. Be careful to interpret those instructions so as to place code in the category, not in the main body of VRMainWindowController as you were instructed to do at that point in the development of the application. However, the forward declaration of `@class VRSliderModel` does go at the top of the VRMainWindowController.h header file.

4. To help manage your files, create a new group in the Groups & Files pane called Window Controllers, and move all of the VRMainWindowController files into it.

5. It would be a good idea to build the application before proceeding, just to make sure you added all the correct imports, forward declarations, instance variables, and methods. If you receive any error messages, review the code in VRButtonModel and VRButtonController to discover what you left out of their Slider counterparts. If you get stuck, download the complete Vermont Recipes project files at the Stepwise Web site, www.stepwise.com, and see what the slider controller category should look like.

1.4 Write the Code for the Slider in Project Builder

Use Project Builder to write the code required to make the new slider work.

1. **USER CONTROL OUTLET VARIABLES AND ACCESSORS.** In the header file VRMainWindowController.h, declare an outlet variable after the existing variable declarations near the top of the file, as follows:

```
// Personality slider
IBOutlet NSSlider *personalitySlider;
```

Still in MyWindowController.h, also declare an accessor method for the outlet at the end of the ACCESSORS section of the new VRSliderController category at the bottom of the file, as follows:

```
// Personality slider
- (NSSlider *)personalitySlider
```

Turn to the new category source file VRSliderController.m and define the accessor method at the end of the ACCESSORS section, as follows:

```
// Personality slider

- (NSSlider *)personalitySlider {
    return personalitySlider;
}
```

2. **DATA VARIABLES AND ACCESSORS.** In the header file VRSliderModel.h, declare a new instance variable after the existing instance variable declarations, as shown below. The data type represented by a slider is the C float type.

```
// Personality
float personalityValue;
```

Still in VRSliderModel.h, also declare the corresponding accessor methods at the end of the ACCESSORS section, as follows:

```
// Personality

- (void) setPersonalityValue:(float)inValue;
- (float) personalityValue;
```

In the source file VRSliderModel.m, define the accessor methods at the end of the ACCESSORS section, as follows:

```
// Personality

- (void) setPersonalityValue:(float)inValue {
    [[[self undoManager] prepareWithInvocationTarget:self]
        setPersonalityValue:personalityValue];
    personalityValue = inValue;
    [[NSNotificationCenter defaultCenter] postNotificationName:
        VRSliderModelPersonalityValueChangedNotification
        object:[self document]];
}

- (float)personalityValue {
    return personalityValue;
}
```

3. **NOTIFICATION VARIABLES.** Return to the header file VRSliderModel.h, after the @end directive at the bottom of the file, to declare the notification variable, as follows:

```
#pragma mark NOTIFICATIONS

// Personality
extern NSString
    *VRSliderModelPersonalityValueChangedNotification;
```

Turn back to the source file VRSliderModel.m, above the **@implementation** directive near the top of the file, to define the notification variable, as follows:

```
#pragma mark NOTIFICATIONS

// Personality
NSString *VRSliderModelPersonalityValueChangedNotification =
    @"SliderModel personalityValue Changed Notification";
```

4. **GUI UPDATE METHODS.** In the header file VRMainWindowController.h, declare a specific interface update method after the ACCESSORS section of the VRSliderController category, as follows:

```
#pragma mark INTERFACE MANAGEMENT - Specific updaters

// Personality
- (void)updatePersonalitySlider:(NSNotification *)notification;
```

In the category source file VRSliderController.m, define this specific update method after the ACCESSORS section, as follows:

```
#pragma mark INTERFACE MANAGEMENT - Specific updaters

// Personality

- (void)updatePersonalitySlider:(NSNotification *)notification {
    [self updateSlider:[self personalitySlider]
          setting:[[self sliderModel] personalityValue]];
}
```

As you see, a new generic updater is required for sliders. In the header file VRMainWindowController.h, declare an interface update method at the end of the "INTERFACE MANAGEMENT - Generic updaters" section, as follows:

```
- (void)updateSlider:(NSSlider *)control setting:(float)inValue;
```

In the source file VRMainWindowController.m, define this update method at the end of the "INTERFACE MANAGEMENT - Generic updaters" section, as follows:

```
- (void)updateSlider:(NSSlider *)control setting:(float)inValue {
    if (inValue != [control floatValue]) {
        [control setFloatValue:inValue];
    }
}
```

5. **NOTIFICATION OBSERVERS.** To register the window controller as an observer of the notification that will trigger the updater method, insert the following statement in the **registerNotificationObserversForSlidersTab** method of the category source file VRSliderController.m:

```
// Personality
[[NSNotificationCenter defaultCenter] addObserver:self
        selector:@selector(updatePersonalitySlider:)
        name:VRSliderModelPersonalityValueChangedNotification
        object:[self document]];
```

6. **ACTION METHODS.** In the header file VRMainWindowController.h, after the WINDOW MANAGEMENT section at the end of the VRSliderController category, add the following:

```
#pragma mark ACTIONS

// Personality
- (IBAction)personalityAction:(id)sender;
```

In the category source file VRSliderController.m, define the action method after the WINDOW MANAGEMENT section, as follows:

```
#pragma mark ACTIONS

// Personality

- (IBAction)personalityAction:(id)sender {
    [[self sliderModel]
            setPersonalityValue:[sender floatValue]];
    [[[self document] undoManager] setActionName:
            NSLocalizedString(@"Set Personality",
            @"Name of undo/redo menu item after \
            Personality slider was set")];
}
```

7. **LOCALIZABLE.STRINGS.** Update the Localizable.strings file by adding Set Personality.

8. **INITIALIZATION.** Leave the Personality data variable uninitialized. Objective-C will initialize it to 0, which in this case stands for a Type A personality.

9. **DATA STORAGE.** In the source file VRSliderModel.m, define the following key at the end of the file:

```
#pragma mark STORAGE

// Keys and values for dictionary

// Personality
static NSString *VRPersonalityValueKey =
    @"VRSliderModelPersonalityValue";
```

Immediately after that, add this method definition:

```
// Saving information to persistent storage:

- (void)addDataToDictionary:(NSMutableDictionary *)dictionary {

    // Personality
    [dictionary setObject:[NSString stringWithFormat:@"%f",
        [self personalityValue]]
        forKey:VRPersonalityValueKey];
}
```

Add this method definition at the end of the file:

```
// Loading information from persistent storage

- (void)restoreDataFromDictionary:(NSDictionary *)dictionary {
    [[self undoManager] disableUndoRegistration];

    // Personality
    [self setPersonalityValue:[[dictionary objectForKey:
        VRPersonalityValueKey] floatValue]];

    [[self undoManager] enableUndoRegistration];
}
```

Since you are working with a new pair of header and source files for the VRSliderModel class, you also have to declare these storage methods in the header file. Add the following declarations at the end of VRSliderModel.h:

```
#pragma mark STORAGE

// Saving information to persistent storage:

- (void)addDataToDictionary:(NSMutableDictionary *)dictionary;
```

```
// Loading information from persistent storage
```

```
- (void)restoreDataFromDictionary:(NSDictionary *)dictionary:
```

Finally, you must add calls to these two storage methods in VRDocument.m, in the **dictionaryFromModel** and **readFromFile:ofType:** methods, respectively. In the **dictionaryFromModel** method, add this line immediately following its **buttonModel** look-alike:

```
[[self sliderModel] addDataToDictionary:dictionary];
```

In the **readFromFile:ofType:** method, add this line immediately following its **buttonModel** equivalent:

```
[[self sliderModel] restoreDataFromDictionary:dictionary];
```

10. **GUI UPDATE METHOD INVOCATION.** In the category source file VRSlider-Controller.m, add the following call at the end of the **updateSlidersTab** method:

```
// Personality
[self updatePersonalitySlider:nil];
```

11. **DESCRIPTION METHOD.** Add a **description** method to VRSliderModel for debugging use. You have learned many ways to convert a value to a string for display in human-readable form. Here, you will learn yet another. Instead of creating a new category method on NSString or using the NSString **stringWithFormat:** class method, you will use some methods from the NSNumber class.

```
#pragma mark DEBUGGING
```

```
- (NSString *) description {
    return [NSString stringWithFormat:@"%@\
\n\tpersonalityValue:%@\n",
        [super description],
        [[NSNumber numberWithFloat:
            [self personalityValue]] stringValue]];
}
```

First, the NSNumber class method **numberWithFloat:** is used to capture the float value represented by the slider, converting it from a standard C type to an NSNumber object type. Then NSNumber's instance method **stringValue** is called to express the value of the new NSNumber object as a string. As a bonus, the string will automatically be formatted according to the conventions of the current locale for displaying floating-point numbers. You will use NSNumber frequently in your programs because it offers capabilities such as this for all standard C numeric types, as well as for Boolean values.

If you implement an NSLog() call in the setPersonalityValue: accessor method, it would be appropriate to use the same NSNumber message to display the value in StdIO.

Note that you did not use this technique in the data storage routines, above. You want your document files to be readable in any country no matter where they are created, so it wouldn't do to save them with numbers in localized format.

12. **HELP TAGS.** Using Interface Builder, provide a Help tag for the slider: "Guess your personality type."

1.5 Implement an Alert Sheet

To enable you to verify that the slider set the data variable to an appropriate value (that is, between 0.0 and 100.0), you will now modify the slider's action method so that it presents a sheet reporting the value every time it changes. This is why you unchecked the Continuous attribute of the slider in Step 1.1, above: You don't want the alert to be presented immediately when you begin dragging the slider but only after the drag is completed.

The key feature of sheets is that they are *document modal;* that is, a user can't do anything in the document window to which a sheet is attached while it is pending. A user can nevertheless continue to work in other windows within the application as well as in other applications. Because the sheet remains attached to the window whose slider was set, the user will have no doubt about which window's slider value the alert is reporting even if many other windows are open at once.

Presenting an alert sheet for the purpose of displaying a slider's value is questionable interface design. Besides, if you have been implementing an NSLog() call in every set accessor method, you have a ready means of verifying that the slider is working, anyway; just run the application in Project Builder and look at the StdIO pane after dragging the slider. In a real application, however, this sheet could be used to present a warning to the user if, say, the value chosen using the slider was incompatible with some other setting. I will present a dummy warning message designed to do something like this here, with confidence that everybody will get the joke in the message. I wanted an excuse to demonstrate sheets, anyway. When Steve Jobs first demonstrated Mac OS X to the public, sheets were among the features that received loud acclaim.

For history buffs, the NSBeginAlertSheet() function used here was introduced in Developer Preview 4 and, by the time of the initial public release of Mac OS X, had replaced the deprecated NSRunAlertPanelRelativeToWindow() function. Documentation for the new function was sparse until recently. It is declared in NSPanel.h, where you will find some cryptic comments regarding its use, and there is some relevant discussion in the Developer Preview 4 and Public Beta AppKit Release Notes, under the heading

"Document-Modal API." More recently, the documentation in the Functions section of the AppKit reference is quite thorough.

The invocation here is the simplest possible, providing information to the user but offering no alternative course of action. It makes no use of the modal delegate or other available parameters, but simply goes away when the user clicks OK. You will learn about these more complex features of sheets, including how to provide multiple buttons and respond to the user's selection, in Recipe 5. For now, just passing NULL or nil in most of the parameters does the trick.

Go back to the slider's action method definition in VRSliderController.m and add the following statements calling the Cocoa NSBeginAlertSheet() function, at the end of the method:

```
{
    NSString *alertMessage =
        [NSString localizedStringWithFormat:
        NSLocalizedString(@"The personality type %f is not \
        compatible with a computer programming career.",
        @"Message text of alert posed by Personality slider \
        to report value set by user"),
        [[self sliderModel] personalityValue]];

    NSString *alertInformation = NSLocalizedString
        (@"0 is Type A, 100 is Type B.", @"Informative text \
        of alert posed by Personality slider to report value \
        set by user");

    NSBeginAlertSheet(alertMessage,
        nil, nil, nil, [self window],
        nil, NULL, NULL, nil, alertInformation);
}
```

Most Cocoa developers declare local variables such as alertMessage and alertInformation at the beginning of a method, then use them elsewhere in the method as needed. This practice grew up because the GCC compiler historically required all variables to be declared at the beginning of an Objective-C code block. Cocoa newcomers often overlooked the fact that this rule allowed you to declare local variables at the beginning of any block, not just at the beginning of a method. You could therefore use curly braces, as here, to create an otherwise pointless block allowing declaration of local variables after other statements within a method.

Now, however, with the new GCC 3.1 compiler in Mac OS X 10.2, the restriction has been removed and you can declare variables anywhere in a method. This is welcome news for developers with backgrounds in other languages where this has always been allowed, because it permits you to group declarations with the code that uses them in a much more intuitive and readable manner. You may therefore remove the enclosing braces from the code shown above if you are working in Mac OS X 10.2 or newer. Doing so will, of course, mean your code won't compile under old versions of the developer tools.

Note the use of the NSString `localizedStringWithFormat:` class method. This is a method you will make heavy use of in your Cocoa applications, as you will its companion method, `stringWithFormat:`. They provide concatenation of multiple string values and, in the case of the former, localization of many data types. Just pass in a formatting string followed by any number of values or variables, separated by commas, and include placeholders for each of the values in the formatting string (such as `%f` for a floating-point value). String versions of the values in the order given will fill the placeholders. The `localizedStringWithFormat:` method is appropriate when one or more of the values you want to convert is a numeric value and you want to use the numeric formatting conventions of the particular computer's locale as set in System Preferences (in many countries, for example, the thousands separator is a period and the decimal separator is a comma).

You are already familiar with the `NSLocalizedString()` function from Recipe 1, Step 3.1.4. You have used it repeatedly when naming undo and redo strings using localization key-value pairs from the Localizable.strings file. Here, you use it for a similar purpose, providing internationalized strings for the message and information text in a sheet. Be sure to put the key-value pairs in the Localizable.strings file now, as shown below. Notice that the printf-style placeholder `%f` continues to serve its purpose even though it is passed through the Localizable.strings file (assuming the localization contractor includes it in the new localized string).

```
/* Alert strings */

/* Personality slider alert */
/* Message text of alert posed by Personality slider to report value
set by user */
"The personality type %f is not compatible with a computer programming
career." = "The personality type %f is not compatible with a computer
programming career.";
/* Informative text of alert posed by Personality slider to report
value set by user */
"0 is Type A, 100 is Type B." = "0 is Type A, 100 is Type B.";
```

1.6 Read the Source Files into the Nib File and Connect Outlets and Actions

Inform the nib file of the new outlet and action you have created in the code files, then connect them to the new slider.

1. In Interface Builder, select the Classes tab in the nib file window, then choose Classes > Read Files. In the resulting dialog, select the header file in which you have created outlets or actions, VRMainWindowController.h, then click the Parse button.

2. Select the Instances tab, Control-drag from the File's Owner icon to the new slider, click its outlet name, and click the Connect button in the Connections pane of the File's Owner Info Panel.

3. Control-drag from the new slider to the File's Owner icon, click the target in the left pane and the appropriate action in the right pane of the Outlets section in the Connections pane of the NSSlider Info Panel, and click the Connect button.

4. In the Attributes pane of the NSSlider Info Panel, set the current value of the slider to 0.0, since the corresponding data variable was left at the default initialization value of 0.0.

1.7 Build and Run the Application

Build and run the application to test the slider. Be sure to explore how undo and redo work, and make sure changes can be saved to disk, restored, and reverted properly.

Also open several windows at once and exercise the slider in each, to confirm that you can leave the sheet open and still switch to another window and open its sheet as well. Note which buttons and menu items are disabled while a sheet is pending, and notice that if you try to quit the application while a sheet is pending, nothing happens. This is correct Mac OS X application behavior with regard to sheets.

If you harbor some lingering doubts about the internationalized key-value pairs used in the Personality slider alert sheet, you do not have to travel to an exotic country or hire a localization contractor to test it. Just change the value associated with the key in your own Localizable.strings file by adding some garbage text while leaving the key unchanged. Then run the application and set a new Personality value. You will now see your garbage text in the alert that's presented. (Don't forget to change the value in the Localizable.strings file back to its original text after completing this experiment.)

Finally, test the navigation buttons you added in Recipe 2, Step 7. Confirm that they disable and enable themselves at the right times, even though you have added a tab view item in this step without updating the code for the navigation buttons.

Step 2: Create a Continuous Slider with an Interactive Text Field

HIGHLIGHTS:

Setting an editable text field from a slider's value continuously as the slider is dragged

Setting a slider from an editable text field

Using a formatter to constrain text entry to a floating-point value within a predefined range

In this step, you will create a horizontal slider with labeled tick marks. It will return a floating-point value within a predefined range, as in Step 1, but the range does not start at 0.0 and must therefore be explicitly initialized. The slider will allow you to set the automatic speed limiter on your Porsche Boxster to a safe and conservative value (Boxster not included).

The slider in this step is associated with a text field, which is a much more useful device than the sheet you used in Step 1 to communicate the final value set by the slider. The value in the text field will always reflect the value of the slider, changing rapidly as the user drags the slider back and forth. For those who prefer to type, you can enter a value in the text field and the slider will snap to the indicated value when you press the Enter key.

This is your first editable text field. It no doubt occurs to you that you may run into a problem if the user types something into the field that isn't a number, such as the word *fast*. The text field is supposed to accept only floating-point numbers. You will therefore associate a Cocoa NSFormatter object with the field to apply the desired constraints on text entry. A formatter can be very complex, but in this introduction to the topic you will find it easy to use one of the two formatters supplied with Cocoa.

The formatter will cause the text field to beep if the user attempts to enter an illegal value (an out-of-range value or text that isn't a valid number). This is adequate for experienced users, but you might not want to leave less-experienced users guessing about what went wrong. You should therefore consider presenting an alert sheet to explain what the problem is and provide an easy way out. However, the alert sheet you would need here is considerably more complex than the simple sheet you created in Step 1. It should provide additional buttons to let the user cancel an illegal entry or substitute the minimum or maximum value for an out-of-range value. You will therefore defer creating the more complex sheet until Recipe 5, concentrating for now on getting the formatter working.

2.1 Create a Slider and an Interactive Text Field in Interface Builder

Use Interface Builder to create a new horizontal slider with a title, tick marks, and labels, along with an associated text field and its label. When you are done with Step 2.1, the group should look like that shown in **Figure 3.3**.

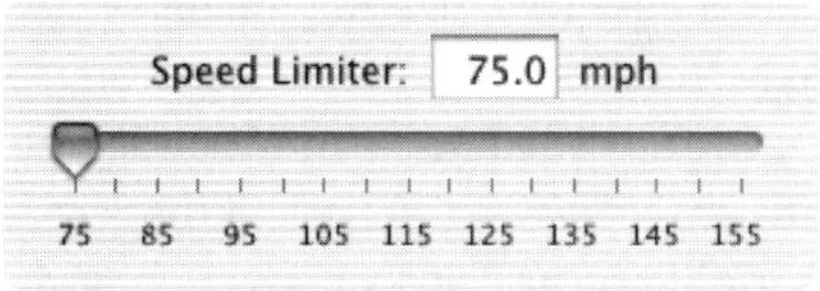

FIGURE 3.3 The Speed Limiter slider and text field.

1. With the Sliders tab view item selected, drag the topmost horizontal slider from the Other palette onto the Sliders pane and place it in the upper-right area of the pane. Drag its left resize handle to the left to make it longer. In the NSSlider Info Panel, type **75.0** as the Minimum Value and **155.0** as the Maximum Value (the current value should automatically assume a value within that range, but type **75.0** for the Current Value, if necessary); check the Continuous checkbox; set the Number of Markers to **17** with Position Below; and uncheck Marker Values Only. This slider must be a *continuous* slider, sending its action message repeatedly as it is dragged back and forth, to update the associated text field while the drag is under way; you will see how this is done in Step 2.3, below.

2. Drag the System Font Text item from the Cocoa Views palette to the Sliders pane twice, naming one **Speed Limiter:** (note the colon) and the other **mph**. Position them above the slider, leaving space between them for a small text field. Choose Layout > Size to Fit, if necessary, to make the entire longer text item visible and to shrink the shorter text item, and line them up on the same text baseline.

3. Drag an NSTextField item from the Cocoa Views palette and position it between the Speed Limiter: and mph labels. Select the text field and type **155.0** as a guide to sizing and positioning the text field so the largest value fits. Then choose Layout > Size to Fit. With the 155.0 text field selected, click the right-alignment button in the NSTextField Info Panel's Attributes pane. Finally, type **75.0** as its default value.

4. Select the Speed Limiter:, 75.0, and mph text fields, and choose Layout > Alignment > Align Baselines. Drag or nudge the 75.0 and mph text fields until the Aqua guides tell you they are separated from one another and from the Speed Limiter: text field by the proper amounts. Then select all three of them and choose Layout > Group.

5. Drag the Label Font Text item to the Sliders pane once, type to replace it with 75, and position it beneath the leftmost tick mark. Create additional mph labels by Option-dragging to duplicate the 75 label; typing 85, 95, 105, 115, 125, 135, 145, and 155, respectively; and positioning each approximately beneath the appropriate tick mark (each tick mark denotes a 5-mph increment).

   Use the Aqua guides to position the first and last labels the correct distance beneath the slider and centered under the left and right tick marks of the slider, respectively. Then select all of the labels and choose Layout > Alignment > Align Baselines to line them up. Using the NSTextField Info Panel, first center the text of each label within its text field, using the Attributes pane, then set the width of all the labels so they are all as wide as the widest label, using the Size pane. Finally, choose Layout > Alignment > Alignment Panel, choose Center from the Align pop-up menu, and select the leftmost button in the Spread area. Since the text of the tick mark labels is of different lengths, you had to center each of them in a standard-width text field before spreading them out. By centering the 75 and 155 labels under their respective tick marks and then spreading the others evenly between them, you caused each of the labels to be centered exactly under its own tick mark.

   Once you have them positioned to your satisfaction, select all of them and the slider and choose Layout > Group.

6. Drag the Speed Limiter: group to the proper distance above the slider. Then Shift-click to add the slider and its tick mark labels to the selection and choose Layout > Alignment > Align Vertical Centers.

7. Select all of the new items, then choose Layout > Ungroup, followed immediately by Layout > Group. Now you can drag the slider and all of its associated items as a group without selecting all of them. This is especially important given how much work you did to line up the tick mark labels.

8. Drag to position the slider group in the upper-right corner of the tab view item so it complies with human interface guidelines.

9. For each of the static text fields, use the NSTextField Info Panel to uncheck the Editable and Selectable checkboxes in the Options area, and check the Enabled checkbox, if necessary.

2.2 Write the Code for the Slider and Text Field in Project Builder

Use Project Builder to write the code required to make the new slider and text field work.

1. **USER CONTROL OUTLET VARIABLES AND ACCESSORS.** In the header file VRMainWindowController.h, declare instance variables after the existing variable declarations near the top of the file, as follows:

```
// Speed slider
IBOutlet NSSlider *speedSlider;
IBOutlet NSTextField *speedTextField;
```

Still in VRMainWindowController.h, declare accessor methods for these instance variables at the end of the ACCESSORS section of the VRSliderController category near the bottom of the file, as follows:

```
// Speed slider
- (NSSlider *)speedSlider;
- (NSTextField *)speedTextField;
```

Turn to the category source file VRSliderController.m and define the accessor methods at the end of the ACCESSORS section, as follows:

```
// Speed slider

- (NSSlider *)speedSlider {
    return speedSlider;
}

- (NSTextField *)speedTextField {
    return speedTextField;
}
```

2. **DATA VARIABLES AND ACCESSORS.** In the header file VRSliderModel.h, declare a new variable after the existing variable declarations, as shown below. You need only the one data variable, because both of the new user controls—the slider and its associated 75.0 text field—represent the same value.

```
// Speed
float speedValue;
```

In VRSliderModel.h, also declare the corresponding accessor methods at the end of the ACCESSORS section, as follows:

// Speed

```
- (void) setSpeedValue:(float)inValue;
- (float) speedValue;
```

In the source file VRSliderModel.m, define the accessor methods at the end of the ACCESSORS section, as set forth below. Include an NSLog() call in the set accessor if you are following that practice, using the NSNumber numberWithFloat: class method about which you learned in the previous step.

// Speed

```
- (void) setSpeedValue:(float)inValue {
    [[[self undoManager] prepareWithInvocationTarget:self]
        setSpeedValue:speedValue];
    speedValue = inValue;
    [[NSNotificationCenter defaultCenter] postNotificationName:
        VRSliderModelSpeedValueChangedNotification
        object:[self document]];
#ifndef VR_BLOCK_LOGS
    NSLog(@"\n\tExiting [VRsliderModel setSpeedValue:], \
        speedValue:%@\n", [[NSNumber numberWithFloat:
        [self speedValue]] stringValue]);
#endif}

- (float)speedValue {
    return speedValue;
}
```

3. **NOTIFICATION VARIABLES.** In the header file VRSliderModel.h, at the bottom of the file, declare the notification variable, as follows:

```
// Speed
extern NSString *VRsliderModelSpeedValueChangedNotification;
```

In the source file VRSliderModel.m, near the top of the file, define the notification variable, as follows:

```
// Speed
NSString *VRsliderModelSpeedValueChangedNotification =
    @"SliderModel speedValue Changed Notification";
```

4. **GUI UPDATE METHODS.** In the header file VRMainWindowController.h, declare specific updater methods at the end of the "INTERFACE MANAGEMENT - Specific updaters" section of the VRSliderController category, as follows:

```
// Speed
- (void)updateSpeedSlider:(NSNotification *)notification;
- (void)updateSpeedTextField:(NSNotification *)notification;
```

In the category source file VRSliderController.m, define these methods at the end of the "INTERFACE MANAGEMENT - Specific updaters" section, as follows:

```
// Speed

- (void)updateSpeedSlider:(NSNotification *)notification {
    [self updateSlider:[self speedSlider]
          setting:[[self sliderModel] speedValue]];
}

- (void)updateSpeedTextField:(NSNotification *)notification {
    if (([[self sliderModel] speedValue] !=
          [[self speedTextField] floatValue]) ||
          ([[[self speedTextField] stringValue]
          isEqualToString:@""])) {
        [[self speedTextField] setFloatValue:
              [[self sliderModel] speedValue]];

    }
}
```

Here, in the **updateSpeedTextField:** method, you don't call a generic text field updater method, as you have done with all of the other specific updater methods until now. The reason for this is that the cell contained in a text field is capable of receiving values of many types. The incoming value might be a string, or it might be a C value such as a **float** or an **int**, or it might be an object of some type, such as NSDecimalNumber or NSCalendarDate. To set the value of a text field, you might therefore use a variety of methods, such as **setFloatValue:**, **setIntValue:**, or **setObjectValue:**. It doesn't make as much sense to apply your specific-generic updater scheme to text fields as it does to, say, checkboxes and radio buttons, because you might end up with as many generic methods as you have specific methods. Although it may make sense to use a generic method in an application that has multiple text fields holding the same type of value, this is not the case with Vermont Recipes.

When you set a text field to hold a particular type of data, it automatically converts the data to a corresponding Foundation object, such as NSNumber, NSString, or NSCalendarDate. A text field knows how to convert the cell's object into a formatted string for display in its cell, and it knows how to convert a string typed in the text field by a user into an object of that type. It converts incoming data into a corresponding Foundation object using NSCell's **setObjectValue:** method behind the scenes. By connecting a custom formatter to the text field—you will learn how to do this in Recipe 6—you can customize the text field's ability to convert between object and formatted string values.

Recall that the original point of setting up the specific-generic updater scheme was to allow you to incorporate a test once in the generic updater, instead of doing so in every specific updater, to avoid having to update a user control onscreen and register with the undo manager if its old value was the same as its new value. Since you won't be using a generic updater for text fields, you have to include the test in every specific text field updater, as you just did in the `updateSpeedTextField:` specific updater method. The test compares the `float` value returned by the Slider model object's `speedValue` accessor method with the Speed Slider text field's `floatValue` method, implemented in the text field's superclass, NSControl. In the case of a text field with a connected formatter, NSControl obtains the latter behind the scenes from the `getObjectValue:forString:errorDescription:` method of the formatter.

In a final tweak, you also have to test whether the text field is empty, as it will be when the document is first opened, and update the field if it is. This does nothing when the text field holds a default value other than `0`, as it does in the case of the Speed Limiter text field, because the inequality test will establish that the default data value is not equal to the initially empty text field value, and the field will be updated anyway. However, in text fields you will create later, where the initial data value and the text field are both `0`, the field would not be updated to display the initial `0` value if it weren't for this additional test. At this point in the development of the Vermont Recipes application, you don't allow any text fields to be left blank, as you will later.

You want to be sure that the text field displays the number by using thousands and decimal separators that are appropriate for the locale of the computer on which Vermont Recipes is running, of course. In this case, you will do that shortly, in Step 2.4, by setting a localization option in the formatter that you will connect using Interface Builder. Later, in Recipe 6, you will learn how to do it programmatically with custom formatters.

In earlier versions of the Vermont Recipes application, I used the NSString `localizedStringWithFormat:` class method, with a `%f` printf-style placeholder, to convert the model object's C `float` value to a localized string object, then set the text field to the formatted string value. Later, I used the **NSNumber** **numberWithFloat:** method to pass an NSDecimalNumber object to the text field, dispensing with a string object. Neither of these approaches was appropriate, however, because a text field converts incoming values of any recognized type to an object, anyway. Now, therefore, I simply pass the model object's value to the text field directly and let the text field's cell do all the work of displaying it and giving it back after the user edits it.

There is a subtle but important point to be made here about these update methods. For the first time, you are arranging to update a text field, which presents many more complexities than a simple button or slider. If several windows are open in the Vermont Recipes application at once, for example, it is possible that a user will start to edit the text field in one window, then switch to another window and begin editing the corresponding text field in it, leaving the edit in the first window pending with an active cursor. Unlike in the case of buttons or sliders, a user can end up with many text fields, each in a different document window, in simultaneous suspended animation. Without careful coding, when the user attempts to commit one of the fields, these update methods might not know in which window the field was committed.

Fortunately, in Recipe 1, Step 6.3, you adopted the practice of registering observers only for notifications containing this particular document. Otherwise, all instances of this text field in every open window would receive and act upon the notification, which would cause all of them to update to the same value at once. To your user, it would look as though the text field in the other windows had aborted their pending edits on their own initiative. Because you have ensured that the notification is observed only by the particular window controller associated with the specific document that posted the notification, you have avoided this puzzling and hard-to-debug behavior.

5. **NOTIFICATION OBSERVERS.** Register the window controller as an observer of the notification that will trigger the updater method. You must register two methods for the same notification, one to update the slider and the other to update the text field. Insert the following statements in the **registerNotification-ObserversForSlidersTab** method of the source file VRSliderController.m, after the existing registrations:

```
// Speed
[[NSNotificationCenter defaultCenter] addObserver:self
        selector:@selector(updateSpeedSlider:)
        name:VRSliderModelSpeedValueChangedNotification
        object:[self document]];
[[NSNotificationCenter defaultCenter] addObserver:self
        selector:@selector(updateSpeedTextField:)
        name:VRSliderModelSpeedValueChangedNotification
        object:[self document]];
```

6. **ACTION METHODS.** In the header file VRMainWindowController.h, at the end of the ACTIONS section of the VRSliderController category, declare two action methods as shown below. Two action methods are needed because, as you will see in Step 2.3, below, when the user operates either of the two controls, the single, shared data variable must be set and the other control must be updated automatically.

```
// Speed
- (IBAction)speedSliderAction:(id)sender;
- (IBAction)speedTextFieldAction:(id)sender;
```

In the category source file VRSliderController.m, define the action methods at the end of the ACTIONS section, as shown below:

```
// Speed

- (IBAction)speedSliderAction:(id)sender {
    [[self sliderModel] setSpeedValue:[sender floatValue]];
    [[[self document] undoManager] setActionName:
            NSLocalizedString(@"Set Speed Limiter",
            @"Name of undo/redo menu item after Speed \
            slider was set")];
}


- (IBAction)speedTextFieldAction:(id)sender {
    [[self sliderModel] setSpeedValue:[sender floatValue]];
    [[[self document] undoManager] setActionName:
            NSLocalizedString(@"Set Speed Limiter",
            @"Name of undo/redo menu item after Speed \
            text field was set")];
}
```

If you were to finish this step and build and run the application using the **speedTextFieldAction:** method as given above, you would encounter one usability issue that is intolerable in a working application. If a user cleared the text field and attempted to enter the resulting blank value by pressing Return, the formatter object that you will apply to the text field in Step 2.4, below, would not catch the improper entry and the model object's instance variable would be set to **0**. This is unacceptable, because the formatter is supposed to constrain entries to the range from 75 to 155. Formatters don't normally prevent blank text field entries, because applications are often designed to allow blank text fields. Here, however, where the text field is associated with a slider having a prescribed range, a **0** or blank entry is inappropriate.

A temporary workaround is simple enough. Enclose the body of the action method in an **if** block testing whether the value entered is an empty string object. If so, the action method will not be sent, the data value will not be changed, and the updater will not be called. The effect will be that the field remains selected for editing, with an active text entry cursor. However, there remains a problem: This workaround bypasses the formatter, so when you later implement a sheet to report improper data entry, the sheet will not be presented in this situation.

You will address this remaining problem later, in Recipe 5. For now, revise the method as shown here:

```
- (IBAction)speedTextFieldAction:(id)sender {
    if (![[sender stringValue] isEqualToString:@""]) {
        [[self sliderModel] setSpeedValue:[sender floatValue]];
        [[[self document] undoManager] setActionName:
            NSLocalizedString(@"Set Speed Limiter",
            @"Name of undo/redo menu item after Speed \
            text field was set")];
    }
}
```

7. **LOCALIZABLE.STRINGS.** Update the Localizable.strings file by adding Set Speed Limiter.

8. **INITIALIZATION.** Initialize the Speed data variable to its minimum value, 75.0, using these statements at the end of the `if` block in the `initWithDocument:` method definition near the top of VRSliderModel.m:

```
// Default settings values
[[self undoManager] disableUndoRegistration];

[self setSpeedValue:75.0];

[[self undoManager] enableUndoRegistration];
```

9. **DATA STORAGE.** In the source file VRSliderModel.m, define the following key in the "Keys and values for dictionary" subsection of the STORAGE section:

```
// Speed
static NSString *VRSpeedValueKey = @"VRSliderModelSpeedValue";
```

Immediately after that, add these lines at the end of the `addDataToDictionary:` method:

```
// Speed
[dictionary setObject:[NSString stringWithFormat:@"%f",
    [self speedValue]] forKey:VRSpeedValueKey];
```

You use the `stringWithFormat:` method here, rather than `localizedStringWithFormat:`, because this method uses a string format only to store the data as a byte stream. You don't want localization of numeric data values for storage.

Then add these lines near the end of the `restoreDataFromDictionary:` method, before the `[[self undoManager] enableUndoRegistration]` message:

```
// Speed
[self setSpeedValue: [[dictionary objectForKey:
    VRSpeedValueKey] floatValue]];
```

10. **GUI UPDATE METHOD INVOCATIONS.** In VRSliderController.m, add the following calls at the end of the **updateSlidersTab** method:

```
// Speed
[self updateSpeedSlider:nil];
[self updateSpeedTextField:nil];
```

11. **DESCRIPTION METHOD.** Revise the **description** method in VRSliderModel.m to read as follows:

```
- (NSString *) description {
    return [NSString stringWithFormat:@"%@\
    \n\tpersonalityValue:%@\
    \n\tspeedValue:%@\n",
        [super description],
        [[NSNumber numberWithFloat:
            [self personalityValue]] stringValue],
        [[NSNumber numberWithFloat:
            [self speedValue]] stringValue]];
}
```

12. **HELP TAGS.** Add Help tags to each of the sliders and the associated text field: "Set maximum allowed speed."

2.3 Confirm That the Slider and the Text Field Remain Synchronized

Cocoa provides built-in methods that allow one user control to take its value directly from another control, without putting you through any convoluted routines to update the control from the value of a data variable. You don't even need to associate a data variable with the second control.

Here, however, you don't need to use these built-in methods, because the notification-based updating scheme you have adopted keeps the slider and the editable text field linked automatically. When the user sets a value using either of these two controls, its action method sets the single shared data value in VRSliderModel by calling the appropriate accessor method. The accessor method then posts a notification signaling that the data value has changed. Finally, since both the slider's and the text field's update methods have been registered to receive that notification, both controls are updated if they don't already show the new value.

You will see an example of Cocoa's automatic control linking methods in Step 3, where the control to be updated is a static text field and therefore isn't implicated in a mutual action-and-updater method network.

2.4 Apply an NSNumberFormatter Object to the Text Field

If you were to connect the outlets and actions in Interface Builder now and use these new controls, you would find that the numbers in the new text field are not formatted appropriately. When you set an exact integer value, no decimal point appears (that is, 75.0 displays as 75), and when you set a noninteger value, many digits to the right of the decimal point may appear, overflowing the text field. To cure this cosmetic problem, you will use one of the built-in formatters supplied with Cocoa, NSNumberFormatter, in Interface Builder.

1. Drag the icon with a dollar-sign ($) badge from the Cocoa Views palette to the VRDocument.nib window. In the VRDocument.nib window, rename it **SpeedFormatter**. If your application were to need multiple text fields, all with the same formatting attributes you are about to give this one, you could reuse the new SpeedFormatter object to keep down memory requirements. For text fields with different formatting requirements, you would add more formatter objects and give them different names.

2. Click the SpeedFormatter icon in the VRDocument.nib window. The NSNumberFormatter Info Panel appears. Uncheck the Add 1000 Separators option and check the Localize option.

3. In the Positive format string field, type **##0.0**. The Info Panel won't let you leave the Negative field blank, so place the same formatting string there that you placed in the Positive field.

   Until the most recent version of the Developer Tools, NSNumberFormatter treated the Zero field as a string constant. You had to leave the Zero field blank in number formatters that constrain values to positive ranges. Otherwise, the formatter would incorrectly accept input of a **0** value identical to that set in the Zero field. I struggled with this issue in earlier versions of the Vermont Recipes application, thinking that some bug in my code was responsible for the fact that the text field accepted unwanted **0** values despite the range settings. I finally discovered that it was not my bug, but Apple's. Apple fixed the bug in Mac OS X 10.2, so this is no longer an issue.

4. Set the Minimum and Maximum values to **75** and **155**, respectively.

5. Control-drag from the text field to the new SpeedFormatter icon, select `formatter` in the Connections pane of the NSTextField Info Panel, and click the Connect button.

When you connect the outlets and actions in Interface Builder and use these new controls with the formatter, you will find that the formatting is just what you want, and that the minimum and maximum values you set in the formatter are enforced by a beep when you attempt to enter an out-of-range or nonnumeric value in the text field. You can live with the beep for now, but you will add a powerful sheet in Recipe 5 to give your users better feedback and increased options.

2.5 Read the Source Files into the Nib File and Connect Outlets and Actions

Inform the nib file of the new outlet and action you have created in the code files, then connect them to the new slider.

1. In Interface Builder, select the Classes tab in the nib file window, then choose Classes > Read Files. In the resulting dialog, select the header file in which you have created outlets or actions, VRMainWindowController.h, then click the Parse button.

2. Select the Instances tab. Control-drag from the File's Owner icon to the new slider and click its outlet name, then click the Connect button in the Connections pane of the File's Owner Info palette. Repeat this procedure with the new text field, connecting its outlet.

3. Control-drag from the new slider to the File's Owner icon. Click the target in the left pane and the appropriate action in the right pane of the Outlets section in the Connections pane of the NSSlider Info palette, then click the Connect button. Repeat this procedure with the new text field to connect its action.

2.6 Build and Run the Application

Build and run the application to test the slider and the text field. Explore how undo and redo work, and make sure changes can be saved to disk, restored, and reverted properly.

Notice how the value in the text field changes continuously as you drag the slider back and forth. If it seems a little slow, this is because it is logging continuous values to StdIO (if you implemented an `NSLog()` call in the `set` accessor). When you compile for deployment without this debugging aid, it will be blindingly fast. Also, type numbers in the text field and watch the slider snap to the corresponding settings once you press the Return or Enter key.

Type an out-of-range value, such as 200 or 0, or the word *fast* into the text field and press Return. You will hear a beep telling you that you made an error, and the text field will still display an active cursor inviting you to edit the erroneous entry.

Observe what happens when you attempt to enter an out-of-range value, such as 10, and then switch to another pane. Whether you click a tab or one of the navigation buttons, you hear a beep. When you return to the Sliders tab, you find that the value in the text field has reverted to what it was before you attempted to enter an invalid value. You will revisit this issue later, in Recipe 5, but it appears that Cocoa is treating your switching tab view items as a signal that you wish to commit the pending data value. It won't let you, because the value is invalid.

If you test even more thoroughly, you will discover one issue with the text field: It doesn't beep when you attempt to enter a blank value. You anticipated this problem in the discussion above. You will fix it and enhance the text field with an alert sheet in Recipe 5, Step 3. Before that, however, you will create one more slider in the next step.

Step 3: Create a Continuous Slider with Push-buttons and a Static Text Field

In this step, you will create a horizontal slider with tick marks in a range, as in Step 2, but the floating-point values it returns are constrained to unit intervals. The thumb of the slider jumps from tick mark to tick mark in discrete increments as you drag it. The slider lets you set the quantum energy levels of electrons, which must assume integer values (at least according to physical laws applicable in Vermont, where life is uncomplicated).

The slider in this step has two associated push-buttons. Clicking one or the other resets the slider to its minimum or maximum value.

A static text field is associated with this slider as well to provide a readout of the slider's numeric value. Unlike the text field in the previous step, this text field cannot be edited; the slider and the buttons are the only means to enter values. However, like the text field in the previous step, this static field's value is updated continuously as the slider is dragged, using a shortcut method in NSControl for linking user controls.

3.1 Create a Slider, a Synchronized Static Text Field, and Push-buttons in Interface Builder

Use Interface Builder to create a new horizontal slider with a title and unlabeled tick marks, along with two push-buttons, a label, and a static text field that the slider will update. When you are done with Step 3.1, the group should look like that shown in **Figure 3.4**.

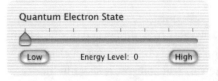

FIGURE 3.4 The Quantum Electron State slider, push-buttons, and text field.

1. With the Sliders tab view item selected, drag the lower of the two horizontal sliders from the Other Cocoa Views palette onto the Sliders pane and place it on the right side, far enough below the Speed Limiter group to allow insertion of some static text above it. In the NSSlider Info Panel, type **0.0** for the Minimum Value, **7.0** for the Maximum Value, and, if necessary, **0.0** for the Current Value; check the Continuous checkbox; set the Number of Markers to **8** with Position Above selected; and check Marker Values Only. Note that Continuous in this Info Panel refers to the frequency with which the control's action message is sent; it is unrelated to the Marker Values Only setting, which determines whether the thumb may be positioned anywhere along the length of the slider or only at tick marks.

2. Drag System Font Text from the Cocoa Views palette to the Sliders pane, placing it above the new slider and naming it **Quantum Electron State**; choose Layout > Size to Fit to make all the text visible. Drag Small System Font Text to the Sliders pane, placing it below the new slider, then type **Energy Level:** with a trailing colon; choose Layout > Size to Fit, and position it beneath the leftmost tick mark. Uncheck the Editable and Selectable checkboxes in the Options area, and check the Enabled checkbox, as necessary, for both of these static text fields.

3. Now drag Small System Font Text to the Sliders pane again, placing it to the right of the Energy Level text field. Type the numeral **0** to match the default setting of the slider, and choose Layout > Size to Fit. This text field, though not editable or scrollable, will contain a value that varies depending on the position of the thumb in the slider. The text field should be marked Selectable in the Info palette to permit the user to select and copy its contents to the clipboard for pasting elsewhere. Use the Alignment submenu and Aqua guides to align the

baselines of the Energy Level and 0 text fields and position them the proper distance apart, then choose Layout > Group. Finally, select the slider, Shift-click to add the new text field group to the selection, and choose Layout > Alignment > Align Vertical Centers.

4. Drag a standard push-button from the Cocoa Views palette and position it below the right end of the new slider. In the NSButton Info Panel, select the Small checkbox to make it a small button, type the name **High** in the Title field, and choose Layout > Size to Fit. With the High button selected, choose Edit > Duplicate or press Command-D to make a duplicate, then name it **Low**. Leave it the same width as the High button, and move it to a position below the left end of the new slider. Position the buttons using the Aqua guides so that they have the same text baselines as the Energy Level text field group.

5. Select all the new items, then choose Layout > Ungroup, followed immediately by Layout > Group. Now you can drag the new items as a group without selecting all of them.

6. Position the group so it complies with human interface guidelines. However, it will look better if it is a somewhat greater distance below the Speed Limiter group, as if it were in a borderless group box.

3.2 Write the Code for the Slider, Text Field, and Push-buttons in Project Builder

Use Project Builder to write the code required to make the new controls work.

1. USER CONTROL OUTLET VARIABLES AND ACCESSORS. In VRMainWindowController.h, declare outlet variables after the existing variable declarations, as follows:

```
// Quantum slider
IBOutlet NSSlider *quantumSlider;
IBOutlet NSButton *quantumButtonLo;
IBOutlet NSButton *quantumButtonHi;
```

Still in VRMainWindowController.h, also declare accessor methods for the outlets at the end of the ACCESSORS section of the VRSliderController category, as follows:

```
// Quantum slider
- (NSSlider *)quantumSlider;
- (NSButton *)quantumButtonLo;
- (NSButton *)quantumButtonHi;
```

In the category source file VRSliderController.m, define the accessor methods at the end of the ACCESSORS section, as follows:

```
// Quantum slider

- (NSSlider *)quantumSlider {
    return quantumSlider;
}

- (NSButton *)quantumButtonLo {
    return quantumButtonLo;
}

- (NSButton *)quantumButtonHi {
    return quantumButtonHi;
}
```

You will declare an instance variable and accessor methods for the text field in Step 3.4, below.

2. **DATA VARIABLES AND ACCESSORS.** In VRSliderModel.h, declare a new variable after the existing variable declarations, as follows:

```
// Quantum
float quantumValue;
```

In VRSliderModel.h, also declare the corresponding accessor methods at the end of the ACCESSORS section, as follows:

```
// Quantum

- (void)setQuantumValue:(float)inValue;
- (float)quantumValue;
```

In VRSliderModel.m, define the accessor methods at the end of the ACCESSORS section, as follows, adding a call to **NSLog()** if you are following that practice:

```
// Quantum

- (void)setQuantumValue:(float)inValue {
    [[[self undoManager]
            prepareWithInvocationTarget:self]
            setQuantumValue:quantumValue];
    quantumValue = inValue;
    [[NSNotificationCenter defaultCenter] postNotificationName:
```

```
            VRSliderModelQuantumValueChangedNotification
            object:[self document]];
}

- (float)quantumValue {
    return quantumValue;
}
```

3. **NOTIFICATION VARIABLE.** In VRSliderModel.h, at the bottom of the file, declare the notification variable, as follows:

```
// Quantum
extern NSString *VRSliderModelQuantumValueChangedNotification;
```

In VRSliderModel.m, near the top of the file, define the notification variable, as follows:

```
// Quantum
NSString *VRSliderModelQuantumValueChangedNotification =
        @"SliderModel quantumValue Changed Notification";
```

4. **GUI UPDATE METHOD.** In VRMainWindowController.h, declare a specific updater method at the end of the "INTERFACE MANAGEMENT - Specific updaters" section of the VRSliderController category, as follows:

```
// Quantum
- (void)updateQuantumSlider:(NSNotification *)notification;
```

In the category source file VRSliderController.m, define the specific update method at the end of the "INTERFACE MANAGEMENT - Specific updaters" section, as follows:

```
// Quantum

- (void)updateQuantumSlider:(NSNotification *)notification {
    [self updateSlider:[self quantumSlider]
            setting:[[self sliderModel] quantumValue]];
}
```

Notice that the existing **updateSlider:** generic update method will be reused.

5. **NOTIFICATION OBSERVER.** Register the window controller as an observer of the notification that will trigger the updater method, at the end of the **registerNotificationObserversForSlidersTab** method in the category source file VRSliderController.m, after the existing registrations:

```
// Quantum
[[NSNotificationCenter defaultCenter] addObserver:self
        selector:@selector(updateQuantumSlider:)
        name:VRSliderModelQuantumValueChangedNotification
        object:[self document]];
```

6. **Action method.** In VRMainController.h, at the end of the ACTIONS section of the VRSliderController category, declare three action methods as shown below. Action methods are needed for the buttons because they will update the slider.

```
// Quantum
- (IBAction)quantumSliderAction:(id)sender;
- (IBAction)quantumButtonLoAction:(id)sender;
- (IBAction)quantumButtonHiAction:(id)sender;
```

In the category source file VRSliderController.m, define the action methods at the end of the ACTIONS section, as shown below.

```
// Quantum

- (IBAction)quantumSliderAction:(id)sender {
    [[self sliderModel] setQuantumValue:[sender floatValue]];
    [[[self document] undoManager] setActionName:
            NSLocalizedString(@"Set Quantum Electron State \
            Slider", @"Name of undo/redo menu item after \
            Quantum slider was set")];
}

- (IBAction)quantumButtonLoAction:(id)sender {
    [[self sliderModel] setQuantumValue:
            [[self quantumSlider] minValue]];
    [[[self document] undoManager] setActionName:
            NSLocalizedString(@"Set Lowest Quantum Electron \
            State", @"Name of undo/redo menu item after \
            Quantum button Low was set")];
}

- (IBAction)quantumButtonHiAction:(id)sender {
    [[self sliderModel] setQuantumValue:
            [[self quantumSlider] maxValue]];
    [[[self document] undoManager] setActionName:
            NSLocalizedString(@"Set Highest Quantum Electron \
            State", @"Name of undo/redo menu item after \
```

```
              Quantum button High was set")];
}
```

Notice that, because you decided early on to set the action name in the action method rather than in the data variable's accessor method, you can use different, more informative names for the Undo and Redo menu items, depending on exactly what action the user performed—clicking the Low or High button, or using the slider.

7. **LOCALIZABLE.STRINGS.** Update the Localizable.strings file by adding Set Quantum Electron State Slider, Set Lowest Quantum Electron State, and Set Highest Quantum Electron State.

8. **INITIALIZATION.** No initialization is required to set the slider's default value to 0.

9. **DATA STORAGE.** In VRSliderModel.m, define the following key in the "Keys and values for dictionary" subsection of the STORAGE section:

```
// Quantum
static NSString *VRQuantumValueKey = @"VRSliderModelQuantumValue";
```

Immediately after that, add these lines at the end of the **addDataToDictionary:** method:

```
// Quantum
[dictionary setObject:[NSString stringWithFormat:@"%f",
        [self quantumValue]] forKey:VRQuantumValueKey];
```

Add these lines near the end of the **restoreDataFromDictionary:** method:

```
// Quantum
[self setQuantumValue:[[dictionary
        objectForKey:VFRQuantumValueKey] floatValue]];
```

10. **GUI UPDATE METHOD INVOCATIONS.** In the category source file VRSliderController.m, add the following call at the end of the **updateSlidersTab** method:

```
// Quantum
[self updateQuantumSlider:nil]
```

11. **DESCRIPTION METHOD.** Update the **description** method in VRSliderModel.m so that it reads as follows:

```
- (NSString *) description {
    return [NSString stringWithFormat:@"%@\
    \n\tpersonalityValue:%@\
    \n\tspeedValue:%@\
```

(continues on next page)

```
\n\tquantumValue:%@\n",
        [super description],
        [[NSNumber numberWithFloat:
            [self personalityValue]] stringValue],
        [[NSNumber numberWithFloat:
            [self speedValue]] stringValue],
        [[NSNumber numberWithFloat:
            [self quantumValue]] stringValue]);
}
```

12. **HELP TAGS.** Add a Help tag to the new slider: "Specify any quantum energy state."
Also add Help tags for the two new buttons: "Specify lowest quantum energy
state" and "Specify highest quantum energy state," respectively.

3.3 Synchronize the Slider and the Text Field

In Step 3.1, above, you used Interface Builder to insert a noneditable text field after
Energy Levels:, to hold a numerical representation of the value of the slider. Now
you need to add code to ensure that the contents of this text field get updated continuously as a user drags the slider back and forth or sets it to its lowest or highest
values using the buttons. In Step 2, you linked a slider and a text field as a fortuitous
side effect of the notification-based updating scheme used in the Vermont Recipes
application. There, the link depended on the fact that the slider and the text field
shared a single data variable, and both controls required action and updater methods
so that you could use both to set the data value.

Here, the text field is not editable, and it therefore has no action or update method
and is not associated with a data value. You need another means to link it to the
slider. It happens that NSControl contains a small set of methods designed precisely
for this situation. You will use NSControl's **takeIntValueFrom:** method to tell the
text field to take its value as an integer directly from the float value of the slider.
Since you set the slider's Continuous option in Step 3.1, above, the updating of both
the slider and the text field will occur continuously as a user drags the slider, because
the slider's action method will be invoked continuously. Note that making a text
field noneditable doesn't mean your code can't change its value.

1. In VRMainWindowController.h, add this declaration of an instance variable for
the text field, at the end of the "Quantum slider variables" section:

```
IBOutlet NSTextField *quantumTextField;
```

2. Also in VRMainWindowController.h, declare the accessor method at the end of
the ACCESSORS section of the VRSliderController category:

```
- (NSTextField *)quantumTextField;
```

3. Define the accessor method in the category source file VRSliderController.m at the end of the ACCESSORS section:

```
- (NSTextField *)quantumTextField {
    return quantumTextField;
}
```

4. Finally, add the following statement at the end of the updateQuantumSlider: specific updater method in VRSliderController.m:

```
[[self quantumTextField] takeIntValueFrom:[self quantumSlider]];
```

This statement goes in the slider's update method, not its action method. If you placed it in the action method, it would be invoked only when the user clicked the slider. But you want the text field to update as well when the document is created or opened, after a Redo or Undo command, and when the document reverts to its saved state. This statement must therefore go in the slider's update method, which will be invoked every time the slider's data value changes, no matter how the user initiated the change. This is why, in Step 1, you went to the trouble of invoking updaters for *specific* user controls in the updateWindow method—namely, so that methods specific to an individual control, such as the takeIntValueFrom: method in the Quantum slider update method, will be invoked even when the document window is first opened and when the document reverts to its saved state. If you had instead invoked the *generic* slider update method in updateWindow, the takeIntValueFrom: method would not have been called in these circumstances.

3.4 Read the Source Files into the Nib File and Connect Outlets and Actions

Inform the nib file of the new outlets and actions you have created in the code files, then connect them to the new slider and push-buttons.

1. In Interface Builder, select the Classes tab in the nib file window, then choose Classes > Read Files. In the resulting dialog, select the header file in which you have created outlets or actions, VRMainWindowController.h, then click the Parse button.

2. Select the Instances tab. Control-drag from the File's Owner icon to each of the new controls in turn and click its outlet name, then click the Connect button in the Connections pane of the File's Owner Info Panel. Don't leave out the Energy Level text field.

3. Control-drag from each of the new controls to the File's Owner icon in turn. Click the target in the left pane and the appropriate action in the right pane of the Outlets section in the Connections pane of the Info Panel, then click the Connect button.

3.5 Build and Run the Application

Build and run the application to test the slider and the two buttons. As usual, explore how undo and redo work, and make sure changes can be saved to disk, restored, and reverted properly. Notice how both the slider and the contents of the static text field change instantly to the lowest or highest value when you press the appropriate push-button. Try copying the value in the text field and pasting it into, say, TextEdit.

Conclusion

You are now done with Recipe 3. In the next several recipes you will explore text fields, first creating a handful of simple text fields and establishing their tab order, then exploring several extras relevant to almost all text fields. In Recipe 5, for example, you will learn how to create complex, interactive alert sheets, and in Recipe 6 you will learn how to implement on-the-fly input filtering as a user types characters into a field, as well as more complex, customized on-the-fly formatters. In subsequent recipes, you will deal with undo and redo in text fields and drag-and-drop editing. Finally, you will implement a variety of other controls that accept text input, such as combo boxes, forms, and tables.

RECIPE 4

Text Fields

This recipe is the first in a series of recipes dealing with text fields. Text fields are jacks-of-all-trades among user controls, able to display in text form all of the values that, if displayed graphically, require a variety of more specialized controls such as checkboxes and sliders. In addition, of course, text fields are indispensable for displaying the infinite variety of textual data that forms the basis of many applications.

You will begin in Step 1 by rearranging the tab view items in the main document window and changing the name on the Text Boxes tab to Text Fields. Then you will create three simple text fields in the Text Fields tab view item, along with a new model object and a new controller category for code relating specifically to the Text Fields tab view item. In Step 2, you will learn how to establish a key view loop that specifies the tab order of these three text fields, as well as how to establish a key view loop for tabbing between nontext controls in the Buttons and Sliders tab view items.

Once these simple text fields are in place, several following recipes will deal with text field extras. Text fields are versatile user controls, with a number of features that enhance their simplest form. In Recipe 5, you will implement alert sheets to deal with invalid contents of text fields at the point when the user has completed an entry. In Recipe 6, you will learn how to create custom on-the-fly formatters—instead of relying only on the two canned formatters that come with Cocoa, NSNumberFormatter and NSDateFormatter—to catch entry errors while the user is typing. Recipe 7 will show you how to implement a feature that should be a built-in feature of Cocoa but is not: undo and redo while editing a text field. Recipe 8 will cover aspects of drag-and-drop editing within text fields. Subsequent recipes will delve into more complex text controls, such as combo boxes, forms, and tables. Figure 4.1 shows how the finished Text Fields tab view item will appear once you have completed all your work in this book, including the three Formatted Data Entry text fields you create in this recipe (**Figure 4.1**).

Before turning to Step 1, you should prepare your project files for Recipe 4. Update the build version in the Info.plist Entries to **4** and the document version code in VRDocument.m to **4**.

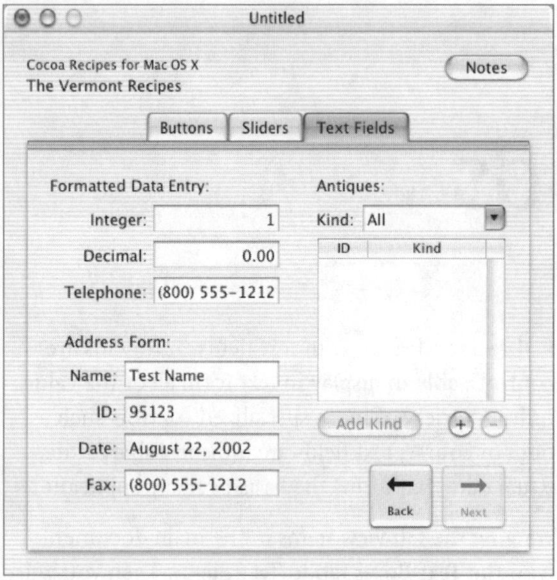

FIGURE 4.1 The finished Text Fields tab view item.

Step 1: Set Up Standard Text Fields

HIGHLIGHTS:

Memory management for instance variables that hold value objects

Accessor method conventions

In Step 1, you will set up the text fields used in many of the subsequent recipes. These are ordinary, standalone text fields, differing from the text field you created in connection with the Speed Limiter slider in Recipe 3, Step 2, only in that you are not linking them to another control. You have at least one new thing to learn, however. In Instruction 2, you learn how to handle memory management issues when an instance variable holds a value object, rather than the simple C data types you have used up to this point.

Before you begin, you should create a new model object and controller category for the Text Fields tab view item, because all of these new text fields will appear on this one tab view item. Follow the instructions in Recipe 3, Step 1.2, to create a new model class for the Text Fields tab view item, naming it **VRTextFieldModel**. Follow the instructions in Recipe 3, Step 1.3, to create a new controller category for the Text Fields tab view item, naming it **VRTextFieldController**.

1.1 Change the Order of the Tab View Items

Before adding the new text fields, it is time to fix a cosmetic issue in the application. When you originally created the document window's tab view with two tab view items, in Recipe 1, Step 2.2, you named the first tab Text Boxes and the second tab Buttons. Later, in Recipe 3, Step 1.1, you added a third tab view item to their right, named Sliders. Although the order of the tabs from left to right thus suggests that the topic of Text Boxes comes first in *Vermont Recipes*, you are only now starting to deal with them seriously. You will therefore make the Text Boxes tab come third in order from left to right, instead of first, to reflect the order of these recipes. While you're at it, you will rename this tab view item Text Fields.

1. Open VRDocument.nib in Interface Builder, if necessary.

2. Click the Text Boxes tab once to select the tab view item.

3. Press the right-arrow key on the keyboard twice to move the Text Boxes tab to the right of the other two tabs.

4. Double-click the Text Boxes tab's title to select it for editing, and change it to `Text Fields`.

If you were to compile and run the application now, you would find that the navigation buttons enable and disable themselves as expected even though you've moved a tab view item to a new position. The code you wrote for these buttons in Recipe 2, Step 7, was sufficiently robust to make this happen automatically.

1.2 Add Assertions as Reminders of Required Application Settings

Remember that you disabled the Next button in Interface Builder on the assumption that you'd build the application with the last tab view item showing. If you built it with another tab view item selected, the navigation buttons would not be appropriately enabled and disabled when the window is first created, but only after the user selected another pane. In anticipation of your application's final setup, where the first, or leftmost, tab will be selected when a new window is created, use Interface Builder's NSButton Info Panel now to disable the Back button and enable the Next button. Hereafter, you must always remember to build the application with the first tab view item selected, especially before releasing the product publicly.

Since memory isn't necessarily reliable, especially on a large team project, you should consider including something in the application's code to ensure that the active tab view item and the enabled or disabled state of the navigation buttons are properly configured in the nib file. You have been taking care of the initial state of the window in VRMainWindowController's `awakeFromNib` method. One possibility would be to insert code there to set the state of the tab view programmatically. For example, you might add these statements:

```
[[self tabView] selectFirstTabViewItem:nil];
[[self backButton] setEnabled:NO];
[[self nextButton] setEnabled:YES];
```

This may not be the best approach, however. For one thing, the nib file can and, in the absence of countervailing considerations, normally should be configured to set the state of features such as these. More important, calling the `selectFirstTabViewItem:` method here would automatically trigger any delegate method you may later implement to respond to the user's selection of panes in the tab view, and it might be hard to track down any resulting misbehavior that occurs when the window opens.

Therefore, instead of inserting the code just shown, it is better to call upon Cocoa's `NSAssert()` function to log a message to StdIO if the nib file is improperly configured. `NSAssert()` is designed to provide checks and reminders of just this sort during application development. When you finally build the application for public release, you will use Project Builder's deployment build style to optimize this code out so it will not adversely affect performance. Add the following to the end of the `awakeFromNib` method in VRMainWindowController.m:

```
NSAssert((([[[self tabView] tabViewItemAtIndex:0] tabState]
        == NSSelectedTab),
        @"First tab view item should be \
        selected in VRDocument.nib.");
NSAssert((![[self backButton] isEnabled]),
        @"Back button should be disabled in VRDocument.nib.");
NSAssert(([[self nextButton] isEnabled]),
        @"Next button should be enabled in VRDocument.nib.");
```

1.3 Create Three Text Fields in Interface Builder

Use Interface Builder to create three new editable text fields in the Text Fields tab view item, along with four static text fields to serve as labels. You will create all three editable fields now.

1. Select the Text Fields tab view item by clicking the Text Fields tab.

2. Drag System Font Text from the Views palette to the upper-left corner of the Text Fields pane, using the Aqua guides to position it, and change the text to `Formatted Data Entry:` as the group label. Choose Layout > Size to Fit, if

necessary, to make all the text visible. Use the NSTextField Info Panel to uncheck the Editable and Selectable checkboxes in the Options area, since this is to be a static text field, and check the Enabled checkbox, as necessary.

3. Repeat the process three more times to create three additional text field labels aligned to the left beneath the title you just created and indented slightly. Type so that the labels read `Integer:`, `Decimal:`, and `Telephone:`, respectively, and set their attributes as directed above.

4. Drag NSTextField items from the Views palette three times and align the text baseline of each so that it lies to the right of its associated label. Make sure they are sized identically and aligned with one another vertically. This requires using the Aqua guide associated with the longest of the three static text fields to position the editable text fields properly to the right of their labels. You can temporarily type a full telephone number into the Title field of the NSTextField Info Panel, using a wide digit such as 8 and the conventional North American format, to help size the text fields. The format looks like this: **(888) 888-8888**. Once you have resized these fields, remove the dummy telephone number.

5. With each of the text fields you just created selected in turn, click the right-alignment button in the NSTextField Info Panel for the Integer and Decimal text fields, so that digits typed into each text field will fill from right to left and remain aligned against the right edge of the box, and click the left-alignment button for the Telephone text field so that it will fill from left to right. Also check the Editable and Enabled checkboxes in the Options area, since these three text fields are to be editable; selecting Editable automatically turns on Selectable.

6. Choose Layout > Group so that you can drag the new items as a group without selecting all of them.

7. Drag to position the group as necessary so that it complies with human interface guidelines.

1.4 Write the Code for the Text Fields in Project Builder

Now turn to Project Builder to code the editable text fields. You must run through the checklist of tasks you have used repeatedly to implement user controls, as originally developed in Recipe 2, Step 2. This should be almost second nature to you by now, but I will give a bare-bones exposition of the code here for all three of the new editable text fields at once. In Step 2, you will for the first time implement the last of the code items in the checklist, setting the initial first responder and next key views to accommodate the new controls.

This step introduces one new feature, which requires that you perform some of these tasks a little differently than you did when setting up all of the previous fields in the Vermont Recipes application. For the first time, you will create an instance variable for data that holds an object rather than one of the standard C data types you have worked with up to this point. The new Telephone text field will display a telephone number, the data for which will be held in an instance variable of type NSString, an object, in the VRTextFieldModel model object. An instance variable that holds an object requires special handling, including allocating and initializing the new data object when a new document is created, deallocating the object when the document is closed, and attending to memory management while the new object is in use. Each of these points is discussed as it arises, below.

In later recipes, you will learn to use other value objects, such as NSNumber objects, instead of C data types for many text fields, to take advantage of the many benefits of objects in a Cocoa application. The most significant advantage may be that you can easily insert objects into Cocoa collection objects, such as arrays and dictionaries.

1. **USER CONTROL OUTLET VARIABLES AND ACCESSORS.** In the header file VRMainWindowController.h, declare three outlet variables after the existing variable declarations (but before **controlUpdatingDisabled**) near the top of the file, as follows:

```
// Formatted text fields
IBOutlet NSTextField *integerTextField;
IBOutlet NSTextField *decimalTextField;
IBOutlet NSTextField *telephoneTextField;
```

Still in VRMainWindowController.h, also declare an accessor method for each outlet at the end of the ACCESSORS section of the new VRTextFieldController category at the end of the file, as follows:

```
// Formatted text fields
- (NSTextField *)integerTextField;
- (NSTextField *)decimalTextField;
- (NSTextField *)telephoneTextField;
```

Turn to the new category source file VRTextFieldController.m and define the accessor methods at the end of the ACCESSORS section, as follows:

```
// Formatted text fields

- (NSTextField *)integerTextField {
    return integerTextField;
}
```

```
- (NSTextField *)decimalTextField {
    return decimalTextField;
}

- (NSTextField *)telephoneTextField {
    return telephoneTextField;
}
```

2. **DATA VARIABLES AND ACCESSORS.** In the new header file VRTextFieldModel.h,
    declare three new variables after the existing variable declarations, as shown
    below. They hold an **int**, a **float**, and an **NSString**, respectively. Note that the
    second is typed as a **float** for convenience, even though the second text field
    will be displayed as a decimal value without any of the additional exponent
    formatting characteristic of true floating-point values. In Recipe 5, you
    will be introduced to Cocoa's NSDecimalNumber class, which may be more
    appropriate for this purpose in a typical Cocoa programming project.

```
// Formatted values
int integerValue;
float decimalValue;
NSString *telephoneValue;
```

Remaining in VRTextFieldModel.h, also declare the corresponding accessor
methods at the end of the ACCESSORS section, as follows:

```
// Formatted values

- (void)setIntegerValue:(int)inValue;
- (int)integerValue;

- (void)setDecimalValue:(float)inValue;
- (float)decimalValue;

- (void)setTelephoneValue:(NSString *)inValue;
- (NSString *)telephoneValue;
```

In the source file VRTextFieldModel.m, define the accessor methods at the
end of the ACCESSORS section, as shown below. Don't forget to add **NSLog()**
calls to print the new values to StdIO if you are following that practice. In writing NSLog(), you will find it easiest to get the **stringValue** of NSNumber's
numberWithInt: and **numberWithFloat:** methods for the first two and get
[self telephoneValue] for the third.

```
// Formatted values

- (void)setIntegerValue:(int)inValue {
    [[[self undoManager] prepareWithInvocationTarget:self]
        setIntegerValue:integerValue];
    integerValue = inValue;
    [[NSNotificationCenter defaultCenter] postNotificationName:
        VRIntegerValueChangedNotification
        object:[self document]];
}

- (int)integerValue {
    return integerValue;
}

- (void)setDecimalValue:(float)inValue {
    [[[self undoManager] prepareWithInvocationTarget:self]
        setDecimalValue:decimalValue];
    decimalValue = inValue;
    [[NSNotificationCenter defaultCenter] postNotificationName:
        VRDecimalValueChangedNotification
        object:[self document]];
}

- (float)decimalValue {
    return decimalValue;
}

- (void)setTelephoneValue:(NSString *)inValue {
    if (telephoneValue != inValue) {
        [[[self undoManager] prepareWithInvocationTarget:self]
            setTelephoneValue:telephoneValue];
        [telephoneValue release];
        telephoneValue = [inValue copy];
        [[NSNotificationCenter defaultCenter]
            postNotificationName:
            VRTelephoneValueChangedNotification
            object:[self document]];
    }
}

- (NSString *)telephoneValue {
    return [[telephoneValue retain] autorelease];
}
```

Take a close look at the `setTelephoneValue:` and `telephoneValue` accessor methods, above, because they harbor some very important new lessons. Until now, all of the values you have used in model objects have been standard C data types. Now, for the first time, you have used an object instead—here, an NSString object. This requires that you consider several memory management issues that arise in the context of accessor methods. The rules you should follow are simple, with a few simple exceptions. I will explain this in detail over the next several pages.

RULES OF THUMB FOR ACCESSOR METHODS FOR OBJECTS. The rules given here reflect Apple Computer's current recommendations. Some of them may look unfamiliar even to seasoned Cocoa developers, particularly with respect to **get** accessors. The developer community, where other techniques are more common, has not understood Apple to have clearly articulated conventions in this form until recently.

Vermont Recipes follows Apple's recommendations because Apple has begun, with its Worldwide Developers Conference (WWDC) in 2002, to press the case for the rules described here. Most of these points have been in the documentation for years, although in some cases with a little ambiguity. Apple believes that, especially as the Cocoa frameworks are revised and improved over time, these conventions will be more suitable than other common practices.

If you are developing new software or substantially revising existing software for Mac OS X 10.2—especially reusable frameworks made available to others—Apple suggests that you adopt them. See the "Accessor Methods and Memory Management" sidebar for more information, including a summary of opposing views.

A GET ACCESSOR SHOULD NORMALLY RETAIN AND AUTORELEASE THE OBJECT IT RETURNS. The role of a **get** accessor method is to return a value to the caller, hiding from the caller the details of the value's implementation. In the simplest case, the returned object is a simple instance variable, but many other implementations are possible. For example, the object might have been constructed on the spot. It is fundamental in Cocoa that the caller shouldn't have to worry about how the returned value was formed.

In particular, the caller should be able to count on a returned object's remaining valid within the scope of the receiving method. This can be reasonably assured in the widest variety of circumstances if the **get** accessor retains the object. This protects against its being released in the meantime—for example, as an unanticipated side effect of some other operation.

The **get** accessor must also autorelease the returned object to ensure that it is released automatically later, since the receiver may choose not to assume ownership of it. The receiver has the option of assuming ownership by retaining it upon receipt, but it is often the case that the receiver only needs the object temporarily. This policy is familiar from the behavior of AppKit methods, which generally follow a policy of returning objects autoreleased. You see an example of this technique in the telephoneValue accessor method, above.

The principal exception to this rule applies when performance considerations are paramount. If the get accessor will be called thousands of times per second, it should return the object as is, without retaining or autoreleasing it. For most uses, however, Apple's experience is that the overhead associated with retaining and autoreleasing the object is not significant. Apple believes, based on its experience, that past expressions of concern about autorelease overhead have been greatly overstated.

Another common exception is for a get accessor that returns an object from a collection, such as an array. Collections are low-level objects, and their accessor methods have no business using autorelease to extend the life of an object obtained from the collection. Collections have long been documented to release objects that are removed, for performance reasons, and a caller that gets an object from an array must therefore retain it.

The get accessors you have written to obtain references to user controls might be viewed as another exception. The typical user control is a permanent fixture of the application's GUI, and it will not likely be replaced by a new object. Using your get accessors is just a convenient way of getting pointers to them.

Apple urges you to document any get accessors that apply exceptions to this rule, especially in frameworks and other software for reuse by others. The caller must handle retain and release in these exceptional cases and therefore needs to know from the documentation that it is in fact an exceptional case.

A set accessor should retain or copy the new object. A set accessor method should retain or copy the new, incoming object, which will be assigned to an instance variable. Retaining or copying it is necessary to ensure that it stays alive long enough for you to use the instance variable. This goes hand in hand with the rule that get accessors should retain and autorelease the objects they return. The incoming object, obtained from a get accessor, may be disposed of automatically not long after the set accessor assigns it to the instance variable. If the set accessor doesn't retain it, your application will likely crash if it attempts to access the instance variable.

You have the choice of explicitly retaining the new object or copying it. Copying it also has the effect of retaining it. The different uses of retain and copy will be discussed shortly.

A set accessor should release or autorelease the old object. Assigning a new, incoming object to the instance variable raises an issue regarding the fate of the old object to which the instance variable already refers. Something must be done to arrange for disposal of its memory, or your application will suffer a memory leak. The leak will accumulate every time the user assigns a different object, leaving all the old objects occupying memory unnecessarily.

I refer here to disposing of the old object because that is what will happen sooner or later. However, to be precise, the accessor merely releases the old object, decrementing its retain count. Your application may have good reason to keep other references to the old object in other instance variables or collection objects. Cocoa will dispose of its memory only when its retain count reaches 0, which might be at some later time. But the set accessor must release or autorelease it because a new object is being assigned to this instance variable.

The set accessor is your last chance to use this instance variable to ensure that the old object is released or autoreleased before the new object is assigned to the variable. Once the accessor assigns the incoming object to the instance variable, the instance variable's reference to the old object is lost and your application no longer has its address. You must therefore arrange here, in the set accessor, to release or autorelease the old object.

It is important that the set accessor retains or copies the new object before it releases the old object, unless it first checks to make sure the new object is not identical to the old object. Releasing the old object first would work correctly only if the new object were a different object—that is, if the new object occupied a different memory address from the old object. If it were the same object, disposing of the memory occupied by the old object would also dispose of the memory occupied by the new object, since it is the same memory location. The accessor would end up assigning a released object to the instance variable.

There are three common ways to release or autorelease the old object. Apple recommends that a set accessor release the old object if the get accessor autoreleases it and autorelease it if the get accessor does not.

If you release the old object, you can first test whether the new and the old objects are identical. If so, there is no need to waste time with the assignment, memory management, undo registration, or update notification, and the set accessor can immediately exit. This is a potential performance optimization as well as assuring correct behavior. If the objects are not identical, the set accessor can safely release the old object and retain or copy the new one in either order. It turns out to be easier to release the old one first in the case where the accessor copies the new object, as opposed to retaining it, because this avoids having to use an intermediate local variable. You see an example of this technique in the setTelephoneValue: accessor method, above. For a shared reference, just substitute retain for copy in that example.

One of the common alternatives to testing for identity of the old and new objects is to autorelease the old object so that, if it is identical to the new object, the object remains in existence long enough to be retained and reassigned to the instance variable. Apple recommends this pattern to match the case of an exceptional get accessor that does not retain and autorelease the returned object. This pattern might look like this:

```
- (void)setTelephoneValue:(NSString *)inValue {
    [[[self undoManager] prepareWithInvocationTarget:self]
            setTelephoneValue:telephoneValue];
    [telephoneValue autorelease];
    telephoneValue = [inValue copy];
    [[NSNotificationCenter defaultCenter]
            postNotificationName:
            VRTelephoneValueChangedNotification
            object:[self document]];
}
```

Another alternative is to be sure to retain or copy the new object before releasing the old one. In the case of a **copy**, this is awkward, requiring the use of an intermediate local variable. In the case of a **retain**, this very common pattern looks like this:

```
- (void)setTelephoneValue:(NSString *)inValue {
    [[[self undoManager] prepareWithInvocationTarget:self]
            setTelephoneValue:telephoneValue];
    [inValue retain];
    [telephoneValue release];
    telephoneValue = inValue;
    [[NSNotificationCenter defaultCenter]
            postNotificationName:
            VRTelephoneValueChangedNotification
            object:[self document]];
}
```

Releasing the old object is not only an issue that arises when a document has been around for a while and the user has given its instance variables new values. Even in the case of a newly created document, the instance variable points to an old object if the designated initializer allocated and initialized an object—possibly empty—and assigned it to the instance variable. An empty object is a real object, so the old object is taking up memory even in the case of a new document that only allocates the object. You must therefore make arrangements for the disposal of the memory that the old object uses in connection with the assignment of the new object to the instance variable in all cases.

WHETHER TO RETAIN OR COPY THE NEW OBJECT. In some circumstances it is better that a **set** accessor copy the new object than to retain it, as noted above.

A **set** accessor is often used to assign an object that is already in use by the application. In this situation, if the set accessor calls **retain**, the instance variable will point to the same object—that is, the same memory location—that is already in use elsewhere. Two or more variables then *share* the one object. In these circumstances, it is possible that some operation will change the value of one of the other references, and this will also change your instance variable's value. Similarly, if you eventually change your instance variable's value, it will change the value of the other references to the object. This may or may not be what you want, so you must always pay attention to whether a shared object or an independent object is appropriate in the circumstances.

In the case of a *value object* such as a telephone number, you usually want the instance variable to remain independent so you can maintain complete control over its value without having to worry that some other operation will change its value. A value object is a simple data value, and its **set** accessor is often used repeatedly to assign different values of a similar type to different instance variables.

Apple recommends that you use **copy** in a **set** accessor that assigns a value object to an instance variable that is independent of other instance variables. The only alternative is to make sure you create a new object every time you need a new value object; then use **retain**. Using **copy** is the more convenient and reliable technique, because it frees you from having to remember to create a new object. (Note that the compiler sometimes optimizes a **copy** to a simple **retain**, anyway, when it knows it can do so safely—for example, when the object is immutable.) If the instance variable should be shared, use **retain** in the **set** accessor.

So-called *entity objects*—objects that represent complex systems rather than relatively simple data values such as telephone numbers—are usually meant to be shared. You would not use **copy** in the **set** accessor for such an object, and you would not create a new object to pass to it.

CONCLUSION. Both for beginners writing simple applications and for experts and teams of developers writing complex applications, Apple believes it is advisable to apply the rules described above. This is especially so for new software projects and when you're writing reusable components such as classes for use by others.

The appropriate way to write **get** and **set** accessor methods is a subject of some considerable dispute as *Vermont Recipes* goes to press. If you want to consider other approaches, see the "Accessor Methods and Memory Management" sidebar for details.

Accessor Methods and Memory Management

As *Vermont Recipes* goes to press, there appears to be a consensus among many Cocoa developers about the best way to code get and set accessor methods for objects in most situations. A get accessor simply returns the instance variable. A set accessor first retains the incoming object, then releases the existing instance variable, and finally assigns the incoming object to the instance variable. Where a shared object is not wanted, the incoming object is copied, not retained. In Cocoa, this model is followed by Foundation collection classes and other performance-critical objects, as well as some AppKit classes. An alternative is to autorelease the existing object in the set accessor, as some AppKit classes do, but developers have tended to shy away from this because of concerns about performance degradation.

This consensus must be considered fragile, however, because Apple began, with WWDC 2002, to emphasize what it sees as its long-standing recommendation of a different pattern for most situations. You can see examples of this pattern in the "Memory Management" topic under *Application Design* in *Cocoa Programming Topics* on your disk.

Apple's recommendation involves moving from a paradigm based on releasing objects to one based on autoreleasing objects. Further, Apple recommends that objects normally be autoreleased in the get accessor rather than the set accessor. Apple's view can be summarized as set forth below.

For get accessors, return the instance variable retained, and autoreleased. By doing this, in Apple's view, the getter's client can have greater confidence than under the current consensus that the returned object will remain valid in the scope of the calling method. That is, its lifetime will be extended even if the body of the getter directly or indirectly releases the object.

Apple acknowledges exceptions where you should use the simple getter that forms today's developer consensus. The prime example is where performance is a paramount concern. In this case, the developer should document the accessor as an exception so the caller can take care of retaining and releasing the object.

For set accessors, release the existing object and retain or copy the new object, taking care to handle properly the case where the existing object and the new object are identical. Testing whether the incoming object and the existing object are identical is one way to handle the identity issue, and it may provide a performance enhancement no matter which of the techniques you use.

Some AppKit classes follow this getter and setter model today, and it is Apple's intent to expand its use in Cocoa going forward.

Apple believes that existing guidelines in the documentation, both historically and today, are not inconsistent with its position, although admittedly the current documentation is not unambiguous in every respect. In particular, Apple notes that it has never suggested that autorelease not be used in getters to extend the life of an object.

Apple's professed goal is to make the use of getters safer in the broadest range of applications and to keep the number of widely applicable guidelines small, along with a small number of easily identifiable exceptions. Apple's historical understanding and use of accessor methods within the Cocoa frameworks have evolved over time. In general, the tendency has been to eliminate distinctions between accessors and constructors, or properties and computed values. You should be able to use a received object without knowing how it was formed. Apple wants the developer community to move toward this model in new code, at least if it is destined to be reusable by the public—that is, to free callers from having to worry about the objects they receive and, when that is not possible, to document the exception.

Note that thread safety is not addressed by Apple's position, although the getter model would be one element of a thread-safe implementation. Apple is moving toward thread safety in Cocoa.

Until Apple formally publishes its recommendation—which is likely to happen fairly soon—a summary of guidelines that track Apple's recommendations appears in mmalcolm crawford's recent article, *Accessor Methods Revisited*, on the Stepwise Web site at www.stepwise.com/Articles/Technical/2002-06-11.01.html/.

Some experienced Cocoa developers have raised a number of objections to Apple's position. As *Vermont Recipes* goes to press, their counterpoint has not been published, but an article by Marcel Weiher and Marco Scheurer is slated to appear on the Stepwise Web site. Look for it at www.stepwise.com/Articles/.

The debate involves many complex and subtle issues that I cannot hope to cover adequately here. Among other things, the dissenters believe that Apple's new approach is wrong in theory; that it tries to solve a problem that rarely arises; that it will not eliminate bugs but often push them deeper, where they will be harder to find; and that it is easier to solve the real problem by careful coding. They also express concerns about inconsistent usage in the Cocoa community and impacts on maintainability, revision, and optimization of code. They feel that using autorelease is generally unnecessary and exacts an unacceptable performance penalty. In general, they believe that retaining and releasing objects should be left to the client, where the job can be handled correctly and appropriately in circumstances that can be known only to the client.

Apple owns United States Patents 6,304,884, 6,026,415, and 5,687,370 on autoreleasing. See the U.S. Patent and Trademakr Office Web site at www.uspto.gov/patft/.

3. **NOTIFICATION VARIABLES.** Return to the header file VRTextFieldModel.h, at the bottom of the file after the @end directive, to declare the notification variables, as follows:

```
//#pragma mark NOTIFICATIONS

// Formatted values
extern NSString
      *VRTextFieldModelIntegerValueChangedNotification;
extern NSString
      *VRTextFieldModelDecimalValueChangedNotification;
extern NSString
      *VRTextFieldModelTelephoneValueChangedNotification;
```

Turn back to the source file VRTextFieldModel.m, near the top of the file, to define the notification variables, as follows:

```
#pragma mark NOTIFICATIONS

// Formatted values
NSString *VRTextFieldModelIntegerValueChangedNotification =
      @"TextFieldModel integerValue Changed Notification";
NSString *VRTextFieldModelDecimalValueChangedNotification =
      @"TextFieldModel decimalValue Changed Notification";
NSString *VRTextFieldModelTelephoneValueChangedNotification =
      @"TextFieldModel telephoneValue Changed Notification";
```

4. **GUI UPDATE METHODS.** In the header file VRMainWindowController.h, declare specific update methods after the ACCESSORS section of the VRTextField-Controller category, as follows:

```
//#pragma mark INTERFACE MANAGEMENT - Specific updaters

// Formatted text fields
- (void)updateIntegerTextField:(NSNotification *)notification;
- (void)updateDecimalTextField:(NSNotification *)notification;
- (void)updateTelephoneTextField:(NSNotification *)notification;
```

In the category source file VRTextFieldController.m, define these specific update methods after the ACCESSORS section, as follows:

```
#pragma mark INTERFACE MANAGEMENT - Specific updaters

// Formatted text fields

- (void)updateIntegerTextField:
```

```
        (NSNotification *)notification {
    if (([[self textFieldModel] integerValue] !=
        [[self integerTextField] intValue]) ||
        ([[[self integerTextField] stringValue]
        isEqualToString:@""])) {
      [[self integerTextField] setIntValue:
          [[self textFieldModel] integerValue]];
    }
}


- (void)updateDecimalTextField:
      (NSNotification *)notification {
    if (([[self textFieldModel] decimalValue] !=
        [[self decimalTextField] floatValue]) ||
        ([[[self decimalTextField] stringValue]
        isEqualToString:@""])) {
      [[self decimalTextField] setFloatValue:
            [[self textFieldModel] decimalValue]];
    }
}


- (void)updateTelephoneTextField:
      (NSNotification *)notification {
    if (![[[self textFieldModel] telephoneValue]
        isEqualToString:[[self telephoneTextField]
        stringValue]]) {
      [[self telephoneTextField] setStringValue:
            [[self textFieldModel] telephoneValue]];
    }
}
```

These specific updaters are identical in concept to the text field updater you wrote for the Speed Limiter text field in Recipe 3, Step 2.2.

Notice that the last of the update methods sets its text field to a string. This field will be formatted to North American phone number conventions using a custom formatter, which you will write in Recipe 6. It won't require localization because these phone numbers should appear the same to people calling from anywhere in the world. Finally, you are perfectly happy to have the Telephone text field left blank, because the person who is using this application may not have a telephone, so you omit the test for a blank field in its updater.

5. **NOTIFICATION OBSERVERS.** Register the window controller as an observer of the notifications that will trigger the updater methods, by inserting the following statements in the `registerNotificationObserversForTextFieldsTab` method of the category source file VRTextFieldController.m:

```
// Formatted text fields
[[NSNotificationCenter defaultCenter] addObserver:self
        selector:@selector(updateIntegerTextField:)
        name:VRTextFieldModelIntegerValueChangedNotification
        object:[self document]];
[[NSNotificationCenter defaultCenter] addObserver:self
        selector:@selector(updateDecimalTextField:)
        name:VRTextFieldModelDecimalValueChangedNotification
        object:[self document]];
[[NSNotificationCenter defaultCenter] addObserver:self
        selector:@selector(updateTelephoneTextField:)
        name:VRTextFieldModelTelephoneValueChangedNotification
        object:[self document]];
}
```

6. **ACTION METHODS.** In the header file VRMainWindowController.h, at the end of the VRTextFieldController category at the end of the file, add the following:

```
//#pragma mark ACTIONS

// Formatted text fields
- (IBAction)integerTextFieldAction:(id)sender;
- (IBAction)decimalTextFieldAction:(id)sender;
- (IBAction)telephoneTextFieldAction:(id)sender;
```

In the category source file VRTextFieldController.m, define the action methods at the end of the file, as follows:

```
#pragma mark ACTIONS

// Formatted text fields

- (IBAction)integerTextFieldAction:(id)sender {
    [[self textFieldModel]
      setIntegerValue:[sender intValue]];
    [[[self document] undoManager] setActionName:
          NSLocalizedString(@"Set Integer Value",
          @"Name of undo/redo menu item after \
          Integer text field was set")];
```

```
        }

- (IBAction)decimalTextFieldAction:(id)sender {
    [[self textFieldModel]
        setDecimalValue:[sender floatValue]];
    [[[self document] undoManager] setActionName:
            NSLocalizedString(@"Set Decimal Value",
            @"Name of undo/redo menu item after \
            Decimal text field was set")];
}


- (IBAction)telephoneTextFieldAction:(id)sender {
    [[self textFieldModel]
            setTelephoneValue:[sender stringValue]];
    [[[self document] undoManager] setActionName:
            NSLocalizedString(@"Set Telephone Value",
            @"Name of undo/redo menu item after \
            Telephone text field was set")];
}
```

7. **LOCALIZABLE.STRINGS.** Update the Localizable.strings file by adding Set Integer Value, Set Decimal Value, and Set Telephone Value.

8. **INITIALIZATION.** Leave the first two data variables uninitialized. Objective-C will initialize them to 0.

However, in the case of the **telephoneValue** variable, you have to consider where the initial NSString object will come from when a new window is created. The answer for every instance variable that holds an object, rather than a standard C data type, is that you must instantiate it yourself. You typically do this in the model object's designated initializer.

Go to the **initWithDocument:** method in VRTextFieldModel.m and add the following at the end (before the **NSLog()** call, if you implemented it):

```
telephoneValue =
        [[NSString alloc] initWithString:@"(800) 555-1212"];
```

ALLOCATING AND INITIALIZING OBJECTS. The statement above is written for the most general case, to illustrate the pattern you should use to allocate and initialize almost any kind of object. The instance variable was already declared in the **@interface** compiler directive block, and its type was declared there as an NSString object. Now, in the designated initializer, you first allocate memory for it by calling the NSObject **alloc** class method that NSString, like almost all Cocoa objects, inherits. Allocating it implicitly retains it. Then, in the usual pattern for allocating and initializing any Objective-C object in one statement, you call one of NSString's instance methods designed to initialize its value—here, the `initWithString:` instance method, passing a string constant. Convenience methods in Foundation, like NSString's `initWithString:` method, return their objects autoreleased by convention to give clients the opportunity to claim ownership of them by retaining them, but you needn't be concerned with that here because your `alloc` retained the object; it will last at least until you no longer need it and therefore `release` it.

Notice that you did not call the `setTelephoneValue:` accessor method that you have already written. That accessor method does not instantiate a new instance variable; that is, it does not allocate the memory required before a value can be assigned to an object. Therefore, the accessor method cannot be used alone here, in the designated initializer, as it could be for standard C data types that don't require allocation of memory. Because most objects come with a variety of built-in initialization methods similar to NSString's `initWithString:` method, you can generally allocate, initialize, and pass a default value to a new object in a single statement along the lines of the statement you wrote above. Because you do not use the accessor method, you don't have to bracket this statement in calls to NSUndoManager's `disableUndoRegistration` and `enableUndo-Registration` methods.

You could have accomplished the same objective in a variety of other ways. For example, you could have first allocated and initialized an empty string, then used the `setTelephoneValue:` accessor method to set its value. In this case, you would have had to disable undo registration temporarily. While this is more work than you need to undertake here, you should understand the principle. You would do so like this:

```
[[self undoManager] disableUndoRegistration];

telephoneValue = [[NSString alloc] init];
[self setTelephoneValue:@"(800) 555-1212"];

[[self undoManager] enableUndoRegistration];
```

The `[[telephoneValue alloc] init]` message in that code is one of many ways in which you can create an empty string object in Cocoa. You will see several others in a moment. You can use an identical technique to allocate and initialize an empty object of just about any kind, since almost all objects inherit NSObject's `init` method.

ALLOCATING AND INITIALIZING A STRING OBJECT. The NSString class is unusual in providing a special way to instantiate and initialize string objects. Because strings are used so frequently, it has its own compiler directive for creating new strings with specified values. You saw an example of this in the code just written above, where the compiler directive was used to pass a string object containing a specific telephone number to the `setTelephoneValue:` accessor method. In fact, that example did a lot of work that is unnecessary in the special case of string objects. You could simply have written this, without allocating memory for the object and without calling its set accessor:

```
telephoneValue = @"(800) 555-1212"];
```

The `@"any string"` compiler directive creates a string constant that exists throughout the life of the application. You learned about this in Instruction 7 of Recipe 1, Step 3.3. It does not require explicit allocation of memory, nor the use of `retain` and `release`, and for these reasons it is very convenient to use. Nevertheless, you can use `retain` and `release` with a string constant to write string routines without having to consider how they were created. Note, however, that you could not have used your `setTelephoneValue:` accessor method alone in the `initWithDocument:` designated initializer, without first allocating memory for the instance variable, because the accessor would have attempted to release an old object at a time when no such old object has yet been allocated. A `release` without an earlier matching `retain`—for example, from an earlier `alloc`—would crash the application.

ALLOCATING AND INITIALIZING AN EMPTY OBJECT. If you had wanted the document to open without an initial default telephone number in the `telephoneValue` instance variable, you still would have had to allocate and initialize a string object, albeit one containing an empty string. This is true of most objects for which you declare an instance variable in your application. You can, in a manner of speaking, allocate, initialize, and assign an empty string object in Cocoa all at once using a string constant, like this:

```
telephoneValue = @"";
```

Alternatively, you can do it like this, which is typically the right way to allocate and initialize any object other than an NSString object to an initial, empty value:

```
telephoneValue = [[NSString alloc] init];
```

Many Cocoa objects have a class method that explicitly returns an empty instance, so another common way to allocate and initialize a simple object is something like the following.

```
telephoneValue = [NSString string];
```

DEALLOCATING AN OBJECT. Finally, you must release every object that you allocate to avoid memory leaks, so add a **dealloc** override method to VRTextFieldModel.m, after the designated initializer, as shown below. It will deallocate whatever object is currently referred to by the instance variable, including the object assigned by the last call to the **setTelephoneValue:** accessor method described in Instruction 2, above, if the user has typed a new value in the field. As described above, the **release** is valid here even if the string is a string constant created using the **@"any string"** compiler directive.

```
- (void)dealloc {
    [[self telephoneValue] release];
    [super dealloc];
}
```

9. **DATA STORAGE.** In the source file VRTextFieldModel.m, define the following keys at the end of the file:

```
//#pragma mark STORAGE

// Keys and values for dictionary

// Formatted values
static NSString *VRIntegerValueKey =
        @"VRTextFieldModelIntegerValue";
static NSString *VRDecimalValueKey =
        @"VRTextFieldModelDecimalValue";
static NSString *VRTelephoneValueKey =
        @"VRTextFieldModelTelephoneValue";
```

Immediately after that, add this method:

```
// Saving information to persistent storage

- (void)addDataToDictionary:(NSMutableDictionary *)dictionary {

    // Formatted values
    [dictionary setObject:[NSString stringWithFormat:@"%d",
            [self integerValue]] forKey:VRIntegerValueKey];
    [dictionary setObject:[NSString stringWithFormat:@"%f",
            [self decimalValue]] forKey:VRDecimalValueKey];
    [dictionary setObject:[self telephoneValue]
            forKey:VRTelephoneValueKey];
}
```

Again, the `telephoneValue` variable does not require conversion to a string because it is already a string.

And add these lines after that:

```
// Loading information from persistent storage

- (void)restoreDataFromDictionary:(NSDictionary *)dictionary {
    [[self undoManager] disableUndoRegistration];

    // Formatted values
    [self setIntegerValue:[[dictionary
        objectForKey:VRIntegerValueKey] intValue]];
    [self setDecimalValue:[[dictionary
        objectForKey:VRDecimalValueKey] floatValue]];
    [self setTelephoneValue:[dictionary
        objectForKey:VRTelephoneValueKey]];

    [[self undoManager] enableUndoRegistration];
}
```

Again, the parameter passed to `setTelephoneValue:` does not have to be converted to a string because it is already a string.

Since you are working with a new pair of header and source files for the VRTextFieldModel class, you also have to declare these storage methods in the header file. Add the following declarations at the end of VRTextFieldModel.h:

```
//#pragma mark STORAGE

// Saving information to persistent storage:

- (void)addDataToDictionary:(NSMutableDictionary *)dictionary;

// Loading information from persistent storage

- (void)restoreDataFromDictionary:(NSDictionary *)dictionary:
```

Finally, you must add calls to these two storage methods in VRDocument.m, in the `dictionaryFromModel` and `readFromFile:ofType:` methods, respectively. In the `dictionaryFromModel` method, add this line immediately following its `buttonModel` look-alike:

```
[[self textFieldModel] addDataToDictionary:dictionary];
```

In the `readFromFile:ofType:` method, add this line immediately following its `buttonModel` equivalent:

```
[[self textFieldModel] restoreDataFromDictionary:dictionary];
```

10. **GUI UPDATE METHOD INVOCATION.** Finally, in the category source file VRTextFieldController.m, add the following calls at the end of the updateTextFieldsTab method:

```
// Formatted text fields
[self updateIntegerTextField:nil];
[self updateDecimalTextField:nil];
[self updateTelephoneTextField:nil];
```

11. **DESCRIPTION METHOD.** Add a `description` method to VRTextFieldModel for debugging use, before the STORAGE section:

```
#pragma mark DEBUGGING


- (NSString *) description {
    return [NSString stringWithFormat:@"%@\
    \n\tintegerValue:%@\n
    \n\tdecimalValue:%@\n
    \n\ttelephoneValue:%@\n",
        [super description],
        [[NSNumber numberWithInt:
                [self integerValue]] stringValue],
        [[NSNumber numberWithFloat:
                [self decimalValue]] stringValue]
        [self telephoneValue]];
}
```

12. **HELP TAGS.** Using Interface Builder, provide a Help tag for the three text fields: "Enter an integer," "Enter a decimal number," and "Enter a telephone number."

1.5 Read the Source Files into the Nib File and Connect Outlets and Actions

Inform the nib file of the new outlets and actions you have created for the Integer, Decimal, and Telephone text fields, then connect them to the three new text fields.

1. In Interface Builder, select the Classes tab in the nib file window, then choose Classes > Read Files. In the resulting dialog, select the header file in which you have created outlets or actions, VRMainWindowController.h, then click the Parse button.

2. Select the Instances tab. Control-drag from the File's Owner icon to each of the three new text fields in turn and click their outlet names, then click the Connect button in the Connections pane of the File's Owner Info Panel.

3. Control-drag from each of the three new text fields to the File's Owner icon in turn. Click the targets in the left pane and the appropriate actions in the right pane of the Outlets section in the Connections pane of the NSTextField Info Panel, then click the Connect button.

1.6 Build and Run the Application

Build and run the application.

Try typing in each of the three new text fields.

Among other things, observe that you can type anything into any text field—numbers or text—and enter it. You receive no warning that none of the fields accepts letters, for example, or that "Hi, there!" isn't a valid telephone number.

Also, try typing something into one of the text fields, then erasing it, all without pressing Return, Enter, or Tab to commit the value. Then look at the Edit menu and observe that the Undo menu item is not available to restore the characters you just erased.

Finally, try dragging the contents of one of the text fields to another text field. It doesn't work.

Evidently, simply creating a text field does not give you all the power and sophistication your users expect of full-featured text fields in a Mac OS X application. In the next several recipes, you will take care of these deficiencies.

You have now created and wired up three text fields in the Text Fields pane to serve as a test bed for things to come. Before moving on, however, you need to set up the key view loop, or tabbing order, for your new text fields. You will learn in addition that Mac OS X supports tabbing between nontextual user controls.

Step 2: Set Up the Key View Loop

HIGHLIGHTS:

Setting the tab order among text fields and other controls in a window or tab view item

Preventing tabbed text fields from registering with the undo manager when their values are unchanged

Preventing clicked controls from registering with the undo manager when their values are unchanged

Here, you learn the procedure you must follow to establish the tabbing order, or key view loop, between editable text fields within their view. In fact, you should follow this procedure when creating any kind of user control, because the Mac OS X user interface supports a systemwide preference allowing use of the keyboard to navigate and manipulate user controls of all kinds. In System Preference's Keyboard pane, a user can select the Full Keyboard Access pane, then select the "Any control" radio button to enable keyboard navigation and manipulation of all user controls, not only text fields and lists. If this radio button is not selected, tabbing will move the user's selection only among text fields and items in lists, even if all user controls are properly hooked into the key view loop.

When the option is selected, pressing Tab or Shift-Tab moves the user's selection forward or backward from any user control to the next. Pressing the spacebar sets and clears some kinds of control settings, such as checkboxes, and expands others, such as pop-up and pop-down command menus. In addition, when the selection moves to some kinds of controls, such as a tab view or a radio button cluster, it becomes possible for the user to press the arrow keys to highlight different items within the view, such as another tab view item or another radio button, and then use the spacebar to set it. In Mac OS X 10.2, pressing Command-Shift-` sends focus from a window to a drawer, according to the release notes.

For all of this to work, you must connect the initial first responder and the next key view of many views and controls, which you usually do by using Interface Builder.

Wiring up the key view loop is also necessary to ensure a correct user experience with respect to editing text fields. The *Aqua Human Interface Guidelines* indicate that typing in a window's text field should not be allowed until the user has deliberately selected it for editing (the rule for dialogs is different). In addition to selecting a text field by clicking or double-clicking in it, users are accustomed to pressing the Tab key. While no text field is active in a window, pressing Tab should select the first text field for editing (usually the upper-left field on Roman systems). Furthermore, pressing the Tab key while a text field is already selected validates and commits any pending data in that field and causes the insertion point to jump from one to another editable text field in the window in a sensible order, making it easy to enter data in a number of text fields in succession with one's hands on the keyboard. You can and should provide for this behavior by using Interface Builder.

The use of the keyboard for interface navigation and control is documented very briefly and incompletely in the "Using Keyboard Interface Control in Windows" task in the "Windows and Panels" section of the "User Interface Elements" topic in Cocoa Help's *Programming Topics*. The same basic principles govern setting the key view loop in a tab view item. The Cocoa key view loop routines for tab views were broken until the release of Mac OS X 10.1. Now that they've been fixed in Mac OS X 10.2, you can use the new conventions for key view loops in tab views and tab view items that are detailed in the Mac OS X 10.1 AppKit *Release Notes*. Even the *Release Notes* are a little difficult to decipher, so I provide very detailed instructions here.

2.1 Set the Tab Order, or Key View Loop, Using Interface Builder

To specify which text field or other user control in a window or a tab view item will be selected the first time the user presses the Tab key, you must designate an initial first responder for the window or tab view item. You typically do this in Interface Builder, but of course you can handle it programmatically as well, using the `setInitialFirstResponder:` methods declared in NSWindow and NSTabViewItem. To specify the route that the Tab key will follow among other user controls in the view thereafter, you must designate each control's next key view. You also typically do this in Interface Builder, but again you can do it programmatically. When the user clicks or tabs into a user control, that control becomes the view's first responder for the time being. Cocoa will automatically establish a default key view loop for you if you don't provide one, but you will not necessarily find it satisfactory.

Mac OS X 10.1 introduced new concepts, allowing tab views to supplement the typical behavior of a key view loop in a window.

First, a tab view should be the next key view of some other user control in the tab view's enclosing window, and it might be the initial first responder of the window as well.

In turn, the tab view must have as its own next key view some other control in the window, such as a button or a text field. The next key view that you specify initially for a tab view is called its *original next key view*. You usually set it in Interface Builder by connecting the tab view's `nextKeyView` outlet to some user control outside the tab view but within its enclosing window. Cocoa remembers the original next key view for your convenience, but you needn't (indeed, you can't) do anything with it.

Second, once you have the tab view's key loop completely set up, you must set up a separate key view loop for each tab view item within the tab view, specifying both an initial first responder and a valid key view loop for each. A valid key view loop in a tab view item must form a circle; that is, the `nextKeyView` outlet of the last key view in every tab view item's key loop must connect to the view that is that tab view item's initial first responder. Otherwise, the key view loop will not behave correctly.

It is this last point that is key to understanding the new concept of the original next key view. Internally, Cocoa recognizes that the control whose next key view is the initial first responder at the beginning of a tab view item's key loop is the last control in the loop. When the user tabs out of the last control in the tab view item, Cocoa substitutes the remembered original next key view of the tab view, and the selection jumps to that control, which may be, for example, a button or a text field in the window enclosing the tab view.

If you've set up all of this correctly and enabled the "Any control" option, a user can tab into the tab view from somewhere else in the window, causing one of the tabs to become highlighted. Then the user can, if desired, use the arrow keys to select a particular tab view item (perhaps first having to press Tab again to reselect the tab view). With the desired tab highlighted, the user can then tab through successive user controls in the selected tab view item, then tab out of the tab view to its next key view (the original next key view) in the window. The last step is called tabbing "out the other side" in the *Release Notes*. The user can use Shift-Tab to reverse the process. With certain kinds of controls selected, such as a radio button cluster, the user can press arrow keys to highlight different items, then use the spacebar to set them. In other cases, such as checkboxes, the user can set them with the spacebar alone.

This all happens only if the "Any control" option is in force, however. With that option turned off, tabbing only highlights text fields and lists. Continued tabbing between text fields within any one tab view item will proceed in a circular fashion, never going out the other side.

In general, every user control in a window can and normally should be included in the key view loop, and thus potentially be included when the user navigates between and within its controls via the keyboard. Users will come to expect that they can turn on this option in Mac OS X applications, and your application will fail to satisfy if you haven't set it up in Interface Builder to behave this way when your users tell it to do so. You can override a particular view's `acceptsFirstResponder` method to return `NO` so it will automatically be skipped, or you can simply leave a particular control out of the key view loop when you don't want it to appear there under any circumstances.

When adding or removing user controls from a window during design, you must remember to revise the next key views and possibly the initial first responder so as to accommodate the change and maintain the key view loop's integrity. Failing to do so is a frequent source of errors. That's why I included this as an item in the list of tasks required when creating any user control, in Recipe 2, Step 2. I have ignored this task until now, but henceforward I remind you to implement it.

The first four instructions, below, show how to use the Instances tab of the VRDocument.nib window to set up a valid key view loop for the user controls at the top level of the window: namely, the tab view, the Back button, and the Next button. The remaining instructions show how to set up valid key view loops in each tab view item in the tab view. When you have completed Step 1.4, you will have correctly set the tabbing order for all three tab view items in the Vermont Recipes application.

In carrying out the following instructions, you will see that when the Instances tab is in its default Icon View mode, you can only see *top-level* object icons in the window. They represent objects that have been instantiated in Interface Builder, or their proxies. To connect lower-level objects that have been installed in a top-level object—such as the Integer text field, here installed in a tab view item—you can and sometimes must switch to the List View mode of the Instances tab and tunnel down through the outline levels until you find the objects you want. You can Control-drag between objects in the main document window and either mode of the nib window's Instances tab. In some cases, such as when you're setting the initial first responder of a tab view item, List View mode is the only available technique for making connections; you cannot Control-drag from a tab view item in the main document window.

1. In the VRDocument.nib window, select the Instances tab. For now, remain in Icon View mode. Control-drag from the Parent Window icon to the tab view in the document window above the VRDocument.nib window. In the NSWindow Info Panel, select **initialFirstResponder** in the Outlets pane, then click Connect. The tab view is now the initial first responder of the main document window.

2. Control-drag from the tab view in the main document window to the general vicinity of the window's Back button. The Back button is hidden from view while you perform the drag, because it lies in the window behind the tab view, but the drag will still latch onto the location of the Back button and show a ghostly outline around its square shape. In the NSTabView Info Panel, select **nextKeyView** and click Connect. The Back button is now the next key view of the tab view. Cocoa will also remember the Back button as the tab view's original next key view. (If you aren't sure you have found the Back button while Control-dragging, use the Instances tab's List View mode instead.)

3. Deselect the tab view in the main document window by clicking in an empty area within the window, and the Back and Next buttons become visible. Control-drag from the Back button to the Next button, select **nextKeyView** in the NSButton Info Panel, and click Connect. The Next button is now the next key view of the Back button.

4. Control-drag from the Next button to the tab view, select **nextKeyView** in the NSButton Info Panel, and click Connect. The tab view is now the next key view of the Next button. You have defined a complete key loop for the window, from the tab view to the Back button to the Next button and around again.

Next, you must turn to each tab view item and specify a key view loop for each one.

5. Select the Text Fields tab view item in the main document window by clicking the Text Fields tab. Try to Control-drag from the Text Fields tab view item to the Integer text field. The computer beeps at you. You can't initiate a Control-drag from a tab view item in the main document window.

   Instead, go to the Instances tab of the VRDocument.nib window and select its List View mode by clicking the little button at the top of the vertical scroll bar. You see an expandable outline of the Instances tab, which allows you to navigate the entire hierarchy of objects represented in the nib file.

   Find NSWindow at the bottom of the list and expand it, then expand its Content View object. Among other objects contained in the window's content view, you see NSTabView. Expand it, and you see the three tab view items. You may have to scroll down in the window to see everything. (If you expand any of the tab view items, you will see the hierarchy of user controls contained in that pane, including the group boxes you have created in some of them to hold other controls. The outline in the List View reflects the nesting hierarchy of the application's main document window, its tab view, its tab view items, and their controls.)

   Control-drag from NSTabViewItem (Text Fields) to the Integer text field in the main document window. (You could instead have dragged to the Integer text field in the list itself, but it is harder to know which text field is which in the List View because all three currently have values of 0.) Click the `initialFirstResponder` outlet in the NSTabViewItem Info Panel, then click Connect. You have now made the Integer text field the initial first responder for the Text Fields pane of the tab view. As a result, when the user presses the Tab key after selecting the Text Fields pane, the Integer text field will be selected and the user can type over whatever value it contains.

6. Now, in the main document window, Control-drag from the Integer text field to the Decimal text field, select `nextKeyView` in the NSTextField Info Panel, and click Connect. Then Control-drag from the Decimal text field to the Telephone text field and connect its next key view in the same way. Finally, Control-drag from the Telephone text field to the Integer text field and repeat the process to complete the key loop for the Text Fields tab view item.

7. Follow Instructions 5 and 6 in the Sliders text field item. Start with the Personality slider as the initial first responder, then proceed to the Speed Limiter text field, the Speed Limiter slider, the Quantum Electron State slider, the Low button, and the High button, setting each control's next key view to the next. Finally, make the Personality slider the next key view of the Quantum Electron State slider to complete the key loop for the Sliders tab view item.

8. Follow Instructions 5 and 6 in the Buttons tab view item. In Recipe 1, Step 2.6.3, you designated the Checkbox control as its initial first responder. Make the Triangle checkbox in the Pegs for Tots group the next key view of the Checkbox control. (You could have made the box the next key view, but this wouldn't work right because an NSBox object doesn't let you designate one of its controls as initial first responder.) Continue connecting next key views from top to bottom and left to right in this fashion. When you get to the Party Affiliation radio button cluster, you must connect the entire cluster as the next key view of the Classical checkbox; Cocoa will let the user press arrow keys to select a particular radio button and the spacebar to select it. Be sure to complete the key view loop by designating the Checkbox control as the next key view of the Beeper pull-down menu.

That's it. You've set up correct key view loops for the window and all three tab view items.

2.2 Prevent Tabbing Among Text Fields from Registering with the Undo Manager

If you were to build and run the application now, you would discover one last bunch of problems, all related to one another and easily fixed. When you tab from text field to text field in the Text Fields pane, the window is *dirtied*—that is, a dot appears in the close button in the window's title bar, indicating that a change has been made to the data displayed in the window. In addition, the Undo menu item in the Edit menu now indicates, for example, that you may Undo Set Integer Value or Undo Set Decimal Value and so on. Yet you haven't changed the value of any of the text fields in the pane but only tabbed through all of them. What is wrong?

If you set a few strategic breakpoints in the code and run the application in debug mode, you will discover that tabbing past a text field invokes its action method. You will also see this in the StdIO pane in Project Builder if you implemented `NSLog()` calls in your set accessors. The action method sets the data value associated with the text field, but in this case resets it to the same value it already holds. It does this by invoking the set accessor method, which records the "change" in the data value for the undo manager's use. When the accessor method returns, the action method also sets the Undo menu item name. None of this is appropriate when you merely tab through a text field without changing its value.

An obvious way to prevent this behavior is to begin every text field's action method with a test, checking whether the value currently held in the model object's associated data variable is not the same as the value currently displayed in the user control. If they are the same, there is no need to invoke the action method. In VRTextFieldController.m, revise the three text field action methods to read as follows:

```objc
- (IBAction)integerTextFieldAction:(id)sender {
    if ([[self textFieldModel] integerValue] !=
            [sender intValue]) {
        [[self textFieldModel] setIntegerValue:[sender intValue]];
        [[[self document] undoManager] setActionName:
                NSLocalizedString(@"Set Integer Value",
                @"Name of undo/redo menu item after Integer \
                text field was set")];
    }
}


- (IBAction)decimalTextFieldAction:(id)sender {
    if ([[self textFieldModel] decimalValue] !=
            [sender floatValue]) {
        [[self textFieldModel] setDecimalValue:[sender floatValue]];
        [[[self document] undoManager] setActionName:
                NSLocalizedString(@"Set Decimal Value",
                @"Name of undo/redo menu item after Decimal \
                text field was set")];
    }
}


- (IBAction)telephoneTextFieldAction:(id)sender {
    if (![[[self textFieldModel] telephoneValue]
            isEqualToString:[sender stringValue]]) {
        [[self textFieldModel]
                setTelephoneValue:[sender stringValue]];
        [[[self document] undoManager] setActionName:
                NSLocalizedString(@"Set Telephone Value",
                @"Name of undo/redo menu item after Telephone \
                text field was set")];
    }
}
```

Note that the **telephoneTextFieldAction:** method must use NSString's
isEqualToString: method, rather than the direct comparison that is possible with
an **int** and a **float**. You don't want to compare the memory addresses of the objects,
which is what would happen if you used a simple C comparison operator. All you
care about is whether the text is the same, which is what **isEqualToString:** does.

You should also change the Speed Limiter text field's action method in
VRSliderController.m, so that repeatedly pressing the Tab key on that field will not
cause the same problem. In earlier versions of *Vermont Recipes,* I did this by comparing

the associated slider's value to the text field value, but I now suggest you do this by comparing the current value of the data in the model object to the current value of the slider, as in the case of the other text fields, like so:

```
if ([[self sliderModel] speedValue] !=
    [sender floatValue]) {
```

2.3 Prevent Clicked Controls from Registering with the Undo Manager

You might wonder whether any action methods other than text field action methods require modification to suppress registration with the undo manager when resetting them to their previous values by tabbing past them while the "Any control" option is in force. Try it, and you see that tabbing through checkboxes, radio button clusters, sliders, and associated push-buttons without changing their values does not result in their action methods' firing.

It may seem as though the issue is therefore limited to text fields, but it isn't that simple.

Another way to cause unnecessary registration with the undo manager with respect to some kinds of controls is simply to click them. Checkboxes do not present this problem, because whenever you click a checkbox, its value changes, requiring registration with the undo manager. Some thought and a little testing reveal, however, that it is possible to click controls of several other kinds without changing their value, and in each case the document is dirtied inappropriately. These include clicking a radio button that is already on; clicking a slider at precisely its current setting (this can be hard to do with a continuous slider, since the slightest drag changes its value); and using a pop-up menu to reselect its current setting. In these cases, the user probably did not intend to make a change to the document, and in any event no change was made. In some cases, the user may simply have been looking to see what other values are available (for example, in the case of a pop-up menu). You should therefore make similar changes to each of the action methods shown below. In each case, wrap the existing body of the action method in the indicated test.

Some might prefer to have clicks that don't change the value registered with the undo manager, because a user might expect an undo to appear in the stack as a result of clicking the control. While this may be debatable, I prefer consistency with the tabbing behavior built into Cocoa.

In **partyAction:**, use:

```
if ([[self buttonModel] partyValue] !=
    [sender selectedTag]) {
```

In stateAction:, use:

```
if ([[self buttonModel] stateValue] !=
        [sender indexOfSelectedItem]) {
```

In personalityAction:, use:

```
if ([[self sliderModel] personalityValue] !=
        [sender floatValue]) {
```

In speedSliderAction:, use:

```
if ([[self sliderModel] speedValue] !=
        [sender floatValue]) {
```

In quantumSliderAction:, use:

```
if ([[self sliderModel] quantumValue] !=
        [sender floatValue]) {
```

In both quantumButtonLoAction: and quantumButtonHiAction:, it is not the current setting of the sender (a button), but the minimum and maximum acceptable slider settings, respectively, that govern the test. Although these two buttons are secondary controls and you could test them against the current value of the slider, I prefer to test against the current data value in the sliderModel object, in accordance with my consistent practice. In quantumButtonLoAction:, use:

```
if ([[self sliderModel] quantumValue] !=
        [[self quantumSlider] minValue]) {
```

And in quantumButtonHiAction:, use:

```
if ([[self sliderModel] quantumValue] !=
        [[self quantumSlider] maxValue]) {
```

2.4 Build and Run the Application

Build and run the application. You need not read the files into Interface Builder because you haven't created any new outlets or actions.

For the first round of tests, use the Keyboard pane of System Preferences to make sure the "Any control" option is turned off.

Switch to the Text Fields pane and confirm that no text field is active and that you cannot type into a text field. Then press the Tab key to confirm that the insertion point appears in the Integer text field and that typing is now allowed there.

Press Tab again and note that the insertion point jumps to the Decimal text field. Save the document to disk, then make another change to the Integer text field and choose File > Revert. If the Integer text field reverts to the saved value, you know that pressing Tab properly committed the value you first entered.

Press Tab several times and see that each text field in turn is made key, and that you can continue tabbing indefinitely to cycle repeatedly through the fields. Watch the window's close button and look at the Edit > Undo menu item after each press of the Tab key to confirm that the undo manager did not register the action.

Select the Sliders pane and make sure the Speed Limiter text field is made key only after you press the Tab key, and that pressing Tab repeatedly does not register with the undo manager. Set the Quantum slider to its highest or lowest setting, then click the High or Low button to confirm that the undo manager doesn't register this action either.

Select the Buttons pane and reselect the current setting of the Party radio button cluster and the State pop-up menu to confirm that neither action registers with the undo manager.

Next, turn on the "Any control" option in System Preferences. You don't have to quit and relaunch the Vermont Recipes application; the change takes effect immediately. Press Tab repeatedly and watch which controls are highlighted. Experiment with the arrow keys and the spacebar to see how full keyboard control works. Don't forget to turn this option off again when you're done testing, unless you prefer having it turned on.

Conclusion

In Recipe 4 you created several text fields in the Text Fields tab view item, as well as a new model class and controller category to hold code to control their unique features. You also established a key view loop between them, as well as between user controls in other tab view items.

In the next series of recipes, you will add several enhancements to the text fields, including alert sheets, formatters, live undo and redo while editing a field, and drag-and-drop editing.

Text Field Extras: Alert Sheets

This recipe is the first in a series of recipes dealing with enhancements to text fields. Recipe 3 briefly introduced you to text fields, as well as two features of Cocoa that come in handy when you're working with text fields—alert sheets and formatters. In Recipe 4, you created three additional text fields and set their key view loop. Now, in this and the next several recipes, you will learn how to enhance text fields with sheets, formatters, live undo and redo while editing, and drag-and-drop editing, all of which are important for gaining the greatest benefit from the text fields you will implement in your applications. In Recipe 5, you will start by obtaining a thorough grounding in interactive alert sheets.

Before turning to Step 1, you should prepare your project files for Recipe 5. Follow a procedure similar to that in the introduction to Recipe 4, updating the build version in the Info.plist Entries to **5**. You should not update the document version code in VRDocument.m because you will not change the document's file format in this recipe.

Step 1: Create a Complex, Interactive Document-Modal Alert Sheet to Deal with an Invalid Text Field Entry

In Step 1, you will take up the challenge posed in Recipe 3, Step 2. There, you associated an NSNumberFormatter object with the Speed Limiter text field, but you provided the user with nothing more than a beep when an illegal value was entered. Now, you will add code to the application to present a document-modal alert sheet explaining to the user the nature of any data entry problem and

HIGHLIGHTS:
Internationalizing an alert sheet

offering options to resolve it. You saw how to present a simple, one-button sheet in Recipe 3, Step 1, using a single Cocoa function, `NSBeginAlertSheet()`. The sheets you will create in this recipe involve a number of complexities, such as varying the sheet's content depending on the nature of the error and recognizing the choice the user made between multiple buttons in the sheet.

I've deferred text validation and complex alert sheets to this recipe, where your lesson in text field extras begins, because they are often associated with text fields. The other controls you have encountered up to this point, buttons and sliders, have their data types and constraints built in. Your users normally can't accidentally enter an illegal value into a checkbox by clicking it (if setting or clearing a checkbox is improper in a particular context, it should be disabled), and they can't exceed a slider's maximum value by inadvertently dragging it over the top. Although you can use formatters and other techniques to prevent similar errors in text fields, an alert is required if you wish to provide the user with an explanation and helpful options.

Macintosh human interface guidelines have dictated, since as long ago as 1986, that text entered into text fields should be tested for validity and, if valid, committed when the user presses the Return, Enter, or Tab key or clicks anywhere other than in the text field.

You must take the last part of this rule at something less than face value. It may be understood as requiring a validity check when the user clicks anywhere else *on certain enabled objects within the text field's window*. Clicks in many other locations do not require validation of a pending text edit. For example, you must allow clicking another window, including another application's window, or clicking the desktop in the modern, nonmodal Macintosh environment. The ability to work in several windows at once greatly increases the flexibility of Macintosh usage; for example, the user may need to copy some text in a second window to paste into the text field currently being edited. The user's switching to another window or another application suspends the editing of the text field only temporarily, pending the user's return to its window, at which time its cursor will again become active. Clicking an inactive part of the window, such as its background, also normally does not require a validity check for the text field but instead leaves it active and ready to accept typing. Similarly, clicking various other menu items, buttons, sliders, and other controls need not trigger a validity check for the text field because, among other things, these other user controls might alter application settings that affect what is happening in the text field—for example, applying another font or style to a selected word. However, clicking another text field within the window will trigger a validity check on the active text field, since only one text field may have keyboard focus within a window at any one time.

There are other situations that the human interface guidelines don't explicitly cover where you will simply follow Cocoa's default behavior in the absence of more concrete guidance. For example, switching to another tab view item within a window (as opposed to a dialog) requires validating a pending edit and committing it if valid, while you simply discard any pending edits when you close the window or quit the application.

You will therefore test the validity of a text field's pending entry, and present a sheet if the entry is illegal, in two situations: when the user attempts to enter a value by pressing the Return, Enter, or Tab key or clicking another text field in the same window, and when the user attempts to switch to another tab view item in the same window. You will not validate a pending edit when the user attempts to close the window or quit, because Cocoa apparently regards these events as evidence of the user's intent to abandon a pending edit.

1.1 Write the Code to Present a Complex, Interactive Alert Sheet

You will now start creating a comprehensive text validation system for the first editable text field you created in the Vermont Recipes application, using Project Builder to write the code required to associate a document-modal sheet with the Speed Limiter text field in the Sliders tab view item. You use the Speed Limiter text field instead of the new fields you created in Recipe 4 because you have an unanswered challenge to meet for it—namely, to give it a more informative warning than a mere beep. Recall that the Speed Limiter slider has an associated text field, where the user can type a value between 75 and 155 instead of dragging the slider. You provided all the code necessary to handle the data and the text field itself in Recipe 3, Step 2, and you already associated an NSNumberFormatter object with the field to enforce these constraints.

All you have to do here to give the user more useful feedback than a beep is to add some methods to your project files relating to the new sheet and appoint a delegate. The sheet will alert the user when an illegal out-of-range or string value is entered in the Speed Limiter text field and an attempt is made to commit it. While the principles will be relatively easy to comprehend (though more complex than any you have encountered up to this point in *Vermont Recipes*), the implementation is convoluted, involving the use of asynchronous callback routines. Additional apparent complexity stems from the need to keep the implementation of sheets fully internationalized.

See how two versions of the sheet will look (**Figures 5.1** and **5.2**). Once you've completed Step 1 and implemented the basic sheets, you will turn to several related issues in Step 2 and following.

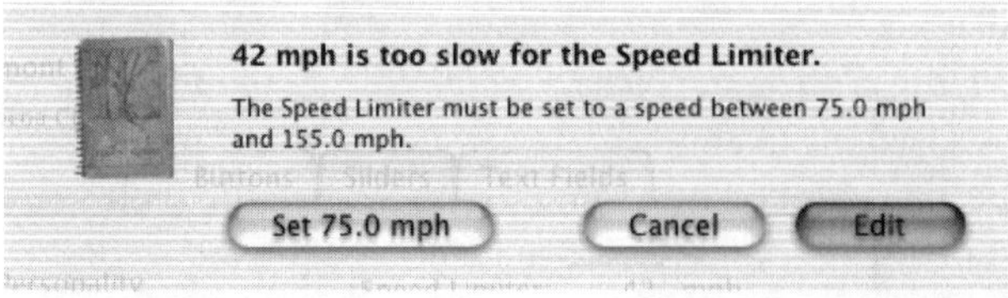

FIGURE 5.1 A three-button alert sheet.

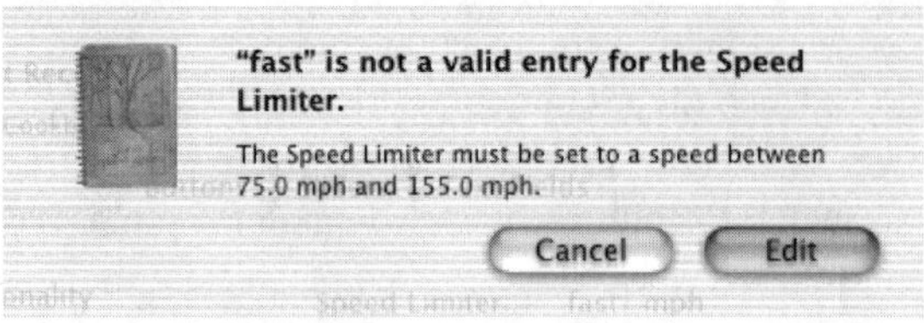

FIGURE 5.2 A two-button alert sheet.

1. **DETECT THE INVALID TEXT ENTRY.** The first issue is how to detect the user's attempt to enter an illegal value. You already associated an NSNumberFormatter object with the text field, and the formatter clearly knows when an error has occurred because it beeps and refuses to accept the entry when you press the Return, Enter, or Tab key. But how can your application find out about the error? There does not appear to be any method in NSFormatter or NSNumberFormatter to do this.

The answer lies in the **control:didFailToFormatString:errorDescription:** delegate method, which the authors of the NSControl class thoughtfully provided as an option for your use. As is the case with all of the many delegate methods in Cocoa, you have to do only two things to take advantage of it: First, implement the delegate method in one of your application's classes, being careful to conform it exactly to the delegate method's signature as declared in NSControl.h, and second, appoint your class as the delegate of the particular control in which you're interested, typically using Interface Builder. Cocoa will then automatically invoke your implementation of the delegate method every time the formatter object attached to the control detects an attempt to enter illegal data. Here, you will appoint VRMainWindowController as the delegate of the Speed Limiter text field and implement the delegate method there.

In the source file VRMainWindowController.m, define the delegate method as shown below, at the end of the file before the **@end** directive. You do not need to declare this method in the header file because it is a delegate method declared and called within the NSControl class.

```
#pragma mark INPUT VALIDATION AND FORMATTING

// Formatter errors

- (BOOL)control:(NSControl *)control
    didFailToFormatString:(NSString *)string
```

```
        errorDescription:(NSString *)error {
    if (control == [self speedTextField]) {
        return [self sheetForSpeedTextFieldFormatFailure:string
            errorDescription:error];
    }
    return YES;
}
```

Once implemented, this delegate method will be invoked indiscriminately by every formatted text field in the application that has appointed VRMainWindowController as its delegate, whenever there is an attempted illegal data entry in any such field. Therefore, the first thing the method must do is to identify which control invoked it on this occasion. If it was not the Speed Limiter text field, the method returns YES. This allows all other controls to accept any attempted data entry, without validation. Your delegate method will not necessarily include a validation test for every control in the application that appoints VRMainWindowController as delegate, so the YES branch is always required to allow unvalidated controls to function. But if the control that triggered the delegate method was the Speed Limiter text field, the delegate method will handle the error, presenting an alert sheet. You will encounter many Cocoa delegate methods that similarly enable you to identify the particular object that sent the message.

You can see why this delegate method should not be implemented in the NSSliderController category. It may be called by an erroneous data entry in any text field in the application, not just those that lie in the Sliders tab view item.

Notice that the delegate method provides two important items, in addition to the control object in the first parameter that identifies which control caused the delegate method to be invoked. The string value in the didFailToFormatString: parameter holds the invalid string that the user attempted to enter, and the error value in the errorDescription: parameter holds a string describing the nature of the error. You may use both items when you present an alert sheet.

2. **PRESENT THE SHEET.** In the event that the Speed Limiter text field generated the data entry error, the delegate method calls the sheetForSpeedTextFieldFormatFailure: errorDescription: method, which you will now write to provide feedback customized for this text field. You pass the invalid string and the error description from the delegate method to this method. As you add text fields requiring validation to your application, you will have to add custom sheet methods for each of them on this model. You will also have to add branches to the test in the control: didFailToFormatString:errorDescription: delegate method, one for each new text field you choose to validate, to call its associated sheet method.

Because each sheet method applies only to a single text field, you can place it in an appropriate controller category—here, the VRSliderController category.

At the end of the VRSliderController category declaration at the end of the header file VRMainWindowController.h, just before its **@end** directive, declare the sheet method that will handle the Speed Limiter text field error, as follows:

```
//#pragma mark INPUT VALIDATION AND FORMATTING

// Formatter errors

- (BOOL) sheetForSpeedTextFieldFormatFailure:(NSString *)string
      errorDescription:(NSString *)error;
```

In the category source file VRSliderController.m, define it as shown below, at the end of the file before the **@end** directive. This is the longest and most verbose method you have yet written in *Vermont Recipes*. I will explain its interesting features in depth immediately following the code.

```
#pragma mark INPUT VALIDATION AND FORMATTING

// Formatter errors

- (BOOL) sheetForSpeedTextFieldFormatFailure:(NSString *)string
      errorDescription:(NSString *)error {
    NSString *alertMessage;
    NSString *alternateButtonString;
    float proposedValue;
    NSDecimalNumber *proposedValueObject;

    NSString *alertInformation =
      [NSString localizedStringWithFormat:
          NSLocalizedString(@"The Speed Limiter must be set to \
          a speed between %1.1f mph and %1.1f mph.",
          @"Informative text for alert posed by Speed Limiter \
          text field when invalid value is entered"),
          [[self speedSlider] minValue],
          [[self speedSlider] maxValue]];
    NSString *defaultButtonString =
          NSLocalizedString(@"Edit", @"Name of Edit button");
    NSString *otherButtonString =
          NSLocalizedString(@"Cancel", @"Name of Cancel \
          button");

    if ([error isEqualToString:
          NSLocalizedStringFromTableInBundle(
```

```
                @"Fell short of minimum",
                @"Formatter",
                [NSBundle bundleForClass:[NSFormatter class]],
                @"Presented when user value smaller than minimum")]) {
            proposedValue = [[self speedSlider] minValue];
            alertMessage = [NSString stringWithFormat:
                    NSLocalizedString(
                    @"%@ mph is too slow for the Speed Limiter.",
                    @"Message text for alert posed by Speed Limiter \
                    text field when value smaller than minimum \
                    is entered"), string];
            alternateButtonString =
                    [NSString localizedStringWithFormat:
                    NSLocalizedString(@"Set %1.1f mph",
                    @"Name of alternate button for alert posed \
                    by Speed Limiter text field when value smaller \
                    than minimum is entered"), proposedValue];

    } else if ([error isEqualToString:
            NSLocalizedStringFromTableInBundle(
            @"Maximum exceeded",
            @"Formatter",
            [NSBundle bundleForClass:[NSFormatter class]],
            @"Presented when user value larger than maximum")]) {
            proposedValue = [[self speedSlider] maxValue];
            alertMessage = [NSString stringWithFormat:
                    NSLocalizedString(
                    @"%@ mph is too fast for the Speed Limiter.",
                    @"Message text for alert posed by Speed Limiter \
                    text field when value larger than \
                    maximum is entered"), string];
            alternateButtonString =
                    [NSString localizedStringWithFormat:
                    NSLocalizedString(@"Set %1.1f mph",
                    @"Name of alternate button for alert posed by \
                    Speed Limiter text field when value larger than \
                    maximum is entered"), proposedValue];
    } else if ([error isEqualToString:
            NSLocalizedStringFromTableInBundle(@"Invalid number",
            @"Formatter",
```

(continues on next page)

```
                [NSBundle bundleForClass:[NSFormatter class]],
                @"Presented when user typed illegal characters - \
                No valid object")]) {
        alertMessage = [NSString
                stringWithFormat: NSLocalizedString(
                @""%@" is not a valid entry for \
                the Speed Limiter.",
                @"Message text for alert posed \
                by Speed Limiter text field when invalid \
                value is entered"), string];
        alternateButtonString = nil;
    }

    [proposedValueObject =
            [[NSDecimalNumber numberWithFloat:proposedValue]
            retain];
    NSBeep();
    NSBeginAlertSheet(
            alertMessage,
            defaultButtonString,
            alternateButtonString,
            otherButtonString,
            [self window],
            self,
            @selector(speedSheetDidEnd:returnCode:contextInfo:),
            NULL,
            proposedValueObject,
            alertInformation);

    return NO;
}
```

The basic approach taken in this method is quite simple in its outline. It examines the value of the **error** parameter value passed in from the delegate method, using a succession of three tests to determine whether it was a below-minimum, above-maximum, or other illegal data entry. Based on this information about the kind of error, it sets the string values of the sheet's message text and the name of its alternate button using local variables. Once the variables are set up, it is just a matter of passing them to the sheet using the same **NSBeginAlertSheet()** function declared in NSPanel.h that you used in Recipe 3, Step 1. The apparent complexity of the method comes mostly from its internationalization code, not its logic.

Now, examine the method in detail.

- First, you declare the `alertInformation` local variable's string value once, since it will be used without change no matter which error the user committed.

  The *Aqua Human Interface Guidelines* recommend more extensive communication with the user than was customary in the classic Mac OS. In addition to a descriptive error message in bold near the top of the alert, you should try to provide useful information in plain text in the middle of the alert to help the user understand what to do. You will provide the message text shortly to describe each of the three possible errors, but you provide informative text here to tell the user in every case that this text field requires a number between fixed minimum and maximum values.

  You use the now familiar `NSLocalizedString()` function to define the key for the informative text and a comment that will help your localization contractors. You will provide the corresponding value for this key shortly in your Localizable.strings file. Your localization contractors will provide alternative versions of the string value for other languages.

  Finally, you pass the `NSLocalizedString()` function's return value as a parameter to an invocation of the NSString `localizedStringWithFormat:` class method. You use printf-style placeholders for the minimum and maximum values; these values will be filled in at run time by invoking the Speed Limiter slider's built-in `minValue` and `maxValue` methods. If your localization contractor uses Interface Builder to change the slider's minimum and maximum values, these error messages and informative strings will still function correctly, picking up the new limits automatically without requiring any change to your code. This is especially important for localization of a speed limiter control, since speed limits and the units in which they are expressed vary widely from country to country.

  The `localizedStringWithFormat:` method is appropriate when placeholders represent values that require localization. Cocoa will automatically use the correct thousands and decimal separators, for example, depending on the preferred language set in the user's System Preferences. If your placeholders don't require localization, you can use the `stringWithFormat:` method instead.

  That may seem like a lot of work to set one variable, but in a single statement you have provided almost everything you need to make this string value fully localizable. This will become second nature to you in no time.

- You next set the names of the default and other buttons, using the `NSLocalizedString()` function again to ensure that they can be localized.

The *Aqua Human Interface Guidelines* recommend using names that describe the dialog button's action, when possible. Here, you use Edit instead of OK as the default button to return the user to the text field for continued editing, with the illegal value and the insertion point left in place. The value is not committed but is left pending as if the user had not yet attempted to commit it. You use Cancel to cancel the invalid entry and restore the original entry, leaving it selected for immediate editing. You will use these two buttons in all branches of this method.

Note that the code refers to Cancel as the *other* button and passes it as the fourth parameter (`otherButton`) to the `NSBeginAlertSheet()` function. The other button appears immediately to the left of the default button in the sheet, whether the sheet holds two or three buttons. The *alternate* button, which you will define shortly, is the optional third button, which, in a three-button sheet, appears some distance to the left of the Cancel button. It is passed as the third parameter (`alternateButton`) to the `NSBeginAlertSheet()` function. In a two-button sheet, you pass the alternate button as `nil` to suppress it.

It is easy to become confused about which is the other and which is the alternate button, since their names mean essentially the same thing. Indeed, the book *Learning Cocoa* has them backward in the example starting on page 186 of the second edition (O'Reilly & Associates, 2001). The example only works because it uses a two-button sheet and the alternate button (Cancel, in that example) therefore moves to the right to fill the vacant position adjacent to the OK button. If the book had used a three-button example, the Cancel button would have appeared to the far left of the sheet because of this mistake.

The confusion worsens because in Cocoa's NSPanel header file, both the `NSAlertAlternateReturn` and `NSCancelButton` enumeration constants equate to `0`, suggesting to a casual reader that the alternate button should be used as the Cancel button. In fact, the `NSOKButton` and `NSCancelButton` constants in the header serve other purposes altogether, and their values are irrelevant here. In the context of the `NSBeginAlertSheet()` function that I am discussing, the `NSAlertAlternateReturn` constant (`0`) is used to detect a user's having clicked the optional third, or alternate, button, and the `NSAlertOtherReturn` constant (`-1`) is used to detect a user's having clicked the second, or other, button, which is usually Cancel. An Apple engineer told me that documentation errors relating to these constants originally arose in the Java documentation.

The *Aqua Human Interface Guidelines,* which added to the confusion in earlier editions, finally got it right on page 118 of the October 2001 edition: "If there's a Cancel button, it should be to the left of the default button.

If there's a third, or *alternate,* button (Don't Save, for example), it should go to the left of the Cancel button." (Emphasis mine.) The `NSBeginAlert-Sheet()` function reference document in the AppKit documentation also now has it right: "The buttons are laid out on the lower-right corner of the sheet, with `defaultButton` on the right, `alternateButton` on the left, and `otherButton` in the middle."

- Now you turn to the three-branched test of the delegate method's error description.

  Here, you encounter the localization problem in reverse. The string Cocoa returned in the `error` parameter to the `control:didFailToFormatString:errorDescription:` delegate method is a meaningful description intended for possible display in the sheet itself; it is not merely a key useful only to programmers in their code. If you are working on a machine configured for the English language, this delegate method will provide the `error` parameter value in English. Cocoa's NSNumberFormatter object provides it. Your first problem, since you didn't write NSNumberFormatter and don't have access to its code, is to figure out what these English string values might be so you can test for them and branch according to the result. Once you solve this problem (which you might do by simple experimentation), you have the even harder problem of finding out what values will be passed to you on machines configured for other languages. If you look at the NSControl documentation where the delegate method is described, you will learn only that the `error` parameter value is a localized string describing the error. For example, it might be in German if one of your users works in Germany, or in any of a dozen or more other languages.

  What should you do if you want your application fully internationalized? If you've been studying Cocoa assiduously, you have begun to realize that just about everything relating to an application or framework bundle is located in the bundle itself—headers, documentation, localized language folders such as English.lproj containing images and sounds, and what have you. It has probably dawned on you that some of Cocoa's framework bundles might contain their own equivalents of your Localizable.strings file. Where would the strings for data formatting errors be located? In the Foundation framework bundle, of course, where NSFormatter is declared.

  Using the Finder, navigate to /System/Library/Frameworks/Foundation.framework/Resources/English.lproj. There, in plain sight if only you know where to look, is a file called Formatter.strings. Drag it to the Project Builder application icon to open it, and you see a perfectly ordinary set of key-value pairs for the very error strings you seek. For example, the key

"Maximum exceeded" is equated to the output string "Maximum exceeded." You will also see several other language folders in the bundle. Look in German.lproj, for example; you find that the key is still in English (this is typical of Cocoa), "Maximum exceeded," but the value is in German, "Maximum überschritten" (Latin is Latin in any language).

But do you really need to look up the string values manually for each language and code them verbatim into your tests? Of course not; Cocoa provides built-in methods to do this for you. All you need is the English-language keys, which you do have to look up manually in the Formatter.strings file.

Looking at the code, above, you see that each branch tests for the value of the incoming error description by using the standard NSString `isEqualToString:` method. However, to get the localized version of the description returned in the error parameter, you call upon the `NSLocalizedStringFromTableInBundle()` function declared in the NSBundle header file. In this function and its siblings, you identify the .strings file by passing it in by name (without the .strings extension) as `@"Formatter"`. You identify the bundle in which the Formatter.strings file lives by invoking NSBundle's `bundleForClass:` method, passing it NSFormatter's `class` method. In this way, you can be assured of obtaining the correct localized string value no matter where Apple may eventually place the Foundation framework bundle in Mac OS X's directory structure.

In each branch, now that you know how to test for the kind of error in every supported language, you provide unique values for the message text and the third, or alternate, button to be shown in your alert sheet.

- You dismiss the alert by returning **NO** as the method's return value. This rejects the attempted illegal entry—that is, it declines to commit it to the data variable in the VRSliderModel model object—and, if you provide no new value, it leaves the insertion point active in the field awaiting the user's entry of the correct value.

The rest of the `sheetForSpeedTextFieldFormatFailure:errorDescription:` method uses the same techniques described above, until you get to the `NSBeginAlertSheet()` function. There, you will find the answer to your next question: How do you tell which button the user clicked to dismiss the sheet, and how do you do something with that information?

First, take a moment to consider why you call **NSBeginAlertSheet()** instead of its sibling, **NSBeginCriticalAlertSheet()**. They work identically, except that the latter superimposes a large caution symbol over your application icon in the sheet. If you were writing an application for the classic Mac OS, you would probably use it here to flag the erroneous data entry as an error. However, for Mac OS X, the *Aqua Human Interface Guidelines* reserve `NSBeginCriticalAlertSheet()` for situations where an impending error may result in extraordinary or permanent harm, such as the loss of data. You should not dilute the impact of the caution symbol by using it too frequently or in mundane situations.

3. **GET THE USER'S RESPONSE TO THE SHEET.** Earlier, prerelease versions of Mac OS X provided a simple technique to get the user's response to a modal sheet: You called a function to present the sheet, and it returned a value representing the button that the user had clicked. However, this didn't work properly when multiple sheets were open simultaneously in different windows—a possibility implicit in the fact that a document-modal sheet is modal only with respect to the document, not with respect to other documents or the rest of the application. Cocoa got confused and sometimes dismissed the wrong sheet.

The last developer preview version of Mac OS X introduced a new technique, and the Public Beta release enhanced the relevant methods. Now, the new `NSBeginAlertSheet()` function returns control to the application immediately upon presenting the sheet, without waiting for the user to press a button. Your application's flow of execution continues while the window where the error occurred just sits there, frozen, with a document-modal sheet in front of it. You must declare and specify a callback method to obtain the information you need regarding the user's actions in the sheet and to dismiss it, bringing the window back to life. Cocoa will invoke the callback method for you asynchronously, when the user finally gets around to pressing a button in the sheet. Between the time the `NSBeginAlertSheet()` function is called and the time the callback method is called, the document window remains in a state of suspended animation while the rest of the application works around it.

This new technique may seem very complex, but you will get used to it. The code is summarized in the next paragraph, then explained in detail in the following paragraphs. Note that the AppKit function reference documentation for the `NSBeginAlertSheet()` function recently, at the end of 2001, caught up with the code. It now provides a full and accurate description of this function's usage. You may still examine the NSPanel header file itself to obtain additional information about the `NSBeginAlertSheet()` function in the comments.

You designate one of your custom application classes as the temporary *modal delegate* for this sheet. The modal delegate may optionally implement one or both of two callback routines, the format for which is specified in NSPanel.h and in the AppKit function reference documentation. Each of these callback methods will know the identity of the button the user clicked and is responsible for acting on that information. You specify the modal delegate class in the `modalDelegate` parameter to the `NSBeginAlertSheet()` function, and you also pass references to either or both of your two callback selectors in the `didEndSelector` parameter and the `didDismissSelector` parameter, respectively. Each of these two parameters, if not `NULL`, must refer to a callback method implemented in your designated modal delegate class, using a special signature described in the NSPanel header file: namely, `sheetDidEnd:returnCode:contextInfo:` and `sheetDidDismiss:returnCode:contextInfo:`. You can name these methods anything you like, as long as they follow the prescribed signature.

Here, you designated VRMainWindowController as the modal delegate, by passing `self` as the `modalDelegate` parameter value to the `NSBeginAlertSheet()` function. You also invoked a custom `speedSheetDidEnd:returnCode:contextInfo:` method in that function, as the selector for the `didEndSelector` parameter (passing `NULL` in the `didDismissSelector` parameter). Now you must implement that callback method.

In VRMainWindowController.h, declare the method as follows, at the end of the "Formatter errors" section of the VRSlidersController category:

```
- (void)speedSheetDidEnd:(NSWindow *)sheet
     returnCode:(int)returnCode
     contextInfo:(void *)contextInfo;
```

In the category source file VRSliderController.m, define the method as follows, at the end of the "Formatter errors" section:

```
- (void)speedSheetDidEnd:(NSWindow *)sheet
      returnCode:(int)returnCode
      contextInfo:(void *)contextInfo {
   if (returnCode == NSAlertOtherReturn) {
      [[self speedTextField] abortEditing];
      [[self speedTextField]
            selectText:[self speedTextField]];
   } else if (returnCode == NSAlertAlternateReturn) {
      [[self sliderModel] setSpeedValue:
            [(NSDecimalNumber *)contextInfo floatValue]];
      [[[self document] undoManager] setActionName:
            NSLocalizedString(@"Set Speed Limiter",
            @"Name of undo/redo menu item after Speed \
            text field was set")];
   }
   [(NSString *)contextInfo release];
}
```

Here's what's going on. The NSBeginAlertSheet() function, in passing a reference to the speedSheetDidEnd:returnCode:contextInfo: selector in the didEndSelector parameter, also populated that method's first two parameters with values you might need: namely, a reference to the sheet and the return code of the button the user clicked. It also populated the third parameter of the method, contextInfo, with any context information you passed in the contextInfo parameter of the NSBeginAlertSheet() function. The speedSheetDidEnd:returnCode:contextInfo: method uses some of this information to recognize which button the user clicked and to reset the value of the text field accordingly. The method is called only when the user clicks one of the buttons in the sheet. This may occur minutes, hours, or days after the sheet was presented, since this sheet is modal only to this document window. The user may continue to work in other windows or even in other applications while the sheet is pending.

- In the speedSheetDidEnd:returnCode:contextInfo: method, you haven't used the selector's reference to the sheet. You could use it to dismiss the sheet yourself in appropriate circumstances with NSWindow's orderOut: method (for example, if you want to dismiss both the sheet and the underlying window simultaneously, as the save and open sheets do), but here you'll just rely on the NSBeginAlertSheet() callback mechanism to dismiss the sheet.

- You use the returnCode parameter to test which button the user clicked, using the constants declared in NSPanel.h for this purpose, NSAlertDefaultReturn, NSAlertAlternateReturn, and NSAlertOtherReturn. (As noted above, you should not use the NSOKButton and NSCancelButton constants here, because they are declared for a different purpose. Indeed, these two constants have values that conflict with those used by the NSBeginAlertSheet() method.)

You don't care if the user clicked the default button (Edit). By doing nothing in that case, you simply rely on the NSBeginAlertSheet() callback mechanism to reject the invalid data entry and leave the insertion point active for editing in the text field. To understand how this works, you need to understand the subtlety involved in the statement, at the beginning of this instruction, to the effect that the NSBeginAlertSheet() function returns control immediately. This means only that the application's flow of control immediately goes on to other tasks. It does not mean that the sheetForSpeedTextFieldFormatFailure:errorDescription: or control:didFailToFormatString:errorDescription: methods return their results immediately. To the contrary, Cocoa holds not only the text field and the sheet but also these methods in suspension while your sheet is pending, waiting to see the result of the callback method. Once the user finally clicks a button in the sheet, the sheetForSpeedTextFieldFormatFailure:errorDescription: method passes its NO return value to the control:didFailToFormatString:errorDescription: method, which also returns NO, thereby rejecting the bad string.

If the user clicked the other button (Cancel), the method invokes NSControl's **abortEditing** method. This restores the text field's displayed value to its original value before editing of the field began, which was the current, unchanged data value in VRSliderModel. Notice that the method does not have to access the VRSliderModel object to obtain the original value; the window's field editor remembers that value during this editing session. The *field editor,* about which you will learn more later, is a shared object that the window normally uses to hold and manipulate text in the currently active text field. The method also invokes NSTextField's **selectText:** method to select the restored text, leaving it in a state for immediate type-over revision by the user.

Finally, if the user clicked the alternate button ("Set to 75 mph" or "Set to 155 mph"), the method invokes the Slider model object's **setSpeedValue:** accessor method to set the model's data value so it matches the button's minimum or maximum value. This results in registration of the change with the undo manager and sending of a notification to update the text field. The design theory behind these alternate buttons is that the user's entering an out-of-range value may have been an attempt to enter the slider's minimum or maximum value. Note that the action name is set here, since this method acts like an action method when the user clicks the alternate button.

- The **contextInfo** parameter also needs explanation. Normally, you should consider using a temporary dictionary object to pass context information through the **contextInfo** parameter, to make it easier to revise the application in the future if you discover a need to pass more or different information. Here, however, for convenience, you have passed a single value, an NSDecimalNumber object representing the minimum or maximum allowed value, depending on whether the user typed a value below the text field's minimum or above its maximum.

It is important to notice that in creating this NSDecimalNumber object in the **sheetForSpeedTextFieldFormatFailure:errorDescription:** method, you retained it, and in the **speedSheetDidEnd:returnCode:contextInfo:** method, you released it. You had to retain it, because otherwise Cocoa would have released it automatically when you exited the **sheetForSpeedTextField:errorDescription:** method. Objects that convenience methods such as NSString's **localizedStringWithFormat:** return are always autoreleased before they are returned to you, and they are therefore always released when the autorelease pool is released, unless you explicitly retain them.

It's worth compiling and running the application without the **retain** just to see what happens. As soon as execution enters the **speedSheetDidEnd:returnCode:contextInfo:** method and attempts to obtain the value of the **contextInfo** parameter, your program crashes because the value is no longer accessible in memory. Look at the crashing behavior and the error messages it generates in

Project Builder; over time, you will come to recognize these as characteristic of a failure to retain an object. By the same token, you must balance the `retain` with a `release` when you are done with the value in the `speedSheetDidEnd:-returnCode:contextInfo:` method, to avoid a memory leak.

A final detail: When the `proposedValueObject` variable was passed in the `contextInfo` parameter, it was cast from an NSDecimalNumber object to a void pointer (`void*`). When it was received in the `speedSheetDidEnd:returnCode:-contextInfo:` method, you had to cast it back to an NSDecimalNumber value to allow its release at the end of that method. Objective-C will not act on void pointers.

4. **SET UP LOCALIZABLE.STRINGS.** Next, add all of the required entries to your Localizable.strings file. Basically, just include an entry for every unique invocation of the `NSLocalizableString()` function.

You should not include an entry for the `NSLocalizedStringFromTableInBundle()` function invocations, since those entries already exist in Cocoa's Formatter.strings file. You also don't have to include Cancel, because it, like OK and many other common strings, appears at least once in the Cocoa frameworks. Look, for example, in Common.strings in the AppKit framework. However, duplicating these is harmless, assuming they are all localized the same way, and doing so will protect you against Apple's someday changing its files.

In this case, the new entries are the following, placed in the "Alert strings" section:

```
/* Common buttons */
/* Name of Edit button */
"Edit" = "Edit"


/* Speed Limiter text field alert */
/* Message text for alert posed by Speed Limiter text field when value
        smaller than minimum is entered */
"%@ mph is too slow for the Speed Limiter." = "%@ mph is too slow for
        the Speed Limiter."
/* Message text for alert posed by Speed Limiter text field when value
        larger than maximum is entered */
"%@ mph is too fast for the Speed Limiter." = "%@ mph is too fast for
        the Speed Limiter."
/* Message text for alert posed by Speed Limiter text field when
        invalid value is entered */
""%@" is not a valid entry for the Speed Limiter." = ""%@" is not a
        valid entry for the Speed Limiter."
```

(continues on next page)

```
/* Informative text for alert posed by Speed Limiter text field when
      invalid value is entered */
"The Speed Limiter must be set to a speed between %1.1f mph and %1.1f
      mph." = "The Speed Limiter must be set to a speed between %1.1f
      mph and %1.1f mph."
/* Name of alternate button for alert posed by Speed Limiter text
      field when value smaller than minimum is entered */
"Set %1.1f mph" = "Set %1.1f mph"
/* Name of alternate button for alert posed by Speed Limiter text
      field when value larger than maximum is entered */
"Set %1.1f mph" = "Set %1.1f mph"
```

1.2 Connect the Delegate in Interface Builder

In Interface Builder, Control-drag from the Speed Limiter text field to the File's
Owner icon. In the NSTextField Info Panel, select **delegate** in the left pane of the
Outlets section, then click the Connect button. If you leave out this essential step
through forgetfulness (a not uncommon experience!), none of this will work as
expected and it may take you a long while to figure out why.

1.3 Build and Run the Application

Build and run the application to test the sheet. If the usual untitled window fails to
open when you run the application, you probably left the Sliders tab view item
selected in Interface Builder when you built it. Look in the StdIO pane and you'll
probably see an assertion failure message telling you that you should select the first
tab in the VRDocument.nib file. This is just why you inserted the assertion code in
Recipe 4. Fix this problem in Interface Builder by selecting the Buttons tab, then
build and run the application again.

Select the Sliders tab view item and enter various legal and illegal values in the
Speed Limiter text field. If you enter a legal value, the text field will accept it and the
slider will snap to it, as before. If you enter an illegal value less than the minimum
value in the acceptable range, a beep will sound and a sheet will descend explaining
exactly what is wrong and, in accordance with the *Aqua Human Interface Guidelines,*
giving you useful information about how to solve the problem. Notice that if you
click Edit, you return to an active insertion point in the text field, waiting for you to
revise the invalid entry. If you click Cancel, the previous value is reinstated and
selected in case you want to attempt to edit it again. In both cases, the slider remains
set to its previous value, as it should, because you haven't committed any new value.

A third button offers to let you set the value to the legal minimum. If you had
entered an illegal value greater than the maximum, this button would offer to let

you set the value to the legal maximum instead. In either case, clicking this alternate button will enter the legal minimum or maximum value in the text field, as indicated, and the slider will snap to that new value because you have committed it.

Try entering a string, such as fast, in the text field. A somewhat different sheet descends, explaining that a number is required and offering only two buttons, Edit and Cancel.

Notice that as of Mac OS X 10.0, Cocoa disables the close button in a window while a sheet is pending, and it disables several menu items as well, which the user could otherwise use to do things to the window in violation of the document-modality principle of sheets.

After trying several illegal values and fixing them, exercise the Undo and Redo commands repeatedly to make sure they work as expected.

Open several windows at once and attempt to enter illegal values in each of them in turn, pressing the Enter key—but don't fix any of them yet; that is, leave all of the sheets open at once. Confirm that, although a document-modal sheet remains open in each window to prevent user interaction there, user interaction is nevertheless allowed in other windows that do not have a pending sheet, as well as in other applications. Also confirm that the correct sheet is dismissed as you resolve the illegal entry in each window and dismiss its sheet in a random order.

Finally, try editing the text field in several windows at once without pressing the Enter key. That is, leave edits pending in several windows at the same time. Everything will work properly. You can enter a value in one window's text field by pressing the Enter key or using its slider, and the text fields in all the other windows will remain pending. If you now close any of the windows with pending entries, or quit the application, the pending entries will be discarded because the user has not yet affirmatively committed them.

Unfortunately, you aren't out of the woods yet. First, try deleting whatever is in the text field, then pressing Enter while the field is blank. Uh-oh—no alert sheet! Although you expected this problem, because you dealt with it in a preliminary way in Instruction 6 of Recipe 3, Step 2.2, you still need to fix it. Second, try switching to another tab view item, using the navigation buttons you created earlier, while an illegal entry, such as 45, is pending. A sheet is presented signaling the attempted illegal entry, but while the sheet is pending, the window underneath switches to the new tab view item, hiding the illegal entry from you. This is a violation of human interface guidelines specifying that a document-modal sheet must not permit user actions in the window. The same thing happens when you click another tab while an illegal value is pending. You need to fix this as well, because Cocoa doesn't take care of it for you.

In the next few steps, you will add code to the application to resolve these remaining problems, starting with the issue of empty text fields.

Step 2: Set Up a Generic Document-Modal Sheet to Require an Entry in a Text Field

In many, if not most, cases, it is desirable to allow a user to delete information found in a text field or to leave an empty field blank. Consider a typical form, spreadsheet, or database in which you can record, say, a fax number or the vehicle identification number of a car. In case a user has no fax machine or doesn't own a car, you have to make it possible to tab through the field without entering any data.

When you design a text field to contain free-form text, implementing the ability to leave it empty is easy; just do nothing. You don't need to attach a formatter to a free-form field, and a blank entry—that is, an empty or zero-length string—is as acceptable as any other text entry.

Even when you format a text field according to an attached formatter, leaving the field blank is often still a desirable option. It is presumably for this reason that, as you have discovered, Cocoa does not invoke an attached formatter when the user commits a blank text field, but only when the user enters data. Thus, even for fields with an attached formatter, allowing the user to delete their contents or leave them empty requires no code.

However, the fact that Cocoa does not invoke a formatter when the user is deleting information or leaving a field empty creates an issue in the case of a text field that does require an entry. In the case of the Speed Limiter text field, for example, the slider is constrained to a range of values from 75 mph to 155 mph, and the text field is expected to match the slider's displayed value at all times. The field initializes to the default value of the slider when the window opens, and a user should not be permitted to leave the field blank under any circumstances. As you have discovered, you can't rely on the attached formatter to detect and prevent a blank entry, since Cocoa does not invoke a formatter in that case.

The fact that the formatter you have attached to the Speed Limiter text field isn't being invoked when the user deletes the field's contents or leaves it empty is easily proved. Remove the temporary code you added to the `speedTextFieldAction:` method to prevent entry of a blank value in Instruction 6 of Recipe 3, Step 2.2. Then set a breakpoint on the `control:didFailToFormatString:errorDescription:` method in VRMainWindowController.m, build and run the application in debug mode, and attempt to enter a blank value. The breakpoint is never hit.

The issue is even more complex in the case of a text field formatted as a floating-point number, such as the Speed Limiter field. You may wonder how it happens that entering a blank value in the Speed Limiter field results in display of a 0 value. The answer has to do with the fact that, somewhere in the process of updating the text field onscreen to reflect the blank entry, NSString's floatValue method is called (your speedTextFieldAction: method explicitly invokes the text field control's floatValue method through the sender parameter, and the NSControl reference document indicates that this is converted to a string, presumably through a call to NSString's floatValue method, via NSControl's validateEditing method). One aspect of NSString's floatValue behavior, according to the NSString class reference document, is that it returns 0.0 if the string doesn't begin with a valid text representation of a floating-point number. Since an empty string doesn't begin with anything, Cocoa interprets a blank entry as 0.0. This is common practice among programming languages, because it allows a default empty value to be stored in a variable that is typed as a float. You must take into account this documented but perhaps obscure side effect of the floatValue method when allowing deletion of the contents of a field formatted as a float.

It is clearly wrong to accept a blank entry that generates a 0 value here, in the face of the range restriction that applies to the Speed Limiter text field. In this step, therefore, you will write some generic routines to suppress blank entries—that is, to require entry of data in a text field. The routines are written generically to allow their reuse by any other text fields that might have similar constraints.

Note that it might be less disruptive to your users' work patterns to dispense with a sheet in these situations and to simply restore the text field to its previous value silently. This is how TextEdit behaves, for example, when the user attempts to delete the values in the text fields for window width and height in its Preferences dialog. Here, it is perhaps even more obvious that 0 is not an acceptable value, since the Speed Limiter is associated visually and interactively with a slider that has a prominently displayed minimum acceptable value of 75 mph. However, other situations might not be so clear, and this is a recipe about creating interactive sheets, so you'll create an interactive sheet here. See **Figure 5.3** to see what the sheet will look like.

The Speed Limiter field is blank.

A value must be entered in this field.

Cancel   Edit

FIGURE 5.3 A sheet to require an entry in a text field.

1. Since NSNumberFormatter isn't invoked when a text field is left blank, you must hunt around for some other hook to catch attempts to enter a blank value. In NSControl, you find just the thing, the control:textShouldEndEditing:

delegate method. If you implement this delegate method in the control's delegate, it will be invoked whenever the user attempts to do something that would cause the text field to relinquish first responder status, such as pressing the Return, Enter, or Tab key—unless an attached formatter intercepts the flow of control first. The `control:textShouldEndEditing:` method is typical of the many delegate methods provided for you in the Cocoa frameworks. You see here how important it is to read the documentation and become familiar with these delegate methods, because they often make it easy to accomplish important tasks.

You have already designated VRMainWindowController as the Speed Limiter text field's delegate, so you will implement this delegate method there. Because every text field that similarly appoints VRMainWindowController as delegate will trigger this method, its first task is to identify the responsible text field. In VRMainWindowController.m, define the delegate method as shown below, at the top of the INPUT VALIDATION AND FORMATTING section. You do not need to declare this method in the header file because it is a delegate method.

```
// Validation of pending edits

- (BOOL)control:(NSControl *)control
     textShouldEndEditing:(NSText *)fieldEditor {
    if (control == [self speedTextField]) {
        if ([[fieldEditor string] isEqualToString:@""]) {
            return [self sheetForBlankTextField:control
                    name:NSLocalizedString(@"Speed Limiter",
                    @"Name of Speed Limiter text field")];
        }
    }
    return YES;
}
```

A Cocoa delegate method with the word *should* in its name is usually a request for permission to perform some work. If you implement the delegate method and return NO, you have exercised your veto power and the work will not be performed. You must return YES to allow the work to go forward. Here, the sheet method, which you will write in a moment, will return NO to prevent entry of the invalid value, and it will modify the contents of the text field depending on the user's response to the sheet. However, if the value the user entered is valid (that is, the attached formatter did not intercept it because it is a number within the prescribed range), then this method will return YES to allow the entry to be committed. It will also return YES if some other field is key, because other fields may appropriately allow deletion of their contents.

After determining that it is the Speed Limiter text field whose editing session is about to end, this method tests whether the contents of the current field editor are empty. The window's field editor, which the text field currently having focus uses as a shared editing object, is passed into the `control:textShouldEndEditing:` delegate method so that you can use it to access the string currently being edited; you can't use the contents of the text field itself for this purpose, because its value hasn't yet been committed. You could check whether the field editor is blank by testing the length of the string against `0`, but you chose the more common technique of testing whether it is equal to `@""`. Remember that Cocoa relies heavily on Unicode, where multibyte sequences can represent individual characters. Testing whether the length is `0` or the string is empty, however, is a safe way to make sure the field is blank.

2. Next, you must implement the custom `sheetForBlankTextField:name:` method you just invoked, presenting a sheet using the same techniques you used in Step 1. You will design this method for reuse by any and all text fields that require a value, so you should not put it in a separate category but in the main body of the window controller. The alert message and informative text are very general, but you provide for an option to pass a name in the `name` parameter to customize the sheet to some extent. You can pass `nil` if the field has no name or if you don't wish to show it in the sheet.

    In VRMainWindowController.h, declare the method as follows, at the end of the main body immediately before the VRButtonController category interface:

```
//#pragma mark INPUT VALIDATION AND FORMATTING

// Validation of pending edits

- (BOOL)sheetForBlankTextField:(NSControl *)control
      name:(NSString *)fieldName;
```

Define it in VRMainWindowController.m, after the `control:textShouldEndEditing:` method you just added:

```
- (BOOL)sheetForBlankTextField:(NSControl *)control
      name:(NSString *)fieldName {

   NSString *alertMessage;

   NSString *alertInformation =
         NSLocalizedString(@"A value must be entered in \
         this field.",
```

(continues on next page)

```
            @"Informative text for alert posed by any text \
            field if empty when attempting to resign first \
            responder status");
    NSString *defaultButtonString =
            NSLocalizedString(@"Edit", @"Name of Edit button");
    NSString *otherButtonString =
            NSLocalizedString(@"Cancel", @"Name of Cancel \
            button");

    if (fieldName == NULL) {
        alertMessage =
                NSLocalizedString(@"The field is blank.",
                @"Message text for alert posed by any unnamed \
                field if blank when attempting to resign first \
                responder status");
    } else {
        alertMessage = [NSString stringWithFormat:
                NSLocalizedString(@"The %@ field is blank.",
                @"Message text for alert posed by any named text \
                field if blank when attempting to resign first \
                responder status"), fieldName];
    }

    NSBeginAlertSheet(
            alertMessage,
            defaultButtonString,
            nil,
            otherButtonString,
             [self window],
            self,
            @selector(blankTextFieldSheetDidEnd:
                    returnCode:contextInfo:),
            NULL,
            control,
            alertInformation);

    return NO;
}
```

As in Step 1, the `NSBeginAlertSheet()` function here designates VRMain-WindowController as modal delegate and passes in a **didEndSelector** reference so the user's choice of buttons in the sheet can be processed. The alternate button name is passed as `nil` because this is a two-button sheet. Instead of passing a string object in the `contextInfo` parameter, it passes a reference to the text field object. Since the text field object is already instantiated, there is no need to bother with `retain` and `release`.

You don't call `NSBeep()` here, as you did in `sheetForSpeedTextFieldFormat-Failure:errorDescription:`, because `control:textShouldEndEditing:`, which you use to trigger this sheet, calls NSTextField's `textShouldEndEditing:` delegate method, which beeps for you.

3. Now declare the `didEndSelector` callback method in VRMainWindow-Controller.h, immediately after the `sheetForBlankTextField:name:` method declaration you just added, as follows:

```
- (void)blankTextFieldSheetDidEnd:(NSWindow *)sheet
        returnCode:(int)returnCode
        contextInfo:(void *)contextInfo;
```

Define the callback method in VRMainWindowController.m, immediately after the `sheetForBlankTextField:name:` method definition you just added, as follows:

```
- (void)blankTextFieldSheetDidEnd:(NSWindow *)sheet
        returnCode:(int)returnCode
        contextInfo:(void *)contextInfo {
    if (returnCode == NSAlertOtherReturn) {
        NSTextField *field = (NSTextField *)contextInfo;
        [field abortEditing];
        [field selectText:field];
    }
}
```

The `contextInfo` parameter value is cast from a void pointer to an NSTextField object here and assigned to a local variable to invoke the following two methods, which abort editing in the field and select it for correction.

4. Now that you have implemented a means to check for blank text field entries and present an alert sheet, you can remove the temporary fix you inserted in Instruction 6 of Recipe 3, Step 2.2. In the `speedTextFieldAction:` method in the category source file VRSliderController.m, remove the `if` block wrapper, promoting the statements it contains to the top level of the method. It doesn't get in the way because the `control:textShouldEndEditing:` method preempts it, but you shouldn't leave useless code lying around.

5. Don't forget to add the localized strings used in these methods to the Localizable.strings file, as follows:

```
/* Field names */
/* Name of Speed Limiter text field */
"Speed Limiter" = "Speed Limiter"

/* Blank text field alert */
/* Message text for alert posed by any unnamed field if blank when
attempting to resign first responder status */
"The field is blank." = "The field is blank."
/* Message text for alert posed by any named text field if blank when
attempting to resign first responder status */
"The %@ field is blank." = "The %@ field is blank."
/* Informative text for alert posed by any text field if blank when
attempting to resign first responder status */
"A value must be entered in this field." = "A value must be entered in
this field."
```

6. Build and run the application to test the sheet. With the Sliders tab view item selected, try deleting whatever is in the text field, then pressing the Enter key. Confirm that a sheet warns you that you must provide a value. Also confirm that clicking Cancel restores the previous value, while clicking Edit leaves the blank field pending, awaiting your further editing.

Step 3: Prevent Tab View Navigation While an Invalid Text Entry and Sheet Are Pending

HIGHLIGHTS:

Human interface considerations relating to invalid text field entries

At this point, you have in place good validity checking for the text field when the user presses the Return, Enter, or Tab key, and it would also work properly if you added another text field to the Sliders pane and the user clicked in it. But I alluded to still another situation previously, in which the text field's behavior should be reviewed.

The issue arises when the user attempts to switch to another tab view item. Cocoa's default behavior is to treat the attempted selection of a second tab view item as a signal to validate and commit any pending edit in the first tab view item—that is, to attempt to force the text field in which the edit is pending to resign first responder status. You can see the effect of this by clicking another tab while a blank or out-of-range value is pending in the text field: The sheets you created previously are immediately presented, as if you had pressed the Enter key or clicked in another text field. You can also see this behavior by setting a breakpoint on the `control:textShouldEndEditing:` and `control:didFailToFormatString:errorDescription:` delegate methods. When you run the application in the debugger while a blank or out-of-range value is pending in the text field, you see that either of these methods is invoked when you click another tab. In other words, a text field is tested for validity whenever the user attempts to switch tab view items, and the switch is prevented if the field is invalid.

Surprisingly, however, if you attempt to switch tab view items by clicking another tab or using the navigation buttons you added in Recipe 2, Step 7, the destination tab view item appears even if the pending text field entry in the first tab view item is blank or otherwise illegal. Your users see a sheet telling them about the illegal entry in the text field, but the tab view item is nevertheless switched out from under them while the sheet is open and before they can respond to it. The navigation button's action method is apparently invoked before Cocoa can present the sheet and place the document into its modal state. This is a violation of the human interface guidelines, which describe document-modal sheets as blocking all user actions on a window until they are dismissed. Cocoa usually takes care of this for you—for example, by disabling the close box on a window and disabling several menu items while a sheet is pending. You must now do something to make tab view switching behave appropriately.

If you are beginning to get the drift of Cocoa delegate methods, you know you should look for a delegate method in NSTabView that will let you intercept and thwart the attempt to select another tab view item if an illegal entry is pending. The delegate method you need to force a validity check on the field is NSTabView's `tabView:shouldSelectTabViewItem:` method. This is similar to the `tabView:willSelectTabViewItem:` method you invoked in Recipe 2, Step 7, to enable and disable the navigation buttons selectively in the event that the user was selecting the first or last tab in the tab view. Here, however, you use the *should* variant of the delegate method because you want to be able to veto the switch.

In VRMainWindowController.m, define the delegate method as shown below, at the top of the "Validation of pending edits" subsection of the INPUT VALIDATION AND FORMATTING section. As a delegate method, it does not need a declaration.

```
- (BOOL)tabView:(NSTabView *)tabView
     shouldSelectTabViewItem:(NSTabViewItem *)tabViewItem {
   return [[self window] makeFirstResponder:[self window]];
}
```

Invoking the `makeFirstResponder:` method on the window, as you did here, is the standard Cocoa way to force validation of a pending text field entry, recommended in the documentation. This method attempts to designate the window itself as first responder, implicitly forcing the text field to attempt to resign first responder status because there can be only one first responder at a time. The method returns YES if successful and NO otherwise, so it makes a perfect test of the validity of a pending text field entry. By placing it in the `tabview:shouldSelectTabViewItem:` method, you cause it to be invoked by any other tab-switching user controls or menu items you may later add to the application, such as the command pop-down menu button or radio button cluster recommended as options in the human interface guidelines.

The attempt to force the window itself to become the first responder immediately triggers the `control:textShouldEndEditing:` delegate method, which tests for a blank entry, and the `control:didFailToFormatString:errorDescription:` delegate method in the case of any other invalid entry. Since either of these methods returns NO in the case of a blank or invalid entry, preventing the text field from relinquishing first responder status, the command to make the window first responder fails and `tabView:shouldSelectTabViewItem:` also returns NO. The end result is to overrule the attempted selection of a different tab view item. The sheet presented lets the user decide how to resolve the issue, whereupon the user can again switch tab view items.

You don't need a means to disable the navigation buttons while the sheet is pending, because Cocoa implements the modal aspect of a document-modal sheet for you: All controls in the window become unresponsive once a sheet is pending for that window. Cocoa does not put the controls into a visually disabled state, presumably because the sheet is so obvious. Cocoa does, however, disable some menu items that could otherwise affect the window while the sheet is pending, perhaps because the association between the window and the menu items is not so obvious.

Human Interface Considerations

What becomes of data that is pending in a text field when the user selects another tab view item or closes the window or quits the application before pressing the Enter key to commit that data?

Selecting another tab view item. Cocoa's default behavior is to perform a validity check on a pending edit when a new tab view item is selected. This behavior makes it clear that switching panes in a tab view is regarded as a signal that the user intends to commit any pending edit. The user is not interrupted with a notice that the data will be committed, because this is the way things are supposed to work.

This seems sensible from a human interface perspective. Switching panes does not have the same negative connotation as closing the window or quitting the application; it does not suggest that the user is abandoning work on the document and wants to discard pending edits, as those other two actions do. At the same time, it does suggest an intent to move on to other aspects of the document.

Furthermore, the alternative—leaving an edit session live in a text field that's hidden behind another tab view item—could become confusing. After a while, the live text field would tend to be forgotten, yet at any moment the user's clicking in a text field in the current tab view item would force the other text field to commit, since only one text field can have focus in a window. Better to get the validity check out of the way as soon as the user switches to a new pane. Several things protect the user: The user is still within the same window and can therefore easily return to the first tab view item to check the value; the Undo menu item allows the user to restore the previous value of the text field, even without returning to its tab view item; and built-in Cocoa routines will ask the user whether to save changes when closing the window.

The *Aqua Human Interface Guidelines* do not advocate a contrary approach in this statement: "In a dialog that has multiple panes (selected by tabs or a pop-up menu), avoid validating data when a user switches from one pane to another." You should interpret this in the context of the general injunction, in the same section of the *Guidelines,* to validate data entries immediately in dialogs: "In general, all changes a user makes in a dialog should appear to take effect immediately." In other words, the data should already be validated before the user attempts to select another tab view item. Even in a dialog, therefore, you should forbid switching tab view items until the validation has succeeded.

CLOSING A WINDOW OR QUITTING. A similar user interface issue arises when the user attempts to close the window holding the text field or to quit the application. Closing a window or quitting after committing a change to a text field naturally causes Cocoa to ask the user whether to save it. However, by default Cocoa simply discards a pending *uncommitted* edit to a text field when the user closes the window or quits the application.

Cocoa allows an attempt to close the window or to quit while an edit is pending, legal or illegal, without giving any warning that the pending edit will be discarded and without offering to let the user save it. The unfinished edit in the text field is aborted and the new value is lost. The theory implicit in this behavior is that data isn't data until the user presses Enter or takes other steps recognized as evidence of an intent to end editing and commit the value. As noted above, switching tab view items is regarded as evidence of such an intent, but closing a window or quitting a document is regarded as evidence of an intent to abandon pending edits. This behavior is deeply ingrained in Cocoa. A few examples: The Window menu places a check-mark in front of unsaved window names only after the user has committed a change to a text field; the automatic save sheet descends only when the user closes a window in which he or she has committed changes; the review-all-changes dialog is posed upon quitting only if the user has committed changes; the close button in a window's title bar only acquires its dot when the user has committed changes; and the Undo menu item is enabled only when the user has committed changes. In the context of these interface signals, Cocoa simply doesn't recognize a pending, uncommitted edit as real data.

If you were to attempt to override Cocoa's default behavior when the user closes a window or quits, you would discover that there is no straightforward way to do so. There are methods to intercept these events. Examples are NSWindow's `windowShouldClose:` delegate method, NSDocument's `shouldCloseWindowController:delegate:` `shouldCloseSelector:contextInfo:` method, and NSApplication's `application-ShouldTerminate:` delegate method. You can use all of them to catch invalid pending edits before the window closes or the application quits, but doing so makes little sense if you can't also commit a valid pending edit and give the user the option to save it. Extensive testing reveals that Cocoa invokes all of these methods too late in the process of closing a window or quitting the application to raise a save sheet or dialog on a pending, valid edit that wasn't committed before one of these methods was invoked.

Enough is enough; you should do it Cocoa's way.

Build and run the application. Try switching to another tab view item while an invalid entry is pending, to confirm that you cannot do so until the entry is fixed. Try closing the window or quitting while an invalid entry is pending, and you will see that Cocoa instantly obeys your command.

You have now learned enough about sheets to make use of them throughout your application. You can also build custom sheets and dialogs in Interface Builder, so that you can include within them a variety of user controls in addition to the buttons provided by the `NSBeginAlertSheet()` function and its siblings, but you will defer doing this until you get to Section 5 dealing with windows in general.

Before moving on to additional text field examples, you will first take another detour, this time to study text field formatting in Recipe 6.

Conclusion

You now have the skills you need to associate informative alert sheets with text fields whenever an error condition might require giving the user an explanation and information that will enable recovery, as well as provide additional options.

In Recipe 6, you will learn how to connect custom formatters to a text field. I hope this will lessen the need for the alert sheets you just learned how to create. With on-the-fly formatters to prevent the user from entering invalid characters in the first place, you won't so often need to give the user a means of error recovery.

Text Field Extras: Formatters

This recipe is the second in a series of recipes dealing with text field enhancements. In Recipe 5, you implemented alert sheets to deal with invalid text field contents at the point when the user has completed an entry. In this recipe, you will learn how to create custom formatters that filter text on the fly as it is typed. This makes it unnecessary to perform some kinds of validation after an entry is complete, by screening out unwanted characters while a user types.

Custom formatters can also force entries in a text field to assume a specified format, either on the fly or after the entry is complete. You had a brief introduction to formatters in Recipe 3, Step 2, where you used Interface Builder to connect a built-in Cocoa number formatter to the Speed Limiter text field. Cocoa also provides a built-in date formatter. Custom formatters allow you to venture far beyond NSNumberFormatter and NSDateFormatter to many other data formats, such as Social Security numbers and telephone numbers.

In this recipe, you will learn how to implement specialized custom formatters, one for on-the-fly filtering and two for on-the-fly filtering and formatting.

Documentation

To understand the background for coding custom formatters, you should read the "Data Formatting" section of the "Data Management" topic under *Programming Topics* in Cocoa Help, as well as the NSControl, NSCell, NSCharacterSet, and NSFormatter class reference documents. In addition, you will need to read the Foundation *Release Notes* for Mac OS X 10.0, which contain a short section explaining in detail the usage of an important new method added to NSFormatter in that version of Mac OS X.

Before turning to Step 1, you should prepare your project files for Recipe 6. Update the build version in the Info.plist Entries to **6**. You don't need to change the document version code in VRDocument.m because the file format will remain unchanged.

Step 1: Set Up On-the-Fly Input Filtering for Integers

HIGHLIGHTS:

Writing a custom formatter by subclassing NSNumberFormatter

Using a built-in character set for membership testing

Substring searching and manipulation

Limiting typing in a text field to a specific set of characters (filtering for numeric digits)

Now you are ready to implement on-the-fly input filtering for the first of the three new text fields you created in Recipe 4, the Integer text field.

The filter applied to the Integer text field here accepts only the digits 0 to 9 and will prevent typing or pasting any other character. Among other characters, it does not allow the user to insert a minus sign (-), so negative numbers are excluded. This filter might be suitable for a text field representing an all-numeric serial number, for example.

On-the-fly filtering and formatting require that you write your own formatter, because the two formatters built into Cocoa do their formatting only after the user commits an entry—for example, by pressing Enter.

Normally, a custom on-the-fly formatter requires you to override, at a minimum, three methods of NSFormatter. For number or date filtering, however, you can subclass NSNumberFormatter or NSDateFormatter to take advantage of the fact that they already implement the two required methods that handle the completed entry, leaving you to override only a single method to implement on-the-fly filtering and formatting. You will learn the simplest case, a filter that does no formatting, in this step.

Writing a formatter is not the end of the work. You must also instantiate and release the formatter, and you must write a delegate method that is triggered when the formatter detects an illegal entry. You might also have to write a method to present a sheet informing the user about the nature of the problem and offering options. You will start in this step with the simplest approach, a filter that simply beeps at the user without presenting a sheet.

1.1 Write a Delegate Method to Catch Input Errors Detected by a Formatter

First, in the source file VRMainWindowController.m, add the following delegate method in the "Formatter errors" subsection of the INPUT VALIDATION AND FORMATTING section, following the `control:didFailToFormatString:errorDescription:` method. It is a delegate method and doesn't require a declaration.

```
- (void)control:(NSControl *)control
      didFailToValidatePartialString:(NSString *)string
      errorDescription:(NSString *)error {
    if (control == [self integerTextField]) {
        NSBeep();
    }
}
```

As you have already learned, when you implement one of the delegate methods declared in NSControl to catch formatter errors, you must begin by checking whether it was the control you are interested in that caused the delegate method to be called. This is because other controls may also appoint VRMainWindowController as their delegate, and they may also invoke on-the-fly input filters. Filtering errors in all of them will trigger this delegate method. You therefore have to be careful to differentiate between the controls if, as will be the case here, you want to provide different responses to filtering errors in different controls. For Integer text field filtering errors, the application will simply beep, but in Steps 2 and 3 you will add branches to the `if` block of this method to detect input errors in the Decimal text field and the Telephone text field and to cause the application to present sheets in response.

For the same reason, you should not place the delegate method in one of the specific window controller categories you have created but instead in the main body of the controller. You may need to use it for text fields in other parts of the application.

1.2 Connect the Delegate

Remember that, since this is a delegate method, NSControl will call it automatically—but only if you remember to appoint VRMainWindowController as the delegate of this control. You had best get this out of the way right now, because it is easy to forget. In Interface Builder, Control-drag from the Integer text field to the File's Owner icon, which you may recall is a proxy for the VRMainWindowController object, then connect its `delegate` target.

1.3 Instantiate and Connect the Formatter

Before writing the formatter, you will write the code to instantiate it and connect it to the Integer text field. In Recipe 3, Step 2, you used Interface Builder to accomplish this, making use of its built-in facilities for instantiating an NSNumberFormatter object and connecting it to a user control. Here, you will perform these steps programmatically. You will leave the best part—writing the custom formatter class—for last in Steps 1.4 and following.

1. You will create the formatter as a separate object in its own header and source files. Let's say that you'll name the class VRIntegerNumberFilter, and that it will be declared as a subclass of NSNumberFormatter in order to inherit all the methods and number-handling capabilities of that built-in Cocoa class. The only method you will have to implement in the subclass is the `isPartialStringValid:newEditingString:errorDescription:` method or its sibling, `isPartialStringValid:proposedSelectedRange:originalString: originalSelectedRange:errorDescription:`.

    With these points in mind, you can write a method in the VRTextFieldController category that will instantiate an instance of the VRIntegerNumberFilter class and call it in VRMainWindowController's `awakeFromNib` method.

    In VRMainWindowController.m, before the "Formatter errors" subsection of the INPUT VALIDATION AND FORMATTING section, declare the method that will instantiate a VRIntegerNumberFilter object and connect it to the Integer text field, as set forth below. You should not place constructor methods such as this in a category, because you might want to instantiate this formatter for text fields located anywhere in the application.

    ```
    // Formatter constructors

    - (void)makeIntegerNumberFilter {
        VRIntegerNumberFilter *integerNumberFilter =
                [[VRIntegerNumberFilter alloc] init];
        [integerNumberFilter setFormat:@"##0"];
        [[[self integerTextField] cell]
                setFormatter:integerNumberFilter];

        [integerNumberFilter release];
    }
    ```

    This is very straightforward. You use the now-familiar standard means to allocate and initialize an instance of the VRIntegerNumberFilter class in a single line. Since it will be a subclass of NSNumberFormatter, you know that you can call the `setFormat:` method it inherits from NSNumberFormatter to define a template string controlling the appearance of the numbers that will be entered in the Integer text field. Then you call the `setFormatter:` method, built into every AppKit cell, to connect the new formatter to the text field.

The NSCell class reference document states that `setFormatter:` retains the formatter. Since this makes the cell the owner of the formatter, the cell also takes on the responsibility to release it when the text field goes away or you set another formatter on the same field. You therefore `release` the formatter here, in the same method where you created it, because you have no further use for it aside from its use in the text field. The formatter remains alive in the text field's ownership until the text field itself goes away when the document is closed. In general, `setFormatter:` acts very much the way similar methods in Cocoa's collection classes act, assuming ownership of objects that are inserted into the collection. To instantiate, or construct, a formatter, you allocate it temporarily and then release it in the same method, following a familiar Cocoa pattern.

In another application, there might be a good reason to wait until the window controller's `dealloc` method is called to release the formatter. For example, if you will connect the same formatter to multiple text fields, you could save yourself the overhead of instantiating it again, only to connect it to another text field and immediately release it. Instead, you would just connect it to each new text field. There would be only the one formatter taking up memory in this situation, although it may have been retained many times, so you would lose nothing by postponing the release until the document is deallocated.

Note that no range checking is done to ensure that the value typed can safely be converted to an integer data type internally. That is an exercise for another day. If you tackle this issue, note that the NSCell class reference document lists the constants that define the range limitations of all of the data types that a text field can accommodate, along with the methods you can use to determine the type of a particular text field's contents.

Declare this method in VRMainWindowController.h after the "Validation of pending edits" subsection of the INPUT VALIDATION AND FORMATTING section:

```
// Formatter constructors
- (void)makeIntegerNumberFilter;
```

Also, because the implementation of the method calls methods of the VRIntegerNumberFilter class or its superclass, you must import that class into the source file VRMainWindowController.m by adding the following line to the end of the import directives at the top of the file:

```
#import "VRIntegerNumberFilter.h"
```

2. In anticipation of writing several custom formatters for the application, you might want to follow your previous practice of writing an umbrella method where you can collect all of your calls to similar methods, as you did when you wrote the `registerNotificationObservers` and `updateWindow` methods in earlier recipes. Create a method to collect formatter constructors such as `makeIntegerNumberFilter` and call it `makeFormatters`. In VRMainWindowController.m, before the `registerNotificationObservers` method, insert the following:

```
- (void)makeFormatters {
    [self makeIntegerNumberFilter];
}
```

Declare it in VRMainWindowController.h, before the `registerNotification-Observers` method:

```
- (void)makeFormatters;
```

3. A text field's formatter can be instantiated at the same time its window is created or, in the case of a window, instantiated in a nib file, as soon as it has been fully unarchived from the nib file. Therefore, add the following line to the `awakeFromNib` method in VRMainWindowController.m, before the call to `registerNotificationObservers`:

```
[self makeFormatters];
```

1.4 Write a Formatter to Detect Input Errors

You are now ready to write the new formatter. It is very simple, after all that preparation. However, you will explore two incorrect solutions here before settling on the final version, to help you understand the variety of situations a formatter can encounter in the real world.

In general outline, you create an on-the-fly formatter by implementing NSControl's `control:didFailToValidatePartialString:errorDescription:` delegate method in a control's delegate, along with one of these two methods in the formatter to check and possibly modify the new contents of a connected text field: either the `isPartialStringValid:newEditingString:errorDescription:` method or a more powerful sibling that was added to NSFormatter in Mac OS X 10.0, `isPartialStringValid:proposedSelectedRange:originalString:originalSelectedRange:errorDescription:`. The documentation makes clear that the latter is preferred; the former exists for backward compatibility only. Cocoa automatically calls whichever of the two formatter methods you implement every time the user types or deletes characters using the keyboard and every time the user cuts or pastes characters from the keyboard or the Edit menu, or adds or removes characters from the text field in some other manner, or even just moves characters around within the text field using drag-and-drop editing.

In any custom formatter that you write, it is your responsibility to supply one or the other of these two methods to implement on-the-fly filtering or formatting. If you provide neither of them, your formatter will not do on-the-fly filtering or formatting.

You have already satisfied some of these prerequisites by implementing the `control:didFailToValidatePartialString:errorDescription:` delegate method in VRMainWindowController in Step 1.1 and appointing VRMainWindowController as the control's delegate in Step 1.2. You will now write the formatter itself.

1. Using Project Builder techniques that you have now applied several times, create new Cocoa header and source files and name them `VRIntegerNumberFilter.h` and `VRIntegerNumberFilter.m`, respectively. In the Groups & Files pane of the Project Builder window, create a new subgroup in the Classes group and name it `Formatters`. Then choose Project > Add Files, add the two new files, and drag their icons into the new Formatters group. In each file, add any comments you customarily place in your code files to identify them.

2. Set up the header file VRIntegerNumberFilter.h so that it imports the Foundation umbrella framework and inherits from NSNumberFormatter. Formatters are creatures of the Foundation frameworks because they are not specific to applications; you might want to use a formatter in software that does not make use of the AppKit. The skeleton should look like this:

```
#import <Foundation/Foundation>

@interface VRIntegerNumberFilter : NSNumberFormatter {
}

@end
```

3. Set up the source file VRIntegerNumberFilter.m so that it imports its header file and provide the implementation skeleton, as follows:

```
#import "VRIntegerNumberFilter.h"

@implementation VRIntegerNumberFilter

@end
```

4. Finally, add the following definition of the filter method, as a tentative first stab at it:

```
// Input filter

- (BOOL)isPartialStringValid:(NSString *)partialString
    newEditingString:(NSString **)newString
    errorDescription:(NSString **)error {
  if (!([[NSCharacterSet decimalDigitCharacterSet]
      characterIsMember:[partialString
      characterAtIndex:[partialString length] - 1]])) {
    *newString = nil;
    *error = NSLocalizedString(
        @"Input is not an integer.",
        @"Presented when user value not a numeric digit");
    return NO;
  }
  *error = nil;
  return YES;
}
```

As an override method, this does not require a declaration. In fact, for this formatter, the header file will be empty.

Here, you use the **isPartialStringValid:newEditingString:errorDescription:** method, one of the two methods mentioned above. On entry, the **partialString** parameter value is the string the user has been typing into the text field, including the last character the user typed—which may be an illegal character. You obtain the last character by using NSString's **characterAtIndex:** method, using the index of the last character in the string, [**partialString length**] - 1. This is a mistake, of course, because the user might be editing an existing string, starting somewhere other than at its end. To keep things simple for the moment, you begin on the assumption that the user is typing into an empty field.

The **newString** value in the **newEditingString** parameter is for your use in passing another string back to the text field. Typically, **newString** will be a revised version of the **partialString** object, altered within the method before it is returned to the caller by reference. You would use it to substitute a string object of your own devising for the string object typed by the user, if your formatter is intended to provide formatting on the fly as well as filtering. Here, you won't use it for this purpose because this formatter does nothing but filter the user's input.

The **error** value in the **ErrorDescription** parameter allows you to return to the caller, by reference, another string object containing a displayable description of any error discovered when the user typed the last character. The error value should be localized.

To test the validity of the last character typed, you check it for membership in the `decimalDigitCharacterSet` object, using NSCharacterSet's `characterIsMember:` method. The `decimalDigitCharacterSet` method is a class method that returns an instantiated character set object, one of several character sets provided in Cocoa's NSCharacterSet class. This character set consists solely of the characters 0 through 9 (in several script systems), which is just what you want.

If the last character typed is determined to be invalid because it is not a member of the character set, you set `newString` to `nil` and return it by reference and you define an error description string that you also return by reference. You then return `NO` as the method result to indicate that `partialString` is unacceptable. Cocoa will display the previous contents of the text field without the last character.

Although you are not making use of the capability to return an edited string here, you could do so and it would be displayed in the text field in place of the string the user has typed. You define an `error` string here, just in case you might redesign the application later to present an alert sheet, but in this version you will only sound a beep.

If the last character passes the validity test, you simply return `YES` to indicate that `partialString` is acceptable and return `nil` in the `errorDescription` parameter. Cocoa will go ahead and display it in the text field as the user typed it, including the last character.

If you were to hook up everything in the nib file and build and run the application now, you would discover that the formatter works—sort of. If you start typing in an empty Integer text field or after selecting its entire existing contents, any illegal characters are indeed rejected with a warning beep, as you expected. However, if you place the insertion point at the front or in the middle of the text field's existing contents before you start typing, illegal characters are accepted without complaint. The reason is immediately apparent: Your formatter explicitly tests the last character in the entire field—that is, the character at the right end— not the character that was most recently typed. As you have just discovered, they are not always the same. There are other problems with this approach, too, as you will see further along in this step.

5. I discovered early in the development of the Vermont Recipes application that NSFormatter's old `isPartialStringValid:newEditingString:errorDescription:` method is inadequate to resolve some of the problems you encounter in writing even the simplest on-the-fly formatter. As a result of communications among Apple and several developers, including me, regarding these problems during the Developer Preview days of Mac OS X, NSFormatter was revised in Mac OS X 10.0 to add a new method. You will use the new method in this instruction and the next to solve problems you can't solve by using the old method. The old

method is still included in NSFormatter for compatibility with older software, according to the class reference document. A comment in the NSFormatter header file notes that the old method always leaves the insertion point at the end of the field if changes are made to its contents and that the new method should therefore be used whenever you need to control the location or length of the insertion point or selection on exit. The Foundation *Release Notes* for Mac OS X 10.0 make clear that you should only override one or the other in a custom formatter, not both.

The *Release Notes* suggest that the new, enhanced sibling of the method you used in Instruction 4 will be useful for the Integer field's formatter, so you will try it next in your ongoing effort to perfect the formatter.

The new method offers a much more powerful approach, for both simple and complex on-the-fly filtering and formatting. Among other things, it provides you with the current location of the insertion point every time the user inserts or deletes characters. This allows you to track the most recent printable character that was typed, even if it is not at the end of the text field. In addition to the original location and length of the insertion point or selection, this method gives you the original string itself, as it existed before any new text was inserted or deleted. The method also offers enhanced facilities for editing the string and tracking or altering the user's selection.

All you need in this step is the location of the insertion point before and after the user typed or pasted new characters into the text field. You will explore the finer points of the new method later.

One way to deal with the problem presented by your last approach might be to override this new, enhanced NSFormatter method as a substitute for the approach you took in Instruction 4:

```
- (BOOL)isPartialStringValid:(NSString **)partialStringPtr
      proposedSelectedRange:(NSRangePointer)proposedSelRangePtr
      originalString:(NSString *)origString
      originalSelectedRange:(NSRange)origSelRange
      errorDescription:(NSString **)error {
   if (!([[NSCharacterSet decimalDigitCharacterSet]
         characterIsMember:[*partialStringPtr
         characterAtIndex:origSelRange.location]])) {
      *error = NSLocalizedString(@"Input is not an integer.",
            @"Presented when user value not a numeric digit");
      return NO;
   }
   *error = nil;
```

```
    return YES;
}
```

As you see, the new NSFormatter method's parameters are considerably more complex than those of the old method, tracking both the original string before another character was typed (the `origString` parameter value) and the new string after the character was typed (the `partialStringPtr` parameter value), as well as tracking the selection range both before (the `origSelRange` parameter value) and after (the `proposedSelRangePtr` parameter value) typing. A proposed revised string and selection can be returned by reference to the caller in the `partialStringPtr` and `proposedSelRangePtr` values.

The only change you have made in this approach is to use the `location` element of the new `originalSelectedRange` parameter to examine the character inserted by the user anywhere in the text field, not just at its end.

The `origSelRange` parameter value is of type NSRange. This is a C structure, declared in Foundation's NSRange.h header file, consisting of the `location` and `length` of a range of characters within a string. Its use in Cocoa, including the dot notation familiar to C programmers for accessing individual elements of a structure, is one of the reasons why newcomers to Cocoa development are urged to learn standard C as well as the Objective-C extensions. The `location` of the user's selection in the text field just before typing another character is the position of the insertion point, whether the user had selected a range of characters for replacement or merely placed the insertion point with a mouse click. This is precisely the value you need to obtain the new character last typed by the user, wherever in the string the user might have typed it, and to test it for membership in `decimalDigitCharacterSet` using the `characterIsMember:` method. You know that new characters are typed at the insertion point, or at the beginning of the original selection that new typing replaces, and the `origSelRange.location` element makes this information available to you painlessly.

Although it appears more complex, using this new NSFormatter method actually makes your implementation simpler than it was before. Instead of returning a `nil` value in the old `newEditingString` parameter, you just leave the new two-way `partialStringPtr` parameter value undisturbed. By returning `NO` as the method result, Cocoa knows that you wish to reject the newly typed character and display only the previous version of the text field entry. The only other change in your implementation, besides using `origSelRange.location` instead of the index of the new string's last character, is to obtain the user's proposed new string by dereferencing the new `partialStringPtr` parameter value instead of getting the old `partialString` parameter value.

6. Unfortunately, the need to accommodate typing at the beginning or in the middle of the text field was not the only problem with your initial approach. In addition, if the user were to paste a multicharacter string into the field and the pasted string contained invalid characters in any position, the invalid characters would be accepted without generating an error. This is because even your latest approach to designing the Integer field's formatter tests only a single new input character, overlooking the fact that whole strings can be pasted into a text field. You need to fix this problem, too.

To provide a complete solution, you must try yet another approach, this time testing the entire selection range rather than the single character at the insertion point. By giving you the selection as a range, the new NSFormatter method accommodates this need.

The bottom line is that every formatter designed to filter out illegal characters must test a string, rather than a single character, because the user might at any time paste a string of characters rather than typing only one. It turns out to be easy to accommodate this need; you alter the code you have already developed only as much as is required to test an input string instead of an input character. This requires two new code snippets, one to obtain the user's input of one or more characters in the form of a string, and another to test all of the characters in the string for membership in the character set.

Substitute the following final approach in VRIntegerNumberFilter.m:

```
- (BOOL)isPartialStringValid:(NSString **)partialStringPtr
        proposedSelectedRange:(NSRangePointer)proposedSelRangePtr
        originalString:(NSString *)origString
        originalSelectedRange:(NSRange)origSelRange
        errorDescription:(NSString **)error {
    if ([[*partialStringPtr substringWithRange:
            NSMakeRange(origSelRange.location,
            (*proposedSelRangePtr).location -
            origSelRange.location)] rangeOfCharacterFromSet:
            [[NSCharacterSet decimalDigitCharacterSet]
            invertedSet] options:NSLiteralSearch].location !=
            NSNotFound) {
        *error = NSLocalizedString(@"Input is not an integer.",
                @"Presented when user value not a numeric digit");
        return NO;
    }
    *error = nil;
    return YES;
}
```

That complicated `if` test is not meant to show off how convoluted an Objective-C statement can be made to appear but only to cram as much work as possible into a single Boolean statement. I will break it into pieces to explain what it does.

The first part of the test extracts what the user typed or pasted in the field, in the form of a string. The string may contain a single character if the user typed on the keyboard, or one or more characters if the user pasted in something from the pasteboard, or nothing if the user pressed the Delete key or the Forward Delete key. By getting the user's input all at once in a string, whether it was typed, pasted, or deleted, you save yourself the bother of getting it one way if typed, a second way if pasted, and a third way if deleted.

It was very easy to extract the typed or pasted string using the information provided by the new NSFormatter method introduced in Mac OS X 10.0. The dereferenced `partialStringPtr` parameter value gives you the entire contents of the field after the user edited it, including any newly added character or characters. NSString's `substringWithRange:` method is used to extract from it the portion of the text field's proposed new contents that was just added by a typing or pasting operation. This works even if the extracted string is empty because the user deleted something, due to the way the Cocoa string handling methods are designed.

The range you use to extract the substring is created using Cocoa's `NSMakeRange()` function, a macro defined in NSRange.h and documented in the *Functions* section near the end of the Foundation reference document. Cocoa makes this macro available, so you might as well use it, although you could just as well have used standard C to write the method in curly braces and cast it to an NSRange like this: `(NSRange){origSelRange.location, (*proposedSelRangePtr).location - origSelRange.location}`. The dereferenced `proposedSelRangePtr` parameter value contains, in its `location` element, the proposed new `position` of the insertion point after the user's entry, which falls at the end of the newly typed or pasted characters (its `length` is `0`, because the newly typed or pasted characters are not selected). The `location` element of the `origString` parameter value contains the original location of the insertion point before the user's entry. The difference between these two positions defines the range that marks the character or characters just inserted: namely, the substring within the text field's contents that the user just typed or pasted in.

Having the input string in hand, you need only filter every character in it. Since you need to detect whether any one of the characters in the string is illegal, you cannot test whether any character in a valid character set is found. You must instead test whether any character in an illegal character set is found. For this, you need the inverse of Cocoa's built-in `decimalDigitCharacterSet`—that is, a set containing every character *other than* the decimal digits. For these purposes,

NSCharacterSet provides the `invertedSet` method. It uses a very efficient bit manipulation technique for immutable character sets like the one you employ here, so you needn't worry about overhead.

You also need a method that tests every character in a string for membership in the inverted character set. NSString provides this in the `rangeOfCharacterFromSet:options:` method. It works by reporting the range of the first appearance of any character or characters in the set. You set the `options:` parameter to `NSLiteralSearch`. It is worth looking at the NSString reference document for an explanation of how this method works and to review the several alternatives, because they are quite useful for string processing. This method returns an NSRange structure defining the `location` and `length` of the substring for which it is searching within the target string, if one is found. If the substring is not found, the `location` element of the structure is returned as the value of the `NSNotFound` constant, along with a `length` of `0`. This is all accomplished by the second part of the test in your formatter method, which boils down to testing whether the reported location of an illegal character in whatever the user typed or pasted is not equal to `NSNotFound`. If this double negative is true, then an invalid character was found somewhere in what was typed or pasted in and your formatter method returns `NO` to reject it.

Finally, you return `nil` by reference in the `errorDescription:` parameter if there is no error. This neatly solves a cosmetic issue in earlier versions of the Vermont Recipes application, which did not return `nil` in the `errorDescription:` parameter. When the user typed some numbers into the field and then deleted all of them, one at a time, the insertion point disappeared in our old implementation—but only if all of the following conditions were met: The text field was right-aligned, the last character to be deleted was not selected at the time, and the Delete key (not the Forward Delete key) was used to remove it. I don't understand why returning `nil` by reference in the `errorDescription:` parameter resolves this issue, but it does. It seems in retrospect that returning `nil` is the right thing to do when there is no error, anyway.

7. Don't forget to add the "Input is not an integer" error message to the Localizable.strings file:

```
/* Formatters */
/* Presented when user value not a numeric digit */
"Input is not an integer" = "Input is not an integer"
```

1.5 Require an Entry in the Text Field

For the perfectionists among you, one more matter demands your attention. The Integer text field allows you to delete its contents. When you do this and tab or click out of the field, the blank entry is accepted. You recall that formatters are not invoked when fields are left blank.

Let's assume this field is not supposed to be left blank. The solution is easy: Just add this field to those checked by the `control:textShouldEndEditing:` delegate method you wrote in Recipe 5, Step 2. A sheet will be presented telling you that the field cannot be left empty.

In VRMainWindowController.m, add this code to the `control:textShouldEndEditing:` delegate method, after the block that deals with the Speed Limiter text field:

```
else if (control == [self integerTextField]) {
    if ([[fieldEditor string] isEqualToString:@""]) {
        return [self sheetForBlankTextField:control
                name:NSLocalizedString(@"Integer",
                @"Name of Integer text field")];
    }
}
```

You must add the Integer field name to Localizable.strings.

1.6 Build and Run the Application

Build and run the application.

Type one or more digits. Then type a character that is not included in the digits 0 through 9, and note that the computer beeps at you and does not display the illegal character. Try typing an illegal character in several locations, not just at the end of the text field. Also try pasting a string of characters into the field at any location, using both a string of digits and a string that includes one or more nonnumeric characters. The latter will be rejected with a beep.

You have now learned how to apply a simple character-filtering, on-the-fly formatter to a text field. In the next step you will take this knowledge a step further, applying a slightly more complex custom formatter and adding the ability not only to filter but also to format a text field entry on the fly.

Step 2: Set Up On-the-Fly Input Filtering and Formatting for Decimal Values

HIGHLIGHTS:

Obtaining localized user defaults from NSUserDefaults

Creating and using a custom character set for membership testing

Limiting typing in a text field to positive decimal values (filtering for numeric digits plus localized thousands and decimal separators)

Creating and using a scanner to remove unwanted characters from a string

Formatting a text field on the fly by inserting thousands separators automatically and adjusting the insertion point

Creating a category to work around Cocoa bugs

Recognizing a control character or function key typed on the keyboard

In Step 1, you implemented simple on-the-fly input filtering, without formatting, for the first of three text fields. In this step, you will implement a more complex formatter for the Decimal text field. It will let the user type positive decimal values using the numeric digits plus localized thousands and decimal separators. Typing any other character will cause the computer to not only beep but also present a sheet explaining the input error. You will also provide formatting on the fly by inserting localized thousands separators in the correct locations automatically as the user types, deletes, forward-deletes, cuts, pastes, and drags and drops individual characters and strings.

This step and the next are quite complex. If you prefer to skip them for now, you will suffer no inconvenience as you proceed through the remainder of *Vermont Recipes*. I chose to tackle the issue of formatters here to show you that they are of great value in adding a polished user experience to a completed application. But formatters are difficult and time-consuming to write, and they might better be left to the final stages of developing an application. If you skip these two steps now, be sure to mark them for a return visit later, because many text fields should make use of formatters.

You already created the Decimal text field in Recipe 4, so you can get right to work on the custom formatter.

2.1 Write a Delegate Method to Catch Input Errors Detected by the Formatter

First, in VRMainWindowController.m, revise the **control:didFailToValidate-PartialString:errorDescription:** delegate method in the "Formatter errors" subsection of the INPUT VALIDATION AND FORMATTING section to test whether the Decimal text field was the source of the validation error. If it was, and if you determine that there was in fact a validation error, you will provide the user with both a beep and an alert sheet. You will write the code for the sheet shortly, using the techniques you learned in Recipe 5.

```
- (void)control:(NSControl *)control
     didFailToValidatePartialString:(NSString *)string
     errorDescription:(NSString *)error {
   if (control == [self integerTextField]) {
      NSBeep();
   } else if (control == [self decimalTextField]) {
      if (error != nil) {
         NSBeep();
         [self sheetForDecimalTextFieldValidationFailure:string
               errorDescription:error];
      }
   }
}
```

Here, as in Recipe 5, Step 1, the custom method you are about to write to present the sheet, **sheetForDecimalTextFieldValidationFailure:errorDescription:**, will return **NO** to prevent the invalid string from being displayed. However, the **control:didFailToValidatePartialString:errorDescription:** delegate method does not need to return that result to the caller, as did the **control:didFailToFormatString:errorDescription:** method in Recipe 5, so you ignore the result here.

The new section of this method tests the **errorDescription** parameter to determine whether the formatter did not return **nil** by reference in the **errorDescription:** parameter. Anticipating some code that you will write at the end of this step, this reflects a convention you will adopt of returning **nil** instead of an error description string from an on-the-fly formatter to signal that no error has occurred. This is necessary when the formatter substitutes some text that it has edited for the text that the user actually typed, because Cocoa invokes the **control:didFailToValidatePartialString:errorDescription:** method to display the substituted string even though there has not been an error. You don't want to display an alert sheet when there is no error.

2.2 Connect the Delegate

To ensure that NSControl will call this delegate method automatically, you must appoint VRMainWindowController as the text field's delegate. In Interface Builder, Control-drag from the Decimal text field to the File's Owner icon, which you recall is a proxy for the VRMainWindowController object, then connect the **delegate** target.

2.3 Instantiate and Connect the Formatter

Next, connect the formatter to the control, leaving the code for the sheet and the formatter itself until later.

1. When you create the formatter, you will call it VRDecimalNumberFilter, a subclass of NSNumberFormatter. In VRMainWindowController.m, in the new "Formatter constructors" section after the **makeIntegerNumberFilter** method that you wrote in the previous step, declare the method that will instantiate a VRDecimalNumberFilter object and connect it to the Decimal text field, as follows:

```
- (void)makeDecimalNumberFilter {
    VRDecimalNumberFilter *decimalNumberFilter =
        [[VRDecimalNumberFilter alloc] init];
    [decimalNumberFilter setFormat:@"#,##0.00"];
    [[[self decimalTextField] cell]
        setFormatter:decimalNumberFilter];
    [decimalNumberFilter release];
}
```

Declare this method in VRMainWindowController.h after the **makeInteger-NumberFilter** declaration:

```
- (void)makeDecimalNumberFilter;
```

2. You must also import VRDecimalNumberFilter.h into VRMainWindow-Controller.m by adding the following line to the end of the import directives at the top of the source file:

```
#import "VRDecimalNumberFilter.h"
```

3. In the **makeFormatters** method you added to VRMainWindowController.m in the previous step, insert the following to create the new formatter when the window opens:

```
[self makeDecimalNumberFilter];
```

2.4 Present an Alert Sheet for Input Errors

Now create the sheet that will explain what's wrong when the user types an invalid character. This sheet is very simple, requiring only some informative text and an OK button. No callback method is required because the sheet presents the user with no options other than to click the OK button when an illegal character is typed; NULL is passed in both callback selector parameters to the NSBeginAlertSheet() function.

You could have defined the message text for the sheet in this method, as you have done with your other sheets, but here you want the formatter you will shortly create to supply the message text. So instead, you simply accept the **error** string value that the formatter will pass in and pass it along to the sheet as the first parameter of the NSBeginAlertSheet() function.

Only the Decimal text field in the Text Fields tab view item will use the alert sheet, so you can place it in the VRTextFieldController category. If you anticipated using the same sheet in several tab view items, you could place it in the VRMainWindowController.m file instead after generalizing the text. Add this method at the end of the VRTextFieldController.m category source file:

```
#pragma mark INPUT VALIDATION AND FORMATTING


// Formatter errors


// Decimal text field


- (BOOL)sheetForDecimalTextFieldValidationFailure:
        (NSString *)string errorDescription:(NSString *)error {

    NSString *alertInformation =
            NSLocalizedString(@"Type any of the digits "0"-"9" and a \
            single decimal point for a decimal number, such \
            as "1,472.34".",
            @"Informative text for alert posed by Decimal text \
            field when invalid character is typed");

    NSBeginAlertSheet(error, nil, nil, nil, [self window],
            self, NULL, NULL, nil, alertInformation);

    return NO;
}
```

You could have defined the OK button's title explicitly, like so: `NSString *defaultButtonString = NSLocalizedString(@"OK", @"Name of OK button")` and passed it in the second parameter to `NSBeginAlertSheet()`. However, this is such a common alert sheet configuration that Cocoa does it for you if you pass `nil` in the second parameter.

Make sure to add the informative text for the sheet to the Localizable.strings file. Add the following at the end of the Localizable.strings file:

```
/* Decimal text field alert */
/* Informative text for alert posed by Decimal text field when invalid
character is typed */
"Type any of the digits "0"-"9" and a single decimal point for a decimal
number, such as "1,472.34"." = "Type any of the digits "0"-"9" and a
single decimal point for a decimal number, such as "1,472.34"."
```

2.5 Write a Formatter to Detect Input Errors and Format Output

You are now ready to write the new formatter.

Before you turn to the code, consider what your strategy will be. First, from the broadest view, the formatter should do two things: filter out invalid characters (characters other than the decimal digits, the thousands separator, and a decimal separator) and insert thousands separators automatically. In addition, it should do these things in a manner that is intuitive and transparent to the user. For example, if the user deletes or cuts something, it should be possible to retype it or paste it back in immediately without using the arrow keys or the mouse to reposition the insertion point. It is probably beginning to dawn on you that accomplishing this may involve some additional work not required in the Integer text field formatter you just completed, such as adjusting the location of the insertion point to accommodate the automatic formatting done by the formatter.

It seems reasonable to tackle the filtering and formatting tasks sequentially, as independent sections of code, although each section will have to keep in mind what the other section does.

The filter section should be similar to what you wrote in Step 1, but you have to consider some complexities that you didn't need to address there. For one thing, what if the user cuts some part of the contents of this text field, including one or more of the thousands separators that the formatter will add automatically, and then tries to paste that part back into the field? Usability considerations suggest that you will have to write the filter in such a way that it doesn't reject pasted thousands separators, so perhaps typed thousands separators should be accepted too. Finally, this is a decimal number formatter, and the user may therefore type or paste in a decimal separator. But what if the user types two decimal separators or pastes a string that would give the field two or more of them? The filter will obviously have to count decimal separators and reject any effort to insert characters that would leave more than one of them in the field.

The formatter section is also a can of worms. From the moment the user first types or pastes characters in the text field, you not only have to consider filtering out invalid characters but also where to place the automatic thousands separators that are the formatter's responsibility. Furthermore, the second time the user inserts, removes, or moves something in the field, you have to consider moving the thousands separators that were added the first time around, because they are now probably positioned incorrectly relative to the edited text. Also, both deleting and inserting thousands separators will require careful monitoring and adjustment of the insertion point's location. Finally, you may not anticipate it now, but you will soon discover that the user's typing of the Delete key or the Forward Delete key can present subtle problems when positioning the insertion point.

In short, writing a formatter is no easy task. You must take care to write a formatter so that it makes no assumptions about where the insertion point is (the beginning, end, or middle of the text field), or about what was selected (all of the text field, nothing, or a substring), or about whether the user is typing, cutting, deleting, forward deleting, pasting, or dragging and dropping. To do this, you must evaluate a snapshot of the contents of the text field after each edit. It can be quite difficult to design an algorithm that will work in all possible scenarios and even more difficult to simplify and generalize it instead of dealing with every issue as a special case. Trial and error is not only inevitable but also necessary to make sure you haven't left a bug that a user is bound to discover.

1. Create new Cocoa header and source files and name them **VRDecimalNumber-Filter.h** and **VRDecimalNumberFilter.m**, respectively. Choose Project > Add File, add the two new files, and drag their icons into the Formatters group in the Groups & Files pane of the Project Builder window. Add any customary comments.

2. Set up the header file VRDecimalNumberFilter.h so that it imports the Foundation umbrella framework and inherits from NSNumberFormatter. The skeleton should look like this:

```
#import <Foundation/Foundation.h>

@interface VRDecimalNumberFilter : NSNumberFormatter {
}

@end
```

Add the following instance variable declarations, which you will use shortly, inside the curly braces of the interface declaration in VRDecimalNumberFilter.h:

```
@protected
NSString *localizedDecimalSeparatorString;
NSString *localizedThousandsSeparatorString;
NSCharacterSet
        *invertedDecimalDigitPlusLocalizedSeparatorsCharacterSet;
```

You can probably deduce from the instance variables how the formatter is going to handle its filtering function. It will first learn which character is used in the machine's locale as the decimal separator and which as the thousands separator, and it will set up a string version of each of them for use with the Cocoa methods you will use in the formatter. Then it will create a custom character set, which you call invertedDecimalDigitPlusLocalizedSeparatorsCharacterSet, consisting of every character *except* the ten numerical digits and these localized decimal and thousands separator characters. Each character that the user types into the text field will be tested for membership in this custom character set and rejected if it falls within the set. Because of this logic, as you learned in Step 1, it is convenient to use an inverted set instead of the set of decimal digits and separators. In that step, you did not have to create a custom character set to be inverted, because Cocoa comes equipped with a prebuilt character set for the numeric digits; here, you will first create a custom character set, then invert it.

You may be surprised to see that the filter will allow the user to type and paste thousands separators, since the formatter will automatically supply them in the correct positions. This turns out to be the easiest way to solve the problem, mentioned above, of letting the user cut a portion of the field that contains thousands separators and paste it right back into the field. You simply make thousands separators legal and reposition them as necessary in the formatting block, should the user choose to type or paste one of them. The user's experience will be that typing a thousands separator, though permissible, accomplishes nothing, because the thousands separator will instantly disappear or be repositioned by the formatter the moment it is typed.

The character set is created when the formatter is initialized, to minimize the amount of processing required while the user is typing. Machines are fast enough these days so that this precaution may seem antediluvian, but it is a good idea to minimize the processing load during typing, if for no other reason than to reserve as much time as possible for background tasks. You should read the NSCharacterSet reference document to see what steps Apple recommends you take to avoid slowdowns that can occur if you misuse character sets. Here, the formatter will be created when a new window is opened, which is an occasion when a little time is available to take care of things like setting up a character set. You will also create the inverted character set when the formatter is initialized; although the inversion process was apparently fast enough in the Integer filter so that it could safely be performed every time the user typed a character, you might as well take care of it once in the **init** method of the formatter.

Notice that you have not declared any accessor methods for the instance variables. The formatter will be called upon to validate every character as the user types it, and another way that you can avoid using up processor time unnecessarily is to dispense with accessor methods and call the instance variables directly while the user is typing. Accessor methods are not needed here because there are no undo registration or view updater requirements to take into account and you needn't worry about memory management. You used the **@protected** compiler directive to allow any subclass inheriting from this formatter to access the same instance variables despite the absence of an accessor method.

3. Set up the source file VRDecimalNumberFilter.m so that it imports its header file, and provide the implementation skeleton, as follows:

```
#import "VRDecimalNumberFilter.h"

@implementation VRDecimalNumberFilter

@end
```

4. Add the **init** and **dealloc** methods to VRDecimalNumberFilter.m:

```
//Initialization

- (id)init {
    if (self = [super init]) {
        NSMutableCharacterSet *tempSet;
        NSCharacterSet
            *decimalDigitPlusLocalizedSeparatorsCharacterSet;

        localizedDecimalSeparatorString =
            [[NSUserDefaults standardUserDefaults]
            objectForKey:NSDecimalSeparator];
        localizedThousandsSeparatorString =
            [[NSUserDefaults standardUserDefaults]
            objectForKey:NSThousandsSeparator];
```

(continues on next page)

```
        tempSet =
                [[NSCharacterSet decimalDigitCharacterSet]
                mutableCopy];
        [tempSet addCharactersInString:
                [localizedDecimalSeparatorString
                stringByAppendingString:
                localizedThousandsSeparatorString]];
        decimalDigitPlusLocalizedSeparatorsCharacterSet =
                [tempSet copy];
        [tempSet release];

        invertedDecimalDigitPlusLocalizedSeparatorsCharacterSet =
                [[decimalDigitPlusLocalizedSeparatorsCharacterSet
                invertedSet] retain];
        [decimalDigitPlusLocalizedSeparatorsCharacterSet
                release];
    }
    return self;
}


- (void)dealloc {
    [invertedDecimalDigitPlusLocalizedSeparatorsCharacterSet
            release];
    [super dealloc];
}
```

As override methods, these do not require declaration.

First, you set up two of the instance variables to refer to the localized decimal and thousands separators. The NSUserDefaults class reference document contains information about important localized user defaults that are built into Cocoa. You can obtain these default values by using the provided constants, such as `NSDecimalSeparator` and `NSThousandsSeparator`, as keys to determine what values are being used on the computer based on its current locale. The values you obtain for the decimal and thousands separators are strings, which is just what you need for the Cocoa methods you will use here.

Second, you create the custom inverted character set. You do this in two steps, one to create an intermediate character set containing the decimal digits and both separators, and a second to create the inverse of that set. The logic of the filter you are about to write requires the inverted set.

The technique used to create the intermediate character set comes straight out of the NSCharacterSet documentation. You first create a mutable copy of the built-in Cocoa `decimalDigitCharacterSet` character set, which you used in the previous step, using NSObject's `mutableCopy` method, and assign it to a temporary local variable whose declared type is NSMutableCharacterSet. Next, you add the localized decimal and thousands separator strings to it using an NSCharacterSet method designed for this purpose, `addCharactersInString:`. You then copy the temporary mutable character set into another intermediate local variable, `decimalDigitPlusLocalizedSeparatorsCharacterSet`, this one declared as an immutable character set. Finally, you release the temporary mutable character set because it is no longer needed. By using NSObject's `copy` method to assign the new character set to the intermediate local variable, you ensure that it holds an immutable character set. You want the intermediate character set to be immutable because, according to the NSCharacterSet reference document, it is much faster to invert an immutable character set than a mutable character set.

Creating the second character set is a simple matter of calling NSCharacterSet's `invertedSet` method on the intermediate character set, retaining the result and assigning it to the instance variable you have already declared in the interface file as an immutable character set, `invertedDecimalDigitPlusLocalized-SeparatorsCharacterSet`. You then release the intermediate local variable because it won't be needed. You make the final instance variable immutable because the documentation tells you that an immutable character set is much faster when used in a membership test than the temporary mutable character set you had to create so you could add the separators to it.

The `mutableCopy` method that assigned the initial, temporary object to the temporary variable, like the allocation of a new object, implicitly retained it, thus requiring you to release it. You do that here before execution leaves the `init` method. Similarly, the `copy` method used to assign a value to the intermediate variable also performed an implicit `retain` and therefore requires a matching `release`. Finally, you explicitly retained the instance variable to ensure that it will remain in memory for use when the user types in the text field to which the formatter is connected. The character set will last for the life of the formatter, and the formatter will live for the life of the document. Thus, the `dealloc` method must release the new character set when the formatter is deallocated as the window is closed.

You don't release the two NSString instance variables in the formatter's `dealloc` method. You didn't `retain` them; if you had, you would have to `release` them. The reason you can get away without retaining them here is that objects in the user defaults database, like objects in any dictionary or other Cocoa collection object, are retained when they are added to the database and stay retained as long as they remain there. Because an object is released when it is removed from a collection, you would normally have to worry about memory management for objects obtained from a collection. However, the decimal and thousands separator strings in the user defaults database are subject to a special constraint that eliminates the risk; namely, the system requires you to relaunch the application before a change to the system preference takes effect.

5. Start writing the input filtering and formatting method. This method is complex, and you will take it one step at a time.

First, add the method name, its block, and its local variable declarations to VRDecimalNumberFilter.m:

```
// Input validation and formatting

- (BOOL)isPartialStringValid:(NSString **)partialStringPtr
      proposedSelectedRange:(NSRangePointer)proposedSelRangePtr
      originalString:(NSString *)origString
      originalSelectedRange:(NSRange)origSelRange
      errorDescription:(NSString **)error {

   NSString *tempPartialString;
   int tempProposedSelRangeLocation;

   NSString *insertedString;

   NSScanner *scanner;

   int thousandsSeparatorLocation;
   int decimalSeparatorLocation;
   int remainingIntegerPart;

   BOOL deleting;

   // Insert remaining code here
}
```

The tempPartialString and tempProposedSelRangeLocation variables are temporary stand-ins for the *partialStringPtr and proposedSelRange->location parameter values, respectively, used only during the section of the method in which thousands separators are restored. Using placeholders allows you to alter their values within the method while leaving the parameters unchanged and therefore always accessible. I find that doing this helps to keep concepts straight when working out complex algorithms.

The `insertedString` variable will hold the string of characters typed or pasted in the text field by the user. It will be empty if the user cut or deleted characters.

The `scanner` variable will hold a Cocoa object used to strip thousands separators from the text field contents.

The `thousandsSeparatorLocation`, `decimalSeparatorLocation`, and `remainingIntegerPart` variables keep track of the locations of the separators and the length of the integer part of the text field's contents still remaining to be processed while inserting new thousands separators.

Finally, the `deleting` variable indicates whether the user pressed the Delete key, which requires special handling in the algorithm used here.

6. Next, fill the method's outermost code block by inserting the following at the position indicated in Instruction 5:

```
if ([*partialStringPtr length] == 0) {
    [self emptyBugfix:*partialStringPtr];
    return YES;
} else {
    // Insert remaining code here
}
```

This bypasses all of the method's computations in the case where the user has pressed the Delete or Forward Delete key or cut characters so as to leave the text field empty. That case obviously requires no filtering or formatting. The method therefore immediately returns YES to signal Cocoa to accept the new contents of the field: namely, an empty string.

I will explain the call to the `emptyBugfix:` method later, in Step 2.6. Suffice it to say that a bug in NSFormatter results in an anomalous selection in the text field in some cases when its contents have been deleted. The insertion point either disappears or is left with an odd appearance and location. This method cures the problem but otherwise has no effect on the computation.

7. Before you are ready to write the guts of the formatter, insert a couple of preliminary statements where indicated in Instruction 6, to set up some preconditions for further processing:

```
origSelRange = [self deleteBugfix:origSelRange];
deleting = (origSelRange.location -
    proposedSelRangePtr->location) == 1;
```

I will explain the call to the `deleteBugfix:` method later, in Step 2.6. It compensates for another bug in NSFormatter. When the Delete key is pressed, the `origSelRange.location` parameter element holds the position of the insertion point in the text field *after* the user pressed Delete, instead of the position *before* the user pressed Delete, as NSFormatter is specified. This method corrects the selection range when the Delete key is pressed so that the algorithm can work as it should.

The other statement simply sets the deleting local variable to YES if the Delete key was pressed, or NO if not. The Delete key is distinguished from the Forward Delete key for this purpose. You could have set this value by using NSEvent to decode the actual key press, but formatters are supposed to require only the Foundation umbrella framework, not the AppKit where NSEvent lives. Therefore, you rely on simple arithmetic to detect the Delete key. The Delete key is the only user action that triggers this method and results in the proposedSelRangePtr->location being one position to the left of the origSelRange.location.

8. You are now ready to write the working part of the formatter. You will start with the filter section, which detects and rejects invalid characters. You will take this in pieces.

First, you need to obtain the new text inserted by the user, to determine whether it contains any invalid characters. Add the following immediately after the statements you just added in Instruction 7:

```
if (proposedSelRangePtr->location <= origSelRange.location) {
    insertedString = @"";

} else {
    insertedString = [*partialStringPtr substringWithRange:
            NSMakeRange(origSelRange.location,
            proposedSelRangePtr->location - origSelRange.location)];
    // Insert code from instructions 9 and 11 here
}
// Insert remaining code here
```

This code obtains and places in the insertedString local variable whatever the user typed or pasted in the field, in the form of a string. You already used this technique in Step 1, where it was buried in a complicated if test. Here, you have pulled it out and used a local variable to hold the user's input. It is set to an empty string if the user cut or deleted text instead of typing or pasting in text.

Note that the location element of the proposed selection range is accessed here using the optional C structure pointer operator, in proposedSelRangePtr->location, instead of the structure member operator that you used in Step 1, (*proposedSelRangePtr).location. Either form is acceptable.

9. The next step is to filter the contents of the `insertedString` variable for invalid characters that are to be rejected. Insert the first part of the filter section where indicated in Instruction 8:

```
if ([insertedString rangeOfCharacterFromSet:
        invertedDecimalDigitPlusLocalizedSeparatorsCharacterSet
        options:NSLiteralSearch].location != NSNotFound) {
    *error = [NSString stringWithFormat:NSLocalizedString(
            @""“%@” is not allowed in a decimal number.",
            @"Presented when typed or pasted value contains \
            a character other than a numeric digit \
            or localized thousands or decimal separator"),
            insertedString];
    return NO;
}
```

This code is self-explanatory, given your experience with this technique in Step 1. The very useful **rangeOfCharacterFromSet:options:** method from NSString determines whether the **insertedString** variable contains any character from the inverted set you created earlier. If so, it must be rejected with an error message and a return value of **NO**.

10. The **errorDescription** parameter value is, of course, localized. Add the following to the new **Formatters** section of the Localizable.strings file:

```
/* Presented when typed or pasted value contains a character other
than a numeric digit or localized thousands or decimal separator */
""“%c” is not allowed in a decimal number" = ""“%c” is not allowed in a
decimal number"
```

11. The first part of the formatter's filtering code is only the beginning. It is now properly filtering out all characters except the digits and the localized separators. However, it allows the user to type an unlimited number of decimal separator characters, which is, of course, inappropriate for a field that is to contain a valid decimal number.

A reasonable approach to ensure that the field contains only a single decimal separator is to test the entire contents of the text field after insertion of the input string to see whether it contains the decimal separator and, if it does, to search the remainder of the field to see whether it contains a second decimal separator.

Complete the section of the method you wrote in Instruction 9, above, by adding the following **else** clause after the existing **if** clause:

```
    else {
        decimalSeparatorLocation = [*partialStringPtr
                rangeOfString:localizedDecimalSeparatorString
                options:NSLiteralSearch].location;
        if ((decimalSeparatorLocation != NSNotFound) &&
                ([*partialStringPtr length] - 1 >
                decimalSeparatorLocation) &&
                ([[*partialStringPtr substringFromIndex:
                decimalSeparatorLocation + 1]
                rangeOfString:localizedDecimalSeparatorString
                options:NSLiteralSearch].location != NSNotFound)) {
            *error = [NSString stringWithFormat:NSLocalizedString(
                    @""%@" can't be entered more than once.",
                    @"Presented when typed or pasted value \
                    contains a second decimal separator"),
                    localizedDecimalSeparatorString];
            return NO;
        }
    }
}
```

This clause analyzes the entire contents of the text field in ***partialStringPtr**, rather than analyzing only the most recent input string, because the text field may already contain a decimal separator that was added earlier, when it was legal to do so. Two or more decimal separators anywhere in the field would be illegal, however, so you start by checking whether there is any decimal separator in the field. Two calls to NSString's **rangeOfString:options:** method, which you first saw in Step 1, handle evaluation of the string.

Here, three tests are made in the **if** clause. First, if a decimal separator is found nowhere in the text field, the flow of execution leaves the **if** clause. Otherwise, if a decimal separator is found, then its location in the field is tested; if it is at the end of the field, execution leaves the **if** clause because by definition there can't be a subsequent decimal separator in the field. Otherwise, finally, the portion of the field remaining after the first decimal separator is extracted using NSString's **substringFromIndex:** method and the **rangeOfString:options:** method is used again to detect a second decimal separator, if any. If one is found, an error message is generated and the method returns **NO**.

12. The **errorDescription** parameter value is again localized. Add the following to the Formatters section of the Localizable.strings file:

```
/* Presented when typed or pasted value contains a second decimal
separator */
```

""%c" can't be entered more than once" = ""%c" can't be entered more than once"

13. What remains is to fulfill the promise to provide automatic, on-the-fly localized thousands separators as the user types. The technique used will be similar in concept to that employed above to filter the text field. You have already defined the thousands separator instance variable. Using it, your strategy will be to strip any existing thousands separators from the contents of the text field, because they are now out of position, then insert new thousands separators wherever needed, adjusting the insertion point backward and forward at every stage to keep it synchronized with the contents of the field.

Before proceeding, you must add a test that earlier versions of the Vermont Recipes application omitted, which determines whether the user's system preferences specify that thousands separators are not to be used at all. If that is the case, you should skip all of the remaining computations and simply return YES to accept the text field as is. The previous version of the application crashed when the user's preferences were set to omit thousands separators because it was designed on the assumption that the `localizedThousandsSeparatorString` variable held a character.

Insert the following at the end of the code you added in Instruction 11:

```
if ([localizedThousandsSeparatorString isEqualToString: @""]) {
    return YES;
} else {
    // Insert remaining code here
}
```

14. The rest of the method will be inserted within the `else` clause where indicated in Instruction 13. You will tackle it in three stages.

First, insert the following code to strip existing thousands separators:

```
tempPartialString = @"";
tempProposedSelRangeLocation = proposedSelRangePtr->location;

scanner = [NSScanner
        localizedScannerWithString:*partialStringPtr];
[scanner setCharactersToBeSkipped:[NSCharacterSet
        characterSetWithCharactersInString:@""]];

while (![scanner isAtEnd]) {
    NSString *tempString;
    if ([scanner scanUpToString:
            localizedThousandsSeparatorString
```

(continues on next page)

```
            intoString:&tempString]) {
        tempPartialString = [tempPartialString
            stringByAppendingString:tempString];
    } else if ([scanner scanString:
        localizedThousandsSeparatorString intoString:nil]) {
        if ([scanner scanLocation] <=
            proposedSelRangePtr->location +
            [insertedString length]) {
            tempProposedSelRangeLocation--;
        }
    }
}
```

This is your first encounter with a scanner, a fascinating and useful Cocoa object. A scanner may not be appropriate in every situation where you might consider using one, because more efficient special-purpose methods may be available, but a scanner can be very useful indeed for some purposes. Scanners are useful because of their generality; they make it easy to do something such as stripping thousands separators from a string, without requiring you to dive very deeply into management of indices. In this context, this scanner is quick enough to let a fast typist work the keyboard without hindrance. Be sure to read the NSScanner reference document in conjunction with this code.

You may find a statement in the documentation suggesting that scanners are deprecated in favor of formatters. On the authority of a lead Apple engineer, this is not accurate. Formatters are often preferred over scanners when you have a choice between them, but scanners are fully supported—and very useful when writing formatters.

In this section, you first create a scanner object using one of the provided convenience methods: in this case, a method that instantiates a scanner and initializes it with the string forming the current contents of the text field. Once the string is safely copied into the scanner, the code uses the empty temporary string to hold numbers that are concatenated into it from the copy of the original string now residing in the scanner.

The scanner does this using a while loop, which will terminate when the NSScanner isAtEnd method returns YES. In the while loop, the scanner first scans a run of valid digits or decimal separators into a second temporary string variable and concatenates it into the first temporary variable. Then it scans a thousands separator, if one is found, into oblivion. Whenever a thousands separator is found and discarded, the insertion point is decremented if the thousands separator was located to the left of the insertion point, to move the insertion point to the left in sync with the left shift of all characters located to the right of the discarded thousands separator. (The insertion point will be incremented again when thousands separators are added back to the field in the next block of code.) The second temporary string variable is concatenated into the first on each pass until the first temporary variable is fully reconstituted, minus the thousands separators, and the insertion point remains adjacent to the digit to which it was initially adjacent.

The conditions for decrementing the insertion point are very sensitive. The scanner's `scanLocation` is used to determine how much progress has been made. Since the string within the scanner is not altered as the scanner operates, the values of `scanLocation` are measured in every iteration from the original beginning of the text field. For this reason, these values are measured against the starting insertion point, which is calculated as the sum of the original insertion point before the user typed or pasted, `origSelRange.location`, and the length of the `insertedString` string. It isn't appropriate to use the constantly changing adjusted selection point, `proposedSelRangePtr->location`. I chose the "less than or equal to" inequality operator based on visualization of what is happening to the string dynamically as the code executes.

Note that the second line of this code snippet sets the scanner so it will not skip any characters. This is necessary because by default Cocoa sets up all new scanners to skip white space and the newline character. As a result of this default, earlier versions of the Vermont Recipes application did not work correctly if the user set system preferences to use a space for the thousands separator, as I understand is standard practice in some language systems. In any event, it isn't normally appropriate for a scanner used in a formatter to skip white space, so you now reset the scanner's default to a null character set here.

15. Next, you must add thousands separators back into the text field in appropriate positions.

A constraint you must observe is to work only with the integer part of the decimal number in the text field, which you do by noting the location of the decimal separator, if any.

One way to position thousands separators appropriately is to apply a log function to the numerical value of the string. Here, however, you have already stripped out the old thousands separators, so you can instead position the new separators by counting characters by threes in the integer part of the decimal number. You will do this by using the standard C modulus operator, a percent sign (%). The hardest part of this is to set the location of the insertion point correctly after inserting the thousands separators.

Add the following section after the one you just completed:

```
thousandsSeparatorLocation = 1;
decimalSeparatorLocation = [tempPartialString
        rangeOfString:localizedDecimalSeparatorString
        options:NSLiteralSearch].location;
remainingIntegerPart = (decimalSeparatorLocation == NSNotFound)
        ? [tempPartialString length] - 1 :
        decimalSeparatorLocation - 1;


while (remainingIntegerPart > 2) {

    if (remainingIntegerPart % 3 == 0) {
        tempPartialString = [NSString
                stringWithFormat:@"%@%@%@", [tempPartialString
                substringToIndex:thousandsSeparatorLocation],
                localizedThousandsSeparatorString,
                [tempPartialString substringFromIndex:
                thousandsSeparatorLocation]];
        if ((thousandsSeparatorLocation <=
                proposedSelRangePtr->location) &&
                !(deleting && [[tempPartialString
                substringWithRange:NSMakeRange(
                proposedSelRangePtr->location, 1)]
                isEqualToString:
                localizedThousandsSeparatorString])) {
            tempProposedSelRangeLocation++;
        }
        thousandsSeparatorLocation++;
    }
    thousandsSeparatorLocation++;
    remainingIntegerPart--;
}
```

This block first defines an intermediate variable and two working local variables;
one of the latter, thousandsSeparatorLocation, tracks the location where the
next thousands separator is to be inserted, and one, remainingIntegerPart,
tracks how many characters following that remain to be processed in the
integer part of the string. The C conditional expression ? is used to set the
remainingIntegerPart variable concisely, depending on whether a decimal
separator is present in the string. The first thousands separator will be inserted
at location 1 when a total of four characters have been processed, with three
characters following the first thousands separator location. In a while loop that
terminates when the remaining length is whittled down to 2, a thousands separator is added in every iteration in which the remaining length modulo 3 is 0.

In all iterations, the two working local variables are incremented and decremented, respectively, in preparation for the next iteration. When an iteration is reached that requires insertion of a thousands separator, the NSString class method `stringWithFormat:` is called to concatenate the two substrings on either side of the thousands separator location, with a localized thousands separator sandwiched between them. In addition, the `thousandsSeparatorLocation` is incremented an extra notch on account of the new separator.

The insertion point is incremented every time a thousands separator is inserted to the left of the currently proposed insertion point, to move the insertion point to the right in sync with the right shift of the remaining characters.

One insertion point consideration was difficult to resolve: namely, the effect of the user's pressing the Delete key or the Forward Delete key. The basic algorithm accommodates the effect of the Forward Delete key. The action of the Delete key is treated as a special case. If the `deleting` variable detects the Delete key and the character at the proposed insertion point is a thousands separator, the proposed insertion point is not incremented even if it would have been incremented otherwise. In both cases, the effect is that the insertion point skips over a thousands separator without deleting it whenever the Delete or Forward Delete key is pressed. This is the desired behavior, because each key press in this on-the-fly formatter is supposed to leave thousands separators in the correct location. Although the user is allowed to type or delete a thousands separator, the formatter controls the field's appearance and the user always sees thousands separators only where they belong.

16. Finally, the method must return some values. Insert the following code after the code in Instruction 15:

```
*partialStringPtr = tempPartialString;
*proposedSelRangePtr =
        NSMakeRange(tempProposedSelRangeLocation, 0);

[self emptyBugfix:*partialStringPtr];

*error = nil;
return NO;
```

The method result is returned as `NO`. As the NSFormatter reference document describes, this result, in conjunction with a new string value passed by reference in the `partialStringPtr` parameter, tells Cocoa to display the edited string. This result also triggers the `control:didFailToValidatePartialString:errorDescription:` method, however, and without something more, it would sound a beep and trigger an alert sheet in the Vermont Recipes application.

As described near the beginning of this step, you therefore adopt the convention of returning `nil` by reference in the `errorDescription` parameter, to signal that no error has occurred and nothing should be done to disturb the peace.

The `emptyBugfix:` method is called to work around a Cocoa bug and will be explained next.

2.6 Create a Category to Fix Bugs in NSFormatter

In Step 2.5, I mentioned two bugs in Cocoa's current implementation of NSFormatter and you called two methods to fix them, `deleteBugFix:` and `emptyBugfix:`. My first instinct was to code the workarounds in VRDecimalNumberFilter directly, but I soon realized that they were also needed in VRTelephoneFormatter, which you will write in Step 3, and that they might, of course, be needed in other formatters as well. It therefore makes sense to code them once in a separate file so that they can be imported and called in any formatter that needs them. What better place than a category on NSFormatter, so that they will be associated directly with the class in which the bug exists? I have it on good authority that Apple, itself, uses categories to fix bugs.

A category cannot ordinarily be used to enhance an existing method in the base class but only to add new methods or completely replace existing methods. Since you don't have access to the source code for NSFormatter, it makes no sense to try to rewrite the offending method. Instead, you will write two new methods in the category. Once the category is imported into your custom formatter, the formatter can call the category's methods.

1. Follow the instructions in Recipe 2, Step 2.7, to create the new category, naming it `NSFormatter+VRFormatterBugfixes`. Import <Foundation/NSFormatter.h>.

2. Declare the two methods in the category header file NSFormatter+VRFormatterBugfixes.h, as follows:

    ```
    - (NSRange)deleteBugfix:(NSRange)origSelRange;
    - (void)emptyBugfix:(NSString *)partialString;
    ```

3. Define the first of the two methods in the category source file NSFormatter+VRFormatterBugfixes.m, as follows:

    ```
    - (NSRange)deleteBugfix:(NSRange)origSelRange {
        if ((([[NSApp currentEvent] type] == NSKeyDown) &&
            ([[[NSApp currentEvent] characters]
            characterAtIndex:0] == NSDeleteCharacter)) {
            return [(NSText *)[[NSApp keyWindow]
    ```

```
                firstResponder] selectedRange];
    } else {
        return origSelRange;
    }
}
```

Because the implementation uses methods from some Cocoa classes, the source
file must import Cocoa, as follows:

`#import <Cocoa/Cocoa.h>`

Thus, any formatter that imports this category will work only in applications
that have access to the AppKit.

The bug this method works around causes the `origSelRange` parameter of
NSFormatter's `isPartialStringValid:proposedSelectedRange:originalString:`
`originalSelectedRange:errorDescription:` method to yield an incorrect value
when the Delete key is pressed, as described above. Cocoa acts as if it has
already carried out the actions of the Delete key before invoking the method
and reporting `origSelRange`. The original selection range's `location` is reported
as if it were one less than it actually was before the Delete key was pressed. Also,
the original selection range's `length` is reported as `1` even if there was no selection before the Delete key was pressed. Despite these surprises, the original
selection string still includes the deleted character, as it should.

The first step in the workaround is to find out whether the Delete key was
pressed. The arithmetical technique you used in Step 2.6 works only in the context of the formatter method, where the original and proposed insertion points
are handed to you as parameter values.

In the general case, you must instead consult the application's current event.
The `NSApp` global variable, which you have encountered before, makes the current event available to you everywhere as the return value of the `[NSApp`
`currentEvent]` message. Using this message, you first get the current event's
`type` to make sure it is `NSKeyDown`.

If the user's most recent action was to press a key on the keyboard, the character
last typed by the user is obtained from the resulting event's `characters` method.
You can't use the last printable character inserted in the text field for this purpose, because the Delete key generates a control character, which isn't printable
and so doesn't appear in the text field. NSEvent's `characters` method returns a
string that contains the Unicode character or characters generated by the user's
last key press, including nonprintable characters. Although some key presses can
generate more than one Unicode character, you are only concerned about simple
characters here and can therefore make do with the character at index `0` of the
string. If it is `NSDeleteCharacter`, you know the user pressed the Delete key.

You should read the NSEvent class reference document at this point to see how much information the NSEvent class makes available to you when you need to know what the user is doing with the keyboard or other input devices. You should also read the NSResponder and NSTextView class reference documents, which have useful information about handling user input.

Where did the constant for the Delete key come from? As with much of Cocoa programming, you just have to become familiar with the AppKit and Foundation classes to learn where useful things like this hide. It turns out that the constant for the Delete character (known to older typists as Backspace), along with several other traditional typewriter control characters such as the carriage return, is defined in NSText.h. All of the control character constants there, including the NSDeleteCharacter constant used here, end with Character. In case you need it, the constant for the Forward Delete key is defined in NSEvent.h, along with many computer-oriented function keys, including all of the function keys—F1, F2, and so on. They all end with FunctionKey, including the NSDelete-FunctionKey constant you could use to detect the Forward Delete key.

Once you know the user pressed the Delete key, you can implement the work-around for the NSFormatter bug. To do this, you get the range of text currently selected in the text field and return it. If some other key was pressed, you return the origSelRange value passed in from the formatter in the method's sole parameter.

To get the text field's current selection, you have to access the window's field editor. You have already learned that the window's field editor is a shared text object, which the window recycles for use by whichever text field is currently selected for editing. Whenever a text field is being edited, it is actually the field editor, not the text field itself, that is the window's first responder. Be sure to remember this. It is a frequent source of confusion for beginning Cocoa programmers.

You can therefore overcome this NSFormatter bug by the simple expedient of grabbing the field editor's current selection range. You start by finding the window in which all this is happening, using another message to the application object, [NSApp keyWindow]. The application's *key window* is the window currently receiving keyboard input. You then use the window's firstResponder method to get what looks like the text field being edited, then call selectedRange to get the correct value for the range of text that is actually selected. Since, however, the first responder is in fact the field editor—which is an NSTextView object, not an NSControl object—you must cast the first responder to another type. You could cast it to an NSTextView object, but you use its superclass, NSText, here because that is the class that declares the selectedRange method. (Instead of getting the first responder and coercing it to an NSText object, you could just as well have retrieved the window's field editor from the key window directly by calling [fieldEditor:NO forObject:nil] on the key window.)

You must call this category method in any affected formatter's override of the `isPartialStringValid:proposedSelectedRange:originalString:originalSelectedRange:errorDescription:` method, near the beginning before the value returned in the `OriginalSelectedRange:` parameter is used. By assigning its return value to the `origSelRange` value, you eradicate the effect of the bug.

4. Define the second of the two methods in the category source file NSFormatter+-VRFormatterBugfixes.h, as follows:

```
- (void)emptyBugfix:(NSString *)partialString {
    if ([partialString length] == 0) {
        [(NSText *)[[NSApp keyWindow] firstResponder]
                setSelectedRange:NSMakeRange(0, 0)];
    }

}
```

The bug this method works around may be related to the first bug. When the formatter leaves a text field empty in certain circumstances, it fails to set the revised selection range properly in the field editor. The workaround is therefore, in a sense, the reverse of the workaround for the other bug. If the text field is empty, you simply set the field editor's selected range to {0, 0}.

5. To make these two methods available to your custom formatter, include the following line at the top of the formatter's source file:

```
#import "NSFormatter+VRFormatterBugfixes.h"
```

Because these two methods do nothing more intrusive than reading and writing the field editor's selection range, I believe that any formatter using them will continue to work correctly even after Apple fixes these bugs.

2.7 Require an Entry in the Text Field

In Step 1, you added a little code to the `control:textShouldEndEditing:` delegate method in VRMainWindowController.m to prevent the user from leaving the Integer text field blank. You should do the same thing here to require an entry in the Decimal text field.

Add this code after the block that deals with the Integer text field:

```
else if (control == [self decimalTextField]) {
    if ([[fieldEditor string] isEqualToString:@""]) {
        return [self sheetForBlankTextField:control
```

(continues on next page)

```
                        name:NSLocalizedString(@"Decimal",
                        @"Name of Decimal text field")];
        }
}
```

You must add the Decimal field name to Localizable.strings.

2.8 Build and Run the Application

You took care of connecting the Decimal text field in Recipe 4, so you can build and run the application now. Select the Text Fields pane and press the Tab key twice to move the insertion point to the Decimal text field, or click directly in it.

Type one or more digits. Then type a character that is not included in the digits 0 through 9 and is not the localized thousands or decimal character. Note that the computer beeps at you and presents a sheet, and it does not display the illegal character.

Type some more digits, and watch as localized thousands separators appear in the proper locations automatically. Use the Delete and Forward Delete keys and watch as the thousands separators continue to be positioned correctly. Try selecting various portions of the number and deleting, forward-deleting, typing, cutting, pasting, and dragging. Pasting a string containing illegal characters generates an error message. Note also that traditional means of selecting text, such as holding down the Shift key while using the arrow keys, work as they are supposed to. Verify that all works as you would expect and that the insertion point always ends up at a point that allows you to continue typing or to resume typing where a deletion occurred. Try typing or pasting a thousands separator explicitly, and you will find that, although no error is generated, the thousands separators appear only where they are supposed to, not necessarily where you try to put them.

It is particularly interesting to place the insertion point immediately before or after a thousands separator, then alternately press the Delete and Forward Delete keys. The insertion point moves back and forth to either side of the thousands separator, without deleting it or in any way altering the correct display of thousands separators.

Try typing a decimal separator and additional digits to form a fractional part of the number. Then try all of the above tests again to see whether you are happy with the way on-the-fly formatting works in that case. If so, isn't it remarkable that you achieved this without giving it any significant thought?

Press the Enter key (or click in another text field or tab out of the Decimal field) while a number with several digits in the fractional part is in the field. Notice that this reduces the fractional part to two digits, rounding the second digit appropriately. If you save the file and examine it in Property List Editor, you will see that the precise number you typed is preserved; the rounding occurs only in the display.

This truncation occurred because you called NSNumberFormatter's `setFormat:` method with a template string specifying two-digit decimal display. As you see, the `setFormat:` method provides formatting that applies only when editing in the text field has ended. Depending on your application's design, you might prefer not to invoke any formatting at that point; instead, you can simply accept the text field as the user's typing and the formatter's on-the-fly formatting have left it. The choice is yours.

You now have a working on-the-fly decimal number formatter.

But what do you do when you want to write a formatter that NSNumberFormatter's or NSDateFormatter's built-in templates can't handle? The NSFormatter reference document challenges the reader to write a custom formatter for telephone numbers, part numbers, or Social Security numbers. You will take up the telephone number challenge in the next step. There, you will learn how to write a complete formatter, one that handles both on-the-fly and end-of-editing formatting. You will discover that instead of overriding the one method you overrode in this and the previous step, you must subclass NSFormatter itself and override at least three of its methods.

Step 3: Create a Complete Custom Formatter for Conventional North American Telephone Numbers

In Step 2, you implemented an on-the-fly decimal number filter and formatter that inserts localized thousands separators in the correct positions as the user types, deletes, forward-deletes, cuts, pastes, and drags individual characters and selections. In Step 3, you will use similar techniques to implement a telephone number filter and formatter, enabling users to type a telephone number in the conventional North American form of (800) 555-1212 without having to type any of its delimiter characters.

> **HIGHLIGHTS:**
> *Writing a custom formatter by subclassing NSFormatter*

One of the reasons you will tackle a telephone number formatter is that Apple's formatter documentation more or less challenges you to write one. In addition, this formatter gives you an opportunity to apply what you learned in Step 2 to a more difficult problem, one that requires more general techniques than those you used in Step 2. Using the new techniques you will learn here, you should be able to write virtually any formatter.

A telephone number formatter presents these new issues, among others:

- There are several different delimiter characters to insert on the fly—namely, the open and close parentheses, the space, and the dash—instead of just the one in Step 2, a localized thousands separator. It will not be possible to isolate a single string in your code this time around; you must instead isolate a set of several delimiter characters.

- Two of the delimiters,) and a space, always appear together. You will no longer be able to deal with insertion point position adjustments in increments of a single character but will have to take into account the length of a delimiter string containing multiple characters.

- A telephone number has a fixed, mandatory length of 14 characters, including the delimiters. You must now deal appropriately with the user's attempts to enter strings that are too short or too long.

- Finally, you will subclass NSFormatter, rather than NSNumberFormatter, since a telephone number does not need the various numerical formatting routines provided in NSNumberFormatter. Whenever you subclass NSFormatter directly, you must override at least two additional methods.

Despite these new issues, you will be surprised to discover that the code for the on-the-fly portion of the telephone number formatter is about as short as that for the decimal number formatter. This is mainly because Cocoa's built-in routines for dealing with character sets are just about as simple as those that deal with strings. It is very easy to substitute a character set method for a string method when you must deal with a disparate set of multiple delimiter characters.

Because the basic outline of the telephone number formatter is already familiar to you, I will provide the repetitious code here with very little comment, in the same order in which Step 2 presented it. As usual, I will highlight and explain the new techniques.

You already created the Telephone text field in Recipe 4, so you can get right to work on the custom formatter.

3.1 Write a Delegate Method to Catch Input Errors Detected by the Formatter

In VRMainWindowController.m, revise the `control:didFailToValidatePartial String:errorDescription:` delegate method again, as follows:

```
(void)control:(NSControl *)control
    didFailToValidatePartialString:(NSString *)string
```

```
             errorDescription:(NSString *)error {
        if (control == [self integerTextField]) {
            NSBeep();
        } else if (control == [self decimalTextField]) {
            if (error != nil) {
                NSBeep();
                [self sheetForDecimalTextFieldValidationFailure:string
                        errorDescription:error];
            }
        } else if (control == [self telephoneTextField]) {
            if (error != nil) {
                NSBeep();
                [self sheetForTelephoneTextFieldValidationFailure:string
                        errorDescription:error];
            }
        }
    }
}
```

You will also revise `control:didFailToFormatString:errorDescription:` in Instruction 6 of Step 3.5, because you will discover that some kinds of filtering can't be done on the fly.

3.2 Connect the Delegate

Appoint VRMainWindowController as the delegate of this control. In Interface Builder, Control-drag from the Telephone text field to the File's Owner icon, then connect the **delegate** target.

3.3 Instantiate and Connect the Formatter

Connect the formatter to the control.

1. When you create the formatter, you will call it MyTelephoneFormatter, a subclass of NSFormatter. In VRMainWindowController.m, in the "Formatter constructors" section after the `makeDecimalFilter` method, declare the method that will instantiate a VRTelephoneFormatter object and connect it to the Telephone text field, as follows:

```
- (void)makeTelephoneFormatter:(NSControl *)control {
    VRTelephoneFormatter *telephoneFormatter =
            [[VRTelephoneFormatter alloc] init];
```

(continues on next page)

```
        [[[self telephoneTextField] cell]
            setFormatter:telephoneFormatter];
        [telephoneFormatter release];
}
```

This method is essentially identical to its counterparts from Steps 1 and 2, except that you don't call NSNumberFormatter's `setFormat:` method since you aren't subclassing NSNumberFormatter.

In an older version of the Vermont Recipes application, I passed to this formatter a reference to the user control to which it will be connected, writing a designated initializer for the purpose named `initWithControl:`. This allowed the formatter to capture the user's keystrokes from the control's window, rather than from the application itself as you did in Step 2. It also gave the formatter access to the window's field editor for direct manipulation of its contents, and it would have allowed the formatter to take its cues from the current state of other controls in the same window. As you saw in Step 2.6, however, it is easy to gain access to all these things by using the `NSApp` global variable, so it became obvious that this diversion was unnecessary.

In addition, there was a cost associated with passing the user control to the formatter. You had to instantiate a new formatter for each individual text field that held a formatted telephone number, so that each would have a reference to its own text field.

Declare this method in VRMainWindowController.h after the makeDecimalNumberFilter declaration:

```
- (void)makeTelephoneFormatter;
```

2. Import VRTelephoneFormatter.h into VRMainWindowController.m by adding the following line to the end of the import directives at the top of the file:

```
#import "VRTelephoneFormatter.h"
```

3. In the `makeFormatters` method that you added to VRMainWindowController.m in Step 1, insert the following in order to create the new formatter when the window opens:

```
[self makeTelephoneFormatter];
```

3.4 Present an Alert Sheet for Input Errors

Now create a sheet identical to that created in Step 2 except for the informative text. Add this method at the end of the VRTextFieldController.m category source file:

```
// Telephone text field

- (BOOL)sheetForTelephoneTextFieldValidationFailure:
        (NSString *)string errorDescription:(NSString *)error {


    NSString *alertInformation =
            NSLocalizedString(@"Type ten digits "0"-"9" for a \
            telephone number, such as "(800) 555-1212".",
            @"Informative text for alert posed by Telephone \
            text field when invalid character is typed");


    NSBeginAlertSheet(error, nil, nil, nil, [self window],
            self, NULL, NULL, nil, alertInformation);


    return NO;
}
```

Add the declaration at the end of the VRTextFieldController category declaration in VRMainWindowController.h:

```
// Telephone text field

- (BOOL)sheetForTelephoneTextFieldValidationFailure:
        (NSString *)string errorDescription:(NSString *)error;
```

Add the informative text for the sheet to the Localizable.strings file.:

```
/* Telephone text field alert*/

/* Informative text for alert posed by Telephone text field when
invalid character is typed */

"Type ten digits "0"-"9" for a telephone number, such as "(800) 555-
1212"." = "Type ten digits "0"-"9" for a telephone number, such as
"(800) 555-1212"."
```

3.5 Write a Formatter to Detect Input Errors and Format Output

You are now ready to write the new formatter, using a strategy essentially identical to that applied in Step 2.

1. Create new Cocoa header and source files and name them **VRTelephoneFormatter.h** and **VRTelephoneFormatter.m**, respectively.

2. Set up the header file VRTelephoneFormatter.h so that it imports the Foundation umbrella framework and inherits from NSFormatter (not NSNumberFormatter this time). This is the skeleton:

```
#import <Foundation/Foundation.h>

@interface VRTelephoneFormatter : NSFormatter {
}

@end
```

Add the following instance variable declarations inside the curly braces of the interface declaration in VRTelephoneFormatter.h:

```
@protected
NSCharacterSet *telephoneDelimitersCharacterSet;
NSCharacterSet
      *invertedDecimalDigitPlusTelephoneDelimitersCharacterSet;
```

3. Set up the source file VRTelephoneFormatter.m so that it imports its header file, and provide the implementation skeleton, as follows:

```
#import "VRTelephoneFormatter.h"

@implementation VRTelephoneFormatter

@end
```

4. Add the **init** and **dealloc** methods to VRTelephoneFormatter.m:

```
// Initialization

- (id)init
    if (self = [super init]) {
        NSMutableCharacterSet *tempSet;
        NSCharacterSet
            *decimalDigitPlusTelephoneDelimitersCharacterSet;
```

```
            telephoneDelimitersCharacterSet =
            [[NSCharacterSet characterSetWithCharactersInString:
                @"() -"] retain];

            tempSet =   [[NSCharacterSet
                decimalDigitCharacterSet] mutableCopy];
            [tempSet addCharactersInString:@"() -"];
            decimalDigitPlusTelephoneDelimitersCharacterSet =
                [tempSet copy];
            [tempSet release];

        invertedDecimalDigitPlusTelephoneDelimitersCharacterSet =
                [[decimalDigitPlusTelephoneDelimitersCharacterSet
                invertedSet] retain];
            [decimalDigitPlusTelephoneDelimitersCharacterSet
                release];
    }
    return self;
}

- (void)dealloc {
    [telephoneDelimitersCharacterSet release];
    [invertedDecimalDigitPlusTelephoneDelimitersCharacterSet
        release];
    [super dealloc];
}
```

The init method requires only a little explanation. It initializes the two character sets used via instance variables in this formatter, telephoneDelimitersCharacterSet and invertedDecimalDigitPlusTelephoneDelmitersCharacterSet, retaining both, using techniques you learned in Step 2.

5. VRTelephoneFormatter must override two additional methods, stringForObjectValue: and getObjectValue:forString:errorDescription:, because you are subclassing NSFormatter. You didn't have to override them for your previous formatters because NSNumberFormatter overrides these two methods for you.

You need not override a third, similar method, attributedStringForObjectValue: withDefaultAttributes:, if, as here, your text field does not provide text attributes such as color. The default version returns nil to inform Cocoa that the field doesn't implement text attributes. You need not override a fourth method, editingStringForObjectValue:, if, as here, the string being edited is to be displayed as is when editing is complete.

The stringForObjectValue: method should verify that the object passed in its parameter is of the correct type, returning nil if it is not, then do whatever formatting is necessary to return the object as a formatted string ready for display and possible editing in the text field. The getObjectValue:forString: errorDescription: method should convert the text field's formatted string to its native object value. The former is called whenever Cocoa needs to display the text field; the latter, whenever Cocoa needs the text field's value. The latter can generate an alert sheet if something is wrong with the string's format as finally committed by the user. In a formatter that does no on-the-fly formatting, these two methods do all the work of the formatter.

In this formatter, both of the required methods can be quite simple because the native format of a telephone number is already a string. No conversion between object types is required. Write these two override methods now. You don't need to declare them in the header file.

In VRTelephoneFormatter.m, add the following:

```
// Output validation

- (NSString *)stringForObjectValue:(id)object {
    if (![object isKindOfClass:[NSString class]]) {
        return nil;
    }
    return object;
}


- (BOOL)getObjectValue:(id *)object forString:(NSString *)string
        errorDescription:(NSString **)error {
    if (([string length] == 0) || ([string length] == 14)) {
        *object = string;
        return YES;
    } else if ([string length] < 14) {
        *error = NSLocalizedString(
                @"Telephone number is too short.",
                @"Presented when telephone number is too short");
        return NO;
    } else {
        *error = NSLocalizedString(
                @"Telephone number is too long.",
                @"Presented when telephone number is too long");
```

```
            return NO;
      }
}
```

The first of these, `stringForObjectValue:`, is taken straight from the NSFormatter class reference document. Its only function is to return `nil` if the incoming object is not of the correct class for the field; otherwise, it returns the object as it finds it. Here, the incoming object is always the formatted string itself, either already formatted on the fly as the user typed or provided as a pre-formatted string in an initialization routine, so no additional formatting is required.

The second, `getObjectValue:forString:errorDescription:`, is somewhat more complex. It takes the incoming string from the text field and returns by reference a corresponding object in its native form, indicating success or failure by returning a method result of `YES` or `NO`. Here you can catch any improper formatting or other error relating to the incoming string and turn it into an error signal to the window controller's `control:didFailToFormatString:errorDescription:` delegate method when the user commits the data. The incoming string is known to be in the proper format in the sense that all delimiters are in the correct places, because it has been filtered and formatted on the fly by the formatter's `isPartialStringValid:proposedSelectedRange:originalString:originalSelec tedRange:errorDescription:` method, which you are about to write.

A poorly documented aspect of the use of a custom formatter is that the object returned by the `getObjectValue:forString:errorDescription:` method must conform to the NSCopying protocol if it is to be used in connection with a cell. Since most, if not all, formatters are for use with cells in text fields and other text based controls, this is a near-universal requirement. The reason for this requirement is that NSCell's `setObjectValue:` method specifies a parameter of type `id <NSCopying>`; that is, the object passed in the parameter must conform to the NSCopying protocol. This issue is only relevant to writers of custom formatters that return nonstandard object types, since most Foundation objects, such as the NSString and NSCalendarDate objects used here, do adopt the NSCopying protocol.

There are two tests the `isPartialStringValid:proposedSelectedRange: originalString:originalSelectedRange:errorDescription:` method can't perform. One is to determine whether a string is too short, forming an incomplete telephone number. It can't know that the user has typed too few characters until the user presses the Enter key or otherwise terminates editing of the field, so the `getObjectValue:forString:errorDescription:` method must perform this job. If the string is the correct length, the method returns it by reference as the object parameter value and returns YES as the function result; if the string is too short, the method returns an error message by reference and returns NO, which will trigger the `control:didFailToFormatString:errorDescription:` delegate method.

The other test the `isPartialStringValid:proposedSelectedRange:originalString:originalSelectedRange:errorDescription:` method can't perform is to determine whether a string is too long. True, it can count the characters the user has typed and see that there are too many. However, an on-the-fly formatter must allow the temporary presence of too many characters in the field to support pasting of characters cut from the field itself and drag-and-drop editing within the field. Pasting requires temporarily exceeding the proper length of a telephone number to allow excess delimiters, included in the cut, to be pasted back in even though the formatter supplied additional delimiters after the cut. The reason why drag-and-drop editing requires allowing excess characters is more arcane but equally compelling: This type of editing occurs in two phases, and the paste phase comes before the cut phase, potentially leaving the telephone number too long for a moment.

For these reasons, the `getObjectValue:forString:errorDescription:` method instead of the `isPartialStringValid:proposedSelectedRange:originalString:originalSelectedRange:errorDescription:` method handles both the too-short and the too-long scenarios.

The case of a zero-length telephone number is also accepted as valid, permitting the user to tab past the field without entering any telephone number. You don't want to trap a user by forcing the entry of a telephone number, since the user might not be able to find the right number to enter until later or the subject of the entry might not have a telephone.

6. To complete the picture painted by these two methods, now is a good time to update the `control:didFailToFormatString:errorDescription:` delegate method to provide additional alert sheets for the case of a telephone number that is too short or too long. These are self-explanatory. In the "Formatter errors" section of VRMainWindowController.m, revise the delegate method to read as follows:

```
- (BOOL)control:(NSControl *)control
      didFailToFormatString:(NSString *)string
      errorDescription:(NSString *)error {
   if (control == [self speedTextField]) {
      return [self sheetForSpeedTextFieldFormatFailure:string
            errorDescription:error];
   } else if (control == [self telephoneTextField]) {
      NSBeep();
```

```
        return [self sheetForTelephoneTextFieldFormatFailure:
                string errorDescription:error];
    }
    return YES;
}
```

And at the end of the VRTextFieldController.m category source file, add the method for the new sheet. You use the same informative text for a telephone number that is too long or too short. You already provided different message text to distinguish between them in the formatter.

```
- (BOOL)sheetForTelephoneTextFieldFormatFailure:
        (NSString *)string errorDescription:(NSString *)error {

    NSString *alertInformation = NSLocalizedString(
            @"Type ten digits "0"-"9" for a telephone \
            number, such as "(800) 555-1212".",
            @"Informative text for alert posed by Telephone \
            text field when incomplete phone number is entered");

    NSBeginAlertSheet(error, nil, nil, nil, [self window],
            self, NULL, NULL, nil, alertInformation);

    return NO;
}
```

Add the declaration at the end of the VRTextFieldController category declaration in VRMainWindowController.h:

```
- (BOOL) sheetForTelephoneTextFieldFormatFailure:
        (NSString *)string errorDescription:(NSString *)error;
```

Finally, add the necessary items to the Localizable.strings file:

```
/* Presented when telephone number is too short */
"Telephone number is too short" = "Telephone number is too short"

/* Presented when telephone number is too long */
"Telephone number is too long" = "Telephone number is too long"
/* Informative text for alert posed by Telephone text field when
incomplete phone number is entered */
"Type ten digits "0"-"9" for a telephone number, such as "(800) 555-
1212"." = "Type ten digits "0"-"9" for a telephone number, such as
"(800) 555-1212"."
```

7. Start writing the input filtering and formatting method. It is very similar in structure to the same method in VRDecimalNumberFilter.

First, add the method name and block and its local variable declarations to VRTelephoneFormatter.m:

```
- (BOOL)isPartialStringValid:(NSString **)partialStringPtr
proposedSelectedRange:(NSRangePointer)proposedSelRangePtr
originalString:(NSString *)origString
originalSelectedRange:(NSRange)origSelRange errorDescription:(NSString
**)error {
    NSString *tempPartialString;
    int tempProposedSelRangeLocation;

    NSString *insertedString;

    NSScanner *scanner;
    NSString *accumulatedDigits;
    NSString *discardedDelimiters;

    int index;
    BOOL deleting;

    // Insert remaining code here
}
```

The only new local variables are `accumulatedDigits` and `discardedDelimiters` to accumulate scanner output when stripping delimiters and `index` to serve as a loop variable when restoring delimiters.

8. Next, fill the method's outermost code block by inserting the following at the position indicated in Instruction 7:

```
if ([*partialStringPtr length] == 0) {
    [self emptyBugfix:*partialStringPtr];
    return YES;
} else {
    // Insert remaining code here
}
```

This bypasses all of the method's computations in a case familiar from Step 2: An empty string needs no filtering or formatting, but it does need one of the bug fixes you wrote in Step 2.6.

9. Before writing the core routines of the formatter, insert the same two preliminary statements that you inserted in Instruction 7 of Step 2.5 for VRDecimalNumberFilter, where indicated in Instruction 8, above.

```
origSelRange = [self deleteBugfix:origSelRange];
deleting = (origSelRange.location -
    proposedSelRangePtr->location) == 1;
```

10. You can now begin to write the working part of the formatter, starting with the filter section. Insert the following immediately after the statements you just added in Instruction 9.

```
if (proposedSelRangePtr->location <= origSelRange.location) {
    insertedString = @"";

} else {
    insertedString = [*partialStringPtr substringWithRange:
        NSMakeRange(origSelRange.location,
        proposedSelRangePtr->location - origSelRange.location)];
    // Insert code from instruction 11 here
}
// Insert remaining code here
```

This is identical to the Decimal number formatter, obtaining the string that the user input by either typing one character or pasting one or more characters.

11. Next, filter the insertedString variable to reject invalid characters. Insert the following where indicated in the previous instruction:

```
if ([insertedString rangeOfCharacterFromSet:
        invertedDecimalDigitPlusTelephoneDelimitersCharacterSet
        options:NSLiteralSearch].location != NSNotFound) {
    *error = [NSString stringWithFormat:NSLocalizedString(
        @""“%@” is not allowed in a telephone number.",
        @"Presented when typed or pasted value contains \
        a character other than a numeric digit \
        or telephone delimiter"),
        insertedString];
    return NO;
}
```

This code is also nearly identical to the Decimal number formatter, differing only in the character set used and the text of the error description and comment.

12. The `errorDescription` parameter value should be localized. Add the following to the Formatters section of the Localizable.strings file:

/* Presented when typed or pasted value contains a character other
than a numeric digit or telephone delimiter r6s3 */

""%@" is not allowed in a telephone number" = ""%@" is not allowed in
a telephone number"

13. You will add automatic, on-the-fly telephone delimiters as the user types using
the same strategy as in the Decimal number formatter: Strip any existing telephone delimiters from the contents of the text field, then insert new telephone
delimiters wherever needed, adjusting the insertion point backward and forward
at every stage to keep it synchronized with the contents of the field.

As you will see, the fact that there are several different telephone delimiters
requires you to use a character set rather than a string to hold the delimiters. In
addition, since two of the delimiters always come as a pair, adjusting the insertion point requires some extra gymnastics.

First, insert the following code where indicated in Instruction 10:

```
tempPartialString = @"";
tempProposedSelRangeLocation = proposedSelRangePtr->location;

scanner = [NSScanner scannerWithString:*partialStringPtr];
[scanner setCharactersToBeSkipped:[NSCharacterSet
characterSetWithCharactersInString:@""]];
while (![scanner isAtEnd]) {
    if ([scanner scanCharactersFromSet:
            telephoneDelimitersCharacterSet
          intoString:&discardedDelimiters]) {
        if ([scanner scanLocation] <=
                proposedSelRangePtr->location) {
            tempProposedSelRangeLocation =
                tempProposedSelRangeLocation -
                [discardedDelimiters length];
        } else if ((([scanner scanLocation] -
                [discardedDelimiters length]) <=
                proposedSelRangePtr->location) {
            tempProposedSelRangeLocation =
                tempProposedSelRangeLocation -
                ([discardedDelimiters length] -
                ([scanner scanLocation] -
                proposedSelRangePtr->location));
        }
    }
```

```
        if ([scanner scanCharactersFromSet:
            [NSCharacterSet decimalDigitCharacterSet]
            intoString:&accumulatedDigits]) {
        tempPartialString = [tempPartialString
                stringByAppendingString:accumulatedDigits];
        }
}
```

This block differs from the corresponding block in the decimal number filter in several ways. First, it doesn't scan *up to* a delimiter to accumulate valid characters and then use an `else if` block to discard delimiters in the next iteration of the `while` loop but instead scans *from* exclusively, discarding delimiters and accumulating valid characters within each iteration of the `while` loop. This is slightly more efficient but works essentially the same way.

Also, this method does not scan telephone delimiters into oblivion immediately but instead scans them into a temporary local string variable. It discards the contents of the variable as soon as it is done with that variable, but it uses the string briefly to determine how many delimiter characters were scanned at once, so it can decrement the insertion point by that number of positions. As a result, when you use this formatter, you will observe that deleting or forward-deleting over the two-character delimiter following the area code,) and a space, will cause the insertion point to jump two characters forward or backward at once.

Finally and most important, this code uses a character set to hold the delimiters required by a telephone number, instead of a single-character string to hold the one thousands separator as in the decimal number filter. The only change this requires is to call `scanCharactersFromSet:intoString:` instead of `scanString:-intoString:`.

14. Next, you must add telephone delimiters back into the text field in appropriate locations. Unlike the decimal number filter, which formats only the integer part of the string, the telephone formatter formats the entire string. It uses a `for` loop instead of a `while` loop.

Add the following after the block you just completed:

```
for (index = [tempPartialString length] - 1;
        index >= 0; index–) {
    NSString *delimiterString;
    switch (index) {
        case 0: delimiterString = @"("; break;
        case 3: delimiterString = @") "; break;
```

(continues on next page)

```
        case 6: delimiterString = @"-";  break;
        default: delimiterString = @""; break;
    }

    if ([delimiterString length] > 0) {
        tempPartialString = [NSString stringWithFormat:
                @"%@%@%@", [tempPartialString
                substringToIndex:index], delimiterString,
                [tempPartialString substringFromIndex:index]];
        if ((index <= tempProposedSelRangeLocation) &&
                !(deleting && ([telephoneDelimitersCharacterSet
                characterIsMember:[tempPartialString
                characterAtIndex:(tempProposedSelRangeLocation +
                [delimiterString length] -1)]]))) {
            tempProposedSelRangeLocation =
                    tempProposedSelRangeLocation +
                    [delimiterString length];
        }
    }
}
```

This block uses a **for** loop to traverse the current contents of the text field (now stripped of its telephone delimiter characters), including the most recently inserted character or characters, one character at a time. It uses a switch statement to set the local variable **delimiterString** to whatever telephone delimiter string should be inserted in specific iterations. Note that the delimiter string is a two-character sequence at position **3**. In iterations where no telephone delimiter belongs, the delimiter string is set to an empty string. The length of the delimiter string is used to determine when the insertion point requires adjustment and by how many character positions.

The special handling of the Delete key is almost the same as in the decimal number filter. Note that the incrementing of the insertion point is only pre-empted once because the user pressed the Delete key for any eligible delimiter, even if multiple delimiters have been inserted at once.

15. Finally, the method must return some values. Insert the following code after the code in Instruction 14. It is identical to the code in Instruction 16 of Step 2.5.

```
*partialStringPtr = tempPartialString;
*proposedSelRangePtr =
        NSMakeRange(tempProposedSelRangeLocation, 0);
```

```
[self emptyBugfix:*partialStringPtr];


* error = nil;
return NO;
```

3.6 Build and Run the Application

You took care of connecting the Telephone text field in Step 1, so you can build and run the application now. Select the Text Fields pane and press the Tab key three times to move the insertion point to the Telephone text field or click directly in it.

Type a telephone number and watch as telephone delimiters appear in the proper locations automatically. Use the Delete and Forward Delete keys and watch as the delimiters continue to be positioned correctly. Try selecting various portions of the number and deleting, forward-deleting, typing, cutting, pasting, and dragging. Typing or pasting a string containing illegal characters generates an error message. Note also that traditional means of selecting text, such as holding down the Shift key while using the arrow keys, work as they are supposed to. Verify that all works as you would expect and that the insertion point always ends up in a position that allows you to continue typing or to resume typing where a deletion occurred. Try typing or pasting a telephone delimiter explicitly, and you find that, although no error is generated, the characters appear where they are supposed to, not necessarily where you try to put them.

It is particularly interesting to place the insertion point immediately before or after the paired delimiter string of (and a space, then alternately press the Delete and Forward Delete keys. The insertion point moves back and forth to either side of the pair, without deleting it or either character in it. If you deliberately place the insertion point in the middle of the pair, between (and the space, then press the Delete or Forward Delete key, the insertion point jumps only a single position to get to the next numerical digit on either side.

Finally, press the Enter key (or click in another text field, or tab out of the Telephone field) while a number with too few or too many characters are in the field. Notice that an appropriate alert sheet is presented. On the other hand, you are allowed to delete the entire contents of the field and move on to another field because the Telephone text field does not require an entry.

There is another on-the-fly telephone formatter available on the Web for comparison with the one you have just completed. The Omni Group, longtime master of OpenStep and Cocoa programming, makes its Omni Frameworks available for public study and use. One of its frameworks, OmniFoundation, contains a large number of custom formatters, including OFTelephoneFormatter. It is worth taking a look at the Omni version, because it overrides the old, pre–Mac OS X 10.0 `isPartialStringValid:newEditingString:errorDescription:` method, rather than the new, more powerful `isPartialStringValid:proposedSelectedRange:originalString:originalSelectedRange:errorDescription:` method you used here. The difference is striking; your code is much shorter and simpler than that of the Omni version, thanks to the fact that Cocoa now does even more of the work for you.

Conclusion

You are not yet finished with the subject of custom formatters, but you now have the skills required to write your own. In Recipe 7, you will learn how to add live undo and redo to a text field, something that Cocoa doesn't provide automatically.

In the process, you will learn a little more about formatters. One thing you will learn, in Recipe 9, Step 4, is that many different text fields within a window can use a single instance of a custom formatter repeatedly, thus conserving memory and making your code shorter.

RECIPE 7

Text Field Extras: Undo and Redo

In Recipe 7, you will implement an enhancement that will bring substantial additional
usability to your applications: live multiple
undo and redo of editing actions taken in a
text field before the user has committed the
field's final contents.

HIGHLIGHTS:

Creating additional field editors

Manipulating the undo and redo stacks

Manipulating a document's change counter

Subclassing NSTextField

The Vermont Recipes application already
implements undo and redo for text fields in which the data has been committed.
Just type something into, say, the Integer text field, press Enter to commit it, and
then choose Edit > Undo Set Integer Value to retrieve the field's previous value. You
implemented this aspect of undo support in Recipe 1, Step 6. But if you type something into the field and then delete or edit it *before* pressing Enter, the Undo menu
item remains disabled; you can't get back what you typed before deleting or editing
it. Here, you will fill this gap in Cocoa's built-in undo support.

The Cocoa documentation discloses that NSTextView, the AppKit class that presents
the public interface for text editing, comes with full undo management built in.
Cocoa has it turned off by default because text views can be used in contexts where
undo and redo might not be appropriate, but you can turn it on very easily by sending
a single message to a text view. If you read between the lines, however, you get the
impression that the built-in undo support is designed primarily for use in full-blown
text views, such as the scrolling NSTextView widget available in Interface Builder's
Data Palette. Little is said about undo in text fields.

The documentation does state, without elaboration, that undo management applies
to text fields, but it does not explain clearly how to make this work. A text field is not
itself a text view, so you can't directly turn on a text field's undo support by sending
the text field a message. In this step, you will learn that the solution is to work with the
window's field editor, a shared text view object that Cocoa uses to optimize editing

of text fields. Although you must first jump a few hurdles, you will learn that you can install undo and redo of live text fields in your application by simply sending the field editor a message to turn on undo support.

Undo support for text editing as it is built into Cocoa works very well in text fields. When you turn on undo support in a text field's field editor and try it out, you discover that the Edit menu's Undo and Redo item titles are preset to appropriate strings such as Undo Typing, Redo Paste, and—new in Mac OS X 10.2—Undo Drag, depending on what editing actions the user has taken, which is just what you want. Furthermore, all of these commands pile up in the undo stack where they remain available so you can backtrack through editing actions that require undoing or redoing, because Cocoa supports multiple undo and redo. When you are finally satisfied with the contents of the text field and you press Enter, a new Undo command appears in the Edit menu, entitled something like Undo Set Integer Value, because of the undo support for committed text field values that you implemented in Recipe 1, Step 6.

After using it for a while, however, you will discover some issues you might have failed to appreciate initially. Robust, convenient support for live undo and redo in text fields requires a little more work.

- For one thing, turning on undo support in the window's field editor turns it on for all text fields and other text cells that use the field editor. You may want it turned on only for some of them.

  To implement live undo support selectively in text fields, you will create a separate field editor for their exclusive use. This is not nearly as hard as it sounds. You will do it in Step 2.

- In addition, Cocoa's built-in undo support leaves the intermediate undo items on the stack after the user is done editing the field and has committed the entry. In a text field that implements live undo and redo of editing, the user has to choose Edit > Undo repeatedly after committing the data, backing through each of the intermediate edits before returning to the previously committed value. This is in sharp contrast to undoing committed text in a text field that lacks live undo support, where a single undo command returns the user immediately to the previously committed text.

  After committing a value, having to backtrack through all intermediate edits before undoing previously committed text makes undo in text fields tedious and unworkable. One thing that distinguishes a text field from a long, scrollable text window is the ability to commit changes. The act of committing the text is a watershed in the use of a text field, representing a degree of finality that has no equivalent in the editing of a larger text view. It is important to maintain this distinction between text fields and text views.

An important objective of this recipe, therefore, is to clear the undo and redo stacks of all intermediate editing actions once the text field is committed, leaving in their place only the one undo command that allows the user to restore the value of the field as it was last committed. Accomplishing this will not be easy, because any previous undo and redo actions left over from changes to other user controls must remain in the undo and redo stacks. The solution requires implementing a subclass of NSTextField, which you will do in Step 1, and implementing a few methods, which you will do in Step 3.

- Turning on undo support in the field editor has an unwanted side effect: It causes the document to become "dirtied" when the user starts typing, so that the document thinks it needs saving. Since the text field has not been committed yet, the user interface considerations you thought about in Recipe 5, Step 3, tell you that the document shouldn't be dirtied yet. In Step 4, you will suppress changes to the document's change counter while the user is editing the field, to prevent this effect.

- In Step 5 you fix a problem that prevents the stack from unwinding when the last redo operation leaves the text field's value equal to its starting value.

- Finally, there is one limitation on the approach this recipe takes, imposed by the current state of Cocoa's text view undo support, which you cannot work around.

  Live undo and redo do not work correctly in a text field that has an on-the-fly formatter connected. The undo support built into NSTextView takes no account of the manipulations that an on-the-fly formatter carries out. If you turn on undo support for a text field with an on-the-fly formatter, the contents of the text field and of the undo stack quickly become corrupted as the user undoes and redoes changes repeatedly. This has to do with the somewhat complex implementation of undo and redo in text views generally, and it probably stems in part from the fact that text view undo support is designed for separate windows and large, scrolling text views that do not use formatters.

  Until Apple revises undo support for text views to provide better support for text fields and their formatters, you must choose between on-the-fly formatting and live undo support in any one text field. Formatters that do their work only after a text field is committed work perfectly well with live undo and redo, however, as do on-the-fly filters that merely exclude sets of characters. You will see this here, where you will implement live undo and redo in the Integer text field even though it has an attached filter to prevent typing of nonnumeric characters into the field.

The strategy you will pursue here is designed to make it very easy to add live undo support to any text field, subject to the formatter limitation just mentioned. Although inventing and developing the solution is difficult, once it is completed you will not have to revisit the implementation details. You will subclass Cocoa's NSTextField, naming the new subclass VRUndoableTextField, to clear the redo stack when the user commits a final text field value. To make a text field in your application undoable, you need only declare it as type VRUndoableTextField, use Interface Builder to set its Custom Class to VRUndoableTextField, and add a couple of routines to your window controller to create a separate field editor and turn on its undo support.

This recipe, like some of the steps in Recipe 6, teaches advanced techniques. You can bypass Recipe 7 for now if you prefer to get on with coding other kinds of user controls and application features. You don't have to write your application to support live undo and redo in text fields—most Mac OS X applications don't. If you do skip this recipe, however, make a note to come back to it when you're ready.

Let's get started. First, prepare your project files for Recipe 7 by updating the build version in the Info.Plist Entries to **7**. You will begin coding by setting up the infrastructure for undoable text fields. Then you will make the first of the existing text fields in the Text Fields tab view item, the Integer text field, support live undo and redo.

Step 1: Subclass NSTextField

The first job is to create the VRUndoableTextField class header and implementation files. The new subclass will inherit from NSTextField because it needs to do everything a normal text field can do, plus some new tricks. You will also make a couple of changes to VRMainWindowController to make it possible to declare text fields of type VRUndoableTextField.

1. You already know how to create a new class using Project Builder. Choose File > New File, select Objective-C class in the New File assistant, click Next, give the new class a name, and click Finish. The name of the implementation file should be **VRUndoableTextField.m**, and check the checkbox to create the header file automatically. Make sure the header file imports the Cocoa umbrella framework and inherits from NSTextField. Also insert any comments you customarily use to identify your work.

2. In VRMainWindowController.h, you must import the VRUndoableTextField header file. Add the following above the **@interface VRMainWindowController** directive:

    ```
    #import "VRUndoableTextField.h"
    ```

Step 2: Allocate and Initialize a Separate Field Editor

Before you begin to write the VRUndoableTextField class, you need to resolve the fundamental question of how you will turn on undo support in the text view that will provide an undoable text field's editing capabilities.

You know from previous recipes that a single, shared text view object, known as the window's *field editor,* normally handles text editing in all of the text fields in a window. Using a shared object for editing promotes efficient use of memory, and it is made possible by the fact that only one text field can have keyboard focus at any one time. The window simply recycles the field editor for reuse with each new text field as it gains focus. Since the field editor is a text view, it implements the built-in undo support that you want for your text fields. A first approach might therefore be to simply turn on the field editor's undo support, using the NSTextView method `setAllowsUndo:YES`, when any window containing undoable text fields is opened.

This approach is not satisfactory, however, precisely because this one field editor services every text field in the window. All of the text fields in the window would immediately acquire undo and redo capability, even if some of them were not typed as VRUndoableTextField and therefore lacked the code you will write shortly to deal with some of the problems described in the introduction to this recipe. For example, the undo and redo stacks would not be cleared when the user committed the text. One important reason for creating a separate VRUndoableTextField class is to allow you to make some text fields undoable while leaving others without live undo capability.

Another approach might be to turn on undo support in the field editor just before it is needed, then to turn it off again just after it is used—that is, to turn on the field editor's undo feature when an undoable text field acquires focus and to turn it off when it loses focus. In principle, this should be workable, but I can't find suitable hooks for this purpose. There are delegate methods and notifications to tell you when the user has begun to edit a text field, but this is too late because the user has already typed the first character. If you don't turn on the field editor's undo support until then, the undo manager will not record the first character and it will not be undoable. What you need is a hook to find out when the text field acquires focus before the user types in it. NSResponder's `becomeFirstResponder` method could be overridden, but it doesn't seem to provide a workable solution. At the other end, you would also need a suitable hook to turn off the field editor's undo support, but that would also require proper timing to make sure all the cleanup code you are about to write works correctly.

No matter. You might not have thought it possible, but it is actually much easier to simply create another field editor and turn on its built-in undo support permanently for the life of the window. Then you need only make sure that undoable text fields always use this second field editor for their editing, while unenhanced text fields continue to use the window's standard field editor. You won't have to puzzle out what hooks to use to turn a single field editor's undo support on and off at strategic times. While there is a modest memory penalty for instantiating a second field editor, it isn't costly enough to make this approach unreasonable. And it offers a big gain: an easy way to make some text fields undoable while leaving others without that capability. Furthermore, if none of your text fields is undoable, Cocoa won't create the window's field editor at all because it normally gets created only when needed. You won't suffer any penalty.

NSWindow comes equipped from the factory with a delegate method to do exactly what you want, `windowWillReturnFieldEditor:toObject:`. VRMainWindowController is already the window's delegate, so you will define this delegate method in its existing UNDO MANAGEMENT section, right after your implementation of its sister delegate method, `windowWillReturnUndoManager:`. As a delegate method, it does not require a declaration.

The window's `fieldEditor:forObject:` method calls the `windowWillReturnFieldEditor:toObject:` method every time any Cocoa object needs a reference to its field editor. Experimentation in the debugger makes it clear that one occasion when this method is called is when a text field acquires focus but before the user types in it. This is perfect. Your definition of the delegate method can therefore ensure that it will always return your new field editor for undoable text fields whenever a user is about to edit an undoable text field, by testing the `toObject:` parameter to see whether it is (or descends from) the VRUndoableTextField class. If so, return the custom field editor; if not, return `nil`, which tells Cocoa to use the standard field editor. As an added twist, you will create the second field editor lazily in this delegate method, if one does not already exist, as a way to make windows open faster if they don't immediately need the second field editor. Cocoa opens the standard field editor lazily in this manner for the same reason.

1. Here is the delegate method in its entirety:

```
- (id)windowWillReturnFieldEditor:(NSWindow *)sender
      toObject:(id)object {
   if ((sender == [self window]) && ([object isKindOfClass:
         [VRUndoableTextField class]])) {
      if (![self fieldEditorForUndoableTextField]) {
         [self setFieldEditorForUndoableTextField:
               [[NSText alloc] init]];
         [[self fieldEditorForUndoableTextField]
```

```
                setFieldEditor:YES];
            [[self fieldEditorForUndoableTextField]
                setAllowsUndo:YES];
        }
        return [self fieldEditorForUndoableTextField];
    }
    return nil;
}
```

A call to NSObject's **init** method, not to the designated initializer for text views, initializes this new field editor, because the text system's built-in support for field editors will take care of everything you need. The **setFieldEditor:YES** message simply sets a flag so this text view will interpret certain keys as navigation commands instead of character insertion commands (for example, interpreting the Tab key as a signal to move to the next text field). The **setAllowsUndo:YES** message, of course, is the key to the rest of what you will do in this recipe.

2. In the delegate method, you assigned the new field editor to an instance variable, **fieldEditorForUndoableTextField**. You must declare this instance variable at the end of the instance variable declarations in VRMainWindowController.h, as follows:

```
// Field Editors
NSTextView *fieldEditorForUndoableTextField;
```

3. Declare corresponding accessor methods at the end of the ACCESSORS section of VRMainWindowController.h, as follows:

```
// Field Editors
- (void)setFieldEditorForUndoableTextField:(NSTextView
    *)fieldEditor;
- (NSTextView *)fieldEditorForUndoableTextField;
```

4. Define the accessor methods in VRMainWindowController.m at the end of the ACCESSORS section, like this:

```
// Field editors

- (void)setFieldEditorForUndoableTextField:
    (NSTextView *)fieldEditor {
    fieldEditorForUndoableTextField = fieldEditor;
}

- (NSTextView *)fieldEditorForUndoableTextField {
    return fieldEditorForUndoableTextField;
}
```

5. Finally, you must release the new field editor when the window closes. Since you arranged for the window controller to create it lazily, it might never have been created at all. However, since Objective-C permits sending messages to null objects, you do not have to precede the **release** message with a test to determine whether it exists. In the **dealloc** method of VRMainWindowController.m, add this line before the [**super dealloc**] message:

```
[[self fieldEditorForUndoableTextField] release];
```

Your window controller can now create a field editor on demand whose built-in undo support is turned on, and any text field declared as an undoable text field will automatically use it. This means editing actions such as inserting and deleting text, cutting, pasting, and dragging are automatically registered with the undo manager. They also automatically receive appropriate Undo and Redo menu item titles, such as Undo Typing and Undo Cut. When you choose an Undo or Redo menu item, you in fact undo or redo the corresponding editing action. Thus, your application now benefits from all that support for any text field you choose to declare as VRUndoableTextField.

But you aren't yet ready to move on to the next recipe. A number of problems remain to be solved. You can take care of most of these by adding suitable code to the VRUndoableTextField class you created in Step 1, above. You will now turn to the first of these problems.

Step 3: Clear the Undo and Redo Stacks

The first problem is how to clear the undo and redo stacks when the user commits the data in an undoable text field. NSUndoManager declares two methods normally used to accomplish tasks such as this, **removeAllActions** and **removeAllActionsWith-Target:**, but you can't use either of them here.

You are familiar with the first of them from Recipe 1, Step 6.1, where you called **removeAllActions** when saving a document. It clears the entire contents of the undo and redo stacks for a document, which is appropriate when you save a document since it should then no longer be possible to undo or redo any changes to it. That isn't the case here, however; you only want to clear those changes that relate to the user's editing of the current text field, not any pending undo or redo actions left over from changes made earlier to other user controls in the document's window. The latter must remain undoable or redoable.

It would be very convenient if you could use `removeAllActionsWithTarget:` here. This method is designed to clear only those undo and redo actions that operate on a specified target. Unfortunately, you have no convenient way to know what objects are the targets of the undo and redo actions created by the field editor when undo support is turned on. A lot of magic is working behind the scenes to support undo of text editing, involving numerous different classes, many of which are private and inaccessible to you.

One approach might be to subclass NSUndoManager and override the method in it that registers undo actions. In this way, you could arrange to watch all of the undo actions as NSTextView's undo support routines register them and maintain an array of their targets. When the user commits the text field, you could play out this array through the `removeAllActionsWithTarget:` method to clear only the proper undo and redo actions. My efforts to implement this approach foundered, in large part because of a bug in that method that failed to clear the stacks completely. That bug has been fixed in Mac OS X 10.2, but in the meantime I developed the technique you will learn here.

The approach you will use instead seems simpler, at least once you have it working. You will write your VRUndoableTextField class so it's registered to receive certain notifications posted by the undo manager. Responding to these notifications, you will simply maintain an up-to-date count of all of an undoable text field's editing actions adding or removing items from the undo stack.

When the user eventually commits the data in the text field, you will send an undo message to the undo manager in a loop for every action remaining on the undo stack that was placed there since the user began editing this field, based on the current value of the count. This clears the undo stack of the appropriate actions, and only these actions, because each undo message automatically causes the undo manager to transfer an action from the undo stack to the redo stack. Of course, you don't want these undo messages to change the value of the text field, so you preserve its starting value in a temporary variable before unwinding the undo stack, then restore it afterward. You aren't sending any action methods as a result of these undo messages, so you don't affect the data values in the application's model objects, and none of these manipulations is registered with the undo manager.

Note that you only unwind the *undo* stack. Any actions that were on the *redo* stack will remain there for the moment, and all the undo actions you unwind from the undo stack will be added to the redo stack. You don't want these redo actions to remain on the redo stack, however. How will you clear them? The answer is that the user's committing the text field finally invokes the text field's action method. Among other things, this causes a new undo action to be registered with the undo manager. This happens because you have already written the text field's action method to invoke the model object's accessor method, which in turn registers the action with the undo manager. In response, the undo manager automatically clears the redo stack of actions relating to this field. You will take advantage of this fortuitous effect.

Credit for the idea of using this technique for clearing the redo stack belongs to Greg Titus of Omni Group, who suggested it during a private e-mail exchange while I was developing this recipe. Now for the implementation.

None of the methods defined here requires declaration in the header file. Two of them are override methods already declared in the superclass, NSTextField. The rest are notification methods, invoked directly as selectors using Cocoa's notification mechanism.

1. You will name the undo action counter **undoCount**. You need to declare a variable for it, but you will dispense with accessor methods because no other objects will need to access this value. You can declare it as a protected variable, not a private variable, in case you ever want to subclass VRUndoableTextField and need access to the value. In the **@interface** block of VRUndoableTextField.h, insert the following:

   ```
   @protected
   int undoCount;
   ```

   Later, in Recipe 9, Step 5, you will revise this and other variables that are declared here as standard Objective-C instance variables, making them C static variables instead.

2. The counter must be reset to **0** every time the user begins to edit an undoable text field. To do this, you must override NSTextField's **textDidBeginEditing:** method, taking care to invoke super's **textDidBeginEditing:** method at the end so it can perform its normal duty of posting the corresponding notification to the default notification center for the benefit of any observers. Now is also a good time to register the text field for the notifications it will need to observe; you will learn why you need to observe each of them shortly. After the **@implementation** directive in VRUndoableTextField.m, insert the following:

   ```
   #pragma mark EDITING

   - (void)textDidBeginEditing:(NSNotification *)notification {
       undoCount = 0;
       [[NSNotificationCenter defaultCenter] addObserver:self
               selector:@selector(handleWillCloseUndoGroup:)
               name:NSUndoManagerWillCloseUndoGroupNotification
               object:nil];
       [[NSNotificationCenter defaultCenter] addObserver:self
               selector:@selector(handleDidUndo:)
               name:NSUndoManagerDidUndoChangeNotification
   ```

```
        object:nil];
    [[NSNotificationCenter defaultCenter] addObserver:self
        selector:@selector(handleDidRedo:)
        name:NSUndoManagerDidRedoChangeNotification
        object:nil];
    [super textDidBeginEditing:notification];
}
```

You pass nil in the object: parameter of each registration, because you don't need to filter out notifications with this name from any other object. You will unregister the observer as soon as the user commits the data in this field, and only one field can have keyboard focus at a time.

3. The first notification you registered to observe is NSUndoManagerWillCloseUndo-GroupNotification. You will have to read the NSUndoManager documentation to understand the details of how undo works. Suffice it to say that the undo manager opens a new undo group when editing in the text field begins, it accumulates various user actions in the group as editing proceeds (such as the typing of a string of successive characters or the cutting of a selection), and it closes the undo group when the event loop comes to an end. By the time the undo group closes, a new action has been added to the undo stack. This, therefore, is the notification you need to observe so you know when to increment the undo group counter.

Since you wrote the notification registration statement to trigger a handleWillCloseUndoGroup: method, add the following to VRUndoable-TextField.m after the textDidBeginEditing: method:

```
#pragma mark NOTIFICATION METHODS

- (void)handleWillCloseUndoGroup:
    (NSNotification *)notification {
    undoCount++;
}
```

4. Next, you need to adjust the counter downward or upward if the user chooses the undo or redo menu item, respectively, while editing the text field. Undo removes a group from the undo stack and Redo adds a group to it. You wrote your notification registration statements to invoke handleDidUndo: and handleDidRedo: methods in response to the NSUndoManagerDidUndoChangeNotification and NSUndoManagerDidRedoChangeNotification notifications, respectively, posted by the undo manager.

Add these two methods to VRUndoableTextField.m after the handleWillClose-UndoGroup: method:

```
- (void)handleDidUndo:
      (NSNotification *)notification {
    undoCount--;
}

- (void)handleDidRedo:
      (NSNotification *)notification {
    undoCount++;
}
```

5. Now you are ready for the hard part, unwinding the undo stack when the user commits the text field. When the user presses Return or Enter or otherwise indicates an intent to commit the field, Cocoa calls NSTextField's **textDidEndEditing:** method. You override it to unwind the undo stack by sending an undo message repeatedly, using the strategy outlined above. This will cause the undo manager to transfer to the redo stack all of the remaining undo actions added to the undo stack since the user began editing this field, while you preserve and afterward restore the field's value. The redo stack will automatically be cleared of these redo actions, and all others added since the user began editing this field, when the next undo action for the field is registered, as discussed below.

You might be tempted to use the **undoCount** variable as the loop counter for unwinding the undo stack, but you can't do this here. Because an undo message is sent within the loop, a notification is posted that calls your **handleDidUndo:** notification method, which decrements the variable. Therefore, if you used it as the loop counter, you would reduce the number of times the undo message is sent within the loop and the undo stack would not fully unwind. You have to use a local loop counter variable instead to control the number of loop iterations. The **undoCount** variable is therefore not reduced to **0** when editing ends. This is why you have to reinitialize it to **0** every time editing in this field begins.

In addition, since editing of the text field is now complete, you should remove the text field as a notification observer. You can remove it as an observer of all of these notifications at once with NSNotificationCenter's **removeObserver:** method.

Finally, you invoke super's method so it can go on with its normal duties of posting a corresponding notification to the default notification center and calling the text field's action method.

Add the following to VRUndoableTextField.m after the **textDidBeginEditing:** method:

```
- (void)textDidEndEditing:(NSNotification *)notification {
    int index;
    NSObject *savedObjectValue = [self objectValue];
```

```
            for (index = undoCount; index > 0; index--)
                [[self undoManager] undo];
            [self setObjectValue:savedObjectValue];
            [[NSNotificationCenter defaultCenter] removeObserver:self];
            [super textDidEndEditing:notification];
        }
```

6. If a class registers notification observers, it must always remove itself as an observer when it is deallocated. This is easily overlooked, but your application will crash when the window is closed if you don't do it.

    Although you removed VRUndoableTextField as an observer of notifications in the **textDidEndEditing:** method, that method is not called if the window is closed before the text field is committed. At the beginning of VRUndoableTextField.m, add the following to handle that situation:

    ```
    #pragma mark INITIALIZATION
    ```

    ```
    - (void)dealloc {
        [[NSNotificationCenter defaultCenter] removeObserver:self];
        [super dealloc];
    }
    ```

Step 4: Suppress Changes to the Document's Change Counter

You are now clearing the undo and redo stacks when the user commits the text field, but you have a few more problems to tackle.

First, if you were to create a field typed as an undoable text field and build and run the application at this point, you would discover that the document becomes dirtied as soon as the user begins typing in an undoable text field. In addition, it is cleaned and dirtied alternately from time to time as editing continues. The little dot in the close button of the window's title bar appears and disappears, and you are asked whether to save changes when you close the window, depending on the sequence of editing actions, even though you have not called an action method to alter the document's data. This is inconsistent with the objectives you identified above for an undoable text field. The user's editing of an undoable text field, as for standard text fields, should not dirty the document until the user has explicitly committed the field.

The document is being dirtied because the undo manager increments and decrements a change counter in your subclass of NSDocument behind your back whenever a user makes changes to the text field while editing it. The undo support built into NSTextView assumes that changes to the text view reflect changes to the document, even though you are not in fact invoking the action methods that would change the data values. This is a consequence of the undo manager's assumption that undo and redo normally relate to changes in the application's model object—that is, to its data—not to its user interface. Whenever the document's change counter changes from 0 to a positive number, the window manager puts the dot in the window's close button; whenever the document's change counter changes from a positive number to 0, the undo manager removes the dot.

To overcome this behavior, you must countermand every one of the undo manager's changes to the document's change counter, so the change counter will retain its beginning value at all appropriate times, including when editing in the text field ends.

NSDocument's updateChangeCount: method is available to perform this job. It takes one of three constants as a parameter to control what should be done to the document's change counter: NSChangeCleared to set it to 0, NSChangeDone to increment it, and NSChangeUndone to decrement it. This method is normally used to implement undo support yourself when you don't want to use NSUndoManager. It perfectly suits your purpose here, which is to reverse or countermand NSUndoManager's efforts to update the document's change counter. At every point where NSUndoManager increments the counter—namely, after the user makes or redoes a change—you call the updateChangeCount: method with the NSChangeUndone parameter constant to decrement it, and at every point where NSUndoManager decrements the counter— after an undo operation—you pass NSChangeDone to increment it. It should come as no surprise that you do this at the same places where you have already incremented or decremented the undoCount variable, except that you move the document's change counter in the opposite direction.

The document's change counter will return to its beginning value when the undo stack is unwound, after the user ends editing in the field. By calling undo repeatedly to clear the undo stack, you trigger your handleDidUndo: method repeatedly, which decrements the change counter appropriately, leaving it at the original value when editing of the field began.

1. At the end of the handleWillCloseUndoGroup: notification method of VRUndoableTextField.m, add this statement:

    [[[self delegate] document] updateChangeCount:NSChangeUndone];

2. At the end of the handleDidUndo: method, add this:

    [[[self delegate] document] updateChangeCount:NSChangeDone];

3. And at the end of the handleDidRedo: method, add this:

    [[[self delegate] document] updateChangeCount:NSChangeUndone];

Step 5: Enable Undo Registration for Unchanged Fields

For many applications, you are now done, except for declaring some VRUndoableTextField objects and setting them up properly in Interface Builder.

But for Vermont Recipes and applications based on its architecture, there remains one more problem. In Recipe 4, Step 2, you added a test to most of your text field action methods, preventing their execution if the current value of a field was identical to the corresponding data value in the model object. You did this to allow the user to tab through all the text fields and certain other controls in a window without dirtying the document or leaving behind a trail of useless undo menu items if none of them was edited. Unfortunately, VRUndoableTextField objects depend on the act of setting up a new undo action for the field to clear out the redo stack. If the user undoes changes to an undoable text field to the point where the value being edited is identical to its corresponding model object data value, this will not happen.

A solution for this problem is to set up a mechanism in VRUndoableTextField that keeps track of whether the field is currently being edited, somewhat on the model of NSUndoManager's `isUndoing` and `isRedoing` accessor methods. Call this new accessor method `isEditing`. Then, in every undoable text field's action method, you will add a test to determine whether it is currently being edited. If so, the action method should execute even if the displayed value of the field is identical to the corresponding data value. This generates an Undo menu item such as Undo Set Integer Value even if a field's value has not changed since the value was last committed; this seems appropriate when the user has been editing the field and might not remember the previous committed value. It has the more important advantage of ensuring that the redo stack will always be cleared of intermediate redo items once the user has finished editing it.

Set up the `isEditing` mechanism now.

1. In the `@interface` block of VRUndoableTextField.h, declare the `isEditing` variable, as follows:

   ```
   @private
   BOOL isEditing;
   ```

2. An accessor method to retrieve the value of the variable is required because another class, NSWindowController, will use it.

   An accessor to set the value is not required because nobody else should be allowed to set this value. The mechanism is private to the VRUndoableTextField class.

Just after the **@interface** block, declare the associated accessor method, as shown below:

```
#pragma mark ACCESSORS
- (BOOL) isEditing;
```

3. Turn to VRUndoableTextField.m and take care of setting and resetting the value of the **isEditing** variable.

First, near the beginning of the **textDidBeginEditing:** method, insert the statement shown below to set the variable's value to **YES**. Objective-C automatically initialized the value to **NO** when the text field was created, and you will shortly reset it to **NO** again as soon as editing of the text field ends. It is important to note that its value will always therefore be **NO** when the user first tabs or clicks into the field. The technique you established in Recipe 4, Step 2, for preventing execution of the action method when the user simply tabs through text fields will still work, because the **isEditing** value will be **NO** until **textDidBeginEditing:** is called, if and when the user starts typing in the field.

```
isEditing = YES;
```

4. You can reset the value of **isEditing** to **NO** in the existing **textDidEndEditing:** method. Because super's **textDidEndEditing:** method calls the action method, you must be careful to reset **isEditing** to **NO** *after* the call to super. You can safely reset the value of **isEditing** to **NO** here, because it won't happen until after NSWindowController uses it in the action method.

At the end of the **textDidEndEditing:** method in VRUndoableTextField.m, after the call to **super**, insert the following;

```
isEditing = NO;
```

This awkward solution would not be necessary if Apple enhanced NSUndoManager by adding a mechanism for unwinding the undo and redo stacks to a particular point in time. For example, Apple could add a **mark** method to let you mark the point to which you want the undo and redo stacks unwound and a **removeAllActionsToMark** method to do the unwinding. With such a mechanism, you would not have to add the **isEditing** mechanism to VRUndoableTextField and, more important, you would not have to test it in every text field action method in your window controller. Adding text field undo and redo to your application would then be a simple matter of declaring text fields to be of type VRUndoableTextField, implementing the **windowWillReturnFieldEditor:toObject:** method to the window controller, and releasing the separate field editor when the window closes. I have made this suggestion to Apple; stay tuned to see whether it happens.

Step 6: Make the Integer Text Field Undoable

You are now ready to turn an NSTextField object into an undoable text field. The Integer text field is eligible because, although it has a connected formatter, that formatter does on-the-fly filtering, not on-the-fly formatting.

In VRMainWindowController.h, change the declared class of the Integer text field, as follows:

```
IBOutlet VRUndoableTextField *integerTextField;
```

In the VRTextFieldController category of the same file, change the declared class of the return value of the accessor method accordingly:

```
- (VRUndoableTextField *) integerTextField;
```

In VRTextFieldController.m, change the declared class of the return value of the accessor method to (VRUndoableTextField *) to match the declaration.

Also in VRTextFieldController.m, add a test to the action method for this field, integerTextFieldAction:, by changing its first line to read as follows:

```
if ((([[self textFieldModel] integerValue] != [sender intValue])
      || [sender isEditing]) {
```

In the event that you later decide to reverse the process and turn an undoable text field back into a normal text field, you have only to reverse each of the changes made in Step 6 with respect to that text field and then use Interface Builder to read the VRMainWindowController.h file back into the nib file and reset the text field's custom class to NSTextField.

Step 7: Read the Source Files into the Nib File and Connect Outlets and Actions

Inform the nib file of the revised outlet, then tell Interface Builder that its custom class is VRUndoableTextField.

1. In Interface Builder, select the Classes tab in the nib file window, then choose Classes > Read Files. In the resulting dialog, select the revised VRMainWindowController.h and VRUndoableTextField.h header files, then click the Parse button.

2. Select the Integer text field, go to the Custom Class pane of the Info Panel, and designate its class as VRUndoableTextField.

3. As long as you are in Interface Builder, make sure the Integer text field names the window controller as its delegate. (This should have been set up in an earlier recipe.)

Step 8: Build and Run the Application

Compile and run the application to test the undoability of the Integer text field. Satisfy yourself that any combination of undo, redo, typing, cutting, pasting, and dragging works as expected. Confirm that the editing undo and redo menu items are stripped from the Edit menu when you commit a value to the field and that prior undo and redo menu items relating to other user controls remain pending and available.

Conclusion

In Recipe 7, you have subclassed NSTextField to create VRUndoableTextField, a standard text field with one remarkable addition: the ability to undo and redo while the user is editing the field. You have implemented this capability in a manner that allows you to pick and choose which text fields in the application will support live undo and redo. Although this raises a danger that the behavior of similar user controls will be inconsistent, careful interface design on your part can prevent this from happening. Making this behavior optional is unavoidable until Apple implements live undo and redo in Cocoa, itself, and removes the current impediment to creating a text field that supports both live undo and on-the-fly formatting. In Recipes 9 and 11 you will extend live undo and redo to forms and table views.

In Recipe 8, you will learn about the last of the text field extras, drag and drop editing.

RECIPE 8

Text Field Extras: Drag and Drop

You've already seen that the text fields you've created for the Vermont Recipes application allow you to drag characters from one position in the field and drop them in another position in the same field. This required literally

HIGHLIGHTS:

Creating an informal protocol

no programming on your part beyond creating the text field itself, because drag-and-drop support for text editing is built into the Cocoa text system.

If you perform a little experiment right now, you will discover that you can also drag characters from a text field in the Vermont Recipes application to another application that supports text dragging. For example, you can drag the contents of the Telephone text field to a TextEdit window. When you drag the contents of the field to the Finder, a clipping file containing the telephone number is created.

However, if you drag characters *to* a text field in the Vermont Recipes application, the attempt usually fails. This is so whether you drag and drop, say, a clipping file from the Finder, a text selection from TextEdit, or the contents of another Vermont Recipes text field. The dragged item slides back to its source, and nothing happens in the destination. Evidently, dropping text onto a Cocoa text field requires a little programming on your part. The one exception is a text field that is already selected; it will accept dropped text from another application.

In Recipe 8, you will learn how to enable drag and drop from any source, within or outside the Vermont Recipes application, to almost any text field in the application. Drag-and-drop support in Cocoa goes far beyond text, of course, allowing dragging and dropping of graphic images and other data types, but implementing drag and drop requires less effort for text fields. Text fields should often support dropping of dragged text, and implementing it presents a very simple introduction to the topic. In fact, it requires only about a dozen lines of code.

There are three principal programming interfaces for drag and drop in Cocoa, all of them in the AppKit. Two are the NSDraggingSource and NSDraggingDestination informal protocols, and the third is the NSDraggingInfo formal protocol. In the case of text fields, you need not bother with the methods in the NSDraggingSource protocol because, as you have seen, you can already drag text from a text field. You do, however, have to deal with methods in the NSDraggingDestination and NSDraggingInfo protocols to extract the text from the application's pasteboard and drop it into a text field.

A text dragging session extends from the initial selection and dragging of characters away from the source, through their continued dragging across the screen, to their acceptance at the destination when dropped or their rejection and slide-back to the source. Only a window or view object can be a source. Visual feedback consists of the onscreen movement of a graphic image of the dragged text, the addition of a plus (+) badge to the cursor when it hovers over a destination that can accept a drop, and usually some form of highlighting of the destination (an insertion point in the case of text, and highlighting and a focus ring around a text field). The actual text represented by the image is on a special dragging pasteboard, separate from the cut-and-paste pasteboard, so that the dragging and dropping operation does not interfere with data you've already cut or copied that awaits pasting.

Here, as noted above, Cocoa takes care of the source, so you will not consider the methods declared in the NSDraggingSource protocol in this recipe. You will be concerned here with the dragging operation performed by the destination, requiring you to work with the NSDraggingDestination informal protocol and the NSDraggingInfo formal protocol.

Protocols

Protocols are, like categories, a feature of the Objective-C extensions to the C programming language. Although their use is optional, they play an important role in the Cocoa frameworks, accounting for much of the intensely object-oriented nature of Cocoa programming. You should look at the AppKit and Foundation tables of contents in Cocoa Help. Scrolling to the bottom, you see listed, at this writing, 26 protocols in the AppKit and 13 in Foundation. For Cocoa beginners, it is almost as easy to overlook these protocols as it is to overlook the even more deeply hidden Cocoa functions, types, and constants. You should make a point of becoming familiar with all of them.

Protocols declare methods that aren't associated with any particular class. Thus, they fall outside the normal class hierarchy. You can use a protocol many times in many different classes, without regard to their inheritance structure, and any class can adopt multiple unrelated protocols. For this reason, you can think of protocols as forming another network of data types, separate from the class hierarchy. Classes can be grouped conceptually both according to their inheritance structure and according to the protocols they adopt. The language offers the means of ascertaining whether any class uses a particular protocol and of identifying all of the classes that use it. The language even creates protocol objects that Cocoa can pass as arguments to methods.

One use for protocols is to implement something very like the multiple inheritance capability that exists in some other object-oriented languages. If you examine the NSCopying protocol in Foundation, for example, you discover that it declares a method that must be implemented by any object that supports copying. A great many Cocoa classes adopt the NSCopying protocol. By doing so, they enable the compiler to ensure that objects you attempt to copy implement the required method. Other protocols declare larger sets of required methods. If declared in subclasses or categories, these could be used only within a class hierarchy; implementing them as protocols means they can be used anywhere.

There are two kinds of protocols, *formal* and *informal*. Neither has an implementation part, because only a protocol's clients implement the protocol's declared methods.

A formal protocol is declared using the @protocol directive. A client class or category adopts it by importing its header file and including its name, or a comma-delimited list of protocol names, in angle brackets at the end of the @interface directive. Adopting a formal protocol constitutes a promise to implement all of the protocol's declared methods, and the compiler complains if you don't. A class or category adopting a formal protocol does not include declarations of the protocol's methods in its interface, because the adoption of the protocol in the @interface directive guarantees that they were all implemented.

An informal protocol is typically declared as a category without an implementation part. To use the methods that it declares, a client class or category does nothing more than implement those of its declared methods that it needs, just as it would the methods of any category. There is no special type checking to verify that you have done so correctly.

Protocols as a feature of the Objective-C language are discussed in Chapter 4 of *Inside Mac OS X: Object-Oriented Programming and the Objective-C Language*. Their use in the Cocoa frameworks to support drag and drop is discussed in the "Drag and Drop" section of the "Events and Other Input" topic in Cocoa Help's *Programming Topics*. In addition, very important guidance on the human interface requirements for drag and drop is given in Chapter 12 of *Inside Mac OS X: Aqua Human Interface Guidelines*.

Support for dropping on a destination requires that you implement in the destination object some or all of seven methods declared in the NSDraggingDestination protocol. The principal methods are these:

- **draggingEntered:**, called when the image first enters the destination, tests whether the destination can accept data of the type being dragged and whether it can perform the kind of dragging operation that the source permits. If so, it implements some of the visual feedback described above (for example, a focus ring around the text field).

- **draggingUpdated:**, called repeatedly as you move the image around in the destination, implements some of the visual feedback described above (for example, an insertion point under the mouse pointer).

- **draggingExited:**, called when the image leaves the destination, removes the visual feedback.

- **performDragOperation:**, called when you drop the image, extracts the data from the pasteboard and inserts it in the destination with any required formatting and other work.

Additional methods are available to provide refinements to this model, such as **prepareForDragOperation:** and **concludeDragOperation:**.

Each of these methods has a single parameter, **sender**. The **sender** is a protocol object of type **id <NSDraggingInfo>** that gives you access to information about the source. Among other things, this includes the nature of the dragging operations that the source will permit (for example, moving or copying) and the type of data that is on the dragging pasteboard (for example, **NSStringPboardType** for text). The destination object tests both of these before deciding whether it can accept a drop.

One additional step is required to implement drag and drop. The destination object must register for the types of data it can accept, using NSWindow's or NSView's **registerForDraggedTypes:** method. When you implement drag-and-drop support in a subclass of a window or view object, Cocoa normally calls this method from the subclass's initialization method. In other circumstances, Cocoa can call it from, for example, a window controller's **awakeFromNib** method. If you forget to register a destination or choose not to, drag and drop simply won't work for that destination; you won't even see any of the visual feedback.

If you had to implement a drag operation for text entirely by yourself, you would have to go through some very complicated gymnastics. For example, during the updating phase of a dragging session, you would have to call methods to translate the window coordinates of the mouse pointer to a point in the destination object's coordinate system. Then you would have to convert that point to a character index in the text storage object's contents, taking into account the font and its size, glyphs, kerning, and so on. Then you would have to place an insertion point under the cursor.

Fortunately, Cocoa does all this for you in its implementation of drag and drop for text. In fact, as it turns out, a technique implemented in Instruction 3, below, leaves you with nothing to do but implement the `draggingEntered:` protocol method and register particular text fields for the data they will accept. I stumbled onto this technique almost by accident—the lack of documentation about drag and drop for text fields at that time forced me to fall back on trial and error.

First, prepare your project files for Recipe 8 by updating the build version in the Info.Plist Entries to **8**.

1. Begin by considering how to implement the NSDraggingDestination protocol. The means you choose will have profound consequences.

One possibility is to subclass NSTextField and implement the protocol methods in the subclass. This is the way drag and drop is usually taught—for example, to drag images to an image well or colors to a color well. You might name the subclass VRDragDestinationTextField and declare those text fields in the Vermont Recipes application that should accept dropped text as this type. Then you would register the fields and be done with it. This technique works perfectly well for a one-off drag destination such as a color well.

A little reflection reveals that such an approach might create a serious problem in the case of text fields. You have already written a VRUndoableTextField subclass. It inherits from NSTextField, so the only way you can make an undoable text field—such as your Integer text field—support drag and drop is to revise VRUndoableTextField so that it inherits from VRDragDestinationTextField. Fortunately, you wrote VRUndoableTextField yourself and therefore have access to its source, so you can do this easily enough. But what will you do if you want to implement a secure text field that accepts dropped passwords? NSSecureTextField is provided as part of Cocoa—but it inherits from NSTextField, and you don't have access to its source. You will have to subclass it and reimplement the NSDraggingDestination protocol in this subclass. This could become tedious if you have a lot of NSTextField subclasses and have to duplicate the implementation of the protocol in all of them.

For this reason, Cocoa allows you to implement the NSDraggingDestination protocol methods in the window's delegate. Here, however, I will demonstrate another possibility.

What you want here is multiple inheritance, so that VRUndoableTextField, for example, can partake of both NSTextField's capabilities and drag and drop at the same time. The Objective-C solution is to write a category on NSTextField instead of subclassing it. You have already used categories, once in Recipe 2, Steps 2, 4, and 5, to create several convenient new methods for converting strings to Booleans and other data types, and once in Recipe 6, Steps 2 and 3, to provide three new methods to overcome bugs in an NSFormatter object.

Here, you can create a category for still another purpose, to make your implementation of the NSDraggingDestination protocol methods automatically available to all NSTextField objects as well as objects descended from NSTextField. Categories let you extend the functionality of existing classes even if you don't have access to their source code, and categories can adopt and implement protocols. Furthermore, because the protocol methods are declared in Cocoa and need not be redeclared in clients, all NSTextField objects will become drag-enabled without even requiring that you import the category's header file. Once the category is written, you have to take only a single step to make any text field in the application drag aware: Register it for its data type in the window controller's **awakeFromNib** method. Don't register a field if you don't want it to accept dragged text.

Choose File > New File and create new category files named **NSTextField+- VRDragTarget.h** and **NSTextField+VRDragTarget.m**. Place them in the Categories group, and insert any customary identifying comments.

2. Write the header file NSTextField+VRDragTarget.h, as follows:

```
#import <AppKit/NSTextField.h>

@interface NSTextField (VRDragTarget)

@end
```

Because NSDraggingDestination is an informal protocol, you conform to it simply by implementing one or more of its methods. No special directive is required in the header file.

3. In the source file NSTextField+VRDragTarget.m, import the header file and Cocoa, and implement the method as follows:

```
#import "NSTextField+VRDragTarget.h"
#import <Cocoa/Cocoa.h>

@implementation NSTextField (VRDragTarget)

- (unsigned int)draggingEntered:(id <NSDraggingInfo>)sender {
    NSDragOperation sourceDragMask =
      [sender draggingSourceOperationMask];
    NSPasteboard *sourcePasteboard =
      [sender draggingPasteboard];
    if ([[sourcePasteboard types]
          containsObject:NSStringPboardType]) {
        if (sourceDragMask & NSDragOperationCopy) {
```

```
            [[self window] makeFirstResponder:self];
            return NSDragOperationCopy;
        }
    }
    return NSDragOperationNone;
}
```

@end

In the first two lines of the method body, you get two items of information from the **sender**: a mask indicating what kinds of dragging operations the **sender** will permit the destination to perform and an array indicating what kinds of data the **sender** put on the dragging pasteboard. You are interested only in text here, so you reject the drop by returning **NSDragOperationNone** if the pasteboard includes no data of type **NSStringPboardType**. If it does contain text, you accept it only if the source permits it to be copied to the destination. You determine this by performing a logical **and** operation on the mask, then return **NSDragOperationCopy** if the result is acceptable.

The trick lies in making the text field the window's first responder when the drag session enters the text field. As a result, the field editor for the text field takes over the entire remainder of the dragging session, until you drag the image back out of the text field without dropping it. Once the field editor is active, its built-in support for drag and drop handles all of the visual feedback required during the updating phase of the dragging session, the termination of feedback when you exit the text field without dropping, and the insertion of the dropped data into the text field when you do drop it. The field editor highlights the text in the field; it provides an insertion point that moves as the cursor moves within the field; and it adds the + badge to the cursor to indicate that a drop is allowed. When you drop the image, the field editor terminates the visual feedback and inserts the text at the insertion point, first triggering any on-the-fly formatter and rejecting the drop if the formatter finds illegal text. The dragging session is complete at this point, and you are left with a pending edit in the text field, which you can continue to edit or commit in the usual fashion. If the drag session exits the text field instead, the field editor hands control back to your protocol method until you enter the next text field.

You can see the field editor alternately take over control and relinquish control by implementing stub methods for all of the NSDraggingDestination protocol methods and placing **NSLog()** calls in each. After doing this, comment out the line that makes the text field the first responder and build and run the application. As you drag some text from one text field to another, you see each of the protocol methods logged in turn to StdIO. If you then uncomment the line and build and run the application again, you see that StdIO stops logging after the first **draggingEntered:** call because the field editor has taken control. Then, when you drag out of a text field and into another, you see another **draggingEntered:** call logged, demonstrating that the field editor surrendered control to you when you exited the first field. While you move the cursor around within any text field, you see the insertion point move with it under the field editor's control, but you don't see any logging to StdIO because you no longer have control of the dragging session.

Because the field editor handles everything except the **draggingEntered:** method, you don't have to implement the other protocol methods. In fact, you can't, because the field editor preempted them. Note that this technique works only in fields that use a field editor for text processing.

4. In VRMainWindowController.m, add the following method to the WINDOW MANAGEMENT section, after **registerNotificationObservers**, to register all four existing text fields for text drag and drop:

```
- (void)registerDragTypes {
    [[self speedTextField] registerForDraggedTypes:
            [NSArray arrayWithObject:NSStringPboardType]];
    [[self integerTextField] registerForDraggedTypes:
            [NSArray arrayWithObject:NSStringPboardType]];
    [[self decimalTextField] registerForDraggedTypes:
            [NSArray arrayWithObject:NSStringPboardType]];
    [[self telephoneTextField] registerForDraggedTypes:
            [NSArray arrayWithObject:NSStringPboardType]];
}
```

You must also declare it in the header file VRMainWindowController.h:

```
- (void)registerDragTypes;
```

Call it in **awakeFromNib** by inserting this line:

```
[self registerDragTypes];
```

This was a quick-and-dirty way to get this technique working, so that you wouldn't have to wait too long to try it out. To maintain separation of window controller categories for each tab view item, however, you should break this method into separate pieces, as you did with the **registerNotification Observers** and **updateWindow** methods. I'll leave this as an exercise; just put the speed text field's registration into a **registerDragTypesForSlidersTab** method in the VRSliderController category and the others into a **registerDragTypesFor TextFieldsTab** method in the VRTextFieldController category.

5. Build and run the application. Drag text to any of the application's text fields from any source, be it another text field within the Vermont Recipes application, a selection in a TextEdit window, or a Finder clipping file (bearing in mind the restriction noted at the end of this instruction). Watch how the visual feedback works, and see what happens when you drop text into various fields. One nice detail is that the dropped characters are highlighted after a drop, again as recommended by the Human Interface Guidelines, so you can immediately delete them or drag them elsewhere without having to select them. Try dropping illegal entries and watch how they respond. All in all, this appears to be a good solution with full *Aqua Human Interface Guidelines* compliance.

Notice, among other things, that drag and drop obeys the *Interface Guidelines* regarding when to copy and when to move text. The general rule is that dragging and dropping within a container should always move the data, deleting it from the source and inserting it in the destination, while dragging and dropping from one container to another should copy the data, leaving it in the source while inserting it in the destination. The *Guidelines* give a window as the example of a container when the text fills the window, but they are careful to point out that you'll need to apply some interpretation to understand what the container is in other cases. In the case of text fields, it is clear that the container is the text field, so dragging and dropping from one text field to another, even within a single window or tab view item, should perform a copy instead of a move. Sure enough, your implementation here does exactly that, while performing a move when dragging and dropping within a single text field.

It is particularly interesting to note that all of this works appropriately even if you are dragging something from an external source and dropping it into Vermont Recipes while the Vermont Recipes window is in the background. You don't see a focus ring around the destination text field, of course, because the window is in the background. But you do see the insertion point move appropriately, and you see the text appear when you drop it. The window doesn't come to the foreground, so you can continue to select and drag text from the source without having to reactivate it. In fact, if you drop illegal text from another application, a sheet appears but, because Vermont Recipes remains in the background, the application's icon starts bouncing in the Dock to signal its need for attention. You can reactivate the window and dismiss the sheet with a single click on the sheet's OK button, because a sheet accepts click-through in this circumstance.

I have observed only three interface issues with this scheme. Two are minor, and I can live with both of them:

- If you drop illegal text on one of the text fields, you don't see the slide-back behavior that normally tells you a drop was rejected. However, you do see or hear whatever feedback you wrote into your formatters: a beep from the Integer text field, for example, and a beep and a sheet from the others. You could consider this correct behavior, because it gives you exactly the custom feedback you wrote into the application for these situations.

- If you drag numbers into the Telephone text field, it becomes too long. You haven't committed it yet, so that's not a problem. But if you drag some numbers into another text field, the new text field becomes the window's first responder, which commits the data in the Telephone text field. Since it is too long, you are presented with a sheet advising you that the Telephone text field isn't right. This sudden interruption of your train of thought, focused now on the second text field, can be confusing. This is only distracting when you are dragging from another application to the Vermont Recipes application in the background, and even then it is easy to figure out what happened if you wrote an informative sheet.

The third interface issue presents a serious problem. While you can successfully drag and drop text between the Integer field and either of the other two fields without incident, glitches occur when you drag and drop text between the Decimal field and the Telephone field in the same document window. The formatting in those windows may obscure the defect if you drag a single character. To see the problem, enter the number 1234.00 in the Decimal field, then drag the characters 1234 and drop them at the end of the default phone number in the Telephone field. You notice that the first few numbers in the Telephone field disappear.

I won't ask you to do the sleuthing required to discover the cause of this problem, because it is quite obscure. Basically, if you drag and drop text between two text fields that share the same field editor, the Cocoa text system thinks you are dragging text from one position to another within a single text field. As a result, thinking it is acting in accordance with the *Aqua Human Interface Guidelines*, Cocoa attempts to *move* the dragged text instead of *copying* it. It does this by using character indexing within the field editor, which results in cutting the text from the destination field that was in the position occupied by the dragged text in the source field.

The Decimal and Telephone fields both use the window's standard field editor. You can drag between the Integer field and either the Decimal field or the Telephone field, because in Recipe 7 you implemented live undo and redo by giving the Integer field a separate field editor. You can also drag and drop between any fields in separate document windows, because each window has its own field editor. You will read more about this issue and work around this limitation in Recipe 9, Step 6, where you will implement drag and drop in a Cocoa form.

Conclusion

You have now finished your long detour through text field enhancements. You know how to create text fields that present alert sheets in response to illegal entries, that filter and format text on the fly, that support live undo and redo, and that fully support drag and drop (subject to the problem just discussed).

Several other controls available in Cocoa work with text, and you will explore some of them next. You will start with the simplest, NSForm, which is nothing more than a matrix containing multiple text field cells. After that, you will explore combo boxes and tables. You will implement drag-and-drop editing in all of them.

RECIPE 9

Forms

In this recipe, you will implement a Cocoa form simulating a record in a simplified address book. Each record has four fields displaying data entries: a name, an ID, a date, and a fax number. Some of the fields will be connected to built-in or custom formatters; some will support live undo and redo; and they will all accept drag-and-drop text.

HIGHLIGHTS:
Working with objects of various data types
Creating a formal protocol
Using include files
Using static variables
Reusing a custom formatter on multiple fields

A Cocoa form is an NSForm object containing multiple fields for text, each with an associated title, in a fixed, vertical, formlike arrangement. After NSTextField, NSForm is the simplest of the Cocoa view classes that contain fields for text, so it is a good place to start as you delve into the more complex text-based user controls, which include tables, outlines, and browsers. The form will also serve as a test bed for extending to other controls the alert sheet, formatting, live undo and redo, and drag-and-drop techniques you developed initially for text fields. You will also use it to explore additional issues arising from the use of objects instead of C data types to hold data in your model object.

Like the radio cluster you implemented in Recipe 2, Step 4, a form is a matrix of component cells, to which you can assign tags. Each form field, consisting of an editable area for text and its associated title, is a separate cell of type NSFormCell. You can use the NSFormCell Info Panel in Interface Builder to assign each cell a unique tag value, which you can use in your code to specify a particular cell. These tags can be any value in any order, giving you great flexibility. A common technique is to simply equate each tag to its cell's 0-based ordinal position within the matrix. Select the "Cell tags = Positions" checkbox to accomplish this for all the cells at once (the tags for the first two cells are already set to their index values by default, but you have to set the tags of additional cells manually).

Using a form is a convenient way to set up a group of related fields that need to be stacked in a vertical orientation with titles. NSForm manages the field interactions for you, so you can do less coding of the boring details. For example, it guarantees that tabbing from field to field within the form takes place in the correct order, top to bottom, without requiring that you hook up the connections in Interface Builder as you did with the stand-alone text fields in Recipe 4. Typically, you have a single outlet for the form and none for its individual fields; you access the fields by their indices or tags using methods for this purpose provided by the NSForm class. This makes it easy, for example, to walk the cells in order. Because only one field of a form can have keyboard focus at any one time, Cocoa lets you code most of the uses of a form as if you were coding a single text field; the form automatically assumes that your messages to the form are messages to its current key field. As a result, adding a form to your application is remarkably similar to adding a single text field.

Unlike a radio cluster, a form does not have a single value that completely specifies the data it represents. A radio cluster's integer index indicates which radio button is selected. Each of a form's multiple fields, on the other hand, has a separate value of its own. It is therefore usually necessary to have an action method for each cell in a form. You can also assign an action method to the form itself. If an individual cell does not have an action method, the form's action method will be invoked; if an individual cell's action method does not have a target, it will be sent to the form's target.

Examples using forms often treat the form as a unitary entity, clearing or committing the data values for all of the fields in the form only when the user explicitly commits the form as a whole—perhaps by pressing a Submit button or the like. The ability to do this is one of the primary uses of forms. Here, however, you will treat the form as little more than a device for grouping text fields. Each field's associated data value will be validated and updated when the user commits that field.

You will start with the familiar outline for implementing every user control, designing it in Interface Builder and filling out the code in Project Builder by using the checklist you developed in Recipe 2, Step 2.

First, prepare your project files for Recipe 9 by updating the build version in the Info.Plist Entries to **9**. Because you are changing the document format by adding four data fields, you should also update the document version in VRDocument.m to **5**.

Step 1: Create a Form in Interface Builder

Use Interface Builder to create a form. When you are done, the form should look like **Figure 9.1**.

1. Open VRDocument.nib in Interface Builder and select the Text Fields tab view item.

2. From the Views palette, drag a System Font Text item onto the Text Fields pane and position it below the three text fields you added in Recipe 4, Step 1, using the Aqua guides to position it. Rename it **Address Form:**.

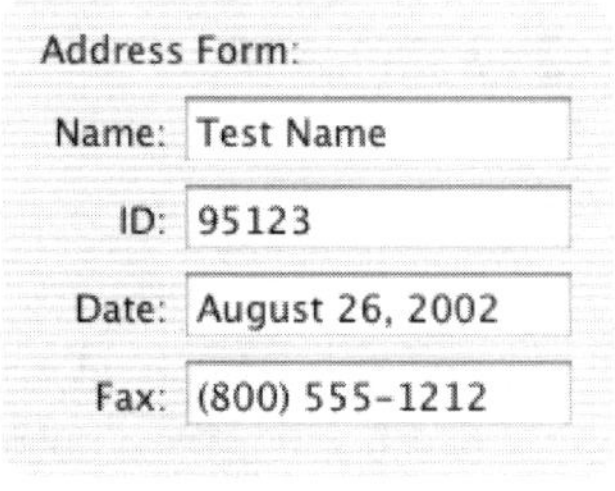

Address Form:

Name:	Test Name
ID:	95123
Date:	August 26, 2002
Fax:	(800) 555-1212

FIGURE 9.1 The finished Address form.

3. From the Views palette, drag an NSForm item onto the Text Fields pane and position it below the Address Form: heading, again using the Aqua guides to position it. The form is the icon illustrating two fields with accompanying titles, Field1: and Field2:.

4. Initially, the form has two cells. Create a third and a fourth cell by Option-dragging one of the form's bottom resize handles downward. The new cells appear in the form below the original two cells as you drag.

5. If you aren't happy with the default spacing between cells, you can change it by Command-dragging the same handle. Do this to close up the rows vertically until they match the spacing of the text fields above them. Aqua guides do not appear to help you with the spacing of cells in a form. The *Aqua Human Interface Guidelines* indicate that the spacing between text fields should be at least 10 pixels, although the Aqua guides in Interface Builder at this writing still suggest 8; either seems a reasonable standard for form cells as well. (There appears to be a bug in Mac OS X at this writing that causes an error under certain circumstances if form fields are too close together, so don't close them up tighter than 8 pixels, to be safe.)

6. Widen the form by dragging its right resize handle until its right edge aligns with the right edge of the text fields above it, as indicated by the Aqua guidelines.

7. Rename the cell titles, from top to bottom, `Name:`, `ID:`, `Date:`, and `Fax:`. To select a form title for editing, you must first double-click a cell to select it, then double-click a title to select its text for editing. Then you can tab to the remaining titles and text fields in order.

8. In the Attributes pane of the NSForm Info Panel, make sure that, in accordance with the *Aqua Human Interface Guidelines* preference for centering of control layouts, Title Alignment is set to right align and Text Alignment is set to left align, by clicking the appropriate buttons. Also make sure the Enabled, Editable, Selectable, and Scrollable checkboxes are selected under Options. The Scrollable checkbox controls whether text within individual form cells will scroll horizontally when it overflows the cell boundaries, not whether the form will scroll its selected cell into view if the form is embedded in a scrollable view. You can set both features programmatically.

Step 2: Write the Code for the Form in Project Builder

All of the data variables you will create in this recipe will hold objects as opposed to standard C data types. Two of them will hold NSString objects, which you learned how to code in Recipe 4, Step 1. However, the new ID text field will hold a number of type NSNumber and the new Date text field will hold an NSCalendarDate object. As in the case of an NSString object, these objects require special handling, including allocating and initializing the new objects when a new window is created, deallocating the objects when the window is closed, and attending to memory management while the new object is in use. In addition, you will learn how to use methods of objects other than NSString to compare values, to update the view objects, and to get and set object values. Interestingly, you will discover that you can save objects such as NSNumber and NSCalendarDate to persistent storage and retrieve them in their several native object forms without converting them to and from NSString objects.

1. **USER CONTROL OUTLET VARIABLES AND ACCESSORS.** In the header file VRMainWindowController.h, declare a new outlet to access the form, after the "Formatted text fields" section, as follows:

    ```
    // Form
    IBOutlet NSForm *addressForm;
    ```

    Still in the header file, also declare an accessor for this outlet after the "Formatted text fields" subsection of the ACCESSORS section of the VRTextFieldController category, as follows:

    ```
    // Form
    - (NSForm *)addressForm;
    ```

    In the category source file VRTextFieldController.m, define the accessor after the "Formatted text fields" subsection of the ACCESSORS section, as follows:

    ```
    // Form

    - (NSForm *)addressForm {
        return addressForm;
    }
    ```

    As in earlier recipes, this **get** accessor does not concern itself with memory management because it relates to a permanent user control.

2. **DATA VARIABLES AND ACCESSORS.** All of the text fields within the form require corresponding variables in VRTextFieldModel to hold the data they represent.

Having gotten an initial taste of using objects rather than C data types for data values in Recipe 4, Step 1, you already know how to write all four values in the form of Cocoa objects. Here, however, two of them will not be NSString objects. The form itself, of course, does not require a data variable in VRTextFieldModel, unlike the radio group cluster, whose value represented the one radio button that was selected.

In the header file VRTextFieldModel.h, declare four new variables after the "Formatted values" section, as follows:

```
// Form values
NSString *formNameValue;
NSNumber *formIdValue;
NSCalendarDate *formDateValue;
NSString *formFaxValue;
```

Still in VRTextFieldModel.h, also declare the corresponding accessor methods after the "Formatted values" subsection of the ACCESSORS section, as follows:

```
// Form values

-(void)setFormNameValue:(NSString *)inValue;
-(NSString *)formNameValue;

-(void)setFormIdValue:(NSNumber *)inValue;
-(NSNumber *)formIdValue;

-(void)setFormDateValue:(NSCalendarDate *)inValue;
-(NSCalendarDate *)formDateValue;

-(void)setFormFaxValue:(NSString *)inValue;
-(NSString *)formFaxValue;
```

Turn to the source file VRTextFieldModel.m and define the accessor methods after the "Formatted values" subsection of the ACCESSORS section, as follows:

```
// Form values

- (void)setFormNameValue:(NSString *)inValue {
    if (formNameValue != inValue) {
        [[[self undoManager]
                prepareWithInvocationTarget:self]
                setFormNameValue:formNameValue];
        [formNameValue release];
```

(continues on next page)

```
            formNameValue = [inValue copy];
            [[NSNotificationCenter defaultCenter]
                    postNotificationName:
                    VRTextFieldModelFormNameValueChangedNotification
                    object:[self document]];
        }
    }

    - (NSString *)formNameValue {
        return [[formNameValue retain] autorelease];
    }

    - (void)setFormIdValue:(NSNumber *)inValue {
        if (formIdValue!= inValue) {
            [[[self undoManager]
                    prepareWithInvocationTarget:self]
                    setFormIdValue:formIdValue];
            [formIdValue release];
            formIdValue = [inValue copy];
            [[NSNotificationCenter defaultCenter]
                    postNotificationName:
                    VRTextFieldModelFormIdValueChangedNotification
                    object:[self document]];
        }
    }

    - (NSNumber *)formIdValue {
        return [[formIdValue retain] autorelease];
    }

    - (void)setFormDateValue:(NSCalendarDate *)inValue {
        if (formDateValue!= inValue) {
            [[[self undoManager]
                    prepareWithInvocationTarget:self]
                    setFormDateValue:formDateValue];
            [formDateValue release];
            formDateValue = [inValue copy];
            [[NSNotificationCenter defaultCenter]
                    postNotificationName:
                    VRTextFieldModelFormDateValueChangedNotification
                    object:[self document]];
        }
```

```
        }

    - (NSCalendarDate *)formDateValue
        return [[formDateValue retain] autorelease];
    }


    - (void)setFormFaxValue:(NSString *)inValue {
        if (formFaxValue!= inValue) {
            [[[self undoManager]
                    prepareWithInvocationTarget:self]
                    setFormFaxValue:formFaxValue];
            [formFaxValue release];
            formFaxValue = [inValue copy];
            [[NSNotificationCenter defaultCenter]
                    postNotificationName:
                    VRTextFieldModelFormFaxValueChangedNotification
                    object:[self document]];
        }
    }


    - (NSString *)formFaxValue {
        return [[formFaxValue retain] autorelease];
    }
```

Make sure to add NSLog() function calls to the set accessors if you are following
that practice.

Notice that the formIdValue variable holds a new type of object, an NSNumber
object instead of an NSString object. There can be good reasons for using an
NSNumber object instead of a C int value, beyond simply illustrating the consequences of using object values of various types to hold data. In a real application,
you might very well want to accumulate address form information in an array
or other collection object for various purposes. In addition, NSValue and its
descendants, especially NSDecimalNumber, make available some very useful
math and other operations. Starting out now with it in object form will make
future development that much easier. Notice also that the formDateValue object
holds a value of type NSCalendarDate. This holds considerable potential advantage, because the NSCalendarDate class implements a variety of methods for
calculating, comparing, and manipulating date values. None of this has an effect
on the structure of the access methods, however, since they merely set and get
an object without caring about its inner structure. All of these accessor methods
use the new technique you learned in Recipe 4, Step 1, for dealing with memory
management issues when writing accessor methods for object values.

3. **NOTIFICATION VARIABLES.** Return to the header file VRTextFieldModel.h, at the bottom of the file, to declare the notification variables used in the **set** methods, as follows:

```
// Form values
extern NSString
        *VRTextFieldModelFormNameValueChangedNotification;extern
NSString
        *VRTextFieldModelFormIdValueChangedNotification;extern NSString
        *VRTextFieldModelFormDateValueChangedNotification;extern
NSString
        *VRTextFieldModelFormFaxValueChangedNotification;
```

Turn back to the source file VRTextFieldModel.m, near the top of the file, to define the notification variables, as follows:

```
// Form values
NSString
        *VRTextFieldModelFormNameValueChangedNotification
        = @"TextFieldModel formNameValue Changed \
        Notification";
NSString
        *VRTextFieldModelFormIdValueChangedNotification
        = @"TextFieldModel formIdValue Changed \
        Notification";
NSString
        *VRTextFieldModelFormDateValueChangedNotification
        = @"TextFieldModel formDateValue Changed \
        Notification";
NSString
        *VRTextFieldModelFormFaxValueChangedNotification
        = @"TextFieldModel formFaxValue Changed \
        Notification";
```

4. **GUI UPDATE METHODS.** Go now to the header file VRMainWindowController.h to declare methods to update the graphical user interface in response to these notifications, after the "Formatted text fields" subsection of the "INTERFACE MANAGEMENT - Specific updaters" section of the VRTextFieldController category, as follows:

```
// Form
- (void)updateFormNameEntry:(NSNotification *)notification;
- (void)updateFormIdEntry:(NSNotification *)notification;
- (void)updateFormDateEntry:(NSNotification *)notification;
- (void)updateFormFaxEntry:(NSNotification *)notification;
```

In the category source file VRTextFieldController.m, define these specific update methods, after the "Formatted text fields" subsection of the "INTERFACE MANAGEMENT - Specific updaters" section, as follows:

```
// Form

- (void)updateFormNameEntry: (NSNotification *)notification {
    if (![[[self textFieldModel] formNameValue]
          isEqualToString:[[[self addressForm]
          cellAtIndex:0] stringValue]]) {
        [[[self addressForm] cellAtIndex:0]
              setStringValue:[[self textFieldModel]
              formNameValue]];
    }
}

- (void)updateFormIdEntry: (NSNotification *)notification {
    if ((([[[self addressForm] cellAtIndex:1] objectValue]
          == nil) || (![[[self textFieldModel]
          formIdValue] isEqualToNumber:
          [[[self addressForm] cellAtIndex:1]
          objectValue]])) {
        [[[self addressForm] cellAtIndex:1]
              setObjectValue:[[self textFieldModel]
              formIdValue]];
    }
}

- (void)updateFormDateEntry:
        (NSNotification *)notification {
    if ((([[[self addressForm] cellAtIndex:2] objectValue]
          == nil) || (![[[self textFieldModel]
          formDateValue] isEqualToDate:
          [[[self addressForm] cellAtIndex:2]
          objectValue]])) {
        [[[self addressForm] cellAtIndex:2]
              setObjectValue:[[self textFieldModel]
              formDateValue]];
    }
}

- (void)updateFormFaxEntry:
```

(continues on next page)

```
        (NSNotification *)notification {
    if (![[[self textFieldModel] formFaxValue]
         isEqualToString:[[[self addressForm]
         cellAtIndex:3] stringValue]]) {
       [[[self addressForm] cellAtIndex:3]
            setStringValue:[[self textFieldModel]
            formFaxValue]];
    }
}
```

There are several important points to understand about this code.

- You are not using a generic view updater method to simplify these specific view updater methods. Recall that you originally resorted to generic view updaters simply as a convenience. Certain portions of every specific view updater method for a particular kind of user control could be abstracted out and implemented just once, saving on repetitious code. This made sense for user controls that might be reused repeatedly, such as buttons and stand-alone text fields. Now, however, you are working with a kind of user control, a form, that is not as likely to be used repeatedly for different kinds of forms in any one application. Furthermore, because each cell or pair of cells in this particular form represents a different class of object, it is clear that efficiency cannot be served by using a generic view updater method; you would need almost as many generic methods as you need specific methods.

- Look at the first of these specific view updaters, **updateFormNameEntry:**. Most of it should be familiar. You use NSString's **isEqualToString:** method to make sure the NSString object currently held in the VRTextFieldModel **formNameValue** object is not equal to the NSString object currently displayed in the first field of the form, before updating the view. Then you use NSCell's **setStringValue:** method to update the view.

  What is new here is the way you obtain a reference to the field displaying the Name value. Instead of using an accessor method to reference a specific instance variable for a particular text field, you use the one accessor method for the form as a whole that you created moments ago, then use NSForm's **cellAtIndex:** method. This is essentially identical to the technique you used when creating a radio button cluster in Recipe 2, Step 4. NSForm provides a variety of methods to access cells within a form by referring to their indices or to any tags you may have assigned them. There is no need whatsoever for a separate instance variable for each cell within the form.

  Using the cell's index is safe here, because you don't plan to revise this form in a future version of the application. In a real application, however, you might be better off using the cell's tag. A tag will not change its value if the cells are reordered, and you'll have less work because you won't have to revise any code that refers to the indices.

- Look at the second and third of these specific view updaters, **updateFormIdEntry:** and **updateFormDateEntry:**. In all of your previous work, you either updated a text field with a C data type using a method such as **setIntValue:** or, as in the **updateFormNameEntry:** method just discussed, you worked with a string object using **setStringValue:**. Now you have an NSNumber object and an NSCalendarDate object in your VRTextFieldModel model object, and you need to display them using these specific view updater methods. It would be nice to be able to display them directly, without having to convert them to a string beforehand. You're in luck! NSCell provides a **setObjectValue:** method, a sort of catchall that allows you to work generically with objects of any type.

  As is often the case in Cocoa, you get a kind of free lunch when you use **setObjectValue:**. If you don't provide a formatter to display the object exactly as you want it to appear, Cocoa will automatically use the object's **description** method to display its value in a default format. All built-in Cocoa value objects come with a suitable description method for this and other purposes. If you aren't happy with Cocoa's default display format for a value object, you simply connect a formatter to it, and whenever Cocoa is told to update the cell's view, it calls upon the formatter to turn the object into an appropriate string for display. Likewise, when Cocoa is told to retrieve the cell's displayed string as an object of the original type, it will use the formatter to make the conversion. These are the functions of NSFormatter's **stringForObjectValue:** and **getObjectValue:forString:errorDescription:** methods; you wrote overrides of each in Recipe 6.

  As an aside, note that **setObjectValue:** requires that its parameter support the NSCopying protocol. This usually isn't an issue because built-in Cocoa types do support NSCopying.

  To make the **updateFormIdEntry:** and **updateFormDateEntry:** methods work as you want them to, use Interface Builder to attach formatters to the ID and Date cells of the form. You learned how to do this in Recipe 3, Step 2.4. In Interface Builder, drag an NSNumberFormatter icon and an NSDateFormatter icon from the Cocoa Views palette to the VRDocument.nib window and name them **FormDateFormatter** and **FormIDFormatter**, respectively. Select each in turn and, using the Info Panel, set up their display strings as desired (use an integer for the ID field, with a minimum value of 1 and a maximum value of 99999, and a date in the form August 24, 2002, for the Date field). Then Control-drag from each of these two fields in turn to the appropriate formatter instance in the VRDocument.nib window and click the Connect button in the Info Panel.

Because built-in Cocoa formatters do not check for blank text field entries, you must prevent the user from leaving the ID and Date fields empty. Add the following to the `control:textShouldEndEditing:` method in the VRMainWindowController.m source file:

```
else if (control == [self addressForm]) {
    if ((([[self addressForm] indexOfSelectedItem] == 1 ||
        [[self addressForm] indexOfSelectedItem] == 2) &&
        ([[fieldEditor string] isEqualToString:@""])) {
        return [self sheetForBlankTextField:control name:nil];
    }
}
```

Leave the Fax field unformatted for now. You will connect a custom formatter to it shortly.

- Both `updateFormIdEntry:` and `updateFormDateEntry:` use specialized methods to compare the value of the data object and the value currently showing in the cell of the form: `isEqualToNumber:` and `isEqualToDate:`. Like the `isEqualToString:` method used in the other two specific view updater methods, these methods are specialized variants of the `isEqual:` method of the NSObject protocol. The specialized methods perform a variety of evaluations appropriate for comparing the kinds of data to which they relate.

  In using these specialized methods, note that you obtain the current value displayed in the cell of the form by using NSCell's `objectValue` method. This method returns an untyped object in its raw form, which, if it in fact contains data of the right type, can be compared to, for example, an NSNumber or NSCalendarDate object.

- Finally, in the `updateFormIdEntry:` and `updateFormDateEntry:` methods, you first tested the two cells in the form to see if they were `nil`. This is necessary because when the window first opens, these cells contain no objects. Without this test, when the `updateWindow` method in VRMainWindowController calls either update method during initialization of the window, the second test would cause an error.

5. **NOTIFICATION OBSERVERS.** Now register the window controller as an observer of the notifications that will trigger these updaters, by inserting the following statements in the `registerNotificationObservers` method of the category source file VRTextFieldController.m, after the "Formatted text fields" registrations:

```
// Form
[[NSNotificationCenter defaultCenter] addObserver:self
    selector:@selector(updateFormNameEntry:)
    name:VRTextFieldModelFormNameValueChangedNotification
    object:[self document]];
[[NSNotificationCenter defaultCenter] addObserver:self
    selector:@selector(updateFormIdEntry:)
    name:VRTextFieldModelFormIdValueChangedNotification
    object:[self document]];
[[NSNotificationCenter defaultCenter] addObserver:self
    selector:@selector(updateFormDateEntry:)
    name:VRTextFieldModelFormDateValueChangedNotification
    object:[self document]];
[[NSNotificationCenter defaultCenter] addObserver:self
    selector:@selector(updateFormFaxEntry:)
    name:VRTextFieldModelFormFaxValueChangedNotification
    object:[self document]];
```

6. **ACTION METHODS.** Next, add action methods. In the header file VRMainWindow-Controller.h, after the "Formatted text fields" subsection of the ACTIONS section of the VRTextFieldController category, add the following:

```
// Form
- (IBAction)formNameEntryAction:(id)sender;
- (IBAction)formIdEntryAction:(id)sender;
- (IBAction)formDateEntryAction:(id)sender;
- (IBAction)formFaxEntryAction:(id)sender;
```

In the category source file VRTextFieldController.m, define these action methods, after the "Formatted text fields" subsection of the ACTIONS section, as follows:

```
// Form

- (IBAction)formNameEntryAction:(id)sender {
    if (![[[self VRTextFieldModel] formNameValue]
        isEqualToString:[sender stringValue]] ||
        [sender isEditing]) {
        [[self VRTextFieldModel]
            setFormNameValue:[sender stringValue]];
        [[[self document] undoManager] setActionName:
            NSLocalizedString(@"Set Form Name Value",
            @"Name of undo/redo menu item after \
            Form Name text field was set")];
```

(continues on next page)

```objc
        }
    }

- (IBAction)formIdEntryAction:(id)sender {
    if (![[[self VRTextFieldModel] formIdValue]
            isEqualToNumber:[sender objectValue]] ||
            [sender isEditing]) {
        [[self VRTextFieldModel]
                setFormIdValue:[sender objectValue]];
        [[[self document] undoManager] setActionName:
                NSLocalizedString(@"Set Form ID Value",
                @"Name of undo/redo menu item after \
                
                Form ID text field was set")];
    }

}

- (IBAction)formDateEntryAction:(id)sender {
    if (![[[self VRTextFieldModel] formDateValue]
            isEqualToDate:[sender objectValue]] ||
            [sender isEditing]) {
        [[self VRTextFieldModel]
                setFormDateValue:[sender objectValue]];
        [[[self document] undoManager] setActionName:
                NSLocalizedString(@"Set Form Date Value",
                @"Name of undo/redo menu item after \
                Form Date text field was set")];
    }
}

- (IBAction)formFaxEntryAction:(id)sender {
    if (![[[self VRTextFieldModel] formFaxValue]
            isEqualToString:[sender stringValue]] ||
            [sender isEditing]) {
        [[self VRTextFieldModel]
                setFormFaxValue:[sender stringValue]];
        [[[self document] undoManager] setActionName:
                NSLocalizedString(@"Set Form Fax Value",
                @"Name of undo/redo menu item after \
                Form Fax text field was set")];
    }
}
```

Again, the `formIdEntryAction:` and `formDateEntryAction:` methods require a slightly different implementation than was required for the C data types or NSString values you have used until now. Because the ID text field contains an NSNumber object and the Date text field contains an NSCalendarDate object, you obtain the value held in each field by invoking NSCell's `objectValue` method, which returns an untyped object containing the NSNumber and NSCalendarDate data you need. This method is used both to compare the text fields' contents with the current data values in VRTextFieldModel and to provide the new values to be stored in VRTextFieldModel. The `isEditing` test anticipates adding live undo support in Step 5.

7. **LOCALIZABLE.STRINGS.** Don't forget to update the Localizable.strings file with the undo and redo menu titles in the previous instruction.

8. **INITIALIZATION.** Instantiate objects for each of the new data values in the model object's designated initializer. To make it easy to test these routines, the objects will be initialized to arbitrary values. Go to the `initWithDocument:` method in VRTextFieldModel.m and add the following lines before the call to the undoManager's `enableUndoRegistration` method:

```
formNameValue = @"Test Name";
formIdValue = [[NSNumber alloc] initWithInt:95123];
formDateValue = [[NSCalendarDate calendarDate] retain];
formFaxValue = @"(800) 555-1212";
```

Examine the initialization statements for `formIdValue` and `formDateValue`. Notice that `formIdValue` is initialized by allocating memory for it and immediately calling one of its specialized initializer methods, `initWithInt:`. However, `formDateValue` is allocated and initialized with the convenience method `calendarDate`, which returns the current date and time. This is called a *convenience* method because it takes care of allocating memory; you just call the method and you have a new, initialized object. These convenience methods all return their objects autoreleased; an object will disappear at the end of the current event loop, and any instance variable to which you thought you had assigned the new object will point to thin air unless you explicitly retain it as part of the assignment, as you did here. (NSString objects are a special case; using the @"" compiler directive causes the compiler to set up a permanent string constant in the file, and you don't need to worry about its retain count.)

You must release every object that you allocate or retain, so add the following lines to the **dealloc** override method in VRTextFieldModel.m. These lines will deallocate whatever object the instance variable currently refers to. This includes the last object of any of the accessor methods described in Instruction 2, above, assigned to the instance variable if the user has typed a new value into the field.

You release the string variables as well as the object variables because while the application is running, they may acquire values that are not constants but real objects. Releasing a string constant does no harm, in any event.

```
[[self formNameValue] release];
[[self formIdValue] release];
[[self formDateValue] release];
[[self formFaxValue] release];
```

9. **DATA STORAGE.** In the source file VRTextFieldModel.m, define the following keys in the "Keys and values for dictionary" subsection of the STORAGE section:

```
// Form values
static NSString *VRFormNameValueKey =
        @"VRTextFieldModelFormNameValue";
static NSString *VRFormIdValueKey =
        @"VRTextFieldModelFormIdValue";
static NSString *VRFormDateValueKey =
        @"VRTextFieldModelFormDateValue";
static NSString *VRFormFaxValueKey =
        @"VRTextFieldModelFormFaxValue";
```

Immediately after that, add these lines at the end of the **addDataToDictionary:** method:

```
// Form values
[dictionary setObject:[self formNameValue]
        forKey:VRFormNameValueKey];
[dictionary setObject:[self formIdValue]
        forKey:VRFormIdValueKey];
[dictionary setObject:[self formDateValue]
        forKey:VRFormDateValueKey];
[dictionary setObject:[self formFaxValue]
        forKey:VRFormFaxValueKey];
```

The **VRFormNameValue** and **VRFormFaxValue** variables do not require conversion to strings because they are already strings. They are saved as is, in their native NSString object format.

For the first time, however, you will save a nonstring object value in its native format, instead of converting it to a string before saving it. Until now, you have been using standard C data types and one NSString object, and it has seemed natural to convert and save all of them as strings using NSString's convenient **stringWithFormat:** method. Cocoa is much smarter than that. Cocoa dictionaries can accommodate many object values that are not strings, and it can save these values to persistent storage and retrieve them as they are, without conversion. Thus, in the code snippet above, you placed the `formIdValue` object into the intermediate dictionary as an NSNumber object without converting it to a string and you similarly placed the `formDateValue` object into the intermediate dictionary as an NSCalendarDate value without converting it to a string.

Once you have hooked up everything and compiled the application, save some ID and Date values to disk, then open the files in Property List Editor. You will see that these new values are recognized on disk as number and date objects.

By the same token, Cocoa permits you to retrieve nonstring objects from persistent storage. Add these lines near the end of the `restoreDataFromDictionary:` method, before the `[[self undoManager] enableUndoRegistration]` message:

```
// Form values
[self setFormNameValue:
    [dictionary objectForKey:VRFormNameValueKey]];
[self setFormIdValue:
    [dictionary objectForKey:VRFormIdValueKey]];
[self setFormDateValue:
    [dictionary objectForKey:VRFormDateValueKey]];
[self setFormFaxValue:
    [dictionary objectForKey:VRFormFaxValueKey]];
```

10. **GUI UPDATE METHOD INVOCATIONS.** Add calls to the control update methods in the window controller. In the category source file VRTextFieldController.m, add the following calls at the end of the `updateTextFieldsTab` method:

```
// Form
[self updateFormNameEntry:nil];
[self updateFormIdEntry:nil];
[self updateFormDateEntry:nil];
[self updateFormFaxEntry:nil];
```

11. **DESCRIPTION METHOD.** Add the values of the new data variables to the model object's description method, in VRTextFieldModel.m, so that it looks like this:

```
- (NSString *) description {
    return [NSString stringWithFormat:@"%@\
\n\tintegerValue:%@\
\n\tdecimalValue:%@\
\n\tteleponeValue:%@\
\n\tformNameValue:%@\
```

(continues on next page)

```
\n\tformIDValue:%@\
\n\tformDateValue:%@\
\n\tformFaxValue:%@\n",
      [super description],
      [[NSNumber numberWithInt:
            [self integerValue]] stringValue],
      [[NSNumber numberWithFloat:
            [self decimalValue]] stringValue],

      [self telephoneValue],
      [self formNameValue],
      [[self formIdValue] stringValue],
      [[self formDateValue] description],
      [self formFaxValue]];
}
```

12. **Help tags.** Add Help tags in Interface Builder to each of the form fields: "Enter a name," " Enter an ID number," "Enter the date," and "Enter a fax number." The form is a user control apart from its fields, so enter a Help tag for the entire form as well: "Address form."

13. **Initial first responder and next key view.** Use Interface Builder to integrate the form into the key view loop for the Text Fields tab. For this purpose, you need only be concerned with the form itself. It handles the tabbing order of the fields within the form for you. Disconnect the current next key view for the Telephone text field and reconnect it to the form. Then connect the form to its next key view, the Integer text field.

Step 3: Read the Source Files into the Nib File and Connect Outlets and Actions

Now that you have the basic code for the Address form completed, go ahead and connect outlets and actions in Interface Builder so you can verify that it works. When you are satisfied, you will go on to add extras to the form's fields.

1. In Interface Builder, select the Classes tab in the VRDocument.nib window, then choose Classes > Read Files. In the dialog, select the header file in which you have created outlets or actions, VRMainWindowController.h, then click the Parse button.

2. Select the Instances tab and Control-drag from the File's Owner icon to the form. Be careful to end the drag on the form, not on one of the form fields, because you only need an outlet to the form as a whole. Click the `addressForm` outlet in the File's Owner Info Panel, then click Connect.

3. Control-drag from each of the four form fields to the File's Owner icon in turn, click the targets in the Outlets section and the appropriate actions in the Actions section of the Connections pane of the NSFormCell Info Panel, then click the Connect button.

Now try entering some data in the form fields, saving them, reading them back from disk, and testing whatever else you think is important. You will see, of course, that the new form fields do not support a custom format for the Fax number, or live undo and redo, or the dropping of text dragged from a text field in the window. You will attend to those extras next.

Step 4: Add a Custom Formatter to the Fax Form Field, with Alert Sheets

Now that you have the Address form set up and working, you should give its constituent fields all the extra capabilities you gave text fields in Recipes 5, 6, 7, and 8. A field of a form is not a text field, but instead a combination of a static title and an editable text entry area, so you might anticipate some difficulty implementing features originally designed to work with text fields. But Cocoa will once again surprise you with its ease of use and power.

Start with formatters. The Fax field of the Address form holds a telephone number. Since you wrote an excellent custom telephone number formatter in Recipe 6, Step 3, it would be nice to use it with the Fax field of the form, too.

You can skip this step for now if you skipped Recipe 6. Custom formatters are an advanced topic.

1. You can't connect the telephone formatter to the Fax field using Interface Builder, as you did with the number and date formatters in Instruction 4 of Step 2, above, because you haven't installed it in an Interface Builder palette. However, you can easily connect it programmatically by adding the following line to the `makeTelephoneFormatter` method you wrote in Recipe 6, Step 3. In the Formatter Constructors subsection of the INPUT VALIDATION AND

FORMATTING section of the main VRMainWindowController.m file, after the line that sets the formatter for the Telephone text field, add this line:

```
[[[self addressForm] cellAtIndex:3]
        setFormatter:telephoneFormatter];
```

Note that you use the same formatter you used for the Telephone text field, without having to re-create it.

2. In the same file, you must add a branch to the `control:didFailToValidate-PartialString:errorDescription:` delegate method to catch on-the-fly entry errors in the Fax field. Insert the following branch near the end of the delegate method:

```
else if ((control == [[self addressForm] cellAtIndex:3])
        && ([[self addressForm] indexOfSelectedItem] == 3)) {
    if (error != nil) {
        NSBeep();
        [self sheetForTelephoneTextFieldValidationFailure:
                string errorDescription:error];
    }
}
```

You must also add a branch to the `control:didFailToFormatString:-errorDescription:` delegate method to catch attempts to commit a telephone number that is too short or too long. In the same file, insert the following branch near the end of the delegate method:

```
else if ((control == [self addressForm]) &&
        ([[self addressForm] indexOfSelectedItem] == 3)) {
    NSBeep();
    return [self sheetForTelephoneTextFieldFormatFailure:
            string errorDescription:error];
}
```

Note that, in both cases, you tested whether the control that generated the validation or format error was the Address form, because the fields within a form are not themselves controls. Once you know that the Address form generated the error, however, you do have to make sure the Fax field was at fault. You do this by employing NSForm's `indexOfSelectedItem` method to make sure that field 3, the Fax field, is currently selected. If you were to omit this second leg of the test, you would find that input errors in the Date form field present alert sheets containing informative text intended for telephone number entry errors. If you add additional telephone number fields to the Address form, you can apply the formatter to them as well and enhance these two tests to check for their indices too. Remember that if you add or remove fields in the Address form or change their order, you will have to revise every method in your code that refers to the fields by index.

You don't need to write new methods to present alert sheets in the event of an input error in the Fax field, because the sheets you wrote in Recipe 6, Step 3.4 and Step 3.5, Instruction 6, are worded generally enough for any field containing a telephone number. For the same reason, you don't have to add anything to the Localizable.strings file for the Fax field.

3. Finally, you must make the window controller the Address form's delegate so the validation and format checking delegate methods will be invoked when their time comes. Although you are concerned only with the Fax field within the form, the form itself is a control capable of having a delegate. In Interface Builder, Control-drag from the Address form to the File's Owner icon, then connect the delegate target.

That's all there is to extending the telephone number formatter you wrote in Recipe 6, Step 3, to other fields in the application that hold telephone numbers. The fact that these other fields are form fields within an NSForm control did not make your task materially more difficult.

In general, any field that has a formatter connected, whether it be a custom formatter or one of the two built-in Cocoa formatters, needs your help to provide feedback to the user. This is a tutorial, however, and you have already learned how to write alert sheets. Rather than repeat the process here, you will just make the ID and Date fields beep when the user attempts to commit an entry that violates the constraints imposed by the built-in Cocoa formatters you connected to them in Instruction 4 of Step 2, above. Revise the branch you added to the `control:didFailToFormat-String:errorDescription:` delegate method a moment ago so that it beeps when any field in the form detects an illegal entry but presents a sheet only for the Fax field, as follows:

```
else if (control == [self addressForm]) {
    NSBeep();
    if ([[self addressForm] indexOfSelectedItem] == 3) {
        return [self sheetForTelephoneTextFieldFormatFailure:
            string errorDescription:error];
    }
    return NO;
}
```

Step 5: Add Live Undo and Redo Support to the Form

Next, add support for live undo and redo to the form fields in the Address form. You can skip this step for now if you skipped Recipe 7. Live undo and redo is an advanced topic.

This step may at first seem more complicated than adding a formatter to the Fax field, because you will use three new Cocoa techniques: a formal protocol, static variables, and an include file. In fact, however, you will end up implementing live undo and redo for form fields using almost exactly the same code that you wrote for live undo and redo in VRUndoableTextField in Recipe 7, so most of your work is already done. The major difference lies in the packaging.

In Recipe 7, you made text fields undoable while they are being edited by implementing a single override method in your window controller, `windowWillReturnFieldEditor:-toObject:`, to create a separate field editor whose built-in undo support is turned on. There is nothing special about text fields in this regard. All text-based cells in a window use a field editor for editing, even if the cells are embedded in a control such as a form. All of them use the window's field editor by default, but you can provide a separate field editor for any of them. Therefore, you can easily make any of them undoable by modifying your `windowWillReturnFieldEditor:toObject:` method so that any text-based cell uses the same separate field editor with its undo feature turned on.

The harder part is figuring out how to implement the ability to clear the undo and redo stacks of intermediate editing actions once the user commits the data. In Recipe 7, you did this for the single cell in a text field by writing VRUndoableTextField, a sub-class of NSTextField. It implements a number of notification methods that track editing, undo, and redo actions in the field and unwind them when the data is com-mitted. VRUndoableTextField relies principally upon the `textDidBeginEditing:` and `textDidEndEditing:` methods of NSTextField, and you probably assume that you can't use these methods for an NSForm.

In fact, however, a method with the same name and purpose exists in NSMatrix, on which forms are based. This is a characteristic design feature of Cocoa, where meth-ods with the same name may be implemented in several different classes. The point of it is precisely to allow use of methods with the same name in disparate but similar situations. You can therefore solve the problem for forms using exactly the same code you used for text fields, but because you will subclass NSForm, you will get the NSMatrix version of the method. It knows that only one form field can be key at any one time in a form, and so by knowing which form field is key it produces exactly the same result as the NSTextField version of the method, without requiring any effort on your part to tell it which field you're interested in.

You can't use the same subclass here because the fields in a form are not text fields. However, you can easily create a similar subclass of NSForm to do the same thing for form fields, with only slight modifications to account for the fact that a form has multiple fields.

In implementing live undo and redo in the form, you will generalize your code so that you can reuse it as much as possible in other text-based controls. In fact, once you have it working, you will revise VRUndoableTextField to make use of the new techniques. In subsequent recipes, you will use them again in still other text-based controls.

The first leg of your strategy will be to restructure the `windowWillReturnFieldEditor:-toObject:` method slightly so it's easy to add additional controls to the set of controls that will use the separate undoable field editor. At the same time, you will make it easy to turn off undo and redo capability for individual fields in a multifield control. You learned in Recipe 7 that live undo and redo doesn't work with fields to which an on-the-fly formatter is attached, and you have attached one to the Fax field in your form. You can see that you need a general ability to turn off live undo and redo in individual fields of multifield controls.

The second leg of your strategy will be to implement the functionality of VRUndoableTextField in a new subclass of NSForm, VRUndoableForm.

To make this functionality as reusable as possible, you will employ two new techniques, one of them a Cocoa technology and the other a common C programming technique. First, to avoid having to duplicate the interface part of the subclass many times over for other controls, you will write a formal protocol that declares the interface for every undoable text control subclass, and you will have all of your undoable text control subclasses adopt the protocol. Second, to avoid having to duplicate the implementation part of the subclass many times over for other controls, you will write it in a text file and use an `#include` preprocessor command to include the text file in the implementation part of all your undoable text controls. You will use a third technique, static variables, to declare two variables in the include file used in the implementation part, so that you don't have to redeclare them in the interface of every undoable subclass of a text-based control. By using these three techniques, you make both the header file and the source file of all of your undoable subclasses essentially empty (unless you decide to add other unrelated functionality to them).

The advantage of having a separate subclass for each kind of undoable text control is that you can make a separate decision about undoability for each instance of each kind of control. For example, you can declare any form that is not to be undoable as type NSForm, while you declare any form that is to be undoable as type

VRUndoableForm, with appropriate corresponding custom class connections in Interface Builder in both cases.

1. Start by revising the `windowWillReturnFieldEditor:toObject:` method in the UNDO MANAGEMENT section of the source file VRMainWindowController.m to read as follows:

```
- (id)windowWillReturnFieldEditor:(NSWindow *)sender
        toObject:(id)object {
    if ((sender == [self window]) &&
            ([object isKindOfClass:[VRUndoableTextField class]]
            || [object isKindOfClass:[VRUndoableForm class]])) {

        if (![self fieldEditorForUndoableTextControl]) {
            [self setfieldEditorForUndoableTextControl:
                    [[NSText alloc] init]];
            [[self fieldEditorForUndoableTextControl]
                    setFieldEditor:YES];
        }
        [[self fieldEditorForUndoableTextControl]
                setAllowsUndo:YES];

        if ((object == [self addressForm]) &&
                ([object indexOfSelectedItem] == 3)) {
            [[self fieldEditorForUndoableTextControl]
                    setAllowsUndo:NO];
        }

        return [self fieldEditorForUndoableTextControl];
    }
    return nil;
}
```

The first `if` test checks first to make sure your window invoked the method. It then checks whether the object requesting a field editor is one of your undoable text controls by testing its class. As you create additional kinds of undoable text controls, you will add them to this list to make them undoable. If the requesting control is of an undoable class, the method returns the undoable field editor you first set up in Recipe 7 (renamed `fieldEditorForUndoableTextControl` for generality), creating it if necessary.

The second `if` test turns off the separate field editor's undo feature if the specific field within the control is one you do not want to be undoable. You can't simply return the window's normal, nonundoable field editor in this case, because Cocoa does not take kindly to efforts to switch field editors for individual fields within a

multifield text control. As you make more controls undoable in your application, you will add other fields to this list if they are not supposed to be undoable.

2. Because you changed the name of the variable holding the separate undoable field editor, you should change its declaration accordingly. In the header file VRMainWindowController.m, revise the declaration to read as follows:

`NSTextView *fieldEditorForUndoableTextControl;`

You also have to change the names of both accessor methods in both the header and the source files, and everywhere else where they are called. To be sure you make all of the changes everywhere they are required, use Project Builder's global change feature to change the variable's name and both accessor names everywhere in the project. To do this, select the Find tab near the top of the main Project Builder window, then change the pop-up menu options to "This project, no frameworks" and Textual. Then type each name and its replacement name in turn in the Find and Replace fields and click the Replace button.

3. Create the formal protocol. First create a new Cocoa Objective-C class file, naming it `VRUndoableTextControl.h`. A formal protocol does not have a corresponding source file, because it is up to classes that adopt the protocol to implement the methods it declares, so uncheck the box to create a sibling file. It would be a good idea to keep your project organized by creating a new group in your project called `Protocols` and dragging the new protocol file into it.

A formal protocol is declared similarly to a class. In this case, apart from your customary identifying comments, the entire protocol file should look like this:

`@protocol VRUndoableTextControl`

`- (BOOL) isEditing;`

`@end`

Every class you write that adopts this protocol must implement the `isEditing` method. Each implementation can be different, although here they will be identical. In addition, as noted above, each subclass will implement additional methods adopted from the VRUndoableTextField class you wrote in Recipe 7. These classes should not declare the `isEditing` method in their interface parts, because the adoption of the protocol takes care of informing the class of the method names.

4. Now you can create the undoable form subclass. Create another new Cocoa Objective-C class, this time creating both a header and a source file named, respectively, `VRUndoableForm.h` and `VRUndoableForm.m`. To keep the project organized, create a `Controls` group in the project and drag the new VRUndoableForm files into it. Also drag both existing VRUndoableTextField files into it.

Because the subclass adopts the protocol, and because you will shortly use static variable declarations in the source file instead of declaring instance variables in the header file, the new header file will be even emptier than the protocol file. Apart from comments, the entire header file should look like this:

```
#import <Cocoa/Cocoa.h>
#import "VRUndoableTextControl.h"

@interface VRUndoableForm : NSForm <VRUndoableTextControl> {
}

@end
```

Placing the name of the protocol in angle brackets at the end of the **@interface** directive and importing the protocol's header file are all you have to do to adopt the protocol. You also import the Cocoa umbrella headers, as you would in any class header file.

5. Next, write the implementation part for the undoable form subclass. The entire source file VRUndoableForm.m should look like this:

```
#import "VRUndoableForm.h"

@implementation VRUndoableForm
#include "VRUndoableTextControl.include"
@end
```

6. This is beginning to look pretty simple. Now you finally have to write the include file containing the implementation part of the VRUndoableForm subclass, but even this will be mostly a matter of cutting and pasting.

First create a new Empty File using the Project Builder New File Assistant. This should be a single file named **VRUndoableTextControl.include**. There is no magic to the .include extension; I just made it up for clarity's sake. To keep the project organized, create a new group in the project, name it **Includes**, and drag the new include file into it.

Then open the existing VRUndoableTextField.m source file that you wrote in Recipe 7, copy all of its method implementations to the clipboard, return to the VRUndoableTextControl.include file, and paste the contents of the clipboard into it.

7. You do have to make a few changes to the code you purloined from VRUndoableTextField.m to make it serve its broader purpose here. Start by inserting the following static variable declarations at the top of the include file:

```
static BOOL isEditing;
static int undoCount;
```

In Objective-C, as in C, *external* variables like `isEditing` and `undoCount`, declared outside any function or method, are permanent. That is, they retain their values across execution of functions and methods. The `extern` declaration is optional because it is implicit in the fact that the declarations lie outside any function or method. Their behavior as external variables is consistent with their behavior in VRUndoableTextField, where they were declared as instance variables. Because these are declared as `static`, their scope is limited to the source file in which they are declared (here, VRUndoableForm.m, since the preprocessor includes them in it, but other sources will include the include file as well).

The important point here is that they don't have to be declared in the header file and are thus invisible to users of the VRUndoableForm subclass. I find this an attractive feature in the present context, not only because implementation details should not be of interest to clients but also because I want to minimize the opportunity for developer errors implicit in having to redeclare identical instance variables in undoable subclasses of multiple text-based controls. Declaring them once in an include file guarantees that their implementation in all similar subclasses will be the same, much as the use of the formal protocol to declare the `isEditing` accessor method once for all subclasses that adopt the protocol will guarantee that they will be declared the same way in all similar subclasses.

It is important, however, to keep in mind this passage from *The C Programming Language* by Kernighan and Ritchie (second edition, 1988), pages 33 and 34: "Relying too heavily on external variables is fraught with peril since it leads to programs whose data connections are not at all obvious—variables can be changed in unexpected and even inadvertent ways, and the program is hard to modify."

8. Another required change to the include file is to bracket the operative statements in the `textDidBeginEditing:` and `textDidEndEditing:` methods in tests to determine whether the field editor is set to provide undo support. This is necessary because you have provided a means to turn off undo support for some fields in multifield controls. For clarity, I give the complete revised forms of both methods here:

```
- (void)textDidBeginEditing:(NSNotification *)notification {
    if ([(NSTextView *)[self currentEditor] allowsUndo]) {
        undoCount = 0;
        isEditing = YES;
        [[NSNotificationCenter defaultCenter]
                addObserver:self
                selector:@selector(handleWillCloseUndoGroup:)
                name:NSUndoManagerWillCloseUndoGroupNotification
                object:nil];
```

(continues on next page)

```
            [[NSNotificationCenter defaultCenter]
                    addObserver:self
                    selector:@selector(handleDidUndo:)
                    name:NSUndoManagerDidUndoChangeNotification
                    object:nil];
            [[NSNotificationCenter defaultCenter]
                    addObserver:self
                    selector:@selector(handleDidRedo:)
                    name:NSUndoManagerDidRedoChangeNotification
                    object:nil];
        }
        [super textDidBeginEditing:notification];
}


- (void)textDidEndEditing:(NSNotification *)notification {
    if (isEditing &&
            [(NSTextView *)[self currentEditor] allowsUndo]) {
        int index;
        NSObject *savedObjectValue = [self objectValue];
        for (index = undoCount; index > 0; index--)
                [[self undoManager] undo];
        [self setObjectValue:savedObjectValue];
        [[NSNotificationCenter defaultCenter]
                removeObserver:self
                name:NSUndoManagerWillCloseUndoGroupNotification
                object:nil];
        [[NSNotificationCenter defaultCenter]
                removeObserver:self
                name:NSUndoManagerDidUndoChangeNotification
                object:nil];
        [[NSNotificationCenter defaultCenter]
                removeObserver:self
                name:NSUndoManagerDidRedoChangeNotification
                object:nil];
    }
    [super textDidEndEditing:notification];
    isEditing = NO;
}
```

The calls to **super** are left outside the test blocks, because fields that do not meet the tests also require the services of the superclass. The **isEditing = NO** statement is left outside the test block for two reasons: one, it guarantees an appropriate default value for the variable; and two (this is of greater importance), it must come after the [super textDidEndEditing:notification] message is sent because that message triggers the field's action method, which in turn consults the non-default value of the accessor method.

In both methods, you obtain the required reference to the current field editor by calling NSControl's currentEditor method on self. This is more convenient than getting a reference to the field editor from this control's window by calling NSWindow's fieldEditor:forObject: method. In either case, it is necessary to cast the return value to NSTextView* or it won't compile, because the allowsUndo method used here is declared in NSTextView. For historical reasons that you needn't worry about, both the currentEditor and fieldEditor:forObject: methods return objects of type NSText, NSTextView's parent.

The rest of the implementation methods remain unchanged from VRUndoableTextField. Consult Recipe 7 to be reminded of what they do and why.

9. All that remains in Project Builder to make this work is to change the declaration of the addressForm instance variable from NSForm to VRUndoableForm and import the VRUndoableForm header file into the window controller class. In VRMainWindowController.h, change the existing instance variable declaration to this:

```
IBOutlet VRUndoableForm *addressForm;
```

Also change the return type of the addressForm accessor method to VRUndoable-Form in the VRTextFieldController category declaration in VRMainWindow-Controller.m and the category source file VRTextFieldController.m.

Finally, add this at the top of the VRMainWindowController.h header file, after the other import commands:

```
#import "VRUndoableForm.h"
```

10. In Interface Builder, select the Classes tab of VRDocument.nib and read in the VRUndoableForm.h and VRMainWindowController.h files. Then select the Address form in the main document window, go to the Custom Classes pane of the NSForm Info Panel, and select VRUndoableForm.

11. Because you have generalized the protocol method and the include file, you can now go back to VRUndoableTextField and conform it to the changes you made for VRUndoableForm.

Revise the header file VRUndoableTextField.h so that it declares no instance variables or methods but adopts the VRUndoableTextControl protocol and imports its header file.

Revise the source file VRUndoableTextField.m so that it defines nothing but includes the VRUndoableTextControl.include file.

You now have a general system in place for making text fields in text-based controls support live undo and redo. It is working in several existing text fields and in the Address form, and it will be very easy to implement for other controls in future recipes. You will have only to create nearly empty subclass header and source files for each undoable subclass and make minor changes to the window controller. The protocol and the include file you just wrote handle everything else.

Step 6: Add Full Drag-and-Drop Support to the Form

Finally, all of the fields in the Address form should be able to receive dragged-and-dropped text. You recall from Recipe 8 that you created a category on NSTextField to enable text fields to act as dragging destinations. Because you implemented Cocoa's NSDraggingDestination informal protocol in a category, the capability automatically became available to all text fields, whether they were simple NSTextFields or subclasses such as NSUndoableTextField. All that was required was that individual text field controls be registered for the NSStringPboardType drag type.

You want all form fields to have full drag-and-drop capability as well. Having succeeded with the category approach in Recipe 8, you will create a similar category on NSForm. Then you can make any form field capable of acting as a dragging destination by simply registering the form to receive the NSStringPboardType drag type.

You can't simply copy the code from the NSTextField+VRDragTarget category, because forms contain multiple fields, but you will find that dragging is almost as easy to implement. In summary, you must take steps to ensure that each field in the form is highlighted independently as a user drags the mouse over it. Cocoa's dragging protocols work with windows and other views, not with cells. Realizing this, you will understand that instead of implementing the **draggingEntered:** method, you will have to implement the **draggingUpdated:** method to track the mouse location continuously as it moves within the form relative to the bounds of each of its fields. Instead of making the form the window's first responder when the mouse enters the form, you will select the form cell over which the mouse is hovering. This will result in a focus ring's appearing around that form field, together with all the other visual feedback that results when the form's field editor takes over management of the drag session.

In the course of making this work, you discovered in Recipe 8 that errors occur when dragging takes place between fields that share the same field editor. For one thing, drag and drop within one field editor causes the dragged text to be moved, whereas the *Aqua Human Interface Guidelines* require that it be copied. Even a committed value in the dragging source is cleared when the new value in the dragging destination is committed—something that may surprise the user. More fundamental errors can also occur, usually corrupting the dragging destination's contents due to range errors.

By definition, these errors are confined to drags within a single window, since other windows use different field editors. In most cases, therefore, you would be well advised to make a virtue of necessity by restricting the drag-and-drop feature of your application to dragging sessions involving two separate windows (whether within the same application or involving a drag from a separate application such as the Finder). Here, however, you will take advantage of the fact that some Vermont Recipes document windows use two different field editors, one for undoable fields and the other for nonundoable fields. You will allow dragging sessions to take place between fields of these disparate types even if they are within a single window. While this may present documentation issues in an application designed like Vermont Recipes, where users aren't likely to see it as a rational distinction, the technique is worth understanding for designs where it might come in more handy. For example, I can imagine a structured text editor with a single dragging destination for the composed text, represented by a field editor of its own, with one or more dragging sources in the same window from which the user might drag special tags to the destination.

1. Begin by creating a new category to add dragging destination capability to forms. Create two new Cocoa Objective-C class files, one named NSForm+VRDragTarget.h and the other named NSForm+VRDragTarget.m. Place each in the existing Categories group, and add your customary identifying comments to them.

2. The header file NSForm+VRDragTarget.h consists entirely of the following lines:

```
#import <AppKit/NSForm.h>

@interface NSForm (VRDragTarget)

@end
```

3. The source file NSForm+VRDragTarget.m is as follows:

```
#import "NSForm+VRDragTarget.h"
#import <Cocoa/Cocoa.h>

@implementation NSForm (VRDragTarget)

- (unsigned int)draggingUpdated:(id <NSDraggingInfo>)sender {
```

(continues on next page)

```
        if ([[[sender draggingPasteboard] types]
              containsObject:NSStringPboardType]) {
            if ([sender draggingSourceOperationMask]
                  & NSDragOperationCopy) {
                int row, column;
                NSPoint mouseLocation = [self convertPoint:
                        [sender draggingLocation] fromView:nil];
                if ([self getRow:&row column:&column
                        forPoint:mouseLocation]) {

                    [self selectCellAtRow:row column:column];
                    if ([sender draggingSource] == [self currentEditor]) {
                        [self abortEditing];
                    } else {
                        return NSDragOperationCopy;
                    }
                }
            }
        }
    }
    return NSDragOperationNone;
}


@end
```

This isn't much more complicated than the corresponding category on
NSTextField that you wrote in Recipe 8. It imports the same Cocoa headers,
it returns the same constants, and it is structured similarly.

One difference is the innermost **if** block. Here, you test whether the sender's
draggingSource is identical to this form's field editor. In the case of text-based
cells, a little experimentation reveals that the dragging source is always a field
editor. Once you understand that a cell's field editor is actually a text view
superimposed directly on top of the cell, you see that this has to be the case;
when you click in the cell, you are actually clicking in the field editor in front of
the cell. By virtue of this test, a dragging copy operation will be permitted only
if the dragging source is different from the destination's field editor. This will
always be the case when the source and the destination are in different windows
or applications, and it will sometimes be the case within a single window if it
uses more than one field editor. If the dragging source and the field editor are
identical, you simply abort editing in the destination.

The other **if** blocks perform tests identical to those in the corresponding text
field category, although the code has been cleaned up a little by eliminating the
local variables and sending the messages inline.

At the core of the method, you find code that tests the current mouse coordinates within the form against the bounds of each form cell. An NSForm control descends directly from the NSMatrix class, and, as you would expect, NSMatrix gives the form a method designed to make just this sort of mouse comparison easy to do: getRow:column:forPoint:. By feeding this method the point representing the mouse's current location, you can retrieve the row and column numbers of any cell lying under the mouse. If the mouse is within the form but not hovering over a cell, the method returns NO and otherwise YES. The NSDraggingInfo protocol's draggingLocation method supplies the current mouse coordinates. These are in the window's coordinate system, so they must be converted to the form's coordinate system using the standard NSView convertPoint:fromView: method (passing nil in the fromView: parameter signifies the window's coordinate system). Finally, the row and column numbers are used to select the cell over which the mouse is hovering, to give it the telltale focus ring and cause the form's field editor to take over editing and drag-and-drop responsibilities. If the mouse leaves the cell's bounds without dropping its text, this method resumes management of the dragging session until the mouse leaves the form or the text is dropped.

4. Finally, you register the Address form to receive dropped text by adding the following line to the end of the registerDragTypesForTextFieldsTab method in the category source file NSTextFieldController.m:

```
[[self addressForm] registerForDraggedTypes:
    [NSArray arrayWithObject:NSStringPboardType]];
```

5. I described near the beginning of this step a problem that occurs when the same field editor represents both the dragging source and the dragging destination. The innermost if block you just wrote for the NSForm category solves this problem for drags destined for a form field, but you need to insert the same test in the NSTextField category you wrote in Recipe 8. Insert the following line in place of return NSDragOperationCopy in NSTextField+VRDragTarget.m:

```
if ([sender draggingSource] == [self currentEditor]) {
    [self abortEditing];
} else {
    return NSDragOperationCopy;
}
```

Step 7: Build and Run the Application

Build and run the application to test the behavior of each of the four fields in the new address form. You have already made the necessary Interface Builder connections.

Go ahead and exercise the four form fields. Notice that the Fax field's on-the-fly filtering and formatting works identically to the filtering and formatting of the Telephone text field and generates identical alert sheets for errors. Notice that you can undo and redo editing of three of the form fields before the final value is committed and that the intermediate undo and redo actions are cleared when the final value is committed. And notice that you can drag text from any location onto any of the form fields (with the exception that you can't drag text from other fields in the same window that use the same field editor).

Conclusion

Using an NSForm object to add four new text-based fields to the Text Fields tab view item is more efficient than adding four independent text fields. NSForm takes care of some of the coding you would otherwise have to do repetitively for each text field, and NSForm includes optimizations to make execution more efficient as well. You might as well use forms whenever you can—that is, when lining up same-size fields vertically is feasible—because you now know how to add the same extras to fields whether they stand alone or are included within a form: on-the-fly formatters, alert sheets, live undo and redo, and full drag-and-drop support.

You are now ready to add another text-based control to the Vermont Recipes application, a combo box. It will introduce you to a new feature that you must implement when you create some complex user controls: the data source.

RECIPE 10

Combo Boxes

In Recipe 10, you will implement a Combo Box, or Combination Box, a cross between a pop-up menu and an editable text field. It is associated with a list of predefined choices from which the user can choose in much the same way a menu item is chosen from a pop-up menu. The predefined choices can appear as either menu

HIGHLIGHTS:

Using an external data source to provide a list of choices for a combo box

items or, if there are more than 12 choices, a scrollable list. In addition, in case none of the predefined choices is suitable, the user can type some other value into the text field that forms the main body of the control. For example, if the predefined choices are "Dell," "HP," "Gateway," and "IBM," the user who thinks different can type "Apple." NSComboBox is in fact a subclass of NSTextField and inherits all of its methods for handling text. In addition, it optionally supports autocompletion; if the user types the first part of one of the predefined choices, the full text of that choice is automatically inserted into the text field as a candidate for selection.

The *Aqua Human Interface Guidelines* make it clear that a typed value should not be added automatically to the permanent list of predefined menu items. They give no explanation for this restriction, but it seems obvious that indiscriminately adding custom-typed values could quickly generate an unmanageable list containing many rarely used items. The *Guidelines* are apparently telling you that a combo box is appropriate only in situations where the application designer can anticipate the most common choices but needs to leave the user some flexibility to enter less common values by hand. The burden of typing a custom value is justified because the need should rarely occur.

Despite the *Guidelines'* suggestions, it is technically feasible to allow user modification of the predefined list, and you may find this attractive if you anticipate that this option will serve individual users' convenience. The *Guidelines* do not offer any interface design advice should you choose to do this, but it is clear that you should at least secure the user's permission beforehand. Many of the methods implemented in NSComboBox explicitly support adding items to the list programmatically, and comments in the SimpleComboBox example application provided with Apple's Developer Tools suggest that you may do it in appropriate circumstances. In this recipe, however, you will follow the approach suggested by the *Guidelines,* deferring a more daring approach until Recipe 11.

Interface Builder offers a simple way to define an internal list of predefined strings your application will use to provide choices to the user when it launches for the first time, much like listing menu items for a pop-up menu. In addition, the NSComboBox class provides methods to construct an internal list programmatically from objects of any type and an alternate mechanism for implementing lists using an external *data source* object. You can use either an internal list or an external data source for combo boxes whether they offer fixed or user-modifiable choices. Which mechanism you choose to use is a matter of convenience, flexibility, and efficiency.

An external data source can be an object of any kind, so long as it implements certain required methods and can identify the choices with an integer index. For example, the data source can be a separate object with only one purpose, or it can be an existing window controller or other object sharing the role of data source with many other functions. You may base the mechanism for holding the list on any Cocoa collection object, such as an NSArray, or you might use a separate database. The required methods for a data source are declared in the NSComboBoxDataSource and NSComboBoxCellDataSource informal protocols. Because other kinds of controls, such as tables, use a data source in a similar fashion, you will implement a combo box in this recipe using a data source, to give you a simple introduction to the concept. You will do this by implementing the methods declared in the NSComboBoxDataSource informal protocol.

In this recipe, you will create a combo box that will become part of an antique dealer's inventory management system. The combo box will act as a filter, allowing the user to select one of several kinds of antiques to display in a table that you will create in Recipe 11. When the user chooses, say, "Rag Dolls" in the combo box, the table will display all of the rag dolls in the inventory, hiding everything else. The decision to use a combo box to select the filter is dictated by the fact that the user will be able to define custom categories of antiques when entering new inventory items in the table. To filter the inventory by one of these new categories, the user must be able to type the new kind into the combo box. In Recipe 11, you will think about letting the user add these custom categories to the combo box's permanent list, saving them with the table, but for now you will assume that the user has to type custom values into the combo box manually.

Note that a bug in Mac OS X 10.1 causes a crash if a view contains more than one disabled but editable combo box and the user clicks one of them. A workaround was published in Apple Technical Q&A QA1142. This bug is fixed in Mac OS X 10.2, and the workaround is omitted here because Vermont Recipes uses only one combo box.

First, prepare your project files for Recipe 10 by updating the Build Version in the Application Settings to **10**. You will use this combo box only to control how the table is filtered for display, so there is no need to save it as a persistent data value in the document. You therefore don't have to increment the document version in VRDocument.m.

Step 1: Create a Combo Box in Interface Builder

Use Interface Builder to create a combo box. When you are done, the combo box should look like **Figure 10.1**.

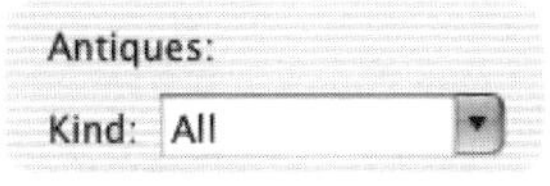

FIGURE 10.1 The finished combo box.

1. Open VRDocument.nib in Interface Builder and select the Text Fields tab view item.

2. From the Other palette, drag a combo box onto the Text Fields pane and position it near the upper right corner, leaving room above it for a static text field.

3. Drag a System Font Text item from the Views palette, position it to the left of the combo box, and make it a label for the combo box with the text **Kind:**.

4. Drag another System Font Text item into the Text Fields pane and position it above the label. Name this static text item **Antiques:**.

5. Position all of the new items appropriately using the Aqua guides, and group the combo box and its labels so they will not become separated when dragged.

6. With the combo box selected, set the Options in the NSComboBox Info panel to Editable, Selectable, Enabled, "Uses data source," and Completes. You will learn the significance of the "Uses data source" and Completes settings in Step 3. In the Layout area, make sure it is Scrollable so that long entries will scroll into view as the user types.

    Finally, in the Send Action area, select the "Only on enter" send action if it isn't already selected. "Only on enter" is the default for combo boxes because a combo box is both a text field and a button. From the programming topic: "NSComboBox relies heavily upon its cell class, NSComboBoxCell. NSComboBoxCell is a NSTextFieldCell subclass, which combines a text field cell with a button cell." To the extent that it is a text field, it is an unusual text field in that it is meant to act as if it were a button. That is, it's supposed to send an action message when you press Enter, but it's supposed to act like a text field and move focus to the next key view without sending an action message when you press Tab or click elsewhere. Its pop-up menu is a button, pure and simple, so the action message is sent when the user chooses a menu item, too. You will connect the action method in Step 4.

Step 2: Write the Code for the Combo Box in Project Builder

The steps for implementing the combo box follow a severely truncated version of the checklist you first created in Recipe 2, Step 2. The interesting new material in this recipe is the creation and use of the data source, which you will deal with in Step 3.

1. USER CONTROL OUTLET VARIABLES AND ACCESSORS. In the header file VRMainWindowController.h, declare a new outlet to access the combo box, after the Form section, as follows:

    ```
    // Combo Box
    IBOutlet NSComboBox *antiqueKindComboBox;
    ```

    Still in the header file, also declare an accessor for this outlet after the Form subsection of the ACCESSORS section of the VRTextFieldController category, as follows:

    ```
    // Combo Box
    - (NSComboBox *)antiqueKindComboBox;
    ```

    In the category source file VRTextFieldController.m, define the accessor after the Form subsection of the ACCESSORS section, as follows:

    ```
    // Combo Box

    - (NSComboBox *)antiqueKindComboBox {
        return antiqueKindComboBox;
    }
    ```

    Because this combo box will be used only to specify how the table is filtered, there is no need for data variables and accessors, notification variables and observers, GUI update methods, or storage methods. In this respect, this combo box is similar to the Beeper command pop-down menu button you created in Recipe 2, Step 6. It serves only to send an action message that will control the table's display.

2. ACTION METHODS. In Recipe 2, Step 6, you wrote two action methods for the Beeper pull-down menu, one for each of its two menu items. Here, you will take a different course and write a single action method for the combo box as a whole, basing the action to be taken on the text of the menu item the user chose.

    In the header file VRMainWindowController.h, after the Form subsection of the ACTIONS section of the VRTextFieldController category, add the following:

```
// Combo Box
- (IBAction) filterAntiqueRecordsAction:(id)sender;
```

In the category source file VRTextFieldController.m, define this action method, after the Form subsection of the ACTIONS section, as follows:

```
// Combo Box

- (IBAction)filterAntiqueRecordsAction:(id)sender {
    NSBeep();
}
```

The call to the NSBeep() function is a temporary placeholder to allow you to compile and run the application when you have finished this recipe. When you get around to creating the table itself in Recipe 11, you will come back to this action method and provide code to tell the table to display its contents according to the chosen filter.

3. **HELP TAGS.** Add a help tag to the combo box: "Choose the kind of antiques to display."

4. **INITIAL FIRST RESPONDER AND NEXT KEY VIEW.** Use Interface Builder to integrate the combo box into the key loop for the Text Fields tab. Disconnect the current next key view for the Address form and reconnect it to the combo box. Then connect the combo box to its next key view, the Integer text field.

Step 3: Create a Data Source for the Combo Box

Because the role of this combo box is simply to choose a string representing one of several kinds of antiques, by far the simplest way to define the list of available choices would be to use Interface Builder to insert names into the combo box's internal list. To see how you would do this, go to the Attributes pane of the NSComboBox Info panel and deselect the "Uses data source" option. The controls that appear in the Items area at the bottom of the pane enable you to add items to the combo box's internal list. You can click the plus sign (+) and type a new item in the editable text box as many times as you have items to add, and you can reorder the items in the list area by dragging them. NSComboBox implements several methods that let you work with internal list items created in this manner.

However, in this recipe you will do it the hard way for the sake of the learning experience, so reselect the "Uses data source" option and create a data source programmatically.

1. In Step 1, you used Interface Builder to specify that this combo box will use an external data source to hold and manage the user's choices, instead of its own internal list, and in Step 4, you will use Interface Builder to connect the window controller as the combo box's data source. You will now instantiate an NSMutableArray object in the window controller to hold the available choices, because a mutable array has exactly the properties you want: namely, the ability to hold an open-ended number of NSString objects, the ability to access them by index, and the ability to add and delete elements once you have set up an interface for letting the user expand or contract the choices that are permanently available as combo box menu items. (You will not implement the ability to modify the available choices until Recipe 11.)

   In the SimpleComboBox example provided with the Developer Tools, the data source is the application's NSDocument subclass. That example is very simple, and the user's choice is saved in the document. Here, the data source will service a combo box that does nothing more than control the display of another object in the GUI, and the user's choice will not be saved. Therefore, it makes more sense for you to use VRMainWindowController as the data source in the Vermont Recipes application.

   Start by declaring an instance variable for the data in VRMainWindowController.h immediately after the `antiqueKindComboBox` outlet, as follows:

   `NSMutableArray *antiqueKinds;`

   There is no need to give other classes access to this array, and it will not be saved or support undo and redo. Therefore you will not declare accessor methods for it but instead simply use the instance variable itself in those few places where the window controller must access it. You will revisit this decision in Recipe 11.

2. The initial list of choices available in the combo box should be established when the window opens, so you should accomplish this initialization in the window controller's `init` method. The array is not a user interface object, so its initialization does not have to wait until the `awakeFromNib` method is called after the nib file is fully initialized.

   In the `init` method of VRMainWindowController.m, after the [self setShouldCloseDocument:YES] message, insert these statements:

```
// Combo Box
antiqueKinds = [[[NSArray arrayWithObjects:
        @"All", @"Rag Dolls", @"Milking Stools", @"Quilts",
        @"Dry Sinks", @"Game Boards", @"Pocket Knives", nil]
        sortedArrayUsingSelector:@selector(caseInsensitiveCompare:
        )] retain];
```

NSArray's `sortedArrayUsingSelector:` method produces an array sorted according to the comparator selector used in the parameter. Here, you use NSString's `caseInsensitiveCompare:` method to sort the array alphabetically without regard to case.

NSArray's `arrayWithObjects:` class method is a convenience method that allocates a new array object and populates it with the objects listed in the parameter. Notice that the parameter list ends with `nil`; the `arrayWithObjects:` method requires `nil` as the final item in the list.

You did not internationalize this code. You have learned enough to know how to do this yourself. I leave out the required code here because this implementation will be changed in Recipe 11 and internationalized there.

Like all such convenience methods, `arrayWithObjects:` returns an autoreleased object, so you must explicitly retain it to keep it alive while the window is open. This in turn gives you the responsibility to deallocate it, which you will do when the window closes. Add this statement to the `dealloc` method in VRMainWindowController.m:

```
[antiqueKinds release];
```

3. An initial default choice should be displayed in the combo box when the Text Fields tab view item is first selected. Because this does depend on the nib file's having been fully unarchived and initialized, you must take care of it in the `awakeFromNib` method of VRMainWindowController.m. The ideal default value is All. This choice appears first in the array as you initialized it, so you might be tempted to simply set the default string value in the combo box to array element 0. However, you have to consider the possibility that the array might eventually contain a value that alphabetizes before All, so you should choose the All item by name instead. If you were programming paranoically rather than just defensively, you might also take account of the possibility that the array might not always contain the value All, but you can avoid that here because you will later take steps to make sure the user cannot delete the All choice.

In addition, you should set the combo box to use a pop-up menu without a vertical scroll bar because there are only 5 choices in the initial list. A combo box defaults to show a vertical scroll bar, but according to the *Aqua Human Interface Guidelines,* you should use this default only if the list contains more than 12 items. To avoid any problems if you add built-in choices in a later version of Vermont Recipes, it makes sense to test the number of methods at initialization time before turning off the default.

Add these statements at the beginning of the **awakeFromNib** method:

```
if ([antiqueKinds count] <= 12)
    [[self antiqueKindComboBox] setHasVerticalScroller:NO];
[[self antiqueKindComboBox] setStringValue:
    [antiqueKinds objectAtIndex:
    [self comboBox:[self antiqueKindComboBox]
    indexOfItemWithStringValue:@"All"]]];
```

You will write the **comboBox:indexOfItemWithStringValue:** method used here in the next instruction.

If you were creating the combo box programmatically, you would also have to call **setUsesDataSource:YES** and **SetDataSource:self** here, in that order. However, in Vermont Recipes, you are using Interface Builder to tell the combo box that it uses an external data source instead of its internal list and to connect its **dataSource** outlet to the window controller.

4. Finally, you must implement the data source methods. The first two are required whenever you use an external data source.

First, add a method to your data source (the window controller) named **numberOfItemsInComboBox:**; the combo box will call this method to determine how many items are available for display. The AppKit's NSComboBoxDataSource informal protocol declares this method, so you should not declare it in your window controller's header. Because all combo boxes in your application that use external data sources will call this method, you must test which combo box is requesting the information before you respond. In the source file VRMainWindowController.m, add this method definition before the ACTIONS section:

```
#pragma mark DATA SOURCES

// Combo Boxes

- (int)numberOfItemsInComboBox:(NSComboBox *)comboBox {
    if (comboBox == [self antiqueKindComboBox]) {
        return [antiqueKinds count];
    }
    return 0;
}
```

Second, add a method in the same place to tell the combo box how to retrieve the object at a specified index. The NSComboBoxDataSource informal protocol declares this method, as well. Immediately after the definition of the **numberOfItemsInComboBox:** method, insert this definition:

```
- (id)comboBox:(NSComboBox *)comboBox
      objectValueForItemAtIndex:(int)index {
    if (comboBox == [self antiqueKindComboBox]) {
        return [antiqueKinds objectAtIndex:index];
    }
    return nil;
}
```

The NSComboBoxDataSource informal protocol also declares two optional data source methods. They are relevant only if you have turned on autocompletion, as you have done in Interface Builder for this combo box. Autocompletion will still work if you do not implement these two methods, but it will work faster with them. Furthermore, as you will implement these methods here, autocompletion will also work without regard to the case of the text typed by the user.

Immediately after the definition of the `comboBox:objectValueForItemAtIndex:` method, insert the definition below. The combo box will use it to perform a fast search for a matching string as the user types. If a match is found, it will synchronize the selected item with the text field's contents. It returns -1 if no match is found.

```
- (unsigned int)comboBox:(NSComboBox *)comboBox
      indexOfItemWithStringValue:(NSString *)string {
    if (comboBox == [self antiqueKindComboBox]) {
        return [antiqueKinds indexOfObject: string];
    }
    return -1;
}
```

Immediately after the `comboBox:indexOfItemWithStringValue:` method, define the method that the combo box will use to extract a proposed completed string from the data source when it finds a partial match with what the user is typing. Since you have turned on autocompletion, the combo box will send this message to the data source every time the user types a character into the combo box. This method returns the entire contents of the first item in the list whose leading characters match the partial string typed by the user, without regard to case. The `comboBox:indexOfItemWithStringValue:` method uses this completed string to select the matching item in the list. (Note that the `completedString:` parameter is mislabeled; in reality, it is the incoming partial string typed by the user. The method's return value is the matching completed string. The current documentation for the protocol fudges this misnomer by referring to the parameter value as `uncompletedString`, although the protocol's header file does not use this term. I prefer `partialString`, derived from the NSFormatter terminology.)

```
- (NSString *)comboBox:(NSComboBox *)comboBox
      completedString:(NSString *)partialString {
    if (comboBox == [self antiqueKindComboBox]) {
        int idx;
        for (idx= 0; idx< [antiqueKinds count]; idx++) {
            NSString *testItem =
                [antiqueKinds objectAtIndex:idx];
            if ([[testItem commonPrefixWithString:partialString
                options:NSCaseInsensitiveSearch] length] ==
                [partialString length]) {
                return testItem;
            }
        }
    }
    return @"";
}
```

In this method, you have followed a different strategy for finding a case-insensitive match from that used in Apple's SimpleComboBox example. Here, you use NSString's convenience method, `commonPrefixWithString:options:`, to find any common prefix, then you test its length against that of the text the user has so far typed to detect a potential match. Your code here is simpler than that in Apple's example. It has not been tested for comparative speed with an array containing many choices, but a combo box would be a poor user interface choice anyway if the list contains enough items to affect its responsiveness.

Step 4: Add Full Drag-and-Drop Support to the Combo Box

There is no need for a formatter or live undo and redo in the combo box, but one extra that might be useful is the ability to drag text onto the combo box. Implementing this capability is a simple matter of adapting the techniques you learned in Recipe 8 and Recipe 9, Step 6.

1. Begin by creating a new category to add dragging destination capability to the combo box. Create two new Cocoa Objective-C class files, one named NSComboBox+VRDragTarget.h and the other named NSComboBox+VRDragTarget.m. Place each in the existing Categories group, and add your customary identifying comments to them.

2. The header file NSComboBox+VRDragTarget.h consists of the following lines:

```
#import <AppKit/NSComboBox.h>

@interface NSComboBox (VRDragTarget)

@end
```

3. The source file NSComboBox+VRDragTarget.m is as follows:

```
#import "NSComboBox+VRDragTarget.h"
#import <Cocoa/Cocoa.h>

@implementation NSComboBox (VRDragTarget)
- (unsigned int)draggingEntered:(id <NSDraggingInfo>)sender {
    NSDragOperation sourceDragMask =
        [sender draggingSourceOperationMask];
    NSPasteboard *sourcePasteboard =
        [sender draggingPasteboard];
    if ([[sourcePasteboard types] containsObject:
        NSStringPboardType]) {
        if (sourceDragMask & NSDragOperationCopy) {
            [[self window] makeFirstResponder:self];
            if ([sender draggingSource] == [self currentEditor]) {
                [self abortEditing];
            } else {
                return NSDragOperationCopy;
            }
        }
    }
    return NSDragOperationNone;
}

@end
```

4. Finally, you register the combo box to receive dropped text by adding the following line to the end of the registerDragTypesForTextFieldsTab method in the category source file NSTextFieldController.m:

```
[[self antiqueKindsComboBox] registerForDraggedTypes:
    [NSArray arrayWithObject:NSStringPboardType]];
```

Step 5: Read the Source Files into the Nib File and Connect the Actions

You must inform the nib file of the new outlet and action you have created, then connect them to the new combo box.

1. In Interface Builder, select the Classes tab in the nib file window, then choose Classes > Read Files. In the resulting dialog, select the header file in which you have created the outlet and action, VRMainWindowController.h, then click the Parse button.

2. Control-drag from the File's Owner icon to the combo box, select the **antiqueKindComboBox** outlet in the File's Owner Info panel, and click Connect.

3. Control-drag from the combo box to the File's Owner icon, select the target outlet, select the **antiqueKindAction:** action, and click Connect.

Step 6: Build and Run the Application

Build and run the application and test the operation of the new combo box.

If you click the combo box and hold down the mouse, the combo box acts like an ordinary pop-up menu. If you click and release, the menu stays open as you would expect. In either case, it shows only 5 items at a time but allows you to scroll to see others (you selected the 5-item limit in Interface Builder in Step 1). If it contained more than 12 items, it would have a vertical scroll bar to make scrolling of a long list easier.

Try typing something in the box. If you start with a letter that coincides with the first letter of one of the built-in choices, the entire matching choice appears in the box. The letters added by autocompletion are selected, so that you can keep typing if you meant to type a different word or phrase. If you continue typing a word or phrase that does not appear in the list, the autocompletion text disappears and you are allowed to enter a custom value. If you start by typing some other letter, no autocompletion text appears at all and you can enter a value as if this were a standard text field.

Conclusion

Some people disparage combo boxes as poor user interface design. But the use of a combo box here and in the next recipe demonstrates that they do have a legitimate place in your portfolio of user controls.

In Recipe 11, you will create a table displaying the description and kind of every item in an imaginary antiques inventory. In the process, you will finish writing the action method for the combo box so that it will actively filter the inventory items displayed in the table. Although the user will be free to enter custom kinds in the inventory, the combo box can still filter them by virtue of its unique ability to accept typed values that do not appear in its built-in list or data source.

You will also learn in Recipe 11 one way to let the user add items to the combo box's permanent list of choices.

RECIPE 11

Table Views

A table view—or table, for short—is an instance of Cocoa's NSTableView class. It is designed to display potentially large amounts of data in a grid or spreadsheet, usually scrollable, representing an unlimited number of records (the rows) containing multiple fields (the columns).

Like the combo box you worked with in the previous recipe, a table displays data by using a helper object known as a *data source*. While the use of a data source is optional in the NSComboBox class you studied in Recipe 10, it is mandatory in a table view. A table has no internal data store analogous to a combo box's internal list. The table view is, as its name emphasizes, strictly a view object, separate and apart from its data store.

The data source with which you will work in this recipe is more complex than the one you engineered in Recipe 10. Because of this, you will find it necessary to distinguish between the data itself and the data source. The data a user adds to the

table in Recipe 11 is held in an NSMutableArray object in the application's model (unlike the fixed display option strings made available to the user through the combo box in Recipe 10, which an array in the window controller housed). The table's data source, on the other hand, is simply a set of methods for accessing the data and is therefore treated as a controller object.

Because the user can modify the table's contents and save them to disk, the table requires this more careful distinction between the role of the data and the role of the data source in accordance with the Model-View-Controller (MVC) paradigm. As you learn about these complexities, you will also apply techniques developed here to the combo box to make it, too, user-modifiable.

The data displayed by the table in this recipe will be an imaginary antique dealer's inventory, and your users (not to mention the IRS and state tax authorities) will want the data to be saved in persistent storage for later use and examination. The NSMutableArray object holding the inventory data will therefore be declared in one of the application's model objects, VRTextFieldModel. Similarly, although some of the combo box's choices will remain coded in the window controller, an array of user additions to the fixed list of antique kinds will be held in another NSMutableArray object in the same VRTextFieldModel model object that holds the table's data.

Neither these arrays nor the model object that holds them is the data source, as Cocoa defines that term. Instead, the data source is the object in which the methods required by the data source protocol are defined. This is apparent from the fact that you connect the **datasource** outlet in Interface Builder to the object that implements the data source protocol methods, not necessarily to the object that contains the data itself. Although the documentation loosely refers to the data source as the object holding the data, you will see in this recipe that you can use multiple objects containing alternative versions of the data, and they can be located in any object. The table's data source methods, declared in the NSTableDataSource informal protocol, serve as a funnel through which you pour data into the view object for display. They function as a controller, not a model.

You can define both the data and the protocol methods in the same Cocoa class, as you did in Recipe 10, but you're not required to. Because Recipe 10 had fixed combo box choices, it was easy to think of them as part of the controller rather than as pieces of data. However, the data with which you'll deal in Recipe 11 is modifiable, and MVC design principles suggest that you separate it from its controller. The data source methods mediate between view objects—here the combo box and the table view— and the model objects that hold the data to display. Applying the MVC paradigm, you will therefore declare the data source protocol methods in the main window controller, along with the code that controls the associated combo box and table view. You will code the arrays and their accessors in a separate model object, where they will be readily available for storage to disk using the document's storage facilities.

Recipe 11 will wrap up Section 2 of *Vermont Recipes*. Although Cocoa offers additional user controls, such as outlines, browsers, steppers, and progress bars, you will have learned more than enough to create them yourself in your own applications.

First, prepare your project files for Recipe 11 by updating the Build Version in the Application Settings to **11**. You'll use the table to add data, so you'll need to save it to persistent storage in the document. However, you'll defer the document storage code to Recipe 12, where you will learn a new Cocoa technique for saving data, known as *keyed archiving*. You therefore needn't increment the document version in VRDocument.m for Recipe 11.

Step 1: Create a Table View and Three Push-buttons in Interface Builder

Use Interface Builder to add a table view and three buttons to the Text Fields tab view item. When you're done, you'll have placed this new group of controls below the combo box, as in **Figure 11.1**.

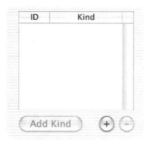

FIGURE 11.1 The table and three buttons.

The table view will display multiple rows, each corresponding to a record in an antique dealer's inventory. The inventory can be quite large, so you'll enable the table's vertical scroll bar to allow the user to view all of the records. The table will have only two columns, one showing each inventory item's unique identification number and the other showing the item's kind or classification. In a real inventory application, such a table would have many additional columns to display data such as an item's age, provenance, cost, and markup. You can easily extrapolate what you learn here to create tables with more fields. The two columns included in this table are special: One illustrates a way to assign a unique ID number to each item added to the inventory, and the other is used to filter the records to display selected kinds of antiques. The combo box you wrote in Recipe 10 will enable a user to select any one kind of antique for display.

Two of the buttons, bearing plus (+) and minus (–) signs, will add and remove items from the inventory. The words Add and Remove might make the buttons more descriptive, but users have become accustomed to + and – for these purposes. You will also code alternative means by which the user can add and remove antiques: Namely, to add an item, you can press the Command-plus (+) combination on the keyboard, and to delete an item, you can select it and press Command-minus (–) or Delete.

One important feature of the table you will create in this recipe is the ability to add new records to the table and edit them in place—that is, within the table itself. Until very recently, other examples of Cocoa table views have instructed the reader to provide a separate text field in which to enter data for a new record, which requires the user to click a button to transfer the data from the text field into a new row in the table. Years ago, Microsoft Excel required its users to enter spreadsheet data in a separate text field, but Excel eventually implemented in-cell editing. Here you will learn how to implement this more modern user interface technology in your own applications, saving the screen real estate that a separate text field unnecessarily consumes.

The third button, labeled Add Kind, allows the user to add choices to the combo box's pop-up menu. You learned in Recipe 10 that while combo boxes allow typing of custom choices into the control's integral text field, the *Aqua Human Interface Guidelines* counsel against automatically making such additions permanent. Nothing in the *Guidelines* prohibits giving the user the option to add choices permanently, however. In this recipe, you will learn one unobtrusive technique for doing this. Whenever the user selects a row in the table, the Add Kind button becomes enabled if the selected antique's kind is not already present in the combo box's list of choices. The user won't see a distracting alert sheet and can easily ignore the button, but the ability to add a classification will be apparent and easily exercised. A user who notices a frequent need to filter the table by a custom kind not provided as a built-in classification can simply select an antique exemplifying that classification and click the Add Kind button. The new filtering classification will be saved to disk with the document and restored when the document is read back from disk.

1. Open VRDocument.nib in Interface Builder and select the Text Fields tab view item.

2. From the Data palette, drag an NSTableView item onto the Text Fields pane of the main application window and position it below the combo box, using the Aqua guides to line it up with the left edge of the combo box's label and the proper distance below it. Drag the lower-right resize handle to widen the table until its right edge is the proper distance from the right edge of the tab view item. Leave room below the bottom of the table for a standard push-button, and make sure the dummy text in the table is not cut off in the middle of a row. You will have to click in an empty area of the window to make the tab view navigation buttons visible so you can prevent the new buttons from overlapping them.

3. Configure the table view so that it contains two columns with column headers and a single vertical scroll bar. A table view is a little tricky to manage in Interface Builder because the palette embeds it within a scroll view. You should watch the title of the Info Panel to make sure you are working with the table view. A fresh Interface Builder table view comes with two columns and two scroll bars, so all you have to do is deselect the Horizontal Scrollbar checkbox in the Attributes pane of the Info Panel. Set up the attributes pane so that the only selected check boxes are Allows Empty Selection, Vertical, Allows Reordering, and Display Column Headers.

4. Next, configure the table's two columns. First, select the left column header. You will have to experiment with a combination of clicks and double-clicks until you see the NSTableColumn Info Panel. In the Info Panel's Attributes pane, give the left column a Column Title of `ID` and an Identifier of `antiqueID`. Do the same thing to give the right column a Column Title of `Kind` and an Identifier of `antiqueKind`. The Column Title is cosmetic, but the Identifier is the key—literally—to a technique known as *key-value coding*, which you will encounter in Step 3. It is very important that the identifier of each column be identical to the name of its instance variable, declared in the corresponding code file for antiques records.

5. Drag a push-button from the Views palette and place it below the table using the Aqua guides. The left edge of the button should align with the left edge of the table. Entitle the button `Add Kind` and size it to fit. Deselect the Enabled button in the NSButton Info Panel. The button should start out disabled so your code can enable it when the user selects an antique in the table whose kind is not yet installed in the combo box's list of filtering choices.

6. Drag two round buttons from the Cocoa Views palette and place them below the table to the right of the Add Kind button. The buttons are too big, so turn them into small round buttons by selecting the Small checkbox in the NSButton Info Panel's Attributes pane. This makes them the same height as the Add Kind button.

The prettiest + and − buttons use graphic images for the + and − signs, but it is easier to use text. Select the title field of the round button on the left for editing and type **+**; do the same with the button on the right and make its title **-**. I will refer to these as the New and Delete buttons. Select the centered button in the Alignment section of the NSButton Info Panel to enter the text in both round buttons. The + and − signs are still not centered vertically, and they are too small. For each button, select the title, choose Format > Font > Show Fonts, and in the dialog change the size to 14 points. Position the Delete button in line with the right edge of the table and the proper distance below it, and position the New button the proper distance to the left of the Delete button and on the same line.

Finally, deselect the Enabled button in the NSButton Info Panel for the Delete button, since you can't delete a record from the table until you've selected that record. Leave the New button enabled.

Step 2: Write the Basic Code for the Table and Buttons in Project Builder

You will write the basic code for the table and the three push-buttons all at once in this step, using the standard checklist you first created in Recipe 2, Step 2.

The code for the three push-buttons will be minimal, as was the code for the Quantum Slider buttons you created in Recipe 3, Step 3.2, and the combo box you created in Step 2 of this recipe, because these buttons are action-oriented controls. They initiate changes to the GUI rather than modifying the data.

Even the code for the table will be somewhat truncated for now, because you will not write the data storage routines for the antiques inventory until Recipe 12.

I'll defer the interesting code in Recipe 11 to subsequent steps. This will include, for example, the table view's data source protocol methods, methods to implement the display of a filtered subset of the antiques inventory, and methods to add custom choices to the built-in combo box pop-up menu.

1. **USER CONTROL OUTLET VARIABLES AND ACCESSORS.** In the header file VRMainWindowController.h, declare new outlets to access the table view and all three new buttons after the Combo Box section, as follows:

    ```
    // Antiques table
    IBOutlet VRAntiquesTableView *antiquesTable;
    IBOutlet NSButton *newAntiqueButton;
    IBOutlet NSButton *deleteAntiqueButton;
    IBOutlet NSButton *addAntiqueKindButton;
    ```

    You haven't yet declared the VRAntiquesTableView class referred to in the first instance variable declaration. You will declare it as a sub-subclass of NSTableView in Step 13, where you will learn how to intercept **keyDown** events in the table to implement a Command-key equivalent to delete a selected antiques record. You won't be able to compile the application until you declare this class. (If you insist on compiling before then, just declare the **antiquesTable** instance variable's type as NSTableView for now, and do the same in the accessor methods you are about to write. Remember to change these references back to VRAntiquesTableView when you get to Step 13.)

    At the top of the VRMainWindowController.h header file, import the VRAntiquesTableView header file by adding the following line at the end of the

#import directives above the @interface compiler directive. (Comment it out for now if you are temporarily referring to NSTableView instead of VRAntiquesTableView.)

```
#import "VRAntiquesTableView.h"
```

Near the end of the header file, at the end of the ACCESSORS section of the VRTextFieldController category, declare the accessors for these four instance variables, as follows:

```
// Antiques table
- (VRAntiquesTableView *)antiquesTable;
- (NSButton *)newAntiqueButton;
- (NSButton *)deleteAntiqueButton;
- (NSButton *)addAntiqueKindButton;
```

In the category source file VRTextFieldController.m, define the accessor methods after the Combo Box subsection of the ACCESSORS section, as follows:

```
// Antiques table

- (VRAntiquesTableView *)antiquesTable {
        return antiquesTable;
}

- (NSButton *)newAntiqueButton {
        return newAntiqueButton;
}

- (NSButton *)deleteAntiqueButton {
        return deleteAntiqueButton;
}

- (NSButton *)addAntiqueKindButton {
        return addAntiqueKindButton;
}
```

The three buttons are used only to issue commands affecting the GUI, so you don't need to write data variables and accessors, notification variables and observers, GUI update methods, or storage methods for them. The next few instructions, until you get to the action methods instruction, therefore deal only with the table view.

2. **DATA VARIABLES AND ACCESSORS.** In the header file VRTextFieldModel.h, declare an instance variable for the antiques array after the existing instance variable declarations, as shown below. This is declared as a mutable array so the user can

add and remove records. You will write a separate class for the records themselves in Step 3. For now, you can design and code the GUI and the basic table routines without knowing how you'll structure the records contained in the array.

```
// Antiques table values
NSMutableArray *antiques;
```

Declare the corresponding accessor method at the end of the ACCESSORS section of the header file, as shown below. You do not need a **set** accessor method for the array because you will never create more than one of these arrays in the document. You will allocate and initialize the one empty **antiques** array in the Initialization instruction, below. Later, in Step 4, you will write code to add new records to the array and to delete records from the array when the user clicks the New and Delete buttons below the table view.

```
// Antiques array values

- (NSMutableArray *)antiques;
```

Define the accessor at the end of the ACCESSORS section of the source file VRTextFieldModel.m as follows:

```
// Antiques array values

- (NSMutableArray *)antiques {
        return antiques;
}
```

3. **NOTIFICATION VARIABLES.** The values stored in the array will change from time to time as the user adds and deletes records. These changes will require the application to update its GUI, as do changes to any other model object data variable. Therefore, to maintain a separation between the model and view objects, you need to use notifications to inform the window controller that the **antiques** array has changed.

In the header file VRTextFieldModel.h, declare the notification variable after the **@end** directive at the bottom of the file, as follows:

```
// Antiques table values
extern NSString
        *VRTextFieldModelAntiquesArrayChangedNotification;
```

Near the top of the source file VRTextFieldModel.m, define the notification variable at the end of the NOTIFICATIONS section before the **@implementation** directive, as follows:

```
// Antiques table values
NSString *VRTextFieldModelAntiquesArrayChangedNotification =
    @"TextFieldModel antiquesArray Changed Notification";
```

4. **GUI UPDATE METHODS.** In the header file VRMainWindowController.h, declare a specific interface update method at the end of the "INTERFACE MANAGEMENT - Specific updaters" section of the VRTextFieldController category, as follows:

```
// Antiques table
- (void)updateAntiquesTable:(NSNotification *)notification;
```

Define the update method in the category source file VRTextFieldController.m at the end of the "INTERFACE MANAGEMENT - Specific updaters" section, as follows:

```
- (void)updateAntiquesTable:(NSNotification *)notification {
    [self filterAntiqueRecords];
}
```

You haven't yet done enough design work on the application to know exactly how you will update the table view when records are added to or deleted from the **antiques** array. You do know, however, that the **antiques** array will have to be filtered at least some of the time—namely, when the user has employed the combo box to choose a specific kind of antique for display. It is reasonable to anticipate that you will perform the filtering operation in a single method and that the same method might easily handle the job when the user chooses no filtering at all (that is, filtering for all of the records). You therefore temporize for now and simply call a **filterAntiqueRecords** method that you will write later, in Step 7.

5. **NOTIFICATION OBSERVERS.** Register the window controller as an observer of the notification that will trigger the GUI updater method. Insert the following message at the end of the **registerNotificationObserversForTextFieldsTab** method in the WINDOW MANAGEMENT section of the category source file VRTextFieldController.m.

```
// Antiques table
[[NSNotificationCenter defaultCenter] addObserver:self
    selector:@selector(updateAntiquesTable:)
    name:VRTextFieldModelAntiquesArrayChangedNotification
    object:[self document]];
```

6. **ACTION METHODS.** All three of the new buttons associated with the table view require action methods, but the table view itself does not. The user will be able to edit cells in the table by double-clicking them and typing, and the user will also be able to add records to the table by clicking the New button or pressing

the Command-plus (+) key combination, but you'll handle both of these user actions in new ways in later steps. So for now you'll just write action methods for the three buttons.

The declarations are easy. At the end of the ACTIONS section of the VRTextFieldController category in the VRMainWindowController.h header file, add the following:

```
// Antiques table
- (IBAction)newAntiqueRecordAction:(id)sender;
- (IBAction)deleteAntiqueRecordAction:(id)sender;
- (IBAction)addAntiqueKindAction:(id)sender;
```

As in the case of the table view's GUI update methods, you don't yet know enough about the implementation of individual antiques records to flesh out the definitions of the action methods that add and remove records. All you know is that the user can click the New or Delete button or take certain alternative steps to accomplish these tasks. Similarly, you haven't yet designed a mechanism for adding new choices to the combo box. For now, therefore, you will simply write stub action method definitions and make a note to return to them later, in Steps 6 and 9, respectively.

```
// Antiques table

- (IBAction)newAntiqueRecordAction:(id)sender {
}

- (IBAction)deleteAntiqueRecordAction:(id)sender {
}

- (IBAction)addAntiqueKindAction:(id)sender {
}
```

Because you haven't filled in the stub action methods, you don't know yet what undo menu item titles will require localization via the Localizable.strings file.

7. **INITIALIZATION.** You have declared one instance variable, **antiques**, and it requires initialization. The initialization is easy, because the array always starts out empty when the user creates a new document, even if it will be filled shortly later by reading data from disk or obtaining data from the user at the keyboard.

    Near the end of the `initWithDocument:` method in the source file VRTextFieldModel.m, just before the preprocessor directive, insert this line:

    ```
    antiques = [[NSMutableArray array] retain];
    ```

The **array** method is a class method that allocates and returns an empty array. It is known as a *convenience method* because it performs the allocation and initialization tasks for you. Like all such convenience methods in Foundation, it returns the array to you autoreleased. That is, the array will disappear automatically in the next event loop if you don't retain it. Since you will use this array to hold antiques records as long as the document is open, you must retain it.

Because you retained the array, you own it and you are responsible for releasing it. You will do this when the document is closed, in its **dealloc** method. At the end of the **dealloc** method in VRTextFieldModel.m, insert this line:

```
[[self antiques] release];
```

You will defer data storage issues to Recipe 12, where you will learn about keyed archiving.

8. **GUI UPDATE METHOD INVOCATION.** Records from disk may fill the **antiques** array as soon as the document opens, so you must ensure that the GUI is updated. In the category source file VRTextFieldController.m, add the following call at the end of the **updateTextFieldsTab** method:

```
// Antiques table
[self updateAntiquesTable:nil];
```

9. **DESCRIPTION METHOD.** You can add an entry for the antiques array to the **description** method in VRTextFieldModel.m, although the antiques array will always be empty at initialization. You don't need to see the entire method reproduced again here. Just append a line, **antiques,** to the long text string, with appropriate formatting characters, and add this message at the end:
```
[[self antiques] description].
```

10. **HELP TAGS.** Using Interface Builder, provide Help tags for the table ("Displays antiques by kind") and each of the three buttons (from left to right: "Add the selected antique's kind to the Kind menu," "Add a new antique," and "Delete a selected antique").

You have now set up the foundation on which you can finish coding the antiques inventory. The table view is far more complex than any user control you have created up to this point, yet the road map you devised in Recipe 2, Step 2, remains viable as a standardized and therefore less error-prone way to support this new user control.

The feature that differentiates a table from the other user controls you have encountered is that a table can hold a large number of complex data items. It is true that radio buttons, pop-up menus, and combo boxes, for example, offer a variety of options from which the user may choose, but the result of the user's choice is a single value. A table holds multiple complex values at once. It is like a form in this respect but unlimited in the number of items it can display.

Because of this difference, you need additional mechanisms in your code to handle a table and the data it displays. Chief among these are a separate data structure for the individual records in the table and separate user interaction mechanisms to add and remove the individual records from the table. You will tackle these in the next two steps.

Step 3: Create a New Model Class for Records

Before you write any code to add and remove individual antiques records and manipulate them in the table, you will provide a data structure for the records themselves. You could approach the task from the other end, simply deciding in the abstract, say, that each inventory item will be an instance of an undefined class named VRAntiqueRecord having standard accessors, then proceed directly to write methods to handle such a data structure. However, I find it more comfortable to deal first with the concrete job of defining the data structure.

One reason for my preference is that attempts to implement a new data structure sometimes lead to the realization that my initial design is fundamentally wrong. In this case, for example, I might eventually discover that it is better to code the record data structure as a Cocoa dictionary or array within the existing VRTextFieldModel class, as some examples do, rather than as a separate class of its own. If I write code to manipulate records as separate objects before making this discovery, I may have wasted a lot of time. In my mind, data comes before process.

You will therefore begin by creating a new model class for individual antique records. In the future, perhaps after beta testers of your application have had a chance to try it out, you may realize this data structure isn't appropriate. Perhaps, for example, your users have enormous inventories, and the use of a separate Cocoa object for each antique involves so much overhead that processing all of them is too slow. In such a scenario, you may have to make fundamental changes in any event, perhaps by adopting one of several available third-party SQL database products. It is very hard to predict performance in advance, however. Here you will assume that your target market is the typical ma-and-pa antiques dealer with no more than a few hundred items in the shop. It is unlikely that execution speed will become an issue, and considerations like ease of code maintenance are more important to your product's success.

A class to represent a single antique should be quite simple. It will need an instance variable for each attribute of the antique, where each instance variable corresponds to a field in the abstract idea of a record. In a real-world application, there might be many of these fields, such as age, provenance, markup, and price. To simplify this recipe, however, you will implement only two, the unique identification number of the antique and its kind or classification. You can easily flesh out the record later by adding instance variables using the same techniques. In addition to instance variables, a record will need initialization methods, accessor methods to get and set the value of each variable, a means to notify observers such as the window controller when a variable has changed value, access to the document's undo manager for undo support, and some means of rapid access to the variables in response to queries. You will also need storage methods, but you will defer those to Recipe 12.

In coding this small set of methods, bear in mind that you are creating a model object. It holds data. It doesn't care how the data is represented in the GUI.

1. You already know how to create a new pair of header and source files in Project Builder. Choose File > New File and use the Assistant to create a new Cocoa Objective-C class consisting of the two files VRAntiqueRecord.h and VRAntiqueRecord.m. Place them in the Models group in the project window's Groups & Files pane.

2. The header file VRAntiqueRecord.h is short and simple, as described above. This is the entire declaration of the antiques record class:

```objc
#import <Cocoa/Cocoa.h>

@class VRDocument;

@interface VRAntiqueRecord : NSObject {
    @private
    VRDocument *document;

    NSNumber *antiqueID;
    NSString *antiqueKind;
    // Insert other fields here.
}

#pragma mark INITIALIZATION

- (id)initWithDocument:(VRDocument *)inDocument;
- (id)initWithID:(NSNumber *)inID
        document:(VRDocument *)inDocument;
        // designated initializer

#pragma mark ACCESSORS
```

(continues on next page)

```
- (VRDocument *)document;
- (NSUndoManager *)undoManager;

- (void)setAntiqueID:(NSNumber *)inValue;
- (NSNumber *)antiqueID;

- (void)setAntiqueKind:(NSString *)inValue;
- (NSString *)antiqueKind;

@end

#pragma mark NOTIFICATIONS

extern NSString *VRAntiqueRecordChangedNotification;
```

You should, as usual, insert your standard comments and disclaimers at the beginning of the header file and at the top of the source file as well.

Only a few items in the header deserve mention.

You need a forward reference to the VRDocument class because some of the method declarations refer to this type. You will import the VRDocument class in the source file. You could just as well have imported it in the header file instead of using the forward reference, but it is generally preferable to hide as many implementation details as possible.

Two custom initialization methods are provided, one to create a record with a reference to its document but no ID, and the other, the designated initializer, to create a record with both. In this design, a unique ID and kind or classification of antique are required fields fundamental to the design of the application, so both are normally provided as parameters during initialization of the object. Other fields you might add to the record, such as price and markup, play no special role in database management and need not be included as parameters to initialization methods.

Turn now to implementation of each of these methods.

3. In the source file VRAntiqueRecord.m, import VRDocument.m and define the notification variable by adding these lines after the directive importing the header file:

```
#import "VRDocument.h"

#pragma mark NOTIFICATIONS

NSString *VRAntiqueRecordChangedNotification =
        @"AntiqueRecord Changed Notification";
```

4. In the same file, after the @implementation directive, add the following INITIALIZATION section:

```
#pragma mark INITIALIZATION

- (id)init {
    return [self initWithDocument:nil];
}



- (id)initWithDocument:(VRDocument *)inDocument {
    return [self initWithID:nil document:inDocument];
}

- (id)initWithID:(NSNumber *)inID document:(VRDocument *)inDocument {
    // Designated initializer.
    if (self = [super init]) {
        document = inDocument;

        [[self undoManager] disableUndoRegistration];
        [self setAntiqueID:inID];
        [self setAntiqueKind:NSLocalizedString(
                @"New", @"Kind of new antique record")];
        [[self undoManager] enableUndoRegistration];
    }
    return self;
}


- (void)dealloc {
    [[self antiqueID] release];
    [[self antiqueKind] release];
    [super dealloc];
}
```

There is nothing new here. The initialization methods, with a simple **init** method, a designated initializer, and a **dealloc** method, are familiar from several earlier recipes. The incoming **inID** object assigned to **antiqueID** will be created elsewhere, as you will see in Steps 4 and 5. Both of the instance variables, **antiqueID** and **antiqueKind**, are objects that will survive for the life of the document, so they require release in the **dealloc** method.

The **antiqueKind** is always initialized to the word New or its localized equivalent, to reflect a design decision that all new, unclassified antiques will be flagged as falling in a special New category. Empty **antiqueKind** fields will not be allowed. Make sure you add the string New to Localizable.strings.

Calls to **disableUndoRegistration** and **enableUndoRegistration** bracket the code initializing the **antiqueID** and **antiqueKind** variables as usual.

5. The accessor methods are almost standard. They include a method to access the document to which this record belongs and a method to access the document's undo manager. Insert the entire ACCESSORS section at the end of the source file VRAntiqueRecord.m, as follows:

```
#pragma mark ACCESSORS

- (VRDocument *)document {
    return document;
}

- (NSUndoManager *)undoManager {
    return [[self document] undoManager];
}

- (void)setAntiqueID:(NSNumber *)inValue {
    if (antiqueID != inValue) {
        [[[self undoManager] prepareWithInvocationTarget:self]
            setAntiqueID:antiqueID];
        [antiqueID release];
        antiqueID = [inValue copy];
        [[NSNotificationCenter defaultCenter]
            postNotificationName:
            VRAntiqueRecordChangedNotification
            object:[self document]];
    }
}

- (NSNumber *)antiqueID {
    return [[antiqueID retain] autorelease];
}

- (void)setAntiqueKind:(NSString *)inValue {
    if (antiqueKind != inValue) {
        [[[self undoManager] prepareWithInvocationTarget:self]
            setAntiqueKind:antiqueKind];
        [antiqueKind release];
```

```
          antiqueKind = [inValue copy];
          [[NSNotificationCenter defaultCenter]
                postNotificationName:
                VRAntiqueRecordChangedNotification
                object:[self doucment]];

     }
}


- (NSString *)antiqueKind {
    return [[antiqueKind retain] autorelease];
}
```

Here you code the two **set** accessor methods just as you have coded model object accessors throughout *Vermont Recipes*. In addition to assigning a new value to the instance variable and taking care of memory management, each of the **set** accessors records the action with the undo manager and posts a notification that the data has changed. The only implementation novelty is that you post the same notification, **VRAntiqueRecordChangedNotification**, in each **set** accessor, instead of posting a unique notification for each field as you did, for example, for the data associated with the NSForm object in Recipe 9. This is because you're treating the table as a single user control, whereas you treated the form as a matrix of individual text fields. Whenever a user modifies any field of any record in the table, the table view itself must be updated (Cocoa actually updates only that part of the table view that is currently visible, to maximize performance).

You must of course register the window controller to observe this notification, so that the **updateAntiquesTable:** method will be called to display the change in data when the user edits a record. The **updateAntiquesTable:** method will therefore be called both when the user edits a record and when the user adds or deletes records by virtue of the separate **VRTextFieldModelAntiques-ArrayChangedNotification** you registered in Step 2. At the end of the **registerNotificationObserversForTextFieldsTab** method in the WINDOW MANAGEMENT section of the VRTextFieldController.m category source file, add this message:

```
[[NSNotificationCenter defaultCenter]
    addObserver:self
    selector:@selector(updateAntiquesTable:)
    name:VRAntiqueRecordChangedNotification
    object:[self document]];
```

Although the record object's accessor methods are thus essentially identical in structure to those of any other model object, you will use them very differently.

As you'll see in Step 8, you will never call any of these accessors explicitly in your code except here, during initialization. How can this be? How will your application change the values of these data fields when the user edits cells in the table view? How will your application obtain the current values of these data fields when the table view needs to display them?

The answer to these questions lies in a remarkable feature of the Cocoa frameworks known as *key-value coding*. Newcomers usually find this Cocoa feature astonishing when they first come across it.

You saw a related notion earlier, in Recipe 1, Step 4.2.1, where you accessed the values of items in a Cocoa NSDictionary object by using their associated keys. However, the use of keys, or labels, for random access to unordered values in a dictionary of key-value pairs is not a radical idea. NSDictionary objects are implemented with hash tables to assure fast access to any value without regard to its position in a collection. So far as it goes, this is a nice idea but not particularly surprising.

What *is* surprising about key-value coding is that you can employ it to access the values of instance variables in a Cocoa object by using the variable's names as keys. Cocoa makes this possible by the manner in which it compiles objects, turning their instance variable names and associated values into a hashed dictionary. As you will see in Step 8, table views and other Cocoa view objects use this important Cocoa feature to access an object's variables with an `identifier`, which is nothing more than a string matching the name of the variable in your code. You usually specify a column's identifier in Interface Builder, as you did in Step 1 for the antiques table. This technique allows the user to look up the value of a particular variable very rapidly by name, at hash table speed, without regard to its position in the compiled object and no matter what column of the table it occupies. In fact, the user can drag the columns of a table into a different order, and the lookups will still succeed because the identifier moves with the column.

To tell the application which variable's value is wanted, you do not have to write specialized code in the table view to read the instance variable or call its accessor method for each column. Instead, a single pair of generic key-value methods, declared in Foundation's NSKeyValueCoding informal protocol and implemented in NSObject, handles the lookup. These methods take a couple of forms, but the two most often used are `valueForKey:` and `takeValue:forKey:`. Because these methods are implemented in NSObject, they are available to every descendant of NSObject, such as the VRAntiqueRecord object you have implemented here. These key-value coding methods allow you to write very simple, generalized code to obtain data values for a variety of complex user controls such as tables. They allow objects with instance variables or accessor methods to rival more traditional structures in data-handling speed, and they dramatically simplify the code required to manipulate data. In addition, the key-value coding mechanism automatically returns an object of the correct type, so you don't have to cast it to the desired type yourself.

An important detail of key-value coding is that the `takeValue:forKey:` method attempts to execute the `set` accessor associated with an instance variable before resorting to the instance variable itself. Among other things, this means the code in your `set` accessor that records it with the undo manager and posts a notification runs automatically every time your application calls `takeValue:forKey:` on any field of any record in the table. You will learn more about key-value coding and its use in Step 8.

That takes care of the VRAntiqueRecord class. Since a new document does not initialize any records but instead reads them in from disk or waits for the user to add them at the keyboard, the document class has no need to allocate or initialize a new record in its own initializers. What the document does need is methods to create and delete record objects when the application requires it. In the Vermont Recipes application, this is a job for the VRTextFieldModel object, managed by the VRDocument class. You will do this in the next step.

Step 4: Add and Remove Records in the Model Object

At the end of Step 2, after setting up the basic foundation for the table view, you decided that you next had to provide for two important items, the data structure of an individual record and a means to add and remove records from the inventory. You set up the record data structure in Step 3, and in this step you will write methods by which the model object can add and delete individual records. You wrote the VRAntiqueRecord class so as to make this task quite simple.

You will write code to display the records in the table view later, in Steps 6, 7, and 8.

1. In the header file VRTextFieldModel.h, after the existing `#import` directive near the beginning of the file, insert this line:

   ```
   #import "VRAntiqueRecord.h"
   ```

2. Still in the header file, add the following method declarations after the ACCESSORS section:

   ```
   #pragma mark ANTIQUES ARRAY METHODS

   - (void)newAntiqueRecord;
   ```

```
- (void)deleteAntiqueRecord:(VRAntiqueRecord *)record;
- (void)undeleteAntiqueRecord:(VRAntiqueRecord *)record;
```

3. In the source file VRTextFieldModel.m, define these three methods after the ACCESSORS section, as follows:

```
#pragma mark ANTIQUES ARRAY METHODS

- (void)newAntiqueRecord {
    VRAntiqueRecord *record = [[VRAntiqueRecord alloc]
            initWithID:[self uniqueAntiqueID]
            document:[self document]];
    [[[self undoManager] prepareWithInvocationTarget:self]
            deleteAntiqueRecord:record];
    [[self antiques] addObject:record];
    [record release];
    [[NSNotificationCenter defaultCenter] postNotificationName:
            VRTextFieldModelAntiquesArrayChangedNotification
            object:[self document]];
}

- (void)deleteAntiqueRecord:(VRAntiqueRecord *)record {
    [[[self undoManager] prepareWithInvocationTarget:self]
            undeleteAntiqueRecord:record];
    [[self antiques] removeObject:record];
    [[NSNotificationCenter defaultCenter] postNotificationName:
            VRTextFieldModelAntiquesArrayChangedNotification
            object:[self document]];
}

- (void)undeleteAntiqueRecord:(VRAntiqueRecord *)record {
    [[[self undoManager] prepareWithInvocationTarget:self]
            deleteAntiqueRecord:record];
    [[self antiques] addObject:record];
    [[NSNotificationCenter defaultCenter] postNotificationName:
            VRTextFieldModelAntiquesArrayChangedNotification
            object:[self document]];
}
```

These methods demonstrate some techniques that are interesting in their own right.

CREATING A NEW RECORD AND ADDING IT TO AN ARRAY. The newAntiqueRecord method follows a familiar pattern in creating a record and adding it to the antiques array.

It begins by allocating a new VRAntiqueRecord object and calling its designated initializer. It passes to the newly allocated record object a reference to the document and a unique identification number. You will learn how to generate the unique ID in Step 5. It then adds the new record to the `antiques` array by calling NSMutableArray's `addObject:` method, and it promptly releases the new record.

Allocating a new object and then releasing it in the same method is standard practice for adding a new object to a collection like the `antiques` array. Your invocation of NSObject's `alloc` method automatically retained the new record and gave you ownership of it. The standard methods for adding an object to a collection, such as NSMutableArray's `addObject:`, always retain the added object again and thereby give the collection ownership of it. You no longer need to control it yourself, so you release it to balance the `retain` of the `alloc` method. The record doesn't go away, because the array's `retain` has not yet been matched by a `release`.

UNDO AND REDO OF ADDED AND DELETED RECORDS. Let's deal next with the way this method handles undo registration for the actions of adding and deleting a record. Until now, you have set the values of simple data structures such as checkboxes that have binary `YES` or `NO` values and text fields that set a specific value. You accomplished undo registration for these in a single `set` accessor method by recording the same accessor method with the current data value.

You can't undo and redo adding and deleting records the same way. Take a delete operation, for example. Once you've added a record object to the `antiques` array, a `deleteAntiqueRecord:` method that calls the NSMutableArray method `removeObject:` can delete it. But you can't undo the delete operation by calling the same `deleteAntiqueRecord:` method with a different parameter. Instead, you must call a separate `undeleteAntiqueRecord:` method that adds the previously deleted record back into the array by calling the NSMutableArray `addObject:` method.

To implement undo of the deletion operation, you therefore record a separate method, the `undeleteAntiqueRecord:` method, along with the record object you're deleting. Both the `undeleteAntiqueRecord:` method and the deleted record itself are recorded into the undo stack, waiting for the user to choose Edit > Undo. When that happens, the undo manager calls the recorded `undeleteAntiqueRecord:` method to reinstate the deleted record saved on the undo stack. It also records the first method, `deleteAntiqueRecord:`, with the same record into the redo stack. One of the marvels of the undo mechanism in Cocoa is that it saves the deleted record for you indefinitely on the undo or redo stack, without requiring that you write code to set up any sort of deleted records cache. The deleted records that accumulate on the undo and redo stacks take up memory, of course, as would any undo caching mechanism. When the user saves or closes the document, they all disappear from memory as your application removes all pending undo actions.

You might at first wonder why you don't record the `newAntiqueRecord` method in the `deleteAntiqueRecord:` method instead of recording the special `undeleteAntiqueRecord:` method. The explanation should be apparent from the code. When the user chooses Edit > Undo to restore a deleted record to the array, the record already exists. Cocoa saved it on the undo stack, so you don't need to allocate and initialize it. But you do need this third method, `newAntiqueRecord`, to allocate and initialize a new record in the first place. The `newAntiqueRecord` method prepares for a possible undo by recording the `deleteAntiqueRecord:` method with the new record object, and thereafter the `newAntiqueRecord` method drops out of the undo/redo cycle.

You now have all the machinery in place for the application to create records for the array and delete them, with full undo and redo support for these actions. Because you have implemented undo and redo of record addition and deletion, you don't have to make any special effort to dirty the document when changes are made. Most available code examples for table views advise you to send a `[self udpateChangeCount:NSChangeDone]` message at critical points. Here, implementing undo and redo allows Cocoa to take care of this for you.

One aspect of creating a record still needs clearing up, however—namely, the generation of a unique identification number. Notice that `newAntiqueRecord` passes a unique ID to the new record, which it obtains by calling the `uniqueAntiqueID` convenience method. As you will see in the next step, this method returns a unique ID as an auto-released NSNumber object.

Step 5: Assign a Unique ID to Each New Record

In Step 4, `uniqueAntiqueID` was passed to the antique record's designated initializer. In this step, you will learn one way to generate and use a unique identification number. The technique I teach here is simple and serviceable, but it might not suit all circumstances.

You'll assign each antique in a Vermont Recipes document's **antiques** inventory what you might call a use-once-and-retire serial number, starting with 1 and proceeding sequentially. To implement this scheme, you need to initialize an instance variable to 0 in a new document. You will call it, aptly, `lastAntiqueID`. Every time a user at the keyboard adds a new antique to the database, the method assigns that item a unique antique ID 1 greater than `lastAntiqueID` and increments `lastAntiqueID`. An antique's ID is saved with it to disk and read back from disk, and `lastAntiqueID` is also saved with the document. When the user deletes an antique, its ID is deleted along with it and permanently retired; that is, lastAntiqueID does not change and the method does not keep a pool of unused IDs for reassignment.

In the Vermont Recipes application, a user can edit an antique's unique ID, but you'll institute safeguards to prevent the user from reusing or duplicating an ID less than or equal to lastAntiqueID. Allowing the user to edit the ID is, to speak plainly, nuts as a matter of application design, but I implement this feature here to show you how to code editing of multiple columns in a table view.

In your own applications, you should consider encapsulating the machinery to generate a unique ID in a small class of its own. Treating such a class as a black box for generating unique IDs would make it much easier to modify the ID scheme in the future. Here, you will just do it with code scattered throughout the existing application classes.

1. Start by adding the lastAntiqueID instance variable and corresponding accessor methods to VRTextFieldModel. These are data values and belong in the model.

    In the header file VRTextFieldModel.h, add this line after the declaration of the **antiques** array in the "Antiques table values" section of the instance variable declarations:

    ```
    int lastAntiqueID;
    ```

    You might want to use a data type with greater capacity than an integer for a more ambitious application, but this will do for your typical ma-and-pa antiques shop.

    Still in the header file, declare the accessor methods at the end of the "Antiques array values" subsection of the ACCESSORS section, as follows:

    ```
    - (void)setLastAntiqueID:(int)inValue;
    - (int)lastAntiqueID;
    ```

    Define the accessors in the ACCESSORS section of the source file VRTextField-Model.m, as follows:

    ```
    - (void)setLastAntiqueID:(int)inValue {
        lastAntiqueID = inValue;
    }

    - (int)lastAntiqueID {
        return lastAntiqueID;
    }
    ```

    There is no reason to provide for undo and redo or notifications because the generation of the lastAntiqueID value occurs entirely under the hood and doesn't involve the user.

In the `initWithDocument:` method of the VRTextFieldModel.m source file, initialize `lastAntiqueID` to 0. The next instruction will increment it.

```
[self setLastAntiqueID:0];
```

2. Next, provide methods to supply a new unique ID and, because you will need it to help the user edit IDs in the table, to test whether a given ID is unique.

In the header file VRTextFieldModel.h, at the top of the ANTIQUES ARRAY METHODS section, add these declarations:

```
- (NSNumber *)uniqueAntiqueID;
- (BOOL)isUniqueAntiqueID:(NSNumber *)inValue;
```

Add their definitions at the top of the ANTIQUES ARRAY METHODS section of the source file VRTextFieldModel.m, as follows:

```
- (NSNumber *)uniqueAntiqueID {
    int newID = [self lastAntiqueID] + 1;
    [self setLastAntiqueID:newID];
    return [NSNumber numberWithInt:newID];
}


- (BOOL)isUniqueAntiqueID:(NSNumber *)inValue {
    return ([inValue intValue] > [self lastAntiqueID]);
}
```

These methods switch back and forth between a standard C `int` data type and a Foundation NSNumber type, because you declared the `lastAntiqueID` variable as the former, while you declare a record object's unique ID as the latter in anticipation of implementing archiving in Recipe 12. Take care to keep the data types straight here. A less error-prone technique would use NSNumbers for the `lastAntiqueID` value throughout, but this method appears to be implemented correctly.

CONVENIENCE METHODS AND THE AUTORELEASE POLICY. Notice that the `uniqueAntiqueID` method returns an NSNumber without retaining it. A policy that applies throughout the Foundation classes, and that you should normally follow as well, is that convenience methods return the objects they create autoreleased. That is, the objects are automatically deallocated shortly after the calling method exits unless the calling method explicitly retains them. This is a useful policy, because convenience methods very often create temporary variables that do not have to remain alive after the client method exits. Because they're autoreleased, you don't have to remember to release them explicitly. Rigid adherence to this policy makes it possible for you to code memory management in your applications efficiently and reliably. Here, NSNumber's `numberWithInt:` convenience method returns an autoreleased NSNumber object, and your **uniqueAntiqueID** convenience method passes it along in the same form.

In this case, you noted in Step 3 that the object returned by the **uniqueAntiqueID** method was immediately copied when the **newAntiqueRecord** method called it. This is a standard use of the policy, whereby the client of the convenience method—here, a new VRAntiqueRecord object—can assume ownership of the object by copying or retaining it. This centralizes ownership of the object where it's needed, in the record object, and the record object assumes the obligation to release it. It does this in the VRAntiqueRecord **dealloc** method when the record is deleted, as you saw in Step 3.

With the means to create and delete records in the inventory finally behind you, you are now ready to return to the table view and implement the action methods and other routines that will empower the user to make this happen. After you've written the action methods in Step 6, you will address the filtering function in Step 7 and the all-important data source protocol methods, which do the actual work of filling in the table view from the data held in the inventory, in Step 8.

Step 6: Write Action Methods and Supporting Code to Add and Delete Records in the Table

In Step 2, you added stub implementations of two action methods, **newAntiqueRecord Action:** and **deleteAntiqueRecordAction:**, to the VRTextFieldController category. You held off filling in the stubs at that time, pending a more complete definition of the data structures for the antiques inventory and methods for managing the data. You have now taken care of the data, so it is time to begin fleshing out the user interface. In this step, you will keep the task as simple as possible, making the New and Delete buttons work. The next two steps will cover display of the records.

The most interesting achievement in this step is the ability to begin editing a newly added record in place, directly in a table cell, without using a separate text field as an assistant.

1.   You'll connect the **newAntiqueRecordAction:** stub method in the VRTextFieldController.m category source file to the New button (the + button) in Interface Builder. Complete the stub method as follows:

```
- (IBAction)newAntiqueRecordAction:(id)sender {
    VRAntiquesTableView *table = [self antiquesTable];
    int newRow = [table numberOfRows];
    NSMutableArray *antiques = [[self textFieldModel] antiques];

    [[self textFieldModel] newAntiqueRecord];
    [[[self document] undoManager] setActionName:
            [NSString stringWithFormat:@"%@%@",
            NSLocalizedString(@"Add Antique ID ",
            @"Name of undo/redo menu item after antique record \
            was added"), [[[antiques lastObject] antiqueID]
            stringValue]]];

    [table selectRow:newRow byExtendingSelection:NO];
    [table editColumn:columnToEdit row:newRow
            withEvent:nil select:YES];
}
```

Two of the three local variables declared at the top of the method—**table** and **antiques**—are conveniences to make the remainder of the code easier to read. The third, newRow, computes the index of the table row in which you'll install the new record. Since row indices are 0-based, the current number of rows is identical to the index for the new row to be added at the end.

The next two statements tell the model to add a new record to the **antiques** array and set up the undo action name. Recall that the method will assign a new record a unique ID automatically and set its Kind to New. If you had additional fields in your antique record object, they would be left blank, ready for user input.

The undo action name will include the unique record ID, so each of several undo or redo menu items will specifically identify the affected record. Make sure you add the common part of this menu item title, Add Antique ID (note the trailing space), to Localizable.strings.

To wrap up the addition of a new record to the table, the final statements select the new row and set up the designated cell of the new row for editing. It is this last feat that hasn't until recently been demonstrated in other examples of table view code. The documentation for NSTableView notes that the **editColumn:row:withEvent:select:** method is designed for this purpose, although Cocoa usually calls it internally. You must select the row before this will work, according to the documentation, which is why you called NSTableView's **selectRow:byExtendingSelection:** first.

When you run the application at the end of this recipe, you will find that it assigns newly added records New as their kind. The cell containing the word New will be selected, ready for the user to type over it and assign a real kind to this antique. This version of Vermont Recipes will accept any word the user types, but you will shortly add code to make sure the user can never leave the cell blank. In your own applications, you may want to consider offering entry aids, such as a pop-up menu of recognized kinds.

Because of Cocoa's built-in support for table editing, the user can double-click any cell of records already installed in the table to edit them, without your having to provide any additional code. You will, however, have to write a very small amount of code shortly so the application will recognize when the user's done editing a cell, in order to update the affected **antiques** record. You will also have to write some code to disable the New button while the user's editing a cell, then reenable it afterward and to enable and disable the Add Kind and Delete buttons when rows in the table are selected and deselected, since these two buttons operate only on selected rows. First, write the action method for deleting selected records.

2. You'll connect the **deleteAntiqueRecordAction:** stub method in the VRTextFieldController.m category source file to the Delete (–) button in Interface Builder. Complete the stub as follows:

```
- (IBAction)deleteAntiqueRecordAction:(id)sender {
    VRAntiquesTableView *table = [self antiquesTable];
    NSMutableArray *whichArray = ([self filteredAntiques]) ?
            [self filteredAntiques] :
            [[self textFieldModel] antiques];
    VRAntiqueRecord *record =
            [whichArray objectAtIndex:[table selectedRow]];

    [[self textFieldModel] deleteAntiqueRecord:record];
    [[[self document] undoManager] setActionName:
            [NSString stringWithFormat:@"%@%@",
            NSLocalizedString(@"Delete Antique ID ",
            @"Name of undo/redo menu item after antique record \
            was deleted"), [[record antiqueID] stringValue]]];
}
```

The first statement declares a convenience variable, **table**, for easy readability of the following code.

The next two statements, declaring the **whichArray** and **record** local variables, are much more than conveniences. They offer a hint of the technique you will use in Vermont Recipes to display a filtered subset of the **antiques** array in the table. A brief outline of the technique will help you understand what is happening in this deceptively simple method.

Whenever the user chooses a kind of antique other than All in the combo box, the `filterAntiqueRecords` method you will write in Step 7 scans the model `antiques` array and populates a second array, `filteredAntiques`, with references to any records meeting the filtering criterion. The data source protocol methods you will write in Step 8 use the `filteredAntiques` array to display records in the table, instead of the full `antiques` array, whenever a filtering criterion other than All is in effect. The application determines when to use one array or the other for display by testing whether the `filteredAntiques` array exists. Since this array is deallocated whenever the All criterion is in effect, its nonexistence signals that the table should display the full `antiques` array.

Here, the `whichArray` local variable is set to the `filteredAntiques` array if it exists; otherwise it's set to the full `antiques` array. This array reference, assigned to the `whichArray` local variable, then obtains from the appropriate array the record corresponding to the selected row of the table, which is assigned to the `record` local variable. With the record object in hand, you can easily delete it from the `antiques` array using the model object's `deleteAntiqueRecord:` method, which you wrote in Step 4. That method posts a notification telling the window controller that the data in the model array has changed, and in response the window controller calls its update method to refilter the model array. This re-creates and updates the `filteredAntiques` array if a filter criterion is in effect and reloads the table from the appropriate array without the deleted record. You will read more about this filtering technique, including why it is surprisingly efficient, in Step 7.

Finally, the `deleteAntiqueRecord:` method you wrote in Step 4 tells the model object to delete the record, and it tells the undo manager to set a descriptive undo action title. Make sure you add the common part of this menu item title, Delete Antique ID (note the trailing space), to Localizable.strings.

3. Now that the application knows how to delete a selected record, you need to enable the button that will trigger this action method. Recall from Step 1 that you used Interface Builder to disable the Delete button initially, when you created the document. Since the user must select a record first to identify it for deletion, the act of selecting it should enable the Delete button. When it is deleted, or whenever no record is selected, the Delete button should revert to its disabled state.

You know enough by now to anticipate that Cocoa declares a delegate method you can use as a hook to detect the act of selecting a row in a table. Open the NSTableView class reference document and, near the bottom, examine the delegate methods it declares.

Here's an enticing one: `tableView:shouldSelectRow:`. If you implement this delegate method in your window controller—you will appoint the window controller as the table's delegate at the end of this recipe—it will be called every time the user clicks a row in the table to select it. This is a *should* delegate method, so it will have to return YES to allow the selection to occur, but this isn't a problem. Unfortunately, however, if you implement this delegate method, you will discover a problem: It is limited to exactly the circumstances implied by its name. It fires only when the user attempts to select a row, not when the user attempts to deselect a row. It therefore gives you no way to disable the Delete button when the user deselects a row.

Looking again at the class reference document, you find the right delegate method: `tableViewSelectionDidChange:`. The smart people who wrote Cocoa anticipated that developers would need to know both when a row was selected and when it was deselected. A single method reporting any change in the row's selection state easily captures this information.

Like many delegate methods in Cocoa, this method is simultaneously a delegate method and a notification method. Since you're passing in the notification as a parameter, you can test its `object` to determine whether the table in which you are interested posted it.

At the very end of the VRMainWindowController.m source file, implement the delegate method as shown below. It belongs in the main source file, not the text field controller category, because any other table you might add to your application in some other tab view item will trigger it.

```
#pragma mark CONTROL VALIDATION


- (void) tableViewSelectionDidChange:
    (NSNotification *)notification {
  if ([notification object] == [self antiquesTable]) {
    [self validateAntiquesTableButtons];
  }
}
```

You could have put the code to enable and disable the Delete button here in the delegate method, but you will see shortly that you need to invoke the same code under other circumstances, so it makes sense to encapsulate it in a separate method. You'll have to enable and disable the Add Kind button in various circumstances, too. It will be best to consolidate as much as possible of the enabling and disabling code in one place—the `validateAntiquesTableButtons` method you will write now.

Declare this method in the VRTextFieldController category of VRMainWindow-Controller.h, at the end of the "Antiques table" subsection of the ACTIONS section:

```
- (void)validateAntiquesTableButtons;
```

Insert the following definition in the VRTextFieldController.m category source file, immediately following the deleteAntiqueRecordAction: method:

```
- (void)validateAntiquesTableButtons {

    NSTableView *table = [self antiquesTable];

    [[self deleteAntiqueButton]
        setEnabled:([table selectedRow] != -1)];
}
```

The documentation explains that NSTable's selectedRow method returns -1 if no row is selected.

The name of this method includes the word *validate*. In Cocoa, validation usually has to do with enabling and disabling menu items and user controls. The word doesn't often describe testing whether data is valid (for example, in a certain range); for that, you should use a formatter. A familiar example of correct usage of the term is the NSMenuValidation protocol's validateMenuItem: method. You should note that there is also a NSUserInterfaceValidations protocol that might provide a better way to validate the Delete button here. User interface validation is an advanced topic that *Vermont Recipes* does not cover. See the "User Interface Validation" section in Cocoa's *Programming Topics* for more information.

4. Finally, you will disable the New and Delete buttons while the user is editing any cell in the record.

Disabling these buttons during editing is advisable because it avoids troublesome issues regarding the implementation of undo and redo when editing table cells, a subject you will take up in Step 12. The *Aqua Human Interface Guidelines* do not address the design issues. One can argue that adding a new record to a table is analogous to editing a new text field and that the user should therefore be allowed to add a new record while editing another record just as the user is allowed to start editing a text field while editing another field. In either case, the user's work in the new record or field would be treated as a signal to commit the pending edit in the last record or field. One can just as easily argue, however, that adding a new record within a single user control, the table view, is not the same as starting to edit a new text field and that it shouldn't be allowed until the user has unambiguously completed editing in a cell—by pressing the Enter key, for example. Since the human interface issues don't have a definitive correct answer, convenience wins out.

In the Control Validation section you just added at the end of the VRMainWindowController.m source file, add these two delegate methods. They will be called when editing begins and ends in the antiques table, because the window controller is the table's delegate.

```
- (void)controlTextDidBeginEditing:
        (NSNotification *)notification {
    if ([notification object] == [self antiquesTable]) {
        [[self newAntiqueButton] setEnabled:NO];
        [[self deleteAntiqueButton] setEnabled:NO];
    }
}


- (void)controlTextDidEndEditing:(NSNotification *)notification {
    if ([notification object] == [self antiquesTable]) {
        [[self newAntiqueButton] setEnabled:YES];
        [[self deleteAntiqueButton] setEnabled:YES];
    }
}
```

You must also tweak the updateAntiquesTable: method in the "INTERFACE MANAGEMENT - Specific updaters" section of the VRTextFieldController.m category source file. Although you have disabled the Delete button while a field in a record is being actively edited (that is, after the user has started typing in the field), the button is still enabled after the user has selected a field for editing by double-clicking but hasn't yet begun typing. Updating a record in this state after the user deletes it or chooses Undo Add Antique Record will generate an array bounds error. Can you see why? The table view would think it had to update the row containing this record, but the record would already have been removed from the array in the model object by the time the updateAntiquesTable: method attempted to get its value. To prevent this, add the following message to the beginning of the updateAntiquesTable: method:

```
[[self antiquesTable] abortEditing];
```

Step 7: Filter the Array for Display in the Table

Up to this point in Recipe 11, you have heard only promises of a technique to filter the model **antiques** array to display a subset of records based on their kind. You read a summary of it in Step 6. Now you will finally implement this feature of the Vermont Recipes application. This will require implementing the action method connected to the combo box. In Recipe 10, Step 2, you wrote a stub for the action method, which just sounded a beep. Here, you will fill it in.

1. You read in Step 6 that a temporary array called **filteredAntiques** would hold the records meeting the filtering criterion chosen in the combo box. Because this array is temporary and used only for display of records, you will declare it in the window controller instead of the model object. There is no need to store it to disk, because all of the records in the inventory are stored to disk in the model object's **antiques** array. The **filteredAntiques** array is more a part of the application's controller than of its model, since it mediates between the full **antiques** array in the model and its display in the table view. In the future, you will be able to alter the filtering mechanism without touching the model class.

    In the VRMainWindowController.h header file, at the end of the "Antiques table" section of the instance variable declarations, insert this line:

    `NSMutableArray *filteredAntiques;`

    In the same header file, declare this accessor method at the end of the ACCESSORS section of the VRTextFieldController category, as follows:

    `- (NSMutableArray *)filteredAntiques;`

    In the category source file VRTextFieldController.m, define the accessor method at the end of the ACCESSORS section, as follows:

    ```
    - (NSMutableArray *)filteredAntiques {
        return filteredAntiques;
    }
    ```

2. Now write the body of the action method for which you wrote a stub in Recipe 10, Step 2. In the category source file VRTextFieldController.m, substitute the following statement for the **NSBeep()** call that currently forms the body of the **filterAntiqueRecordsAction:** method in the ACTIONS section:

    `[self filterAntiqueRecords];`

Next, you will finally come to the **filterAntiqueRecords** method. It is a separate method because the **updateAntiquesTable** method you wrote in Step 2 must execute the same code.

3. In the VRTextFieldController category of the header file VRMainWindow-Controller.m, declare the method at the end of the "Antiques table" subsection of the ACTIONS section, as follows:

```
- (void)filterAntiqueRecords;
```

In the category source file VRTextFieldController.m, at the end of the ACTIONS section, define the method as follows:

```
- (void)filterAntiqueRecords {
    NSString *kind = [[self antiqueKindComboBox] stringValue];

    if ([kind isEqualToString:NSLocalizedString(@"All",
            @"Kind of all antique records")]) {
        if ([self filteredAntiques]) {
            [[self filteredAntiques] release];
            filteredAntiques = nil;
        }
    } else {
        NSMutableArray *antiques =
                [[self textFieldModel] antiques];
        NSEnumerator *enumerator = [antiques objectEnumerator];
        VRAntiqueRecord *record;

        if ([self filteredAntiques]) {
            [[self filteredAntiques] removeAllObjects];
        } else {
            filteredAntiques = [[NSMutableArray alloc] init];
        }
        while (record = [enumerator nextObject]) {
            if ([[record antiqueKind] isEqualToString:kind] ||
                    [[record antiqueKind] isEqualToString:
                    NSLocalizedString(@"New",
                    @"Kind of new antique record")]) {
                [filteredAntiques addObject:record];
            }
        }
    }
    [[self antiquesTable] reloadData];
}
```

The first thing to notice about this method is that it does one important thing about which you have already read. If the user sets the combo box's filter criterion to All, this method makes sure any existing `filteredAntiques` array is deallocated and, for good measure, sets its instance variable to `nil`, then falls through to the end to call NSTableView's `reloadData` method. When the user doesn't want any filtering, the `filteredAntiques` array must be deallocated and set to `nil`; this signals the data source protocol methods you will write in Step 8 to use the full model `antiques` array to supply the records the table will display when `reloadData` is called.

If the chosen filtering criterion is something other than All, the `else` block handles the actual work of filtering. First, if the `filteredAntiques` array exists because another filtering criterion was in effect previously, the `filteredAntiques` array is emptied to make way for the new filtering operation. If the `filteredAntiques` array doesn't exist because the previous filtering criterion was All, a new, empty `filteredAntiques` array is allocated and initialized.

The allocation retains the array. This same method will release the array the next time a user chooses the All criterion, because you just wrote that code into the `if` block. But what if a filtering criterion other than All is still in effect when the window closes? In that event, the window controller's `dealloc` method must release the array. Take care of this pesky memory management detail right now, before you forget. Add this line near the end of the `dealloc` method in the source file VRMainWindowController.m:

```
// Antiques table view
[[self filteredAntiques] release];
```

As you know, messages to `nil` do nothing in Objective-C. You therefore don't have to test for the existence of the `filteredAntiques` array before releasing it. If it was already released and set to `nil` by the `filterAntiqueRecords` method, nothing will happen.

Returning to the `filterAntiqueRecords` method, you see that it simply walks the model `antiques` array record by record using a Cocoa enumerator object, examining each record and adding some of them to the temporary `filteredAntiques` array for display in the table. You created the enumerator object a few lines earlier by using NSArray's `objectEnumerator` convenience method. Like all convenience methods, the `objectEnumerator` method gives you the `enumerator` object autoreleased. Because you will be done with it before exiting this method, you need not retain or release it yourself.

In determining whether a record should be added to the `filteredAntiques` array, the method checks whether the record is of the kind chosen as the filtering criterion. In addition, because the application specification requires all records of kind New to display in the table no matter what filtering criterion is in effect, the method adds all New antiques to the `filteredAntiques` array. As a convenience, New is also offered as a filtering criterion so the user can display all of the New antiques at once for reassignment of real kinds.

When the filtering is complete, the method calls the table's `reloadData` method to mark the table as needing update and display. The application accomplishes this by calling the data source protocol methods you will write in Step 8.

Take careful note of an important point about the use of the `filteredAntiques` array. When you add records to it using NSMutableArray's `addObject:` method, the method doesn't duplicate those records. Instead, it installs a pointer to the record in the array and retains the record. The record itself occupies only a single location in memory, which the `antiques` array and the `filteredAntiques` array share. This means employing a second array to hold filtered records is an efficient way to use memory.

The use of two arrays does raise potential speed issues while applying a filter, but it doesn't appear to be a problem for this intended use of the Vermont Recipes application, where you won't encounter more than a few hundred antiques. The issue is that the `filterAntiqueRecords` method will scan the entire model `antiques` array once as it fills the `filteredAntiques` array, then Cocoa's `reloadData` method will scan the latter array to display its contents in the table. The second array requires a shorter scan than the first by definition, and on average the more categories there are, the shorter the second scan will be. You might avoid a second scan by implementing the filtering mechanism directly in the data source protocol methods or by using a delegate method. I haven't explored these possibilities, because the trade-offs discussed below clearly favor using a second array for this application.

The most significant advantage of using a separate array is that you can obtain a reference to a specific filtered record by simply indexing into the second array using the record's row number in the table. A second array therefore makes operations such as editing or deleting a specific record selected in the table much faster. Without a second array, you would have to scan the entire model array for a record having the same field values every time the user wanted to edit or delete a specific record.

The most remarkable aspect of the use of two arrays with shared record memory appears when the user edits a record. You don't have to write any extra code to update the record's instance variables in the model `antiques` array when the data source protocol methods change the record in the `filteredAntiques` array. Changing the data in the record in one array takes care of the same record in the other array because they are one and the same record, sharing the same memory location.

After all this talk of data source protocol methods, it is finally time to write them.

Step 8: Write the Table's Data Source Protocol Methods

The last code you need to write to display and edit the records in the inventory is the table view's data source protocol methods. The NSTableDataSource informal protocol declares several methods that have functions similar to those of the NSComboBoxDataSource protocol methods you implemented in Recipe 10, Step 3. Each method is called very frequently as the table is displayed, scrolled, and filtered, so each must be short and fast.

The one significant difference between the data source methods you will implement here and those you implemented in Recipe 10 is that you must deal with two different arrays here. You already saw how to do this when you wrote the code for the **whichArray** variable in Step 6.

1. Start with the **numberOfRowsInTableView:** protocol method, which you should place after the combo box's data source protocol methods at the end of the DATA SOURCES section of the source file VRMainWindowController.m. Data source methods belong in the main window controller source file, not in one of its category source files, because Cocoa will call them for every table in your application, wherever it's located.

```
// Table views

- (int)numberOfRowsInTableView:(NSTableView *)tableView {
    if (tableView == [self antiquesTable]) {
        NSMutableArray *whichArray = [self filteredAntiques] ?
                [self filteredAntiques] :
                [[self textFieldModel] antiques];
        return [whichArray count];
    }
    [NSException raise:NSInvalidArgumentException
            format:@"Exception raised in VRMainWindowController \
            -numberOfRowsInTableView: - tableView not known"];
    return -1;
}
```

This is straightforward. If the **antiques** table calls this method, it determines whether the **filteredAntiques** array exists and accordingly assigns it or the **antiques** array to the **whichArray** local variable. It then returns the chosen array's count. Because the purpose of the data source method is to display every record from the array in the table, the array's count is the table's count.

You are already familiar with the exception handling shown here, from Recipe 2, Step 4.3.

2. Follow this with the `tableView:objectValueForTablecolumn:row:` method. Cocoa will use this to obtain the value to display in each visible cell of the table whenever it is needed.

```
- (id)tableView:(NSTableView *)tableView
       objectValueForTableColumn:(NSTableColumn *)tableColumn
       row:(int)row {
    if (tableView == [self antiquesTable]) {
        NSMutableArray *whichArray = [self filteredAntiques] ?
                [self filteredAntiques] :
                [[self textFieldModel] antiques];
        NSParameterAssert(row >= 0 && row < [whichArray count]);
        return [[whichArray objectAtIndex:row]
                valueForKey:[tableColumn identifier]];
    }
    [NSException raise:NSInvalidArgumentException
            format:@"Exception raised in VRMainWindowController \
            -tableView:objectValueForTableColumn:row: \
            - tableView not known"];
    return nil;
}
```

This method follows the same pattern as the previous method. Instead of returning the appropriate array's count, however, it returns the object for the specified field of the record displayed in the specified row of the table. The call to Cocoa's **NSParameterAssert()** macro is recommended in the table view documentation as a reality check on the validity of the row parameter.

The method obtains the cell's value by calling NSArray's **objectAtIndex:** method to get the record corresponding to that row of the table, then calling the record's **valueForKey:** method inherited from NSObject, as described in Step 3. The key you pass to the **valueforKey:** method is the column's **identifier** string, which you set in Interface Builder in Step 1. Using the column's identifier instead of its index supports applications that allow the user to reorder the columns in the table, as does Vermont Recipes.

Consider the role of Cocoa's key-value coding technology in this method. The **valueForKey:** method is generic. It allows the application to obtain the value of any instance variable in the VRAntiqueRecord object by simply specifying its key as a string identical to the name of the variable. Because key-value coding looks first for an accessor method with the same name as the instance variable (and accessors with **get** prepended, for good measure), the correct accessor method is called to obtain the value of the instance variable. You do not have to write a long C **switch** statement with hard-coded variable or method names and data type management to get the field value. Instead, Cocoa looks it up in a fast hash table. You don't even have to write the key into the code, since you associated it with the column in Interface Builder. Key-value coding takes care of returning a value of the correct type for you.

Key-Value Coding

Key-value coding is a patented Apple technology implemented in every Cocoa object descended from NSObject—that is, almost every object in the Cocoa frameworks. Cocoa uses it in many areas, including table views. For example, it forms the underpinnings of AppleScript in Cocoa. Key-value coding is also an important feature of the Enterprise Objects framework, which is not currently available in Objective-C as part of the Cocoa frameworks.

The basic idea behind key-value coding is that it can obtain the properties of any object indirectly by name, instead of directly by reading the object's instance variables or calling its accessor methods. Because key-value coding is implemented through hashed dictionaries, the lookup of a value for a key is very fast.

This ability is particularly useful in object-oriented database systems, where a client object may know little about the implementation of the data store, such as its structure, the order in which it stores properties, whether they are accessible through instance variables or accessor methods, or what their data types might be. As long as you know the name of the instance variable, you can obtain its value, and the value will be returned as the proper type. Furthermore, since the key is a simple string, you can pass it into a single method to find any keyed value. To query the database, you don't have to write a long switch statement that reads specific instance variables or calls specific accessor methods; instead, you simply ask for the value associated with the key.

The *Data Management* topic in the *Cocoa Developer Documentation* describes key-value coding. It is important to read and understand this material to appreciate more fully what you can do with tables, outlines, and other complex user controls in Cocoa.

The patent is United States Patent 5,898,871, entitled "Dynamic Object Communication Protocol," issued to Williamson, et al., on April 27, 1999, and assigned to NeXT Software. The original application was filed in 1994. Apple acquired the patent when it acquired NeXT Software. It makes interesting reading, especially if you have a law degree, because it explains key-value coding in language you don't often see in a software manual. Go to the Patents section of the U.S. Patent and Trademark Office Web site at www.uspto.gov/patft/ and use the Patent Number Search page to search for the patent by number. Here are a few excerpts that might help you understand what it's all about.

The patent asserts ten claims. The first is: "A method for communicating data from a data source to an object oriented object, said object oriented object having a method or an instance variable, said method for communicating data comprising the steps of: retrieving column headings and rows from said data source; creating a dictionary of key-value pairs for each of said rows, said key representing a property name of one of said column headings and said value representing a data value from one of said rows; obtaining one of said key-value pairs from said dictionary; searching said object oriented object for a method of the name 'set' plus the property name of said key; loading said value into said object oriented object when said object oriented object has a method of the name 'set' plus said property name; searching for an instance variable with the same name as said property if no method of the name 'set' plus the property name of said key is found; loading said value into said object oriented object when said object oriented object has an instance variable with said property name."

The remaining claims are generally similar, covering communication in both directions and with databases and enterprise objects. The third claim introduces an important additional feature: "The method of claim 1 further including the steps of: determining the argument type of said method when said object oriented object has a method of the type 'set' plus said property name; converting said value to said argument type when said value is not of said argument type; calling said method with said value as an argument."

The key paragraph in the summary of the invention is this: "Key-value pairs are used to examine an object at runtime. An object is examined by comparing its method(s) and/or instance variable(s) with key-value pairs. The dynamic object communication protocol provides the ability to make a run time determination of communication requirements for any object regardless of the object's implementation. Further, the dynamic object communication protocol provides a uniform method to communicate with an object."

The patent spells out the specific algorithms for implementing key-value coding in excruciating detail. As a bonus, it briefly describes the algorithm for implementing undo and redo in Cocoa.

3. Next, write the `tableView:setObjectValue:forTableColumn:row:` method immediately following this. Cocoa will invoke it to set the specified record's field value in the appropriate array whenever the user ends editing in a cell in the table.

```
- (void)tableView:(NSTableView *)tableView
    setObjectValue:(id)object
    forTableColumn:(NSTableColumn *)tableColumn
    row:(int)row {
  if (tableView == [self antiquesTable]) {
    NSString *identifier = [tableColumn identifier];
    VRAntiqueRecord *record;

    NSMutableArray *whichArray = [self filteredAntiques] ?
        [self filteredAntiques] :
        [[self textFieldModel] antiques];
    NSParameterAssert(row >= 0 && row < [whichArray count]);
    record = [whichArray objectAtIndex:row];

    if ((![[[self document] undoManager] isUndoing] &&
        ![object isEqual:
        [record valueForKey:identifier]]) ||
        [[self antiquesTable] isEditing]) {
      [record takeValue:object forKey:identifier];
      [[[self document] undoManager] setActionName:
        [NSString stringWithFormat:
        NSLocalizedString(@"Set %@ of Antique ID %@",
        @"Name of undo/redo menu item after antique \
        record was edited"),
        [[tableColumn headerCell] stringValue],
        [record valueForKey:@"antiqueID"]]];
    }
  }
}
```

Because you're using the **VRAntiqueRecord** type here, you also have to import the VRTextFieldModel class header. At the end of the **#import** directives at the top of VRMainWindowController.m, add this line:

```
#import "VRTextFieldModel.h"
```

The `tableView:setObjectValue:forTableColumn:row:` data source protocol method plays the role of a **set** accessor method, as the **set** in its **setObjectValue:** parameter label suggests. However, it is not a primitive accessor because it sets the value of the instance variable indirectly, by using key-value coding to call VRAntiqueRecord's primitive `set` accessor method for the instance variable associated with the specified identifier. The latter takes care of registering the change to the data with the undo manager and posting a notification so the window controller can update the GUI.

The `tableView:setObjectValue:forTableColumn:row:` method also plays the role of an action method, since Cocoa calls it automatically when the user ends editing in a table cell. This is why you have not written a separate action method for the table view. Therefore, in addition to following the pattern of the previous methods in identifying the table and array involved, it sets the undo action name as any good action method should. Here, the undo action menu item title will include the title of the column and the ID of the row so that users will know exactly which cell any undo or redo action will affect. Don't forget to set up localization for this menu item title in Localizable.strings.

The complicated `if` block enclosing the operative statements of this method have to do with implementation of live undo and redo in table cells. I'll discuss this later, in Step 12.

4. The final method you will write in this step is not a data source protocol method but a simple NSTableView delegate method, `tableView:willDisplayCell:forTableColumn:row:`. However, because it typically controls the appearance of text and other cell attributes, and because Cocoa calls it automatically whenever the cell displays, it seems appropriate to discuss it in the context of the `tableView:setObjectValue:forTableColumn:row:` data source protocol method.

You have seen that the Vermont Recipes application uses the antique kind New to flag a table entry whose kind has not yet been set. You want the word New to appear in boldface once it is entered in a record's Kind column in the table, to emphasize that the user hasn't yet assigned a real kind. Rather than accomplish this by setting the font of the text when it is added to the cell upon initializing a new record and worrying about how to change it when the user assigns a new kind, you will implement the delegate method, which will automatically set up a cell's appearance every time the cell displays.

Following the last data source protocol method, add this method to VRMainWindowcontroller.m:

```
- (void)tableView:(NSTableView *)tableView

    willDisplayCell:(id)cell
    forTableColumn:(NSTableColumn *)tableColumn
```

(continues on next page)

```
      row:(int)row {
    if (tableView == [self antiquesTable]) {
        [cell setFont:([[cell stringValue] isEqualToString:
            NSLocalizedString(@"New", @"Kind of new antique \
            record")] ? [NSFont boldSystemFontOfSize:
            [NSFont systemFontSize]] :
            [NSFont controlContentFontOfSize:
            [NSFont systemFontSize]])];
    }
}
```

If the text in a cell that is about to display is New, it displays using whatever font is currently the user's bold system font in that font's size. Otherwise, the text in the cell displays in the standard user control font in the system font size. You can use similar techniques to make the text another color or to control other features of the cell's appearance. You'll be calling this method on every cell, so it must specify an appearance for every cell that does not meet the criteria, as well as every cell that does. The C ternary operator is perfectly suited to this.

The table view is now doing almost everything you set out to make it do. The only major omissions at this point are live undo and redo in table cells and the ability (promised in Recipe 10) to add additional antique kinds of antiques to the pop-up menu in the combo box. You will add filtering by menu for custom kinds of antiques in the next step. Later, you will deal with live undo and redo and a few minor loose ends, such as a keyboard command for deleting records.

Step 9: Implement a Customizable Combo Box Menu

In Recipe 10, you hard-coded the list of kinds of antiques that would appear in the combo box's pop-up menu as standard criteria for filtering the kinds of antiques displayed in the antiques table. Because they were specified in code and unchangeable, you treated these criteria as part of the controller and declared them in VRMainWindowController.h.

In this step, you will add features to the application to allow the user to define custom kinds of antiques for filtering. This is important to the design of the application, because the table view allows the user to assign any kind whatever to new antiques, without limitation. The range of things people are willing to buy as antiques is virtually unlimited—you have to know a few collectors to appreciate the breadth of their passion. Although the combo box provides the flexibility to allow a user to type in any kind absent from the hard-coded list of criteria, this will become drudgery for any user who has bought a lot of antiques of some other kind and wants to filter for them using the simpler pop-up menu.

You will not entirely abandon the original approach in this step. The hard-coded kinds will remain hard-coded. However, you'll add an instance variable to the model object to hold an array of custom kinds added by the user. You'll make provisions in the code to combine the hard-coded and custom kinds into a single list, alphabetize them, prepend a couple of special categories (All and New) to the beginning of the list, and display the list when the pop-up menu is selected. The idea underlying this design is that the application should present a simple, standard, preprogrammed interface for dealers who don't feel comfortable customizing the application, while giving a more computer-savvy user the ability to add functionality and convenience.

1. In the Recipe 10 version of the combo box, you defined an instance variable in VRMainWindowController.m named **antiqueKinds** as an array of several strings representing various categories of antiques: rag dolls, milking stools, and that sort of thing. Now, in this recipe, you will add two more instance variables to the window controller and one to the model object to hold additional kind strings.

One of the new window controller variables, **antiqueKindCommands**, will hold the special hard-coded kinds All and New, which you can think of as commands to display something rather than a kind of antique, strictly speaking. You'll move one of these, All, here from the original variable, and enhance the original variable with a few additional strings. You need a separate variable for the commands, because they will be added to the top of the final, combined list after it is alphabetized. The second new window controller variable, **antiqueKindsForMenu**, will hold the final list. This is the array that the combo box data source protocol methods will load into the pop-up menu in response to the **reloadData** message.

The new instance variable in the model object, **antiqueAddedKinds**, will hold new kinds added to the list when the user clicks the Add Kinds button. You'll place it in the model object because it will be saved to disk as part of the document and read back from disk when a user opens or reverts the document. In Vermont Recipes, you can think of each document as a separate antiques inventory or collection, so you might expect each to have a different set of custom kinds of antique based on the nature and variety of items in the inventory.

In the header file VRMainWindowController.h, add these two instance variables following the declaration of the existing **antiqueKinds** variable from Recipe 10:

```
NSArray *antiqueKindCommands;
NSMutableArray *antiqueKindsForMenu;
```

Declare accessor methods for all three at the end of the ACCESSORS section of the VRTextFieldController category in the source file VRTextFieldController.h, as shown below. In Recipe 10 you chose not to declare an accessor method for **antiqueKinds**, but now that you will be manipulating these variables more extensively, it seems prudent to do so.

```
- (NSArray *)antiqueKinds;
- (NSArray *)antiqueKindCommands;
- (NSMutableArray *)antiqueKindsForMenu;
```

Define the three accessor methods at the end of the ACCESSORS section of the category source file VRTextFieldController.m:

```
- (NSArray *)antiqueKinds {
    return antiqueKinds;
}


- (NSArray *)antiqueKindCommands {
    return antiqueKindCommands;
}


- (NSMutableArray *)antiqueKindsForMenu {
    return antiqueKindsForMenu;
}
```

In the header file VRTextFieldModel.h, declare this instance variable:

```
NSMutableArray *antiqueAddedKinds;
```

Declare its accessor method at the end of the ACCESSORS section of the same file:

```
- (NSMutableArray *)antiqueAddedKinds;
```

Define the accessor method at the end of the ACCESSORS section of the source file VRTextFieldModel.m:

```
- (NSMutableArray *)antiqueAddedKinds {
    return antiqueAddedKinds;
}
```

2. In the **init** method of the VRMainWindowController.m source file, remove the initialization of the existing **antiqueKinds** instance variable and substitute the following three variable initializations. The **antiqueKinds** strings are not internationalized, on the pretense that these are distinctively American kinds of antiques called by the same names in every language. You must localize the **antiqueKindCommands** so that users speaking other languages will understand All and New. Don't forget to add these to Localizable.strings if you haven't already done so. The third variable is initialized to an empty array for a new document.

```
// Combo Box
antiqueKinds = [[NSArray arrayWithObjects:@"Dry Sinks",
        @"Game Boards", @"Milking Stools", @"Pocket Knives",
        @"Quilts", @"Rag Dolls", nil] retain];
antiqueKindCommands = [[NSArray arrayWithObjects:
        NSLocalizedString(@"All", @"Kind of all antique records"),
        NSLocalizedString(@"New", @"Kind of new antique record"),
        nil] retain];
antiqueKindsForMenu = [[NSMutableArray alloc] init];
```

All three arrays are retained (the third by virtue of **alloc**) because they will live as long as the document lives, so they must be released when the document closes. You wrote the first release into the **dealloc** method in Recipe 10. After that line, add these two additional statements:

```
[antiqueKindCommands release];
[antiqueKindsForMenu release];
```

Near the end of the **init** method of the VRTextFieldModel.m source file, initialize its new variable to an empty array. There is more than one way to get an empty array, as the following line, using an NSMutableArray convenience method, illustrates. The convenience method returns the empty array autoreleased, so you must explicitly retain it to keep it alive.

```
antiqueAddedKinds = [[NSMutableArray array] retain];
```

Release it in the source file's **dealloc** method:

```
[[self antiqueAddedKinds] release];
```

3. You have learned in many contexts that you can't place some kinds of initialization code in an object's initialization method because it depends on the nib file's having been loaded and fully initialized. In Recipe 10, Step 3, for this reason, you placed statements in the window controller's **awakeFromNib** method to initialize the appearance and contents of the combo box's pop-up menu when a document first opens. You must now revise those methods slightly to refer to the new **antiqueKindsForMenu** variable.

    In addition, because you have revised the combo box routines to use three variables as sources of the menu's contents, you must add a new routine to **awakeFromNib** to do the work of assembly. Call the new method **prepare-AntiqueKindsForMenu** and write it first.

    In the VRTextFieldController category in the header file VRMainWindowController.h, at the end of the "Antiques table" subsection of the ACTIONS section, add the declaration shown below. You place this method here because it's basically a helper method for the **addAntiqueKindAction:** method you wrote in Step 2.

```
- (void)prepareAntiqueKindsForMenu;
```

Define it in the corresponding location of the VRTextFieldController.m category source file, as follows:

```
- (void)prepareAntiqueKindsForMenu {
    NSMutableArray *tempKinds = [[NSMutableArray alloc] init];

    [tempKinds addObjectsFromArray:[self antiqueKinds]];
    [tempKinds addObjectsFromArray:
        [[self textFieldModel] antiqueAddedKinds]];
    [tempKinds sortUsingSelector:
        @selector(caseInsensitiveCompare:)];

    [[self antiqueKindsForMenu] removeAllObjects];
    [[self antiqueKindsForMenu]
        addObjectsFromArray:[self antiqueKindCommands]];
    [[self antiqueKindsForMenu] addObjectsFromArray:tempKinds];
    [tempKinds release];
}
```

This method allocates and, at the end, releases a temporary mutable array where the full combo box menu list is built up. First, it inserts the hard-coded kind strings and any user-added strings into the empty temporary array using NSMutableArray's **addObjectsFromArray:** method and alphabetizes the result using NSMutableArray's **sortUsingSelector:** method with the **case-InsensitiveCompare:** method selector. Then it empties and reassembles the **antiqueKindsForMenu** array with the **antiqueKindCommands** (All and New) on top, followed by the sorted list of kind strings from the temporary array.

With this method written, you can now call it from the window controller's **awakeFromNib** method, along with slightly modified versions of the combo box initialization statements you wrote in Recipe 10, Step 3. They must now work with the **antiqueKindsForMenu** variable, not the **antiqueKinds** variable. Also, they now obtain the kind strings through the variable's accessor method. Insert the following lines at the top of the **awakeFromNib** method in the VRMainWindowController.m source file, replacing the two similar lines already there:

```
[self prepareAntiqueKindsForMenu];
if ([[self antiqueKindsForMenu] count] <= 12)
    [[self antiqueKindComboBox] setHasVerticalScroller:NO];
[[self antiqueKindComboBox] setStringValue:
    [[self antiqueKindsForMenu] objectAtIndex:
```

```
[self comboBox:[self antiqueKindComboBox]
indexOfItemWithStringValue:NSLocalizedString(@"All",
@"Kind of all antique records")]]];
```

These routines only set up the combo box's menu when the document first opens. The menu must be prepared again when the user adds a new custom kind by clicking the Add Kind button. You will take care of this shortly, when you write the **addAntiqueKindAction:** action method.

4. You wrote the data source protocol methods for the combo box in Recipe 10, Step 3. You recall that the fundamental purpose of data source methods, whether for combo boxes, tables, or other complex views, is to funnel information from a data store, typically a collection object such as an array, to the view. Originally, you wrote the combo box data sources to obtain information from the **antiqueKinds** array. Now you must rewrite them to obtain data from the new **antiqueKindsForMenu** array, which holds the combination of hard-coded kind and command strings and user-added kind strings. While you're at it, you will add routines to raise exceptions in case the incoming reference to this combo box is wrong, as you have done with similar methods previously. These require no further explanation. Here are the new versions of the combo box data source protocol methods:

```
- (int)numberOfItemsInComboBox:(NSComboBox *)comboBox {
    if (comboBox == [self antiqueKindComboBox]) {
        return [[self antiqueKindsForMenu] count];
    }
    [NSException raise:NSInvalidArgumentException
            format:@"Exception raised in VRMainWindowController \
            -numberOfItemsInComboBox: - comboBox not known"];
    return 0;
}


- (id)comboBox:(NSComboBox *)comboBox
        objectValueForItemAtIndex:(int)index {
    if (comboBox == [self antiqueKindComboBox]) {
        return [[self antiqueKindsForMenu] objectAtIndex:index];
    }
    [NSException raise:NSInvalidArgumentException
            format:@"Exception raised in VRMainWindowController \
            -comboBox:objectValueForItemAtIndex: \
            - comboBox not known"];
    return nil;
```

(continues on next page)

```
        }

        - (unsigned int)comboBox:(NSComboBox *)comboBox
                indexOfItemWithStringValue:(NSString *)string {
            if (comboBox == [self antiqueKindComboBox]) {
                return [[self antiqueKindsForMenu]
                        indexOfObject: string];
            }
            [NSException raise:NSInvalidArgumentException
                    format:@"Exception raised in VRMainWindowController \
                    -comboBox:indexOfItemWithStringValue: \
                    - comboBox not known"];
            return -1;
        }


        - (NSString *)comboBox:(NSComboBox *)comboBox
                datasource:(NSString *)partialString {
            if (comboBox == [self antiqueKindComboBox]) {
                int idx;
                for (idx = 0; idx < [[self antiqueKindsForMenu] count];
                        idx++) {
                    NSString *testItem = [[self antiqueKindsForMenu]
                        objectAtIndex:idx];
                    if ([[testItem commonPrefixWithString:partialString
                            options:NSCaseInsensitiveSearch] length] ==
                            [partialString length]) {
                        return testItem;
                    }
                }
            }
            [NSException raise:NSInvalidArgumentException
                    format:@"Exception raised in VRMainWindowController \
                    -comboBox:dataSource: - comboBox not known"];
            return @"";
        }
```

5. You are now ready to write the action method that you'll connect to the Add
    Kind button. This is the third of three action methods for which you wrote
    stubs in Step 2. You can now fill in the implementation of this method, in the
    "Antiques table" subsection of the ACTIONS section of the category source file
    VRTextFieldController.m, as follows:

```
- (IBAction)addAntiqueKindAction:(id)sender {
    NSTableView *table = [self antiquesTable];
    NSString *selectedKind = [[table dataSource] tableView:table
            objectValueForTableColumn:
            [table tableColumnWithIdentifier:@"antiqueKind"]
            row:[table selectedRow]];

    [[[self textFieldModel] antiqueAddedKinds]
            addObject:selectedKind];
    [self prepareAntiqueKindsForMenu];
    [[self antiqueKindComboBox] reloadData];

    [[self antiqueKindComboBox] setHasVerticalScroller:
            [[self antiqueKindsForMenu] count] > 12];
    [[self addAntiqueKindButton] setEnabled:NO];

}
```

The theory of operation of the Add Kind button is this: The user first clicks a
row in the antiques table to select it. The Add Kind button, which started out
disabled because you set it up that way in Interface Builder in Step 1, is immediately enabled if, and only if, the kind of the selected antique is not already in
the combo box's menu. The enabling of the Add Kind button is not intrusive,
in compliance with the *Aqua Human Interface Guidelines* regarding new menu
items in a combo box. However, the user can click the button, and this action
method then adds the kind of the currently selected antique to the menu. No
typing is required, and only kinds that already exist in the antiques inventory can
be added to the menu for easy filtering of the inventory displayed in the table.

The action method implements this theory of operation by first obtaining the
kind of the selected antique using one of the table's data source methods with
the @"antiqueKind" identifier and NSTableView's selectedRow method. No test
is included here to determine whether an antique is in fact selected, because the
routines you will write shortly will guarantee that the button is enabled only
when the user selects an antique.

The kind of the selected antique is then added to the model object's antiqueAddedKinds
variable; it is added to the window controller's antiqueKindsForMenu variable
by calling of the prepareAntiqueKindsForMenu method you just wrote; and the
NSComboBox reloadData method is called to reconfigure the menu itself. (If
you omit the reloadData command, the menu will still work, but the new kind
will appear only as you drag the cursor over the position where you're adding it.
This is not the effect you want.) Finally, a scroll bar is added if the number of
kinds exceeds 12, and the Add Kind button is immediately disabled because the
menu now includes the kind of the currently selected antique.

6. You must now implement the just-mentioned guarantee that the Add Kind button will be enabled only when an antique is selected in the table and its kind is not already installed in the combo box's pop-up menu. You wrote a method in Step 6, `validateAntiquesTableButtons`, to validate the Delete button, and that is a suitable place to validate the Add Kind button as well. The validation of both buttons depends, at least in part, on whether the user has selected an antique in the table.

In the `validateAntiquesTableButtons` method you wrote in Step 6 in VRMainWindowController.m, after the declaration of the `table` local variable, add these lines:

```
NSString *selectedKind;
if ([table selectedRow] != -1) {
    selectedKind = [[table dataSource] tableView:table
            objectValueForTableColumn:
            [table tableColumnWithIdentifier:@"antiqueKind"]
            row:[table selectedRow]];
}
```

This checks whether a row in the table is selected and, if so, obtains its kind string. Next, at the end of the method, add this line:

```
[[self addAntiqueKindButton] setEnabled:
        (([table selectedRow] != -1) &&
        (![[self antiqueKindsForMenu]
        containsObject:selectedKind]))];
```

This is self-explanatory. It carries out the guarantee that the button will be enabled only if a table row is selected, and it enables the button only if in addition the selected antique's kind is not already in the menu.

7. Validation of the buttons requires a final tweak. A little experimentation with the completed application reveals that adding a new record to the table does not trigger the `tableViewSelectionDidChange:` delegate method you implemented in Step 6, even though the `newAntiqueRecordAction:` method you wrote earlier in Step 6 explicitly calls `selectRow:byExtendingSelection:` just before setting up the new row for editing. This causes a problem if the user commits the data in the new row by clicking another cell in the same row. The row remains selected, but the Delete button is not enabled, and the Add Kind button is not enabled even if the user has entered a custom kind that does not appear in the combo box menu.

The fix is simple. Add this message at the end of the `if` block in the `tableView:-setObjectValue:forTableColumn:row:` data source protocol method in the source file VRMainWindowController.m:

```
[self validateAntiquesTableButtons];
```

You have now implemented all of the primary functionality planned for the antiques table and the associated combo box and push-buttons. All that remains are a number of details that make for a more polished application and a more satisfying user experience. In the following steps to wrap up Recipe 11, you will apply filtering and formatting to data entry in the table's cells, including routines to prevent the user from leaving any ID or Kind cell blank; implement drag and drop for table cells; implement live undo and redo in table cells; and add command-key shortcuts as alternative means for power users to add and delete rows in the table.

Step 10: Apply Data Entry Filtering and Formatting in Table Cells

In cells in a table view, as in a text field, you can filter data entry for valid characters and format it. In the antiques table, four issues fall under the topic of data entry filtering and formatting: Every antique's ID must be an integer; the integer must be unique; no antique can have a blank identification number; and no antique can have a blank kind. You will start with the need to filter entry of characters in the ID column to allow only numerals.

1. You created a custom integer number formatter in Recipe 6, Step 1, and it perfectly suits cells in the ID column of the antiques table as well. To apply this existing formatter to cells in the ID column, you need only connect the formatter to every cell in the ID column.

   But how can you do this? Every table column contains a potentially unlimited number of cells, and you obviously can't connect a formatter to each of them in advance.

   If you examine the table in Interface Builder, you discover that the only way to add a formatter using the Connections pane of the Info Panel is to apply a formatter to the entire table. If you select the ID column, you find that the NSTableColumn info panel doesn't support a **formatter** outlet. Interface Builder apparently also doesn't let you work with individual cells in a table. You don't want to make every cell in the entire table hold an integer, so Interface Builder would not be useful even if you had installed the integer formatter in a custom Interface Builder palette.

   If you examine the NSTableColumn class specification document and header, you don't find a **formatter** outlet. This explains why you don't see such an outlet in Interface Builder. You seem to be stuck.

You might think of the `tableView:willDisplayCell:forTableColumn:row:` method you used in Step 8 to set every cell containing the word New to bold-face. But this method only sets formatting attributes such as color and font style after the user has made an entry. It does not filter the entry on the fly.

Don't give up. The trick is to understand that Cocoa reuses a single cell instance to display every cell value in a table column. For every column, there exists a sort of Platonic idea of a perfect cell, which Cocoa uses to control data entry and display in every cell in the column. This prototype cell is called a *data cell,* and certain methods in NSTableColumn let you work with it. The data cell mechanism is very powerful. You can even use these methods to substitute, say, an NSImageCell for the NSTextFieldCell normally used in a table. Here, you will take advantage of the fact that the NSTextFieldCell instance in the ID column's data cell has a formatter outlet to attach your custom integer filter.

In the existing `makeIntegerNumberFilter` method in VRMainWindow-Controller.m, which you wrote in Recipe 6, Step 1, add this one line just before the last line releasing the filter object:

```
[[[[self antiquesTable] tableColumnWithIdentifier:@"antiqueID"]
        dataCell] setFormatter:integerNumberFilter];
```

You recall from Recipe 6 that formatters such as the integer number filter work by triggering a delegate method, `control:didFailToValidatePartialString:errorDescription:`. You implemented this method in VRMainWindowController.m and applied it to beep and present alert sheets to catch various data entry filter and formatter errors in three text fields in Recipe 6, Steps 1, 2, and 3, and a form object in Recipe 9, Step 4. Since you already know how to present alert sheets in these circumstances, you will just make the application beep when the user types a nonnumeric character into a cell in the ID column of the antiques table.

At the end of the `control:didFailToValidatePartialString:errorDescription:` method, add the following `else if` clause:

```
else if ((control == [self antiquesTable]) &&
        ([[self antiquesTable] editedColumn] == [[self
        antiquesTable] columnWithIdentifier:@"antiqueID"])) {
    NSBeep();
}
```

2. You'll deal with the other three issues simultaneously without using a formatter. You don't need a formatter to prevent the user from entering a blank value in a cell. You only need to test the value in the cell when the user finishes editing and, if it is blank, prevent editing from ending. You learned how to do this in Recipe 5,

Step 2, and you did it again in Recipe 6. You will use the same technique here, and you will include a statement to ensure that the user enters a unique ID.

At the end of the `control:textShouldEndEditing:` delegate method in the source file VRMainWindowController.m, add the following `else if` block:

```
else if (control == [self antiquesTable] &&
        ![[self antiquesTable] isUndoing]) {
    if ([[self antiquesTable] editedColumn] ==
            [[self antiquesTable]
            columnWithIdentifier:@"antiqueID"]) {
        if ([[fieldEditor string] isEqualToString:@""]) {
            return NO;
        } else if (![[[self document] textFieldModel]
                isUniqueAntiqueID:[NSNumber numberWithInt:
                [[fieldEditor string] intValue]]]) {
            return NO;
        } else {
            [[[self document] textFieldModel] setLastAntiqueID:
                    [[fieldEditor string] intValue]];
            return YES;
        }
    } else if ([[self antiquesTable] editedColumn] ==
            [[self antiquesTable]
            columnWithIdentifier:@"antiqueKind"]) {
        if ([[fieldEditor string] isEqualToString:@""]) {
            return NO;
        }
    }
}
```

The last few lines, covering the case of a blank entry in the kind column, are easiest to understand. This block simply tests the field editor, where the editing is actually taking place, to see whether it is blank and, if so, returns NO. This causes the application to beep and prevents editing in the cell from ending. You don't bother presenting an alert sheet here in this teaching application because you've already learned how to do this.

The first subsidiary `else if` block is more complex.

First, it tests the field editor to see whether the entry is blank and, if so, returns NO. Then it tests to make sure a nonblank entry is unique, using the `isUniqueAntiqueID:` method you wrote in Step 5, returning NO if it is not. If the flow of execution has reached this point, then all is well and the `lastAntiqueId` variable must be incremented. Notice that the `isUniqueAntiqueID:` test only prevents entry of an ID equal to or less than the last ID saved in `lastAntiqueID`. The user may assign an arbitrarily high ID to any antique, and thereafter no lower ID may be entered. You will likely want to use some more elaborate test in your applications to prevent a prankster from incrementing the ID by a million.

The test of whether the table is currently in the midst of an undo operation at the beginning of this code block has to do with live undo and redo. The remaining tests in this block are relevant only if the `control:textShouldEndEditing:` delegate method is called while the user is trying to commit data just typed into a cell in the table. You will see in Step 12 that this delegate method will also be called while the user is undoing live editing of a cell, and in that case it is not appropriate to perform these tests. You will implement the `isUndoing` method in Step 12.

Step 11: Implement Drag and Drop for Table Cells

There are two aspects to drag-and-drop editing in tables: dragging entire rows into and out of the table and dragging the contents of individual cells. Other available examples, such as the DragNDropOutlineView example project installed with the Developer Tools, cover the former topic well, so I won't cover it. You will learn how to drag the contents of individual table cells here, however.

You first addressed dragging and dropping the contents of a text field in Recipe 8, and you will use the same technique here. Basically, you just add a registration message for the table to the method that registers the dragging types any control will recognize and create a category on NSTableView that implements the necessary NSDraggingInfo protocol method. Since you have done this for other text field cells recently, I will just offer the code here without additional explanation. See Recipe 8 for more information.

1. In the VRTextFieldController.m category source file `registerDragTypesForText FieldsTab` that you wrote in Recipe 8, add the following line at the end:

   ```
   [[self antiquesTable] registerForDraggedTypes:
       [NSArray arrayWithObject:NSStringPboardType]];
   ```

2. Use Project Builder to create new header and source files for an NSTableView+ VRDragTarget Cocoa Objective-C class and place them in the VRDragTarget subgroup of the Categories group in the Groups & Files pane of the project window.

3. In the new header file, after any standard description and disclaimer comments you may wish to insert, add these lines:

```
#import <AppKit/NSTableView.h>

@interface NSTableView (VRDragTarget)

@end
```

4. In the new source file, after your comments, add the following lines:

```
#import "NSTableView+VRDragTarget.h"
#import <Cocoa/Cocoa.h> // r11s11

@implementation NSTableView (VRDragTarget)

- (unsigned int)draggingUpdated:(id <NSDraggingInfo>)sender {
    if ([[[sender draggingPasteboard] types]
            containsObject:NSStringPboardType]) {
        if ([sender draggingSourceOperationMask] &
                NSDragOperationCopy) {
            NSPoint mouseLocation = [self convertPoint:
                    [sender draggingLocation] fromView:nil];
            int row = [self rowAtPoint:mouseLocation];
            int column = [self columnAtPoint:mouseLocation];
            if (row != -1 && column != -1) {
                [self selectRow:row byExtendingSelection:NO];
                [self editColumn:column row:row
                        withEvent:nil select:YES];
                if ([sender draggingSource] == [self currentEditor]) {
                    [self abortEditing];
                } else {
                    return NSDragOperationCopy;
                }
            }
        }
    }
    return NSDragOperationNone;
}

@end
```

Step 12: Implement Live Undo and Redo in Table Cells

You have implemented live undo and redo of editing in text fields and form fields. For the sake of completeness, try the same trick with cells in a table view. The technique is identical, except for one difficult wrinkle unique to tables.

This issue arises from the fact that you can't undo the addition of a record to a table. Recall from Recipes 7 and 9 that live undo and redo depend crucially on the user's committing the edited data by pressing Enter or taking another action to indicate that editing is complete. Committing the data ends editing and triggers the unwinding of the edited field's live undo stack, then invokes a **set** accessor that registers an undo action. This last step causes Cocoa to clear the redo stack of all live editing actions, leaving behind only the new **set** undo action.

This works correctly when the user is editing a table cell and presses Enter or commits the edit in some other recognized way. However, if the user instead undoes all the editing and then undoes the addition of the record or the setting of a prior record value, the final step—clearing the redo stack—does not happen because the user hasn't committed the editing session. To overcome this problem, you will have to intercept the user's choice of Edit > Undo Add and invoke the **set** accessor programmatically before the command actually deletes the record.

A similar problem would exist if the user added or deleted a record without first committing a pending cell edit, but you avoided having to deal with it by disabling the New and Delete buttons during editing in Step 6.

1. Use Project Builder to create new header and source files for a Cocoa Objective-C class named VRUndoableTableView and place them in the Controls group in the Groups & Files pane of the project window.

2. In the new header file, after your standard comments, add the lines shown below. As was the case with the undoable subclasses you created for text fields and form fields, the file is virtually empty. It just implements the VRUndoableTextControl formal protocol you wrote in Recipe 9, Step 5.

```
#import <Cocoa/Cocoa.h>
#import "VRUndoableTextControl.h"

@interface VRUndoableTableView : NSTableView
        <VRUndoableTextControl> {
}

@end
```

3. In the new source file, after your comments, add the lines shown below. This just imports the VRUndoableTextControl.include file you wrote in Recipe 9, Step 5.

```
#import "VRUndoableTableView.h"

@implementation VRUndoableTableView

#include "VRUndoableTextControl.include"

@end
```

4. Revise the first `if` test in the `windowWillReturnFieldEditor:toObject:` method in the **UNDO MANAGEMENT** section of the source file VRMainWindowController.m to read as follows, so the new class will use the separate field editor required for live undo and redo:

```
if ((sender == [self window]) &&
      ([object isKindOfClass:[VRUndoableTextField class]] ||
      [object isKindOfClass:[VRUndoableForm class]] ||
      [object isKindOfClass:[VRUndoableTableView class]])) {
```

5. Now you are ready to deal with the problem described at the beginning of this step. You must write some code to force the application to generate an undo action clearing the redo stack when the user undoes all edits and then chooses Edit > Undo Add to undo the addition of the record or Edit > Undo Set to undo a prior committed edit.

The user action that must trigger this code is the user's choosing an Undo menu item having a particular title. As you have come to expect, Cocoa offers a notification allowing you to capture the user's choosing any menu item, `NSMenuWillSendActionNotification`, so you can execute code of your own before the menu item's action message is sent. You must register an observer of this notification and write a method to generate the needed undo action.

Where to put this code? So far, you have succeeded in encapsulating almost all of your live undo and redo code in the VRUndoableTextControl.include file, and that's where you should add the new code. By placing it in the include file, you ensure that only subclasses of controls you've explicitly declared undoable, such as VRUndoableTableView, can use it.

In VRUndoableTextControl.include, you already register controls that include it as observers of three notifications issued by the undo manager, in the `textDidBeginEditing:` method that is called as soon as the user starts typing into an undoable field. You will register for `NSMenuWillSendActionNotification` here, too. This notification is only of interest to an undoable table view, which is the only control that needs to take special action when the user chooses the Undo menu item. Since other kinds of controls will use this include file as well, you need to enclose the registration inside an `if` block testing whether this control is a subclass of NSTableView. Insert this code after the three existing registrations:

```
if ([self isKindOfClass:[NSTableView class]]) {
    [[NSNotificationCenter defaultCenter] addObserver:self
        selector:@selector(handleWillSendAction:)
        name: NSMenuWillSendActionNotification object: nil];
}
```

Similarly, you must remove this control as an observer of this notification in the `textDidEndEditing:` method, after the existing removals:

```
if ([self isKindOfClass:[NSTableView class]]) {
    [[NSNotificationCenter defaultCenter] removeObserver:self
        name: NSMenuWillSendActionNotification object: nil];
}
```

Finally, you must write the method that Cocoa will invoke in response to the notification. You can place it at the end of the include file:

```
- (void)handleWillSendAction:(NSNotification *)notification {
    if (undoCount == 0 &&
            [self isKindOfClass:[NSTableView class]]) {
        NSString *menuItemTitle = [[[notification userInfo]
            valueForKey:@"MenuItem"] title];
        NSString *undoActionName = [[self undoManager]
            undoActionName];
        if ([menuItemTitle hasPrefix:NSLocalizedString(@"Undo",
                @"Undo menu item prefix")] &&
                ([undoActionName hasPrefix:
                NSLocalizedString(@"Add",
                @"Add antique record menu item prefix")] ||
                [undoActionName hasPrefix:
                NSLocalizedString(@"Set",
                @"Set antique record cell menu item prefix")])) {
            if ([[self window] makeFirstResponder:
                    [self window]]) {
                [[self undoManager] undo];
            }
            isUndoing = NO;
        }
    }
}
```

Don't forget to add the localized strings to Localizable.strings, if you haven't done so already.

In summary, this method checks first to make sure that the undo stack has been unwound and that this is a table view. Then it obtains the menu item title (looking for Undo) and the undo action name (looking for one that starts with Add or Set). It uses the `userInfo` dictionary sent along with the notification to get the title. It calls an NSUndoManager method to get the name. It uses NSString's `hasPrefix:` method to capture the first part of the strings.

The method then performs its critical role of clearing the redo stack. It uses the standard technique to end editing in a field programmatically, making the table view's window the first responder. This calls the model's `set` accessor and registers an undo action, which causes Cocoa to clear the redo stack.

NSMenu provides the notification you registered to observe, `NSMenuWillSend-ActionNotification`, so your application can execute some code of its own between the time when the user chooses a menu item and the time when Cocoa executes the action method connected to the menu item. Since the Undo Add menu item that the user invoked to begin this whole process will therefore be carried out right after this method has completed its work and immediately moved to the redo stack, it is necessary to move the new Undo Set action to the redo stack first to maintain the correct order of redo actions. You accomplish this by having the undo manager actually perform the new Undo Set action before it carries out the Undo Add action. The leftover live undo actions have already been unwound from the undo stack and cleared from the redo stack, and calling undo moves the Undo Set action to the redo stack. Calling undo is harmless here because the value doesn't change—it is the original value typed by the user because the user has just undone all edits.

All this may seem very devious, but it works and it uses standard Cocoa methods. The application would be simpler to write if Cocoa had live undo and redo built in, but for the time being you must roll your own.

6. There is one remaining issue, which you wouldn't have encountered if you hadn't written a unique-ID requirement into the Vermont Recipes application specification. In Step 10, you added an `else if` block to the `control:textShouldEndEditing:` delegate method, which, among other things, rejects an attempt to enter an antique ID that is not unique. The delegate method works fine if it is invoked after the user types a new ID, but it fails if it is invoked during an undo operation because by definition the ID reinstated by the undo operation is no longer unique. That is, it was used once before, when this record was first created. Since it's the same record, there is nothing wrong with reinstating this ID.

Somehow, you have to prevent this delegate method test from running during an undo operation. It turns out that you can't use NSUndoManager's isUndoing method for this purpose, because it doesn't return YES until the Undo Add action method is invoked. The isUndoing method isn't invoked while your live undo code is running, because the NSMenuWillSendActionNotification notification temporarily suspended it so you could get some work of your own done. So you will have to implement your own isUndoing method to return YES at the right time. This requires adding a new static variable to the VRUndoableTextControl.include file, exposing it through a new isUndoing method declared in the VRUndoable-TableView formal protocol so your main window controller can call it, and setting its value at appropriate times.

In VRUndoableTextControl.include, add this definition at the end of the static variable definitions:

```
static BOOL isUndoing;
```

In the same file, define the isUndoing method after the definition of the isEditing method:

```
- (BOOL)isUndoing {
    return isUndoing;
}
```

Declare the new method in the VRUndoableTextControl.h protocol file:

```
- (BOOL) isUndoing;
```

Returning to the VRUndoableTextControl.include file, set the value of the static variable in several places. In the textDidBeginEditing: method, set it to NO after setting isEditing to YES:

```
isUndoing = NO;
```

Set it to NO again at the end of the textDidEndEditing: method:

```
isUndoing = NO;
```

Set it to YES in the handleDidUndo: method:

```
isUndoing = YES;
```

You already set it to NO in the handleWillSendAction: method in Instruction 5, above.

Now, when the isUndoing method is tested in the control:textShouldEndEditing: delegate method, it will prevent the antiques table else if block from executing during an undo operation.

Step 13: Add a Keyboard Shortcut for Deleting a Record

You need to learn how to capture key events because most applications offer keyboard shortcuts and power users demand them. Now is as good a time as any. In this step, you will override NSResponder's **keyDown:** method in the table view so the user can press the Delete key to delete a selected row from the table without having to use the mouse.

A common technique for implementing a keyboard shortcut for a user control is to subclass the control and override its **keyDown:** method. Therefore, you will write a new class, derived from the VRUndoableTableView subclass of NSTableView you created in the previous step. At the end of this step, you will learn a little about alternative techniques.

1. Use Project Builder to create new header and source files for a Cocoa Objective-C class named VRAntiquesTableView and place them in the Controls group in the Groups & Files pane of the project window.

2. In the new header file, after your standard comments, add the lines shown below. As you see, the header file is essentially empty, simply importing a couple of required header files and indicating that this subclass inherits from VRUndoableTableView.

```
#import <Cocoa/Cocoa.h>
#import "VRUndoableTableView.h"
#import "VRUndoableTextControl.h"

@interface VRAntiquesTableView : VRUndoableTableView {
}

@end
```

Remember that you first referred to this new class, VRAntiquesTableView, in Step 2, where I told you that you'd declare it in Step 13. If you temporarily referred to NSTableView instead in Step 2 in order to compile the application, you now have to change every such reference back to VRAntiquesTableView. Project Builder's batch search-and-replace function is perfect for doing this.

3. In the new source file, after your comments, add these lines:

```
#import "VRAntiquesTableView.h"
#import "VRMainWindowController.h"

@implementation VRAntiquesTableView

- (void)keyDown:(NSEvent *)event {
    unichar key = [[event charactersIgnoringModifiers]
            characterAtIndex:0];
    unsigned int flags = [event modifierFlags];
    if (key == NSDeleteCharacter && flags == 0 &&
            [self numberOfRows] > 0 && [self selectedRow] != -1) {
        [[[self window] windowController]
                deleteAntiqueRecordAction:self];
    } else {
        [super keyDown:event];
    }
}

@end
```

Cocoa declares the **keyDown:** method in NSResponder, which is the parent class from which user controls such as a table view inherit. NSResponder's version of the method simply passes the message up the responder chain to the next responder. Each responder in the chain will do likewise until one is found that overrides the method. If the table view doesn't override it, the next responders in the chain are likely to be its containing scroll view, perhaps its containing tab view, and thereafter its window. If nothing else in the responder chain overrides the application, the application will beep. By overriding it in this table view subclass, you can do anything you like in response to the **keyDown:** event and then either stop it or pass it along for additional handling further up the responder chain.

Here, you start by examining the event object passed in the **event** parameter to determine what key the user pressed. You do this by first calling NSEvent's **charactersIgnoringModifiers** method and getting the initial character—that is, the character at index 0. Next you get the event's **modifierFlags**, so you can determine whether the user held down any modifier key while pressing the first key. Finally, if the key is **NSDeleteCharacter**, the user didn't hold down any modifier keys, and a row in the table is currently selected, you call the **deleteAntiqueRecordAction:** action method you wrote in Step 6, passing the table itself as the sending object.

If none of these conditions is true, the method calls **super** to pass the **keyDown:** event to the next responder, which will eventually cause the application to beep if nothing else up the responder chain intercepts it. For example, the application will beep if no row in the table was selected or if the user was holding down the Command key when he or she pressed the Delete key.

Notice that the method made no effort to determine whether the table view had focus when the user pressed the Delete key. This is unnecessary, because if the antiques table is the first responder at the time a user presses any key and the user isn't currently editing any of its cells, the antiques table will be the only control in the responder chain and only it will receive the event. If some other control is the first responder, the table will not see the event because the table is not in the current responder chain. Its **keyDown:** method will not be called.

This method will continue to work even if you add a second instance of VRAntiquesTableView to the application. Cocoa will always know which instance of the table view is in the current responder chain, based on which control the user last clicked or tabbed into. Cocoa will invoke that instance's **keyDown:** method, which will in turn send its **self** to the window's action method to delete the row in the correct table.

Cocoa experts will often admonish you to avoid subclassing to override a method. This is good advice, but it is not a hard-and-fast rule. It flows from the original design goals of the Objective-C language, and from the Cocoa frameworks and their predecessors. If you understand what you're getting into, you can implement something like the Delete key in a subclass as you did here.

What trouble might you get into when you do it this way? Objective-C was designed as a lightweight language, and it does not implement multiple inheritance. This can put you in a bind if you subclass inappropriately. Suppose, for example, you want to implement another antiques table in Vermont Recipes for, say, a separate inventory but for some reason you don't want it to support live undo. You would, of course, write it as a subclass of NSTableView, not VRUndoableTableView. Then, however, you wouldn't be able to use the VRAntiquesTableView class to make it recognize the Delete key, because this subclass inherits from VRUndoableTableView. You would have to write another subclass of NSTableView and implement the same **keyDown:** method in it.

There is a way to implement keyboard shortcuts so as to avoid this issue, and you should generally use it instead. In Cocoa, you can often do things by alternative means instead of subclassing—for example, you can implement a delegate method or a category. In the case of **keyDown:** and other events, you can take advantage of the responder chain. If a view in the responder chain or the window doesn't catch the event, Cocoa will look in the window's delegate to see if it is implemented there.

In other words, the normal path of events up the Cocoa responder chain includes the window's delegate. Since in Vermont Recipes the window controller is the window's delegate, you can simply implement **keyDown:** in VRMainWindowController. Because the event may have come from any user control in the window, you will have to do a little extra work to determine which view was the window's first responder.

You will not see a full example of the window delegate technique here, but you can prove to yourself that it works by implementing a simple test routine. Temporarily place the following method anywhere in VRMainWindowController.m. When you have finished this recipe, run the application and press any key. When you check the run log, you will see a report showing the key you pressed and the view that was the window's first responder at that time. To see that the antiques table is the first responder when you press any key, click first in an empty area of the antiques table.

```
- (void)keyDown:(NSEvent *)event { // TEMP
    unichar key = [[event charactersIgnoringModifiers]
      characterAtIndex:0];
    NSLog(@"Pressed key:%c", key);
    NSLog(@"First responder:%@", [[self window] firstResponder]);
    [super keyDown:event];
}
```

In the case of the antiques table, you can assign a keyboard shortcut in still another way, which is even easier than the two techniques just described. Use Interface Builder to assign the Delete key as the Delete button's command-key equivalent. Select the Delete button and, in the NSButton Info Panel, use the pop-up menu to select Delete. That's all there is to it! Of course, you won't always have a button or a menu item available, so this simplest of all techniques won't always be feasible. Also, this technique only allows you to assign one command-key equivalent to a button.

To justify having written a method implementing the Delete key as a keyboard shortcut, go ahead and assign some other keys as command-key equivalents for the New and Delete buttons—say, the plus sign (+) and the minus sign (−). For each button, just type its command key equivalent in the Equiv text field in the Info Panel and select the Command key checkbox. Now the user can type Shift-Command-plus (+) on the main keyboard, or Command-plus on the keypad, and a new record will appear in the table view. With a record selected, Command-minus on the keyboard or the keypad will delete it, as will the Delete key.

Note that a button's command-key equivalent must be unique. It doesn't depend on any view's being the window's first responder but instead triggers the action method associated with this one button. You can't reuse the command-key combination to trigger different actions in other controls.

Step 14: Prepare the Table View for the Key View Loop

The Mac OS X 10.2 AppKit release notes mention several bugs in NSTableView that were caught too late to be fixed before release. One of the bugs mentioned in the release notes affects the Vermont Recipes application, so you will fix it now. Since the release notes imply that this bug will be fixed in a future release, you will need to monitor future releases to see whether this fix should be removed or rendered inoperative in a future release.

The AppKit release notes report that in Mac OS X 10.2 a table view will not be included in the key view loop. Although the release notes do not say so, this bug only affects the key view loop when the System Preferences Keyboard Full Keyboard Access pane is set to "Text boxes and lists only." The key view loop does include table views when the Preferences pane is set to "Any control." The bug still exists in Mac OS X 10.2.1.

The release notes recommend subclassing NSTableView to fix the bug: "NSTableView returns NO from **needsPanelToBecomeKey.** This means by default a user that navigates using the tab key will skip over tables and outline views. To work around this, you can subclass NSTableView and return YES from **needsPanelToBecomeKey.**"

However, you already know a better way to implement bug fixes: write a category on the offending Cocoa class. To do this, create new header and source files named NSTableView+VRTableViewBugfixes.h and NSTableView+VRTableViewBugfixes.m and place them in the Categories group in the Groups & Files pane of the project window.

In fact, the Categories group is getting a little crowded. You might want to create some new subgroups within it and rename the existing VRDragTarget subgroup. How about new subgroups named Bug Fixes, Drag Targets, and Utilities? Then move the header and source files into their corresponding subgroups.

According to the release notes, you need only reimplement the needsPanelToBecomeKey method. In addition to your usual comments and disclaimers, the new header file should look like that shown below. The needsPanelToBecomeKey method is declared in Cocoa so you needn't redeclare it here.

```
#import <Cocoa/Cocoa.h>

@interface NSTableView (VRTableViewBugfixes)

@end
```

The source file should look like this:

```
#import "NSTableView+VRTableViewBugfixes.h"

@implementation NSTableView (VRTableViewBugfixes)

- (BOOL)needsPanelToBecomeKey {
    return YES;
}

@end
```

When the user tabs to the table view, the first item in the view will become highlighted. If the table view is empty, it will not be given a focus ring, but it will be the current first responder nonetheless.

Step 15: Read the Source Files into the Nib File and Connect the Actions

You need to read several new outlets and actions into the nib file and make several connections.

1. In Interface Builder, select the Classes tab in the nib file window, then choose Classes > Read Files. In the resulting dialog, select the header file in which you have created the new outlets and actions, VRMainWindowController.h, then click the Parse button.

2. Using now familiar Interface Builder techniques, make the following connections:

   Connect the File's Owner to these outlets: antiquesTable, addAntiqueKindButton, newAntiqueButton, and deleteAntiqueButton.

   Connect the VRAntiquesTableView **datasource** and **delegate** outlets to File's Owner.

   Connect the Add Kind button's **target** outlet to File's Owner (this connects the addAntiqueKindAction: method).

   Connect the New button's **target** outlet to File's Owner (this connects the newAntiqueRecordAction: method).

Connect the Delete button's **target** outlet to File's Owner (this connects the **deleteAntiqueRecordAction:** method).

3. If you haven't already done so, insert the new table and three buttons into the **key** view loop.

Step 16: Build and Run the Application

Build and run the application, then test the operation of the antiques table and its three related buttons. There is a lot to test.

Start simply. Click the New button or press Command-+ to add a record. The default kind, New, is selected, so start typing something, such as **Chess Sets**. You don't have to click in the cell first, because it's already selected and ready for data entry. This is how adding and editing records in place within the table works. Note that the New and Delete buttons became disabled as soon as you started typing.

Choose Edit > Undo Typing and make sure you can do live undo and redo in table cells. Choose Edit > Undo Add Antique ID 1 to remove the record from the table. Then choose Redo repeatedly until you're back to the cell's original state when you finished typing. Notice that the last redo menu item was not Redo Typing, but Redo Set Kind of Antique ID 1. This is because the new code you added in Step 12 forces a pending edit to commit when the user chooses Undo Add while editing a cell. The data value in the cell doesn't change in response to choosing Redo Set Kind of Antique ID 1 because that was the last value you set by undoing the live editing session. Notice that the New key became reenabled when the editing session ended.

Click repeatedly to select and deselect the record. This enables and disables the Delete button repeatedly. Click the Delete button while the record is selected. This removes it from the table. Choose Edit > Undo Delete Antique ID 1, and it returns. While it is selected, press the Delete key or the Command-– key on the keyboard to remove it again.

Double-click the record's ID and type **a**. Since you typed a nonnumeric character, the computer beeps at you immediately due to the on-the-fly formatter you connected to cells in this column. Type **0** or **1** and press Enter. The computer beeps because it doesn't consider these unique.

Create several new records and assign them various kinds, such as **Tools** and **Violins**, pressing the Enter key or clicking in an empty part of the table to commit each entry before adding the next.

Type Tools in the combo box and press Enter. All records disappear from the table except those whose Kind is Tools or New. Type Q in the combo box. Before you can type u, the entire word *Quilts* appears, ready for you to press Enter. This is the combo box autocompletion feature at work. Choose All from the combo box pop-up menu to bring all of the records back into view.

Select a record whose Kind is Tools, then click the Add Kind button. Open the combo box pop-up menu and see that Tools has been added as one of the permanent filtering classifications. Type T in the combo box. Autocompletion fills in the full word *Tools* for you. Press Enter and see all Tools records in the table.

Finally, drag one of the column headers over the other to reverse the column order. Repeat some of the tests you already ran to see that they still work properly.

Conclusion

You have reached the end of Section 2 of *Vermont Recipes*. There are many more user controls available in Cocoa, but I don't have room to cover all of them here. The ambitious treatment of table views that you just completed will help you get through outlines and browsers easily yourself, and other methods, such as progress indicators and steppers, will also come easily to you.

In Section 3, which consists only of Recipe 12, you will learn how to store objects to disk using keyed archiving. The vehicle to demonstrate keyed archiving will be the antiques table you just created, for which you haven't yet written any storage routines. Archiving has been a part of Cocoa for a long time, but keyed archiving is new in Mac OS X 10.2, and it's an important advance.

Data Storage

In Recipe 1, Steps 4 and 5, you learned how to write the Vermont Recipes application's data to persistent storage and read it back. The techniques you learned there used standard-issue Cocoa technology, but I promised you a new technique eventually. You will learn the new technique, keyed archiving and unarchiving, in Recipe 12, the sole recipe in Section 3.

Archiving has been a staple of Cocoa for years, but until now it has imposed some limitations on how you can write and read documents. The techniques you learned in Recipe 1 were not based on archiving but instead implemented a technique that took advantage of the flexibility of dictionaries, with their inherent use of key-value pairs.

Now, with Mac OS X 10.2, Apple has upgraded Cocoa to include a new form of archiving, known as keyed archiving. This is what Recipe 12 will teach. Keyed archiving is similar to the techniques you learned in Recipe 1, which also associated the data with keys. In fact, you'll reuse the keys you already declared in Recipe 1 and throughout Section 2.

Keyed archiving requires Mac OS X 10.2 or newer, both for building an application and for running its data storage routines.

RECIPE 12

Keyed Archiving

In Recipe 1, Steps 4 and 5, you learned two techniques to save a document's data to persistent storage. You implemented one of them throughout Section 2 of *Vermont Recipes* as you added new user controls—and therefore the associated data—to the application, until you got to the antiques array in Recipe 11. Using these techniques as you added new kinds of data to the application was easy up to Recipe 11 because the data values were simple. You

HIGHLIGHTS:

Using keyed archiving to save data to persistent storage and retrieve it

Using the userInfo parameter when posting notifications

could use standard NSDictionary methods in a straightforward way because each instance variable represented a single value that could be saved and read using a single statement.

If you had tried to tackle saving and reading the antiques array using these techniques, however, you would have had to do more work—for example, looping through every record in the array to take care of each array item separately. This would not have been an insuperable obstacle by any means, but naturally you'd prefer a method that takes less work and conveys at least the same advantages.

Almost from the beginning of *Vermont Recipes,* I've been promising you another way to save data, and the time has come to explore it. In Recipe 12, you will learn how to save your application's data using *archiving.* One of the more remarkable Cocoa enabling technologies, archiving—like undo and redo support in the AppKit—gives you a bigger return on your investment than you might expect. When you implement undo and redo, you get automatic tracking of document changes for free. Similarly, you can use archiving to get several other benefits with little additional effort, including a foundation on which you can more easily implement pasteboard types, services, and distributed objects. Here, archiving is used strictly for data storage.

Archiving has long been an important feature of Cocoa, but it has suffered from several limitations that could make the use of alternative techniques, such as those developed in Recipe 1, more attractive. However, Mac OS X 10.2 has greatly enhanced this feature with the addition of *keyed* archiving. This approach eliminates the restrictions on traditional Cocoa archiving and will improve your ability to maintain both backward and forward compatibility with documents created in older or newer versions of your application. Furthermore, keyed archiving is as easy to implement as the techniques you learned in Recipe 1 for simple data values, and much easier in the case of a complex data object like the array that holds the antiques inventory created in Recipe 11. In view of the power and easy implementation of keyed archiving, any new Cocoa document-based application written for Mac OS X 10.2 and later should implement it. (For discussion of the issues presented by existing Cocoa applications that need to maintain compatibility with document formats employed in earlier application versions, see the Foundation release notes for Mac OS X 10.2.)

If some of this sounds familiar, it is because the document storage routines you wrote in Recipe 1, Steps 4 and 5, also used keys to identify individual data items. In those routines, you used keys in conjunction with NSDictionary objects, achieving some of the advantages now available through keyed archiving. Keyed archiving is superior, however, because it does much more of the work for you, especially with respect to complex data objects like arrays. In addition, it is capable of optimizations that may reduce the size of your saved documents.

You will begin Recipe 12 by implementing a keyed archiving mechanism to store the antiques inventory and other data structures you created in Recipe 11. You will first implement old-style archiving, then revise the code to take advantage of the new keyed archiving capabilities of Mac OS X 10.2. Toward the end of Recipe 12, you will change all of the data storage routines you wrote in Recipe 1 and Section 2 so that they use keyed archiving as well. You'll find this conversion remarkably easy to accomplish, because keyed archiving dovetails nicely with the keyed dictionaries you used until now.

The techniques you will learn here require Mac OS X 10.2 or newer for both building the application and running its data storage routines. It's not difficult to include system version checks in the application and keep the older code for execution when it runs on older systems, but I do not address backward compatibility issues in *Vermont Recipes*.

Before beginning, you should prepare your project files for Recipe 12. Update the build version in Info.Plist Entries to **12**. You should also increase the **VRDocumentVersion** static variable in VRDocument.m to **6**, to reflect the fact that the storage format of the document will once again change.

Since you will replace some existing code in several classes in this recipe, you will probably find it safer and easier to follow along if you do the additional preparatory work of commenting out the old code now. You can delete it altogether when you get to the end of this recipe and confirm that everything works as advertised. In each of the VRDocument.h, VRButtonModel.h, VRSliderModel.h, and VRTextFieldModel.h header files, comment out the entire STORAGE section. In the VRDocument.m source file, comment out all of the STORAGE section except the "Keys and values for dictionary" subsection and the **keepBackupFile** method. In each of the VRButtonModel.m, VRSliderModel.m, and VRTextFieldModel.m source files, comment out the entire STORAGE section except the "Keys and values for dictionary" subsection.

Step 1: Encode and Decode the Antiques Inventory

Archiving involves two steps: You must first encode the application's data, along with other information about your application's classes and their interrelationships, into a flat byte stream known as an archive. Then you must write the archive to persistent storage. Unarchiving reverses this process, reading the archive from persistent storage, then decoding it to restore the application's data. Cocoa provides convenience methods that accomplish archiving and saving to disk and then do the reverse, each in a single step. Cocoa also provides lower-level routines that allow you to break down the process into more detailed steps and customize it. Here you will see examples of both techniques, the former for old-style archiving and the latter for keyed archiving.

In this step, you will learn how to encode and decode the data using methods declared in Foundation's abstract NSCoder class and the NSCoding formal protocol declared in NSObject.h. NSCoder and NSCoding haven't changed so much in Mac OS X 10.2 that radically different techniques are required, so this step will look familiar to experienced Cocoa developers.

You will learn in Step 2 that you accomplish keyed archiving by walking the *object graphs* of your application. A keyed archive consists of encoded data from one or more objects at the archive's uppermost level, as well as data encoded from every subsidiary object referenced in each top-level object and in all lower-level objects to any depth. Because archiving is object-based, you must encode the data on an object-by-object basis. Each object in your application that holds data to be saved must encode its own data. The data consists, of course, of the values held in the object's instance variables, although you need not encode all of the instance variables. Unarchiving reconstitutes the application's data by loading the archive from disk and walking the object graphs to decode each object's data and restore the values to the instance variables. Again, each object decodes its own data values and reassigns them to the proper instance variables.

For an object to encode and decode its data, it must implement the two methods declared in the NSCoding formal protocol, `encodeWithCoder:` and `initWithCoder:`. As with all formal protocols, an object that implements these methods must declare that it conforms to the protocol by including the protocol's name in angle brackets in the object's `@interface` directive.

Cocoa method names generally describe what they do, and these two methods are no exception. The first encodes data in the object when the user saves changes made during a working session. The second decodes the data during the object's initialization when it is read from persistent storage, both when an existing document is opened and when an open document is reverted to its last saved state. In each case, a *coder* supplied in the method's parameter does the work. The coder object supplied to the encodeWithCoder: method is known as an **encoder** because encoded data will fill it as your implementation of the protocol method encodes the object. The coder object supplied with the initWithCoder: method is known as a **decoder** because it supplies the encoded data from disk that your implementation of the protocol method will decode. You will learn more in Step 2 about where the supplied coder comes from for each method, but you can anticipate that it is an object descended from NSCoder.

The NSCoder abstract class declares a variety of basic methods and convenience methods, such as encodeObject: and decodeObject:. You call them in your implementation of the two protocol methods to encode and decode various types of instance variables. Normally, you call them through concrete Cocoa classes such as NSArchiver and NSUnarchiver or NSKeyedArchiver and NSKeyedUnarchiver, all of which are subclasses of NSCoder.

1. Begin by declaring that the VRAntiqueRecord class you wrote in Recipe 11 conforms to the NSCoding formal protocol. Change the **@interface** directive in the header file VRAntiqueRecord.h to read as follows:

   ```
   @interface VRAntiqueRecord : NSObject <NSCoding> {
   ```

   If you were to attempt to build the application now, you would receive several compiler warnings, including these: "method definition for '-initWithCoder:' not found," "method definition for '-encodeWithCoder:' not found," and "'VRAntiqueRecord' does not fully implement the 'NSCoding' protocol." Your next step, obviously, is to implement the two missing protocol methods.

2. At the end of the source file VRAntiqueRecord.m, implement the initWithCoder: protocol method initially in the old, pre–Mac OS X 10.2 way, without keys, as follows:

   ```
   #pragma mark STORAGE

   - (id)initWithCoder:(NSCoder *)decoder {
       self = [super init];
       [self setAntiqueID:[decoder decodeObject]];
       [self setAntiqueKind:[decoder decodeObject]];
       return self;
   }
   ```

   The unarchiving routines you will write in Step 2 will call this initWithCoder: method automatically, once for every antiques record object read from the document on disk. These unarchiving routines will create a temporary NSCoder object and pass it to this method in its **decoder** parameter. Here in the protocol method, you simply call each of an antique record object's accessor methods to set the associated instance variable's value to the object returned by the coder's `decodeObject` method. Finally, as with any initializer, you return `self`, which is a fully restored antiques record.

You recall from earlier recipes that initializers usually call **super**'s designated initializer to let inherited objects initialize themselves first. The `initWithCoder:` protocol method normally has a similar requirement—namely, that it call **super**'s implementation of the protocol method first. You would therefore normally begin this method with a statement like this: `self = [super initWithCoder:decoder]`. However, this requirement applies only if **super** conforms to the NSCoding protocol—that is, only if it implements the `initWithCoder:` method. NSObject does not conform to the protocol, and VRAntiqueRecord is an immediate descendant of NSObject. You therefore cannot call super's `initWithCoder:` method here, because it doesn't declare such a method. Instead, you set `self` to `[super init]`.

One consequence of using the antiques record's **set** accessors to set the object's instance variable values is that the objects returned by the coder's `decodeObject` method are retained upon receipt. When an antiques record was first created, its designated initializer, `initWithID:document:`, was called to allocate and thus retain an **antiqueID** and an **antiqueKind** object. The **set** accessors, like all of the application's **set** accessors for object values, releases this old value and copies the new value. If you did not call the **set** accessors in the protocol method but instead assigned the decoded value directly to an instance variable, you would have to release and retain these objects in line.

You must copy or retain the returned objects, although the reasons are different in Mac OS X 10.1 and earlier than in Mac OS X 10.2. In the latter, the `decodeObject` method that you invoke in the `initwithCoder:` protocol method implementation returns the object autoreleased, as do most Foundation methods that return objects. As with all autoreleased objects, you must retain it if you want it to stick around for the life of your document.

The fact that the object is returned autoreleased is new in Mac OS X 10.2. In earlier versions of Mac OS X, the `decodeObject` method was an exception to the usual Foundation policy on this point—the returned object lived exactly as long as the unarchiver object. You still had to retain it if you wanted to keep it, so your code is not affected by this change.

3. In versions of Mac OS X older than 10.2, the order in which you decoded objects in the `initWithCoder:` protocol method was critical. You had to decode them in exactly the same order in which they were originally encoded and saved to disk. Encoding the data *serialized* it in the given order, and there was no way to know while decoding it what data went with which instance variable except by doing it in the same order.

This fact had limiting consequences. Applications always had to read all the data in a document. They couldn't read it for selected pieces of data. They also couldn't check the document to see whether it held a particular piece of data that wasn't there. Together, these issues made it difficult to write new versions of an application that could read documents created by older versions, which didn't necessarily save the same kinds of data in the same order, and to read newer documents using older versions of the application.

To fix these problems, Mac OS X 10.2 introduced keyed archiving. In this type of archiving, the new NSKeyedArchiver class gives every encoded item in an archive a string name and the new NSKeyedUnarchiver class lets you use the saved string to decode objects from disk without regard to the order in which they were saved.

The old, nonkeyed archiving classes will remain in Cocoa for backward compatibility for some time. Existing applications that are being upgraded can intermix keyed and nonkeyed data so long as they follow some fairly complicated rules. The Mac OS X 10.2 Foundation release notes explain these rules, and I will not discuss them here.

Since you are writing the Vermont Recipes application strictly for use in Mac OS X 10.2 and later, you will take advantage of these important improvements and exclusively implement keyed archiving. To get started, you will now change the implementation of the **initWithCoder:** protocol method you just wrote to make use of the new keyed unarchiving capability. Your previous implementation of document storage used keyed dictionaries, so you can reuse the keys you have already written in most of the application's model classes. However, you did not previously write keys for the antiques inventory, so you will have to do so now.

At the beginning of the new STORAGE section of the source file VRAntique-Record.m, insert these keys:

```
// Keys and values

static NSString *VRAntiqueIdKey =
     @"VRAntiqueRecord Antique ID Key";
static NSString *VRAntiqueKindKey =
     @"VRAntiqueRecord Antique Kind Key";
```

4. Next, replace the **initWithCoder:** method you wrote in Instruction 2 with the following new version:

```
- (id)initWithCoder:(NSCoder *)decoder {
    self = [super init];
    [self setAntiqueID:
```

```
                    [decoder decodeObjectForKey:VRAntiqueIdKey]];
        [self setAntiqueKind:
                    [decoder decodeObjectForKey:VRAntiqueKindKey]];
        return self;
}
```

As you see, the only difference is that you now call a new method provided in NSKeyedArchiver, decodeObjectForKey:, in place of the old decodeObject: method, and you pass the new key to it. You will save the key along with the value so that it can be unarchived when read from disk without regard to the order in which the data values were saved.

5. In tackling the initWithCoder: protocol method first, you took things in reverse order, from the document's point of view. You must encode the object's data before it can be decoded.

   Initially using the old, pre–Mac OS X 10.2 technique (without keys), implement the encodeWithCoder: protocol method as follows, at the end of the VRAntique-Record.m source file:

```
- (void)encodeWithCoder:(NSCoder *)encoder {
    [encoder encodeObject:[self antiqueID]];
    [encoder encodeObject:[self antiqueKind]];
}
```

   Notice that you're encoding the instance variables in the order in which they will be decoded and that you don't ask **super** to encode itself first.

6. Now upgrade the implementation to take advantage of the new keyed archiving techniques introduced in Mac OS X 10.2. Replace the method you just wrote with the following:

```
- (void)encodeWithCoder:(NSCoder *)encoder {
    [encoder encodeObject:[self antiqueID]
            forKey:VRAntiqueIdKey];
    [encoder encodeObject:[self antiqueKind]
            forKey:VRAntiqueKindKey];
}
```

   The only difference is that a new parameter, labeled **forKey:**, allows you to pass in the key associated with the value. When the file is read from disk, Cocoa will return the value associated in the file with this key.

7. You have now implemented the NSCoding formal protocol for antiques records. You aren't done with encoding and decoding the antiques inventory, however. For one thing, you need to encode and decode the entire array of antiques records, not just its individual records. In addition, you need to save other data values associated with the inventory: namely, the antiques added kinds you arranged for in Recipe 11, Step 9 and the `lastAntiqueID` value from Recipe 11, Step 5, which governs the generation of unique IDs. To take care of these, you need to make the VRTextFieldModel model object as a whole, as well as the VRAntiqueRecord object, conform to the NSCoding protocol.

For now, you will do this as though the antiques inventory were the only data in the text field model object that required saving to persistent storage. Later, in Step 3, you will convert all of the other data in the text field model to archiving and unarchiving. Finally, in Step 4, you will invite the button model and slider model objects to join the party.

Start by declaring that VRTextFieldModel conforms to the NSCoding protocol. Revise the `@interface` directive in the VRTextFieldModel.h header file to read as follows:

```
@interface VRTextFieldModel : NSObject <NSCoding> {
```

8. At the end of the VRTextFieldModel.m source file, implement the `initWithCoder:` protocol method first the old way, without keys, as follows:

```
- (id)initWithCoder:(NSCoder *)decoder {
    self = [super init];
    [self setAntiques:[decoder decodeObject]];
    [decoder decodeValueOfObjCType:@encode(int)
            at:&lastAntiqueID];
    [self setAntiqueAddedKinds:[decoder decodeObject]];
    return self;
}
```

You see something new in this implementation, the `decodeValueOfObjCType:at:` method. You originally declared the `lastAntiqueID` instance variable as a simple C integer type, rather than a Cocoa NSNumber object. You pay the price for that decision now by having to treat this variable specially when encoding and decoding it, since you can't use the `decodeObject` method. Because C types are frequently used in Objective-C programming, NSCoder provides standard methods for encoding and decoding them, and Objective-C provides a special compiler directive, `@encode`, to assist you in getting the type string's specifier right. Using the `decodeValueOfObjCType:at:` method allows you to stuff the decoded value directly into the instance variable, bypassing its `set` accessor.

You didn't write **set** accessors for the two array objects, **antiques** and **antiqueAddedKinds**, in Recipe 11 because you thought you would never need to set the entire array at once. No matter; you can write them now. You will not register the initialization of these arrays with the undo manager, and for this reason you don't need to bracket the decoding messages in calls to **disableUndoRegistration** and **enableUndoRegistration**.

The **decodeObject** method as implemented in NSUnarchiver will recognize that these are array objects. It will automatically call the **initWithObject:** protocol method you wrote a few moments ago on each antiques record in the array, saving you the trouble of writing any code to loop through the array. Since **decodeObject** returns it as a complete NSArray object, you can pass it directly to the **set** accessor.

At appropriate places in the ACCESSORS section of the header file VRTextFieldModel.h, declare the two **set** accessor methods as follows:

```
- (void)setAntiques:(NSMutableArray *)inValue;
- (void)setAntiqueAddedKinds:(NSMutableArray *)inValue;
```

In the ACCESSORS section of the source file VRTextFieldModel.m, define them as follows:

```
- (void)setAntiques:(NSMutableArray *)inValue {
    [inValue retain];
    [antiques release];
    antiques = inValue;
}

- (void)setAntiqueAddedKinds:(NSMutableArray *)inValue {
    [inValue retain];
    [antiqueAddedKinds release];
    antiqueAddedKinds = inValue;
}
```

9. That was the old way to do it. The new, keyed way will still use your new **set** accessors, and the handling of the simple C data type will also use a **set** accessor, which you wrote in Recipe 11. First, however, declare the keys you will need, at the end of the existing "Keys and values" subsection of the STORAGE section of VRTextFieldModel.m, as shown in the following code. (You should shorten the name of the subsection, since you are no longer using a dictionary.)

```
// Antiques
static NSString *VRAntiquesKey =
        @"VRTextFieldModel Antiques Key";
```

(continues on next page)

```
static NSString *VRLastAntiqueIDKey =
    @"VRTextFieldModel AntiqueID Key";
static NSString *VRAntiqueAddedKindsKey =
    @"VRTextFieldModel AntiqueAddedKinds Key";
```

10. Now upgrade the implementation to employ keyed unarchiving. Substitute the following for the **initWithCoder:** method you wrote in Instruction 8:

```
- (id)initWithCoder:(NSCoder *)decoder {
    self = [super init];
    [self setAntiques:
        [decoder decodeObjectForKey:VRAntiquesKey]];
    [self setLastAntiqueID:
        [decoder decodeIntForKey:VRLastAntiqueIDKey]];
    [self setAntiqueAddedKinds:
        [decoder decodeObjectForKey:VRAntiqueAddedKindsKey]];
    return self;
}
```

You see that the method name for decoding simple C data types takes a different form for keyed archiving. The model for these new method names, such as the **decodeIntForKey:** method you used here, is the same as that of the **decodeObjectForKey:** method you saw earlier. It allows you to use the value's **set** accessor when decoding, instead of stuffing the value directly into the instance variable. Similar methods are provided for other common C data types. Less commonly used C data types are not provided for, and the Foundation release notes explain how to deal with them if you need to use them.

A potential gotcha lurks in the new decoding methods for C data types. If you are converting an application from another storage technique to keyed archiving, you must remember to retain the value returned by any new call to **decodeObjectForKey:** that replaces one of the old **decodeValueOfObjCType:at:** and similar calls, because the former returns an autoreleased object. This warning only applies if you convert the instance variable that holds the returned value from a C data type to an object. If it remains a C data type and you use a new keyed archiving call such as **decodeIntForKey:**, as was done here, you have nothing to worry about.

11. Now implement the **encodeWithCoder:** protocol method at the end of the VRTextFieldModel.m source file, using the old, nonkeyed methods first as follows:

```
- (void)encodeWithCoder:(NSCoder *)encoder {
    [encoder encodeObject:[self antiques]];
    [encoder encodeValueOfObjCType:@encode(int)
```

```
            at:&lastAntiqueID];
    [encoder encodeObject:[self antiqueAddedKinds]];
}
```

This is the mirror image of the `initWithCoder:` method, encoding the instance variables in the order in which they will be decoded.

12. Next, upgrade to keyed archiving. Substitute this new, keyed version of the method:

```
- (void)encodeWithCoder:(NSCoder *)encoder {
    [encoder encodeObject:[self antiques] forKey:VRAntiquesKey];
    [encoder encodeInt:[self lastAntiqueID]
        forKey:VRLastAntiqueIDKey];
    [encoder encodeObject:[self antiqueAddedKinds]
        forKey:VRAntiqueAddedKindsKey];
}
```

You see a similar change in the form of the method name for handling simple C data types, in the `encodeInt:forKey:` method. You encode and decode the data in the same order only because it is natural to organize the code in this way, but it is no longer required.

You have now written all the code you need to encode and decode the antiques inventory's data for Cocoa's archiving and unarchiving routines. The VRTextFieldModel and VRAntiqueRecord classes are the only model classes involved in holding data values for the antiques inventory.

Recall that the VRDocument class you created long ago serves in the Vermont Recipes application as a controller of the model objects, not as a model object itself. VRDocument holds no data of its own to write to disk but only tells the model objects it controls to take care of data storage. You are now ready to turn to VRDocument to implement archiving and unarchiving routines and accomplish that goal for the antiques inventory. You will upgrade the storage routines for other application data in Steps 3 and 4.

Step 2: Archive and Unarchive the Antiques Inventory

Throughout Section 2 of *Vermont Recipes*, the document wrote its data to persistent storage using the override of NSDocument's `writeToFile:ofType:` method you originally wrote in Recipe 1, Step 5. It read its data from storage using your override of NSDocument's `readFromFile:ofType:` method. Both of these methods did their

actual work by calling routines you wrote for each model object, `restoreData-`
`FromDictionary:` and `addDataToDictionary:`. Each of these methods used keys in the
form of fixed string values to differentiate among individual items of saved data.

These latter methods foreshadowed the keyed archiving technique you will use in
this step. The dictionary object you employed until now relied on keys to access
associated values without regard to their order within the dictionary. You were thus
able to declare and implement those methods in any order; that is, the order for
writing and the order for reading could differ. This would not have been possible
had you used old-style archiving instead, but now that keyed archiving is available
in Mac OS X 10.2, you can implement archiving and achieve similar benefits. You
can reuse the old keys you wrote for the dictionaries.

In old-style archiving, it was necessary to create a separate archive for each object
graph. In other words, each archive could have only a single root object. When you
called a Cocoa method, such as the NSArchiver `archiveRootObject:toFile:` or
`archivedDataWithRootObject:` convenience class method, to archive the root object,
that method began by archiving the specified root object using NSArchiver's
`encodeRootObject:` method, then it archived every object to which the root object
referred, then it archived every object to which each of *them* referred, and so on,
until the process reached its end. The documentation cautioned you never to call
`encodeRootObject:` more than once on the same archive.

In Mac OS X 10.2, archives can hold multiple objects at the root level and the
process of archiving each object is the same no matter what its level. In Vermont
Recipes, you will encode each of the three model objects—VRButtonModel,
VRSliderModel, and VRTextFieldModel—into the top level of a single archive for
reading and writing.

In implementing keyed archiving, you will revert to the use of the `data-`
`RepresentationOfType:` and `loadDataRepresentation:ofType:` methods that you
first implemented in Recipe 1, Step 4. They are based on the same NSData objects
the archiving methods use, and in Mac OS X 10.2 they support writing archives in
XML format, if desired.

You will start by implementing archiving routines for the antiques inventory. Since it
exists in a model object, VRTextFieldModel, you will start by archiving and unarchiving
the top-level model object. It is important to be aware that doing this entails creating
a new version of the model object and that the old version will be released as soon
as the process is complete. While archiving or unarchiving is under way, the old
model object should be regarded as invalid and the new model object may not be
complete or may hold different values. It is important to avoid depending on values
in either version of the model object until the archiving or unarchiving process is
completed. You will see in Recipe 17 that this precaution is particularly important
when archiving and unarchiving objects in the Cocoa text system.

In the following discussion, you will first write methods that access the model object using old-style archiving to see how it would have worked using pre-Mac OS X 10.2 techniques. You will then turn to the new, keyed way of archiving so you can see the difference. This will require writing keys as well as the archiving methods themselves, since you did not provide for storage of the antiques inventory in Recipe 11. Later, you will replace the existing methods of file storage for other data in Vermont Recipes, which use a dictionary and already have associated keys.

1. At the end of VRDocument.m, add the implementation of dataRepresentation-OfType:, as follows. This initial version creates an archive with a single root object, the text field model, and it will therefore work in versions of Mac OS X older than 10.2. Later in this recipe, when you expand this method to include archives of the button model and the slider model, it will encode multiple root objects and require at least Mac OS X 10.2.

```
- (NSData *)dataRepresentationOfType:(NSString *)type {
    if ([type isEqualToString:VRDocumentType]) {
        [[self undoManager] removeAllActions];
        return [NSArchiver archivedDataWithRootObject:
                [self textFieldModel]];
    } else {
        return nil;
    }
}
```

The outline of this method is familiar from Recipe 1, Step 4, which you should review briefly to remember the role that dataRepresentationOfType: plays in the Cocoa Document-based Application template. The only difference between this method as you implemented it in Recipe 1 and as it appears here lies in the return value. In Recipe 1, the method returned a dictionary object it built up using a custom helper method, dictionaryFromModel, which stored class and document version information and then called a model object's custom addDataToDictionary: method. After building the dictionary, the method returned it to the caller as an NSData object.

Here, the method returns an NSData object it obtains by calling NSArchiver's convenience class method, archivedDataWithRootObject:, passing to the latter the text field model object. Implementing the dataRepresentationOfType: method is all you need to do to save the antiques inventory to persistent storage, assuming you have completed the text field object's encoding methods as instructed in Step 1. Cocoa automatically calls this method when the user chooses to save a document.

It works like this. The NSArchiver convenience method archivedDataWith RootObject: first creates a temporary archiver, a specialized subclass of NSCoder that knows how to walk the specified root object's object graph and build an optimized form of it that avoids redundancy and maintains extraneous object references if needed. It does this by calling the instance methods `initForWritingWithMutableData:` to initialize the archiver and `encodeRootObject:` to walk the object graph and return it as an encoded NSData object. The latter begins to walk the object graph by calling the `encodeWithCoder:` method you wrote in Step 1 for the root object, VRTextFieldModel.

Wherever the root object's `encodeWithCoder:` method encodes another object, such as the text field model's `antiques` array, it tells the latter object to run its own `encodeWithCoder:` method. In the case of the `antiques` array, as with most Foundation objects, you know that NSMutableArray implements the `encodeWithCoder:` method because NSMutableArray declares that it conforms to the NSCoding protocol. NSMutableArray's implementation of the protocol method calls each array element's implementation of it: namely, the `encodeWithCoder:` method you wrote in Step 1 in the VRAntiqueRecord class. In this way, the `archivedDataWithRootObject:` convenience class method returns the required NSData object encoding the text field model's entire object graph, doing almost all of the hard work for you behind the scenes. (At present, of course, the text field model only encodes the antiques inventory and related instance variables, but in Step 3 you will expand it to encompass the other instance variables in the text field model.)

The previous paragraph referred to certain optimizations that the archiver's `encodeRootObject:` method implements. One of these is to remove any space-consuming redundancy that might occur if the object graph refers to an instance of an object multiple times. Instead of encoding the entire object multiple times, it only encodes a reference to it after the first time. In addition, there is a more complicated optimization having to do with the encoding of objects that might not be part of the object graph but that it might reference. Refer to the documentation for information about the latter form of optimization, including the `encodeConditionalObject:` method you would use to help with it.

Next, you will learn the old way to unarchive the text field model object.

2. At the end of VRDocument.m, add the implementation of `loadDataRepresentation:ofType:`, as follows:

```
- (BOOL)loadDataRepresentation:(NSData *)data
      ofType:(NSString *)type {
   if ([type isEqualToString:VRDocumentType]) {
      [self setTextFieldModel:
            [NSUnarchiver unarchiveObjectWithData:data]];
      return YES:
   } else {
```

```
        return NO;
    }
}
```

This is the mirror image of the `dataRepresentationOfType:` method. Cocoa calls it after reading the document from disk, when the user opens the document or reverts it to its saved state. After Cocoa reads the byte stream from disk into an NSData object and passes it to the `dataRepresentationOfType:` method, that method passes the NSData object along to NSUnarchiver's `unarchiveObjectWithData:` convenience class method in its **data** parameter. This method unarchives the saved object graph from the **data** object, calling the root object's `initWithCoder:` method. Whenever it encounters a coded object, it tells that object to call its own version of `initWithCoder:` and, in that fashion, restores the entire root object and every object it references from disk.

Once again, you find that you needed to write a set accessor for an object after all. Insert the following declaration in the ACCESSORS section of VRDocument.h:

```
- (void)setTextFieldModel:(VRTextFieldModel *)inValue;
```

In the ACCESSORS section of VRDocument.m, define it as follows:

```
- (void)setTextFieldModel:(VRTextFieldModel *)inValue {
    [inValue retain];
    [textFieldModel release];
    textFieldModel = inValue;
}
```

If you were to trace the logic flow in the debugger, you would find that reading a document from disk causes the document's `loadDataRepresentation:ofType:` method to read and unarchive the object graph into an NSData object as described earlier, then pass the NSData object to the `setTextFieldModel:` accessor method you just wrote. When passed to the accessor, the NSData object is a fully reconstituted text field model object containing the restored values of all the instance variables in all its objects and subobjects, however deeply nested. The accessor simply retains the new text field model object, releases the old text field model object, and replaces the old object with the newly unarchived object. Once the `loadDataRepresentation:ofType:` method returns YES, the program flow causes the window controller's `awakeFromNib` method to run, which updates the GUI to reflect all the newly loaded values. As you learned in Recipe 1, Step 7.1, the accessor also notifies the GUI to update itself if the document is read during a revert operation.

Now that you've made archiving work for the antiques inventory the old way, let's change it to the new, keyed way.

3. First, you need a key for the text field model object. While you're at it, you will write keys for the button and slider model objects as well, for use in Step 4. At the end of the "Keys and values" subsection of the STORAGE section of the VRDocument.m source file, create the keys, as follows. Also, remove the "for dictionary" part of the subsection's title.

```
static NSString *VRDocumentButtonModelKey =
        @"VRDocument button model";
static NSString *VRDocumentSliderModelKey =
        @"VRDocument slider model";
static NSString *VRDocumentTextFieldModelKey =
        @"VRDocument text field model";
```

4. Next, in the same file, substitute the following new version for the method you wrote in Instruction 1 to archive the text field model for writing to disk:

```
- (NSData *)dataRepresentationOfType:(NSString *)type {
    if ([type isEqualToString:VRDocumentType]) {
        [[self undoManager] removeAllActions];

        NSMutableData *data = [NSMutableData data];
        NSKeyedArchiver *archiver = [[NSKeyedArchiver alloc]
                initForWritingWithMutableData:data];

        [archiver setOutputFormat:NSPropertyListXMLFormat_v1_0];

        [archiver encodeInt:VRDocumentVersion
                forKey:VRDocumentVersionKey];
        [archiver encodeObject:[self textFieldModel]
                forKey:VRDocumentTextFieldModelKey];
        [archiver finishEncoding];

        [archiver release];
        return data;
    } else {
        return nil;
    }
}
```

Focus first on the core of this new version. Instead of using the `archivedDataWith RootObject:` class convenience method, you call `initForWritingWithMutableData:` and encode objects yourself. You could have done this prior to Mac OS X 10.2,

because both NSArchiver and NSKeyedArchiver implement each of these lower-level methods to grant you the ability to customize the archiving process.

In old-style archiving, you (or the convenience method) would have called encodeRootObject: once to encode a single root object into the archive after initializing it. In Mac OS X 10.2, the concept of a root object has no importance. Instead, you call the basic encodeObject: method as many times as you like, because a keyed archive can hold multiple objects at the root level. You can anticipate that you will add calls to encodeObject: in Step 4 to add the button and slider model objects to the archive. You call a new method, finishEncoding, when you have encoded as many objects as you need, to tell the archiver to clean up after itself.

Here, you take advantage of the multiple-root capability of keyed archiving by encoding both the document version and the text field model object. The encodeInt: method that handles the document version is familiar from Step 1. It works by converting the C integer into an object to store in the archive.

Looking at the rest of the dataRepresentationOfType: method, you see that a little preparation and cleanup are required to make it work. First, you create a temporary, empty, autoreleased data object to hold the archive by calling NSMutableData's convenience class method, data. Then you create the keyed archiver by allocating it and calling NSKeyedArchiver's initForWritingWithMutableData: method. After encoding the data, you release the archiver and return the now-full data object to Cocoa for writing to disk.

After initializing the archiver but before encoding any data, you have an opportunity to configure the archive. In this case, you call the important new NSKeyedArchiver method setOutputFormat:. In addition to letting you write old-style OpenStep archives, in Mac OS X 10.2 this method lets you write either XML files or new binary format files by passing one of these constants: NSPropertyListOpenStepFormat, NSPropertyListXMLFormat_v1_0, or NSPropertyListBinaryFormat_v1_0. These are declared in NSPropertyList.h. Here, you select XML format to maintain the XML capability you wrote into the application in Recipe 1, Step 5. In your applications, you might prefer to make this a user-settable preference. New in Mac OS X 10.2 is the NSPropertyListSerialization class, providing methods for saving and restoring property lists from the three supported formats; you don't use them here.

I should mention a couple of other points. First, you call the undo manager's removeAllActions method because, as you learned in Recipe 1, saving the document should clear the undo and redo stacks. In addition, the document version you save to disk here is the same old VRDocumentVersion constant you have been using all along, incremented to 6 for this recipe. You already coded both the key and the constant in VRDocument.m.

You should be aware that in Mac OS X 10.2, archiving no longer uses Cocoa's class versioning mechanism (which you may have read about in other Cocoa tutorials), so you must roll your own document versioning system if you want to maintain some means by which later versions of your application can detect documents written by earlier versions. You aren't actually implementing the ability to detect older document versions in Vermont Recipes, but the ongoing use of a document versioning scheme means you'll be able to do so in the future.

Finally, since archiving saves class information automatically, you no longer need the VRDocumentClassKey key you added to VRDocument.m in Recipe 1, Step 4.2.1. Delete it now.

5. Next, upgrade the `loadDataRepresentation:ofType:` method you wrote in Instruction 2 to use keyed archiving to read the text field model from disk. Substitute this new version of the method in VRDocument.m:

```
- (BOOL)loadDataRepresentation:(NSData *)data
      ofType:(NSString *)type {
   if ([type isEqualToString:VRDocumentType]) {
      NSKeyedUnarchiver *unarchiver =
            [[NSKeyedUnarchiver alloc]
            initForReadingWithData:data];

      [self setTextFieldModel:[unarchiver
            decodeObjectForKey:VRDocumentTextFieldModelKey]];
      [unarchiver finishDecoding];

      [unarchiver release];
      return YES;
   } else {
      return NO;
   }
}
```

This is the mirror image of the **dataRepresentationOfType:** method and hardly requires explanation. You don't have to create a **data** object, because the **data** value that Cocoa read from disk before calling this method is passed in to you. Note that, as advised earlier, you don't bother to read the document version from disk. If you needed that information, you would add a call to NSKeyedArchiver's **decodeIntForKey:**, either before or after the line that reads in the text field model object. The fact that you can decline to read a piece of the file, or that you can read it in a different order than the one in which it was written, is unique to the new keyed archiving mechanism.

All this has proven somewhat easier to write than the various custom dictionary routines you wrote in Recipe 1 and Section 2. Access to the antiques array in particular was much easier to write than it would have been using your custom dictionary techniques, because NSArray already implements the necessary loop routines required by the NSCoding protocol, which you would otherwise have had to write yourself. Furthermore, with keyed archiving in Mac OS X 10.2, you get all the benefits of the dictionary key system you originally wrote. As Apple enhances keyed archiving in the future, you will gain the benefits of Apple's work with little or no additional effort on your part.

Before moving on to the next step to extend archiving to the rest of Vermont Recipes, take note that the new NSKeyedArchiver and NSKeyedUnarchiver classes declare several new delegate methods. These allow you to appoint a delegate such as the window controller for an archiver or unarchiver, so it can watch the archiver complete various steps in the archiving or unarchiving process. You might do this, for example, to update a progress indicator in your application's window that tracks how much of a large document has been written or read, or to update part of the GUI before the entire file has been read. You will learn about another use of the delegate methods in Recipe 17.

Step 3: Apply Archiving and Unarchiving to the Rest of the Text Field Model

Now that you have archiving and unarchiving working for the most complicated object in the application, the antiques inventory, you can easily extend it to the remaining data in the text field model object.

1. In the source file VRTextFieldModel.m, revise `initWithCoder:` and `encodeWithCoder:` to use keyed archiving and unarchiving for all of the text field model object's data, as shown in the following code. You've already declared all of the keys you use here, most of them in Section 2. Although the two methods list the data encoding and decoding in the same order, this is only because it helps when you're proofreading the code to make sure you've covered everything. With keyed archiving, the order in the two methods need not be the same.

   ```
   - (id)initWithCoder:(NSCoder *)decoder {
       self = [super init];
       [self setIntegerValue:[decoder
   ```

(continues on next page)

```
            decodeIntForKey:VRIntegerValueKey]];
    [self setDecimalValue:[decoder
            decodeFloatForKey:VRDecimalValueKey]];
    [self setTelephoneValue:[decoder
            decodeObjectForKey:VRTelephoneValueKey]];
    [self setFormNameValue:[decoder
            decodeObjectForKey:VRFormNameValueKey]];
    [self setFormIdValue:[decoder
            decodeObjectForKey:VRFormIdValueKey]];
    [self setFormDateValue:[decoder
            decodeObjectForKey:VRFormDateValueKey]];
    [self setFormFaxValue:[decoder
            decodeObjectForKey:VRFormFaxValueKey]];
    [self setAntiques:[decoder
            decodeObjectForKey:VRAntiquesKey]];
    [self setLastAntiqueID:[decoder
            decodeIntForKey:VRLastAntiqueIDKey]];
    [self setAntiqueAddedKinds:[decoder
            decodeObjectForKey:VRAntiqueAddedKindsKey]];
    return self;
}


- (void)encodeWithCoder:(NSCoder *)encoder {
    [encoder encodeInt:[self integerValue]
            forKey:VRIntegerValueKey];
    [encoder encodeFloat:[self decimalValue]
            forKey:VRDecimalValueKey];
    [encoder encodeObject:[self telephoneValue]
            forKey:VRTelephoneValueKey];
    [encoder encodeObject:[self formNameValue]
            forKey:VRFormNameValueKey];
    [encoder encodeObject:[self formIdValue]
            forKey:VRFormIdValueKey];
    [encoder encodeObject:[self formDateValue]
            forKey:VRFormDateValueKey];
    [encoder encodeObject:[self formFaxValue]
            forKey:VRFormFaxValueKey];
    [encoder encodeObject:[self antiques]
            forKey:VRAntiquesKey];
    [encoder encodeInt:[self lastAntiqueID]
```

```
        forKey:VRLastAntiqueIDKey];
    [encoder encodeObject:[self antiqueAddedKinds]
        forKey:VRAntiqueAddedKindsKey];
}
```

Step 4: Apply Archiving and Unarchiving to the Remaining Model Objects

In this step you will revise the button model object and the slider model object to use archiving. The document object will read and write all of its data from all of its model objects at once as a single NSData archive.

Each model object can become what Step 1 referred to as a *root object* in a single archive. In versions of Mac OS X older than 10.2, this wasn't possible. Each archive could contain only a single root object. In version 10.2, archives can contain multiple root objects. Since this somewhat dilutes the whole idea of a root object, you could say more simply that Mac OS X 10.2 archives can contain multiple objects at every level.

You will start by adding the initWithCoder: and encodeWithCoder: methods to the two model objects, then you'll revise the document to archive and unarchive them.

1. In the source file VRButtonModel.m, add these initWithCoder: and encodeWithCoder: methods:

```
- (id)initWithCoder:(NSCoder *)decoder {
    self = [super init];
    [self setCheckboxValue:[decoder
        decodeBoolForKey:VRCheckboxValueKey]];
    [self setTrianglePegsValue:[decoder
        decodeBoolForKey:VRTrianglePegsValueKey]];
    [self setSquarePegsValue:[decoder
        decodeBoolForKey:VRSquarePegsValueKey]];
    [self setRoundPegsValue:[decoder
        decodeBoolForKey:VRRoundPegsValueKey]];
    [self setPlayMusicValue:[decoder
        decodeBoolForKey:VRPlayMusicValueKey]];
```

(continues on next page)

```
    [self setRockValue:[decoder
        decodeBoolForKey:VRRockValueKey]];
    [self setRecentRockValue:[decoder
        decodeBoolForKey:VRRecentRockValueKey]];
    [self setOldiesRockValue:[decoder
        decodeBoolForKey:VROldiesRockValueKey]];
    [self setClassicalValue:[decoder
        decodeBoolForKey:VRClassicalValueKey]];
    [self setPartyValue:[decoder
        decodeIntForKey:VRPartyValueKey]];
    [self setStateValue:[decoder
        decodeIntForKey:VRStateValueKey]];
    return self;
}


- (void)encodeWithCoder:(NSCoder *)encoder {
    [encoder encodeBool:[self checkboxValue]
        forKey:VRCheckboxValueKey];

        [encoder encodeBool:[self trianglePegsValue]
            forKey:VRTrianglePegsValueKey];
    [encoder encodeBool:[self squarePegsValue]
        forKey:VRSquarePegsValueKey];
    [encoder encodeBool:[self roundPegsValue]
        forKey:VRRoundPegsValueKey];
    [encoder encodeBool:[self playMusicValue]
        forKey:VRPlayMusicValueKey];
    [encoder encodeBool:[self rockValue]
        forKey:VRRockValueKey];
    [encoder encodeBool:[self recentRockValue]
        forKey:VRRecentRockValueKey];
    [encoder encodeBool:[self oldiesRockValue]
        forKey:VROldiesRockValueKey];
    [encoder encodeBool:[self classicalValue]
        forKey:VRClassicalValueKey];
    [encoder encodeInt:[self partyValue]
        forKey:VRPartyValueKey];
    [encoder encodeInt:[self stateValue]
        forKey:VRStateValueKey];
}
```

2. In the source file VRSliderModel.m, add these `initWithCoder:` and `encodeWithCoder:` methods:

```
- (id)initWithCoder:(NSCoder *)decoder {
    self = [super init];
    [self setPersonalityValue:[decoder
        decodeFloatForKey:VRPersonalityValueKey]];
    [self setSpeedValue:[decoder
        decodeFloatForKey:VRSpeedValueKey]];
    [self setQuantumValue:[decoder
        decodeFloatForKey:VRQuantumValueKey]];
    return self;
}


- (void)encodeWithCoder:(NSCoder *)encoder {
    [encoder encodeFloat:[self personalityValue]
        forKey:VRPersonalityValueKey];
    [encoder encodeFloat:[self speedValue]
        forKey:VRSpeedValueKey];
    [encoder encodeFloat:[self quantumValue]
        forKey:VRQuantumValueKey];
}
```

3. Before augmenting the `dataRepresentationOfType:` and `loadDataRepresentation:-ofType:` methods in VRDocument.m, you must add **set** accessors for the button and slider models. In the VRDocument.h header file, declare them as follows:

```
- (void)setButtonModel:(VRButtonModel *)inValue;
- (void)setSliderModel:(VRSliderModel *)inValue;
```

In the VRDocument.m source file, define them as follows:

```
- (void)setButtonModel:(VRTextFieldModel *)inValue {
    [inValue retain];
    [buttonModel release];
    buttonModel = inValue;
}


- (void)setSliderModel:(VRTextFieldModel *)inValue {
    [inValue retain];
    [sliderModel release];
    sliderModel = inValue;
}
```

4. Next, you can revise the actual archiving methods. Revise the data-RepresentationOfType: and loadDataRepresentation:ofType: methods in VRDocument.m by adding two lines to each. In the dataRepresentationOfType: method, add these lines just before the similar line encoding the text field model object:

```
[archiver encodeObject:[self buttonModel]
        forKey:VRDocumentButtonModelKey];
[archiver encodeObject:[self sliderModel]
        forKey:VRDocumentSliderModelKey];
```

In the loadDataRepresentation:ofType: method, add these lines just before the similar line decoding the text field model object:

```
[self setButtonModel:[unarchiver
        decodeObjectForKey:VRDocumentButtonModelKey]];
[self setSliderModel:[unarchiver
        decodeObjectForKey:VRDocumentSliderModelKey]];
```

You already declared the keys used here, in Step 2.

5. Finally, you must declare that the VRButtonModel and VRSliderModel classes conform to the NSCoding formal protocol. Change the @interface directive in the header file of each to include the <NSCoding> declaration, as shown here:

```
@interface VRButtonModel : NSObject <NSCoding> {
```

```
@interface VRSliderModel : NSObject <NSCoding> {
```

Step 5: Add Support for Revert, Undo, and Redo

If you were to build and run the application now, almost everything would work nicely. Thorough testing would reveal, however, that attempting to revert an edited document to its last saved state doesn't work correctly for most of the user controls, and once an existing document is read from disk, undo and redo don't work at all.

The key to the problem lies in this easily overlooked fact: The unarchiver that the application creates in the VRDocument object actually creates a new model object when it unarchives a saved document. You see this in each unarchiver call in loadDataRepresentation:ofType:, where a typical step looks like this:

```
[self setButtonModel:[unarchiver
        decodeObjectForKey:VRDocumentButtonModelKey]];
```

The unarchiver's `decodeObjectForKey:` method returns a new object, which you then assign to an instance variable using the `setButtonModel:` accessor method. You can see that it is a separate object by stepping through the code in the debugger and examining the objects; the addresses of the old and new model objects are different. For this reason, in the `setButtonModel:` accessor method to which the new object is passed, you retain it and then release the old model object.

This arrangement works well for most purposes. However, most of the subsidiary data objects in the model refer to their values in the course of being decoded, usually so the window controller can decide whether to update the GUI. These references are to the values in the old model object that is about to be released, because the instance variable referring to each model object still points to the old model object until unarchiving is complete. It's the new model object being built up in the unarchiver that contains the data just read from disk, so mistakes will occur while updating the GUI.

This problem doesn't affect all of the data objects, but it does affect many of them. For example, most data objects in the Button, Slider, and TextField model objects are told to update themselves on screen when their **set** accessors post a notification that the value has changed. But the updaters in the window controller that fire in response to the notification don't update on screen if their new values are identical to the values already held in the model object. It is the new value read from disk that should be used in the comparison, but only the old value is available to the updater until the unarchiving process has been completed. As currently written, all of the notifications are posted by the model object as soon as the data is changed—this is required, as you already learned, in order to make undo and redo update the screen immediately, and perhaps in response to AppleScript commands—but it comes too early if the **set** accessor is called during an unarchiving operation.

A related problem, easily fixed, is that the new model object created by the unarchiver is initialized only with those values that were stored on disk. There are usually instance variables in model objects that are not stored, and the unarchiver therefore cannot initialize them from disk. Often these values are pointers to memory locations that are not valid the next time the application is run. In Vermont Recipes, for example, each model object contains a reference to its document, but the address of the document in memory may be different every time the application is run. Leaving the document reference as `nil` after unarchiving has devastating consequences, of course, making it impossible for the model object's **set** accessors to locate the document's undo manager in order to record undo actions. Thus, after unarchiving a model object, you must explicitly set each model object's document instance variable to the current address of its document, and other initializations may be required.

Deal with the latter problem first, as it is easiest to solve.

1. In the ACCESSORS section of VRDocument.m, you just wrote **set** accessors for each of the four model objects. Add the following nearly identical line at the end of each of them, changing buttonModel to sliderModel and textFieldModel as needed:

```
[buttonModel initAfterUnarchivingWithDocument:self];
```

This calls a new initialization routine after a model object is unarchived, which you will now write. In VRButtonModel.m, add this method at the end of the INITIALIZATION section:

```
- (id)initAfterUnarchivingWithDocument:
        (VRDocument *)inDocument {
    document = inDocument;
    [[NSNotificationCenter defaultCenter]
            postNotificationName:
            VRButtonModelUnarchivedNotification
            object:[self document]];
    return self;
}
```

As you see, the first line sets the document instance variable in the model object to the current document. By doing this, you allow undo recording to work on documents that have been read from disk.

Before you puzzle over the second line in this method, add a similar method to the INITIALIZATION section of the other two model objects, changing only the name of the notification to refer to the Slider and TextField models. Also, declare each in the appropriate header file, using this declaration in the INITIALIZATION section of VRButtonModel.h as a model:

```
- (id)initAfterUnarchivingWithDocument:(VRDocument *)inDocument;
```

There is one other class that also refers to the document: VRAntiqueRecord. Every antiques record object in the text field model object must be told to update its **document** instance variable when the document is unarchived, or antiques records read from disk on Open or Revert commands will fail to undo and redo subsequent changes. To fix this, add the following to the **initAfterUnarchivingWithDocument:** method in VRTextFieldModel.m, after the first line:

```
[[self antiques] makeObjectsPerformSelector:
        @selector(setDocument:) withObject:document];
```

This requires a change to VRAntiqueRecord. Add this **set** accessor declaration near the beginning of the ACCESSORS section of VRAntiqueRecord.h:

```
- (void)setDocument:(id)inDocument;
```

Define it as follows near the beginning of the ACCESSORS section of VRAntiqueRecord.m:

```
- (void)setDocument:(id)inDocument {
    document = inDocument;
}
```

The `inDocument` parameter can't be typed as a pointer to VRDocument because the `makeObjectsPerformSelector:` method requires it to be typed as id.

2. The notification that is posted in the second line of each `initAfter-UnarchivingWithDocument:` method simply announces that a model object has been unarchived from disk. Delegate methods that perform a similar task are provided in VRKeyedUnarchiver, but they don't get called at the right time for your purposes here. Since your initialization method that posts the new notification is called by the document after unarchiving is complete, and even after the document's instance variable has been updated to point to the newly read model object, you have enabled GUI updater methods in the window controller to register to observe the notification and update the user interface after the model object and all its subsidiary data objects have been fully loaded. The old notifications posted by **set** accessors will continue to be used, as well, since they are needed for undo, redo, and AppleScript support.

The notification does nothing when a document is being opened from disk because there is as yet no window to receive it. But it does perform its assigned task in the case of a revert operation, because the window is then already open.

The notification names must be declared and defined, of course. At the end of the NOTIFICATIONS section at the bottom of each of the model object header files, add a declaration like this in VRButtonModel.h, varying the name of the model object as appropriate:

```
extern NSString *VRButtonModelUnarchivedNotification;
```

At the end of the NOTIFICATIONS section at the top of the model object source files, add a definition like this in VRButtonModel.m, varying the model names again:

```
NSString *VRButtonModelUnarchivedNotification =
    @"ButtonModel Unarchived Notification";
```

3. The next step is to register the window controller to observe these unarchiving notifications. Start with the VRButtonController.m category source file, adding these lines to the existing `registerNotificationObserversForButtonsTab` method in the WINDOW MANAGEMENT section.

Near the top of the method, add the following after the first statement:

```
[[NSNotificationCenter defaultCenter]
    addObserver:self
    selector:@selector(updateCheckbox:)
    name:VRButtonModelUnarchivedNotification
    object:[self document]];
```

At the beginning of the Pegs subsection, following the first statement:

```
[[NSNotificationCenter defaultCenter]
    addObserver:self
    selector:@selector(updateTrianglePegsCheckbox:)
    name:VRButtonModelUnarchivedNotification
    object:[self document]];
```

You must make almost identical additions to the rest of the **register-NotificationObserversForButtonsTab** method, one for each user control in the Buttons category that displays a data value (the Beeper command pop-down menu does not). You must also make almost identical additions to the corresponding methods in the other window controller category source files. The language in every case is identical to the registrations you just wrote for the Buttons category, except that the name of the updater method to be invoked differs in each.

If you examine the generic and specific updater methods in these files, you see that they make comparisons to model object values to determine whether to perform an update, and some also do this to decide whether to enable or disable other view objects. Thus, all of them need to be registered to respond to notifications posted when the model object has been unarchived.

You must make similar changes in the other window controller category source files. The language in every case is identical to the registrations you just wrote for the Buttons category, except that the name of the updater method to be invoked differs. Write similar lines into the **registerNotificationObserversForSlidersTab** method in the VRSliderController.m category source file for the **updateSpeed TextField:** updater method. Do the same for the **registerNotification ObserversForTextFieldsTab** in the VRTextFieldController.m category source files for these updater methods: **updateIntegerTextField:**, **updateDecimal TextField:**, **updateTelephoneTextField:**, **updateFormNameEntry:**, **updateForm IdEntry:**, **updateFormDateEntry:**, and **updateFormFaxEntry:**.

4. These new notifications do not require you to revise any of the updater methods that will be called when the controllers receive the new notifications, since the updaters already refer to the model objects' data values in order to update the GUI. The only thing that has changed is that the new notifications arrive later

than the old notifications, at a time when the references to the model object data values are valid because the files have now been fully unarchived.

But what of the old notifications? They are still posted and registered, in part because they are needed for undo, redo, and AppleScript support. While in those cases they will never be posted while unarchiving is going on, they are nevertheless also called during unarchiving. For some data objects this is needed to update the GUI. In other cases, it will be duplicative because the new notifications will be posted shortly later. This duplication is at minimal cost in execution time, so there isn't reason to redesign the application to eliminate it. You do, however, need to change the way the updaters respond to the old notifications, to get the new data values being read from disk during an unarchiving operation.

To do this, you will change the way the old notifications are posted. All of the model objects' set accessors will now be revised to use the alternative posting method in NSNotificationCenter, `postNotification:Name:object:userInfo:`, using the `userInfo:` parameter to transmit the new data value to the updater methods. The updater methods must also be revised to read this data in `userInfo:`. What makes this work is the fact that, when the `set` accessors are called during an unarchiving operation, they are called by the new model object. This is so even though the new model object being read from disk hasn't yet been returned to the document because the operation hasn't yet completed.

There is an important lesson here. The documentation says with good reason that the longer method, with the `userInfo:` parameter, is the preferred way to post notifications. It encapsulates the notification and its data in a way that allows any other object to observe it and use the data without having to know where it came from. In Recipe 1, Step 6.3, you thought you could get away without transmitting the data in `userInfo:`, because you thought the model object would always be its sole client. As you now see, it isn't always possible to anticipate future changes to your application, and it therefore often pays to code defensively. Use the `userInfo:` parameter whenever possible.

Start by revising the first `set` accessor in the button model. In the `setCheck-BoxValue:` method in the VRButtonModel.m source file, replace the existing NSNotificationCenter call with the following:

```
[[NSNotificationCenter defaultCenter]
      postNotificationName:
      VRButtonModelCheckboxValueChangedNotification
      object:[self document]
      userInfo:[NSDictionary dictionaryWithObject:
      [NSNumber numberWithBool:checkboxValue]
      forKey:VRButtonModelCheckboxValueChangedNotification]];
```

This is identical to the old version except for the new **userInfo:** parameter and value. It calls the NSDictionary class method **dictionaryWithObject:** to create a temporary dictionary to be passed to the controller's updater method via the notification center. Since the data value associated with the checkbox is a simple C data type, it must first be converted to an NSNumber object using NSNumber's **numberWithBool:** class method. Dictionaries require keys, and keys should normally be held in variables. Here, it is convenient to use the existing keys defined for changes to this very checkbox.

All of the other set accessors in all three of the model objects require a similar change to pass a **userInfo:** value to the corresponding updater methods. You will figure out how to revise these **set** accessors yourself, using the example just given and this additional advice: In each case, of course, the reference to the model value to be passed in the notification and the name of the notification must be changed to match the accessor. **Set** accessors using other simple C data types, **int** and **float**, are encapsulated in objects using the NSNumber **numberWithInt:** and **numberWithFloat:** methods before being ensconced in a dictionary object. The enumeration constants used in the **setPartyValue:** and **setStateValue:** accessors are treated as integers and use **numberWithInt:**. Those principles cover the button and slider model objects.

The text field model object uses string and date objects, not C data types, and they are added to the notification even more easily, by placing of the object itself in the temporary dictionary. For example, the revised line in **setTelephoneValue:** is this:

```
[[NSNotificationCenter defaultCenter]
        postNotificationName:
        VRTextFieldModelTelephoneValueChangedNotification
        object:[self document]
        userInfo:[NSDictionary dictionaryWithObject:
        telephoneValue forKey:
        VRTextFieldModelTelephoneValueChangedNotification]];
```

5. Finally, to complete these changes, you must revise the updater methods in the window controller. The form you will adopt is illustrated by this new line, replacing the old version, in **updateCheckBox** in the "INTERFACE MANAGEMENT – Specific updaters" section of the VRButtonController.m category source file:

```
[self updateTwoStateCheckbox:[self checkbox]
        setting:([notification userInfo]) ?
        [[[notification userInfo] objectForKey:
        VRButtonModelCheckboxValueChangedNotification] boolValue]
        : [[self buttonModel] checkboxValue]];
```

This is the same as before except for the new C ternary operator providing the `setting:` parameter value. First, the notification's `userInfo:` parameter is tested to determine whether it is `nil`. If it is not `nil`, it must have come from a model object's `set` accessor, since you just added `userInfo:` parameters to each of the notification postings in the `set` accessors. You therefore use the appropriate key with NSDictionary's `objectForKey:` method to retrieve the object in the `userInfo:` parameter and convert it to a C bool type using NSNumber's `boolValue:` method. If the `userInfo:` parameter is `nil`, then you know it came either from the new notifications posted when the unarchiving operation is finished or the window controller's `updateWindows` method. You can therefore safely retrieve the value from the model object.

The same pattern is used in all of the updater methods in all three window controller categories. You will use `intValue:` and `floatValue:` in place of `boolValue:` in some cases. In others, you will just accept the object without converting it to a C data type. For example, the `updateTelephoneTextField` method uses this line:

```
[[self telephoneTextField]
    setStringValue:([notification userInfo]) ?
    [[notification userInfo] objectForKey:
    VRTextFieldModelTelephoneValueChangedNotification] :
    [[self textFieldModel] telephoneValue]];
```

You now have a rather complex scheme for changing the application's data values and updating its GUI to match. Sometimes notifications with a `userInfo:` parameter are used, sometimes notifications without a `userInfo:` parameter are used, and sometimes the window controller calls the updater methods directly, passing `nil` in the `notification` parameter. It is certainly possible to simplify this scheme by relying always on notifications with `userInfo:` parameters. Don't bother revising the Vermont Recipes application to do this, because it is working. But keep it in mind when designing your own applications.

Step 6: Build and Run the Application

Build and run the application and test the operation of the new keyed archiving techniques. You haven't declared any new outlets or actions, so there is no need to read the files into Interface Builder and make new connections.

Change data values at random throughout all three of the tab view items in the main window, then save the document. Close the window and reopen it, then view all the tab view items to satisfy yourself that the new values have been restored and displayed correctly. Also experiment with revert, undo, and redo to make sure they work.

If you are satisfied that everything works as it should, delete the old storage code you commented out at the beginning of this recipe.

You can see what a new-style keyed archive looks like on disk in XML format by opening the document in TextEdit.

As noted at the beginning of this recipe, the Vermont Recipes application now requires Mac OS X 10.2 to work correctly. It will run in earlier versions of Mac OS X, but if you try to save data to disk, the application will quit unexpectedly. In Recipe 21 you will add some routines to check the system version and fail more gracefully if the latter's too old.

I said that the application will run in earlier versions of Mac OS X, but this is only true if you set your Interface Builder preferences and resave your nib files to use the new options to save for Mac OS X 10.1, or for both Mac OS X 10.1 and 10.2. If you save your nib files only for Mac OS X 10.2, your application will not work under Mac OS X 10.1 and earlier. These new Interface Builder preferences reflect the fact that almost all of the built-in Cocoa classes now implement keyed archiving.

Conclusion

Section 3 consisted of the single, relatively short Recipe 12, upgrading the Vermont Recipes application to use the keyed archiving technology Apple introduced to Cocoa in Mac OS X 10.2. Next, you will move into new territory, adding a number of features to the application, many of them standard features of almost every application. I already promised some of the new features, such as a drawer and a separate window for viewing text. Others, such as custom menus and menu items, are surprises.

SECTION 4

Menus

Every application that has a graphical user interface (GUI) needs a menu bar. A Cocoa document-based application comes with one, and it is already populated with several menus, each with the standard hodgepodge of menu items.

However, the built-in menu bar is not sufficient for any but the most humdrum applications. In Section 4, you will learn how to add several kinds of menus to your application. In Recipe 13, you will add a menu to the application's menu bar. In Recipe 14, you will add a contextual menu to one of the application's views. And in Recipe 15, you will add items to the application's Dock menu.

All of these tasks are remarkably easy, and these three recipes are therefore short. You'll accomplish many tasks in Interface Builder, with only a few excursions into Project Builder to write code.

There is in Cocoa another kind of menu, known as the status bar menu. NSStatusBar allows you to place menus in the menu bar at its right end, alongside Apple's own menu extras. Status bar menus aren't covered here because Apple discourages their use by third parties.

RECIPE 13

Application Menus

A standard Cocoa document-based application comes with a number of menus built in, such as File, Edit, and Window. These are useful, but how do you go about adding more menus and menu items to control your application's unique functions? Surprisingly, the documentation doesn't explain this in any detail, and I haven't found many tutorials spelling it out.

HIGHLIGHTS:

Using Interface Builder to add an application menu and menu items to the menu bar

Enabling and disabling application menu items

The process is very simple, though not obvious.

Before proceeding, update the target's Info.plist Entries by incrementing its build version to **13**.

Step 1: Add an Application Menu and Menu Items Using Interface Builder

The antiques table you created in Recipe 11 offers several means by which the user can add and delete records, including the New and Delete buttons and several keyboard equivalents. Wouldn't it be nice if the user could also use menu items—say, New Antique and Delete Antique? Depending on the overall design of the graphical user interface (GUI), you might reasonably place these in one of the built-in menus. However, manipulation of a database often involves several commands that you can more conveniently centralize in one dedicated menu. You'll learn how to do so in this recipe by adding an Antiques menu to the menu bar.

1. Expand the Resources group in the Groups & Files pane of Project Builder and double-click to open MainMenu.nib in Interface Builder. You haven't revisited this file since you first customized some of its built-in menu items in Recipe 1,

Step 9. It is a very important file nonetheless. In fact, it is the application's main nib file, controlling one interface element that every application with a GUI is supposed to have—namely, a menu bar. If you look at the File's Owner Info Panel, you will see that the owner of this nib file is NSApplication.

Look at the Menus palette. Each of the oblong blocks you see there represents an NSMenuItem instance. Most of them, including the Edit and Text blocks, are system menu items, predesigned and prewired with menu items suitable for their purposes. The fact that these are NSMenuItem objects indicates that what you normally speak of as a menu is, in Cocoa, not an NSMenu object but an NSMenuItem object. You can drag any of these system menu items into the menu editor that opens in its own MainMenu window when you open MainMenu.nib. You can drop them in either the menu bar or any of the individual menus, making them either menus or hierarchical submenus, at your discretion.

But the system menu items will not fill your present need. Two of the remaining blocks—the blank one whose Help tag identifies it as a separator, and the block labeled Item—seem inappropriate for the menu bar. In fact, if you attempt to drag either of them onto the menu bar, they fly back to the palette. The NSMenu item doesn't work either.

This leaves only the Submenu block. Despite its misleading name, this is exactly what you want. Drag it onto the menu bar in the MainMenu window and drop it between the Edit and Window menus. Those menus move apart, and you find a new menu in the menu bar named Submenu. Click it, and it opens to show a single menu item named Item (**Figure 13.1**). You're in business!

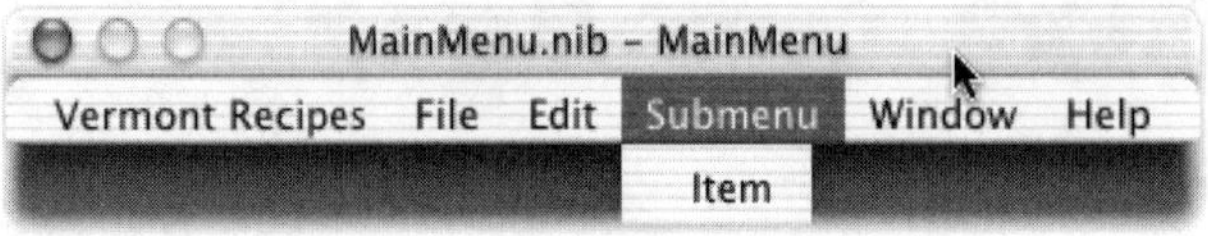

FIGURE 13.1
The Submenu menu installed in MainMenu.nib.

2. Double-click the menu's title and type **Antiques** to rename it.

3. Open the new Antiques menu and double-click its only item, then type to rename it **New Antique**.

4. With the New Antique menu item selected, turn to the NSMenuItem Info Panel and type a plus sign (+) in the Key Equivalent box. Also type **25000** in the Tag box.

5. Drag the block named Item from the Menus palette and drop it in the expanded Antiques menu, below the New Antique item. Then rename it **Delete Antique**, give it the minus sign (-) as its Key Equivalent, and set its tag to **25001**, using the same techniques.

6. Select the Classes tab in the MainMenu.nib window and select FirstResponder, near the top of the list of classes. Then choose Classes > Add Action to

FirstResponder. In the FirstResponder Class Info Panel, select the Actions pane then click the Add button at the bottom, if necessary. Type over the new MyAction: method to name it `newAntiqueRecordAction:` (note the trailing colon). Click the Add button again and name another new action `deleteAntiqueRecordAction:`.

You may recognize these as the names of the action methods you wrote in the window controller in Recipe 11, which are connected to the New and Delete buttons beneath the table view in the Text Fields tab view item. This probably seems puzzling. The MainMenu.nib file knows nothing of the VRWindowController class, whose header you have never read into this nib file. How will the menu items in MainMenu.nib find the action methods in the window controller? The answer lies in Cocoa's first responder mechanism. When the user chooses one of these menu items, Cocoa will search the responder chain using the two action names you just typed into the MainMenu.nib file to recognize the actual action methods in the window controller. You don't have to create another action method; you simply provide the name of an existing action method. The action method itself may have been created in any object that will find itself in the responder chain at run time. You'll get a full explanation of how this works shortly.

7. All you have to do to get the first responder mechanism working is connect the two new menu items to the MainMenu.nib's First Responder icon, using the two new action method names. Select the Instances tab of the MainMenu.nib window, then Control-drag from the New Antique menu item in the MainMenu window, dropping the connection on the First Responder icon. In the NSMenuItem Info Panel's Connections pane, select the **target** outlet, select the **newAntique RecordAction:** action, and click Connect. Repeat the process with the Delete Antique menu item, using the **deleteAntiqueRecordAction:** action (**Figure 13.2**).

8. Save MainMenu.nib and build the application.

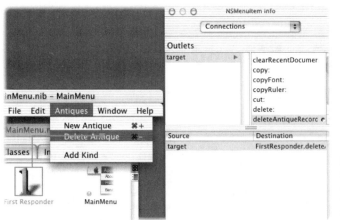

FIGURE 13.2
Connecting the Delete Antique menu item to First Responder.

If you run the application now, you will find that the menu bar has a new Antique menu with two new menu items. Best of all, the menu items work! With the Text Fields tab view item selected, choosing Antiques > New Antique creates a new antique record, and choosing Antiques > Delete Antique while the record is still selected removes it. What could be simpler?

Here is what happens when the user selects Antiques > New Antique.

Because the menu item is connected to the special First Responder icon in Interface Builder, the application knows that it must begin searching the application's responder chain from the current first responder, which might be any view in the window. Since you connected the menu item using the name `newAntiqueRecordAction:`, the application knows it must keep searching the responder chain until it finds a responder that declares a `newAntiqueRecordAction:` action method. This is the special role of the First Responder icon in Interface Builder. It is a proxy for whatever object happens to be the current first responder at run time. No matter what view is currently the key view in the application, the application will start by looking in that view.

Since there is no view that declares such an action method, the application continues looking up the responder chain through the tab view item and the window, finding nothing.

It eventually looks in the window's delegate—this is always part of the responder chain—and there it finds the action method it seeks. You long ago designated VRMainWindowController as the window's delegate, and the action method is declared here. The action method does just what you wrote it to do in Recipe 11: It creates and adds a new antique record and notifies the window controller to display it in the antiques table.

You could stop now, but there is a little matter of user convenience to consider in the next step.

Step 2: Enable and Disable the New Menu Items

The New Antique and Delete Antique menu items are enabled all the time, as things now stand. A user may find it confusing to be able to choose a New Antique menu item while the Buttons or Sliders tab view item is showing, and even more confusing to be able to choose a Delete Antique menu item. You really should disable those menu items until the user has selected the Text Fields tab view item and can see the antiques table. You should also keep the Delete menu item disabled unless an antiques record is selected in the antiques table, since the application won't know which record to delete while none is selected. Finally, you must also disable both new menu items while the user is editing a record.

Although you will disable the menu items when they aren't needed, you will always leave the Antiques menu itself enabled. It is considered good application design to allow the user to see at all times what capabilities are potentially available, even if they aren't available just now.

You experimented in Recipe 1, Step 7.2, with the `validateMenuItem:` method, which is declared in the NSMenuValidation informal protocol and controls the enabling and disabling of menu items. There, you added the method temporarily to the VRDocument class, because the action method for the Revert menu item is declared in NSDocument. Here, you declared the action method in the VRMainWindowController class, so the `validateMenuItem:` method must be declared in the window controller as well. It must always be declared in its menu's **target** object.

Before defining the method, it is advisable to set up a system to keep track of all the menu item tags you might end up using in the application. Recall that in Step 1 you used Interface Builder to set the tags of these two menu items to 25000 and 25001. To avoid potential conflicts with other menu items, you should use a unique tag for each menu item in the application. It is useful to define names for each of them and to test each tag by its defined name in the `validateMenuItem:` method. In Recipe 1, Step 7.2, you used the localized menu item's title to distinguish it. Using tags is easier.

There are many ways to do this, but they have in common the idea of keeping all of the tags in one place, where you can glance at them whenever you need to generate a new unique tag. You'll define the two macros shown here at the top of the VRMain-WindowController.m source file:

```
#pragma mark MENU ITEM TAGS


#define newAntiqueMenuItemTag 25000
#define deleteAntiqueMenuItemTag 25001
```

Now insert the following method in VRMainWindowController.m, just before the DATA SOURCES section, as a first attempt:

```
#pragma mark MENU MANAGEMENT


- (BOOL)validateMenuItem:(NSMenuItem *)menuItem {
    int tag = [menuItem tag];
    NSString *identifier = [[[self tabView]
            selectedTabViewItem] identifier];
```

(continues on next page)

```
        if (tag == newAntiqueMenuItemTag) {
            return ([identifier isEqualToString:@"text fields"]);
        } else if (tag == deleteAntiqueMenuItemTag) {
            return ([identifier isEqualToString:@"text fields"] &&
                    [[self antiquesTable] selectedRow] != -1);
        }
        return YES;

    }
```

Since NSDocument already declared a validateMenuItem: method itself to handle the document's Revert menu item, you had to override it and call **super** in Recipe 1, Step 7.2. NSWindowController does not declare a validateMenuItem: method of its own, so there isn't a **super** to call here.

You don't have to declare validateMenuItem: in the header, because it implements the NSMenuValidation informal protocol.

The first thing the method does is obtain the tag of the menu item passed in through the parameter. In either case, the method checks the identifier of the currently selected tab view item. It returns YES for the New Antique menu item if the result is true; otherwise it returns NO. In the case of the Delete Antique menu item, it also checks whether there is a selection in the antiques table. If the menu item that triggered this method is neither of the Antiques menu's items, the method returns YES.

The method distinguishes the selected tab view item by its identifier. To finish setting this up, turn to Interface Builder and, in the NSTabViewItem Info Panel, assign each tab view item an identifier string identical to its name but in lowercase letters. I chose these names strictly for easy identification. Using identifiers eliminates localization issues that arise when you're relying on the GUI names of objects.

That was good for a start, but the two new menu items remain enabled when a user begins editing a record in the table view. In Recipe 11, Step 6, you disabled the New and Delete buttons in these circumstances using two delegate methods you implemented there, controlTextDidBeginEditing: and controlTextDidEndEditing:. You should achieve the same effect with respect to these two menu items by revising the validateMenuItem: method you just wrote.

A simple way to do this is to add a test in both branches of the if clause to test whether the corresponding button is enabled. Revise the if clause of the validateMenuItem: method to read as follows:

```
        if (tag == newAntiqueRecordMenuItemTag) {
            return ([identifier isEqualToString:@"text fields"] &&
                    [[self newAntiqueButton] isEnabled]);
        } else if (tag == deleteAntiqueRecordMenuItemTag) {
```

```
        return ([identifier isEqualToString:@"text fields"] &&
                ([table selectedRow] != -1) &&
                [[self deleteAntiqueButton] isEnabled]);
}
```

Step 3: Build and Run
the Application

Build and run the application. Test the operation of the new menu and menu items.
Select the Buttons tab view item and open the Antiques menu, noting that both its
menu items are disabled. Select the Text Fields tab view item, and note that the New
Antique menu item is enabled, while the Delete Antique menu item is still disabled.
Choose Antiques > New Antiques and make sure it works. Select the new antiques
record in the antiques table; choose Antiques > Delete Antique, noting that it is now
enabled; and see the record disappear.

In the next recipe, you will implement the same two commands in a contextual menu.

RECIPE 14

Contextual Menus

You may not have noticed it, but a standard Cocoa document-based application comes with a built-in contextual menu. Run the Vermont Recipes application, click in any text field in the Sliders or Text Fields tab view item, and Control-click. A contextual menu pops up, giving you several choices, including Cut, Copy, Paste, Spelling, and Speech. Choose Speech > Start speaking, and the application does.

HIGHLIGHTS:

Using Interface Builder to add a contextual menu and menu items to the antiques table

Enabling and disabling contextual menu items

In this recipe, you will learn how to add your own contextual menus to other views. The process is very similar to what you did in Recipe 13 to add an application menu and menu items to the menu bar.

Before proceeding, update the target's Info.plist Entries by incrementing its build version to **14**.

Step 1: Add a Contextual Menu and Menu Items Using Interface Builder

In this step, you will create a contextual menu and connect it to the antiques table you created in Recipe 11, with the same commands you added to the Antiques menu in Recipe 13. For good measure, you will add one more command to the contextual menu, then add it to the Antiques menu as well.

1. Expand the Resources group in the Groups & Files pane of Project Builder and double-click to open VRDocument.nib in Interface Builder. You use VRDocument.nib instead of MainMenu.nib because that's where the table view is located.

From the Menus palette, drag the NSMenu item into the Instances pane of the VRDocument.nib window. A contextual menu is a separate NSMenu object, just as the application's menu bar in MainMenu.nib is an NSMenu object (**Figure 14.1**).

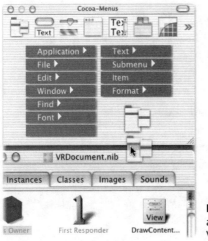

FIGURE 14.1 Dragging an NSMenu item into VRDocument.nib.

Double-click the NSMenu icon's name and type `Antiques Table Menu` to rename it.

2. Double-click the new Antiques Table Menu icon. It opens in a separate window and reveals two menu items.

3. Double-click the first item, then type to rename it `New Antique`.

4. With the New Antique menu item selected, turn to the NSMenuItem Info Panel and type a plus sign (+) in the Key Equivalent box. Also type `25000` in the Tag box. You give it the same tag that you gave the corresponding menu item in the Antiques menu because they are associated with the same action method.

5. Rename the second menu item `Delete Antique`, give it a minus sign (–) as its key equivalent, and set its tag to `25001`, using the same techniques. This item, too, has the same tag as the corresponding menu item in the Antiques menu.

6. To add a third menu item, first drag the blank separator block from the Menus palette and place it below the Delete Antique menu item. Then drag the Item block to the bottom of the contextual menu and name it `Add Kind`. It will perform the same action method as the Add Kind button you wrote in Recipe 11. Do not assign it a key equivalent, but give it a tag of `25002`.

7. To get the first responder mechanism working, connect the three new menu items to the VRDocument.nib's First Responder icon, using the three action methods `newAntiqueRecordAction:`, `deleteAntiqueRecordAction:`, and

addAntiqueKindAction:. Select the Instances tab of the VRDocument.nib window, then Control-drag from the New Antique menu item in the Antiques Table Menu window, dropping the connection on the First Responder icon. In the NSMenuItem Info Panel's Connections pane, select the **target** outlet, select the **newAntiqueRecordAction:** action, and click Connect. Repeat the process with the Delete Antique menu item, using the **deleteAntiqueRecordAction:** action, and the Add Kind menu item, using the **addAntiqueKindAction:** action.

You did not have to add these three action method names to the First Responder, because they were already declared in VRMainWindowController in Recipe 11. The window controller's header was read into the VRDocument.nib file, so it already knows about them.

8. Finally, you must connect the antiques table view to the new Antiques Table Menu. Select the table view in the main document window and Control-drag from it to the Antiques Table Menu icon. In the VRAntiquesTableView Info Panel (**Figure 14.2**). Then select the **menu** outlet and click Connect.

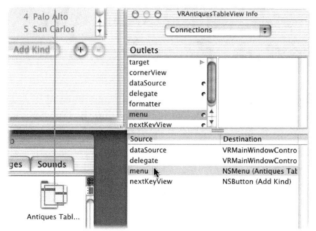

FIGURE 14.2
Connecting the table view to the Antiques Table Menu icon.

9. Save VRDocument.nib and build the application.

If you run the application now and Control-click the antiques table view in the Text Fields tab view item, you'll see that almost everything works. The contextual menu pops up, and the Delete Antique menu item is even enabled and disabled at the right times. (The New Antique menu item is enabled whenever you look at it, since you can't see this contextual menu at all when one of the other tab view items is selected.) These work because you wrote the necessary **validateMenuItem:** method in Recipe 13, and you gave these two menu items the same tags the corresponding menu items have in the Antiques menu in the menu bar (**Figure 14.3**).

FIGURE 14.3 The contextual menu in use.

The only thing that doesn't work is the enabling and disabling of the Add Kind menu item, because you haven't modified the `validateMenuItem:` method to take care of this detail. You will do that in the next step.

Step 2: Enable and Disable the New Contextual Menu Items

The Add Kind contextual menu item should obey the same enabling and disabling rules as the Add Kind button you wrote in Recipe 11. To accomplish this, you will simply steal some code from the `validateAntiquesTableButtons` method you wrote in the VRTextFieldController.m category source file in Recipe 11, Step 9, and add it to the `validateMenuItem:` method you wrote in VRMainWindowController.m in Recipe 13, Step 2.

Revise the latter method so it reads as follows:

```
- (BOOL)validateMenuItem:(NSMenuItem *)menuItem {
    int tag = [menuItem tag];
    NSString *identifier =
        [[[self tabView] selectedTabViewItem] identifier];

    NSTableView *table = [self antiquesTable];

    NSString *selectedKind;
    if ([table selectedRow] != -1) {
        selectedKind = [[table dataSource] tableView: table
            objectValueForTableColumn:
            [table tableColumnWithIdentifier:@"antiqueKind"]
```

```
            row:[table selectedRow]]);
    }

    if (tag == newAntiqueRecordMenuItemTag) {
        return ([identifier isEqualToString:@"text fields"] &&
            [[self newAntiqueButton] isEnabled]);
    } else if (tag == deleteAntiqueRecordMenuItemTag) {
        return ([identifier isEqualToString:@"text fields"] &&
            ([table selectedRow] != -1) &&
            [[self deleteAntiqueButton] isEnabled]);
    } else if (tag == addAntiqueKindMenuItemTag) {
        return ([identifier isEqualToString:@"text fields"] &&
            ([table selectedRow] != -1) &&
            [[self newAntiqueButton] isEnabled] &&
            ![[self antiqueKindsForMenu]
            containsObject:selectedKind]);
    }
    return YES;
}
```

Don't forget to define the new macro for the new menu item in the MENU ITEM TAGS section of the VRMainWindowController.m category source file, as follows:

```
#define addAntiqueKindMenuItemTag 25002
```

Step 3: Add a Menu Item to the Antiques Menu in the Menu Bar

There is no reason not to add the new Add Kind menu item to the Antiques menu in the menu bar as well.

1. Open MainMenu.nib in Interface Builder.

2. Drag a separator block and an Item block from the Menus palette to the bottom of the Antiques menu.

3. Name the new menu item Add Kind.

4. In the NSMenuItem Info Panel, give it a tag of 25002.

5. Because you are back in MainMenu.nib, you have to teach it about the name of the action method for which the application should search in the responder chain.

Switch to the Classes tab, select FirstResponder, and choose Classes > Add Action to FirstResponder. In the FirstResponder Class Info Panel, select the Actions pane, click Add, and name the new action **addAntiqueKindAction:** with a trailing colon.

6. Control-drag from the Add Kind menu item to the First Responder icon in the Instances tab of the MainMenu.nib window, select the **target** outlet in the Connections pane of the File's Owner Info Panel, select the **addAntiqueKindAction:** action, and click Connect.

7. Save MainMenu.nib.

You don't have to make any changes to the **validateMenuItem:** method, because you've already rewritten it to handle a menu item with this tag.

Step 4: Build and Run the Application

Build and run the application and test the operation of the new contextual menu and menu items. The tests you perform should be the same as those you performed in Recipe 13, Step 3, except that you will also check out the Add Kind menu item in the Antiques menu, as well as all of the menu items in the new contextual menu.

RECIPE 15

Dock Menus

In Mac OS X 10.1, Cocoa acquired the ability to give an application access to its Dock menu. The Dock menu is a menu attached to the application's icon in the Dock while it is running.

HIGHLIGHTS:

Using Interface Builder to add static Dock menu items

Using Project Builder to add dynamic Dock menu items

Creating an application delegate

Unless you implement this new feature, a Cocoa application's Dock menu contains only items provided by the system. At the top of the Dock menu, a list of the application's open application windows appears, allowing the user to bring any open window to the front and indicating the frontmost window with a checkmark. At the bottom, the menu contains three additional items, Keep in Dock, Show in Finder, and Quit. The Dock menu is dynamic. The list of open windows expands and contracts as the user opens and closes windows, and the Keep in Dock item disappears once you've set the application to appear in the Dock even when it's not running.

Now you can add your own menu items to the Dock menu. They will appear between the window list and the other built-in Dock menu items. You can see an example of this capability in action in Project Builder's Dock menu, which includes New Project, New File, Open, and Open Quickly items. The added Project Builder menu items are static, and you can easily add static menu items to your own application's Dock menu using Interface Builder. In addition, you can implement a new NSApplication delegate method to create and manage a dynamic Dock menu that allows you to add and remove your own menu items in the Dock menu, just as the system does.

Apple provided the new Dock menu API so that developers could implement a global application menu capability where there is ample room. The Mac OS X 10.1 release notes affirm that Apple does not make available a public API to add iconic menus to the right end of the menu bar. Although Cocoa does somewhat inconsistently provide the NSStatusBar API, Apple reserves that space for its own use to avoid overcrowding. Although a few developers have managed to add their own menus there (CE Software's QuicKeys and Aladdin Systems' Magic Menu, to name two), Apple does not support this in Mac OS X 10.2.

In Step 1 of this recipe, you will add static Dock menu items to bring up the About Vermont Recipes window, open a new file, and open an existing file. You won't have to write any code for these; you will do it almost entirely in Interface Builder. In Step 2, you will add and remove another menu item dynamically using the delegate method (**Figure 15.1**).

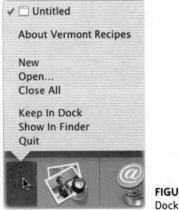

FIGURE 15.1 The finished Dock menu in use.

Before proceeding, update the target's Info.Plist Entries by incrementing its build version to **15**.

Step 1: Add Static Menu Items to the Dock Menu Using Interface Builder

In this step, you will add three static menu items to the Vermont Recipes application's Dock menu. Except for the last instruction, you need only use Interface Builder.

1. First, create a new nib file to hold the menu. A Dock menu isn't used all that often, so an application should create it lazily. By putting it in a separate nib file and loading it only when needed, you can speed up the application's launch.

   In Interface Builder, chose File > New to open the Starting Point dialog. There, select the Empty nib template under the Cocoa heading and click New. A new nib file opens, holding only File's Owner and First Responder icons.

2. From the Cocoa Menus palette, drag the NSMenu item into the Instances pane of the main nib file window. A Dock menu, like a contextual menu, is a separate NSMenu object.

Double-click the NSMenu icon's name and type `Dock Menu` to rename it.

3. Double-click the new Dock Menu icon. It opens in a separate window and reveals two menu items.

4. Double-click the first menu item, then type to rename it `About Vermont Recipes`.

5. Rename the second menu item `New`.

6. To add a third menu item, drag the Item block from the Menus palette to the bottom of the new menu and name it `Open...`. The three-dot ellipsis is Option-semicolon (;) on the U.S. keyboard.

7. Drag the blank separator block from the Menus palette and place it between the About Vermont Recipes and New menu items.

8. Before you can connect action methods to the menu items, you must set the nib file's owner. Select the File's Owner icon, and in the Custom Class pane of the File's Owner Info Panel, select NSApplication. Ignore any error message you may receive.

9. Control-drag from the File's Owner icon to the Dock Menu icon in the main nib window. In the File's Owner Info Panel, select the `dockMenu` outlet and click Connect. This sets the NSApplication `dockMenu` instance variable to your new Dock Menu NSMenu object.

10. To get the first responder mechanism working, connect the three new menu items to their action methods. Menu items with the same names are built into a standard Cocoa document-based application, so the action methods already exist.

First, Control-drag from the About Vermont Recipes menu item in the Dock Menu window, dropping the connection on the File's Owner icon in the main nib window. In the File's Owner Info Panel's Connections pane, select the `target` outlet, select the `orderFrontStandardAboutPanel:` action, and click Connect.

You Control-dragged to the File's Owner icon instead of the First Responder icon because the File's Owner is NSApplication, where the `orderFrontStandard` `AboutPanel:` action is implemented. You could just as well have used the First Responder icon, because the application is in the responder chain. However, in that case, you would have had to take an extra moment to type the action's name into the FirstResponder as you did in Recipe 13, Step 1.

11. Repeat the process with the New and Open menu items, but connect each of them to the First Responder icon instead of the File's Owner icon. Use the `newDocument:` action for the New menu item, and use the `openDocument:` action for the Open menu item.

You did not have to add these two action method names to the First Responder, because they were already declared in VRMainWindowController in Recipe 11. The window controller's header was read into the VRDocument.nib file, so it already knows about them.

12. Save the nib file as DockMenu.nib in the English.lproj subfolder of the project folder. Uncheck the Hide Extension checkbox first. A sheet appears, asking if you want to add the nib file to the project. Click Add.

13. You must perform one final task in Project Builder to finish this step. Open the Targets pane for the Vermont Recipes target. Select the Application Settings pane and click the Expert button. Then click the New Sibling button. Name the new setting AppleDockMenu, and set its value to DockMenu. This is the name of the Dock menu's nib file without the .nib extension.

The AppleDockMenu key in Application Settings informs Cocoa that your application implements static menu items for the Dock menu. Cocoa does the rest, loading your new DockMenu.nib file lazily the first time the user opens the Dock menu while the application is running. When the user chooses one of your menu items, Cocoa causes the application object to trigger the connected action method.

Step 2: Add Dynamic Menu Items to the Dock Menu Using Project Builder

To learn how to set up dynamic Dock menu items, you will make a few changes to the DockMenu.nib file you created in Step 1 and implement the new delegate method added to NSApplication in Mac OS X 10.1, applicationDockMenu:. In the process, you will learn how to create an application delegate object to hold the method implementation.

The Mac OS X 10.1 AppKit release notes indicate that you must use either the Interface Builder technique shown in Step 1 or the delegate method. If you implement both, the delegate method will take precedence. You can nevertheless load static menu items from a separate nib file, as you did in Step 1, by including standard nib-loading code in the delegate method, then modify or add to the Dock menu dynamically. You will use this hybrid technique here.

1. Start by using Project Builder to create an application delegate object to hold the delegate method. You can make any object the application delegate, but it is

usually convenient to create a separate application delegate. The nature of the delegate methods declared in NSApplication is such that they don't fit particularly well in something like the window controller.

You know the drill. In Project Builder, choose New > File, select the Cocoa Objective-C class template, and click Next. Name the new files VRAppDelegate.h and VRAppDelegate.m and complete the process. When you're done, drag them to the Class group in the Groups & Files pane of the project window.

Add your standard comments and disclaimers to the header and source files. NSAppDelegate should descend directly from NSObject. Change the header's **#import** directive to import the Cocoa umbrella class instead of Foundation.

2. From the Resources group in the project window, open MainMenu.nib in Interface Builder. You know from Recipe 14 that MainMenu.nib is the application's main nib file and that NSApplication is its file's owner.

    Select the Classes tab and choose Classes > Read Files, select VRAppDelegate.h, and click Parse. Then, in the same Classes tab, select the new VRAppDelegate item that has appeared and choose Classes > Instantiate VRAppDelegate. You must instantiate it to have a real object to which you can make connections.

    Finally, switch to the Instances tab and Control-drag from the File's Owner icon to the new VRAppDelegate icon that has appeared. In the File's Owner Info Panel, select the **delegate** outlet and click Connect. Your application now has a delegate.

3. In VRAppDelegate.h, declare a single instance variable between the curly braces of the **@interface** directive, as follows:

    ```
    IBOutlet NSMenu *dynamicDockMenu;
    ```

    This outlet variable will provide the delegate object with access to the NSMenu object in DockMenu.nib holding the static Dock menu items. As its name suggests, it will also hold a dynamic Dock menu item that you will create programmatically.

    Save VRAppDelegate.h. Interface Builder's Read Files command will read the header file into the DockMenu.nib file from disk in the next instruction, so you must save the changes beforehand.

4. Before implementing the delegate method, you should return to Interface Builder and revise the DockMenu.nib file you created in Step 1. You normally create dynamic menu items programmatically in the delegate method, but there is no reason not to use a nib file for the menu items that will remain fixed in the Dock menu. For that matter, once you've loaded the nib file, you can make changes to its menu items at run time as well.

    You must change the DockMenu.nib file's owner from NSApplication to NSAppDelegate to use it here. First open DockMenu.nib. In Interface Builder, select its Classes pane and select the VRAppDelegate item. Then choose Classes > Read VRAppDelegate.h. This specific menu item appears because you selected VRAppDelegate first, saving you the trouble of locating it in the standard Open File dialog.

The DockMenu.nib file now knows about the application delegate and its outlet variable, `dynamicDockMenu`. To make the application delegate its file's owner, select the File's Owner icon, select the Custom Classes pane of the File's Owner Info Panel, and select VRAppDelegate. If you are warned that this will break connections, go ahead and break them.

Lastly, you must connect the new `dynamicDockMenu` outlet to the NSMenu object you added to DockMenu.nib in Step 1. Control-drag from the File's Owner icon to the NSMenu icon, select the `dynamicDockMenu` outlet in the File's Owner Info Panel, and click Connect. Now, when the delegate method loads the Dock-Menu.nib file, it will automatically assign the NSMenu instance in the nib file to the outlet variable in the application delegate so that the delegate method you are about to implement can access it.

5. One detail remains in Interface Builder. You need to reconnect the About Vermont Recipes menu item in DockMenu.nib, because the previous instruction broke its connection to the application's action method.

Because VRAppDelegate now owns the DockMenu.nib file, it no longer knows about the `orderFrontStandardAboutPanel:` action method declared in NSApplication. You need to add the action method's name to the DockMenu.nib using the technique you learned in Recipe 13. Select the Classes pane, select the FirstResponder item, then choose Classes > Add Action to FirstResponder. In the FirstResponder Class Info Panel, select the actions pane, click the add button at the bottom if necessary, and type `orderFrontStandardAboutPanel:`.

Finally, Control-drag from the About Vermont Recipes menu item to the first Responder icon in the Instances pane, select the `target` outlet in the NSMenu Info Panel, select the new `orderFrontStandardAboutPanel:` action method name in the actions pane, and click Connect. Since the application is always in the responder chain, the application will call this action method when the user chooses About Vermont Recipes from the Dock menu.

6. You are finally ready to write the delegate method. First, of course, it will use standard techniques to load the DockMenu.nib file and assign its NSMenu object to the application delegate's `dynamicDockMenu` instance variable.

In VRAppDelegate.m, add the following initial implementation of the delegate method:

```
#pragma mark DOCK MENU

- (NSMenu *)applicationDockMenu:(NSApplication *)sender {
    if (dynamicDockMenu == nil) {
        if (![NSBundle loadNibNamed:@"DockMenu" owner:self]) {
            return nil;
        }
    }
}
```

The application calls this delegate method, since you implemented it in the application's delegate, whenever the user clicks and holds your application's Dock icon for a moment. Quickly clicking the Dock icon brings the application to the front without opening the Dock menu, while pressing the icon opens the Dock menu and leaves the application in the background (if that's where it was). Because every time the Dock icon is pressed, this method is called, it must be reasonably efficient. The release notes recommend maintaining the changing state of the Dock menu during execution of the application rather than creating it in the delegate method, but the delegate method allows a fair amount of manipulation without causing delay.

The code you just added to the delegate method checks the instance variable and, if it is `nil`, loads DockMenu.nib. This automatically assigns the NSMenu object in the nib to the delegate's instance method, which will no longer be `nil`. The nib file's contents will thereafter remain loaded, so on subsequent invocations the nib file will not reload. If loading the nib file fails, the delegate method returns `nil`. In this case, the application will open the standard system version of the Dock menu.

7. What would you like to add as a dynamic Dock menu item? It should be something that a user might usefully choose from the Dock menu while the Vermont Recipes application is running even if it is in the background, so the user can perform an action in the application without bringing it to the front. Two of the static menu items you wrote in Step 1, New and Open, relate to windows. Perhaps it would be useful to add a Close All menu item so the user can close all open Vermont Recipes windows without bringing the application to the front.

Write the code to add a dynamic menu item, Close All, to the end of the menu items added to the Dock menu from the nib file's NSMenu object. Insert the following at the end of the `applicationDockMenu:` delegate method:

```
BOOL visibleWindows = NO;
NSEnumerator *windowEnumerator =
        [[sender windows] objectEnumerator];
```

(continues on next page)

```
NSWindow *window;
while (window = [windowEnumerator nextObject]) {
    if ([window isVisible]) {
        visibleWindows = YES;
        break;
    }
}


NSMenuItem *closeAllMenuItem =
        [dynamicDockMenu itemWithTitle:
        NSLocalizedString(@"Close All",
        @"Name of Close All dock menu item")];
if (!visibleWindows) {
    if (closeAllMenuItem != nil) {
    [dynamicDockMenu removeItem:closeAllMenuItem];
    }
} else {
    if (closeAllMenuItem == nil) {
        [dynamicDockMenu addItemWithTitle:
                NSLocalizedString(@"Close All",
                @"Name of Close All dock menu item")
                action:@selector(closeAllWindowsAction:)
                keyEquivalent:@""];
    }
}
```

To know whether to include the Close All menu item when the user opens the Dock menu, the method must first determine whether the application has any open windows. The Cocoa application object maintains a list of all application windows in an array, exposed through its **windows** accessor method. However, this method includes windows that are currently offscreen, and Cocoa typically places windows offscreen when they are closed, for efficiency in case they are reopened. You must therefore look at all of them until you find one that is onscreen.

The delegate method walks the windows array and looks for one that is visible using NSWindow's **isVisible** method. It initializes a local **visibleWindows** variable to **NO**, creating an object enumerator, which it uses to walk the array; setting the local variable to **YES**; and exiting the loop with a **break** statement if any window's **isVisible** method returns **YES**.

If there is no visible window, the Close All menu item should not appear in the Dock menu. However, it might currently be in the menu object from a previous use of the Dock menu, in which case it must be deleted. The delegate method therefore first obtains a reference to a Dock menu item with the title Close All (or its localized equivalent), using NSMenu's `itemWithTitle:` method. This returns `nil` if no such menu item exists in the menu object. If the menu item is not `nil`, the method calls NSMenu's `removeItem:` method to remove it.

If there is at least one visible window, you must add the Close All menu item to the Dock menu if it isn't already present from a previous use of the Dock menu. If it is `nil`, therefore, the method calls NSMenu's `addItemWithTitle:` method to add the menu item and assign it an action method you haven't yet written. You don't need a key equivalent for this menu item, which the method indicates by passing `@""` as the last parameter (not `nil`).

You must localize the name of the menu, of course, so don't forget to add the appropriate entry in Localizable.strings.

8. You must add the action method that actually closes open windows. Since you're implementing this capability only in the Dock menu, you might as well place the action method in the application delegate. Add this method at the end of VRAppDelegate.m:

```
- (void)closeAllWindowsAction:(id)sender {
    [[NSApp windows] makeObjectsPerformSelector:
            @selector(performClose:)];
}
```

This uses an NSArray method that calls the designated selector on every object in an array. It is the `performClose:` method that catches dirtied windows and makes the dock icon bounce when your application needs attention. Since you're invoking the `closeAllWindowsAction:` action method as a selector, you needn't declare it in the header file. It is not declared as an IBAction because there is no need to connect it in Interface Builder. In Mac OS X 10.2 the `sender` parameter is the NSMenuItem that triggered the action method (before, it was NSApp), but you don't need to use it here.

9. For extra credit, consider how you might add a checkmark to the About Vermont Recipes menu item if the About window is open and in front of the application's other windows. This would be a nice touch, complementing the checkmark Cocoa uses to designate the frontmost document window.

When a panel such as the About window is in front, it is the application's key window. That is, it can receive user keystrokes. You can easily identify the key window by calling NSApplication's `keyWindow` method. But how do you determine whether the key window is the standard application About window? I asked this question on Apple's Cocoa developers mailing list and got a thoughtful answer from Andy Lee. The About window has as its delegate a private object called NSSystemInfoPanel.

Here's how you might use that information to solve this puzzle. Add the following to the end of the delegate method:

```
int menuItemIndex =
        [dynamicDockMenu indexOfItemWithTarget:nil
        andAction:@selector(orderFrontStandardAboutPanel:)];
[[dynamicDockMenu itemAtIndex:menuItemIndex]
        setState:([[[[sender keyWindow] delegate] description]
        hasPrefix:@"<NSSystemInfoPanel:"])
        ? NSOnState : NSOffState];
```

The first statement gets the index of the menu item that is connected to the orderFrontStandardAboutPanel: action method. This is convenient because you don't have to worry about the menu item's localized title. The second statement sets the state of that menu item to **NSOnState** or **NSOffState**, which normally gives a menu item a checkmark or removes the checkmark. This statement makes the decision about which state is desired based on whether the current key window's delegate has a description beginning with **<NSSystemInfoPanel:**. I have it on good authority that no other system application panels use NSSystemInfoPanel as delegate. You can't ask directly whether the key window's delegate is NSSystemInfoPanel, because that is a private class and the compiler won't let you use it.

Unfortunately, when Mac OS X 10.1 introduced dynamic Dock menus, it didn't include the ability to display the state of dynamic Dock menu items. This code does no harm, however, and there is a good chance it will work and show the checkmark once Apple adds this ability. It hasn't yet happened as of Mac OS X 10.2.1.

Step 3: Build and Run the Application

Build and run the application and test the operation of the new Dock menu and menu items. Vermont Recipes must be running for the Dock menu to appear.

Select About Vermont Recipes from the Dock menu. The application's About window immediately opens. Even if the application was behind some other application and remains there, the About window appears in front so you can easily read it. Consistent with standard Mac OS X behavior, if you click the About window's close box, it closes without bringing Vermont Recipes to the front.

Select New from the Dock menu. A new Vermont Recipes document immediately opens, although the application remains behind any other applications it was already behind. Depending on how many other application windows are open and how they are positioned, you may or may not be able to see the new window. To bring it to the front, just click the Dock icon.

Select Open from the Dock menu. A standard Open File dialog appears, behind other applications if Vermont Recipes is not in front. If it was behind other applications, the Vermont Recipes Dock icon starts bouncing to alert you that the application needs attention.

This behavior is what Cocoa design principles counsel. Try the Project Builder Dock menu to satisfy yourself that its behavior is consistent.

Finally, make sure that the Close All menu item appears in the Dock menu when Vermont Recipes windows are open and that it disappears when no application windows are open. With one or more windows open, choose Close All and see them close.

Conclusion

You have now completed Section 4 of Vermont Recipes, having learned how to add three different menu types to your application—an application menu in the menu bar, a contextual menu in a view, and a Dock menu.

In Section 5, you will tackle several important application features that I've put off for a long time. In Recipe 16, you will finally set up the drawer I promised you from the beginning. It will contain a scrolling text area in which a user can enter notes. You will also add a button to open and close the drawer. In Recipe 17, you will finally create the long-promised separate document window, which will provide a separate window for viewing and editing the notes that appear in the drawer. You'll need a button to open the window. The window will provide more editing features than the scrolling text area, and of course it will offer a resizable, movable window.

SECTION 5

Windows

Another feature found in virtually every application with a GUI is the window. Windows come in several forms. You have already worked extensively with the standard Cocoa NSWindow object throughout Vermont Recipes. In Section 5, you will encounter several other Cocoa view objects that look and act more or less like windows, broadly defined, and that serve a similar purpose.

In Recipe 16, you will finally create the drawer I've promised you since early in Recipe 1. Strictly speaking, a drawer is not a window but simply another view object associated with window. However, you must open drawers to see their contents, which can consist of the same variety of views that a window can contain. Although tab views and tab view items, discussed in Sections 1 and 2, have similar characteristics, I held off on discussing drawers until Section 5 because they seem even more like windows. In fact, the Aqua Human Interface Guidelines even refer to a drawer as "a child window."

Drawers exist to display things, of course, so I'll devote much of Recipe 16 to the drawer's contents—namely, a very important Cocoa view object, the text view. Drawers are so easy to implement that I won't dwell long on that topic in Recipe 16; I'll focus primarily on the text view that will be the drawer's principal view object.

Recipe 17 will fulfill another long-standing promise: the creation of a separate window to display some of the document's data in another format. The user will be able to open the drawer's text view in a separate window, making it easier to read and edit the text view's contents in a resizable and movable split-view window.

Recipe 18 will cover dialogs, alerts, and panels.

RECIPE 16

Drawers

In Recipe 1, Step 2.1.3, you used Interface Builder to create the Vermont Recipes application's main window as the parent window of a drawer. However, you have since treated the parent window as if it were nothing more than a simple window, leaving the VRDocument.nib window's NSDrawer and DrawContentView instances to gather dust. This approach may have been useful to demonstrate that a drawer's parent window is in fact neither more nor less than an ordinary NSWindow object, but you're now ready to dust off the drawer and make it work.

HIGHLIGHTS:

Creating a scrollable text view with word-processing features in a drawer

Using Interface Builder's autosizing tool to control the size and position of view objects in a drawer

In Recipe 16, you will add a push-button to the main document window to toggle the drawer open and closed. In the drawer itself, you will create a scrolling text view and another button. The work you do in Interface Builder is easy, and the drawer itself doesn't require any work in Project Builder.

It is the text view within the drawer that will take up most of your time in Recipe 16—to the point where you could subtitle this recipe "Text Views." The drawer will house a general-purpose note-taking view named Notes. Because it resides in a drawer, the Notes view normally stays hidden while a user is working in the Vermont Recipes application. Whenever the need arises to make a few notes, the user can simply click the Notes button to open the drawer, click in the text view to make it first responder, and start typing. When done, the user can hide the notes from view by clicking the Notes button again or dragging it shut and continue working without distraction in the document's main window.

With remarkably little code, the text view will have all the features of a reasonably powerful word processor, including the ability to apply styles such as italics and underlining to selected text, apply color, use multiple fonts and font sizes, cut and copy, choose many of these features from a contextual menu, drag and drop text, and undo and redo. It will also have full spelling-check capability, including continuous spelling checks while the user types and the ability to read selected text aloud from a menu. **Figure 16.1** shows the completed drawer with its text view in use.

FIGURE 16.1 The finished drawer and text view in use.

Before proceeding, update the target's Info.Plist Entries by incrementing its build version to **16**. The document format will also change once again, to accommodate the text in the text view, so increment the `VRDocumentVersion` variable in VRDocument.m to **7**.

Step 1: Add a Button to the Main Document Window to Toggle the Drawer Open and Closed

In this step, you will add a standard push-button to the document's main window to toggle the drawer open and closed.

First, select the NSDrawer icon in the VRDocument.nib window in Interface Builder and examine its attributes in the NSDrawer Info Panel. There is only one attribute, Preferred Edge, which defaults to **Left**. If you make no changes here or programmatically, the drawer will open on the window's left if there is room and on the right if there isn't. This is a matter of personal preference, but I prefer my drawers on the right. Make this change in the Info Panel, or leave it as is if you prefer the left edge.

1. In Interface Builder, drag a standard push-button from the Views palette to the upper-right corner of the main document window and align its right edge with the right edge of the tab view. Name the button **Notes**.

   Add a Help tag saying, "Open and close notes drawer."

2. Control-drag from the Notes button to the NSDrawer icon in the VRDocument.nib window. Then, in the Connections pane of the NSButton Info Panel, select the **target** outlet, select the **toggle:** action, and click Connect. Now, clicking the Notes button will open the drawer if it is closed and close it if it is open—no programming required.

3. Integrate the new Notes button into the window's key view loop. The Next bevel button's **nextKeyView** should be the Notes button. The Notes button's **nextKeyView** should be the tab view to complete the circle. You could try to make the next key view the NSTextView embedded in the DrawContentView, but you haven't put anything in the DrawContentView yet, so you'll have to wait. Once you have added a text view and a button to the drawer, you will try to integrate them into the window's key view loop, in Step 2.

   The drawer's content view is just another view in the main window. You leave it out of the key view loop, however, because it is an invisible container for the drawer's usable views.

Step 2: Add Static Text, a Text View, and a Button to the Drawer

The drawer's content view will contain three view objects: a static text item to serve as the drawer's title, a scrolling text view filling most of the content view, and a button to open the text view's contents in a separate window. You will create the button in Interface Builder now, but you won't make it do anything until Recipe 17.

Before beginning, notice that the DrawContentView appears in a window of its own in Interface Builder, although the DrawContentView itself is not a window but only a view object. Interface Builder acquired the ability to show freestanding views like this relatively recently. It makes creating drawers in Interface Builder easier, and it gives you the ability to construct custom views in Interface Builder that you want to integrate into a window or other view object programmatically. Note that the name DrawContentView is short for Drawer Content View.

In the course of this step, you will for the first time make use of Interface Builder's autosizing feature to help control the size and position of view objects in the drawer.

Unlike the Vermont Recipes application's main document window, the drawer's size at run time might differ from its size while you design it in Interface Builder. This is not only because the user can resize the drawer, which is the usual reason to use autosizing, but also because its height is calculated at run time based on the height of the window to which it is attached. You don't know how Cocoa calculates that height, and the calculation might change in the future anyway. It is difficult to size the drawer in Interface Builder to imitate the run-time dimensions exactly, so you have to assume it will change at least slightly.

To see the autosizing tool, select the DrawContentView icon in the VRDocument.nib window, then select the Size pane in the Info Panel. The bottom of the Info Panel contains a stylized graphical representation of the selected view and its enclosing view, with vertical and horizontal lines both inside and outside the inner box.

Clicking any of these lines turns it into a coiled spring representing a dimension that will change automatically at run time based on the size of the enclosing view. If the lines in the inner box are straight, the selected view's size will remain constant when the enclosing view is resized; if either of these two lines changes to a spring, the selected view's size in that dimension will change as the enclosing view's size changes in that dimension. If the lines in the outer box are straight, the margin between that edge of the selected view and the corresponding edge of the enclosing view will remain constant when the enclosing view is resized; if any of the four lines in the outer box changes to a spring, the margin between the selected view and the enclosing view on that side will change when the enclosing view is resized. Different combinations of straight lines and springs have different effects, changing the size of the selected view or changing its position. You'll generally need to experiment to achieve the behavior you desire.

1. Start by dragging the System Font Text item from the Views palette to the upper-left corner of the DrawContentView window. Position it the proper distance from the left and top edges as indicated by the Aqua guides. Rename the static text item **Notes**, choose Layout > Size to Fit, and reposition it to taste.

    Use the autosizing tool in the Size pane of the Info Panel to make sure the title remains in the proper position within the drawer and its DrawContentView view at run time. The title is preferentially anchored to the bottom edge of the view because the origin in a view's coordinate system is its bottom-left corner. Select the title, then convert the line in the bottom margin of the autosizing tool, between the bottom edge of the inner selected view and the bottom edge of the enclosing view, to a spring. This will allow the bottom margin to vary in size as the vertical dimension of the drawer changes, while leaving the top margin fixed. The title will now appear to be anchored to the top edge of the drawer. The margin between the title and the top edge of the drawer will not change when Cocoa calculates the run-time size of the drawer.

2. Before adding more views to the DrawContentView window, resize the drawer and its DrawContentView in Interface Builder to correspond approximately to the size they will be when in use. This has no effect on their size at run time, but it will assist you in designing the drawer's layout.

The drawer and its DrawContentView view are separate objects. To size the drawer, select the NSDrawer icon in the VRDocument.nib window, then select the Size pane in the NSDrawer Info Panel. Set its width to 300. Note that you can't set its height because, as the Info Panel says, height is a calculated value based on the attached window's height.

Drag the DrawContentView window alongside the main document window, and position its top level with the bottom of the main document window's title bar. Then drag the bottom-right corner of the DrawContentView window down until its bottom edge is roughly level with the bottom of the main document window.

Next, with the DrawContentView selected, open the Size pane of its NSView (Custom) Info Panel. Set the width field to 300 to match the drawer's width. Leave the height as is, relying on the height you just set by dragging.

Setting up the size of the drawer and its DrawContentView in Interface Builder in this way is useful for visualizing the placement of views within the DrawContentView. Because the main document window in the Vermont Recipes application is a fixed size and the drawer has a default width, you can count on the drawer to look approximately like this at run time. If you were designing a resizable window, you wouldn't have this luxury. Instead, you would set the window in Interface Builder to any size representing typical usage and position its contents accordingly. You would then set minimum and maximum sizes for the window to make sure any movable view objects within it could never overlap or spread too far apart.

3. From the Data palette, drag the text view embedded in a scrolling view to the DrawContentView window and drop it in the upper-left corner, below the Notes title. Leave space to the left and between the scrolling text view and the title above it, as indicated by the Aqua guides. Then drag the right corner of the scrolling text view down and to the right to fill most of the DrawTextView content area. Leave a margin on the right according to the Aqua guides, and leave room at the bottom for a push-button.

Open the NSScrollView Info Panel's Size pane and click to establish coiled springs in the innermost box both vertically and horizontally. When the containing drawer and its DrawContentView are resized at run time, the size of the scroll view will change, the right and bottom edges moving to match the new size of the enclosing view. The right and bottom margins between the scroll view and the edges of the drawer will remain constant.

When the size of the scroll view changes, the size of its enclosed text view will change to match. You can see why by selecting the text view and opening the Size pane of the NSTextView Info Panel. Springs control both inner dimensions, indicating that the pane will change size to match the size of the enclosing scroll view—that is, maintaining constant margins of 0 pixels on all four sides. The palette provides the scrolling text view in this form as a convenience.

Open the NSTextView Info Panel's Attributes pane and click to select "Undo allowed." Make sure you've also selected Selectable, Editable, and "Multiple fonts allowed."

4. Drag a push-button from the Views palette to the bottom margin of the DrawContentView window, beneath the scrolling text view, and position it to the right according to the Aqua guides. Entitle it `Open in Window`, choose Layout > Size to Fit, and adjust its position. You won't connect it to an action method until Recipe 17.

5. If you like, you can try setting up the key view loop you started to revise in Step 1. Theoretically, the Notes button should tab to the new text view in the DrawContentView window, the text view should tab to the Open in Window button, and the Open in Window button should tab to the tab view in the main document window. However, you will find that this doesn't work. Once you tab into the scrolling text view, pressing Tab just inserts tabs in the text. I prefer the key view loop as I left it in Step 1.

6. Add Help tags to the text view and the Open in Window button saying, "Type notes here" and "Open notes in a separate window."

Step 3: Add a Text-Formatting Menu to the Menu Bar

Since the text view will allow the user to apply many formatting customizations to its contents, you need to provide a menu in the menu bar to make them conveniently available. Interface Builder has anticipated your need and provides no fewer than three prebuilt menus for your consideration.

The Menus palette includes a Font menu, a Text menu, and a Format menu, each with a variety of built-in submenus and menu items. The Format menu is particularly convenient, because it includes the Font and Text menus as submenus. You will use the Format menu for Vermont Recipes.

1. Open MainMenu.nib in Interface Builder and select the Menus palette.

2. Drag the Format menu block to the menu bar in the MainMenu window and drop it between the Edit and Antiques menus.

That's it. If you were to build and run the application now, you would find that every command in the menu works. You can open the Cocoa Font panel and change the font and other characteristics of characters and paragraphs in the text view. You can open the Color panel to change text color. You can copy and paste fonts. You can even make a formatting ruler appear across the top of the text view.

This happens because all of the menu items in the Format menu are already wired to the associated code built into Cocoa. You can see which built-in action method is wired to each menu item by selecting each menu item in turn in Interface Builder and looking at the Connections pane in the Info Panel.

Step 4: Remove the Find Menu from the Menu Bar

One built-in menu in MainMenu.nib is not set up in advance to work for you: the Find submenu near the bottom of the Edit menu. Hopefully some future version of Cocoa will prewire this submenu to working code, as has already been done for the Format menu, but at the moment the Find submenu does nothing.

Other tutorials are available teaching how to make the Find submenu work, so Vermont Recipes will not address this task. Select the submenu in the MainMenu window and delete it.

If you prefer to make it work, you will find all the code you need in Apple's TextEdit example application source files on your disk. An excellent tutorial by Scott Anguish shows how to make it work in your Cocoa application; see the Stepwise Web site at www.stepwise.com/Articles/Technical/HTMLEditor/HTMLEditor-4.html.

Step 5: Set Up a Window Controller Category for the Drawer and Its Text View

The drawer now works and you have a good text-formatting menu in place in the menu bar, all without writing any custom code. You can therefore turn to the text view itself for the remainder of Recipe 16. You want it to have all the features of a reasonably powerful word processor. This will require writing some code, but surprisingly little.

Before beginning, consider how a text view is used and what differences might therefore exist between coding a text view and coding the controls you created in Sections 1 and 2.

In a text view, you edit text, of course. This requires ancillary capabilities such as reading the text from disk and saving it back to disk; cutting and pasting text; and setting styles, fonts, and font sizes for style runs. But these editing features do not distinguish a text view from many user controls, such as text fields and forms.

What is unique about a text view is the fact that users type long text passages in it. Users tend to work in a text view for lengthy periods of time. It's a place where concepts flow from the mind, through the fingers and the keyboard, and into the view, in a continuous stream. This is very different from text-based user controls, where typing occurs in short bursts. The difference has significant consequences for your code. For example, fast typists generally don't like interruptions, such as having to use the mouse to click buttons.

In fact, a text view is not a user control at all, either by inheritance or in concept. It is not a subclass of NSControl, directly or indirectly. You don't click it or press Enter to make something happen, the way you do with a button, a combo box, and sometimes text fields. You don't use it to control anything the way you do with a push-button, slider, or pop-down command button.

One consequence is that a text view doesn't have a target or an associated action method. Look at its attributes in the NSTextView Info Panel. You won't see a section where you can select whether to send an action "On end editing" or "Only on enter," as you can for text-based controls. Look at its outlets; there is no **target** or **action** outlet. NSControl implements the **target** and **action** methods, and NSTextView does not inherit from NSControl.

These considerations lead to fundamental questions about how to code a text view. How do you arrange to hold the text view's data—the characters and related style attributes—in memory? If you adopt the MVC paradigm as you did with text fields and other user controls, your instinct will be to hold the data as an NSString or NSData object in an instance variable in one of your application's model objects, separate from the text as it appears in the text view. But then how will you arrange to keep the view and the separate model object synchronized? If text views have no target and no action, how will the application know when to transfer the user's edits to the model object? With user controls, this was easy: You would just write a simple action method in your window controller and use Interface Builder to connect the control to the controller and its action method. You can't do that with a text view.

Sometimes these questions are not pursued very deeply, and a developer simply sets up a familiar control-style system for a text view without considering other possibilities. You may have seen examples where the `textDidEndEditing:` delegate method was jury-rigged to play the role of an action method. Perhaps a button is provided— say, a Done Editing button—so the user can tell the application that editing is complete for now and that it should therefore synchronize the model object. Or perhaps code is written to trap the Enter key to convey the same message to the application, instead of treating the Enter key like the Return key and placing a carriage return in the text. In either case, the application might be written so that the button or the Enter key forces the text view to resign first responder status and thus trigger a synchronization operation via the `textDidEndEditing:` delegate method.

As a consequence, the user would have to click the Done Editing button or press Enter to commit the most recent edits in the text view before choosing File > Save to save them to disk. A fast typist, mindful of the need for frequent saves, will have to perform two operations at every save: click the Done Editing button or press Enter, then choose File > Save. This is obviously not an ideal solution. You must consider the different role of a text view, look beyond the user control concept, and find a better way to handle these requirements.

You will implement a first, relatively simple approach in Recipe 16 to deal with these issues. You will then promptly abandon it in Recipe 17 in favor of a solution that is both more sophisticated and more in keeping with the overall design of the Cocoa text system. I find that this trial-and-error approach is useful to help readers appreciate the nuances of the problems presented by the Cocoa text system and their solution.

First, for use both in Recipe 16 and in Recipe 17, you will create a new model object associated with the drawer, much as you have done for data in the application's individual tab view item model objects. In this new model object, you will create an NSData instance variable to hold the text, in rich text format, that the user will type or paste into the text view. This will keep the data under the control of the VRDocument object, which serves to prepare the document's data for writing to disk and to configure the data for display after reading from disk. Thus much is essentially identical to the MVC approach you have taken in previous recipes.

However, instead of requiring the user to commit pending edits explicitly, the application will update the data in the model continuously as the user types, cuts, pastes, drags, and sets styles and fonts. The user's experience will be seamless, as it should be in a word processor. The user will be able to edit for a while, then choose File > Save to save recent progress, edit some more, then save again, and so on, all without having to interrupt the work flow to commit the data by pressing Enter or clicking a Done Editing button before saving.

In Recipe 16, you will accomplish this ongoing coordination of the model object with the text view by implementing a delegate method provided by the Cocoa text system. A text view calls this delegate method automatically every time the user adds, removes, moves, or formats text. The implementation of the delegate method will be simple, replacing the entire contents of the NSData model object with the entire contents of the text view's backing store. This may strike you as a time-consuming process, but the Cocoa text system is very well optimized. You will be able to type or paste large text files into the text view and edit them without noticing any slowdown while Cocoa is continuously synchronizing the model object with the text view.

If you eventually add features or redesign the text view as a vehicle for writing long novels, you might encounter a need for optimization of the approach taken in Recipe 16. In fact, this would happen as soon as you attempted to use this technique to implement the separate window you are leaving for Recipe 17. Therefore, in Recipe 17, you will abandon the Recipe 16 approach and instead use the Cocoa text system's own model object, NSTextStorage, to hold the text showing in the text view. This will obviate the need for a separate model object of your own. The Cocoa text system actually performs the coordination of its model object and its view object without your intervention, so the coordination mechanism you are about to set up in Recipe 16 is an unnecessary duplication—and slower than it has to be. You'll nevertheless find it educational to implement the coordination technique described here so you can more easily understand the reasons behind some techniques you will learn in Recipe 17.

Start by setting up a new category in the window controller. Each of the tab view items in the main document window was given its own category in VRMainWindowController, as a convenient organizing principle for your window controller code. You will now set up a fourth window controller category for the drawer and its principal view object, the text view.

1. Open VRMainWindowController.h and insert near the top a forward declaration to the new model class, which will be named VRDrawerModel. You will actually create the new model class in Step 6.

   ```
   @class VRDrawerModel;
   ```

2. Within the curly braces of the `@interface VRMainWindowController` directive, declare an outlet to the text view, as follows:

```
// Drawer
IBOutlet NSTextView *notesView;
```

3. Add the declaration of a new controller category, VRDrawerController, and its methods at the end of the VRMainWindowController.h header file, as follows:

```
@interface VRMainWindowController (VRDrawerController)

#pragma mark ACCESSORS

- (VRDrawerModel *)drawerModel;
- (NSTextView *)notesView;

#pragma mark INTERFACE MANAGEMENT - Specific updaters

- (void)updateNotesView:(NSNotification *)notification;

#pragma mark WINDOW MANAGEMENT

- (void)registerNotificationObserversForDrawer;
- (void)updateDrawer;


@end
```

You know at a glance what these methods do, because you have already created similar methods for each of the other window controller categories. There is an accessor for the `drawerModel` object so the controller can access the data, and another for the `notesView` object, which is the text view you just created in the drawer, so the controller can access the view. There is a method to register the controller as an observer of `set` accessor methods you will write into the model class in the next step. And there are methods to update the drawer and the notes view in the GUI in response to those notifications. All of this is familiar.

4. Implement the new category in a separate category source file, VRDrawer-Controller.m. You have to create the file first. In Project Builder, choose File > New File and go through the usual procedure to create a source file (but not a header file) for a new Cocoa Objective-C class named VRDrawerController.m. Add your standard comments and disclaimers at the top.

5. Insert the following code at the end of the new VRDrawerController.m category source file:

```objc
#import "VRMainWindowController.h"
#import "VRDrawerModel.h"

@implementation VRMainWindowController (VRDrawerController)

#pragma mark ACCESSORS

- (VRDrawerModel *)drawerModel {
    return [[self document] drawerModel];
}
- (NSTextView *)notesView {
    return notesView;
}


#pragma mark INTERFACE MANAGEMENT - Specific updaters

- (void)updateNotesView:(NSNotification *)notification {
    [[self notesView] replaceCharactersInRange:
            NSMakeRange(0, [[[self notesView] string] length])
            withRTF:([notification userInfo]) ?
            [[notification userInfo] objectForKey:
            VRDrawerModelNotesChangedNotification] :
            [[self drawerModel] notes]];
}

#pragma mark WINDOW MANAGEMENT

- (void)registerNotificationObserversForDrawer {
    [[NSNotificationCenter defaultCenter] addObserver:self
            selector:@selector(updateNotesView:)
            name:VRDrawerModelNotesChangedNotification
            object:[self document]];
    [[NSNotificationCenter defaultCenter] addObserver:self
            selector:@selector(updateNotesView:)
            name:VRDrawerModelUnarchivedNotification
            object: [self document]];
}

- (void)updateDrawer {
    [self updateNotesView:nil];
}

@end
```

The only new material here is in the **updateNotesView:** notification method. This method is triggered when the window controller receives one of the notifications for which it registers in the **registerNotificationObserversForDrawer** method, or it is called directly by the **updateDrawer** method. It is called directly when, for example, a new, empty drawer is created, an AppleScript sets the text data in the model object to a new text passage, or the document is unarchived from disk. The **updateNotesView:** method gathers the entire contents of the **notes** instance variable in the VRDrawerModel model object (which you haven't yet written), either from the **userInfo** dictionary contained in the notification or from the model object itself, depending on how the method was invoked, as you learned in Recipe 12. It then calls the **replaceCharactersInRange:withRTF:** method to replace the entire contents of the text view with the text from the model object.

The **replaceCharactersInRange:withRTF:** method is not declared in NSTextView but in its parent class, NSText. There are similar methods in NSText to use RTFD data (rich text with images) or unstyled strings, but you have chosen to use rich text without images for Vermont Recipes. RTF and RTFD text is held in an NSData object, while plain text is held in an NSString object.

Cocoa's convenience function **NSMakeRange()** calculates the range of text to replace in the text view, starting at location **0** and extending for the full current length of the text view. It calculates the length as that of the data in the text view, considered as a string.

6. You must make arrangements to have some of these methods called at appropriate times.

   At the end of the **registerNotificationObservers** method in the WINDOW MANAGEMENT section of the VRMainWindowController.m source file, add this line:

   ```
   [self registerNotificationObserversForDrawer];
   ```

   At the end of the **updateWindow** method in the same section, add this line:

   ```
   [self updateDrawer];
   ```

7. Now arrange for data to flow in the other direction, not from the data model to the GUI but from the GUI to the data model as the user types and edits text. Recall from the beginning of this step that you will use a Cocoa text system delegate method to update the model as the user types or edits text in the text view. Add the following method to the INPUT VALIDATION AND FORMATTING section of the VRMainWindowController.m source file. As with many delegate methods, this belongs in the main window controller source file, not in one of the controller categories, because text views located in different areas of the application might call it.

```
- (void)textStorageDidProcessEditing:(NSNotification
      *)notification {
  if ([notification object] ==
        [[self notesView] textStorage]) {
     [[self drawerModel] setNotesWhileEditing:
           [[self notesView] RTFFromRange:
           NSMakeRange(0,
           [[[self notesView] string] length])]];
  }
}
```

After determining that the text storage object associated with the **notesView** text view called it, this method calls the mirror image of the **replaceCharactersIn-Range:withRTF:** method, the **RTFFromRange:** method, also declared in NSText. The **RTFFromRange:** method gets the current contents of the text view and returns them as an NSData object. Your code then calls a **set** accessor in the Drawer model (which you haven't yet written), **setNotesWhileEditing:**, to place the text in the model object. Again, the **NSMakeRange()** function obtains the entire contents of the text view.

The delegate method you would ordinarily have expected to implement for this purpose is the **textDidChange:** method declared in NSText. However, for historical reasons, the **textDidChange:** method is not suitable for use in most text views. As it happens, the developers of the Cocoa text system implemented most of its high-level sophistication some time after the older NSText class was written, and NSText itself does not understand undo and redo. Because of this, undo and redo events don't trigger the **textDidChange:** method. If you were to use it to synchronize the model object and the text view, they would become unsynchronized the moment the user chose Edit > Undo or Redo and saved the document. The document on disk would no longer match what appeared in the text view, and in short order Cocoa would raise an exception.

Current Cocoa documentation doesn't explain any of this. Indeed, the documentation admonishes you to use delegate methods declared in NSText and NSTextView interchangeably as if they all worked similarly. This is a dangerous trap for the unwary. If you hadn't learned about it here, the beta testing of your application might have missed the fact that text fields were ignoring undo and redo. This discrepancy has been reported to Apple as a bug.

In the meantime, it is fortunate that other, more modern components of the Cocoa text system fully implement undo and redo. Instead of using the **textDidChange:** method, you used a method declared in NSTextStorage, **textStorageDidProcess-Editing:**. Not only all the edits that trigger **textDidChange:** but also undo and redo actions in a text view trigger this method.

8. There is one little detail you mustn't forget: to designate the window controller as the text storage object's delegate. Without this, the delegate method you just wrote will never be called. The simplest way to designate a delegate for the text storage object is to do so in code, in the window controller's `awakeFromNib` method. Add this line in the middle of that method in VRMainWindowController.m:

```
[[[self notesView] textStorage] setDelegate:self];
```

9. To finish your work with the window controller, be sure to import the VRDrawerModel class. Add this line at the end of the `#import` directives in VRMainWindowController.m:

```
#import "VRDrawerModel.h"
```

Step 6: Set Up a Model Object for the Text Data Represented by the Drawer

Next, create the model object for the data held in the drawer, which consists only of the styled text from the text view.

1. In Project Builder, choose File > New File and create header and source files for a new VRDrawerModel object. Don't forget to insert your standard comments and disclaimers in each. Change the header file so that it imports the Cocoa umbrella headers, not Foundation.

2. Insert the following as the entire code for the header file VRDrawerModel.h:

```
#import <Cocoa/Cocoa.h>

@class VRDocument;

@interface VRDrawerModel : NSObject <NSCoding> {
    @private
    VRDocument *document;

    NSData *notes;
}

#pragma mark INITIALIZATION
```

(continues on next page)

```
- (id)initWithDocument:(VRDocument *)inDocument;
// designated initializer

- (id)initAfterUnarchivingWithDocument:(VRDocument *)inDocument;
#pragma mark ACCESSORS

- (VRDocument *)document;

- (void)setNotes:(NSData *)inValue;
- (NSData *)notes;

- (void)setNotesWhileEditing:(NSData *)inValue;
@end

#pragma mark NOTIFICATIONS

extern NSString *VRDrawerModelUnarchivedNotification;
extern NSString *VRDrawerModelNotesChangedNotification;
```

Almost all of these are familiar to you. You see that the class declares its confor-
mance to the NSCoding protocol. It declares a **notes** instance variable of type
NSData to hold the RTF text from the text view. It has a designated initializer to
create a new, empty document with a reference to its document object and an
initAfterUnarchivingWithDocument: method like those you wrote in Recipe 12.
It has accessor methods for the **notes** instance variable. And it declares notification name variables.

Step 5 referred to the only unfamiliar method, **setNotesWhileEditing:**, and I'll
describe it more fully in conjunction with its implementation in a moment.

3. Take the source file VRDrawerModel.m in pieces. First, insert the following
    immediately after your standard comments and disclaimers. It consists mostly
    of initialization routines:

```
#import "VRDrawerModel.h"
#import "VRDocument.h"

#pragma mark NOTIFICATIONS

NSString *VRDrawerModelUnarchivedNotification =
        @"DrawerModel Unarchived Notification";
NSString *VRDrawerModelNotesChangedNotification =
        @"DrawerModel Notes Changed Notification";
```

```objc
@implementation VRDrawerModel

- (id)init {


    return [self initWithDocument:nil];
}

- (id)initWithDocument:(VRDocument *)inDocument {
    // Designated initializer.
    if (self = [super init]) {
        document = inDocument;
        notes = [[NSData alloc] init];

#ifndef VR_BLOCK_LOGS
        NSLog(@"\n\t%@", self);
#endif
    }
    return self;
}

- (id)initAfterUnarchivingWithDocument:(VRDocument *)inDocument {
    document = inDocument;
    [[NSNotificationCenter defaultCenter] postNotificationName:
        VRDrawerModelUnarchivedNotification
        object:[self document]];
    return self;
}

- (void)dealloc {
    [[self notes] release];
    [super dealloc];
}
```

Everything here is routine and familiar, including the initAfterUnarchiving-
WithDocument: method you learned about in Recipe 12.

4. Next, add the ACCESSORS and DEBUGGING sections:

```objc
#pragma mark ACCESSORS

- (VRDocument *)document {
    return document;
```

(continues on next page)

```
    }
- (void)setNotes:(NSData *)inValue {
    if (notes != inValue) {
        [notes release];
        notes = [inValue copy];
        [[NSNotificationCenter defaultCenter]
                postNotificationName:
                VRDrawerModelNotesChangedNotification
                object:[self document]
                userInfo:[NSDictionary dictionaryWithObject:notes
                forKey:VRDrawerModelNotesChangedNotification]];
    }
}


- (void)setNotesWhileEditing:(NSData *)inValue {
    [inValue retain];
    [notes release];
    notes = inValue;
}


- (NSData *)notes {
    return [[notes retain] autorelease];
}


#pragma mark DEBUGGING


- (NSString *)description {
    return [NSString stringWithFormat:@"%@\
    \n\tnotes\n",
        [super description],
        [[self notes] description]];
}
```

The setNotesWhileEditing: method requires some explanation. This is the
method called from the delegate method in the VRDrawerController.m category source file to synchronize the data model with the text view while the user
is typing. You shouldn't use the setNotes: accessor method for this purpose,
because the posting of a notification that the data has changed would trigger
updating of the text view. This is unnecessary while the user is typing in the text
view, and it would slow the synchronization process. Also, it performs a simple

retain for memory management, because this is faster than copying. Testing for identity is unnecessary because this method is called from a delegate method that is triggered only when the text changes.

5. Finally, add the STORAGE section to bring the VRDrawerModel.m source file to an end:

```
#pragma mark STORAGE

static NSString *VRNotesKey = @"VRDrawerModel Notes Key";

- (id)initWithCoder:(NSCoder *)decoder {
    [self setNotes:[decoder decodeObjectForKey:VRNotesKey]];
    return self;
}

- (void)encodeWithCoder:(NSCoder *)encoder {
    [encoder encodeObject:[self notes] forKey:VRNotesKey];
}

@end
```

You'll use the `initWithCoder:` and `encodeWithCoder:` methods when the document archives and unarchives its several model objects, as discussed in the next step.

Step 7: Archive and Unarchive the Drawer's Text Data

The last bunch of code you must write to finish implementing the text view in the drawer sets up the VRDocument class to manage the new **drawerModel** model object, in particular its methods to archive and unarchive the Drawer model.

1. First, in the VRDocument.h header file, provide a forward declaration for the VRDrawerModel class. At the end of the forward declarations section near the top of the file, add this line:

```
@class VRDrawerModel;
```

2. Within the curly braces of the **@interface** directive, declare the **drawerModel** instance variable, as follows:

```
VRDrawerModel *drawerModel;
```

3. In the ACCESSORS section, declare the accessor methods:

```
- (void)setDrawerModel:(VRDrawerModel *)inValue;
- (VRDrawerModel *)drawerModel;
```

4. Now turn to the VRDocument.m source file. Start by importing the header file:

```
#import "VRDrawerModel.h"
```

5. Add this line at the end of the `if` block in the `init` method:

```
drawerModel = [[VRDrawerModel alloc] initWithDocument:self];
```

6. Add this line near the end of the `dealloc` method:

```
[[self drawerModel] release];
```

7. Implement the accessor methods in the ACCESSORS section:

```
- (void)setDrawerModel:(VRDrawerModel *)inValue {
    [inValue retain];
    [drawerModel release];
    drawerModel = inValue;
    [drawerModel initAfterUnarchivingWithDocument:self];
}

- (VRDrawerModel *)drawerModel {
    return drawerModel;
}
```

8. In the STORAGE section, define the `VRDocumentDrawerModelKey` key:

```
static NSString *VRDocumentDrawerModelKey =
    @"VRDocument drawer model";
```

9. Add an `encodeObject:forKey:` call near the end of the `dataRepresentationOfType:` method:

```
[archiver encodeObject:[self drawerModel]
    forKey:VRDocumentDrawerModelKey];
```

10. Finally, add a `decodeObjectForKey:` call near the end of the `loadData-Representation:ofType:` method:

```
[self setDrawerModel:[unarchiver
    decodeObjectForKey:VRDocumentDrawerModelKey]];
```

Step 8: Read the Source Files into the Nib File and Connect Outlets

Next, you will inform the nib file of the new outlet to the text view and connect the outlets.

1. In Interface Builder, select the Classes tab in the nib file window, then choose Classes > Read Files. In the resulting dialog, select the VRMainWindowController.h header file, then click the Parse button.

2. Control-drag from the File's Owner icon to the text view in the DrawContentView window. Then select the `notesView` outlet in the File's Owner Info Panel and click Connect.

3. Select the text view in the DrawContentView window, Control-drag to the File's Owner icon, select the `delegate` outlet in the NSTextView Info Panel, and click Connect. You must connect the text view's `delegate` outlet or your code won't invoke the `textStorageDidProcessEditing:` delegate method to synchronize editing in the text view with the model object.

Step 9: Build and Run the Application

Build and run the application and test the operation of the new drawer and its text view.

The drawer is not particularly exciting. Click the Notes button, and the drawer opens. Click the button again, and the drawer closes. Try moving the window around on your screen to see what position will induce the drawer to open on the nonpreferred edge. This is particularly interesting if you have more than one monitor. Cocoa attempts to keep the drawer on the same screen that the window occupies.

It is much more interesting to test the text view. Open the drawer, click in the Notes text view, and start typing. You should be able to type as fast as you like without encountering any pauses, even if you're a very fast typist (I have been known to exceed 100 words per minute, and I see no delays).

Test all the features for standard Macintosh text editing that you can think of, including cutting, copying, and pasting; dragging text fragments from one position to another; dragging text to the Finder and dragging the resulting styled text clipping back; and so on. Make use of all the commands in the Edit and Format menus. The live spelling checks are particularly fun, as is the ruler, including its formatting controls. Try copying and pasting fonts as well as copying and pasting rulers to create differently styled sections within the text. Try dragging a very large RTF file into the text view and editing it. Let your imagination run riot.

Above all, try undoing an edit, saving the document, then closing and reopening the object. You will find the undo operation properly saved in the document.

As you can see, the Cocoa text system is remarkably robust, at very little cost in coding to you. But there is a more efficient way to code the text view, which you will undertake in Recipe 17.

RECIPE 17

Multiple Windows

In this recipe, you will tackle another topic promised since Recipe 1, multiple windows in a single document. You will implement a standard Mac OS X window, movable and resizable, affording another view of the contents of the scrolling text view you implemented in Recipe 16. The user can open the window by clicking the Open in Window button you created but did not code in Recipe 16 and close it like any other window. In addition, the window will have a split view, allowing the user to read and edit text in disparate parts of the same document simultaneously. Any text entered or deleted in the drawer's Notes view or either half of the split-view window will appear or disappear simultaneously in all three text views.

HIGHLIGHTS:

Coding a text view using the Cocoa text system

Implementing multiple windows in a single document

Implementing a split-view window for text editing

Using Cocoa's text system to implement multiple text views of a single text-storage object

Before getting into the details of coding the new split-view window and its text-editing features, you will devise a much improved technique for handling the text-editing features of the scrolling Notes text view in the drawer. In Recipe 16, you set up an instance variable in the drawer's model object to hold the text as an NSData object and you used notifications to keep it coordinated with the contents of the text view continuously as the user types. This design proved to be fast enough for one text view, and it had the apparent advantage of organizing the code in the familiar design patterns you learned in Section 2 of *Vermont Recipes*. However, the approach you used in Recipe 16 will lead to a noticeable lag during typing when more than one view of the same text is open. Using the design model you developed for simple user controls turns out to be no advantage at all when writing a text view, because the power and flexibility of the Cocoa text system call for a new approach.

In Recipe 17, you will therefore learn how to make more sophisticated use of the Cocoa text system—particularly its principal components, the NSTextStorage, NSLayoutManager, and NSTextContainer classes—to enhance the speed of text operations and implement multiple views of the same text. In making these changes, you will eliminate the separate NSData object in the drawer's model object and rely instead on the text system's built-in NSTextStorage model object. This will allow you to eliminate the notifications and most of the other baggage of Recipe 16, for a much cleaner implementation of the scrolling text view. You haven't wasted your time with Recipe 16, though—it is much easier to understand the advantages of the Cocoa text system after you have done it once the wrong way.

As was true of Recipe 16, the coding of the scrolling text view in the drawer and the text views in the split-view window will take up most of your time in Recipe 17. **Figure 17.1** shows the completed split-view window with its text views in use.

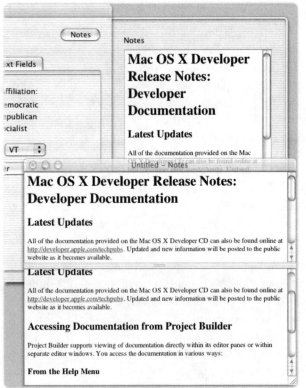

FIGURE 17.1 The finished split-view window in use.

Before proceeding, update the target's Info.Plist Entries by incrementing its build version to **17**. The document format will change slightly, storing its text as an NSTextStorage object rather than an NSData object, so increment the **VRDocument-Version** variable in VRDocument.m to **8**.

Step 1: Redesign the Text-Handling Code for the Drawer's Text View

In this step, you will learn enough about the Cocoa text system to enable you to implement a very advantageous redesign of the application's handling of text in the drawer's scrolling Notes text view. In subsequent steps you will learn still more about the text system, enabling you to create multiple text views displaying the same text-storage object.

The key to the efficiency gains you will realize in Step 1 lies in the abandonment of the NSData object you created in Recipe 16 to hold the text shown in the Notes view. The Cocoa text system is a self-contained MVC network, which already contains a model object holding the text that is shown in the text view—namely, an NSTextStorage object. NSTextStorage is a subclass of NSMutableAttributedString. It is tempting to think of it as little more than a mutable string with rich text format attributes. You encountered NSTextStorage briefly in Recipe 16, when you used two of its methods to extract RTF text from it for storage in your NSData object and to stuff the RTF text back into the NSTextStorage object.

By relying on this built-in text object in Recipe 17, you will eliminate the unnecessary use of additional memory to hold the text as an NSData object. In addition, because Cocoa's NSTextStorage object has built-in links to the other objects that make up the Cocoa text network, ultimately including the text view, Cocoa can handle all of the coordination between the user's typing and the text by itself. Using NSTextStorage eliminates not only the additional memory demand but also the extra processing your earlier approach required to coordinate the model object with the view object.

Using the Cocoa text system will require you to adopt a new pattern for coding the text view. You learned in Recipe 16 that a text view is not a user control, and the resulting absence of a target and action led you to rethink how you might recognize and deal with changes to the text. In Recipe 17, you will learn that Cocoa contains a complete text-handling system of its own, and this will lead you to even better design changes related to text editing. Your effort in Recipe 16 to conform to familiar design patterns led you to an inefficient implementation. By gaining a fuller understanding of the Cocoa text system, you will be able to write leaner, cleaner code, taking full advantage of the text system's built-in features.

In the course of studying *Vermont Recipes* up to this point, you have already met other new Cocoa view objects that required new coding techniques. You may find it useful to review them briefly to appreciate the necessity for an open mind when encountering new Cocoa objects.

At the lowest level, in the first few recipes of Section 2, you dealt with simple user controls such as checkboxes, which don't have any data of their own. Although they do have *state*, you were discouraged from relying on a user control's state as a form of data. Instead, you were expected to provide your own instance variables to hold independent data values. You were also expected to write all of the code required to keep the data model and the view coordinated. You had no particular guidelines or requirements as to how you might structure your code, leaving you to follow customary coding patterns or to strike out on your own, at your discretion. In MVC terms, these simple user controls are view objects and nothing more; the model and controller objects are left to you, without much guidance.

At a higher level, you learned about combo boxes and table views. You still had to provide your own model objects to hold the data associated with these more complex user controls. However, your code for coordinating the views and the model objects had to obey strict rules dictated by their respective data source protocols. Cocoa removed some of your discretion as to the design of the underlying data model and the controller, while relieving you of many very difficult tasks associated with coordinating the view and the model. While these more complex controls are still nothing more than view objects in model-view-controller terms, the protocols carefully guide and constrain your design of the model and controller objects.

When you learned about text fields, you learned still another technique. For efficiency reasons, Cocoa superimposes a special kind of text view known as the field editor on top of text fields when you are editing them. This forced you to adopt new coding techniques.

Now, in full-fledged text views, you encounter a system where Cocoa provides the model, the view, and the controller. It is only a slight exaggeration to say that you have practically nothing left to do except to tell the text system how many layout managers, text containers, and text views to associate with any particular text-storage object. Text systems are among the most complex topics in application programming, but Cocoa has relieved you of almost all of the tedium.

At the same time, the genius of the Cocoa text system gives you great flexibility in how to lay out multiple views of any given text-storage object. With very little effort, you can create complex designs such as multiple columns and pages between which text from a single text-storage object flows, dual views of a single text-storage object in split-view windows, and multitudinous views of a single text-storage object in disparate views (such as the scrolling Notes text view and the separate split-window panes you are about to write). You accomplish this by simply fitting the components of the text system together like pieces of a jigsaw puzzle.

If you need still more flexibility, you can customize everything by using standard Cocoa techniques, including delegate methods, and categories, and, as a last resort, by overriding the text system's components.

Until the release of Mac OS X 10.2, the one major aspect of text views left mostly up to you was reading the text from disk and writing the text to disk. In Mac OS X 10.2, even this is done for you. Every major component of the Cocoa text system now conforms to the NSCoding protocol, so you can use familiar archiving and unarchiving techniques. The new keyed archiving classes you learned about in Recipe 12 contain delegate methods that ease the task of saving and retrieving text in text views. These features, too, will play an important role in the redesign of the Notes text view in the Vermont Recipes application.

With this as background, you can begin rewriting the code you wrote in Recipe 16 to handle the text in the Notes view.

1. Although the key to the redesign is to eliminate the NSData object, **notes**, in the VRDrawerModel object, you won't simply delete it from the code. Instead, you will change it from an NSData instance containing a duplicate copy of the text for the life of the document to an NSTextStorage object used for only one brief moment. Instead of two copies of the text in memory at all times, only one instance will exist in memory at any given time, usually in the Cocoa text system.

    It is necessary to maintain this instance variable in the application model object to act as a placeholder for the text system's model object, to help Cocoa recognize when it must trigger the keyed archiving delegate methods you will read about later. For most of its life, the placeholder will be **nil**, consuming no significant memory, and it will not be used in managing the text. It will be used directly only once in a document's life—while a user is opening the document from disk, when the placeholder will hold the text as it is unarchived until the window controller is created and can move the text into the Cocoa text system.

    In the VRDrawerModel.h header file, change the declaration of the **notes** instance variable's type from NSData to NSTextStorage, like this:

    ```
    NSTextStorage *notes;
    ```

    Make the same change to the type declared in the accessor methods:

    ```
    - (void)setNotes:(NSTextStorage *)inValue;
    - (NSTextStorage *)notes;
    ```

    Make the same change to the signatures of these accessor methods in the source file VRDrawerModel.m:

    ```
    - (void)setNotes:(NSTextStorage *)inValue {
    ```

    ```
    - (NSTextStorage *)notes {
    ```

2. Because the **notes** instance variable will not be used immediately, you don't need to instantiate it when the document is initialized. In the VRDrawerModel.m

source file, remove the statement that allocates and initializes an empty NSData object. In its place, you can (although you don't have to) insert the following statement assigning **nil** to the **notes** instance variable:

```
notes = nil;
```

This also eliminates any need for the **dealloc** method, so remove that from the VRDrawerModel.m source file altogether. Later, you will retain the notes object once and almost immediately release it, so these tasks need not be performed when the document is initialized nor when it is deallocated.

3. The new version of the **setNotes:** accessor method does not need to post a notification, as the old version did. The old **VRDrawerModelNotesChangedNotification** notification was used, as in all of your user control **set** accessors, to tell the window controller to update the view onscreen in response to undo and redo actions. Since the Cocoa text system handles undo and redo for you, you no longer need this notification. (You have not yet implemented AppleScript support in the Vermont Recipes application, so you don't need to investigate at this time whether you might still need the notification to support an AppleScript command to change the contents of the text view.)

    Since you no longer need this notification, you can eliminate it completely from the application's code. Remove its external string declaration from the bottom of the VRDrawerModel.h header file; remove the string definition from the top of the VRDrawerModel.m source file; remove the statement posting this notification from the **setNotes:** method in the VRDrawerModel.m source file; finally, remove the statement registering the window controller to observe this notification from the **registerNotificationObserversForDrawer** method in the WINDOW MANAGEMENT section of the VRDrawerController.m category source file.

4. You will shortly learn how to use one of the new NSKeyedUnarchiver delegate methods to respond to the unarchiving of the Notes text from disk. The availability of this new delegate method makes it unnecessary for the application to post a notification of its own to announce the successful unarchiving of the text, so you can also eliminate all references to the **VRDrawerModelUnarchivedNotification** notification you wrote in Recipe 16. Remove its external string declaration from the bottom of the VRDrawerModel.h header file; remove the string definition from the top of the VRDrawerModel.m source file; remove the statement posting this notification from the **initAfterUnarchivingWithDocument:** method in the VRDrawerModel.m source file; finally, remove the statement registering the window controller to observe this notification from the **registerNotification ObserversForDrawer** method in the WINDOW MANAGEMENT section of the VRDrawerController.m category source file.

In fact, since you no longer require any notifications in the drawer model, you can eliminate the entire `registerNotificationObserversForDrawer` method in both the VRDrawerController.m source file and the VRDrawerController category in the VRMainWindowController.h header file. Also remove the statement calling the `registerNotificationObserversForDrawer` method from the `registerNotificationObservers` method in the WINDOW MANAGEMENT section of the VRMainWindowController.m source file. You would need these registration methods only if you were to add user controls to the drawer.

There is one remaining reference to the `VRDrawerModelNotesChangedNotification` notification, in the `updateNotesView:` notification method in the VRDrawer Controller.m category source file. You will tackle it next.

5. The Notes text view still needs a mechanism to update itself onscreen when a user initially opens a document from disk. You can't use the NSKeyedUnarchiver delegate method at that point because it won't yet have had an opportunity to appoint the window controller as the unarchiver's delegate. A document unarchives its data before it creates its window controller and window.

   You will use the existing `updateNotesView:` method in VRDrawerController for this purpose, with some changes. In Recipe 16, you wrote `updateNotesView:` as a notification method to play this role, in the same way you have done for user controls throughout the application. When the application loaded the document's nib file, the window controller's `awakeFromNib` method called an `updateWindow` method, which in turn called an `updateDrawer` method, which finally called the `updateNotesView:` method. Although you wrote the latter as a notification method to update the screen after undo and redo, `updateDrawer` passed `nil` as the `updateNotesView:` method's notification parameter, since the method was not triggered by a notification but was instead called directly as the user opened the document.

   Now you can change the method to a simple method without a parameter, `updateNotesView`, because you don't need a notification to handle a text view's undo and redo operations. It will only be called directly, when the user opens the document. It will use only the part of its code needed for the direct call, eliminating the part that refers to the `VRDrawerModelNotesChangedNotification` notification, which you have already eliminated everywhere else in the application. Change the method to the following:

```
- (void)updateNotesView {
    [[self notesView] replaceCharactersInRange:
        NSMakeRange(0, [[[self notesView] string] length])
        withRTF:[[[self drawerModel] notes] RTFFromRange:
```

(continues on next page)

```
        NSMakeRange(0, [[[[self drawerModel] notes] string]
        length]) documentAttributes:nil]];
    [[[self drawerModel] notes] release];
    [[self drawerModel] setNotes:nil]
}
```

As you learned in Recipe 16, this simply moves the entire contents of the **notes** instance variable in the drawer model—namely, the text just read from disk—into the text view. To be more precise, it moves the text from the saved NSTextStorage object into the NSTextStorage object maintained by the Cocoa text system in association with the text view.

You have also added new lines after this happens, to release the drawer model's **notes** object and set it to **nil**. This is how you eliminate the duplicate memory usage from Recipe 16. You will learn in a moment how the repurposed **notes** variable acquired the text when it was read from disk, but here you see how it relieves itself of the burden of continuing to hold the text and goes back to its harmless existence for the remainder of the document's life.

You must also change the declaration of **updateNotesView:** in the VRDrawer-Controller category of the VRMainWindowController.h header file to remove the notification parameter.

Finally, you must revise the **updateDrawer** method so that it does not attempt to pass **nil** in the notification parameter you just eliminated. Revise it to read as follows:

```
- (void)updateDrawer {
    [self updateNotesView];
}
```

6. You are now almost ready to code the keyed archiving delegate methods, new in Mac OS X 10.2, which make possible this improvement on the application's handling of text.

Recall first how you wrote the archiving and unarchiving of text in Recipe 16. You won't make any fundamental changes to these basic underpinnings. First, in VRDocument, you wrote **dataRepresentationOfType:** and **loadDataRepresentation: ofType:** methods that created a temporary archiver and unarchiver. The archiver and unarchiver objects used the new **encodeObject:forKey:** and **decodeObject ForKey:** methods to write and read the document's basic model objects. These in turn called **initWithCoder:** and **encodeWithCoder:** methods in VRDrawerModel that actually set the contents of the drawer model's **notes** variable after reading text from disk and extracted the contents of the **notes** variable before writing the text to disk.

You will leave the `initWithCoder:` and `encodeWithCoder:` methods unchanged. However, you are no longer maintaining the **notes** instance variable as an ongoing repository of the Notes view's text, so the issue you face is how to make these two methods work with the Cocoa text system's NSTextStorage object instead of with the **notes** object.

Start by unarchiving the text from disk. You have just read that there are two cases you must handle separately, one when the document opens and the other when it reverts to its saved state. You will take them in order.

When a document first opens, VRDrawerModel's `initWithCoder:` method decodes the text from disk and places it in the **notes** instance variable. This initiates the one brief moment in the life of the document, referred to above, when the notes variable will hold real data. Since objects decoded from disk in this fashion are autoreleased, you must retain the **notes** data so that it will survive the short journey to the **updateDrawerView** method that you just rewrote, where it will be released after transfer to the text view's NSTextStorage object. The `setNotes:` accessor method from Recipe 16 releases the old notes object and retains the new one just read from disk, but you have to change that code for your new design. Modify it to read as follows:

```
- (void)setNotes:(NSTextStorage *)inValue {
    if ([[[self document] windowControllers] count] == 0) {
        [inValue retain];
    }
    notes = inValue;
}
```

You no longer have to release the old object in the **notes** instance variable, because there is nothing in it. This document was just instantiated when the user opened it, and its initialization method merely sets the **notes** instance variable to **nil**. You simply retain the incoming value and assign it to the **notes** variable. The window controller will release the **notes** variable in **updateNotesView** a moment later, as you already arranged, and it will never again be used. You don't even need a **dealloc** method to release it when the document closes.

You should retain the **notes** object only once, when the document opens. Afterward, when the **setNotes:** method is called every time the user reverts the document to its saved state, the **notes** variable should not be retained because the NSKeyedUnarchiver delegate method you are about to write will handle the text from then on. This is why you nested the **retain** call in an **if** block. When a user first opens a document, its contents are decoded before its window controller is instantiated. Determining that there are no window controllers associated with the document is therefore a convenient way to conduct this test. At revert time, although the `initWithCoder:` method will still set the `notes` variable to point to the newly read text, the `notes` variable will not be retained in the drawer model and therefore will not preempt any memory.

7. Now you can finally write the NSKeyedUnarchiver delegate method called when a document reverts to its saved state.

First, you must appoint the window controller as the unarchiver's delegate. You can't do this in Interface Builder, because the unarchiver object is a temporary creature of the `loadDataRepresentation:ofType:` method. Insert the following near the beginning of that method, immediately before its first call to `decodeObjectForKey:`:

```
if ([[self windowControllers] count] > 0) {
    [unarchiver setDelegate:[[self windowControllers]
        objectAtIndex:0]];
}
```

This uses the mirror image of the test you just wrote in `setNotes:`, ensuring that a delegate is designated only when the user chooses Revert, when a window controller is known to exist. You can't appoint the window controller as delegate before then, when the document is opened, because the window controller doesn't yet exist at that time. In Vermont Recipes, the main document window's controller is always the first controller created, so you appoint the window controller at index 0 as the unarchiver's delegate.

Now write the following delegate method at the end of the VRMainWindow Controller.m file. It belongs in the main window controller source file, not in the VRDrawerController.m category source file, because you might have other text views in other parts of the application.

```
- (id)unarchiver:(NSKeyedUnarchiver *)unarchiver
        didDecodeObject:(id)object {
    if ([object isKindOfClass:[[self drawerModel] class]]) {
        [[self notesView] replaceCharactersInRange:
                NSMakeRange(0, [[[self notesView] string] length])
                withRTF:[[object notes] RTFFromRange:
                NSMakeRange(0, [[[object notes] string] length])
                documentAttributes:nil]];
        [object setNotes:nil];
        return object;
    }
    return object;
}
```

This delegate method is called, as its name indicates, just after the temporary unarchiver decodes another object. Because it is called every time another object is decoded, you must first test the incoming `object` parameter value to make sure it is the object you want. The only way to do this here is to make sure it is typed as a VRDrawerModel object, only one of which exists in a Vermont Recipes document. You can't test the incoming object for equality with the document object's `drawerModel` instance variable, because the unarchiver has created a temporary drawer model object while it is unarchiving the drawer model from disk—it hasn't yet called `setDrawerModel:` to substitute the new drawer model for the old. (For this reason, you must always be very careful about referring to any variable in the document or its drawer model while an unarchiving operation is under way. The unarchiver holds a separate instance of the drawer model object and the objects it contains, whose values may be different.)

The delegate method then transfers the contents of the incoming object—the Notes text just decoded from disk—into the text view's associated NSTextStorage object, using code that is almost identical to that which you wrote in `update-NotesView:` for use when the document is first opened. The only difference here is that you grab the text from the `notes` value in the incoming `object` parameter value, which was just read from disk, instead of from the drawer model's `notes` instance variable.

Finally, you set the decoded drawer model object's `notes` instance variable to `nil` and return the incoming drawer model object to the unarchiver. The unarchiver, as you already know, assigns it to the drawer model instance variable. Since the `notes` object has now already been transferred into the text view's associated NSTextStorage object, you no longer need it. You set it to `nil` so the drawer model won't accidentally use it. Since the drawer model won't retain it, either, it won't take up any memory and you can disregard it. The Notes text just read from disk is retained by the Cocoa text system—that is, by the NSTextStorage object associated with the text view where you just placed it. The Cocoa text system takes ownership of it just the way any collection object takes ownership of newly added objects, so you no longer have any responsibility for releasing it. The Cocoa text system has taken over management of the text, which was your objective in redesigning the application's handling of the Notes text view.

Because the delegate method is called after every object is decoded from disk, you must return the object unchanged for all other objects. This you do in the last line of the delegate method.

8. Next, write the delegate method called when the document is saved to disk. Insert this method at the end of the VRMainWindowController.m source file:

```
- (id)archiver:(NSKeyedArchiver *)archiver
    willEncodeObject:(id)object {
  if (object == [self drawerModel]) {
      [object setNotes:[[self notesView] textStorage]];
      return object;
  }
  return object;
}
```

As its name suggests, this delegate method is called just before the temporary archiver encodes the object into itself in preparation for writing itself to disk. Since it is called just before every object in the document is archived, you must determine that the incoming **object** parameter value is the one you want. In this case, you can test for address equality with the **notes** instance variable in the drawer model, because that is the object the drawer model thinks it is going to encode. This is what I meant earlier when I described the **notes** instance variable as a placeholder necessary to trigger the delegate method.

What is remarkable about this delegate method is that it makes a switch behind the back of the drawer model, substituting the text from the Notes view's associated NSTextStorage object for the **nil** text value in the incoming **object** parameter. As you know, the text in the **object** parameter was released a moment after the user opened the document. Now, when the user is saving the document, the delegate method discards that nonexistent value, replacing it with the real text object in the Cocoa text system. The delegate method then assigns the text to the archiver's temporary version of the drawer model's **notes** instance variable and returns it, now modified, to the archiver. The archiver finally writes itself to disk. Using the drawer model's **setNotes:** method in this way does not move any data into the real drawer model—where the **notes** instance variable will remain **nil**—but only into the temporary drawer model used by the temporary archiver object.

The delegate method won't fire unless you appoint a delegate for the temporary archiver. In the **dataRepresentationOfType:** method in the VRMainWindow Controller.m source file, just after setting the archiver's output format, insert this line:

```
[archiver setDelegate:[[self windowControllers]
    objectAtIndex:0]];
```

It isn't necessary to test whether a window controller exists here, because you are saving an open document. You already know it exists.

9. There remain only a few cleanup tasks to complete the redesign of the Notes text view.

First, delete the `textStorageDidProcessEditing:` delegate method from the VRMainWindowController.m source file. You no longer coordinate the text view and its text storage yourself, so this delegate method is not necessary.

Second, delete the line in the VRMainWindowController.m `awakeFromNib` method that designates the window controller as the text-storage object's delegate. This was required only to trigger the `textStorageDidProcessEditing:` delegate method, which you have now deleted.

Third, rewrite the `loadDataRepresentation:ofType:` method in VRDocument.m by moving the `initAfterUnarchivingWithDocument:` method calls from each of the four main `set` accessors in the document to the method that does the unarchiving, `loadDataRepresentation:ofType:`. This doesn't change the operation of the application, but it is a more sensible arrangement, placing the initializations that occur after unarchiving into the unarchiving method itself. Be sure to delete this method call from each of the four `set` accessors in VRDocument.m. You can bunch them together immediately before the `return YES` statement or intersperse them among the `decodeObjectForKey:` calls.

Finally, delete the `setNotesWhileEditing:` method from the VRDrawerModel.h header file and the VRDrawerModel.m source file. You now have one `setNotes:` method that serves all purposes, so you don't need this awkward duplicate.

By redesigning the Notes text view to use the Cocoa text system properly, you have made some remarkable improvements to the operation of the Vermont Recipes application. You no longer waste memory on a duplicate copy of the text view's text in the drawer model, relying instead on the NSTextStorage object associated with the text view, as Cocoa's authors intended. By relying on the NSTextStorage object, you also take full advantage of the highly optimized and very fast processing the Cocoa text system does to coordinate the view object, the Notes text view, with its model object, the NSTextStorage object.

At the same time, you have succeeded in maintaining the basic MVC structure of the Vermont Recipes application. The document object and its associated model objects continue to handle the application's data, and the window controller coordinates the models with the several views, including the Notes text view. You were able to keep the logic for archiving and unarchiving the data in the document and its model objects, where it belongs. Because the Cocoa text system is a self-contained MVC network accessed mainly through its text view, maintaining the application's overall MVC design required a little legerdemain, but the new keyed archiving classes and their delegate methods made this easy to accomplish.

All of this paves the way for creating additional views on the same text in a separate window. You will now turn to this task.

Step 2: Create a Split-View Window in a Separate Nib File in Interface Builder

You can now turn to the main task of Recipe 17, implementing a separate split-view window in which the user can edit the notes in case the small text view in the drawer is inadequate. Over the course of the next three steps, you will use Interface Builder to set up the window in a separate nib file of its own; you will use Project Builder to create a new window controller for it, separate from the main document window's controller; and you will connect the drawer's Open in Window button and code its action method so the user can open the new window at will. After this is done, in Step 5, you will return to the Cocoa text system and take the steps necessary to display and edit the one NSTextStorage object in both panes of the split-view window as well as in the drawer's text view.

Start by using Interface Builder to set up the split-view window in a separate nib file of its own. You should use a separate nib file whenever a window or other view object will likely be used infrequently or will not be used until some time after the document opens. This enables the document to open more quickly, creating a more responsive feel for your application. The separate nib file will load lazily, if and when the user needs it.

1. In Interface Builder, choose File > New to bring up the Starting Point dialog, or just click in the dialog if it is already open. Select the Empty Cocoa template and click New. A new Interface Builder window opens containing only a File's Owner and a First Responder icon.

2. Choose File > Save As. In the standard file dialog, name the new nib file **VRTextWindow** and uncheck the "Hide extension" checkbox to make the file name's .nib extension appear. Then navigate to the English.lproj subfolder of your project folder and click Save.

   In Project Builder's project window, drag the new VRTextWindow.nib file into the Resources group of the Groups & Files pane, if necessary.

3. In Interface Builder, drag a Window item from the Windows palette into the main VRTextWindow.nib window. A new window appears on the Interface Builder desktop. Leave its name (Windows) and all its attributes as you find them.

4. Drag a Custom View item from the Containers palette and drop it in the new window. Position it at the top-left corner of the window, and drag its bottom-right resize handle to the bottom-right corner of the window until it fills the content area, leaving no margins.

For a normal text window, you would have dragged a scrolling text view into the window, but this will be a split-view window holding two scrolling text views. You must therefore embed the two scrolling text views in a split view. In the next instruction, you will convert the custom view into a split view.

5. Ensure that the custom view is selected and, in the NSView (Custom) Info Panel, select the Custom Class pane and select NSSplitView as its class. You now have a split view into which you can drag the two scrolling text views.

    This technique—starting with a custom view and converting its class to something else—is standard Interface Builder procedure for instantiating objects that don't have a ready-made instance in the palette.

6. From the Data palette, drag two scrolling text views into the new text window, dropping one in the upper part of the split view and the other in the lower part.

    Drag the upper scrolling text view to the top-left corner of the split view and drag its lower-right resize handle to the right side of the split view and about halfway down. It should fill the top half of the NSSplitView. You don't have to be precise because you will resize the views before finishing.

    Then drag the lower scrolling text view to the left edge of the split view, and drag it up until an Aqua guide appears about 1/16 inch below the bottom edge of the upper scrolling text view. The narrow gap between the upper and lower text views will become the divider that the user drags up and down to resize the two halves of the split view. Interface Builder will even supply the two short, parallel lines that mark it as a split-view divider. Drag the lower-right resize handle of the lower text view into the bottom-right corner of the split view.

7. Select each scrolling text view in turn and use the NSTextView Info Panel's Attributes pane to check the "Undo allowed" checkbox for each. You may have to click or double-click a couple of times until you have selected a text view instead of its containing scroll view.

8. Select each scroll view in turn and select its Size pane. Click the two lines in the innermost box to change them to springs, ensuring that the scroll views will resize as the split view resizes. Also select the split view. In the Size pane of its Info Panel, click the two inner lines to turn them into springs so the split view will resize as the window resizes. In doing this, make sure you have selected the correct view each time. It is very easy to select the wrong view because there are so many nested views.

9. When the user first opens the window, only the bottom pane should be visible because windows are normally used in single-pane mode. The split-view divider should appear at the top of the window's content region, nestled just under its title bar. The user can drag the divider down to open the top pane if a second view is needed.

Creating this starting arrangement in Interface Builder requires some delicate work. First, you may be surprised to discover that the split view is flipped in Interface Builder. What looks like its top while you design the window actually becomes its bottom at run time, and vice versa. Therefore, to place the divider at the window's top at run time, you must place it at the bottom in Interface Builder. (To avoid confusion, subsequent references in this instruction to upper and lower refer to the appearance of the split view in Interface Builder.) The second difficulty is that the lower scroll view won't let you resize it vertically to 0 pixels high unless you first make a slight change to one of its features, then restore that feature after the scroll view is resized to its final dimensions.

Start by selecting the lower scroll view. In the NSScrollView Info Panel, deselect the Show Scrollbar option. The scroll view won't let you collapse it all the way because it needs room for the scroll bar. Now that the scroll bar is gone, drag the lower scroll view's upper resize handle downward until the scroll view disappears completely. Alternatively, type 0 into the scroll bar's height text field in the Size pane of its Info Panel. It will then be a thin horizontal line at the bottom of the window. If necessary, you can reselect it by enlarging the window and clicking the line. While the scroll view is still selected, reselect the Show Scrollbar option in the Info Panel. At run time, when you drag the divider to make this scroll view visible, it will have a scroll bar.

Finally, drag the lower edge of the upper scroll view downward until the Aqua guide indicates the proper ¹⁄₁₆ inch width for the divider, now located at the bottom of the window in Interface Builder.

10. Choose File > Test Interface and test the window to make sure it's working as desired. Resize the window and observe that its two text views resize with it appropriately. While you're at it, drag the split-view divider up and down and watch the two scrolling text views respond as they should. You can even type a lot of text or carriage returns into each pane to activate their scroll bars.

Step 3: Create a Separate Window Controller for the Split-View Window in Project Builder

There should be a one-to-one correspondence between windows and their window controllers. You therefore need to create a new window controller for the split-view window.

1. In Project Builder, choose File > New File. Select the Cocoa Objective-C NSWindowController template and click Next. Name it `VRTextWindowController.m`, check the option to create a separate header file, and click Finish. Drag it to the Window Controllers group in the Groups & Files pane of the project window, if necessary.

   The NSWindowController template is identical to the bare class template except that it is subclassed from NSWindowController.

2. Add your customary comments and disclaimers to both the header and the source file.

3. Fix the VRTextWindowController.h header file so that it imports Cocoa instead of the AppKit.

4. You can perform many of these steps in a different order, but this time why don't you switch to Interface Builder now to make a preliminary connection? Select the Classes tab in the main VRTextWindow.nib window, then choose Classes > Read Files. Select the VRTextWindowController.h header file and click Parse. The nib file now knows that the VRTextWindowController class exists in the project.

5. Select the Instances tab in the main nib file window and select the File's Owner icon. In the File's Owner Info Panel, select the Custom Class pane and select VRTextWindowController. Your new text window controller is now the new nib file's owner.

6. Write the initial code for the new window controller. Start with the declarations of the instance variables in the VRTextWindowController.h header file. You will dispense with accessor methods in this class because it is so simple. All you need are two instance variables to hold the two split-pane views. The file should look like this:

```
#import <Cocoa/Cocoa.h>

@interface VRTextWindowController : NSWindowController {
    @private
    IBOutlet NSTextView *topNotesView;
    IBOutlet NSTextView *bottomNotesView;
}

@end
```

   Because you will not use accessor methods, you need not define anything in the VRTextWindowController.m source file relating to the instance variables.

7. Add an `init` method to the source file. As in the VRMainWindowController's `init` method, it starts by loading its nib file, as shown here:

```
- (id)init {
    self = [super initWithWindowNibName:@"VRTextWindow"];
    return self;
}
```

Save the VRTextWindowController's files now, because you are about to read them into the nib file again.

8. Return to Interface Builder to connect the two new outlets you wrote and make other connections.

Select the Classes tab in the main nib window and choose Classes > Read Files. Select the VRTextWindowController.h header file and click Parse.

Control-drag from the File's Owner icon to the Window icon, select the Window outlet supplied by NSTextWindowController, and click Connect.

Next, Control-drag from the File's Owner icon to the upper scrolling text view in the split-view window, select the `bottomNotesView` outlet, and click Connect. This appears backward, but—as you learned in Step 2—the split view in which you've embedded the scrolling text views is flipped in Interface Builder. At run time, the `bottomNotesView` will be on the bottom, where it belongs.

Do the same with the lower scrolling text view, connecting the `topNotesView` outlet. This will be difficult to accomplish in the window, because in Step 2 you resized the lower text view to a height of 0 pixels. You should instead use the outline view of the Instances tab in the main VRTextWindow.nib window. Expand the outline topics until both the VRTextWindowController (which is File's Owner) and the `topNotesView` outlet are visible, then Control-drag from the former to the latter.

Control-drag from the Window icon to the upper scrolling text view, select the `initialFirstResponder` outlet, and click Connect.

9. Finally, make sure the new split-view window has a meaningful name. This is a subsidiary window. That is, it shows a subset of the main document window's contents. It should therefore have a name identical to that of the main document window, but with a suffix that identifies it as a notes window. Insert the following method at the end of VRTextWindowController.m to accomplish this:

```
#pragma mark WINDOW MANAGEMENT

- (NSString *)windowTitleForDocumentDisplayName:
        (NSString *)displayName {
```

```
return [[[self document] displayName]
    stringByAppendingString:
    NSLocalizedString(@" - Notes",
    @"String appended to Notes window title")];
}
```

Don't forget to add an appropriate entry to Localizable.strings.

Step 4: Code and Connect the Open in Window Button

In Recipe 16, Step 2, you placed a button at the bottom of the drawer named Open in Window, but you did nothing to make this button work. You will now code it in Project Builder and make the required Interface Builder connections. You will be working with the VRMainWindowController files, of course, and the VRDocument.nib nib file.

1. In the VRMainWindowController.h header file, add an instance variable at the end of the Drawer section, as follows:

    `IBOutlet NSButton *openInWindowButton;`

    Declare its accessor method in the ACCESSORS section of the VRDrawerController category of the VRMainWindowController.h header file, as follows:

    `- (NSButton *)openInWindowButton;`

    Define its accessor in the ACCESSORS section of the VRDrawerController.m category source file, as follows:

    ```
    - (NSButton *)openInWindowButton {
        return openInWindowButton;
    }
    ```

2. Next, the Open in Window button needs an action method so that the new split-view window will actually open when the user clicks the button. In the ACTIONS section of the VRMainWindowController.h header file's VRDrawerController category, define it as follows:

    `#pragma mark ACTIONS`

    `-(IBAction)openInWindowAction:(id)sender;`

Declare it as follows in the ACTIONS section of the VRDrawerController.m category source file:

```
#pragma mark ACTIONS

- (IBAction)openInWindowAction:(id)sender {
    if (![self textWindowController]) {
        [self setTextWindowController:
                [[VRTextWindowController alloc] init]];
        [[self document] addWindowController:
                [self textWindowController]];
    }
    [[self textWindowController] showWindow:sender];
}
```

This is where the important button action takes place. First, if the button has not been used before to open a split-view window for this document, the text window controller will not have been instantiated. You therefore test for the existence of a text window controller. If none is found, you allocate and initialize a new text window controller and you add it to the document's list of window controllers. The main window controller already occupies index position 0 in the document's windowControllers array, so the text window controller will occupy index position 1.

Adding the text window controller to the document's windowControllers array is an extremely important step. A Cocoa document-based application relies heavily on its document's list of window controllers to handle many operations automatically, such as setting each window's edited status in response to undo and redo actions and modifying window titles.

Notice that you have instantiated the text window controller and added it to the document's windowControllers array in an action method. You could have done this instead in the document's makeWindowControllers method, where you created the main document window. However, you have already decided that the text window controller should be instantiated lazily, if and when needed, so you can't create it in the makeWindowControllers method. That method is called as soon as a new document is created.

This is all it takes to create and open the split-view window. In Step 3, you wrote an init method in the text window controller that will be called as soon as the text window controller is instantiated as a result of the user's clicking the Open in Window button. The init method loads the VRTextWindow.nib nib file, which causes the window to open.

The final step of the action method, whether a new text window controller has just been created or one already existed, is to show the window. The `showWindow` method from NSWindowController makes the window key and brings it to the front. The user can thus bring an already opened split-view window to the front, as well as open a new window, by clicking the Open in Window button. Because this code only creates a window controller and loads its nib file once, only one split-view window can be open for any document.

When the user closes the split-view window, Cocoa does not remove it from memory. It just hides the window so that reopening it will take very little time. The `showWindow` method in the Open in Window button's action method is all that is required to make it visible again.

When you build the application and test it, you will discover that closing the main document window automatically closes the split-view window as well if it is open. This is because at the outset of *Vermont Recipes* in Recipe 1, Step 3.3, you had the foresight to call `setShouldCloseDocument:YES` in the main window controller's `init` method. The default value is `NO`, which is why closing the split-view window does not close the main document window. The split-view window is intended to be ancillary to the main document window, so this is desirable behavior.

3. You have blithely referred to the VRTextWindowController object and its accessor methods without creating them. You should take care of these details immediately.

At the top of the VRMainWindowController.h header file, forward-declare the VRTextWindowController class as follows:

```
@class VRTextWindowController;
```

Declare the instance variable for the object at the end of the Drawer section in the same header file, as follows:

```
VRTextWindowController *textWindowController;
```

Define its accessor methods in the ACCESSORS section of the VRDrawer-Controller category near the bottom of the VRMainWindowController.h header file, as follows:

```
- (void)setTextWindowController:
        (VRTextWindowController *)inValue;
- (VRTextWindowController *)textWindowController;
```

Define them in the ACCESSORS section of the VRDrawerController.m category source file, as follows:

```
- (void)setTextWindowController:
     (VRTextWindowController *)inValue {
   textWindowController = inValue;
}

- (NSWindowController *)textWindowController {
   return textWindowController;
}
```

The **set** accessor will only be called once, in the Open in Window button's action method the first time it is clicked, so there isn't any need to worry about releasing an old value and retaining the incoming value.

Don't forget to import the VRTextWindowController.h header file at the top of the VRDrawerController.m source file, as follows:

```
#import "VRTextWindowController.h"
```

4. When you added the text window controller to the document's **windowController** array, the array retained it, as collection objects always do when you add an element to them. You may recall that the document's **makeWindowControllers** method released the temporary window controller used there to create the main document window's controller, as soon as the **windowControllers** array assumed ownership of it. However, the action method here did not promptly release the newly instantiated text window controller. It must stick around to handle future clicks on the Open in Window button. Cocoa will release the text window controller once automatically when the document closes and its **windowControllers** array is released. However, because the main window controller has also maintained shared ownership of the text window controller, it must release the text window controller when the main document window closes.

    Add this line near the end of the **dealloc** method in the VRMainWindow-Controller.m source file:

    ```
    [[self textWindowController] release];
    ```

    This requires you to import the VRTextWindowController.h header file at the top of the VRMainWindowController.m source file, even though you also just imported it into the VRDrawerController.m source file, as follows:

    ```
    #import "VRTextWindowController.h"
    ```

5. You are now ready to return to Interface Builder to connect the Open in Window button and its new action method. Open the VRDocument.nib nib file and select the Classes tab. Choose Classes > Read Files, select VRMainWindowController.h, and click Parse. Select the Instances tab and Control-drag from the File's Owner

icon to the Open in Window button, select the `openInWindowButton` outlet, and click Connect. Also Control-drag from the Open in Window button to the File's Owner icon, select the Target outlet, select the `openInWindowAction:` action method, and click Connect.

If you were to build and run the application now, you would find that you can type and perform other editing operations in both panes of the split-view window. Even undo and redo work, because the Cocoa text system handles them for you. Even more pleasing is the fact that all the commands in the Format menu you added in Recipe 16 work in both panes of the split-view window. Menu items such as those in the Format menu are typically connected to the First Responder icon in a nib file. As a result, whatever object is currently key in the user interface, in any window or view, becomes the target of the menu item's action method. It doesn't matter that the window or view that is key might have come from some other nib file. The Cocoa first-responder system for menu commands has application-wide reach.

One promised feature doesn't yet work, however. Typing in one of the text views— in either pane of the split-view window or in the drawer's Notes view—is not echoed in the other text views. You will attend to this issue next.

Step 5: Coordinate the Three Text Views with One Text Storage

The final step is to ensure that the Notes view in the drawer and the two panes in the split-view window always display text from the same NSTextStorage model object.

When the user first enters text in any one of these text views, it should instantly appear in all of them. Similarly, when the user applies formatting to the text in one of them, the formatting should instantly apply in all of them. In general, any editing in one of them should be reflected in all of them without delay. Depending on the scrolling position in the drawer's Notes view and the panes of the split-view window, of course, the same text might not always be visible in all three. The user's notes may be long enough to overflow the visible regions of the text views. But when the user scrolls the same portion of the user's notes back into view, any changes made in one of them should appear in all of them.

It will prove remarkably easy to accomplish this, now that you have laid the groundwork by ensuring that the application has ready access to the text in the Notes view's associated NSTextStorage object. Before proceeding, however, you have to understand how the main components of the Cocoa text system work together.

There are four principal components in the text system, along with many minor components to deal with details such as rulers and paragraph formatting. These are the four main components:

- NSTextStorage is a subclass of NSMutableAttributedString, so it is mostly just the text and associated formatting. As such, it is considered the MVC model of the text system. It contains a list of its layout managers and other information in addition to the mutable attributed string.

- NSLayoutManager controls the layout of glyphs in the text container, described next. As such, it is considered an MVC controller object. It controls word wrap within the text container and many similar behaviors.

- NSTextContainer provides the onscreen space in which the text will be laid out. It is rectangular, but you can subclass it to provide different shapes. It is also considered an MVC controller object.

- NSTextView is the MVC view object in which the user types and reads the text, makes selections, and performs editing operations.

When writing a Cocoa program, you normally come at it from one or the other end of this list. If you're using Interface Builder, you drag a text view from the Data palette into a window and normally don't have to think about the other components. Interface Builder puts together the network underlying the text view for you, and it all just works. You usually keep a reference to the text view and use it in your code as needed.

If you're using Project Builder to construct a text view programmatically, you usually start by instantiating and initializing a text-storage object, followed by its layout manager, followed by its text container, followed finally by its text view, linking all of these together. You often keep a reference to the text-storage object and use it to get at everything else. In fact, the other components are usually released immediately after you instantiate them and add them to the text-storage object, which thereafter owns them.

You would usually use the latter approach if you need to construct anything more complicated than the simple stand-alone text view you can create in Interface Builder. For example, you can programmatically create combinations of the main text system components that allow a single text storage to flow automatically across page breaks or column boundaries or to appear in multiple panes of a split-view window. One text storage can have multiple text layout managers and one layout manager can have multiple text containers, for example, each resulting in a different combination of features and interrelationships.

All of this is explained, with examples and very useful diagrams, in the Cocoa *Programming Topics* regarding the Cocoa text system. It is essential that you read this documentation before getting very deeply into the subject. In addition, you will find it valuable to study the TextSizingExample project in the AppKit subfolder of the Developer Examples folder on your disk.

Once you understand the organization and mechanics of the text system, you will be able to use it in other ways not covered by the documentation. In this step, for example, you will use both Interface Builder and Project Builder in combination to link the drawer's Notes view and the split-view window's two panes to a single text storage. The result will be what you specified at the beginning of this recipe. Text typed, edited, or formatted in any one of the three text views will appear simultaneously in all of them. The code to accomplish this is short and simple.

1. You have already created a text view and its related text system components in the main document window's drawer, using Interface Builder in Recipe 16. As you learned in Recipe 17, Step 1, the model component of that network is the NSTextStorage object, which the two panes of the split-view window share. Therefore, you must devise a way to make the split-view window aware of the Notes view's NSTextStorage object.

   The standard way to accomplish this is to get a reference to the NSTextStorage object, then pass the reference to the text window's controller when the controller is initialized. You already know how the VRTextWindowController is initialized: In Step 4 you wrote the `openInWindowAction:` action method in the VRDrawer Controller.m category source file, which allocated and initialized the VRText WindowController object. You also called the VRTextWindowController's `init` method. You need to revise that call now so it invokes a new designated initializer, `initWithTextStorage:`, which you will write in a moment.

   In the `openInWindowAction:` action method, revise the first statement in the `if` block to read as follows:

   ```
   [self setTextWindowController:[[VRTextWindowController alloc]
       initWithTextStorage:[[self notesView] textStorage]]];
   ```

2. Revise the existing `init` method and add a new designated initializer to the VRTextWindowController.m source file, as follows:

   ```
   - (id)init {
       return [self initWithTextStorage:nil];
   }


   - (id)initWithTextStorage:(NSTextStorage *)textStorage {
       // Designated initializer
       if (self = [super initWithWindowNibName:@"VRTextWindow"]) {
           notesTextStorage = textStorage;
       }
       return self;
   }
   ```

Also declare the new designated initializer in the VRTextWindowController.h header file, as follows:

```
#pragma mark INITIALIZATION

- (id)initWithTextStorage:(NSTextStorage *)textStorage;
```

3. Still in the VRTextWindowController.h header file, declare the instance variable to which the designated initializer you just wrote assigns the NSTextStorage object passed in from the main document window's controller. This goes within the curly braces in the header file's @interface directive, as follows:

```
NSTextStorage *notesTextStorage;
```

This class is so small and simple that you won't bother with accessor methods.

4. Believe it or not, you are almost done.

Add an awakeFromNib override method to the VRTextWindowController.m source file, at the beginning of the WINDOW MANAGEMENT section, as follows:

```
- (void)awakeFromNib {
    [[topNotesView layoutManager]
            replaceTextStorage:notesTextStorage];
    [[bottomNotesView layoutManager]
            replaceTextStorage:notesTextStorage];
    [[self window] center];
}
```

The classes that make up the Cocoa text system have built-in methods that assist you in piecing together the jigsaw puzzle in just about every way you could ever need. You learned from reading the Cocoa *Programming Topics*, for example, that NSTextStorage includes an addLayoutManager: method to install a layout manager in a text storage when building a network up from the bottom. Similarly, NSLayoutManager contains an addTextContainer: method, and NSTextContainer contains a setTextView: method to build the network still higher.

There are also methods to insert additional components at specified positions in the relevant arrays when it is necessary to add multiple components in a particular order.

In your code here, you proceeded in still another direction. You already had two complete text networks in hand, which you created in Interface Builder when you dragged what became the topNotesView and bottomNotesView text views from the palette into the split-view window. What you want to do here is not to build a new network but to substitute the drawer's NSTextStorage object for the two NSTextStorage objects that Interface Builder placed at the bottom of the topNotesView and bottomNotesView networks.

NSLayoutManager provides just the method you need to do this, `replaceText-Storage:`. As its documentation in the NSLayoutManager class reference document explains, it takes care of reconnecting the entire existing network so that, for example, the existing `topNotesView` text view now refers to its new text storage and all the other components of the network refer properly to one another. Similarly, NSTextContainer includes a `replaceLayoutManager:` method, should you wish to make a different substitution at that level.

You also arrange for the new split-view window to be centered onscreen, as you did with the main document window in Recipe 1, Step 4.3.

The end result is that the split-view window has two text views, each in its own pane, which share a single text storage with each other and with the drawer's Notes text view. You're done!

Step 6: Build and Run the Application

Build and run the application and test the operation of the new split-view window and its twin text views.

When you open the drawer by clicking the Notes button, you see the Notes view you created in Recipe 16. You have already enjoyed the experience of typing into it. Now perform the tests outlined at the end of Recipe 16 again to ensure that the redesign of the Notes view did not alter its operation. Type, cut, paste, undo, redo, save, close, open, type some more, revert, apply formatting, and so on. You will find that everything works as expected.

Then click the Open in Window button to see whether it works. Sure enough, the new split-view window opens, with its divider at the top and only the bottom pane showing. Click in the main document window to bring it to the front, then click the Open in Window button to verify that the split-view window comes to the front again. Close the split-view window and see that it closes but leaves the main document window in place. Open the split-view window again, and this time close the main document window, verifying that both windows close along with the document itself.

Reopen the split-view window in a new document and drag the divider down to make both views visible. Now for the fun part: Type in either pane and watch your prose appear simultaneously in both panes and the Notes view. Try typing in the other pane, then in the Notes view, to verify that they are all linked. Finally, apply every text-editing and formatting technique you know in any and all of the three text views to verify that all three views remain synchronized at all times.

RECIPE 18

Alert and Dialog Panels

Recipe 18 will show you how to present alert and dialog panels. In Recipe 5, you learned how to present document modal alert sheets attached to windows. Here, you are concerned with alerts and dialogs as freestanding panels.

Your work in this recipe will set the stage for Recipe 19, where you will learn how to implement an application preferences system based on Cocoa's

HIGHLIGHTS:

Creating a modal alert panel that does not block background application processing

Using a timer to dismiss an alert panel after a specified interval has elapsed

Creating a modeless dialog panel for use as a Preferences window

Wrapping a C structure in an Objective-C object

NSUserDefaults class. I'll explain here just enough of Cocoa's preferences system to allow you to set up the alert and the dialog that form the subject matter of Recipe 18. Then, in Recipe 19, you will add the underlying preferences system code.

Alerts and dialogs share many features. Alerts provide information to the user, especially about error conditions and potentially dangerous situations. Dialogs elicit information from the user. Application alerts and dialogs come in three basic flavors: modeless, document modal, and application modal.

- Modeless alerts and dialogs do not prevent the user from carrying out other operations in the same document, in other parts of the same application, or in any other application. They may go behind other windows if the user clicks in any document or other window to work in it while the modeless panel is in the background. A find-and-replace dialog is a typical example.

- Document modal alerts and dialogs block the user from performing other operations on the document with which the alert or dialog is associated, but the user can still perform operations on other documents in the same application and in other applications. In Mac OS X, document modal alerts and dialogs should always be sheets attached to the affected document window; they should never be freestanding windows.

- Application modal alerts and dialogs block the user's operations anywhere else in the application, but the user can still work in other applications. These are appropriate for alerts and dialogs that relate to more than one document, such as the alert the system presents when you attempt to quit an application with two or more unsaved documents open. As you will learn in this recipe, though an alert is application modal from the user's point of view, it does not freeze the application's ongoing internal processing.

An alert is typically small and contains little information, so the user can understand the message at a glance. In Mac OS X, as you learned earlier, it should contain a short and punchy message text of only a few words fitting on one or two lines and slightly longer informative text in a smaller font explaining how the situation developed and what the user can do about it. An alert generally has no title in its title bar. User feedback is typically obtained from only one, two, or three buttons. Although you can easily impose a badge over the application's icon at the left side of an alert to identify critically important situations, you should reserve this facility for a very few truly dangerous circumstances to avoid diluting the badge's impact. An impending loss of data is the usual criterion.

A dialog is often more expansive. It generally gives the user one window in which to provide many individual but related pieces of information that the application needs. It should show default values so a user can simply verify information in the typical situation, rather than having to generate new information for even the most common cases. Unlike a document window, if a dialog has text fields or text views for typing, the first text field or text view should display a selection or an active insertion point as soon as the dialog opens so the user can immediately start typing. The standard print dialog is an example; here the user can type a number of copies to print without first clicking in that text field. A freestanding dialog often has a title identical to the menu item the user chose when opening it.

A dialog is usually, but not always, an NSPanel rather than an NSWindow object. As a panel, it does not display the three round buttons at the left end of the title bar to close, minimize, or zoom a window. Instead, it provides push buttons to reject or accept the user's changes and dismiss the dialog and, in some cases, a third button to apply changes. If it provides a Close button, the user can press Escape to close the dialog. It normally cannot be zoomed or minimized, and it generally doesn't appear in the application's Window menu. Except for text fields, changes the user makes to settings in a dialog should appear to take effect immediately, unless you have provided an Apply button making it obvious that they won't take effect until the user clicks that button. As a panel, it can become *key*—that is, it can accept the user's typing and mouse clicks—but it does not become the *main* window—that is, it can't be printed. When some other application comes to the front, it can hide to minimize screen clutter.

New in the June 2002 *Aqua Human Interface Guidelines* is the requirement that dialogs, like all windows, should appear when they are opened for the first time centered horizontally on the user's main screen. They should also be centered vertically in what the *Guidelines* call the "visual" sense, that is, with space above the dialog about half the height of space below the dialog. These requirements are consistent with the long-standing Mac OS X preference for dialogs with center-oriented user controls.

There are still other kinds of windows in Cocoa, but you will not deal with them in *Vermont Recipes.* For example, Cocoa supports utility windows—freestanding windows that float above the main document window in an application but are hidden when a main document window is not open or is behind some ancillary window. These are often used for floating tool palettes. In Mac OS X 10.2, Cocoa even provides new facilities to make such windows float above other applications' windows on a systemwide basis.

Figures 18.1 and **18.2** show the completed alert and dialog panels you will create in this recipe.

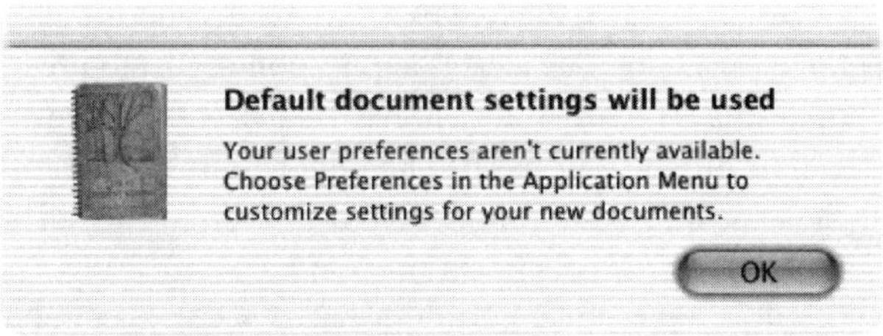

FIGURE 18.1
The alert panel.

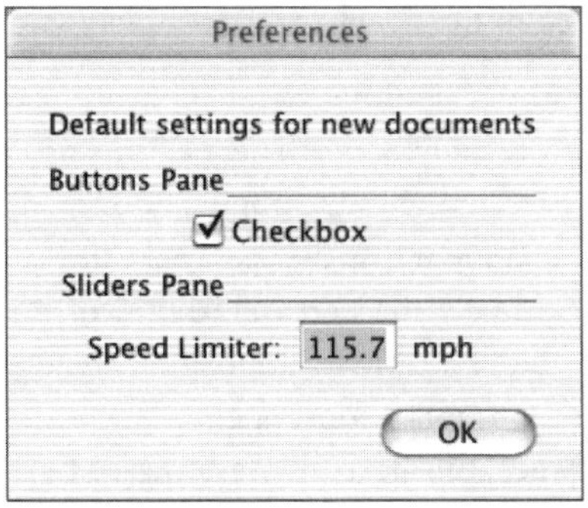

FIGURE 18.2 The
Preferences dialog.

Before proceeding, update the target's Info.Plist Entries by incrementing its build version to **18**. The application preferences you will begin to design in this recipe will be saved to disk, but they will be saved in a special system document, not the main application document. You therefore do not have to increment the `VRDocumentVersion` variable in VRDocument.m for Recipe 18, because the document format is not changing.

Step 1: Create a Freestanding Modal Alert Panel That Doesn't Block Application Processing

In Step 1, you will create a modal alert panel to warn the user if the application's preferences can't be found when the user opens a new document for the first time. Unless you use an installer to provide a prewritten preferences file, the application will present this alert the first time any user runs the application, since it automatically opens a new document at that time. The application will also present the alert if a user opens a new document after the preferences file has been removed. The alert's message and informative text will be crafted so as to be useful on both occasions, informing the user that a Preferences command is available in the Application menu.

Since the new document won't yet be open when the alert appears, you can't use an alert sheet. This is an application issue, not an issue tied to a particular window, so the use of a freestanding panel is appropriate. The alert is application modal to prevent the user from using the application's menus and to prevent the new document window from appearing onscreen before the user has had an opportunity to read and dismiss the alert. Nevertheless, the information presented by the alert is not all that important, so it will dismiss itself after 30 seconds if the user has not already dismissed it. While it is open, the alert will not block behind-the-scenes application processing, such as responding to an AppleScript command to obtain data (which normally does not require that a document be open in the GUI).

The Vermont Recipes application's preferences do not deal with general application settings but instead relate only to a new document's default values. There is thus no reason to present the alert immediately when the user launches the application by double-clicking an existing document. An existing document displays its saved values, not the default values applied to a new document. Normally, the alert will be presented immediately when the application is launched for the first time by double-clicking the application icon, since Vermont Recipes, like most applications, opens a new, untitled window at that time. After its first appearance, the alert will never again be presented unless the preferences file is removed.

This is not a very common application feature because it smacks too much of baby-sitting. Even moderately experienced computer users don't need a reminder that they can set an application's preferences. There is no reason to fear that users will tire of the alert, however, because they will normally only see it the first time they open a new document. It does have the advantage of alerting a user if somebody has removed the preferences file since the last time the application was run. It also serves to inform a novice user at the outset that the Preferences dialog is available to set different defaults for new documents. It might be an appropriate feature in applications for inexperienced computer users or in applications used in public environments or computer labs where jokers up to no good might delete preferences files. Mainly, however, it presents an opportunity to show you how to write an application modal alert panel while introducing you to the topic of application preferences.

To present an alert, you normally use one of several function calls built into Cocoa as conveniences. You learned about a function that presents a document modal alert sheet, `NSBeginAlertSheet()`, in Recipe 5. You can use a similar convenience function, `NSRunAlertPanel()`, to present an application modal alert panel. Both are declared in the NSPanel.h header file and documented in the "Functions" section of the *Application Kit Objective-C API Reference*. Each alert sheet and panel function comes in three forms, the base function to present what is called a simple *attention* alert, a function to present a *critical* alert, and a function to present an *informational* alert. The latter two superimpose distinctive badges on the application's icon in the alert and should be only rarely used.

You can't use the simple `NSRunAlertPanel()` function in Recipe 18, however. Instead, you will use the `NSGetAlertPanel()` function. This function is found in the same NSPanel.h header file and is documented in the same place as the other functions. It takes the same parameters to set up the alert's message text and buttons, but it returns the panel to you without presenting it to the user. Presenting it is your job, and you must take care to clean up after it is dismissed. Using the `NSGetAlertPanel()` function requires more work than the simple functions, but it has the advantage of allowing you to customize an alert panel's behavior. You need this flexibility to add the special features described previously.

Since you don't want to present the alert to a user who has already set custom preferences, you need a way to determine whether the user has in fact done so. Instead of looking for a preferences file by name in the current user's home folder on disk, you will instead ask NSUserDefaults to look for a special preferences item that you will put in the preferences file. This technique will leave all user preferences file handling to Cocoa, where it belongs, allowing you to concentrate on items in the preferences file. You will name this special item `UserPreferencesValidated`. If there is no preferences file for this user, or if there is one but it doesn't contain this special item, the application will present the alert panel described above and then immediately add the `UserPreferencesValidated` item to the preferences file (creating the file if necessary) to prevent the alert from being presented subsequently.

It's time to start coding the application modal alert panel.

1. Start by adding a few lines of code to the VRMainWindowController.m source file's `awakeFromNib` method to determine whether the special `UserPreferencesValidated`

preference item exists. Performing this check in `awakeFromNib` is sensible because you want to present the alert just as a document is created, before its window appears onscreen. Your code will first test whether this document is being opened from disk or is a new document. If it's the latter, the code will look for the special preferences item. If it is not found, the code will open the alert panel.

Add these statements near the end of the `awakeFromNib` method, just before its `NSAssert` calls:

```
if (![[self document] fileName]) {
    NSUserDefaults *defaults =
        [NSUserDefaults standardUserDefaults];
    if (![defaults objectForKey:@"UserPreferencesValidated"]) {
        [defaults setBool:YES
            forKey:@"UserPreferencesValidated"];
        [self openPrefsAlertPanel];
    }
}
```

You learned some time ago that a common way to test whether a document is being opened from disk is to see whether it has a filename. If not, it is a new document. The first line in this code block makes this test and proceeds only if it is a new document.

The second line is the standard way to get a reference to the application's user preferences. The `standardUserDefaults` method is a class method in NSUserDefaults that always returns an NSDictionary object Cocoa has already cached in memory so it will be available shortly after an application is launched. Cocoa takes care of populating this object with values obtained from the user's application preferences file on disk, if it exists, and from any defaults that might have been set in the application's model class that aren't superseded by a setting in the preferences file, or some combination of the two. All you have to do is access the `standardUserDefaults` dictionary and extract settings from it using ordinary NSDictionary methods based on keys.

Here, you ask the `defaults` dictionary for an object having `UserPreferences Validated` as its key. If the returned object is `nil`, it doesn't exist and you know this is the first time this user has tried to create a new document in the application—or at least the first time since somebody deleted the preferences file. You therefore promptly add a Boolean object to the `defaults` dictionary with this key to make sure this test will yield a different outcome the next time this user creates a new document. You then tell the window controller to open the alert panel, using a method you will write next.

Notice that you did not write any code telling the application to save the revised preferences to disk. You don't have to. Cocoa calls the **synchronize** method built in to NSUserDefaults periodically to keep the **standardUserDefaults** cache in memory and the preferences file on disk synchronized, creating the preferences file if necessary. Normally, you needn't lift a finger.

2. Turn next to the openPrefsAlertPanel method that will actually open the application modal alert panel. The version of the method shown here has been stripped of the routines that cause the alert panel to dismiss itself after 30 seconds, because there's a lot to learn even without that complicated NSTimer code. Here is the code you should enter in the VRMainWindowController.m source file, immediately after the awakeFromNib method, for the time being:

```
- (void)openPrefsAlertPanel {
    NSPanel *prefsAlertPanel =
            NSGetAlertPanel(NSLocalizedString
            (@"Default document settings will be used",
            @"Message text for new document alert if preferences \
            for new document settings not found"),
            NSLocalizedString(@"Your user preferences aren't \
            currently available. Choose Preferences in the \
            Application Menu to customize settings for your new \
            documents.",
            @"Informative text for new document alert if \
            preferences for new document settings not found"),
            @"OK", nil, nil);
    NSModalSession prefsAlertModalSession =
            [NSApp beginModalSessionForWindow:prefsAlertPanel];

    int modalResult;
    do {
        modalResult =
                [NSApp runModalSession:prefsAlertModalSession];
        if (modalResult == NSOKButton) {
            [NSApp abortModal];
            [NSApp endModalSession:prefsAlertModalSession];
            NSReleaseAlertPanel(prefsAlertPanel);
        }
    } while (modalResult == NSRunContinuesResponse);
}
```

This method almost exactly duplicates what Cocoa's NSRunAlertPanel() function would do if you had called it in the awakeFromNib method. By doing it yourself, you gain the ability to add some timer routines to make the alert dismiss itself automatically after 30 seconds, which you will do shortly.

There is one important difference, however. NSRunAlertPanel() calls NSApplication's runModalSessionForWindow: method, which blocks application processing while the alert is pending. Here, you call NSApplication's runModalSession: method, which, according to the documentation, does not block application processing. It does, however, prevent the user from working with the application's user interface until it is dismissed, as a modal alert should.

The openPrefsAlertPanel works like this. First, it creates the alert panel using the NSGetAlertPanel() function declared in NSPanel.h. It returns the panel to your code, but it doesn't run it. The parameters to the function are about the same as the parameters to the NSBeginAlertSheet() function you encountered in Recipe 5. One difference is that there you could pass nil in the first of the three button parameters and Cocoa would supply a localized OK button for you. Here, passing nil in all three parameters yields an alert panel with no buttons. This might be appropriate in an informational alert dismissed by some code in your application, but here you want an OK button the user can click to dismiss the alert immediately.

The message and informative text in the alert must be localized, so make sure to add the appropriate entries to the Localizable.strings file.

When you are through with an alert panel created by the NSGetAlertPanel() function, you must release it explicitly by calling the NSReleaseAlertPanel() function. You do this in the do loop after the user clicks the OK button.

Next, this method actually presents the alert panel by calling NSApplication's beginModalSessionForWindow: method. This method sets up the modal event loop, and it presents the alert onscreen. You must match it with an endModalSession: method. You call endModalSession: in the do loop after the user clicks the OK button.

When you use NSApplication's runModalSession: method, as you do here, you must call it repeatedly in a loop that executes frequently enough to maintain the responsiveness of the alert panel. The runModalSession: method acts on any events in its run loop—there may be none—then immediately returns a constant, indicating whether it should run again (NSRunContinuesResponse), whether it was aborted (NSRunAbortedResponse), or whether it was stopped (NSRunStoppedResponse) or a numerical code such as the NSOkButton code returned when the user clicks the OK button in the alert. Here, if the response is NSRunContinuesResponse, you continue to the next iteration of the do loop. If the response is NSOKButton, you execute the code that dismisses the alert, including a call to NSApplication's **abortModal** method. Execution then exits the **do** loop because the **modalResult** is now **NSRunAbortedResponse**, not **NSRunContinuesResponse**, and the application resumes responding to user interaction.

3. Now turn to the NSTimer routines that will cause the alert to dismiss itself after 30 seconds.

First, insert these statements in the **openPrefsAlertPanel** method just before the declaration of the **modalResult** local variable and the **do** loop:

```
NSDictionary *timerInfo =
      [NSDictionary dictionaryWithObjectsAndKeys:
      [NSData dataWithBytes:&prefsAlertModalSession
      length:sizeof(prefsAlertModalSession)],
      @"ModalSessionKey", prefsAlertPanel, @"AlertPanelKey",
      nil];
NSTimer *prefsAlertTimer = [NSTimer
      timerWithTimeInterval:30
      target:self
      selector:@selector(closePrefsAlertPanel:)
      userInfo:timerInfo
      repeats:NO];
[[NSRunLoop currentRunLoop] addTimer:prefsAlertTimer
      forMode:@"NSModalPanelRunLoopMode"];
```

You start by creating a dictionary containing two objects that will be required by the separate method, **closePrefsAlertPanel:**, that the timer will trigger when it fires. You will write the **closePrefsAlertPanel:** method shortly, but you already know that it will need references to the alert panel and the modal session identifier. You just learned in the previous instruction that you have to end the modal session and release the alert panel when the alert is dismissed. You provided code to do this after the user clicks OK, but that code won't execute when the timer dismisses the alert. Because the timer will clean up after the dismissal of the alert in a separate method, you could declare global variables to carry the alert panel and the modal session identifier to the **closePrefsAlertPanel:** method. However, it is much cleaner and more object-oriented to put these objects into the timer's **userInfo** dictionary and let the separate method extract it from the timer's **userInfo** dictionary.

A dictionary can only hold objects, so you must convert any standard C data types into objects before inserting them into the timer's **userInfo** dictionary. The modal session is a C structure, not an object. You have previously used many Cocoa methods designed to ease the task of converting C data types to objects, such as **setFloatValue:** and other NSNumber methods. However, you haven't previously done it with a C structure. Here, you simply call an NSData method, **dataWithBytes:length:**, to stuff the bytes of the C structure into an NSData object. You get the bytes and their length from the **prefsAlertModalSession** local variable you already set up, and the method returns them as an NSData object you can insert into the dictionary. The **prefsAlertPanel** is already an object, and you make up two keys, @**"ModalSessionKey"** and @**"AlertPanelKey"**, as NSString objects. Don't forget the required **nil** ending, or you'll get a bunch of compiler warnings that won't make any sense to you.

Now that the timer's **userInfo** dictionary is ready, you create the timer using NSTimer's **timerWithTimeInterval:target:selector:userInfo:repeats:** class method. The interval is 30 seconds. The selector to call when the timer fires is the **closePrefsAlertPanel:** method you haven't yet written, and the target in which you will implement it is **self**. You pass **NO** in the **repeats:** parameter, because you want this timer to fire only the one time required to dismiss the alert. Because nonrepeating timers invalidate themselves automatically, you won't have to call NSTimer's **invalidate** method. (You will explicitly call the **invalidate** method in the next instruction, in a portion of the code that executes after the OK button is clicked. In that situation, the timer never fires and therefore cannot automatically invalidate itself.)

Finally, you tell the current run loop to add the timer for its **NSModalPanelRun LoopMode** mode. More often, when you use timers you will call the **scheduled-TimerWithTimeInterval:target:selector:userInfo:repeats:** class method. That method is a little easier to use because it adds the timer to the run loop itself. However, it uses the run loop's default mode, which won't work in a modal session. For a modal session, you have to call the **timerWithTimeInterval:-target:selector:userInfo:repeats:** class method to get the timer, then add it explicitly yourself for the correct run loop mode. If you want to know more about run loops and modes, read the documentation—you don't need to know more for *Vermont Recipes*.

4.   At the beginning of the **do** loop, insert this line:

```
[prefsAlertTimer invalidate];
```

As just mentioned, this is required to disassociate the timer from the run loop to make sure it never fires again. You must call this method yourself to clean up after repeating timers and timers that haven't fired but are no longer needed.

5.   You are now ready to write the **closePrefsAlertPanel:** method. Insert it after the **openPrefsAlertPanel** method, as follows:

```
- (void)closePrefsAlertPanel:(NSTimer *)timer {
    [NSApp abortModal];
```

```
    NSModalSession prefsAlertModalSession;
    [[[timer userInfo] objectForKey:@"ModalSessionKey"]
        getBytes:&prefsAlertModalSession];
    [NSApp endModalSession:prefsAlertModalSession];
    NSReleaseAlertPanel([[timer userInfo]
        objectForKey:@"AlertPanelKey"]);

}
```

This is identical to the code in the `if` block within the `do` loop in the openPrefsAlertPanel method called after the user clicked OK, except that here two of the needed data structures have to be extracted from the timer's userInfo dictionary before they can be used. The timer is available in this method's sole parameter, because the selector called when a timer fires always has the timer as its sole parameter.

To extract the modal session C structure, you first declare the local variable prefsAlertModalSession. Then you extract the NSData object from the timer's userInfo dictionary using the ModalSessionKey key, and you call NSData's getBytes: method to stuff the bytes into the local variable.

The alert panel object is extracted from the timer's userInfo dictionary using the AlertPanelKey key and released.

6. You aren't quite done. You must declare the openPrefsAlertPanel and closePrefsAlertPanel: methods in the VRMainWindowController.h header file as follows:

    ```
    - (void)openPrefsAlertPanel;
    - (void)closePrefsAlertPanel:(NSTimer *)timer;
    ```

7. You can compile and run the application now, if you like. The alert panel did not involve any Interface Builder outlets or action methods, so you have no connections to make.

    To test the alert panel, you must open your Preferences folder at ~/Library/Preferences and delete any existing com.stepwise.VermontRecipes.plist file you find there, then run the application. Before a new document window opens, the alert panel will appear. If you look at the application's menus in the menu bar, you will see that most of the menu items are disabled. This is an application modal alert, so it blocks user interaction with the application. If you click the alert's OK button, the panel immediately goes away and the new document window belatedly opens.

    If you quit the application and relaunch it, the alert will not appear, because now there is a preferences file in your Preferences folder and it contains the special

`UserPreferencesValidated` item. You can see this special item by examining the preferences file in TextEdit or Property List Editor.

Quit the application and delete the preferences file again. If you launch the application by double-clicking a saved document, the alert will not appear. If you launch it by double-clicking the application icon, the alert will appear again because the preferences file is missing.

This time, don't click the OK button. Instead, watch the clock. When 30 seconds have passed, the alert will dismiss itself, untouched by human hands.

Step 2: Create a Freestanding Dialog Panel for Entry of User Preference Settings

That may have been the most complex alert panel you will ever write in Cocoa. To make up for all the work you did, I'll keep the Preferences window very simple. About ten data values in the application have non-0 default values for new documents, but you will provide only the ability to set custom defaults for two of them, just to see how it's done.

The Preferences window will be a modeless panel. You learned at the beginning of this recipe that alerts and dialogs can be modeless, document modal, or application modal. You create document-modal panels as sheets and application-modal panels as modal panels. In both cases you normally use certain Cocoa functions to create them. You create and use modeless panels, on the other hand, just as you'd create and use any other window.

You will set up and display the Preferences panel in this recipe and hook it up to the Cocoa preferences system. However, you won't write the code needed to make the application honor user preferences until Recipe 19.

1. Turn to Interface Builder to create the Preferences panel. Start by creating a new nib file for the panel. Choose File > New to open the Starting Point dialog, if necessary. Then select the Cocoa Empty template and click New. Choose File > Save As and save it in the project's English.lproj folder as **VRPreferences**. Don't forget to uncheck the "Hide extension" checkbox before clicking Save.

2. Drag a Panel item from the Windows palette and drop it in the VRPreferences.nib window.

3. In the panel, add some static text items, two horizontal lines, a checkbox and a text field, and an OK button, so the panel looks like Figure 18.2 at the beginning of this recipe. It may be easiest to create the checkbox and the text field group by copying them from VRDocument.nib and pasting them into VRPreferences.nib, then repositioning them as necessary. Be sure to ungroup them before copying them; otherwise, you will copy too many other objects. You can regroup them after pasting them.

4. Turn to Project Builder to create a new window controller subclass for the Preferences panel. Choose File > New File; select the Cocoa Objective-C NSWindowController subclass; click Next; name it VRPreferencesWindowController with both header and source files; and click Finish. Add your customary comments and disclaimers to both files, and make sure the header file imports Cocoa.

5. The whole of the VRPreferencesWindowController.h header file should look like this:

```
#import <Cocoa/Cocoa.h>

@interface VRPreferencesWindowController : NSWindowController {
    @private
    IBOutlet NSButton *checkbox;
    IBOutlet NSTextField *speedTextField;
}

#pragma mark ACCESSORS

- (NSButton *)checkbox;
- (NSTextField *)speedTextField;

#pragma mark ACTIONS

- (IBAction)checkboxAction:(id)sender;
- (IBAction)speedTextFieldAction:(id)sender;
- (IBAction)closeButtonAction:(id)sender;

@end
```

There are two outlets, one for each user control in the Preferences panel, and an accessor method and an action method for each, plus an action method for the close button (which you will label OK).

6. The VRPreferencesWindowController.m source file is almost as simple. First, write its init method:

```
#pragma mark INITIALIZATION

- (id) init {
    self = [super initWithWindowNibName:@"VRPreferences"];
    return self;
}
```

This will load the nib file once the preferences window controller is instantiated.

7. Next, define its accessor methods and action methods, as follows:

```
#pragma mark ACCESSORS

- (NSButton *)checkbox {
    return checkbox;
}

- (NSTextField *)speedTextField {
    return speedTextField;
}

#pragma mark ACTIONS

- (IBAction)checkboxAction:(id)sender {
    [[NSUserDefaults standardUserDefaults]
        setBool:[[self checkbox] state]
        forKey:@"CheckboxValue"];
}

- (IBAction)speedTextFieldAction:(id)sender {
    [[NSUserDefaults standardUserDefaults]
        setFloat:[[self speedTextField] floatValue]
        forKey:@"SpeedValue"];
}

- (IBAction)closeButtonAction:(id)sender {
    [[sef window] makeFirstResponder:[self window]];
    [[self window] close];
}
```

The first two action methods get the now familiar `standardUserDefaults` dictionary, which Cocoa keeps cached in memory and synchronized with the user's preferences file on disk. Then they create new entries having the keys

`CheckboxValue` and `SpeedValue`, if those entries don't already exist, and populate them from the values entered by the user in the two user controls.

The value of the checkbox control is obtained by reading its state, and the value of the text field is obtained by reading its contents as a floating-point number. All this is familiar from Recipe 1 and Section 2.

The `closeButtonAction:` method forces a pending edit in the text field to commit, since a user will expect clicking OK to have this effect even if the Enter key wasn't pressed to end editing. There is no Cancel or Apply button because this dialog follows the *Aqua Human Interface Guidelines* recommendation that changes in dialog settings take effect immediately. Unless you write additional code to restore default values or return to the previous settings, the only way the user can undo changes is to reset them manually. In Interface Builder, be sure to set the key equivalent for the OK button to <no key>; otherwise, when the user presses Enter to end editing in the text field, the window will close, too. The OK button will not have the appearance of a default button when it has no key equivalent.

You don't need to save the preferences, because Cocoa takes care of synchronization with the preferences file for you.

8. Finally, write its `awakeFromNib` method, as follows:

```
#pragma mark WINDOW MANAGEMENT

- (void)awakeFromNib {
    [[self checkbox] setState:
        [[NSUserDefaults standardUserDefaults]
        boolForKey:@"CheckboxValue"]];
    [[self speedTextField] setFloatValue:
        [[NSUserDefaults standardUserDefaults]
        floatForKey:@"SpeedValue"]];
    [[self window] center];
}
```

This does the reverse of the action methods. Just before the Preferences panel appears onscreen, the checkbox and the text field are set to their values as read from the `standardUserDefaults` dictionary. The last line ensures that the Preferences panel is always centered on the main screen, in accordance with the *Aqua Human Interface Guidelines*.

9. What remains to be done in Project Builder is to instantiate the window controller so that it will, through its `init` method, load the nib file.

In Recipe 1, you created the main window controller in the NSDocument subclass. In Recipe 17, you created the text window controller in the `openInWindowAction:` action method in the VRDrawerController category, associated with the drawer's Open in Window button. Where will you create the Preferences panel's window controller?

You should start your search for an answer to this question by asking yourself what the user will do to open the Preferences panel. The answer is to choose the Preferences menu item from the Application menu in the menu bar. The only place in Interface Builder where you can get at the Preferences menu item, to connect an action method to it, is in the main application nib file, MainMenu.nib. You should therefore write an action method to instantiate the preferences window controller in some object that the MainMenu.nib file knows about.

You have already written VRAppDelegate in connection with your work on the application's Dock menu. There's no reason why you can't put the needed action method in that file, even though the action method has nothing to do with the file's role as the application's delegate. If the name bothers you, you could change it from VRAppDelegate to something more descriptive, such as VRAppController, although this would require you to read the file into Interface Builder again and perhaps rename some items in the code files.

Near the top of the VRAppDelegate.h header file, import the preferences window controller as follows:

```
#import "VRPreferencesWindowController.h"
```

Declare an instance variable referring to it in the `@interface` directive, as follows:

```
NSWindowController *preferencesWindowController;
```

Declare the action method in the body of the header file, as follows:

```
#pragma mark ACTIONS

- (IBAction)openPreferencesWindowAction:(id)sender;
```

Finally, define the action method in the VRAppDelegate.m source file, as follows:

```
- (IBAction)openPreferencesWindowAction:(id)sender {
    if (!preferencesWindowController) {
        preferencesWindowController =
            [[VRPreferencesWindowController alloc] init];
    }
    [preferencesWindowController showWindow:sender];
}
```

Once you've connected this action method to the Preferences menu item in MainMenu.nib, it will be triggered when the user chooses the menu item. It first checks whether the preferences window controller already exists, because you only want one Preferences window open at a time. If none exists, it allocates and initializes a window controller, which causes the nib file to load. Whether a window controller already exists or a new one is created, the action method then calls the `showWindow:` method it inherits from NSWindowController to make the Preferences panel key and bring it to the front. In this way, you can use the Preferences menu item both to open the Preferences panel and to bring the Preferences panel to the front if it is already open but hidden behind another window.

10. Turn to Interface Builder to make the required connections and set some attributes.

   Open MainMenu.nib. With its Classes tab selected, choose Classes > Read Files and read in the VRAppDelegate.h header file to capture the new action method. Then Control-drag from the Preferences menu item in the MainMenu.nib – MainMenu window to the VRAppDelegate icon in the MainMenu.nib main window, select the `target` outlet in the Connections pane of the NSMenuItem Info Panel, select the `openPreferencesWindowAction:` action, and click Connect. Save MainMenu.nib and close it.

   Open VRPreferences.nib. With its Classes tab selected, choose Classes > Read Files and read in the VRPreferencesWindowController.h header file to capture the new action methods.

   Control-drag from the File's Owner icon to the Panel icon in the VRPreferences.nib main window, select the `window` outlet, and click Connect. Without this, the `showWindow:` call in the action method won't know what window to open and nothing will happen when the user chooses Preferences from the Application menu.

   Control-drag from each of the three user controls in the Preferences panel to the File's Owner icon and connect their respective action methods.

   Set up the key view loop. The text field should be the Preferences window's initial first responder, so that its contents will be selected when the panel opens, ready for the user to type. Control-drag from the Panel icon to the text field, select the `initialFirstResponder` outlet in the NSPanel Info Panel, and click Connect. Finally, connect the `nextKeyView` outlets of the checkbox and the text field to each other.

   Select the OK button. In the NSButton Info Panel's Attributes pane, select Return in the Equiv pop-up menu. This will cause the OK button to be treated as the Preference Panel's default button, giving it the distinctive Aqua throbbing color and making it respond to the Return key.

Finally, select the Panel icon. In the NSPanel Info Panel, uncheck all three checkboxes in the Controls area. This will cause the three round buttons in the panel's title bar to disappear. Also, check the "Hide on deactivate" checkbox in the Options area. This will cause the Preferences panel to be hidden when some other application comes to the front.

11. You can build and run the application now to make sure the Preferences panel opens when you choose Preferences from the Application menu. You can also examine the preferences file itself using TextEdit or Property List Editor. But don't expect a new document to honor any custom values you may provide for new documents, because you haven't yet written the code needed to apply the user's custom preferences. That is a task for Recipe 19.

Conclusion

You have now learned how to create and use a number of different kinds of Cocoa windows, including standard document windows, drawers, ancillary document windows providing a second view of some of a document's data, alert panels with complex behavior, and dialog panels. There are one or two other kinds of windows you might encounter when writing Cocoa applications, but this tutorial has taken you a good distance down the road toward understanding how to create all of them.

You are also near the end of what *Vermont Recipes* has to teach you. With the long introduction to major application features in Recipe 1 and the subsequent exploration of user controls, keyed archiving, menus, and windows, you have covered almost all the ground you must cover when writing a full-featured Mac OS X Cocoa application. If you don't believe it, just look at the menus and menu items in the Vermont Recipes application. All but one or two of them now work.

You will next turn to Section 6, the last section of this book. It adds a small number of recipes about additional application features that should always be present in a Cocoa application. In Recipe 19, you will finish the work with Cocoa's preferences system you began in Recipe 18, making new documents honor Cocoa's NSUserDefaults system. In Recipe 20, you will explore various forms of online help.

Additional Application Features

There remain a few application features so important or common that no serious application should be without them.

One of these features is user preferences. In Recipe 19, you will pick up where you left off in Recipe 18, implementing an application preferences system that allows the user to override the default values of new documents. The techniques you learn in Recipe 19 will allow you to implement preferences of any degree of complexity in your applications.

Recipe 20 will introduce you to several ways in which you can add online help to your application. You already know how to add static Help tags to user controls and other views. In Recipe 20, you will learn how to make Help tags dynamic, changing with the state of the views to which they are attached. You will also learn how to create larger, styled Help tags. Finally, you will learn how to make the application's Help menu useful, adding a Read Me file and complete online Apple Help.

RECIPE 19

User Preferences

In Recipe 18, Step 2, you created a Preferences panel for the Vermont Recipes application. You wrote an `awakeFromNib` method to display in the Preferences panel two `standardUserDefaults` preference settings for new documents, and you wrote action methods to save new values for those two preference settings in the `standardUserDefaults` dictionary. In other words, the Preferences panel is complete and working, and you can generate real preferences files on disk through NSUserDefaults.

HIGHLIGHTS:

Using Cocoa's user defaults system

However, you haven't yet written any methods to initialize the `standardUserDefaults` dictionary with default values for the two preference settings when the application is first run, before the user has had a chance to enter custom preferences. Nor have you written any code to force a new Vermont Recipes document to honor the `standardUserDefaults` preferences, whether they be default values or custom values entered by a user. In Recipe 19, you will complete the job.

Take care of updating the target's Info.Plist Entries now, to get it out of the way, by incrementing its build version to **19**. You don't have to increment the **VRDocument-Version** variable in VRDocument.m.

What you know at this point about the Vermont Recipes application's preferences is quite limited. You learned in Recipe 18 that the Vermont Recipes application's preferences do not deal with general application settings but instead relate only to a new document's default values. You also know that a new Cocoa object, such as the Buttons model object, sets any instance variable values to **nil** or some other representation of **0** unless you assign a non-**0** value to it. You can easily deduce from these two facts that a new Vermont Recipes document will therefore open with all of its values set to **0**-based default values such as **0**, **NO**, **nil**, or **NULL** unless you provide a non-**0** default value.

You may recall that you did in fact write a few lines of code back in Recipe 1, and also in several recipes in Section 2, to set various model object instance variables to non-**0** values. For example, the **checkbox** value in the Button model is initialized to **YES** in its designated initializer. I told you in Recipe 1, Step 4.1, that this was a temporary measure and that you would eventually develop a new way to do this using Cocoa's NSUserDefaults system. You will do so now.

Before turning to the code, take a moment to meet Cocoa's NSUserDefaults system.

Cocoa normally saves an application's preferences in a property list file in a user's ~/Library/Preferences folder. There is a separate application preferences file for each user on a multiuser machine to let each user have different preferences. The file will be named after the domain you set in the Application Settings in Recipe 1—here, com.stepwise.VermontRecipes.plist. Cocoa creates such a preferences file for each user automatically to save many important bits of user-specific information Cocoa needs behind the scenes. An example of this is the default folder to which a user last navigated when saving a file, so the next save dialog can open to the same folder. When your application uses the NSUserDefaults class for its preferences, it saves a user's application preferences in that file alongside the values that Cocoa stores there. Cocoa provides many methods that make it very convenient for you to use the NSUserDefaults facility in your applications. You should rarely, if ever, need to roll your own preferences system.

Cocoa also provides a defaults initialization scheme you can use if you need to code non-0 default values into your application before a user has set custom preferences. Using this initialization scheme makes it unnecessary to distribute your application with an installer that installs prewritten preference files. You will use this scheme in place of the designated initializer assignments you made earlier in several of the model classes.

The Cocoa defaults initialization scheme is based on the fact that the Cocoa run-time system calls a special class method in NSObject, `initialize`, in every class that implements it, before the application calls any method of that class. You are encouraged to implement an `initialize` method to code default values into an application. Though hard-coded, these values are volatile in the sense that Cocoa will not save them to a user's Preferences folder. They remain in effect only as long as the application is running and only if custom user preferences do not supersede them. They are tied directly into the NSUserDefaults system. An application implementing NSUserDefaults always looks first for these hard-coded, volatile default values and uses them while it is running, unless it finds superseding settings in the user's non-volatile preferences file on disk.

In Recipe 19, you will remove the non-0 default value settings for new Vermont Recipes documents from several model classes' designated initializers and place them instead in a new `initialize` method in each of these model classes. You will also arrange for the application to apply a user's custom preferences saved on disk, if they exist, instead of the volatile defaults set in the `initialize` methods. The model classes will still set affected instance variables to these values in the designated initializer, but they will do so by obtaining them from the `standardUserDefaults` dictionary instead of direct value assignments. In this way, you can be sure that Cocoa will obtain the initial values of non-0 instance variables from either the default values or the user's preferences file, if one exists.

1. Begin by inserting the following `initialize` method at the beginning of the INITIALIZATION section of the NSButtonModel.m source file:

```
+ (void) initialize {
    static BOOL initialized = NO;
    if ( !initialized ) {
        if (self == [VRButtonModel class]) {
            [self setVersion:1];
        }
        NSUserDefaults *defaults =
            [NSUserDefaults standardUserDefaults];
        NSDictionary *initialUserDefaults =
            [NSDictionary dictionaryWithObjectsAndKeys:
            [NSNumber numberWithBool:YES], @"CheckboxValue",
            [NSNumber numberWithBool:YES],
            @"TrianglePegsValue",
            [NSNumber numberWithInt:VRRepublican],
            @"PartyValue",
            [NSNumber numberWithInt:VRVermont], @"StateValue",
            nil];
        [defaults registerDefaults:initialUserDefaults];
        initialized = YES;
    }
}
```

Apple's NSObject class reference document recommends that you always test whether a class has already been initialized using the `initialize` method; if it has been initialized, don't initialize it again. There are apparently circumstances under which the run-time system could call the initialize method more than once, and in any event the application could call it explicitly. Following Apple's recommendation, you should set an internal static variable, `initialized`, to NO before executing the body of the method, then set the static variable to YES at the end. If the method is called again, it will know it has already been initialized.

If you aren't fully conversant with the niceties of the C programming language, you probably doubt this use of the `initialized` variable will work as intended. If the method is called a second time, won't the first line just reset the variable's value to NO and execute the body of the method again? No, it won't. The value of an internal static variable in C is maintained across multiple invocations of a function. Since its scope is limited to the function body, it can only be initialized within the function body. To maintain the ability to initialize it to a value that persists across multiple calls to the method, C executes the initialization statement only once, as if it were executed before the program ran.

Next, the method calls its inherited `setVersion:` method to stamp this as version 1 of the VRButtonModel class. Otherwise, its version would have a default value of `0`. You don't have to implement Cocoa's class versioning system, but if you're writing a complex application and you expect it to go through many releases in its commercial lifetime, it might prove valuable to be able to include diagnostic routines that check a class's version. Check whether `self` is the VRButtonModel class before setting its version, because you don't want subclasses to brand themselves as version 1, too.

Finally, the method gets to NSUserDefaults. As you learned in Recipe 18, the way to access the user's preferences is to get the `standardUserDefaults` dictionary, which Cocoa keeps in a convenient cache. You then call one of NSDictionary's class convenience methods, `dictionaryWithObjectsAndKeys:`, to set a new document's default values. Here, you set the values represented by the `CheckboxValue` and `TrianglePegsValue` keys to the Boolean value `YES`, and you set the values represented by the `PartyValue` and `StateValue` keys to the integer values represented by the enumeration constants `VRRepublican` and `VRVermont`, respectively. All of these are C data types, so you have to wrap them in objects using familiar NSNumber methods before inserting them into the dictionary.

At the end, you call NSUserDefaults' `registerDefaults:` method. This method tells Cocoa to treat these values as if they were user preferences whenever the application attempts to get one of the user's preference values and can't find any. It tells Cocoa not to use these values if the user has already set a specific preference, because persistent user application preferences take precedence over volatile defaults. In no event does Cocoa save these default values to disk. If there are still no saved user preferences the next time the application runs, it will again find these default values via the `initialize` method.

2. Now scroll down in the VRDocumentModel.m source file to the designated initializer, `initWithDocument:`. There, sandwiched between calls to the undo manager's `disableUndoRegistration` and `enableUndoRegistration` methods, you find four methods you wrote a long time ago to set the initial default values of the four instance variables described above. Delete those four statements and replace them with the following:

```
[self setCheckboxValue:[[NSUserDefaults standardUserDefaults]
        boolForKey:@"CheckboxValue"]];
[self setTrianglePegsValue:[[NSUserDefaults
        standardUserDefaults] boolForKey:@"TrianglePegsValue"]];
[self setPartyValue:[[NSUserDefaults standardUserDefaults]
        integerForKey:@"PartyValue"]];
[self setStateValue:[[NSUserDefaults standardUserDefaults]
        integerForKey:@"StateValue"]];
```

Instead of assigning specific values to the instance variables, as your old code did, these statements set the values to whatever they find in the **standardUserDefaults** dictionary for the specified keys. If the user hasn't yet set custom preferences, these will be the default values you just provided in the **initialize** method. If the user has set custom preferences, these are the values the **standardUserDefaults** dictionary will provide from its up-to-date cache of user preferences—in this case, values obtained from the user's preferences file on disk.

Of course, in Recipe 18, you arranged only for the user to set a specific preference for the Button model's **checkbox** instance variable. Thus, only that instance variable will get its value from a user's preferences file on disk. The other instance variables covered by the new code will always get their default values via the **initialize** method. In a real application, you would undoubtedly be more thorough.

You should take care of one little detail before continuing. Long ago, you wrote an **NSAssert()** function call in the designated initializer to show how you might catch a failure to initialize the **checkbox** instance variable to **YES**. Now that you are allowing the user to set a preference of **NO** for the checkbox, you must remove that **NSAssert()** call.

Next, make similar changes in the Slider model and the Text Field model.

3. Insert the following new **initialize** method at the beginning of the INITIALIZATION section of the VRSliderModel.m source file:

```
+ (void) initialize {
    static BOOL initialized = NO;
    if ( !initialized ) {
        if (self == [VRSliderModel class]) {
            [self setVersion:1];
        }
        NSUserDefaults *defaults =
                [NSUserDefaults standardUserDefaults];
        NSDictionary *initialUserDefaults =
                [NSDictionary dictionaryWithObject:
                [NSNumber numberWithFloat:75.0]
                forKey:@"SpeedValue"];
        [defaults registerDefaults:initialUserDefaults];
        initialized = YES;
    }
}
```

4. Insert the following statement in the designated initializer for the VRSliderModel.m source file, `initWithDocument:`, replacing the old assignment of a default value:

```
[self setSpeedValue:[[NSUserDefaults standardUserDefaults]
    floatForKey:@"SpeedValue"]];
```

5. Insert the following new `initialize` method at the beginning of the INITIALIZATION section of the VRTextFieldModel.m source file:

```
+ (void) initialize {
    static BOOL initialized = NO;
    if ( !initialized ) {
        if (self == [VRTextFieldModel class]) {
            [self setVersion:1];
        }
        NSUserDefaults *defaults =
            [NSUserDefaults standardUserDefaults];
        NSDictionary *initialUserDefaults =
            [NSDictionary dictionaryWithObjectsAndKeys:
            @"(800) 555-1212", @"TelephoneValue",
            @"Test Name", @"FormNameValue",
            [NSNumber numberWithInt:95123], @"FormIdValue",
             @"(800) 555-1212", @"FormFaxValue", nil];
        [defaults registerDefaults:initialUserDefaults];
        initialized = YES;
    }
}
```

6. Finally, insert the following statements in the designated initializer for the VRTextFieldModel.m source file, `initWithDocument:`, replacing the old assignments of default values:

```
telephoneValue = [[NSUserDefaults standardUserDefaults]
    objectForKey:@"TelephoneValue"];
formNameValue = [[NSUserDefaults standardUserDefaults]
    objectForKey:@"FormNameValue"];
formIdValue = [[[NSUserDefaults standardUserDefaults]
    objectForKey:@"FormIdValue"] retain];
 formFaxValue = [[NSUserDefaults standardUserDefaults]
    objectForKey:@"FormFaxValue"];
```

Don't delete the statement assigning a value to `formDateValue`, because that instance variable will continue to be initialized to the current date every time a user opens a document.

7. Build and run the application to test it.

The first time you run it, you may see the alert panel you wrote in Recipe 18, reminding you that you can set the application's preferences using the Application menu's Preferences command. Dismiss the alert, and a new document immediately opens. You see that the Checkbox user control is checked, because you set up that value as a new document's default in the Button model's `initialize` method. Select the Sliders tab and see that the Speed Limiter slider and text field are set to 75.0 mph, again because that is the default value you provided in the Slider model's `initialize` method.

Now choose Preferences from the Application menu. Uncheck the Checkbox check box, and type the number 95.0 into the Speed Limiter text field. Press Enter to commit it, and then click the OK button.

Choose File > New. A new Vermont Recipes document opens. This time, the Checkbox user control is unchecked and the Speed Limiter slider and text field are set to 95.0 mph. Congratulations—Cocoa has honored your user preferences.

RECIPE 20

Online Help

Only one menu doesn't yet work as it should in the Vermont Recipes application: the Help menu. The existing Vermont Recipes Help command, provided by the MainMenu.nib file in the Cocoa Document-based Application template, does work, but, as is true of all Cocoa applications by default, it only presents an alert panel explaining that "Help isn't available" for Vermont Recipes. You've probably seen similar alerts on applications undergoing beta testing, but this isn't acceptable for a finished application.

At the very least, even the simplest application should open a read-me document from the Help menu, if only because it's so easy to take advantage of this opportunity to explain and promote your application. In Recipe 20, you will put this finishing touch on the Vermont Recipes application. You will even add a little HTML-based Apple Help that your users can read with Apple's Help Viewer application.

Before turning to the Help menu, you will briefly explore two other forms of online help you can make available to your users: Help tags and context help.

You learned how to add Help tags to a user control or other view in Recipe 1, Step 2.2.4. Using Interface Builder, you simply type a short phrase into a text field in the Info Panel's Help pane. When the application is running, the phrase appears as one short line of text against a yellow background in a small box near the view whenever the mouse hovers over it for a few moments. When the mouse moves somewhere else, the Help tag fades away. This form of online help is perfect for a quick reminder or hint to a user who already knows something about how the application works.

Here, in Step 1, you will take Help tags a step further. Using a convenient method in the AppKit's NSView class, you will arrange to change the wording of a Help tag programmatically to reflect the current state or setting of its associated view. **Figures 20.1** and **20.2** show the Checkbox control in the Buttons pane of the Vermont Recipes application's main document window with Help tags reflecting its On and Off states.

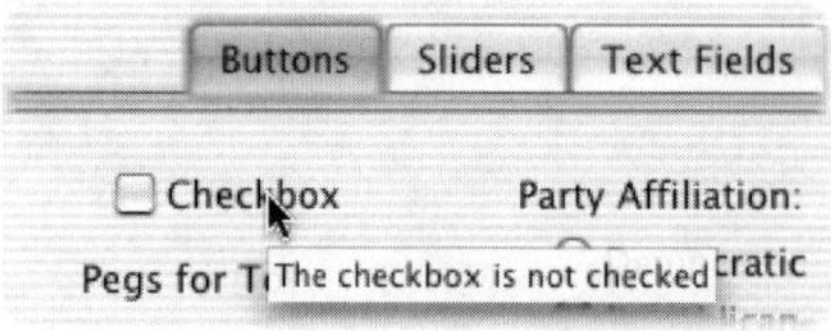

FIGURE 20.1 A Help tag for a checkbox in the On state.

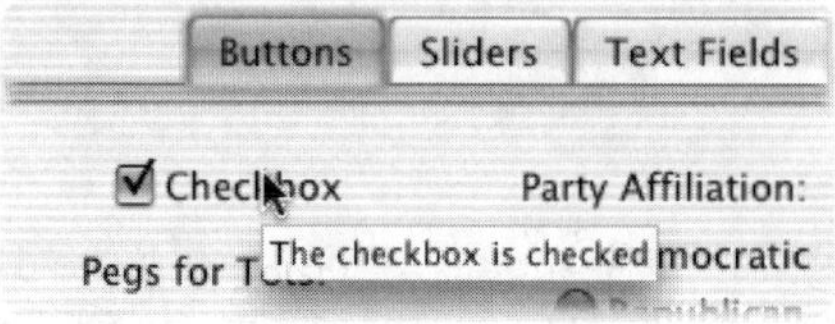

FIGURE 20.2 A Help tag for a checkbox in the Off state.

Notice that the Cocoa frameworks refer to Help tags as tool tips, as does the developer documentation. Help tags is the newer *Aqua Human Interface Guidelines* term. I will try to use it here except when referring to a specific Cocoa method.

Next, in Step 2, you will implement context help, which is similar to Help tags but serves a slightly different purpose. It is presented against the same yellow background in a similar box near the view. However, it only appears when the user asks for it. The user first presses the Help key to turn the cursor into a large question mark (?), then clicks in any view with associated context help to read information about the view. Using Interface Builder, you can arrange to trigger it from a button, menu item, or key combination as well, so PowerBook users can easily read context help even without a Help key. Clicking again causes the context help box to go away. Context help is less intrusive than Help tags because a user isn't likely to trigger it by accident. The main advantage is that a context help box can be much larger than a Help tag and therefore can hold more text, and the text can include a variety of styles, fonts, and even images.

Context help is suitable for more detailed, explanatory help regarding the use of an application's individual features. It can play a role somewhere between the simple reminder a Help tag offers and the manual-style detailed instructional materials found in a comprehensive Apple Help book. **Figure 20.3** shows context help for the Checkbox control.

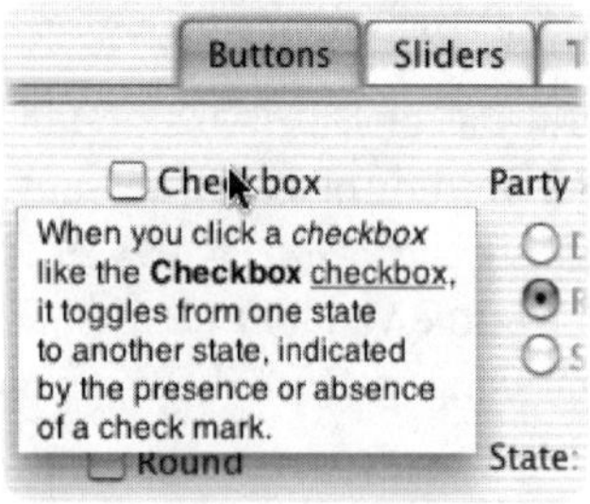

FIGURE 20.3 Context help for a checkbox.

You should bear in mind that context help has no clear sanction in the *Aqua Human Interface Guidelines,* which say only: "Mac OS X supports two user help components: Apple Help and help tags." This statement is ambiguous because you could think of context help as an alternative form of Help tags. The *Guidelines* do note, with apparent approval, that Carbon applications can support an expanded Help tag when the user presses the Command key. Cocoa's context help implements the same concept with a slightly different triggering gesture.

In the final steps of Recipe 20, you will learn how to add additional menu items to the Help menu to present a read-me document and standard, comprehensive HTML-based Apple Help. **Figure 20.4** shows the Vermont Recipes Help menu with the read-me file partially hidden behind it, and **Figure 20.5** shows a page from the application's Apple Help.

FIGURE 20.4
A read-me file presented from the Help menu.

FIGURE 20.5
Comprehensive Apple Help presented from the Help menu.

Update the target's Info.Plist Entries by incrementing its build version to **20**. You don't have to increment the **VRDocumentVersion** variable in VRDocument.m.

Step 1: Create a Dynamic Help Tag Reflecting a View's Current State

NSView manages Help tags, so any and all views can have Help tags associated with them—tags are not limited to user controls. For programmatic control of Help tags, you will most often use NSView's `setToolTip:` method. Just send a particular view a `setToolTip:` message, passing as its only parameter value a string object with a phrase destined to appear in the Help tag.

The `setToolTip:` method does not present the Help tag but only associates the string with the view. The Help tag is presented and fades away when the user moves the mouse over and away from it. You can associate a new string with the view at any time by simply calling `setToolTip:` again. Once associated with a view, a Help tag remains associated with it until it is replaced with a new Help tag or removed.

You won't normally need any of the other Help tag methods in NSView. You can remove a Help tag that's associated with a particular view by calling `setToolTip:` on it with an empty string. Alternatively, you can send it the `removeAllToolTips` message. You could, for example, implement a preferences setting to turn off Help tags by sending either of these messages to every view in the application.

Why, you may ask, is there a method called `removeAllToolTips,` if you have to send it individually to each view? Can a view have more than one Help tag at a time?

The answer is yes. Using the `addToolTipRect:owner:userData:` method, you can associate a Help tag with a particular part of a view and another Help tag with another part of the view. You can then remove all of the Help tags associated with that one view by using the `removeAllToolTips` method. As you would expect, you can remove a single Help tag associated with a multiple-tag view using the `removeToolTip:` method, which takes as its parameter value the special tag returned by the `addToolTipRect:owner:userData:` method. For more complex Help tag scenarios, see the `view:stringForToolTip:point:userData:` method in the NSToolTipOwner informal protocol.

In this step, you will associate two Help tags in alternation with the Checkbox user control in the Buttons pane of the main Vermont Recipes application window. You'll associate one Help tag with the checkbox when it is checked and the other with the unchecked checkbox.

You might at first think an appropriate place to do this would be in the checkbox's action method. However, this would not associate a Help tag with the checkbox until the user clicked it. The checkbox would have no Help tag when the window first opened. The right place to put a dynamic Help tag's code is in the button's specific view updater, which is called every time the checkbox changes state, whether that's when the window opens, when it reverts to its saved state, or when the user clicks it—and even when an AppleScript command toggles it, if you implement AppleScript support in your application.

1. Insert the following statement at the end of the **updateCheckbox:** method in the "INTERFACE MANAGEMENT - Specific updaters" section of the VRButtonController.m category source file:

```
[[self checkbox] setToolTip:([[self checkbox] state] ==
    NSOnState) ? NSLocalizedString(@"The checkbox is checked",
    @"Tool tip for checkbox on state") :
    NSLocalizedString(@"The checkbox is not checked",
    @"Tool tip for checkbox off state")];
```

You must, of course, add these two strings to the Localizable.strings file.

This method uses the C ternary operator because the checkbox is a two-state one. The **setToolTip:** method associates one string or the other with the checkbox whenever its state is set.

You will want to place similar code in the updater method for every view in the application with an associated Help tag whose text should vary depending on the state of the view. As you see, however, this involves some drudgery. You have better things to do with your time, so assign this task to the high-school intern you just hired and move on to more interesting topics.

2. Get editorial help with the text of your Help tags unless you're confident of your writing talent. A programmer's first instincts aren't always very good when it comes to explaining to a nontechnical user how to do something with a computer program. You'll find style guidelines for writing Help tag text in the *Aqua Human Interface Guidelines* and also in Using Help Tags on your computer at /Developer/Documentation/Carbon/pdf/UsingHelpTags.pdf.

Step 2: Create Context Help for a View

Let it be said at the outset that Cocoa context help has known better days. In the summer of 2001, a senior Cocoa engineer at Apple remarked on one of the mailing lists: "Traces of context help have vanished from IB and PB, unfortunately. That was because of the uncertainty in what we wanted to do with it long term. This invalidates some of the description in the NSHelpManager documentation." Sure enough, in

Mac OS X 10.2, the NSHelpManager class reference document still contains several sentences suggesting that you should normally use Interface Builder and Project Builder to implement context help, but those two applications no longer have the facilities required to do so. Instead, you must implement context help programmatically.

Perhaps because of the removal of those facilities, or more likely because the *Aqua Human Interface Guidelines* don't clearly list it among the accepted delivery vehicles for help, very few Cocoa applications implement context help. This is unfortunate for several reasons. First, context help is more informative than Help tags but easier to get at than comprehensive Apple Help, so it can play an important role in introducing your users to the intricacies of your application. I am a strong believer in online help. Second, your application will have a small user interface glitch if you don't implement context help. Run almost any Cocoa application, such as TextEdit; press the Help key on your keyboard to turn the cursor into a question mark; then click on any view in the application. All you get for your trouble is a beep, because TextEdit doesn't implement context help. Few users will notice this incongruity or be bothered by it, but a polished application shouldn't leave a tool like the question-mark cursor unimplemented while allowing a curious user to stumble upon it. Besides, Carbon developers get an expanded form of Help tags that is sanctioned by Apple, and Cocoa developers deserve no less.

Context help is as easy to implement as programmatic Help tags, so it doesn't involve a major cost. In summary, you use TextEdit—or any other editor or word processor capable of saving files in rich text format (RTF), such as Microsoft Word—to write a series of small files. Each file contains the text for a single context help item and can make use of style and font settings and embedded images. Save all these files, with .rtf or .rtfd filename extensions, in the English.lproj subfolder of your project folder (or in the language folder for whatever other language serves as your base development language). You will shortly write a shell script that coalesces all these files into a single property-list file, Help.plist, which will make all of the context help text items available to the application via their NSDictionary keys.

If you don't like clutter in your Project Builder Groups & Files pane, you don't have to add these RTF and RTFD files to the project using the Project > Add Files menu item. Only the shell script uses them, and they will not be loaded into the application bundle when you build it. If you (like me) believe in having the Groups & Files pane reflect the contents of your project folder, you can add them to the project and group them in a separate subgroup of the Resource group in the Groups & Files pane, calling that subgroup, say, Context Help. Just make sure the actual files reside at the root level of the English.lproj subfolder in your project, because that's where the shell script expects to find them.

If you do add them to the project, be sure to uncheck their checkboxes in the left margin of the Groups & Files pane so the final application bundle won't include them. The application won't use the individual files, as it only needs the coalesced Help.plist file, and loading them all when the application launches would waste time. You do want them in the project file, though, so they will be available to your localization contractors.

1. Start by writing a context help RTF file for the Checkbox user control in the Buttons pane of the Vermont Recipes application, in your own words. Use TextEdit or another RTF-capable application. Be sure to italicize or underline some of the text and try using a couple of different fonts. If you can, embed a small image in the file (this requires using the .rtfd filename extension). In a real application, you want your context help to be tasteful, but in this tutorial you can let your imagination run riot.

   Save the file as RTF with the name `checkboxContextHelp.rtf` (the .rtf or .rtfd filename extension is required) in the English.lproj subfolder of your project folder. The final part of the filename, ContextHelp, is merely a convention adopted here to help the shell script identify your context help source files. If you prefer a different naming convention, make sure to change the shell script to match.

   Choose Project > Add Files to add the file to the project. Create a Context Help subgroup in the Resources group in the Groups & Files pane of the main project builder window and drag the file into it. The file itself will remain in the project folder's English.lproj subfolder.

   In a real application, you will have a great many of these RTF and RTFD files, but for the purposes of *Vermont Recipes,* you only need to create one.

2. Write a shell script in Project Builder to coalesce the RTF and RTFD files into a single Help.plist file. *Vermont Recipes* is not a tutorial about how to write shell scripts, but you'll get a small introduction to the topic here.

   Begin by selecting the Targets tab in the main Project Builder window. In the left pane, double-click the target, Vermont Recipes, to open the target editor.

   At the bottom of the target editor's left pane, you see a list of build phases, which normally lists four items. Select the last build phase by clicking it, then choose Project > New Build Phase > New Shell Script Build Phase. A new Shell Script Files build phase appears at or near the bottom of the list. If it isn't at the bottom, click it once to select it, then drag it to the bottom. Shell Script build phases usually come last, to perform postprocessing on the project after Project Builder has largely finished building it. Open the new build phase by clicking its name in the left pane.

   The Shell Script Files section of the target editor contains two text fields and a checkbox (**Figure 20.6**). Leave the "Run only when installing" checkbox unchecked, because you want Project Builder to run this script every time you build the project in case you edit the RTF and RTFD files. In the upper text field, labeled Shell, type **/bin/sh**. This tells Project Builder to run the script in the Bourne shell, one of the Unix shells available in Mac OS X.

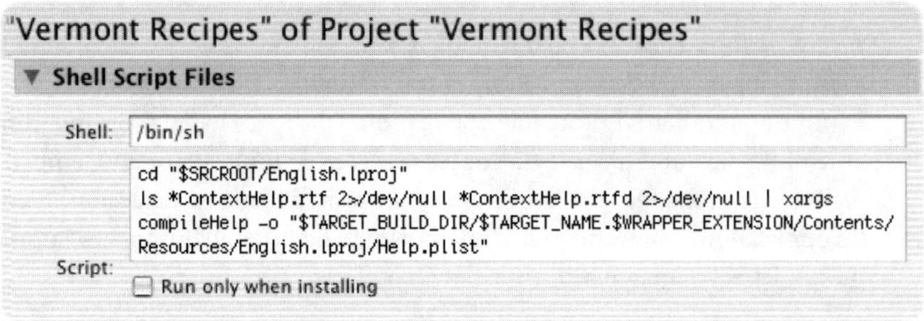

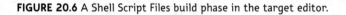

"Vermont Recipes" of Project "Vermont Recipes"

▼ **Shell Script Files**

Shell: | /bin/sh

Script:
```
cd "$SRCROOT/English.lproj"
ls *ContextHelp.rtf 2>/dev/null *ContextHelp.rtfd 2>/dev/null | xargs
compileHelp -o "$TARGET_BUILD_DIR/$TARGET_NAME.$WRAPPER_EXTENSION/Contents/
Resources/English.lproj/Help.plist"
```
☐ Run only when installing

FIGURE 20.6 A Shell Script Files build phase in the target editor.

Type the following shell script into the lower text field, labeled Script, exactly as the text is given below. It contains only two lines, although the second line will wrap because the window isn't wide enough to hold all of it. The slash-delimited path in quotation marks at the end of the script should have no spaces or carriage returns in it.

```
cd "$SRCROOT/English.lproj"
ls *ContextHelp.rtf 2>/dev/null *ContextHelp.rtfd 2>/dev/null
    | xargs compileHelp -o "$TARGET_BUILD_DIR/
    $TARGET_NAME.$WRAPPER_EXTENSION/Contents/Resources/
    English.lproj/Help.plist"
```

You could have written this script in a separate text file with an .sh filename extension and saved it in your project folder. In that case, you would have typed its name into the Scripts text field in Project Builder's target editor, prefaced with a period and slash (./)—say, ./CompileHelpFiles. You'd have to mark the shell script file as user executable by executing this command in the Terminal application: **chmod u+x CompileHelpFiles**. You would not need to include the usual **#!/bin/sh** shebang, which identifies the Bourne shell as the shell in which it should run, at the beginning of the file, because you already provided this in the Shell text field in the target editor.

An example of a project using a separate shell script file is available at Apple's developer sample code Web site under the name ScriptBuildPhases. For examples of complex scripts typed directly into the Scripts text field in the target editor, as you have done here, look at the TextEdit and Sketch project files in your /Developer/Examples/AppKit folder.

Here's a concise explanation of your shell script.

The `cd` command changes the working directory to the designated path. The `$` operator substitutes the value of the built-in **SRCROOT** shell variable for the variable name before the script executes. This variable points to the project folder, so the first line of the script sets the project folder's English.lproj subfolder as the working directory. You can make all subsequent path references relative to the working directory.

In the next statement, the `ls` command lists all the files in the working directory that satisfy the wildcard patterns `*ContextHelp.rtf` and `*ContextHelp.rtfd`. The asterisk at the beginning of each is a wildcard character standing for any number of other characters. In short, the `ls` command generates a list of all the files in the working directory that end in ContextHelp.rtf or ContextHelp.rtfd.

If the English.lproj folder contained no files ending in ContextHelp.rtf or ContextHelp.rtfd, either or both of these wildcard patterns would generate an error interrupting the script and causing the build to fail. To prevent this from happening, the redirection operator, `>`, executes with the file reference **2**, meaning any error output, to redirect the error message to the null device, `/dev/null`. This silences error messages and allows the script and the build to run to conclusion even if there are no qualifying RTF or RTFD files available to process.

Next, the pipe operator, `|`, pipes the list of filenames to the **xargs** command, which in turn parcels them out in bunches to the **compileHelp** command. You could have omitted the **xargs** command, but there may be dozens of context help files in the project folder and **compileHelp** might not be able to handle that many. The **xargs** command is designed to execute other commands with small bunches of input at a time to avoid this problem.

All of the commands described to this point are part of the Bourne shell.

Finally, the **compileHelp** command is a special command provided by Apple solely for use with Project Builder. You can read about its usage by typing man **compileHelp** in Terminal and pressing Return. With the parameters used here, it parses the RTF and RTFD files passed to it and generates a Help.plist file at the designated path. The Help.plist file is a property list file containing all the context help text items from all the input files, using the name (including the file extension) of each file as the key to its text. The values of the shell variables used here—**TARGET_BUILD_DIR**, **TARGET_NAME**, and **WRAPPER_EXTENSION**—are substituted for the variable names to specify the path to the built application bundle in the project's build folder.

In short, this script coalesces all the context help files into a single property list file named Help.plist, then stuffs that file into the Resources subfolder of the application bundle's Contents folder, where the Cocoa code you write next will find it. All this will happen automatically whenever you build the project, and you won't ever have to look at the script again. It will be harmless if you don't implement context help, because it does not generate a Help.plist file if it finds no context help files in the project's English.lproj subfolder.

If your base development language is not English, substitute the correct language lproj subfolder for the English.lproj subfolder wherever it appears in the script.

3. You could insert the code to associate the Cocoa context help with a view in the same **updateCheckbox:** method you used for the Help tag code, but this would be appropriate only if the context help were designed to change with the state of the Checkbox user control. You wrote only one context help file for the Checkbox control, so it will remain unchanged no matter what the control's state. You therefore don't need to waste time executing this code every time the Checkbox control changes state. Instead, insert it in the **awakeFromNib** method.

Near the end of the **awakeFromNib** method in the VRMainWindowController.m source file, insert this code:

```
[[NSHelpManager sharedHelpManager] setContextHelp:
        [[NSBundle mainBundle] contextHelpForKey:
        @"checkboxContextHelp.rtf"] forObject:[self checkbox]];
```

The NSHelpManager.h header file declares all of the context help methods, but it declares some of them as categories on other classes. You will therefore find their documentation in those other classes' reference documents. For example, the AppKit's NSBundleAdditions class reference document describes the **contextHelpForKey:** method, which you just used to retrieve the rich text from the Help.plist file. The key this method uses here, **checkboxContextHelp.rtf**, is the name you gave the original RTF file.

The **sharedHelpManager** object is an instance of a *singleton class*. A singleton instance is shared by all objects that need to use its methods. In Step 3 you will encounter another commonly used Cocoa singleton, NSWorkspace's **sharedWorkspace**. The **sharedHelpManager** singleton is shared by all application objects that need to present context help. It is always available.

NSHelpManager provides a few other methods that you won't exercise here. It also posts notifications when the user turns context help mode on or off, should you want to do something in the application at either of those times. You could, for example, have the Mac read aloud the text of the context help.

You will use one other context help method in the next step. NSApplication provides an action method, **activateContextHelpMode:**, to turn on context help mode. In Step 3, you will connect it to a new item in the Help menu to provide the user with a way to turn on context help without having to press the Help key.

Step 3: Add Menu Items to the Help Menu to Present a Read-Me Document and Turn On Context Help

The *Aqua Human Interface Guidelines* recommend that you place only one menu item in your application's Help menu, consisting of your application's name followed by the localized word "Help," with the question mark serving as its Command-key equivalent. The *Guidelines* don't forbid the use of additional menu items. However, they do insist that the standard item be first if you add others. In what is arguably the most ironic departure from the *Aqua Human Interface Guidelines* in any Apple application, Interface Builder's own Help menu violates this rule. Vermont Recipes, however, will honor it.

The *Guidelines* are somewhat at odds with *Inside Mac OS X: System Overview,* in that the latter encourages conformity to what it calls "the 'all in one place' model of the application package." According to this model, you should package help files and other resources relating to an application in its bundle. In this way, a user can install an application by simply dragging it to the Applications folder, and its associated files, such as read-me documents, won't get lost. Shipping your product with a read-me file hidden inside the application bundle requires that you provide some means to open it, and the Help menu is the most obvious place. Additional menu items are therefore necessary in the Help menu. (If you want your users to see the read-me file before they install and launch the application, you can include an alias to it in your distribution folder. If the alias gets lost, the actual document will still be available inside the bundle.)

In this step, therefore, you will add menu items to the Vermont Recipes application's Help menu. One of the new menu items will open a read-me document in the TextEdit application, and the other will turn on context help. You'll start with the context help menu item, since you've just been working with context help.

1. Open the MainMenu.nib file using Interface Builder. You might as well add both of the new menu items at once. Click the Help menu in the MainMenu.nib – MainMenu window. From the Menus palette, drag an Item block and drop it beneath the existing Vermont Recipes Help menu item. Double-click its title and rename it `Read Me`. Then drag a blank menu item block from the palette and drop it beneath the Read Me menu item to serve as a menu separator. Finally, drag another Item block from the palette and drop it at the bottom of the Help menu. Rename it `Turn Context Help On`.

2. You don't need to write an action method to turn on context help, because NSHelpManager already declares an action method that does this, **activate-ContextHelpMode:**. It is declared in the NSHelpManager.h header file in a category on NSApplication, so you will find it in the MainMenu.nib's File's Owner, NSApplication. You don't want to connect this menu item to the First Responder, because its action is not dependent on whatever view is currently the first responder. Instead, it is a menu item that should always be available and will have an application-wide effect.

Control-drag from the Turn Context Help On menu item to the File's Owner icon. Then select the **target** outlet in the NSMenuItem Info Panel, select the **activateContextHelpMode:** action, and click Connect.

When you build and run the application, the Turn Context Help On menu item will now simply work. Choosing it will turn the cursor into a question mark, and clicking a view that has context help attached (here, the Checkbox control) will display its context help. The next click will cause the context help to go away.

3. Now turn to the Read Me menu item. It doesn't have a built-in Cocoa action method, so you'll have to write your own. But where should you put it?

This menu item, too, should work without regard to the identity of the view that currently has keyboard focus, so you don't want to connect it to the First Responder icon. Since the action method isn't built into Cocoa, you can't connect the menu item to File's Owner, either, as you did with the Turn Context Help On menu item. What is available in MainMenu.nib is the AppDelegate object you created in Recipe 15. Recall that it began to function as an application controller as well as the application delegate when you added an action method to it to support the application's Preferences menu item in Recipe 18, Step 2. You can do the same thing here to support the Read Me menu item. What all these menu items have in common is that they work for the application as a whole, not for a specific view that happens to be first responder when the user chooses the menu item.

At the end of the VRAppDelegate.m source file, insert this action method:

```
- (IBAction)showReadMeAction:(id)sender {
    NSString *path = [[NSBundle mainBundle]
        pathForResource:@"ReadMe" ofType:@"rtf"];
    if (path) {
        if (![[NSWorkspace sharedWorkspace] openFile:path
                withApplication:@"TextEdit"]) NSBeep();
    }
}
```

At the end of the VRAppDelegate.h header file, insert the corresponding declaration, as follows:

```
- (IBAction)showReadMeAction:(id)sender;
```

This method looks in the application's main bundle to find the read-me file, which you will name ReadMe.rtf. It does this using the NSBundle `mainBundle` class method, which is always available to give you an easy reference to the main bundle. A convenient method implemented in NSBundle is `pathForResource:-ofType:`, which you use here to obtain a full path to the ReadMe.rtf file you will shortly add to the project.

You then turn to an important singleton instance that's always available in a Cocoa application: `sharedWorkSpace`. Using the NSWorkspace method `openFile:withApplication:`, passing the read-me file's path to it, you can open the file. TextEdit will launch, and the read-me file will open in it.

You test the return value of the method, `YES` or `NO`, to determine whether the read-me file successfully opened. If not, the application beeps to catch the user's attention. If you are concerned about the possibility that a user might have foolishly removed TextEdit from the computer, you could use a simpler form of the method, `openFile:`, which will try to open the read-me file in whatever application is available that understands RTF files. In fact, this might be the more user-friendly choice, since many users set up their computers to open RTF files in some other application.

4. With the action method in place, you can now connect the menu item to it in Interface Builder. First read the VRAppDelegate header file into the MainMenu.nib file by selecting the Classes pane and choosing Classes > Read Files. Then Control-drag from the Read Me menu item to the VRAppDelegate icon, choose the `target` outlet in the Info Panel, select the `showReadMeAction:` action, and click Connect.

5. All that remains is to supply the ReadMe.rtf file. Create the file in any application that supports RTF, such as TextEdit or Microsoft Word. You've seen read-me files before, so you can write one without further advice. Save it to disk, then in the Finder drag it into the English.lproj subfolder of your project file. It belongs there because you will have to localize it in the event that you distribute your application internationally.

If the read-me file will include images, give it an .rtfd file extension and change the `ofType:` parameter value in your action method accordingly. For that matter, there is no reason why your read-me file can't be any type of file, so long as you are confident that your users' computers will have an application available that knows how to read it. TextEdit is safe because it is installed as part of every normal system installation. In theory, you could write your read-me file as a Microsoft Excel spreadsheet, a QuickTime Player movie, or whatever. Just make sure the file has the proper file extension (for instance, .mov for a movie) and the action method uses the correct type in the `ofType:` parameter of the `pathForResource:-ofType:` method. The Apple Developer Web site's sample code page includes an example application, SimpleCocoaApp, which uses a short HTML file.

One detail to which you might want to attend is protecting the read-me file against tampering. You wouldn't want anybody removing your copyright notice from it, would you? There isn't a lot you can do to stop a determined pirate, but you can impede casual pranksters by setting the file's Everyone permissions to Read Only using the Finder's Get Info panel. You will have to give your localization contractor an editable copy, of course.

You will need to load the read-me file into the application bundle when you build the application, so you have to add it to the project to make Project Builder aware that it exists as a resource. Choose Project > Add Files in Project Builder, then select ReadMe.rtf and add it. In the Groups & Files pane of the main project window, drag it into the Resources group, if it isn't already there, and make sure the checkbox in the left margin is checked so it will be copied into the application bundle at build time.

If you edit the read-me file subsequently, edit the original in the English.lproj subfolder of the project folder. Then clean the project before building it to ensure that Project Builder replaces the old copy of the read-me file in the built application bundle. If you edit the read-me file later, don't edit the copy that opens when you choose it from the Help menu while the application is running—if you do, you'll edit the copy in the executable application bundle and you'll lose your edits the next time you clean and build the project.

Open the Vermont Recipes target in Project Builder's target editor and look at the Bundle Resources Build Phase. There you see the read-me file listed along with the nib files, the Credits.rtf file, images, icons, and other resources. At build time, this build phase will load these listed items into the Resources subfolder of the Contents folder of the application bundle. Because they are in your project folder's English.lproj subfolder, they will be placed in the English.lproj subfolder of the application bundle's Resources subfolder. At run time, NSBundle's `pathForResource:ofType:` method will return this path—the path to the ReadMe.rtf file in this subfolder—to the action method you just wrote and open it in TextEdit when the user chooses Help > Read Me.

Step 4: Implement HTML-Based Comprehensive Apple Help

Apple Help has been Apple's preferred technology for delivering comprehensive online application help for a long time, going back well before Mac OS X. It is HTML-based, with HTML 3.2 as its foundation. Your Apple Help books will work in both the Mac OS X version of an application and Mac OS 9 and earlier Carbon versions.

Using HTML has many advantages, chief among them the fact that it is a mature, standards-based markup language supporting rich and attractive user interface design and presentation capabilities. It gives developers the ability to use a wide variety of existing WYSIWYG HTML editors, such as Adobe GoLive and Macromedia Dreamweaver, to write attractive Apple Help books. It also allows users to view application help in Web browsers other than Apple's own Help Viewer application, whether on the user's computer, on a network, or over the Internet. HTML's hypertext links are ideal in a help book, making it very easy for users to follow cross-references to related topics at any time. HTML's frames feature makes it easy to keep a table of contents in view while reading help text. It can also ease the task of porting help to or from another platform such as Windows, although tools for automating this task are not well developed.

The use of the HTML 3.2 standard goes back to the beginnings of Apple Help technology. The decision not to upgrade Apple Help to a newer version of the HTML standard offers some advantages. The Help Viewer browser application can remain lightweight, for example, and authors of help books do not have to be experts on the more arcane features of newer HTML versions. On the other hand, many complain that the absence of support for style sheets and other modern HTML features is unduly restrictive, and it is cited as one reason for the scarcity of tools that port HTML-based help between the Macintosh and other platforms. Apple Help omits a few features of the HTML 3.2 standard, such as forms, plug-ins, and Java support.

The Apple Help Viewer application supports several features that are not part of the HTML standard, using custom HTML tags that standard Web browsers will ignore. In Mac OS X, one of the more important of these is AppleScript support. You can embed AppleScripts in your help book and provide clickable links enabling the user to perform a variety of automated tasks to illustrate the use of an application. Even if your application is not scriptable, your Apple Help book can include items such as a link to launch the application and a link to reveal it in the Finder. If your application is scriptable, you can provide links enabling your users to exercise specific application features while reading the help book. You can also launch movies and play sounds. Movies are a particularly intriguing possibility, since a utility such as Ambrosia Software's Snapz Pro can record screen activity that a user can then play back from your help book. Instead of *telling* users what to do, you can *show* them what to do. In addition, Apple Help is indexed to allow quick searches.

The Apple Help Viewer in Mac OS X 10.2 is much improved over previous Mac OS X versions of the application. It launches faster, it's prettier, and it incorporates more up-to-date Mac OS X features, such as a drawer for accessing the main Help Center's table of contents. It launches whenever you choose Mac Help from the Finder's Help menu or help from the Help menu of an application that supports Apple Help. It quits automatically whenever you close a help book. If you're curious, you'll find it in /System/Library/CoreServices.

In Mac OS X, the preferred location for your help book files is within your application bundle. To make sure they end up there, place your help folder in the base development language's lproj subfolder in the project folder—say, English.lproj. Add it to the project (turning on the "Create Folder References for any added folders" option to ensure that you'll add its nested subfolders to the right levels). Then check the checkbox in the left margin of the Groups & Files pane, if necessary, to ensure that the help folder is copied into the built application bundle. Placing the help folder in the application bundle means it's included automatically whenever a user installs your application by dragging and dropping it, in keeping with the Mac OS X philosophy of putting everything related to the application in one place. You'll still see your application's Apple Help book listed in the main Help Center table of contents, where you can access it from the Finder and other places even when your application isn't running.

Apple Help is the Mac standard for comprehensive help, and I strongly encourage you to offer it in your applications. It is easier to implement than it looks, so don't let the mystery of an unfamiliar technology deter you.

In this step, you will create a very simple Apple Help book and make it available from the Vermont Recipes application's Help menu. Although a help book should not be as detailed as a traditional printed manual, this help book would be inadequate for a real application by any standard because it leaves out too much needed information. It is offered only to give you a concrete example of the process. For a fuller understanding—especially to learn how to implement some of Apple Help's more complicated features, such as automatic updates over the Internet, AppleScript links and references from your application to specific, anchored pages in your help book—read the documentation cited in the sidebar.

Documentation

Start by reading the "Online Help" topic in the "Program Design" section of the Cocoa Developer Documentation's *Programming Topics*. This is a very short section—just half a dozen short paragraphs—that gives you a very brief introduction to the Project Builder aspects of implementing Apple Help. For an even clearer explanation of the required Project Builder application settings, the current location for your help book, and an HTML snippet for your help book's title page, see Apple Q&A QA1022 at http://developer.apple.com/qa/qa2001/qa1022.html. Next, for the full details of how to design, write, and install your HTML files, including details regarding the custom HTML tags needed in an Apple Help book, read *Providing User Assistance With Apple Help*, a 42-page PDF document on your disk at /Developer/Documentation/Apple Help/Apple Help Reference/Apple Help.pdf. It is almost entirely about how to design and configure the HTML help files and their custom tags. This complete, up-to-date, step-by-step guide should have you up and running with Apple Help very quickly.

Another important source of information is Andrew Stone's article "Help on the Way!" in *MacTech* magazine (April 2001), available on his Web site at www.stone.com/The_Cocoa_Files/Help_On_The_Way_.html. This article details some critical steps that Apple doesn't document, without which your help book will not work. (In the step-by-step instructions that follow, you will learn that some of the more awkward steps recommended in Stone's article are no longer necessary in Mac OS X 10.2.)

A read-me document at /Developer/Documentation/Apple Help/Read Me.htm might lead you to believe that you have to install the Apple Help Reference HTML files in the Help Center to read them. Fortunately, these HTML files are identical to the PDF version of the reference cited in the previous paragraph, so you do not need to do so.

The same Apple Help folder contains several crucial items required to create an Apple Help book. First, it contains an essential tool, the Apple Help Indexing Tool, also aliased in the main /Developer/Applications folder. Every Apple Help book must be indexed using this tool. The Apple Help folder also includes sample books, templates, and a very short tutorial. Speaking from personal experience, I can tell you that the templates are invaluable, given the highly stylized nature of HTML Apple Help authorship even in the new world of Mac OS X. If you want your application's help book to conform to users' expectations and to be internally consistent, it is far more efficient to build on one of these templates than it is to code your own HTML from scratch, even in a WYSIWYG editor. In fact, if you are writing a large help book, you will find it very helpful to develop your own standardized templates.

(continues on next page)

Documentation *(continued)*

Some of Apple's help documentation still suggests that you read the Apple Help Style Guide in the Apple Help SDK. Unfortunately, Apple removed this SDK from its SDK Web site not too long ago, and the Style Guide is no longer officially available. It prescribed very detailed appearance guidelines for Apple Help. Even Apple's own help files have departed substantially from those guidelines since the advent of Mac OS X. The templates in the Apple Help folder provide a more up-to-date indication of the help file appearance Apple favors in its own applications.

I understand that comprehensive, updated documentation is on the way.

The steps required to implement an Apple Help book are as follows:

- Write the HTML content.
- Create a title page.
- Register the help book in the Info.plist file.

You're ready to get started.

1. To write your help content, you will find it easiest to use one of the more powerful WYSIWYG HTML authoring tools. However, if you're familiar with HTML, you can certainly do it in a plain text editor.

    To begin creating an Apple Help book, create a new folder anywhere in the Finder—say, in your Documents folder—bearing the name of the application followed by the word *Help*. Here, name it `Vermont Recipes Help`.

    Within the book, as shown in the example books Apple provides, you will place several files and folders. In this step, you will use Apple's Dynamic Sample Frames sample book as your starting point. In it, you see two files with odd names, rtfmhdy.htm and toctmpl.htm. These are small HTML files that Help Viewer uses to construct tables of contents in your finished help book. Another file, Dynamic Sample Frames Help.htm, is the help book's *title page;* you will read more about this shortly. A folder named gfx, for graphics, contains the image files used in the help book. Finally, there are many other folders, one for each chapter of your help book. Each chapter contains one or more HTML files that form separate pages within that chapter. In a complex help book, you might find other folders, such as a Shared folder containing AppleScripts that could be executed from links in many help pages.

    Open the new Vermont Recipes Help folder you created a moment ago, and copy into it all of the files and folders in Apple's Dynamic Sample Frames folder (except the "About this sample book.txt" file).

2. Change the name of the Dynamic Frames Help file to **index.htm**. This is a common HTML naming convention that identifies the starting point of a Web site. Using this name may make it easier for a standard Web browser to display your help book. Apple's help files use the common file extension .htm instead of the equally common extension .html. Either will do.

3. Open index.htm in your favored HTML authoring tool, and edit it until its HTML source looks like this:

```
<HTML>

    <HEAD>
        <META HTTP-EQUIV="content-type"
                CONTENT="text/html;charset=iso-8859-1">
        <TITLE>Vermont Recipes Help</TITLE>
        <META NAME="AppleTitle" CONTENT="Vermont Recipes Help">
        <META NAME="AppleIcon" CONTENT=
                "Vermont%20Recipes%20Help/gfx/bookIcon.gif">
        <META NAME="AppleFont" CONTENT=
                "Lucida Grande,Helvetica,Arial">
        <META NAME="AppleSearchResultsFont" CONTENT=
                "Lucida Grande,Geneva,Arial">
        <META NAME="ROBOTS" CONTENT="NOINDEX">
    </HEAD>

    <FRAMESET COLS="190,50%" BORDER="0" FRAMESPACING="0"
            FRAMEBORDER="NO">
        <FRAME SRC="toc.htm" NAME="_left" NORESIZE
                FRAMEBORDER="NO">
        <FRAME SRC="rtfmhdy.htm" NAME="_right" FRAMEBORDER="NO">
    </FRAMESET>
    <NOFRAMES>

        <BODY BGCOLOR="#ffffff">This page is designed to be viewed by
                a browser that supports Netscape's Frames extension.
                This text will be shown by browsers that do not support
                the Frames extension.
        </BODY>

    </NOFRAMES>

</HTML>
```

This is not a tutorial on HTML, so I won't offer an explanation here of what all these HTML tags do. Some of them are custom Apple Help tags, such as the `META NAME` tags for `AppleTitle`, `AppleIcon`, `AppleFont`, and `AppleSearchResultsFont`.

The `AppleTitle` tag is particularly important. It must be the same as one of the Project Builder application settings you will create shortly, `CFBundleHelpBookName`. Apple Help uses this, rather than the name of the file, to identify this page as the help book's title page, which will appear first when the user chooses Help > Vermont Recipes Help.

You changed the standard HTML `<title>` tag here to Vermont Recipes Help. The Apple Help Viewer doesn't use this tag, but it will form the title of the page when viewed in another Web browser, so it is worth getting right.

You see in the listing a reference to "toc.htm." Don't create a file with this name. Help Viewer will generate it automatically.

4. Next, open the chp1.htm file in the chapt1 folder, and edit its HTML source to read as follows:

```
<!DOCTYPE HTML PUBLIC "-//W3C//DTD HTML 3.2 Final//EN"
    "http://www.w3.org/MarkUp/Wilbur/HTML32.dtd">
<html>
<head>
    <title>Vermont Recipes Help</title>
    <meta name="AppleTitle" content=
        "About Vermont Recipes">
</head>
<body>
<font size="4" face="Lucida Grande, Helvetica, Arial">
    About Vermont Recipes
</font>
<p>
<font size="2" face="Lucida Grande, Helvetica, Arial">
    Vermont Recipes is....</font>
</body>
</html>
```

Among other things, you have changed the `AppleTitle` tag to About Vermont Recipes. Help Viewer will use this to identify this page's location in the hierarchy of the help book. You have also edited the text in the `<body>` tag to provide the text that will appear on this help page in Help Viewer. Here you see it truncated, but in your own Help book you can make it run on for several paragraphs, complete with links to Web sites, AppleScripts, and other pages in the help book.

5. Change the remaining pages in the other chapters in a manner similar to the changes you made to the chp1.htm page. In most of them, you only need to change the contents of the `<title>` tag, the `AppleTitle` meta name tag, and two text passages in the `<body>` tag. The chp4Web.htm file is different. Near the top it needs a clickable URL pointing to the Stepwise Web site. Those two lines should read as follows:

```
<meta name="AppleURL" content=
      "http://www.stepwise.com/Articles/VermontRecipes/">
<meta name="AppleTitle" content="Vermont Recipes on the Web">
```

If your help book contained a different number of pages or had a different organization, you might want to alter the template files and make other changes. For present purposes, however, you are done editing HTML.

6. In the Finder, drag the finished Vermont Recipes Help folder to your project folder and drop it in the English.lproj folder. It has to be localizable.

7. In Project Builder, choose Project > Add Files and add the Vermont Recipes Help folder and its contents to the project. Make sure you select the "Create Folder References for any added folders" radio button in the sheet before clicking the Add button, to force Project Builder to re-create exactly the folder's nesting hierarchy.

8. In the Groups & Files pane of the main project window, drag the Vermont Recipes Help folder reference into the Resources group, if necessary.

9. Click the Targets tab, double-click the Vermont Recipes target to open the targets editor, and select the Info.plist Entries Expert page. Click the Siblings button twice to create two new settings, `CFBundleHelpBookName` and `CFBundle-HelpBookFolder`. Set the former to `Vermont Recipes Help` because that's the name you used in the `AppleTitle` meta name tag in the title page's HTML source a moment ago. Set the latter to `Vermont Recipes Help` because that's the name you gave your help book folder. You must also have a `CFBundleIdentifier` set here, but you took care of that for other reasons long ago.

10. The `CFBundleHelpBookName` setting is localizable, so also place it on a line in the infoPlist.strings file.

11. In the MainMenu.nib nib file, you must connect the Vermont Recipes Help menu item in the Help menu to the application object's `openHelp:` action method. The Cocoa Document-based Application template already did this for you, so you don't need to worry about it now.

12. You might have read about a few more steps in the Apple Help documentation or in Andrew Stone's *MacTech* article, but in Mac OS X 10.2 (and perhaps earlier) you no longer have to perform all of them. One of them is still required in Carbon applications but was never required in Cocoa applications (although some of the documentation is not very clear about this distinction).

Carbon applications must include explicit code to register the help book so that it will appear in the Help Center. In Cocoa, the Info.plist Entries settings you just completed take care of this chore automatically, so you can skip it.

Stone's article states that you must use a utility such as the SetFile tool to set the creator and type codes of all the HTML files in your help book. This step is quite tedious, but fortunately it is no longer required.

Finally, Stone describes one undocumented step. After building the application, you must open the built application bundle in the Project Builder build folder, open the Resources and English.lproj subfolders, and drag the Vermont Recipes Help folder to the Apple Help Indexing Tool. This will create a required index file in the finished help book. According to Stone, you must perform this task on the help book in its final resting place in the application bundle to ensure that all the index references are relative to the application. As Stone also points out, you must drag a copy of the index file from the built application bundle and drop it in the copy of the help book that is in the project's English.lproj folder to add it to the project. This will ensure that the index is again placed in the right position in the built application bundle should you clean and rebuild the project.

I have been told that indexing no longer must be done on the built application bundle's copy of the help book, but I don't know what the official word on this is currently. In an event, the help book must be reindexed whenever you edit its contents.

13. Build and run the application and choose Help > Vermont Recipes Help. Apple's Help Viewer will launch and your application's help book will appear in its main window. Click the various links you see to read other help book pages, and think how much money you will save on printing costs when you begin to distribute your finished application.

Working with Mac OS X 10.2 (Jaguar)

You have seen references to Mac OS X 10.2 (Jaguar) throughout this book, in connection with new features in the developer tools as well as code for implementing Cocoa features that are new in this release. Chief among these is Recipe 12, which goes into detail about implementing the important new keyed-archiving feature for data storage and retrieval.

In Recipe 21, you will learn several techniques to make sure an application built under Jaguar will run without crashing under older versions of Mac OS X.

RECIPE 21

Ensuring Backward Compatibility for Jaguar Applications

The Jaguar release of Mac OS X, version 10.2, officially became available on August 24, 2002—although Apple advanced the clock a little by starting the process the night before with gala celebrations in the Apple retail stores.

Jaguar is a watershed for Mac OS X. Where version 10.1 brought increased stability, improved speed, and implementation of essential features to advance the operating system to the point where one could fairly recommend it to all users, Version 10.2 has made it the primary operating system for the Macintosh platform now and for many years to come. Not only do new Macs ship with Mac OS X installed as the boot OS, but a Mac OS 9 installation disk isn't even included with the Mac OS X 10.2 retail package. Furthermore, Steve Jobs announced at the Paris Macworld Expo in September 2002 that new Macs will not even boot into Mac OS 9 starting in 2003 (the Classic environment will remain available in Mac OS X). Apple's marketing materials trumpet 150 new features in Jaguar, and the user reception has been enthusiastic.

Jaguar has enhanced Cocoa in many ways. *Vermont Recipes* covers many of the new Cocoa features as they come up in the several topics covered by these recipes. Most notably, Recipe 12 covers the important new keyed archiving feature in depth and Recipe 17 covers additional aspects of keyed archiving—particularly the new delegate methods. For more complete coverage of changes introduced in Jaguar that are of interest to developers, read the AppKit and Foundation release notes and the Mac OS X 10.2 Technical Note TN2053 at http://developer.apple.com/technotes/tn2002/tn2053.html.

Enhancements to Cocoa that Jaguar introduced raise several backward-compatibility issues. How do you ensure that an application built to run in Mac OS X 10.2 will also run correctly in older versions of Mac OS X—or at least fail gracefully instead of crashing? In this final recipe, you will learn several techniques for enabling your application to cope when run in an older version of Mac OS X if it was built to use new Jaguar features.

The first issue is that new Objective-C methods and C functions introduced in the Jaguar version of the Cocoa frameworks won't work in Mac OS X 10.0 or 10.1. An application that implements them will crash unless it takes steps to deal with the fact that the necessary code isn't present in older systems. Cocoa applications require the presence at run time of the Cocoa headers and the compiled and linked implementation code that lies behind them. The declarations and implementations of new features in version 10.2 simply don't exist in older versions of Mac OS X. The application may launch successfully under some circumstances if run on a computer where an older version of Mac OS X is installed, but as soon as the user attempts to do something that causes the application to call a new Jaguar method or function, it will crash. The same problem may appear in the case of applications importing new Jaguar Objective-C classes that don't exist in older systems. Solutions to this problem are described in Steps 1, 2, and 3.

Second, for very different reasons, if the application uses a new Jaguar external variable such as NSFileManager's **NSFileImmutable**, and under some other circumstances, it may simply fail to launch, giving the user no feedback. An external variable is a C variable or constant defined as **external**; C enumeration constants and Objective-C instance variables do not have this problem. This issue is addressed in Step 4.

Third, Cocoa might not unarchive your application's nib files when you run it in older versions of Mac OS X, and in that case no windows or other view objects will appear onscreen. When using Interface Builder to create nib files for your application's windows and other user interface objects, you have the option in Jaguar to save the nib files in one of three formats: "Pre-10.2 format", "10.2 and later format," and Both Formats. You make the selection in Interface Builder's Preferences dialog. If you build the application with a nib file saved in "10.2 and later format," it won't display the window or other user interface objects when running in an older system. For all practical purposes, it will be unusable except in Mac OS X 10.2 and later. The reason is that "10.2 and later format" nib files use Jaguar's new keyed archiving feature, and older versions of the operating system cannot unarchive such a nib file's contents.

Fourth, there are some issues with using the Jaguar tools to build applications to run in Mac OS X 10.1. I won't discuss tool issues since they are obscure and won't affect many developers.

Step 1: Bypass New Jaguar Methods and Functions by Testing the Operating System Version

To run a Jaguar application in older system versions, you must take several steps to ensure compatibility. The easiest of these is to save all of its nib files in "Pre-10.2 format" or Both Formats. The former is an unattractive option for most purposes, since some Jaguar user interface features, such as the spinning progress indicator, won't be available. Although a Both Formats nib file is slightly larger because its contents are archived using both the old and the new archiving technologies, it is usually the preferable choice.

Several techniques are available to ensure that the application does not crash at or after launch in an older system when it encounters Jaguar-only application code. I will describe techniques for dealing with Objective-C methods and C functions in the following instructions, and I will explain another approach that applies only to Object-C methods in Step 2. I will deal with new Objective-C classes in Step 3. Finally, I will discuss the issue of external variables in Step 4.

1. The first thing to do is to find out whether your application calls any Jaguar classes, Objective-C methods, C functions, or external variables that aren't available in older systems. You may already know the answer from paying close attention to the documentation, including the Jaguar release notes. However, there is no reason to risk relying on your memory because it is easy to identify most of them and pinpoint their locations almost automatically.

   Most of the Cocoa headers contain preprocessor directives that mark declarations that are new in Jaguar. These preprocessor directives were added to ensure that Project Builder will compile marked declarations only if the maximum allowed system version for which it is building an application is Mac OS X 10.2 or later. If you do nothing, Project Builder assumes it is building an application for versions 10.0, 10.1, and 10.2 or later, so it does compile the new Jaguar code. However, if you set a compiler flag to compile for version 10.1 or 10.0 as the maximum allowable system version, the marked declarations in the Cocoa headers won't compile. As a result, when you build the application, the compiler will warn you that any calls your application makes to new Jaguar code are invalid. You can use this fact to identify almost every place in your application code where you use new Jaguar features.

   First, set the compiler flag to compile for Mac OS X 10.0 only. To do this, click the Targets tab in Project Builder; select the target, Vermont Recipes, in the left pane; expand the Settings and Simple View topics; and click GCC Compiler Settings. In the Other C Compiler Flags field, enter this flag definition and setting exactly as shown here:

```
-DMAC_OS_X_VERSION_MAX_ALLOWED=MAC_OS_X_VERSION_10_0
```

Next, build the application. After you wade through a lot of warnings about not being able to use the precompiled headers, you should see several warnings about your application code, such as "undefined type, found 'NSKeyedArchiver'" and "'NSPropertyListXMLFormat_v1_0' undeclared." Examining these, you see that most of them relate to the keyed archiving code you added in Recipe 12. Click any of them to jump to the location in your code where you called the offending methods. You see that all the new keyed archiving calls are in VRDocument's `dataRepresentationOfType:` and `loadDataRepresentation:ofType:` methods. You already know that Jaguar introduced the keyed archiving code called in these two methods. This exercise therefore tells you that the Vermont Recipes application will crash if run in Mac OS X 10.0 or 10.1 whenever either of these two methods is encountered—namely, whenever the user attempts to read or write a document.

This technique is documented near the beginning of the Jaguar AppKit release notes, and there is additional useful information in the comments to the new Jaguar system header file AvailabilityMacros.h at /usr/include/AvailabilityMacros.h. The /usr folder is invisible in the Finder, but you can easily open this header file in Project Builder by choosing File > Open and typing the path into the dialog's "Go to" field. The header comments say of the `MAC_OS_X_VERSION_MAX_ALLOWED` compiler setting used here that this is an "upper bound" that controls "which OS functionality, if used, will result in a compiler error because that functionality is not available" on any OS in the specified range.

You can use Project Builder's batch find capability to perform a Textual search on "This project, frameworks only," for the text "10_2" with the Contains setting. You should find 111 occurrences of the search text (two of them are special settings for NSTypesetterBehavior unrelated to the issue under discussion, and one of them marks an old class that is omitted in Jaguar). Clicking each will take you to all 111 Jaguar code changes in the Cocoa frameworks—an interesting and informative exercise in its own right and an easy way to find changes that aren't documented in the release notes.

Note that these techniques do not work for the Address Book framework in Mac OS X 10.2, because that framework is not marked with these preprocessor directives. I understand that this omission was inadvertent.

The header comments suggest that this and similar availability preprocessor directives were originally designed to be embedded in system headers to mark code that was new in Mac OS X 10.1, too, as well as code that is present but deprecated. However, the Jaguar AppKit release notes only mention Mac OS X 10.2 in this connection. This disparity suggests that the Cocoa frameworks in Jaguar support the use of this technique to detect version 10.2 additions but not to detect version 10.1 additions, and in fact code that was new in Mac OS X 10.1 is not marked by similar preprocessor directives. I understand that this is because Apple no longer provides technical support for Mac OS X 10.0 and suggests that all users upgrade. You should consider Mac OS X 10.1 as the oldest Mac OS X system in which your applications may run.

In general, you should test your application's code using the technique described above before distributing any Jaguar application that a user may run in earlier systems, to minimize the chance that you have inadvertently called code that is not available there. If you identify any such code, you will want to take steps to prevent the application from crashing in older systems, using the techniques described below. In fact, since the final deployment build is not when you want to discover a backward-compatibility issue for the first time, you might be well advised to run this test periodically during the development cycle. (You don't want to leave the compiler flag set permanently to compile for Mac OS X 10.0, of course, because you do want your application to run in Jaguar.)

Since you have now identified the areas that raise backward-compatibility concerns in the Vermont Recipes application and are ready to deal with them, remove the `MAC_OS_X_VERSION_MAX_ALLOWED` setting from the compiler flags field in Project Builder.

2. The next step is to enable the application to detect which version of Mac OS X is currently running. You could instead simply bracket the `dataRepresentationOfType:` and `loadDataRepresentation:ofType:` methods in exception handlers, but for present purposes you want to know which version of the OS is running, not merely that attempts to read and write data fail in older systems. You will use the system version information to construct some informative alerts for the user's benefit.

Mac OS X 10.1 introduced a new facility that is suitable for this purpose. The AppKit declares an external variable, `NSAppKitVersionNumber`, which provides the version number of the AppKit framework installed on the computer as well as symbolic constants for the AppKit version in older major releases of the operating system. You can use this facility to determine that your application is running in one of the major public releases, Mac OS X 10.0, 10.1, or 10.2. You could instead use a similar Foundation external variable, `NSFoundationVersionNumber`, declared in NSObjCRuntime.h. (Although `NSAppKitVersionNumber` and its Foundation counterpart are external variables publicly introduced in Mac OS X 10.1, they do not prevent an application from launching in Mac OS X 10.0 because they were defined privately in that version.)

You can count on the reliability of this facility to test whether the application is running in a system containing an AppKit framework that is earlier than, contemporaneous with, or later than some known AppKit milestone. The headers provide no symbolic constants to tell you what AppKit version numbers were assigned to interim "dot" releases of the operating system but only those that were assigned to the first two major releases, Mac OS X 10.0 (577) and 10.1 (620), and a handful of bug fix releases. For example, if you perform a "Contains" batch search of the Cocoa frameworks for "NSAppKitVersionNumber," you find AppKit version numbers for NSAppKitVersionNumberWithPatternColorLeakFix (641.0) and NSAppKitVersionNumberWithDirectionalTabs (631.0). Past practice suggests that Apple will not declare a version constant for the AppKit framework released with Mac OS X 10.2 itself until Mac OS X 10.3 is released, although you can determine by experimenting with NSAppKitVersionNumber that the initial public release of Mac OS X 10.2 included AppKit version 663. This is also the version of the AppKit in Mac OS X 10.2.1. Each new build of the framework is given a new version number, but it wasn't rebuilt for 10.2.1.

The tests shown below enable you to determine with confidence not only whether the application is running in the initial release of Mac OS 10.0, 10.1, or 10.2 but also in any of their interim dot releases, because Apple's policy is to use the same whole number for the AppKit version in every interim release of a given major release of Mac OS X. The AppKit release notes for Mac OS X 10.1 disclose that Mac OS X 10.0 through 10.0.4 all used AppKit version number 577. They suggested that a later dot release would have used a fractionally higher number—say, 577.1—rather than a wholly new number such as 578, if the AppKit were revised, say, for a Mac OS X 10.0.5.

Here is a suggested test for Mac OS X 10.0.x:

```
if (floor(NSAppKitVersionNumber) >= NSAppKitVersionNumber10_0)
    && (floor(NSAppKitVersionNumber)
    < NSAppKitVersionNumber10_1) {
```

Here is a suggested test for Mac OS X 10.1.x:

```
if (floor(NSAppKitVersionNumber) >= NSAppKitVersionNumber10_1)
    && (floor(NSAppKitVersionNumber) < 663) {
```

Finally, testing for Mac OS X 10.2 cannot exclude the possibility of Mac OS X 10.3 or later. Nobody yet knows what AppKit version number will be assigned to them.

```
if (floor(NSAppKitVersionNumber) >= 663) {
```

The Jaguar AppKit release notes recommend using a similar code snippet as a way to determine that the currently running system version is contemporaneous with or newer than a specified major system release—or, phrased from the opposite viewpoint, that the system version is not older than a specified major release. It is suitable for determining that the machine is running a system version that supports some new feature. The Cocoa Dev Central Web site proposes a very similar code snippet in an article by Nick Zitzmann (www.cocoadevcentral.com/tutorials/).

Both the AppKit release notes and Zitzmann's article suggest the use of the **floor** function from the C math library. This function returns a number in the form of a C **double** data type equal to the largest integer less than or equal to the given number. It is appropriate here in light of the indication in the Mac OS X 10.1 AppKit release notes that AppKit version numbers may be incremented fractionally.

The Zitzmann article details three other techniques you can use to determine the current operating system version, but they are not, strictly speaking, Cocoa techniques. In a production environment, you may well prefer to use the gestalt method described by Zitzmann for its greater certitude, until Apple clarifies the proper use of the AppKit version number.

In Vermont Recipes, you will use Cocoa. At the beginning of the body of the VRDocument.h header file, add this declaration for a new method to detect version 10.2 or later of Mac OS X:

```
- (BOOL)isJaguarOrNewer;
```

Define the method at the beginning of the source file VRDocument.m as follows:

```
- (BOOL)isJaguarOrNewer { // Mac OS X 10.2 or newer
    return (floor(NSAppKitVersionNumber) >= 663);
}
```

If this method returns YES, you know that keyed archiving is available and it is safe to call dataRepresentationOfType: and loadDataRepresentation:ofType: and other parts of Vermont Recipes that call new-in-Jaguar methods.

3. You determined in Instruction 1 that dataRepresentationOfType: and loadDataRepresentation:ofType: are the two methods in Vermont Recipes where this test is necessary. Nest the body of each of the data storage methods in VRDocument.m in tests using your isJaguarOrNewer method. Leaving out the existing content, the dataRepresentationOfType: method should look like this:

```
- (NSData *)dataRepresentationOfType:(NSString *)type {
    if ([self isJaguarOrNewer]) {
        if ([type isEqualToString:VRDocumentType]) {
            ....
```

(continues on next page)

```
            return data;
        }
    }
    return nil;
}
```

Make a similar change to the `loadDataRepresentation:ofType:` method:

```
- (BOOL)loadDataRepresentation:(NSData *)data
        ofType:(NSString *)type {
    if ([self isJaguarOrNewer]) {
        if ([type isEqualToString:VRDocumentType]) {
            ....
            return YES;
        }
    }
    return NO;
}
```

With these changes in place, when a user runs the Vermont Recipes application in Mac OS 10.1 or earlier, an error alert panel will appear when the application attempts to open an existing file and an alert sheet will appear when it attempts to save a new document. In both cases, Cocoa provides the alert and its content as a result of these data-storage methods returning, respectively, `nil` and `NO`. You can see both alerts in action by temporarily revising `isJaguarOrNewer` to test against 664 instead of 663. Even if run in Jaguar, the application will now think it is running in an older system and will refuse to read and write documents.

If you were writing an application for the real world and marketing it as compatible with Mac OS X 10.1, you would not be satisfied to stop here, of course. Instead of presenting an alert telling the user that data is inaccessible and unsavable, you would provide an alternative means of reading and writing the data—perhaps one of the methods you learned in Recipe 1, Steps 4 and 5. This would require that the application be able to read and write document files in two formats and to distinguish one from the other when opening documents.

4. Even for present purposes it is not acceptable to leave the user wondering why the Save, Open, and related commands don't work in Mac OS X 10.1. The alerts give no explanation. Rather than devise a means to add this information to the alerts, you will present a warning when the application first launches, so the user won't waste time editing an unsavable document. At the same time, you will block the application from running at all in Mac OS X 10.0.

In Recipe 18, you wrote some code to raise an alert when a new document opens and discovers that preferences haven't yet been set. That isn't the right place for the warning you have in mind now, however, since this new warning is not dependent on opening a document. You will use the VRAppDelegate class, instead, as well as an appropriate NSApplication delegate method.

First, you need a new method to determine whether the application is running in Mac OS X 10.1 or newer. Because it is so simple, first simply duplicate in VRAppDelegate.h and VRAppDelegate.m the isJaguarOrNewer method you just wrote to detect version 10.2 or newer. Then add a nearly identical declaration and definition to detect version 10.1 (whose internal code name was widely known to be Puma) or later, as follows. In the VRAppDelegate.h header file, type this:

```
- (BOOL)isPumaOrNewer;
```

In the VRAppDelegate.m source file, type this:

```
- (BOOL)isPumaOrNewer { // Mac OS X 10.1 or newer
    return (floor(NSAppKitVersionNumber) >=
            NSAppKitVersionNumber10_1);
}
```

The delegate method you will implement is NSApplication's applicationWill-FinishLaunching:. It receives its associated notification just before the NSApplication object is initialized—even before the application object receives the application:openFile: message if the user launched the application by double-clicking the icon of an owned document. This notification is ideal for minimizing the chance that the application will try to execute Cocoa calls that aren't available. Opening a double-clicked document is something the Vermont Recipes application can't do in Mac OS X 10.1, because Vermont Recipes uses keyed archiving. The similar applicationDidFinishLaunching: delegate method is triggered too late, after the application has received the application:openFile: message.

Immediately following the isPumaOrNewer and isJaguarOrNewer method definitions in the VRAppDelegate.m source file, implement this delegate method:

```
#pragma mark DELEGATE METHODS

- (void)applicationWillFinishLaunching:
        (NSNotification *)notification {
    if (![self isPumaOrNewer]) {
        NSString *alertTitle = NSLocalizedString(
                @"Newer version of Mac OS X required",
                @"Title for 10.0 launch alert");
        NSString *alertInformation = NSLocalizedString(
```

(continues on next page)

```
        @"Vermont Recipes will not run in Mac OS X \
        10.0. Mac OS X 10.2 or newer is recommended. Go \
        to www.apple.com/macosx for information about \
        upgrading.",
        @"Informative text for 10.0 launch alert");
    NSRunAlertPanel(alertTitle, alertInformation,
        @"Quit", nil, nil);
    [NSApp terminate:self];
} else if (![self isJaguarOrNewer]) {
    NSString *alertTitle = NSLocalizedString(
        @"Newer version of Mac OS X recommended",
        @"Title for 10.1 launch alert");
    NSString *alertInformation = NSLocalizedString(
        @"Vermont Recipes will not save or read \
        documents in Mac OS X 10.1. Mac OS X 10.2 \
        or newer is recommended. Go to \
        www.apple.com/macosx for information about \
        upgrading.",
        @"Informative text for 10.1 launch alert");
    NSRunCriticalAlertPanel(alertTitle, alertInformation,
        nil, nil, nil);
    }
}
```

Be sure to include these strings in the Localizable.strings file.

This is a straightforward use of the NSRunAlertPanel() and NSRunCriticalAlert-Panel() functions. The critical version is used for the second alert because there is a risk that data will be lost.

The call to NSApplication's **terminate:** action method at the end of the first branch causes the application to quit in an orderly fashion, invoking appropriate Cocoa delegate methods if implemented. This is the same **terminate:** action method that Cocoa calls when the user chooses Quit from the Application menu.

The first alert offers a Quit button, signaling the user that the application will quit as soon as it is clicked. The second alert offers an OK button by virtue of passing **nil** in the default button parameter. Once the user clicks the OK button, an untitled document window will open. Later, if the user attempts to open or save a document, the application will present the error alerts you saw in Instruction 3.

You can test these two alerts by fooling the delegate method into thinking you are running Mac OS X 10.0 or 10.1. For the former, temporarily substitute **664** for the **NSAppKitVersionNumber10_1** constant in **isPumaOrNewer**. For the latter, temporarily substitute **664** for **663** in `isJaguarOrNewer`. (If you conduct this test after the release of Mac OS X 10.3, you will have to substitute its AppKit Version number plus 1 in place of **664**.)

5. In the `applicationWillFinishLaunching:` delegate method you just implemented, you reported information about the identity of the running operating system to the user based on the result of the `isPumaOrNewer` and `isJaguarOrNewer` methods. You have already learned that these methods do not discriminate between dot releases. In Jaguar, a new method, `operatingSystemVersionString` in NSProcessInfo, does this and more, returning a human-readable, localized string identifying the dot release and build number. It is not suitable for parsing as a test but only for display. Since Apple introduced it in Jaguar, of course, it will not work when you run the application in an earlier version of the system.

You could add a third branch to the delegate method to report what major or dot release and build of Jaguar or newer is currently running. At this time, it will be a useless interruption from the user's point of view. As newer versions of the system are released, however, you may want to use this method to better describe what version is currently running while advising the user to upgrade.

To try it out, add this branch to the delegate method's implementation:

```
else {
    NSString *OSVersion = [[NSProcessInfo processInfo]
            operatingSystemVersionString];
    NSString *alertTitle = [NSString stringWithFormat:
            NSLocalizedString(@"Mac OS X %@",
            @"Title for 10.2 launch alert"), OSVersion];
    NSString *alertInformation = [NSString stringWithFormat:
            NSLocalizedString(@"This computer is running Mac OS \
            X %@. Go to www.apple.com/macosx to find out whether \
            a newer version is available.", @"Informative text \
            for 10.2 or newer launch alert"), OSVersion];
    NSRunAlertPanel(alertTitle, alertInformation,
            nil, nil, nil);
}
```

If you do implement this additional alert, make sure you add the one localizable string here to Localizable.strings.

6. The code you wrote in Instructions 4 and 5 works as intended in Mac OS X 10.2. Immediately after you launch the application, if you implemented the third branch of the delegate method, it presents an alert panel identifying the system version and build number. Only when you dismiss the alert does a new document open, untitled unless you double-clicked a document icon. If you

haven't yet set preferences, the application presents the warning alert you wrote in Recipe 19 after you dismiss the system version alert and before a new, untitled window opens.

The application's behavior is not yet desirable in Mac OS X 10.0 or 10.1, however. In version 10.0, a new, untitled document window opens before the user dismisses the system version alert, apparently because the delegate method has a slightly different behavior in that system version. This behavior is inappropriate in the Vermont Recipes application, because the application isn't supposed to work in Mac OS X 10.0. Even worse, since no preferences have been set, the preferences warning alert also appears before the system version alert—and on top of it. This is confusing and unattractive. The application's behavior at launch time is almost as bad in Mac OS X 10.1.

To cure these problems, all you need to do is prevent the application from opening a new, untitled window when it launches in Mac OS X 10.0 or 10.1. This will suppress the preferences alert, too, since that alert is triggered only by a new document. You learned in Recipe 1 that NSApplication declares a delegate method just for this purpose, `applicationShouldOpenUntitledFile:`. Implement this method to return **YES** only in Mac OS X 10.2 or newer and otherwise **NO** at the top of the new DELEGATE METHODS section of VRAppDelegate, as follows:

```
- (BOOL)applicationShouldOpenUntitledFile:
      (NSApplication *)sender {
   return [self isJaguarOrNewer];
}
```

This will suppress the opening of a new, untitled document in any version of Mac OS X older than Jaguar. This means, of course, that a user in Mac OS X 10.1 will not see a new window even after dismissing the system version alert. This is just as well, since the application can't save the document anyway in 10.1.

The techniques you've learned in Step 1 are only some of the available ways to deal gracefully with new Jaguar methods and functions when your application is run in older versions of Mac OS X. The next two steps cover some other techniques.

Step 2: Bypass New Jaguar Methods by Testing Their Availability

Jaguar offers many methods that were not previously available in Cocoa. For example, Cocoa now includes several NSBundle methods with functionality previously available only in Carbon's CFBundle API. Among other things, in Jaguar you can now obtain the localized value of an Info.plist key by calling the new NSBundle method, **objectForInfoDictionaryKey:**. The Jaguar Foundation release notes indicate that use of this new method is preferred over other methods because it provides the localized value for a key, if one is available.

Is there a way to use this new Jaguar method safely without testing the version of the current operating system as you did in Step 1? The solution is to use the **respondsToSelector:** method declared in the NSObject protocol. In fact, this is the preferred technique, since it does not require you to determine what version of the Mac OS is running nor when the method in question first became available. You simply ask Cocoa whether it is available now, on the running system. If so, you call it; if not, you don't.

For example, suppose you wanted to make the localized version of the Vermont Recipes copyright string available to the user in response to a button or menu item. Before Jaguar, you had to duplicate it in your Localizable.strings file so your localization contractor could localize it and obtain the localized version of it there at run time using **NSLocalizedString()**. The process of duplicating the existing copyright string in the **CFBundleGetInfoString** entry in Project Builder's Target pane Info.plist Entries section is prone to error.

To safely retrieve the localized value of the copyright string, you might insert something like the following in some method that needed this information:

```
if ([[NSBundle mainBundle] respondsToSelector:
      @selector(objectForInfoDictionaryKey:)]) {
    myCopyright = [[NSBundle mainBundle] objectForInfoDictionaryKey:
        @"CFBundleGetInfoString"];
} else {
    myCopyright = nil; // or an older call
}
```

There are also some new C functions in Jaguar, especially in the new NSAccessibility.h header file (which is not included in the Cocoa umbrella headers but is nevertheless located in AppKit.framework). Unfortunately, you cannot test for the availability of functions directly and bypass them if not found, as you can for Objective-C methods. You cannot use **respondsToSelector:**, of course, because a C function is not an Objective-C selector.

A veteran C programmer might want to accomplish the same thing by using a statement such as this:

```
if ((void *)newCFunction != NULL) {
```

But this won't work. The reference in the test to the nonexistent function causes the application to refuse to load in pre-Jaguar systems, for the reasons described in Step 4, below, with respect to C external variables. The function is referred to in this test as if it were an external variable containing the address of the function, and the dynamic loader attempts to resolve all external variable references at once when the application is launched. If it fails to find one of them, it won't launch the application.

The only ways to bypass a new Jaguar C function in older versions of the operating system, therefore, are to test for the version of the system in which it was introduced or, if it is in a new Jaguar class, to test for the existence of the class itself as described in Step 3.

Step 3: Bypass New Jaguar Classes by Testing Their Availability

In addition to new features in existing classes, Jaguar offers a number of completely new Objective-C classes. The AppKit has NSGlyphInfo, NSKeyedArchiver, and NSKeyedUnarchiver. Foundation offers NSAppleScript, NSNameSpecifier, and NSUniqueIDSpecifier for AppleScript support, NSNetService and NSNetServiceBrowser to support the new Rendezvous technology, and NSPropertyListSerialization to support new data-storage formats. Outside the Cocoa frameworks, it provides several new Objective-C classes in AddressBook.framework, DiscRecording.framework, and DiscRecordingUI.framework.

Although you can test for the availability of any method or function within one of these classes using the techniques you learned in Steps 1 and 2, there is also a convenient way to test for the availability of an entire class. Just call the Foundation function NSClassFromString(), passing it the name of the desired class as a string object. If it returns the class object, the class is available; if it returns nil, the class is not available.

You could easily have used this function call in Step 1 instead of writing the isJaguarOrNewer method to test for the version of the AppKit. For example, to test for the existence of the NSKeyedArchiver class, you would have written this line:

```
if (NSClassFromString(@"NSKeyedArchiver")) {
```

Step 4: Deal with New Jaguar External Variables

The discussion up to this point has dealt with new Jaguar methods, functions, and classes, and convenient techniques have been found to provide backward compatibility for a Jaguar application that uses any of them. Unfortunately, one kind of new code in Jaguar has no simple backward-compatibility solution: external C variables.

As I write this recipe, there is no convenient way to prevent an application built in Jaguar from attempting to refer to a new Jaguar external variable when you run it in an older version of Mac OS X. The application simply won't launch, and there is no straightforward way to warn your users except in your documentation.

There are only a few new external variables in Jaguar, so this issue is not likely to affect many Cocoa developers. You can find all of the new external variables (except those in the Address Book framework) by using the search technique described in Step 1. The new NSAccessibility category on NSObject in NSAccessibility.h contains a number of them, for example, and NSFileManager contains several.

Here is the reason why an application won't launch in an older system if it refers to a new external variable. When a user launches a Cocoa application, the dynamic loader attempts to load all the application's symbols related to external variables at once. This doesn't affect Objective-C methods, because your code sends Objective-C messages using the facilities of the Objective-C runtime. It also doesn't affect C function calls, because the loader does not attempt to resolve a function until it is called. When the loader discovers a reference to an external variable that isn't available in Mac OS X 10.0 or 10.1, however, the loader can't finish launching the application. The application's icon may appear and bounce once in the Dock, but nothing else happens. The application just goes away, leaving no trace except an error message in console.log. You can't guard against this in your code if you must refer to the new external variable when running in Jaguar, because the guard code never runs in an older system.

Jaguar introduces a new technique that was designed to deal with issues like this, but it doesn't protect Jaguar applications running in Mac OS X 10.1. The new technique is described in the AvailabilityMacros release note on your hard disk in /Developer/Documentation/ReleaseNotes. It involves setting a new C compiler flag, `MAC_OS_X_-VERSION_MIN_REQUIRED`. According to the comments in the AvailabilityMacros.h header file, this is a "lower bound" that "controls which calls to OS functions will be weak-importing (allowed to be unresolved at launch time)." In other words, this setting (at least when combined with another setting described next) is supposed to cause the compiler to build the executable product with weak links instead of the normal strong links. What this means is that the dynamic loader should not complain when, at launch time, it fails to find the symbols for new C functions and external variables. The GCC 3 compiler introduced in Jaguar is required in order to build an application in this fashion.

The Availability Macros solution has limitations, however. Among other things, weak linking doesn't work in applications run in Mac OS X 10.1 and earlier. The dynamic loader in Mac OS X 10.1 and earlier will not recognize weak-linked executables. This technique will therefore only work in the future, to ensure backward compatibility for applications built in Mac OS X 10.3 and later when run in Mac OS X 10.2.

A related mechanism also can't be used easily at this time, involving the `MACOSX_DEPLOYMENT_TARGET` environment variable that is documented in the Jaguar Compiler Tools release notes and in the *ld*(1) man page available through the Terminal application. This environment variable cannot currently be set directly from Project Builder but only when compiling from the command line or using other advanced techniques.

You have other options. For example, if you must refer to new external variables in your Jaguar application and you must also assure backward compatibility, you could include in your application bundle a very small launcher application that runs in all system versions. If it looks around when launched and doesn't like what it sees, it can put up an alert; otherwise, it can launch the main application. A problem with this technique is that the user will see two bouncing icons in the Dock, and there may be issues involving aliases to your application.

This discussion has omitted many highly technical issues. Watch for an Apple technical note dealing with this subject.

The issue discussed in Step 4 does not affect Vermont Recipes, because Vermont Recipes refers to no new external variables. Vermont Recipes will run in Mac OS X 10.1, but without saving or reading documents as described in Step 1, and it will launch in Mac OS X 10.0 sufficiently to present the alert you wrote in Step 1 and then quit. You could overcome these limitations and make the application a full citizen in older versions of Mac OS X by writing a little additional code—so long as you don't refer to any new Jaguar external variables.

Step 5: Build the Application for Deployment

You are now finished writing version 1.0 of the Vermont Recipes application. It is time to build it for deployment and move on to your own projects. You need complete only these simple tasks.

1. In the Targets pane of Project Builder, change several items in Info.plist Entries to indicate that this is version 1.0 of Vermont Recipes, not version 1.0.0d1.

2. In the same place, change the build version to 21.

3. In InfoPlist.strings, make the same changes, as applicable.

4. Change the build style to deployment, not development. Make sure you click the radio button itself, not the name of the build style.

5. Before you build the application the final time, install the August 2002 or later Developer Tools. The Mac OS X 10.2 installation disks shipped with the July 2002 Developer Tools. The August Update included fixes for a number of problems in the July tools, including problems in the compiler, the debugger, and Interface Builder. Apple cautions not to ship a commercial product using the July tools.

6. Check the Apple Developer Connection Web site for the latest information about any other issues that might affect your application.

7. The preferred means to distribute your application is on a disk image file created using Apple's Disk Copy or a similar third-party utility. This will avoid problems with long filenames (perhaps inside your application bundle) and with application privileges that might occur if you use some other utilities. It also lets your customers use an easy installation technique: They just double-click the disk image file to mount it, then drag the finished application from the disk image's window to their Applications folder.

Conclusion

I hope you have found Vermont Recipes *to be everything you expected, and more.*

You have learned how to put together a very full-featured Macintosh application for the Cocoa environment of Mac OS X. Along the way, you have learned many Cocoa techniques, both in the use of the developer tools and in coding the features of the application. Many of these are new in Mac OS X 10.2 (Jaguar). You have also learned something you don't encounter in many other Cocoa books: how to structure the classes and code in the project to enhance your ability to manage and maintain a rather large and complex application.

You still have much to learn, but a book must end somewhere. There are many Cocoa classes I have not covered: These include classes that you will need only when you write special-purpose applications—such as Web browsers, games, or graphics applications— and also many of those that you will need in almost any application such as progress indicators, customized printing setups, and AppleScript support. With all that you have learned here, however, you should find it much easier to learn new Cocoa material. You have learned general techniques that you will find throughout the unexplored regions of Cocoa, such as notifications, delegate methods, categories, and protocols. Of even greater importance, you have found your way around the Cocoa documentation and now know several strategies for finding out how to perform new tricks.

I will end with a challenge. Just as, in the real world, no application ships bug-free, it is also true that no programming book ships without errors. There comes a time when the product simply has to get out the door, whether it's a book or an application. I'm not talking about typographical errors and accidental omissions, although you will surely find some I have overlooked. I'm talking about bugs in the logic and code of the Vermont Recipes application.

I already know of one. There are undoubtedly others, because all except the first few recipes have undergone no beta testing. As errors are discovered and fixed, I will post the news to the Stepwise Web site, so be sure to visit it often at www.stepwise.com. If you find bugs, spend a little time trying to fix them, then tell me about the bugs and your fixes at wjcheeseman@earthlink.net. If, someday, you don't find me at that address, or updates to the book at the Stepwise site, go to www.peachpit.com to find out where we've gone.

Here is the one bug I'm aware of as Vermont Recipes *goes to print:*

When running the application within Project Builder, I occasionally see run-time errors indicating that one class or another does not implement `allocWithZone:`*. This normally means that the class should conform to the NSCoding protocol, but I can't find any reason why the classes named in these error messages should conform to NSCoding. The errors appear to be random. They occur much more frequently when the VRDocument.nib nib file is saved as "10.2 and later format" or Both Formats than they do when it is saved as "Pre-10.2 format." I have brought the nib file connection to Apple's attention but don't yet have any feedback.*

Other issues have been mentioned from time to time in the book. I believe these stem from bugs or design issues in Cocoa, but they could very well be the result of errors on my part. These include the limitation described in Recipe 7, regarding the apparent impossibility of adapting my live undo and redo technique to text fields that have on-the-fly formatters attached, and the backward-compatibility issue regarding external variables discussed in Recipe 21.

I invite you to take a stab at addressing these bugs and issues. All solutions that strike me as valid and interesting will be posted to the Stepwise site, with attribution to you unless you request anonymity.

Index

D

data. *See also* document data
  initializing, 90
data-based primitives, 89, 102
data representation
  methods, 89, 91–98
  and model classes, 77
data storage
  keyed archiving
    adding revert, undo, and redo support,
      578–585
    archiving and unarchiving data, 565–575
    archiving and unarchiving model objects,
      575–578
    encoding and decoding data, 557–564
    overview, 555–556
  saving and retrieving data, 89
  saving data in XML format, 101–109
`dataReprensentationOfType:` method, 89, 91–98
`dealloc` method, 65–68, 83
Debug pane (Project Builder), 138
*DebugApp: Debugging an Application with Project
  Builder,* 137
debugging applications
  documentation, 137
  inserting `description` method, 142–144
  `NSAssert()` macro, 144–145
  `NSLog()` macro, 141–142
  stepping through with breakpoints, 136,
    138–141
Debugging with GDB document, 137
`decodeObject:` method, 558–564
`delegate` methods, 15, 32
  basics, 112
  catching formatter-detected input errors, 351
  dealing with invalid text entries, 336
  documentation, 113
  enabling/disabling bevel buttons, 241–243
  versus notifications, 118
*Delegating Authority—Cocoa Delegation and
  Notification* article, Stepwise Web site, 113
delegation. *See* `delegate` methods
deploying applications, 146–151
  documentation, 137
Deployment build style, 146–151
`description` method, 104
  debugging applications, 142–144
designated initializers, 64, 78, 79, 80
Developer Tools Overview, Project Builder
  documentation, 6
Development build style, 146–151
dialog panels
  creating, 678–684
  overview, 667–669
dictionaries
  basics, 93
  class methods, 94
`dictionaryFromModel` method, 92–95
`dictionaryFromStorage:` method, 105
`dictionaryWithContentsOfFile:` method,
  102, 105

`disableUndoRegistration` method, 114
`displayNameAtPath:` method, 89
Dock menus
  adding menu items
    dynamic, 606–612
    static, 604–606
  overview, 603–604
Document-Based Applications section, *Cocoa
  Developer Documentation*
  classes, superclasses, and subclasses, 32
  saving documents with HFS type and creator
    codes, 53
document data. *See also* data
  displaying, 99–100
  implementing with data representation
    methods, 91–98
  initializing, 90
  Revert menu
    basics, 126–130
    changing behaviors of menu item,
      130–132
  Save menu, 130–132
  saving and retrieving, overview, 89
  saving in XML format, 101–109
    overview, 101–102
  undo and redo features, 109–110
    registering changes with undo manager,
      111–114
    setting menu item titles, 115–116
    updating user interface, 116–126
document icons, 133–134
document-modal alert sheets, 256
  dealing with invalid text entries
    connecting with delegate method, 336
    overview, 319–321
    writing alert sheet code, 321–336
document type definitions (DTDs), XML, 101
documentation
  accessor methods, 66, 297
  applications, building for deployment, 137
  applications, debugging, 137
  bevel buttons, 156
  checkboxes, 156
  classes, superclasses, and subclasses, 32–33
  commmand pop-down menu buttons, 156
  custom formatters, 349
  delegation, 113
  drag-and-drop feature, 427
  exceptions, 137
  Info.plist Entries section, 52
  InfoPlist.strings, 52
  Interface Builder, 13
  key-value coding, 522–523
  Localizable.strings files, 59
  memory management, 66, 297
  notification, 117
  Project Builder, 6
  protocols, 427
  radio buttons, 156
  user controls, 156
`documentDidRevert` method, 128, 129
drag-and-drop features, 425–434